PRINCIPLES OF MICROECONOMICS
FIFTH EDITION

PRINCIPLES OF MICROECONOMICS
FIFTH EDITION

RYAN C. AMACHER
Professor of Economics and
Dean, College of Commerce and Industry
Clemson University

HOLLEY H. ULBRICH
Alumni Professor of Economics
Clemson University

COLLEGE DIVISION   South-Western Publishing Co.
Cincinnati Ohio

Sponsoring Editor: James M. Keefe
Developmental Editor: Alice Denny
Production Editor: Sue Ellen Brown
Production House: Lifland et al., Bookmakers
Cover and Interior Designer: Craig LaGesse Ramsdell
Photo Editor: Diana Robbins Carter
Marketing Manager: Scott D. Person
Cover and Interior Illustrator: Jean Tuttle ©1992

HB67EA2
Copyright ©1992
by South-Western Publishing Co.
Cincinnati, Ohio

ALL RIGHTS RESERVED
The text of this publication, or any part thereof, may not be reproduced or transmitted in any form or by any means, electronic or mechanical, including photocopying, recording, storage in an information retrieval system, or otherwise, without the prior written permission of the publisher.

Library of Congress Cataloging-in-Publication Data

Amacher, Ryan C.
    Principles of microeconomics / Ryan C. Amacher, Holley H. Ulbrich.
  — 5th ed.
    p. cm.
    Includes bibliographical references and index.
    ISBN 0-538-81307-5
    1. Microeconomics.   I. Ulbrich, Holley H.   II. Title.
HB172.A576   1991
338.5—dc20   91-20372
                                                                                                                     CIP

Printed in the United States of America

1 2 3 4 5 6 7   RN   6 5 4 3 2 1

Photo Credits: p. 18: (*top*) Hoover Institution, Stanford University; (*bottom*) Massachusetts Institute of Technology; p. 63: The Bettmann Archive; p. 101: The University of Chicago; p. 138: Historical Pictures Service, Inc., Chicago; p. 153: Bettmann/Hulton; p. 243: The Bettmann Archive; p. 274: Photograph courtesy of The Public Relations Department of Carnegie-Mellon University; p. 283: (*top*) Peter Lofts Photography; (*bottom*) Victor Jorgensen-Scope for Fortune Magazine; p. 301: (*top*) Public Information/University of Chicago; (*bottom*) Photo by Sam Sweezy; p. 342: Brown Brothers, Sterling, Pa.; p. 394: Courtesy of Robert Schalkenback Foundation; p. 413: Courtesy of Thomas Sowell

PREFACE

Each revision of a textbook presents a major challenge. This fifth edition was no exception. We had to decide what to keep, what to change, and what additions or modifications were needed to make the textbook up to date and responsive to changing ideas, methods, and interests. In putting together a fifth edition, we have benefited from comments and suggestions from users of earlier editions, colleagues at Clemson University, and some careful and thoughtful reviewers.

We reiterate our goal that guided the earlier editions. We do not want to make professional economists out of students. A common complaint is that instructors and textbook authors treat the principles of economics course as the first step in work toward a Ph.D. This text is intended not to train professional economists but rather to describe the analytical tools that economic theory offers the policy analyst or adviser to governments and business firms. This book teaches enough theory to enable students to understand policy and presents enough policy situations to give them an understanding of how to apply the theory. In addition, where relevant, we present the historical context of the theory.

CHANGES IN THE FIFTH EDITION

The multi-color format allows us to be more creative with the graphs and to make the book more attractive. The figures have been prepared so that all demand-related curves are blue and all supply-related curves are red. Historical and other nonspecific information is shown in gold. Throughout the text, special features, including the International Perspectives,

Economic Profiles, Economic Insights, and summary boxes, are presented in a consistent color and format.

We have expanded the integration of the international sector in this edition. The gold-colored International Perspective pages in each chapter extend the scope of the material from the purely domestic scene to the worldwide implications and focus on related real-world international issues. Some of the perspectives show what happens to the model or theory when it is placed in the context of an open economy. Thus, we add exports and imports to supply and demand in microeconomics and we look at the antitrust implications of foreign competition. Other perspectives consider how particular problems are addressed or how particular institutions work in other countries. For example, the discussion of poverty programs explores income support programs in Europe.

We recognize that students appreciate having important material summarized frequently, so we continue to include concise summaries of main points in order to make the book as user friendly as possible. Other features that are especially helpful to students have been retained, including key terms and their definitions in the margins and the numbered chapter summaries. Chapter learning objectives have been reintroduced at the request of users. The number of end-of-chapter questions has been expanded, including more problem-solving and brainstorming questions along with those that review chapter material.

On the basis of reviewer recommendations, a major effort was made in this edition to reorganize and streamline the material in the introductory chapters. The number of introductory chapters has been reduced from four to three. Each chapter emphasizes a single model and uses that model to develop basic methodological concepts. Thus, Chapter 1, "Economics, Economic Issues, and Economic Methods," now introduces the production possibilities curve. Chapter 2, "Markets, Governments, and Nations: The Organization of Economic Activity" describes the circular flow model, building on the introductory material on scarcity and choice in Chapter 1 while creating a broad overview of both microeconomics and macroeconomics. This chapter blends some materials from Chapter 2 of the previous editions with a discussion of the role of governments and the international economy, in order to set the stage for the remaining chapters. Some methodological material, which appeared in the opening chapter in earlier editions, is best understood in the context of the circular flow model. Thus, Chapter 3, "Supply and Demand," now incorporates the topics of comparative statics and equilibrium and disequilibrium. The materials that were presented in Chapter 4 in previous editions have been assigned to various chapters as appropriate, but the basic material on the role of government has been incorporated into the new Chapter 2.

Chapter 4, "Applications of Supply and Demand," again reviews the concepts of supply and demand, with new examples and revised material brought together from several chapters of the previous edition. The presentations of elasticity in Chapter 5 and demand and consumer choice in Chapter 6 received strong support from our reviewers. Indifference curve analysis remains as an optional appendix to Chapter 6.

Chapter 7, which introduces the student to the theory of the firm, includes coverage of two new topics: households as firms and nonprofit firms. The optional appendix covering isoquant and isocost curves parallels the Chapter 6 appendix on indifference curves. Chapter 8 presents cost theory and concludes with a discussion of profit maximization. Chapters 9–11, covering perfect competition, monopoly, and monopolistic competition and oligopoly, have been updated with new examples and problems. The final chapter of this section, Chapter 12 on regulation, deregulation, and antitrust policy, includes antitrust and regulatory changes that have occurred since the last edition.

Chapter 13 discusses marginal productivity in the context of labor markets. Chapter 14 follows the labor market theory with a revised and updated discussion of U.S. labor history and the role of unions. All the material on rent, interest, and profit appears in Chapter 15, which now also includes a discussion of the functional distribution of income. Chapter 16, "Income Distribution: Poverty, Discrimination, and Welfare," concludes the section. This chapter includes two new topics: the regional distribution of poverty and transfers to the elderly, an area of great controversy.

Chapters 17 and 18 in turn discuss market failure and government failure, incorporating new material and additional examples on both sides of the argument. A new Chapter 19, "Case Studies in Market Failure and Government Failure," includes the farm problem and urban problems. Also covered in this chapter is a third area of growing interest and concern—the environment. This material is new to the fifth edition.

The international section comprises three chapters. Chapter 20, "International Trade," now includes an introduction to two additional arguments for tariffs: the optimum tariff argument and the theory of the second best. To show the role of services in the balance of payments, Chapter 21 contains an International Perspective that discusses how the United States has become a net exporter of tourism. Chapter 22, which deals with comparative systems, was revised at the last minute to incorporate the rapid changes in Eastern Europe.

IMPORTANT FEATURES OF THE FIFTH EDITION

The previous editions of *Principles of Microeconomics* have been used by thousands of students at hundreds of institutions. The following features have made this text a useful and well-regarded teaching and learning tool.

ORGANIZATION
The length and content of the fifth edition represent a very careful weighing of thoroughness against brevity. Although we did not go quite so far as to apply "zero-based editing" by requiring each item to justify its inclusion, we did carefully rethink what to include and we did some pruning to make room for new material and ideas.

SPECIAL PAGES
Each chapter includes special pages. At least one special page, color-keyed gold, is an International Perspective, extending the scope of the

material in the chapter to a global view. Other special pages may be Economic Profiles of important economists or Economic Insights into important institutions, relevant historical events, or pressing current issues. The special pages are placed close to the relevant chapter material and highlight the development of the theory or its application to current domestic or global problems.

PEDAGOGICAL FEATURES

Each chapter begins with learning objectives, to introduce the students to the materials that will be covered. Key terms and their definitions are highlighted in the margin of the text. A feature introduced in the fourth edition and continued in the fifth edition is the capsule summaries of the preceding section or sections, placed at strategic points in each chapter. We have again expanded the selection of end-of-chapter questions, which can be used for review, homework, or class discussion. Suggested answers are provided in the *Instructor's Manual*. The carefully annotated Suggestions for Further Reading in each chapter have been updated and expanded to include current material. All terms that appear in boldface type and in the margins of the book are defined in the Glossary.

SUPPLEMENTARY MATERIALS

In addition to the pedagogical features in the textbook—the learning objectives, key terms, questions, and summaries—there is also a *Study Guide*, an *Instructor's Manual*, and a *Test Bank*. The *Study Guide* was prepared by Patricia Pando of Houston Baptist University. The revised *Test Bank* for the fifth edition was developed by Ryan Amacher, Holley Ulbrich, and Dennis Placone of Clemson University and has again been expanded to accommodate instructors' needs. The *Instructor's Manual* was prepared by the authors of the textbook.

THE STUDY GUIDE

The *Study Guide* will be a real asset for your students. Each chapter corresponds to a chapter in the textbook. It includes a chapter overview; matching exercises based on the important terms in the chapter; a three-part self-test consisting of true/false questions, problems requiring numerical and/or graphical solutions (where appropriate), and multiple choice questions; a review of the learning objectives for the chapter; complete answers to all questions in the self-test; and chapter exercises. The chapter exercises can be used for homework or for quizzes. (Answers are provided in the *Instructor's Manual*.)

THE INSTRUCTOR'S MANUAL

The *Instructor's Manual* also contains a chapter corresponding to each chapter in the text. Each chapter of the *Manual* includes a short discussion of the purposes of the chapter; the chapter outline, learning objectives, and summary; key terms from the chapter with their definitions; suggestions for lectures, extensions, and applications; suggested answers to all end-of-chapter questions; and answers to the chapter exercises in the *Study Guide*. Transparency masters are also included in the *Instructor's Manual*.

THE TEST BANK

An extensive *Test Bank* is available to adopters. It consists of multiple choice and true/false questions, including those in the *Study Guide* (marked with an asterisk). The *Test Bank* is also available on disk for use with MicroSWAT III test generation software. This easy-to-use, menu-driven software allows instructors to quickly and efficiently produce high-quality tests. Instructors can enter and edit questions, scramble questions and choices, and print graphs as part of a test. Included in the software is a grade book.

TRANSPARENCIES

Important illustrations from *Principles of Microeconomics* have been reproduced on a set of color acetate transparencies available to adopters to enhance classroom presentations. The most critical illustrations appear on overlay transparencies, an innovative teaching tool.

THE MICROCOMPUTER TUTORIALS

Tutorial software, available for IBM® or IBM-compatible machines, contains four modules designed for either individual or group use in reviewing basic concepts.[1] The tutorials have been thoroughly revised in response to suggestions from users and are available to adopters. Copies may be made for student use.

ACKNOWLEDGMENTS

We are grateful to the many colleagues who made specific comments concerning the fourth edition or reviewed drafts of this fifth edition:

Jack E. Adams
University of Arkansas

Andy Barnett
Auburn University

Dan Barszcz
College of DuPage

Greg Brown
Lincoln Memorial University

Heinrich H. Bruschke
St. Louis University

Gary W. Burbridge
Grand Rapids Junior College

Camille P. Castorina
Florida Institute of Technology

Rick L. Chaney
St. Louis University

Abdur Chowdhury
Marquette University

Dave Clark
Marquette University

David L. Cleeton
Oberlin College

Donald A. Coffin
Indiana University Northwest

---

1. IBM® is a registered trademark of International Business Machines Corporation. Any reference to IBM refers to this registered trademark.

Dean S. Dutton
Brigham Young University

Bernard Feigenbaum
California State University–Northridge

David W. Findley
Colby College

Vivek Ghosal
University of Florida

Patricia E. Graham
University of Northern Colorado

Ralph Gunderson
University of Wisconsin-Oshkosh

R. W. Hafer
Southern Illinois University

David L. Hames
University of Hawaii, Hilo

Raza Hamzaee
Missouri Western College

Stephen Happel
Arizona State University

Dannie E. Harrison
Murray State University

Thomas R. Ireland
University of Missouri–St. Louis

David Jobson
Keystone Junior College

Andrew Larkin
St. Cloud State University

Anton D. Lowenberg
California State University–Northridge

Robert McAuliffe
Babson College

Rob Roy McGregor
University of South Carolina

Patrick McMurry
Missouri Western State College

Robert Main
Butler University

John E. Marthisen
Babson College

Richard F. Measell
St. Mary's College

Hamid Milani
University of Wisconsin–Marathon County

Clark Nardinelli
Clemson University

Michael V. Olds
Orange Coast College

Eugene Ottle
McKendree College

John Pisciotta
Baylor University

Dennis Placone
Clemson University

Gary Quinlivin
St. Vincent College

Richard Robertson
Hinds Community College

Barbara Sherman Rolleston
Baldwin Wallace College

Malcolm Russell
Andrews University

Jody L. Sindelar
Yale University

Lawrence G. Smith
Grossmont College

Fred A. Tarpley, Jr.
Georgia Institute of Technology

Percy O. Vera
Sinclair Community College

Doug Wakeman
Meredith College

John Warner
Clemson University

Mellie Warner
Clemson University

Dale Warnke
College of Lake Country

William F. Watson, Jr.
Brunswick Junior College

Donald A. Wells
University of Arizona

Bernard J. Widera
University of Wisconsin, Madison

Arthur L. Welsh
Pennsylvania University

Jehad Yasin
Fort Valley State College

In addition, we owe a significant debt of gratitude to users and reviewers of the earlier editions of the textbook for numerous suggestions and comments. Our team at South-Western Publishing Co. has been a significant part of our textbook life. Our developmental editors—Dennis Hanseman and, for the last two editions, Alice Denny—have greatly improved our work. Sponsoring Editor Jim Keefe and Marketing Manager Scott Person have developed a classy final product. Over the years we have learned a great deal about the market from the College Division publisher's representatives, and we have enjoyed our interactions with them. We also want to thank our spouses, Susan and Carl, who continue to provide encouragement and inspiration through many editions of this textbook.

Finally, we would like to dedicate the fifth edition to the memory of Professor Jack Livingston of Ripon College and Professor Dorothy Goodwin of the University of Connecticut. Their skill and enthusiasm for teaching attracted us to economics as a profession. If they were alive to read this textbook, they would find their inspired teaching living on in its pages.

Ryan C. Amacher
Holley H. Ulbrich

Brief Contents

PART 1
INTRODUCTION TO ECONOMICS 1

1 Economics, Economic Issues, and Economic Methods 2
2 Markets, Governments, and Nations: The Organization of Economic Activity 41
3 Supply and Demand: The Basics of Economic Analysis 69

PART 2
DEMAND AND CONSUMER CHOICE 97

4 Applications of Supply and Demand: The Basic Microeconomic Tools 98
5 Elasticity: The Measure of Responsiveness 125
6 Demand and Consumer Choice 151

PART 3
PRODUCT MARKETS 183

7 Firms and Production 184
8 Costs and Profits 209
9 Perfect Competition 229
10 Monopoly 253
11 Monopolistic Competition and Oligopoly 281
12 Theory in the Real World: Regulation, Deregulation, and Antitrust Policy 307

PART 4
FACTOR MARKETS 339

13 Marginal Productivity Theory and Labor Markets 340
14 The Labor Movement in the United States 365
15 Rent, Interest, and Profit 391
16 Income Distribution: Poverty, Discrimination, and Welfare 407

PART 5
MARKET FAILURE, GOVERNMENT FAILURE, AND PUBLIC CHOICE 435

17 Market Failure and Government Intervention	436
18 Government Failure and Public Choice	459
19 Agriculture, Cities, and the Environment: Case Studies in Market Failure and Government Failure	477

PART 6
THE WORLD ECONOMY 505

20 International Trade	506
21 International Finance	529
22 Comparative Economic Systems in Theory and Practice	549

CONTENTS

PART 1
INTRODUCTION TO ECONOMICS 1

CHAPTER 1 ECONOMICS, ECONOMIC ISSUES, AND ECONOMIC METHODS 2
Introduction 2
What Is Economics? 2
Economics in Relation to Other Fields 3
Why Study Economics? 3
Scarcity: Limited Resources, Insatiable Wants 4
International Perspective: The Nobel Prize for Economics 7
Society's Choices: The Production Possibilities Curve 8
Theories, Hypotheses, and Models 13
Basic Elements of the Economic Approach 17
Economic Profile: Milton Friedman (1912–) and Paul A. Samuelson (1915–) 18
Three Common Fallacies 20
International Perspective: The United States and the Rest of the World 22
Making Policy Choices 23
Summary 25
New Terms 25
Questions for Discussion 26
Suggestions for Further Reading 27
Appendix: Economic Relationships and Graphs 29

CHAPTER 2 MARKETS, GOVERNMENTS, AND NATIONS:
THE ORGANIZATION OF ECONOMIC ACTIVITY 41
Introduction 41
Limited Resources: The Factors of Production 41
The Basic Economic Questions 43
The Circular Flow of Economic Activity 48
The Economic Role of Government 52

International Perspective: Privatization in Britain   54
The Role of the Foreign Sector   59
International Perspective: The Size of the Foreign Sector   60
Economic Profile: Adam Smith (1723–1790)   63
Summary   65
New Terms   65
Questions for Discussion   66
Suggestions for Further Reading   67

Chapter 3 Supply and Demand: The Basics of Economic Analysis   69
Introduction   69
Demand   69
Supply   76
Market Equilibrium   80
International Perspective: Adding Foreign Demand and Supply   81
A Theory of Price Formation   85
Evaluating the Market Process   88
International Perspective: Emerging Markets in Eastern Europe   89
Summary   93
New Terms   94
Questions for Discussion   94
Suggestions for Further Reading   95

Part 2
Demand and Consumer Choice   97

Chapter 4 Applications of Supply and Demand: The Basic Microeconomic Tools   98
Introduction   98
The Economics of Crime: Use of the Self-Interest Assumption   98
Economic Profile: Gary Becker (1930–)   101
Price Ceilings and Price Floors   102
International Perspective: Black Markets   106
Markets as Allocation Mechanisms   109
A Lesson from the Energy Crisis   111
International Perspective: Government Intervention, Japanese Style   113
The Health Care Industry   116
Microeconomics and Social Policy: The Economics of Natural Disasters   119
The Road Ahead   121
Summary   121
New Terms   122
Questions for Discussion   122
Suggestions for Further Reading   123

Chapter 5 Elasticity: The Measure of Responsiveness   125
Introduction   125
Supply and Demand Revisited   125
Elasticity as a General Concept   126
Price Elasticity of Demand   127
International Perspective: The Price Elasticity of Demand for Imports and Exports   132
Economic Profile: Antoine Augustin Cournot (1801–1877)   138
Other Demand Elasticities   141

Price Elasticity of Supply 142
Who Pays the Excise Tax: An Exercise in the Elasticity of Supply and Demand 145
Summary 148
New Terms 149
Questions for Discussion 149
Suggestions for Further Reading 150

CHAPTER 6 DEMAND AND CONSUMER CHOICE 151
Introduction 151
Choice, Value, and Utility Theory 151
Economic Profile: William Stanley Jevons (1835–1882) 153
Some Applications of Utility Theory 161
Consumer Surplus and Utility 164
International Perspective: Tariffs and Consumer Surplus 165
Advertising, Marketing, and Demand 166
Experimental Economics: Economics According to Rats 166
Summary 167
New Terms 167
Questions for Discussion 168
Suggestions for Further Reading 169
Appendix: Indifference Analysis, An Alternative
    Approach to Consumer Choice 170

PART 3
PRODUCT MARKETS 183

CHAPTER 7 FIRMS AND PRODUCTION 184
Introduction 184
The Firm in Theory 184
The Business Firm in Practice 186
International Perspective: Labor-Managed Firms in Yugoslavia 188
The Nonprofit Firm 190
Economic Efficiency 193
Production Functions in the Short and Long Run 194
Economic Insight: Corporate Philanthropy 195
The Choice of Inputs 198
On to Costs 200
Summary 201
New Terms 201
Questions for Discussion 201
Suggestions for Further Reading 202
Appendix: Producer Choice 203

CHAPTER 8 COSTS AND PROFITS 209
Introduction 209
Accounting Profit and Economic Profit 210
Costs in the Short Run 212
Costs in the Long Run 216
International Perspective: Economic Development and Economies of Scale 218
Profit Maximization 221
Present Value 222
Economic Insight: Present Value and Lottery Jackpots 224
Summary 227
New Terms 227

Questions for Discussion 227
Suggestions for Further Reading 228

CHAPTER 9 PERFECT COMPETITION 229
Introduction 229
Characteristics of Perfect Competition 229
Competitive Adjustment in the Short Run 230
The Long Run: Constant, Increasing, or Decreasing Costs 237
International Perspective: Culture, Markets, and Enterprise 238
Economic Profile: David Ricardo (1772–1823) 243
Competitive Equilibrium: What's So Great about Perfect Competition? 245
An Example of Perfect Competition 247
Large Numbers of Buyers: Competition on the Buyer's Side 247
Economic Rent in Perfect Competition 248
Summary 250
New Terms 250
Questions for Discussion 250
Suggestions for Further Reading 251

CHAPTER 10 MONOPOLY 253
Introduction 253
Demand and Marginal Revenue 254
Price and Output Decisions under Monopoly 255
Is Monopoly Bad? 260
International Perspective: Multinational Corporations as Monopolies in Foreign Countries 261
Real-World Monopolies 265
Monopoly Power and Price Discrimination 266
International Perspective: State Trading Monopolies 270
The Costs of Monopoly 271
Who Runs the Firm? Alternatives to Profit Maximization 273
Economic Profile: Herbert Simon (1916–) 274
Fallacies and Facts about Monopoly 276
Contestable Markets 277
Summary 278
New Terms 279
Questions for Discussion 280
Suggestions for Further Reading 280

CHAPTER 11 MONOPOLISTIC COMPETITION AND OLIGOPOLY 281
Introduction 281
Monopolistic Competition 282
Economic Profile: Joan Robinson (1903–1983) and Edward Chamberlin (1899–1967) 283
Resource Allocation in Monopolistic Competition 289
Oligopoly 290
Collusiveness and Oligopolies 290
International Perspective: Commodity Cartels 293
Economic Profile: George Stigler (1911–) and Paul Sweezy (1910–) 301
Market Structures in Review 304
Summary 305
New Terms 305
Questions for Discussion 305
Suggestions for Further Reading 306

Contents

**CHAPTER 12 THEORY IN THE REAL WORLD:
REGULATION, DEREGULATION, AND ANTITRUST POLICY 307**
Introduction 307
What Is an Industry? 307
Industry Structure 309
Concentration and Performance 311
International Perspective: Will Europe Become Monopolized? 315
Policies Aimed at Reducing Monopoly Power 317
Monopoly Regulation 319
Antitrust Laws in the United States 323
International Perspective: Antitrust Abroad 325
Competitiveness 333
Alternatives for Controlling Industry 335
Summary 335
New Terms 336
Questions for Discussion 336
Suggestions for Further Reading 337

**PART 4
FACTOR MARKETS 339**

CHAPTER 13 MARGINAL PRODUCTIVITY THEORY AND LABOR MARKETS 340
Introduction 340
Special Features of the Demand for Labor 341
Economic Profile: John Bates Clark (1847–1938) 342
The Market for Labor with Perfect Competition 343
A Competitive Labor Market with a Monopolistic Product Market 347
International Perspective: U.S. Immigration Policy and Wage Rates 348
Monopsony 351
Determinants of the Elasticity of the Demand for Labor 354
Shifts in the Demand for Labor 355
Productivity and Human Capital 357
Comparable Worth 360
International Perspective: Comparable Worth, Canadian Style 361
Marginal Productivity and Income 362
Summary 363
New Terms 363
Questions for Discussion 363
Suggestions for Further Reading 364

CHAPTER 14 THE LABOR MOVEMENT IN THE UNITED STATES 365
Introduction 365
The Economics of Union Goals 365
Types of Unions 367
Economic Effects of Unions 371
Economic Insight: If You Like Your Job, Thank Your Parents 374
A Short History of the Labor Movement 375
International Perspective: Labor Strikes, Soviet Style 378
International Perspective: The Foreign Policy of the AFL-CIO 384
Forces That Strengthen Unions 387
Forces That Weaken Unions 387
Summary 389
New Terms 389

Questions for Discussion   389
Suggestions for Further Reading   390

CHAPTER 15   RENT, INTEREST, AND PROFIT   391
Introduction   391
Land and Rent   391
Economic Profile: Henry George (1839–1897)   394
Capital and Interest   395
International Perspective: California, the Twenty-Fourth Ward   397
Enterprise and Profits   400
International Perspective: Multinational Corporations   401
The Distribution of Income   403
Summary   405
New Terms   406
Questions for Discussion   406
Suggestions for Further Reading   406

CHAPTER 16   INCOME DISTRIBUTION: POVERTY, DISCRIMINATION, AND WELFARE   407
Introduction   407
The Personal Distribution of Income and Poverty   408
Economic Profile: Thomas Sowell (1930–)   413
Discrimination and the Distribution of Income   414
Income Redistribution   419
Government Transfer Programs in Practice   423
International Perspective: Social Welfare Systems in Other Countries   424
The Welfare Reform Debate   429
Summary   433
New Terms   433
Questions for Discussion   434
Suggestions for Further Reading   434

PART 5
MARKET FAILURE, GOVERNMENT FAILURE, AND PUBLIC CHOICE   435

CHAPTER 17   MARKET FAILURE AND GOVERNMENT INTERVENTION   436
Introduction   436
Law, Economics, and Government   436
Externalities   438
International Perspective: The Japanese Legal System   439
Economic Insight: The Fable of the Bees   444
International Perspective: Paying to Pollute in Europe   449
Public Goods   450
Public Goods in Practice   453
Welfare Economics   455
Summary   455
New Terms   456
Questions for Discussion   456
Suggestions for Further Reading   457

CHAPTER 18   GOVERNMENT FAILURE AND PUBLIC CHOICE   459
Introduction   459
Public Choice Theory   459
Economic Insight: To Vote or Not to Vote—An Economic Decision?   461

Rent Seeking   462
Rent Defending   465
Analysis of the Political Market   465
International Perspective: A Problem with *Perestroika*   469
Other Schools of Thought   471
Summary   474
New Terms   474
Questions for Discussion   475
Suggestions for Further Reading   475

Chapter 19 Agriculture, Cities, and the Environment: Case Studies in Market Failure and Government Failure   477
Introduction   477
The Farm Problem   478
International Perspective: Agricultural Policy, European Community Style   483
Urban Economics   486
The Future of the Environment   492
International Perspective: Chernobyl, a Disaster for the Lapps   495
Summary   501
New Terms   502
Questions for Discussion   502
Suggestions for Further Reading   502

Part 6
The World Economy   505

Chapter 20 International Trade   506
Introduction   506
Why Nations Trade   506
The Why and How of Protection   512
Economic Insight: U.S. Barriers to Imports   516
The Politics of Protection   517
Common Arguments for Protection   518
Sophisticated Arguments for Protection   520
Fair Trade and the Maintenance of the U.S. Market   522
Economic Insight: The United States and Free Trade Pacts   523
Movement of Resources   524
Multinational Corporations   525
Summary   527
New Terms   527
Questions for Discussion   527
Suggestions for Further Reading   528

Chapter 21 International Finance   529
Introduction   529
The Market for Foreign Exchange   529
The Balance of Payments   535
International Monetary Systems   537
International Perspective: Tourism and the Balance of Payments   538
Economic Insight: The Gold Buffs   541
International Perspective: Watching Currencies under Floating Rates   546
Summary   547

New Terms 547
Questions for Discussion 548
Suggestions for Further Reading 548

CHAPTER 22 COMPARATIVE ECONOMIC SYSTEMS IN THEORY AND PRACTICE 549
Introduction 549
Ideologies 550
International Perspective: China, Hong Kong, and Taiwan 552
Marx, Marxists, and Marxism 554
Leaderisms 555
Organization and Decision-Making Approach to
  Comparing Economic Systems 560
Planning 562
Reforms: Economic Freedom and Political Freedom 566
International Perspective: Reform in East Germany, Poland, Hungary, and
  Czechoslovakia 570
Japan 572
Summary 574
New Terms 575
Questions for Discussion 575
Suggestions for Further Reading 575

GLOSSARY G-1

INDEX I-1

PRINCIPLES OF MICROECONOMICS
FIFTH EDITION

INTRODUCTION TO ECONOMICS

1

AFTER STUDYING THIS CHAPTER, YOU SHOULD BE ABLE TO:

1. Define economics and distinguish between microeconomics and macroeconomics.
2. Explain why you should study economics.
3. Discuss how economics is related to other social sciences.
4. Explain the relationship between scarcity and choice.
5. Define and give examples of opportunity cost.
6. Use a production possibilities curve to show:
    a. opportunity cost,
    b. increasing opportunity cost,
    c. economic growth,
    d. unemployment of the factors of production.
7. Identify the basic elements of an economic model and explain how it can be tested.
8. Interpret the self-interest assumption and explain why it is important in economics.
9. Explain and give examples of:
    a. the association-causation fallacy,
    b. the fallacy of composition,
    c. the *ceteris paribus* fallacy.
10. List the steps followed in policy analysis.

CHAPTER 1

ECONOMICS, ECONOMIC ISSUES, AND ECONOMIC METHODS

INTRODUCTION

In this chapter, we explore what economics is, stressing the basic economic problem of scarcity and choice. In order to do that, we introduce you to your first economic model—the production possibilities curve. We then generalize from this model to some properties of models in general. Finally, we explain how economists use models to think about economic problems and develop policies to address those problems. By the end of this chapter, you will have begun to think like an economist.

WHAT IS ECONOMICS?

economics
The study of how people and institutions make decisions about production and consumption and how they face the problem of scarcity.

microeconomics
The study of individual market interactions, focusing on production and consumption by the individual consumer, firm, or industry.

Economics is the study of how people, individually and through institutions, make decisions about producing and consuming goods and services and how they face the problem of scarcity. The word *economics* comes from the Greek *oikonomos*, which means household management. The study of economics is divided into microeconomics and macroeconomics.

Micro, or *mikros*, is a Greek prefix meaning small. **Microeconomics** describes the interactions of producers and consumers in individual markets, such as the market for cars. It also examines interactions between such markets, for example, the impact of changes in the demand for steel on the price of aluminum.

The Greek prefix *macro*, or *makros*, means long or large. So, as you might expect, the study of the economy as a whole is called **macroeconomics**. Macroeconomics is concerned with **aggregates**, or quantities whose values are determined by adding across many markets. Macroeconomics studies the behavior of variables that describe the whole economy, such as the value of the total output that the economy produces in a given time period. Macroeconomics also examines the behavior of such aggregates as the price level and total employment or unemployment. Values of these aggregates are derived from many individual markets taken together.

In both microeconomics and macroeconomics, the most important tools are demand and supply, which are developed in Chapter 3. Demand and supply help to explain prices and outputs in individual markets. These tools also explain the relation between prices and outputs in different markets. In microeconomics, you may look at the demand for the output of a single industry, such as bicycle manufacturing. In macroeconomics, you look at the level of prices and output for the economy as a whole, using aggregate demand and aggregate supply as the main tools. Even though microeconomics and macroeconomics are often studied separately, they are closely related.

macroeconomics
The study of the economy as a whole or of economic aggregates, such as the level of employment and the growth of total output.

aggregates
Quantities whose values are determined by adding across many markets.

ECONOMICS IN RELATION TO OTHER FIELDS

Economics is usually classed as a **social science**. This label makes economics an academic relative of political science, sociology, psychology, and anthropology. All of these fields look at the behavior of human beings, individually and in groups. They study different subsets of the actions and interactions of human beings. (For this reason, they are also sometimes termed *behavioral sciences*.)

social science
An academic field that studies the behavior of human beings, individually and in groups, and examines their interactions.

Economics focuses on the consumption, production, and use of scarce resources by individuals and groups. Economics is also concerned with the processes by which households and firms make decisions about the use of scarce resources. This definition of the "territory" of economics leads to some overlap with the other social sciences. Psychologists and economists share an interest in what causes people to take certain actions. However, economists are primarily interested in actions that are reflected in market activity or in economic decisions made through government. Sociologists are interested in all facets of organized human activity. Economists, however, are interested mainly in organized activities that relate to the production and consumption of goods and services.

In general, economists assume that individuals pursue their own self-interest and respond to various signals or incentives in light of that self-interest. Although that assumption may seem obvious, it is a somewhat different view of human behavior from that of psychologists and sociologists. It often leads economists to draw different conclusions. As you learn more about economics, you will better understand how it overlaps with—and differs from—other social sciences.

WHY STUDY ECONOMICS?

Economics is a required course for many different majors. You may be wondering why this is so. One reason is that economics interacts with almost all other academic subjects. It affects and is affected by current events. Also, it has a major effect on politics, both domestic and international.

A second reason for studying economics is the impact that economic ideas and theories have on world leaders. Much of what political decision makers do is based on economic theory. As John Maynard Keynes, an economist who has had great influence on macroeconomic policy in this century, wrote:

The ideas of economists and political philosophers, both when they are right and when they are wrong, are more powerful than is commonly understood. Indeed, the world is ruled by little else. Practical men, who believe themselves to be quite exempt from any intellectual influences, are usually the slaves of some defunct economist. Madmen in authority, who hear voices in the air, are distilling their frenzy from some academic scribbler of a few years back.[1]

Keynes was saying that if you want to understand what politicians, great or mad, are trying to do, you must understand the economic theories on which they are acting.

A third reason for studying economics is that it provides a better understanding of how society functions. Economic theory is very useful in understanding behavior because it allows the development of models with predictive power. As Alfred Marshall, another noted economist, wrote, "Economics is the study of mankind in the ordinary business of life."[2]

Finally, economics is fun, and people who are trained in economics find rewarding jobs and careers. If you like to think in a logical fashion, you will enjoy studying economics.

SCARCITY: LIMITED RESOURCES, INSATIABLE WANTS

scarcity
The central economic problem that there are not enough resources to produce everything that individuals want.

Whether you are just taking one course or planning a career in economics, the most important single problem you will address is that of **scarcity.** That is, there are not enough resources to produce all the goods and services people would like to consume. The first tool we will develop is an economic model that is used to explain how any economic system deals with the basic problem of scarcity. Human wants and desires are vast, relative to the resources available to satisfy them. Thus, in every economic system, there has to be some method for making choices among different desirable ends.

We live in a world of limited resources. Resources are whatever can be used to produce goods and services for human consumption. Some resources, such as oil and coal, are converted to energy and used up in the course of production or consumption. Others are not used up in that sense but are virtually fixed in quantity. Examples are land, diamonds, and copper. At any given time, even the quantity of resources created by people—roads, factories, machines, and skilled labor—cannot be changed quickly or cheaply.

insatiable wants
The needs and desires of human beings, which can never be completely satisfied.

Limited resources conflict with **insatiable wants**. Human wants are said to be insatiable (unable to be satisfied) because no matter how much peo-

---

1. J. M. Keynes, *The General Theory of Employment, Interest, and Money* (London: Macmillan, 1936), 383.
2. Alfred Marshall, *Principles of Economics*, 8th ed. (Don Mills, Ontario: Macmillan of Canada, 1920), 323.

ple have, they always want more of something. You may know people who seem perfectly content with what they have. If you questioned them carefully, however, you would probably find that they would like cleaner air, more time to play tennis or golf, or more shelters for the homeless. Since not all wants can be satisfied, individuals have to choose which ones to satisfy with limited available resources. In fact, every society is faced with the problem of scarcity and choice. Without scarcity, there would be no need to make choices about what desires or needs to satisfy—and thus no need to study economics.

OPPORTUNITY COSTS

Every decision to produce or consume something means sacrificing the production or consumption of something else. For instance, the cost of going to a football game includes the value of what is given up in order to attend. Economists use the term **opportunity cost** to denote the full value of the best alternative that is given up, or forgone. Part of the cost of attending a football game is the price of the ticket. This price represents the other goods and services you could have purchased with that money instead. However, there is another important part of the cost. This second part is the most valuable alternative use of those three hours, such as studying for a test. The opportunity cost of attending the game consists of both the price of the ticket and the difference in your test grade that three more hours of study would have produced. Even if the ticket had no monetary price, going to the game would still have an opportunity cost.

opportunity cost
The value of the other alternatives given up in order to enjoy a particular good or service.

Many people have problems grasping the concept of opportunity cost because they are used to thinking of cost as price, or the amount of money spent on an item or an activity. In economics, however, the concept of cost is much broader. It includes not only the dollar outlay (the other goods you could have purchased) but also the time cost (the earnings or satisfaction you could have produced for yourself in some other activity) and other sacrifices you might have made. Sometimes it is difficult to place a dollar value on these other costs, but they still play an important role in economic decisions.

SOME APPLICATIONS OF OPPORTUNITY COST

Your everyday life provides many illustrations of the concept of opportunity cost. For example, what is the opportunity cost of attending college? It is not simply the dollar figure given in your college's catalog. Money spent on books and tuition is certainly part of the opportunity cost. However, the expense of your room, meals, and clothing is not, because you would have incurred those costs even if you weren't in college. The catalog may list them as costs, but economists don't count them because they are not opportunity costs.

One important opportunity cost not listed in any college catalog is the income you could have been earning during the years you are spending in classes. For most students, that lost income will eventually be made up in higher future earnings. However, right now it is an opportunity cost that should be included. Even if you can earn only $5 an hour, if you have to cut your working hours by 30 hours a week during the 32 weeks a year you are in school, the lost earnings represent a cost of $4,800 a year.

For some students, the opportunity cost of going to college is even higher. Suppose you are a talented athlete who could play professionally right after high school, as many baseball and tennis players do. Your college education may cost as much as $100,000 a year in lost earnings. After several years of college, many football and basketball players face this dilemma. Even if they are straight-A students, the opportunity cost of completing a degree in terms of lost income is very high. It is not surprising that many of them choose to "turn pro" and postpone or abandon getting a degree.

Another illustration of opportunity cost is provided by the proposal of some politicians that there should be two years of national service for all young adults. This service would be in the military or some other part of the public sector and would pay very low wages. For some, the opportunity cost would be very low because they have few good employment opportunities. But for someone with an engineering or accounting degree, athletic skills, or other potential for good earnings, the opportunity cost would be very high. Universal national service is a tax on being young. Such a tax would be very different for different individuals.

OPPORTUNITY COST AND THE CHOICE CURVE

We can illustrate the concept of opportunity cost and its relationship to choice using a very simple example. Assume that you have $40 to spend and you have two choices: pizza and cola. Pizzas cost $8 each, and colas cost $2 for a six-pack. To keep things simple, we assume that you wish to spend the whole $40. Figure 1 shows the various combinations of pizza and cola that you can buy with $40. If you spend the entire $40 on pizza, you can purchase 5 pizzas (the *y*-intercept in Figure 1). On the other hand, you can

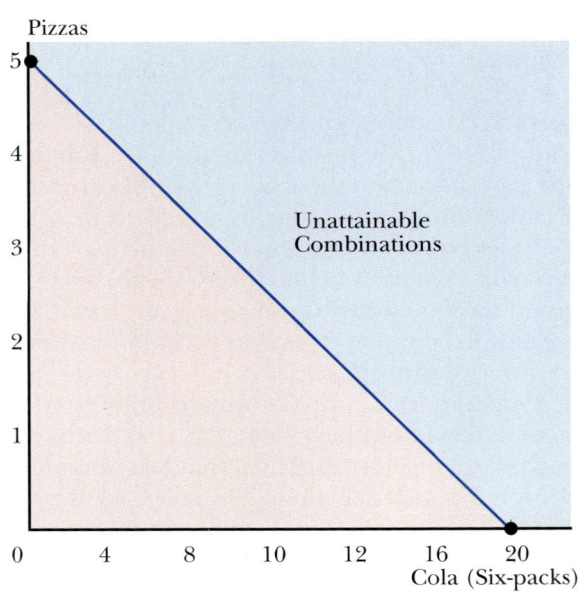

FIGURE 1
CHOICE AMONG ALTERNATIVES
If six-packs of cola cost $2 and pizzas cost $8, a person with $40 to spend has many attainable combinations of cola and pizza. The line *PR* represents the boundary between attainable and unattainable combinations. Along line *PR*, the opportunity cost of 1 pizza is 4 six-packs of cola.

International Perspective

The Nobel Prize for Economics

The Nobel Committee, established by the Swedish Royal Academy of Sciences, awarded the first Nobel Prize in 1901. These prizes include awards for peace, as well as physics, chemistry, literature, and medicine. They were originally funded by a bequest from the inventor of dynamite, Alfred Nobel. It wasn't until 1969, however, that the first Nobel Prize for Economics was awarded. The Bank of Sweden funded this prize to celebrate its 300th anniversary.

The addition of an economics prize puts economics in a distinguished family of academic disciplines. It is the only social science to be so honored. Receipt of a Nobel Prize is a high honor for an economist and financially rewarding.

The Nobel Prize winners in economics have made profound and very diverse contributions to this field. Many of the European winners are noted for their work in international or development economics. These include Myrdal, Meade, Ohlin, and Lewis. More than half the winners have been Americans. The following are the winners of the prize since 1969:

- 1969 Ragnar Frisch, Norway
  Jan Tinbergen, Netherlands
- 1970 Paul A. Samuelson, United States
- 1971 Simon Kuznets, United States
- 1972 Kenneth J. Arrow, United States
  Sir John R. Hicks, Great Britain
- 1973 Wassily Leontief, United States
- 1974 Gunnar Myrdal, Sweden
  Friedrich A. von Hayek, Great Britain
- 1975 Leonid V. Kantorovich, Soviet Union
  Tjalling C. Koopmans, Netherlands/United States
- 1976 Milton Friedman, United States
- 1977 James E. Meade, Great Britain
  Bertil Ohlin, Sweden
- 1978 Herbert A. Simon, United States
- 1979 Sir Arthur Lewis, Great Britain
  Theodore Schultz, United States
- 1980 Lawrence R. Klein, United States
- 1981 James Tobin, United States
- 1982 George Stigler, United States
- 1983 Gerard Debreu, France/United States
- 1984 Sir Richard Stone, Great Britain
- 1985 Franco Modigliani, United States
- 1986 James M. Buchanan, United States
- 1987 Robert Solow, United States
- 1988 Maurice Altais, France
- 1989 Trigve Haavelmo, Norway
- 1990 Harry M. Markowitz, United States
  Merton H. Miller, United States
  William F. Sharpe, United States

buy 20 six-packs of cola with $40 (as shown by the *x*-intercept in Figure 1). Other possibilities lie along the line that connects these two intercepts. The line represents all possible combinations of pizza and cola that total $40.[3] Of course, all combinations in the shaded area of Figure 1 are also attainable. However, these combinations wouldn't exhaust your entire $40.[4] Combinations above and to the right of the line are not attainable because they cost more than $40.

Figure 1 illustrates the array of choices and the concept of opportunity cost. The price of 1 pizza is the same as the price of 4 six-packs of cola. The decision to purchase a pizza means the sacrifice of those six-packs that could have been purchased instead. Opportunity cost is measured by the slope of the choice line.[5]

SOCIETY'S CHOICES: THE PRODUCTION POSSIBILITIES CURVE

From the perspective of the economy as a whole, the choice is not how to spend income between alternative purchases but how to allocate available productive resources between alternative goods that could be produced. This problem is illustrated by a close relative of the choice curve of Figure 1. Society's choice curve is called a **production possibilities curve**. This curve shows the various output combinations of two goods or groups of goods that can be produced in an economy with the available resources. This simple economic model is based on a few assumptions:

production possibilities curve
A graph that depicts the various combinations of two goods that can be produced in an economy with the available resources.

1. All of the economy's productive resources are fully employed. This means that everyone who wants a job has one. Also, factories, land, and other resources are being used to full capacity. (These resources will be discussed in greater detail in the next chapter.)
2. There are only two goods (or types of goods) in the economy.
3. The resources used in production are interchangeable. One worker is the same as another, one machine can be substituted for another, and all land is equally useful for producing the two goods.
4. We are looking at the economy at a specific period of time (the short run). During this time period, both the quantity and quality of resources are fixed, and the technology does not change.

Given these four assumptions, we can look at a simple example of a

---

3. The line *PR* is a continuous line. It is easy to see that points *A* and *B* represent attainable combinations because both contain whole numbers of colas and pizzas. Connecting these points implies that you can purchase fractional units of cola and pizza, for example, half of a six-pack of cola. Since we usually purchase goods in whole units, it might seem strange to show fractional units as attainable combinations. This is merely a convenient assumption. If the numbers on the axes are large enough, for example, hundreds of pizzas and thousands of colas, then there is less problem in visualizing the array of choices as a continuous line.
4. We have ruled out the possibility of saving part of the $40 because we are assuming only two alternative uses of funds: pizza and cola. If saving were an option, there would really be three goods: pizza, cola, and savings. Faced with only two alternatives, we can only choose how to divide the money between them.
5. If you have forgotten how to measure the slope of a line, you should refer to the appendix on graphs to refresh your memory.

Soybeans (Tons)	Missiles
20	0
16	1
12	2
8	3
4	4
0	5

TABLE 1
PRODUCTION POSSIBILITIES SCHEDULE

production possibilities curve. Table 1 shows combinations of missiles and soybeans that an economy can produce. Figure 2 plots the numbers of Table 1 on a graph. Line *PR* in Figure 2 is a production possibilities curve. It represents all the combinations of missiles and soybeans that can be produced in this economy when the available resources are fully employed.

In Figure 2, points *A* and *B* represent two different combinations of missiles and soybeans that both lie on the production possibilities curve. Points *A* and *B* are both output combinations that can be attained in this economy with the available resources. Point *C* is also attainable. Since it lies inside of line *PR*, however, it represents unemployed resources. There are points on *PR* that have to be better than *C* because they represent more missiles, more soybeans, or more of both. The economy can do better, that is, can produce more. Therefore, *C* is inferior to points on the production possibilities curve.

The line *PR* in Figure 2 can also be used to measure opportunity cost for the economy. Line *PR* is a straight line. This fact implies that the opportunity cost of one product in terms of the other is constant. That is, the number of missiles given up to get another ton of soybeans doesn't

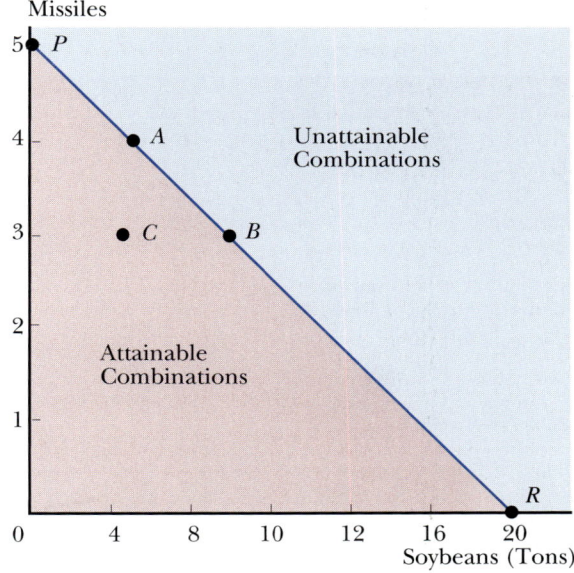

FIGURE 2
PRODUCTION POSSIBILITIES CURVE
A production possibilities curve shows combinations of two goods that can be produced in an economy, with fixed resources and technology. Points on the curve represent the full employment of resources.

change along line *PR*. Each time the production of soybeans is increased by 1 ton, one-quarter of a missile is sacrificed. The opportunity cost of 1 more ton of soybeans is one-quarter of a missile. Conversely, the opportunity cost of 1 more missile is 4 tons of soybeans.

Opportunity cost of one good in terms of another is constant along line *PR* in Figure 2 because we assumed that all resources are alike for production purposes. That is, any unit of resources is just as good as any other unit in producing either soybeans or missiles. This assumption produces a straight-line production possibilities curve.

INCREASING OPPORTUNITY COSTS

After an economist has constructed a model, the next step is to go back and vary the assumptions to see what difference they make. Consider what happens when we drop the third assumption stated above—that productive resources are interchangeable. That is, we no longer assume that one unit of labor or land is just as productive as another for producing either good. Table 2 shows a different set of combinations of missiles and soybeans that can be produced in this economy. These combinations are plotted on the graph in Figure 3. At point *A* in Figure 3, output is 10 missiles and 200 tons of soybeans. At point *B*, output consists of more missiles, 100, but fewer soybeans, only 100 tons.

The production possibilities curve in Figure 3 is bowed, or curved, instead of being a straight line. This new shape reflects the change in the assumption that resources are alike. Here we are being more realistic and assuming that some resources are better suited to the production of missiles and others to the production of soybeans. This change in assumptions produces a model that differs from the first one in what it implies about opportunity cost.

If the economy is at point *A* in Figure 3, we can get another 10 missiles by shifting resources from soybean production to missile production. In moving from point *A* to point *C*, we must give up only a small amount of soybeans, 5 units. But to move from point *B* to point *D*, producing an-

TABLE 2
PRODUCTION POSSIBILITIES SCHEDULE

SOYBEANS	MISSILES
205	0
(A) 200 ⎱ −5	10 ⎱ +10
(C) 195 ⎰	20 ⎰
187	30
179	40
169	50
158	60
146	70
133	80
117	90
(B) 100 ⎱ −23	100 ⎱ +10
(D) 77 ⎰	110 ⎰
50	120
0	130
0	130

Chapter 1 Economics, Economic Issues, and Economic Methods

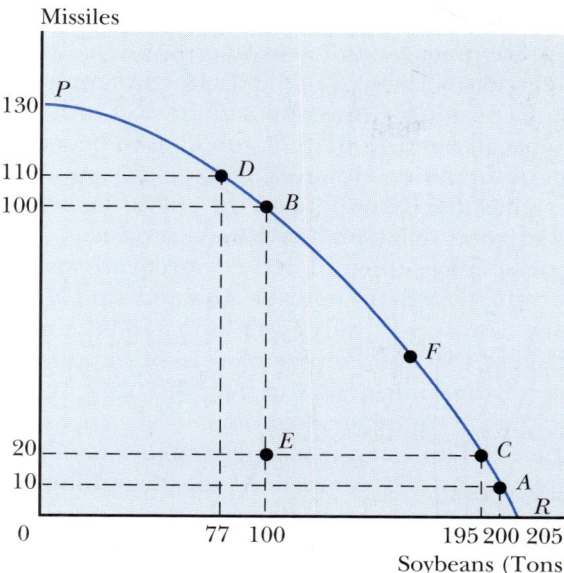

FIGURE 3
PRODUCTION POSSIBILITIES AND INCREASING OPPORTUNITY COSTS
On this production possibilities curve, the opportunity cost of additional units of soybeans increases as the economy becomes more specialized in soybeans: producing each additional unit of soybeans requires a larger sacrifice of missiles than before (increasing opportunity cost). If the economy is inside the production possibilities curve at some point such as E, more of both goods could be produced.

other 10 missiles requires a larger sacrifice of soybeans, 23 units instead of 5. This curved production possibilities curve illustrates the very important principle of **increasing opportunity cost**. That is, the more missiles that are already being produced, the larger the sacrifice of soybeans required to get additional missiles. Table 2 shows that between points A and C, ten more missiles cost 5 units of soybeans. Between points B and D, however, ten more missiles cost 23 units of soybeans.

Increasing opportunity costs are obvious in wartime. As more war goods are demanded, civilian sacrifices increase. Initially, as military production expands, additional labor and other resources are used that are relatively more productive for making missiles and relatively less productive for growing soybeans. As the switch to missiles continues, however, military production takes resources that are relatively less productive for making missiles, although they were highly productive for growing soybeans. Soybean production falls by larger and larger amounts, therefore, because more resources are stripped away from soybeans for every extra missile produced. These resources are increasingly those best suited to producing soybeans and least adaptable to missile production.

increasing opportunity cost The principle that as production of one good rises, larger and larger sacrifices of another are required.

UNEMPLOYMENT
For the straight-line version of the production possibilities curve, another important assumption was that all resources are fully employed. If we drop that assumption, the production possibilities curve can also illustrate unemployment and the effect of reducing it. Suppose the economy is at point E in Figure 3. This point is inside the production possibilities curve because some workers, factories, land, and machines are unemployed. If the economy could move from point E to point C, it would be possible to have more soybeans (195 tons instead of 100) with no sacrifice of missiles.

Moving from point E to point B would mean producing the same amount of soybeans (100 tons) but more missiles (100 instead of 20). Finally, at point F, more of both missiles and soybeans could be produced simply by putting idle resources to work. At point E, the opportunity cost of both soybeans and missiles is zero because none of either good has to be sacrificed to increase production of the other. However, there is an opportunity cost to being at point E rather than elsewhere on the curve. This cost is equal to the output of either good that could have been produced.

From a macroeconomic perspective, unemployed resources are wasteful. They represent extra production that could be attained simply by putting idle resources to work. The opportunity cost of the goods gained is zero. Thus, economists believe that full employment is an important goal. It is important not just for the individual who needs to work in order to earn income, but also for the aggregate economy.

Both World War II and the Vietnam War made Americans aware of the importance of the full employment of resources. At the beginning of World War II, there were unemployed resources. It was therefore possible to produce more war goods (missiles) without a sacrifice of consumer goods (soybeans). Eventually, all the idle resources were employed. Then further expansion of the production of war goods required the sacrifice of consumer goods. No cars were produced for several years during World War II as auto factories switched to making military tanks and trucks. Other consumer goods were also in short supply. The Vietnam War occurred at a time of relatively low unemployment in the late 1960s. Thus, expanding production of military hardware and diverting labor from civilian activities to soldiering led immediately to reduced production of consumer goods. The economy was already on the production possibilities curve when the United States was drawn into the Vietnam War.

One of the main concerns of macroeconomics is explaining how an economy can find itself inside the production possibilities curve at a point such as E in Figure 3. How can an economic system avoid the idleness and waste of unemployed resources? If an economy finds itself at a point such as E, what can be done to get back on the production possibilities curve? These are important questions in the study of macroeconomics. The production possibilities curve is a useful technique for identifying these questions.

ECONOMIC GROWTH

Another macroeconomic issue that can be illustrated by the production possibilities model is economic growth. If technology can improve and the quantity of resources can increase, then output can grow beyond the limits of the production possibilities curve. Better technology or more resources means a change in the fourth assumption stated earlier—that both resources and technology are fixed. As labor becomes more skilled and productive, and as producers acquire new machines and plants embodying the latest technology, the production possibilities curve shifts outward.

An outward shift of a production possibilities curve is shown in Figure 4. If the economy is at point A on PR, production consists of D_1 units of soybeans and C_1 units of missiles. With the shift of the curve to P_1R_1, it is

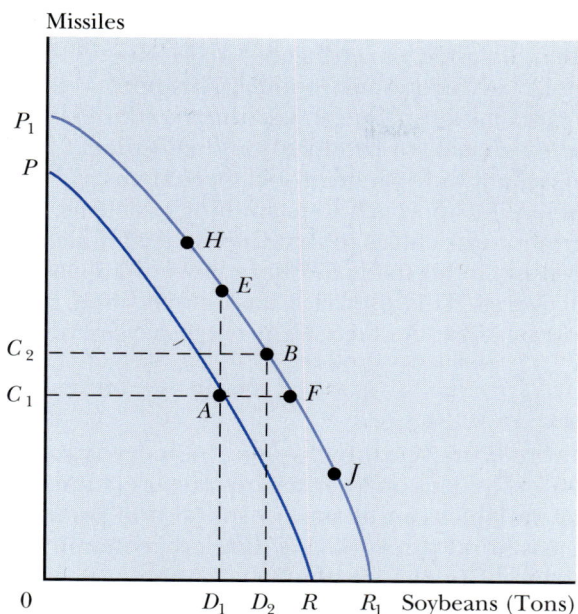

FIGURE 4
SHIFT OF THE PRODUCTION POSSIBILITIES CURVE
An outward shift of the production possibilities curve from PR to P_1R_1 means that the economy can produce more of both goods (economic growth).

possible to reach some point, such as point B, that includes more of both soybeans (D_2 units) and missiles (C_2 units). Other possible combinations on the new production possibilities curve include the same amount of one good and more of the other (such as point E or F) or less of one good and more of the other (such as point H or J). No matter which combination is produced, the important thing about an outward shift of a production possibilities curve is that it increases the economy's capacity to respond to human wants.

Added resources, usually labor or capital, are sources of economic growth. New technology can also shift a production possibilities curve outward and account for economic growth. Invention, innovation, discovery of resources, and improvements in productivity all contribute to economic growth.

THE PRODUCTION POSSIBILITIES CURVE SHOWS:	
• Attainable combinations	Points on the curve
• Opportunity cost	The slope of the curve
• Unemployment of resources	Points below or inside the curve
• Economic growth	A shift of the curve to the right

THEORIES, HYPOTHESES, AND MODELS

The production possibilities curve is a theoretical model. Based on certain assumptions (two products, a brief time period, fixed resources, given technology), we theorized that output of one good would grow in a predictable way if output of the other good was reduced. The production possibilities curve is just one of many economic models. This book will develop and use a variety of these models. You can use them to understand the workings of markets, the behavior of producers and consumers, and the effects of various policies on a wide range of social problems.

A model represents a scientific approach to examining problems. Scientists of all kinds differ from nonscientists in that they deal with facts in a systematic way. Early scientists in all fields did little more than classify the facts they or others uncovered. This approach has limited value, however. It is very easy to get lost in a forest of facts, even when they are neatly filed and classified.

THEORIES AND HYPOTHESES

theory
A set of principles that can be used to make inferences about the world.

Theories play an important role in everything we do. A **theory** is an abstraction from reality that tries to focus on a cause-and-effect relationship between two variables. The variables can be money supply and prices in macroeconomics or labor costs and prices of cars in microeconomics. A theory is useful in that it simplifies observations by clearing away irrelevant details. In a way, a theory allows you to see the forest instead of the trees. Any interpretation of our environment is based on an implicit theory about cause-and-effect relationships. Our senses receive information, and we interpret that information on the basis of some theory about the world we have developed over time. These theories are constantly being revised and improved to better explain the facts. A good theory will develop **testable hypotheses**, which are mini-theories that can be verified or disproved by checking them against facts or experiences. Even small children, for example, quickly develop testable hypotheses based on experience: "My finger will hurt if I touch the hot stove," or "The cat will scratch me if I pull its tail."

testable hypothesis
An inference from a theory that can be subjected to real-world testing.

MODELS

Economic theorists, like other scientists, develop theories that will yield testable hypotheses.[6] Then they test these hypotheses by comparing them with the facts and seeing if they are consistent.

model
A set of assumptions and hypotheses that is a simplified description of reality.

A **model** is a formal statement of a theory, usually in the form of graphs or equations. In the simpler model of the production possibilities curve as a straight line, we assumed that all productive resources were alike. As a result, the relationship between outputs of the two goods was a constant one. In the more complex model, we introduced an alternative assumption—that all resources were not alike. The model then predicted that increased production of one good would require increasing sacrifices of the other.

An economic model will generate one or more "if-then" hypotheses about what will happen in the real world. These hypotheses are then

---

6. Not everyone agrees that economics, or any of the other social sciences, is scientific in the same sense as the natural sciences. This debate has been going on for a century. It started with an essay by Thorstein Veblen in the *Quarterly Journal of Economics* in 1889. For a more recent discussion of this issue, see Alfred Eichner, "Can Economics Become a Science?" *Challenge* (November-December 1986): 4–12.

tested in real situations or experiments. The production possibilities model offers several such testable hypotheses. For example, according to this model, if a larger share of resources is devoted to production of military goods (missiles), then less will be available for consumer goods (soybeans). During the Vietnam War, President Lyndon Johnson was convinced that there were enough idle resources in the U.S. economy to expand both military and civilian output at the same time. As the economy quickly reached full employment, it became apparent that continuing to produce military goods and to divert some productive resources (young men) into fighting could be done only at the expense of producing less housing, education, and other goods and services for consumers.

At the beginning of the 1990s policy makers were anticipating another test of the above hypothesis—in the opposite direction. If reforms in the Soviet Union and Eastern Europe did indeed lead to reduced spending on defense in the United States, most economists expected that the resources released from military use would lead to a large increase in output of civilian goods. Politicians named those released resources the "peace dividend." They were making plans to divert them to such civilian uses as education, housing, anti-drug programs, and bailing out the savings and loan industry, when war broke out in the Persian Gulf. A peace dividend may still occur, but not as soon as many people had hoped.

Assumptions

Unlike physical scientists, economists rarely have the chance to conduct controlled experiments to validate their models. Instead, economists most often test hypotheses by looking at actual experiences in markets. Such experiments are often referred to by economists as *ceteris paribus* experiments. *Ceteris paribus* is a Latin phrase that means "all else being equal." An economist changes one variable in a theoretical model (for example, the technology for producing missiles in the production possibilities model). The economist then predicts what would happen *ceteris paribus*, or if everything else remained constant. The **ceteris paribus assumption**, or holding everything else constant, is the most common and most important assumption in economic models. If the technology of missile production improved but there was no change in the technology of producing soybeans, the production possibilities curve would shift out as in Figure 5, from PR to PR_1. The economist would predict an increase in output of both commodities, but a relatively larger increase in the output of missiles. The economist must then untangle the effects of the change in missile technology on the mix of output (missiles and soybeans) from anything else that changed in the real world in the time period when this model is being tested.

In addition to the *ceteris paribus* assumption, one other assumption is a basic part of most economic models. This assumption is that most people behave in a self-interested way. In general, **self-interested behavior** consists of trying to get the most of something they want (to maximize some goal) out of available resources. For consumers, self-interested behavior means maximizing their satisfaction. For owners of productive resources, self-interest is expressed by seeking to maximize income or wealth. For busi-

ceteris paribus assumption The assumption that everything else will remain constant, used for most economic models. (*Ceteris paribus* is Latin for "all else being equal.")

self-interested behavior A basic assumption of economic theory that individual decision makers do what is best for themselves.

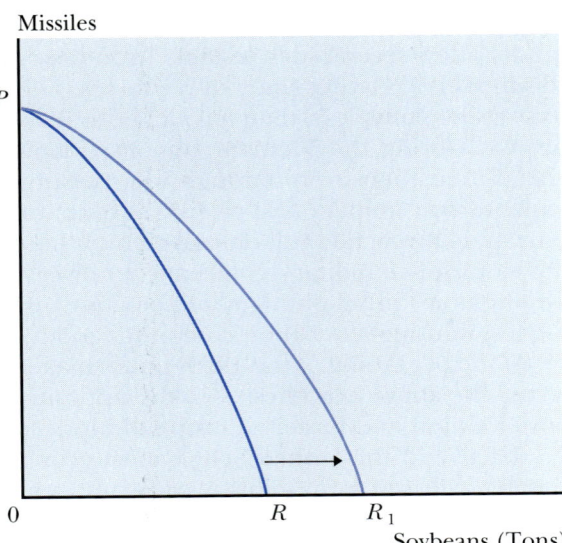

**FIGURE 5
TECHNOLOGICAL CHANGE AND THE PRODUCTION POSSIBILITIES CURVE**
A change in the technology of producing soybeans shifts the production possibilities curve from PR to PR_1. This shows that if all resources were devoted to soybeans, more could be produced. If all resources were devoted to missiles, however, no increase in output could occur. Increases in both are also possible.

ness firms, self-interest means maximizing profits.[7] In the production possibilities model, self-interested behavior will direct the decision as to which combination to produce out of all possible combinations. That combination is the one that maximizes the welfare or satisfaction of consumers.

The self-interest assumption has given economics, and economists, a good deal of undeserved bad press. This has occurred because self-interest is confused with selfishness. Critics of market economies argue that encouraging and rewarding self-interested behavior is a basic flaw in such systems. The ideas of social reformers such as Karl Marx and Mao Zedung have led to many experiments in socialism, such as the Fourier settlements in the United States and the Cultural Revolution in China. These experiments have been attempts to devise alternative ways of organizing economic activity. All of these experiments have tried to rebuild societies in such a way that individuals would act on nobler or higher motives than self-interest.

In fact, concern for others and for the community as a whole is not incompatible with self-interest because individuals define their own self-interest in terms of what is satisfying to them. Some individuals derive their greatest satisfaction from material possessions, others from leisure or enjoyment of the arts, and still others from helping others and building better communities. Some persons may derive satisfaction from all of these! So self-interested behavior is not inconsistent with volunteer work or charitable contributions. Such unselfish activities are not, by our definition, un-self-interested. This definition of self-interest is broad enough to cover the actions of Albert Schweitzer and Mother Teresa as well as those of the most unlovable of "greedy capitalist pigs."

When economists use the self-interest assumption in developing theory, they are simply saying that they expect individual behavior to be

---

7. Maximization of various kinds is a central concern of microeconomics. You can refer to the appendix on graphs to review the geometry of maximization.

influenced by costs and benefits. If the cost of a course of action declines or the benefits rise, relative to alternatives, more people will choose that course of action. For example, if the price of soybeans rises relative to that of missiles, some firms will switch production from missiles to soybeans, attracted by the higher price. If salaries for public school teachers rise relative to those of accountants, more people are likely to prepare for a teaching career and fewer to study accounting. If the penalty for speeding falls, *ceteris paribus*, more people are likely to drive faster than the posted speed limit. If the cost of giving to charity rises because it is no longer tax-deductible, less will be given to charity.

Furthermore, economists do not use the concept of self-interest to predict any one person's or firm's behavior but rather to predict average or group behavior. Such predictions are similar to the use of attributes of certain groups by insurance companies to predict how often certain events will occur. Insurance companies develop norms for various groups—life expectancies, accident rates, or numbers of house fires—and use them to set prices for policies. These norms say nothing about how likely any particular member of a group is to live past the age of 80, run a car off the road, or have a house burn to the ground.

Even economists do not always agree about the best way to develop theories and construct models. Specifically, the role of assumptions has been fiercely debated by two American Nobel Prize winners in economics, Paul Samuelson and Milton Friedman. The traditional view, taken by Samuelson, is that once a theory is demonstrated to be logically correct, its usefulness depends on whether its assumptions are realistic. This view is consistent with the role of theory in the natural sciences. Friedman disagrees, arguing that the true test of the usefulness of a theory is whether it works. That is, does it accurately predict what happens in the real world? In this book, we will be looking for logically correct theories and models that pass both kinds of tests: realistic assumptions, and accurate predictions.

BASIC ELEMENTS OF THE ECONOMIC APPROACH

This discussion of theories and models suggests that economics is much like other sciences in its methods. What is unique or different about the economic approach? There are a few emphases and ideas that help set economics apart.

1. *Like the natural sciences, economic theory is positive, or nonnormative.* **Positive statements** are if-then propositions about *what is*. In contrast, **normative statements** describe *what ought to be*. In other words, economic theory strives to be scientific. However, when economists try to apply economic theory to policy questions, they often find it difficult to keep their work positive. Economic theory is value-free. However, appliers of the theory are often tempted to mix in their values in order to favor a preferred outcome or policy. It is a positive statement to say that production of more missiles will require increasing sacrifices of soybeans. It is a normative statement to say that more missiles and fewer soybeans should be produced.

positive statements
A set of propositions about what is, rather than what ought to be.

normative statements
A set of propositions about what ought to be (also called value judgements).

Milton Friedman and Paul A. Samuelson are two of the best-known contemporary American economists. Both are winners of the Nobel Prize in economics. The two men represent polar extremes with respect to economic policy. Samuelson sees an important role for government in modern industrial society. Friedman advocates a *laissez-faire* economic policy. He argues that the market economy operates very well and that the interventions Samuelson supports do more harm than good. Samuelson is a leader of the Eastern liberal school of economics. Friedman represents the conservative Chicago School.

Samuelson, a professor at the Massachusetts Institute of Technology (MIT), has an A.B. degree from the University of Chicago and A.M. and Ph.D. degrees in economics from Harvard University. His Ph.D. dissertation, *Foundations of Economic Analysis*, written when he was only 23 years old, was published as a book. It still ranks as a monumental work in the application of mathematics to economics. Graduate students still study it. Many of today's economists were introduced to economics with Samuelson's textbook, *Economics*. Samuelson is largely responsible for making MIT's economics department one of the best in the country.

Friedman is retired from the University of Chicago, where he taught for 30 years. He is presently a senior research fellow at the Hoover Institution at Stanford University. Friedman received an A.B. degree from Rutgers, an A.M. degree from the University of Chicago, and a Ph.D. degree from Columbia University. He has made notable contributions to economic theory. His policy ideas are readily available in three popular books: *Essays in Positive Economics* (1953), *Capitalism and Freedom* (1962), and *Free to Choose* (1980). Recently, Friedman has angered some of the conservatives who usually agree with him by arguing that illegal drugs should be legalized. He argues that legalizing such drugs will reduce both the profits in selling them and the crime and violence among sellers and users.

ECONOMIC PROFILE

MILTON FRIEDMAN
1912–
AND
PAUL A. SAMUELSON
1915–

2. *Economic theory cannot predict the future.* It can only explain the effects of certain events. Economic theory consists of statements of the if-*A*-then-*B* type. The prediction that *B* will occur depends on whether or not *A* happens. (Note that theory does not predict the occurrence of *A*. Economists do not have a crystal ball.) In the production possibilities model, an increase in resources will result in economic growth, *ceteris paribus*. In this case, part of the *ceteris paribus* assumption is that the increased resources will be put to work and not left unemployed. There is, however, some difference between what economics *is* and what many economists actually *do*. Many economists, especially macroeconomists, spend a great deal of time forecasting future conditions. To do this, they make use of economic theory. In forecasting, an economist guesses the likelihood that *A* will occur and then uses economic theory to predict the occurrence of *B*. Sometimes, however, forecasts are wrong. This doesn't necessarily mean that the theory is incorrect. The forecaster may have been wrong in expecting *A* to occur.
3. *Most economists look first to market processes for solutions to social problems.* This market bias reflects a preference for the freedom and efficiency arising from decentralized processes. However, most economic theory is applicable to nonmarket systems as well, even though the legal and political institutions differ. Economists can apply tools developed for analyzing market economies to the workings of socialist economies and to a wide variety of nonmarket behavior.
4. *Economists pay a great deal of attention to cost.* The emphasis on opportunity cost, scarcity, and choice is fundamental to economics. Nobel Prize winner Milton Friedman underscored the importance of opportunity cost in this famous remark: "There is no such thing as a free lunch. This is the sum of my economic theory. The rest is elaboration." Harping on the subject of cost often puts economists in conflict with policy makers. Environmentalists don't like to hear economists talk about the opportunity cost of environmental purity in terms of forgone output. College admissions or recruitment officers seeking students don't like economists reminding students that the opportunity cost of a college education includes income not earned while in college.
5. *Economists are very interested in chances to substitute among alternatives.* Substitution and cost are closely related because the decision to substitute is based on the costs of the various alternatives. Sometimes substitutes are obvious, such as plastic for aluminum or electric heat for gas. Other substitutes are less apparent. A tree, for example, can substitute for gas or oil as heat or for aluminum siding on houses. Trees can also substitute for air conditioning or awnings by providing shade. An important task of economic analysis is identifying alternatives that can serve as substitutes and evaluating the costs of substituting one for another.
6. *Economists think in terms of incremental, or marginal, analysis.*[8] The marginal approach means looking at the effects on other variables of small increases or decreases in one important variable. Should we produce another (marginal) missile? If we do, what will be the (marginal) cost in terms of soybeans not produced? Most decisions in economics are

---

8. Remember that *marginal* means extra, or incremental, rather than inferior.

not all-or-nothing choices but are made at the margin. Decisions about how to spend the next hour, whether to eat another slice of pizza, and whether to hire an extra worker are all marginal decisions.

7. *Economists take the individual, rather than the group, the industry, or the community, as the basic decision-making unit.* They regard the behavior of individuals as an important influence on public policy and on decisions made in the private sector. The emphasis on individuals rather than groups reflects the importance of incentives in economics. Changes in prices, costs, profits, wages, substitutes, and opportunities are the driving forces behind individual economic decisions. It is the individual, not the group or community, that responds to incentives.

THREE COMMON FALLACIES

There are three dangerous fallacies, or errors in logical thinking, that can lead to false conclusions in economics. The following three statements could appear in the news and would seem logical to most readers. Each, however, contains a fallacy.

1. "The stock market closed up today in active trading. Analysts attributed the gain to optimism generated by the recent U.S.-Soviet summit on arms control."
2. "Layoffs in the auto industry were attributed to rising imports of cars, especially from Japan. Union leaders called for renewed emphasis on buying American goods, predicting severe unemployment in all manufacturing industries if the tide of imports continues to rise."
3. "The long expected decline in college enrollment, caused by fewer high school graduates since the mid-1980s and sharply rising tuitions, has not taken place. College enrollments appear to be stable or rising, in contradiction to forecasts."

THE ASSOCIATION-CAUSATION FALLACY

association-causation fallacy
The false notion that association implies causality.

The Latin phrase *post hoc, ergo propter hoc* translates as "after this, therefore, because of this." This kind of reasoning is called the **association-causation fallacy**. The fact that A changes and then B changes does not mean that the change in A caused the change in B. Suppose an increase in the number of students taking driver education programs is followed by an increase in accidents involving teenaged drivers. We could not conclude that driver education causes accidents. A statistical or observed association does not imply a causal relationship.

The stock market news item presented above is a familiar example. Newscasters know that the market has either risen or fallen, and they want a cause to offer as an explanation to report to their audiences. They can always find such a reason by identifying another important news event of the same day as *the* cause. The best way to avoid this fallacy is to search for a theoretical explanation for the suggested cause-and-effect relationship. Why, in terms of models and theories, should we expect a change in A to cause B to change in a certain way? There are sound theoretical reasons why an increase in profits or a decline in interest rates might lead to a

> ### THINKING LIKE AN ECONOMIST
>
> As you start to think about problems and policies from an economic perspective, here are some guidelines to help you.
>
> | | |
> |---|---|
> | • Positive, not normative | Try not to confuse what theory tells you will happen with what you *want* to happen |
> | • Can the market solve it? | Economists tend to prefer market solutions because they are more efficient. |
> | • Costs | I know there is no free lunch, but have I really counted all the costs? |
> | • Substitutes | What are the substitutes? Where are they? What are their costs? |
> | • Individuals and incentives | What incentives (positive and negative) does this policy create for individual buyers, sellers, and workers? |
> | • Fallacies | Have I carefully reviewed my analysis to avoid the three common fallacies? |

stock market boom. Is there any reason for an arms agreement to affect the stock market? Avoiding the association-causation fallacy is a good reason for studying and using economic theory.

THE FALLACY OF COMPOSITION

The second news item given above illustrates the **fallacy of composition**. This is the erroneous view that what holds for the parts holds for the whole as well. It is true that rising auto imports hurt auto producers and auto workers as a group. Even if most of the auto industry suffers, that is not true of all manufacturing industries. If Americans import more, some American manufacturers will manage to sell more to foreigners who earn those dollars. Thus, there will be gainers as well as losers. What is true for auto workers and auto producers is not true for the economy as a whole. In fact, the U.S. economy did quite well during some of the worst years for the auto industry in the 1980s.

fallacy of composition The false notion that what holds for the parts holds for the whole.

THE *CETERIS PARIBUS* FALLACY

The third news item offers an example of the *ceteris paribus* fallacy. The ***ceteris paribus* fallacy** occurs when a variable does not change as predicted because the analyst has overlooked the fact that other variables have also changed. When economists make statements or predictions, they qualify them with the phrase *ceteris paribus*, meaning other things being unchanged. What happens to college enrollment when tuition rises, *ceteris paribus*? Economic theory tells us that enrollment should fall. Instead, enrollment in the 1980s held steady and even rose slightly.

ceteris paribus **fallacy** The false notion that arises because an observer fails to recognize that variables other than the one in question have changed.

The rise in tuition and decline in high school graduates, taken together, should have caused a decline in college enrollment. However, at the same time, incomes rose. Even though there were fewer students, they came from smaller families that could more easily afford to educate all their children. Also, a growing population of retired people provided a

From the end of World War II until the mid-1970s, American students learned economics almost as though the United States were on a different planet from the rest of the world. A few textbooks had a chapter or two on international economics at the end. This material was rarely covered in class, however. This approach to economics reflected two common attitudes. The first was that the U.S. economy was so large and the share of foreign trade in U.S. economic activity was so small that the rest of the world could safely be ignored. The second was that it was important for students to learn how the U.S. economy worked, but not necessarily how institutions, policies, and solutions to common problems worked in other countries.

In the 1980s, Americans learned the economic importance of the rest of the world. The rest of the world has had a significant effect on the U.S. economy. The price of the dollar has seen some dramatic ups and downs in the last fifteen years. These fluctuations have affected imports, exports, employment, and price levels in the United States. Clearly, U.S. economists can no longer ignore the macroeconomic effects of the rest of the world.

At the microeconomic level, individual American firms, workers, and consumers have also become increasingly aware of the rest of the world. Americans who eat bananas from Central America on their cereal and drink coffee from Colombia, tea from India, or hot chocolate from Ghana for breakfast start their days in an international market. They may ride to work or school on a Japanese bicycle or in a Japanese car—although the car may have been built in the United States! When students graduate, many take jobs with multinational firms, American or foreign, in the United States or abroad. Their parents may have suffered spells of unemployment related to imports competing with domestic production of steel, autos, shoes, or textiles.

As Americans have become more aware of the impact of the rest of the world on their own economy at both the micro and macro levels, they have also become increasingly interested in learning from others. Europe has taught Americans the benefits of economic integration, which is being applied in the newly created U.S.–Canada free trade area. Americans have looked to Europe and Canada to study experiments in social policy, such as national health insurance and children's allowances. Japan has much to show U.S. firms about management and innovation. Japanese educators have been studying U.S. higher education while Americans are interested in their system of year-round education in the lower grades.

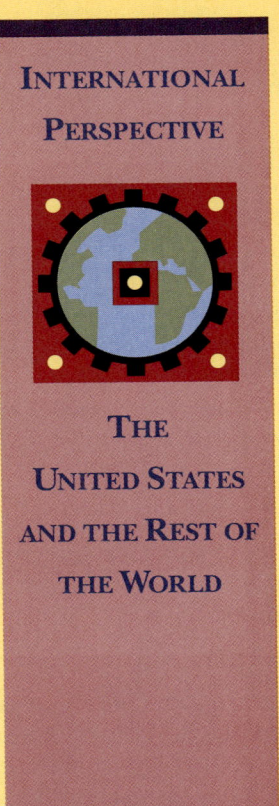

INTERNATIONAL PERSPECTIVE

THE UNITED STATES AND THE REST OF THE WORLD

Recognizing the growing importance of the international economy as both an influence on the U.S. economy and a source of ideas, we have chosen not to relegate the rest of the world to the back of the book. Each chapter offers one or more international perspectives. Some of these extend the material in that chapter to the open, or international, economy. This allows you to see the impact of the rest of the world on economic decisions and events at home. Others look at how a model, analysis, or solution to an economic problem might be different in another environment. You will see how tax systems work in Europe, why antitrust policy in the United States is stricter than in other nations, or why unemployment is always so high in the United Kingdom. Theories and models will explore the similarities between economic systems and the impact of one nation on another. Specific institutions and solutions will highlight the variety of possible approaches to solving the common problem of scarcity and choice.

When you finish this course, you should understand not only how the U.S. economic system operates but also how it appears in perspective with many others. We hope you will use the international perspectives to broaden your horizons and your understanding of the U.S. economy as one among many.

new pool of students. Income, family size, and number of retirees were all assumed to be *ceteris paribus* conditions. However, they did not remain constant but changed. These changes offset the effects of higher tuition and fewer high school graduates. Thus, college enrollments continued to increase. The statement predicting falling enrollment is wrong because the observer failed to examine fully the *ceteris paribus* conditions. In this case, as with the other two, a careful application of economic theory will help avoid the fallacy.

MAKING POLICY CHOICES

When economic models are applied to public policy issues, it is difficult to decide when the economist's task ends and the policy maker takes over. When economic methods are used for policy analysis, there is a five-step process.

1. *State the problem.* The choice of what problem to consider and how to state it is the task of the policy maker. How a problem is stated often determines what tools the economist applies and what solutions are considered. For example, suppose the problem is illegal parking on campus, especially parking by students in faculty spaces. Let's follow that problem through the next four steps.
2. *Apply the relevant economic model.* The economist turns to the toolkit to select the most useful theoretical model. In this case, there is a fairly simple technique called cost-benefit analysis that is not a formal model. This technique simply assumes that people are self-interested, that they are aware of the opportunity costs and benefits of their actions, and that they will choose the course of action that maximizes the excess of benefits over opportunity costs. This simple model predicts that an increase in the opportunity cost of illegal student parking or a reduction in benefits will reduce the amount of such illegal parking.
3. *Identify solutions.* The most common error at this stage is to leave out some solutions. Cost-based solutions to illegal parking might include higher fines. Do you think a student would be less likely to park in a faculty space if the fine were $100 instead of $10? More police officers would raise the cost by increasing the probability of being caught. The university could reduce the benefits of illegal parking by providing more bicycle racks or free bus transportation around campus and to and from commuter parking lots. Campus officials could even sell reserved parking spaces, and let students and faculty bid for parking rights.
4. *Evaluate solutions.* This is the stage where economists are most useful, pointing to costs, substitutes, and incentives. A good economic model predicts how various solutions will affect the amount of illegal parking, who will gain and who will lose, and which solution costs least to implement. For example, more police officers would be more expensive than higher fines. On the other hand, higher fines are a burden on students, many of whom have limited incomes. Bicycle racks are cheaper than shuttle buses. However, racks are not as helpful as buses would be to commuting students, unless they live very close to campus.
5. *Choose and implement one or more solutions.* This step is *not* the task of the

economist, although it is hard to stop after carrying the process this far. The policy maker (who may have been trained as an economist) takes the economist's list of possible solutions and the evaluation and makes a policy choice.

Most arguments among economists occur when they overstep the boundaries of scientific analysis and advocate a particular solution to an economic problem. Newspapers and TV news programs often quote economists who disagree. However, economists agree far more often than they disagree. Disagreements make headlines; agreement isn't news. Throughout this book, we will point out where most economists agree and also where and why they disagree. The models we describe represent a broad range of agreement among most economists on how markets work and how individuals respond to incentives.

Economics is an exciting social science. The individual who understands the economic way of thinking will gain insight into an endless array of interesting policy questions. We wish you well. Let's get on with it!

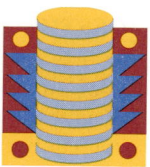

SUMMARY

1. Economics is the study of how decisions about producing and consuming goods and services are made and how individuals and groups face the problem of scarcity.
2. Microeconomics looks at the interactions of producers and consumers in individual markets. Macroeconomics is the study of the economy as a whole and is concerned with aggregates, numbers that are determined by adding across many markets.
3. Economics is one of the social sciences, along with psychology, sociology, and political science. These fields focus on the behavior of individuals in their interactions with one another.
4. Economic theory is an abstract way of thinking that allows the development of principles, or tools, that can be used to study social issues.
5. Resources are finite, but human wants are insatiable. This conflict is the basic economic problem of scarcity. People cannot have everything they want and must make choices.
6. The production possibilities curve illustrates the problem of scarcity. In order to have more of one good, people must settle for less of another. The cost of extra units of one good is the number of units of the other sacrificed, or the opportunity cost.
7. The principle of increasing opportunity cost says that the more of one good people have, the greater the amount of other goods they must sacrifice to obtain one more unit of that good.
8. The production possibilities curve can be used to describe unemployment of resources (points inside the curve) and economic growth (a shift of the curve to the right).
9. Self-interested behavior is a basic assumption of economic theory. Although economists recognize that economic behavior is a complex process, they assume that human beings pursue their own self-interest.
10. Economic theory is positive, or nonnormative. It can't tell us what we should do, but it can make statements of an if-*A*-then-*B* type.
11. Economists tend to rely on the market to solve social problems. In analyzing problems, economists stress identifying options and looking at costs and benefits, particularly at the margin.
12. The association-causation fallacy is the false notion that association implies causality.
13. The fallacy of composition is the false idea that what holds for the parts holds for the whole.
14. The *ceteris paribus* fallacy occurs when changes in one variable fail to have the predicted effect on another variable because the observer has ignored changes in other important variables.
15. A policy decision is analyzed in five steps: state the problem, apply the relevant economic model, identify solutions, evaluate solutions, and choose and implement solutions.
16. Although economists agree on many things, their disagreements are often highlighted. Most of their disagreements are over policy choices rather than economic theory.

NEW TERMS

economics
microeconomics
macroeconomics
aggregates
social science
scarcity
insatiable wants
opportunity cost
production possibilities curve
increasing opportunity cost
theory
testable hypothesis
model
ceteris paribus assumption
self-interested behavior
positive statements
normative statements
association-causation fallacy
fallacy of composition
ceteris paribus fallacy

QUESTIONS FOR DISCUSSION

1. Do you think people exhibit behavior patterns that confirm the self-interest assumption? Does your own behavior confirm this assumption? Is a contribution to charity or volunteer work a contradiction of the self-interest assumption?

2. Why do economists theorize rather than attempt to describe reality exactly?

3. Do assumptions have to be realistic in order for a theory to work?

4. What is the difference between using theory to predict and forecasting?

5. Consider the following simple predictive model: if the speed limit is reduced, fewer highway deaths will occur. What assumptions are being made? What *ceteris paribus* conditions could change and make this prediction invalid?

6. Identify and explain the fallacy in each of the following statements.
   a. "There was a transit strike in April, and unemployment in the city rose in May. Clearly the transit strike created unemployment."
   b. "The new subway system is finally working, but downtown parking spaces are harder to find than before. The subway system hasn't relieved congestion."
   c. "Our state competed heavily to attract industry, and it worked. Unemployment is down. If all states did the same, national unemployment would fall."

7. Which of the following quantities are microeconomic, and which are macroeconomic? Which might fall between the two?
   a. price of shoes
   b. number of men aged 18 to 24 in the U.S. labor force
   c. level of interest rates
   d. unemployment in Tulsa
   e. production of agricultural products
   f. average level of prices
   g. production of butter
   h. average price of imported goods
   i. unemployment in the United States
   j. total output
   k. unemployment of carpenters
   l. number of nurses in the U.S. labor force
   m. unemployment in the northeastern states

8. What is the opportunity cost of working 10 hours a week flipping burgers while in college? If you worked more hours per week, would you experience increasing or constant opportunity cost? That is, would the extra hours require giving up alternative uses of your time that have the same value or an increasing value?

9. a. Given the following data, plot a production possibilities curve and calculate the opportunity cost of bicycles in terms of skateboards.

BICYCLES	SKATEBOARDS
10	0
8	10
6	20
4	30
2	40
0	50

   b. Assume that new technology increases the possible output of both skateboards and bicycles by 50 percent. Draw the new production possibilities curve. Calculate the new opportunity cost of bicycles in terms of skateboards.
   c. Now assume that new technology increases the amount of bicycles that can be produced by 6 units if all resources are devoted to bicycles, but does not change the amount of skateboards that can be produced. Draw a new curve, and calculate a new opportunity cost.

10. You know that the opportunity cost of books in terms of cassettes not produced is 1 book for 2 cassettes and that available resources can produce a maximum of 100 books. Can you draw the production possibilities curve for these two goods? If so, what is the maximum possible output of cassettes? If you choose to produce 40 books, how many cassettes can be produced?

11. Using the following economic data, plot a production possibilities curve for tomatoes and tomahawks:

TOMATOES	TOMAHAWKS
100	0
80	15
60	30
40	45
20	60
0	75

What is the opportunity cost of a tomato? A tomahawk? If 50 tomatoes are produced, how many tomahawks can be produced?

12. Using the data in question 11, suppose a change in technology makes it possible to increase tomato production to a maximum of 150 units. There is no change in the technology of producing tomahawks. Draw the new production possibilities curve. Now what is the opportunity cost of each good? If this economy chooses to produce 60 tomatoes, how many tomahawks can it produce?

13. Try developing a simple economic model to predict how students will respond to an increase in dormitory rents. What are your assumptions? What will happen to the number of dormitory spaces rented? What will happen to the number of off-campus apartments rented and their prices?

14. Which of the following statements are normative, and which are positive? Rewrite the normative statements to make them positive and the positive ones to make them normative.

   a. "Women earn less than men."
   b. "Defense spending has grown too rapidly in the last decade."
   c. "Because their child-care duties interfere with their work, women with children should earn less than men."
   d. "Twenty-three percent of the federal budget is spent on defense."
   e. "An estimated 14 percent of the U.S. population lives in poverty, according to government standards defining poverty."
   f. "The government is not doing enough to reduce poverty."

15. The economy of Southland can only produce two goods: food and clothing. Both are subject to constant costs. Draw a production possibilities curve for Southland that shows the maximum output of food as 50 cartons and the maximum output of clothing as 100 suits. Now locate each of the following on your diagram.

   a. Output of 25 cartons of food and 25 suits of clothing. Label this point *U*. Does it lie on the curve? What does this point represent? What is the opportunity cost of another suit of clothing at this point?
   b. Output of 50 cartons of food and 100 suits of clothing. Label this point *G*. Does this point lie on the curve? Is it attainable? If not, what must happen for *G* to be a possible output combination?
   c. Output of 25 cartons of food and 50 suits of clothing. Label this point *A*. Does it lie on the curve? What is the opportunity cost of another carton of food at this point?

16. a. Suppose the two goods in question 15 are subject to increasing costs, but the end points remain the same. Draw a new production possibilities curve for food and clothing in Southland.
   b. Suppose the economy of Southland has a technological change that increases the capacity to produce food but not clothing. How will the production possibilities curve shift? Is it possible to produce more of both food and clothing after this shift?
   c. Suppose the economy of Southland has an increase in resources that affects both food and clothing production equally. How will the production possibilities curve shift?

SUGGESTIONS FOR FURTHER READING

Boulding, Kenneth. *Human Betterment.* Beverly Hills, CA: Sage, 1985. This recent book by one of America's best known economic philosophers makes a case for normative analysis when the values behind the analysis are clearly spelled out.

Huff, Darrell, and Irving Geis. *How to Lie with Statistics.* New York: W. W. Norton, 1954 (copyright renewed 1982). This classic guide to interpreting and misinterpreting graphs and statistics is must reading for any serious student of the social sciences.

Rhoads, Stephen E. *The Economist's View of the World: Government, Markets, and Public Policy.* New York: Cambridge University Press, 1985. Written by a political scientist, this book looks at both the useful contributions of economics to other social sciences and the limitations of economics.

Stigler, George. *Memoirs of an Unregulated Economist.* New York: Basic Books, 1988. A Nobel Prize–winning economist looks at the training of economists and the uses of economics in an account of his own experiences in the field.

APPENDIX:
ECONOMIC RELATIONSHIPS AND GRAPHS

Economic theories and models are often expressed in the form of mathematical relationships among variables. These relationships can be described by algebraic equations. Economists more often express them visually in the form of graphs. Graphs make it possible to illustrate economic theories and models in ways that make them easier to remember and to apply to the real world. Remember that everything that can be said in graphs can also be said in words. Graphs are only an aid to understanding the theory. Mastering and applying the theory is what you should be trying to achieve. If you can learn to feel comfortable with graphs as visual presentations of economic ideas, reading this textbook and understanding your professor's lectures will be much easier.

RELATIONSHIP BETWEEN TWO VARIABLES

A relationship between two variables, variable x and variable y, can be expressed in a number of ways. One is a table of values of x and y. For example, Table 1A shows the various amounts of fertilizer applied per acre and the corresponding yields of corn per acre. What does this table mean? It means that different amounts of fertilizer were applied to different plots of land and that those plots of land yielded varying amounts of corn.

This relationship could also be expressed in the form of a graph.[a] A

TABLE 1A RELATIONSHIPS BETWEEN TWO VARIABLES

X-VARIABLE, FERTILIZER (100s OF LBS./ACRE)	Y-VARIABLE, CORN (BUSHELS/ACRE)
1	1
2	10
3	40
4	80
5	100
6	110
7	115
8	110
9	100
10	70

a. A third way to represent such a relationship is with an equation, $y = f(x)$. We will be using some equations in this book but will rely more heavily on graphs to display relationships between variables.

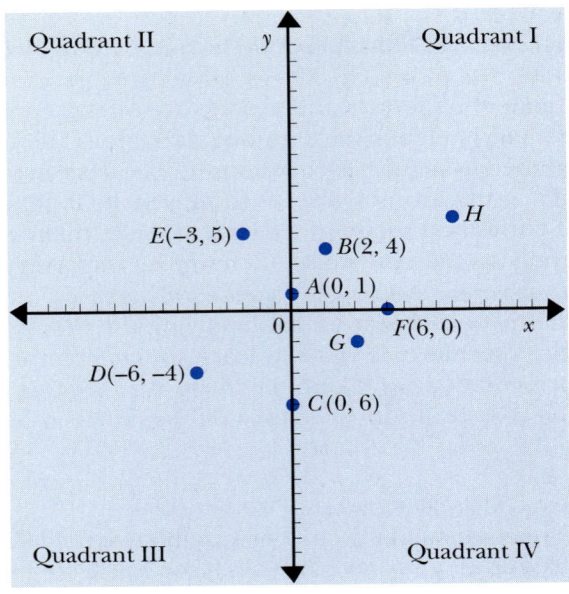

FIGURE 1A
QUADRANT SYSTEM
A four-quadrant system makes it possible to represent combinations of positive and negative values in two dimensions. Point C represents an x-value of 0 and a y-value of −6. The quadrants are labeled I to IV in the counterclockwise direction.

y-axis
The upright line in a coordinate system that shows the values of the dependent variable; the vertical axis.

x-axis
The horizontal line in a coordinate system that shows the values of the independent variable; the horizontal axis.

origin
The intersection of the vertical and horizontal axes of a coordinate system, at which the values of both the x-variable and the y-variable are zero.

coordinates
The values of x and y that define the location of a point in a coordinate system.

graph shows how the quantity of one variable changes when another variable changes. Figure 1A shows the system most commonly used for graphing. The vertical line is referred to as the **y-axis** (or vertical axis). The horizontal line is referred to as the **x-axis** (or horizontal axis). The x-axis and y-axis divide the graph into four quadrants.

The point where the axes cross (or intersect) is the **origin**. At the origin, the values of both the x-variable and the y-variable are zero. Above the x-axis, the y-variable has positive values. Below the x-axis, the y-variable has negative values. To the right of the y-axis, the x-variable has positive values. To the left of the y-axis, the x-variable has negative values. Both x and y have positive values in Quadrant I and negative values in Quadrant III. In Quadrant IV, x takes on positive values, and y takes on negative values. In Quadrant II, x has negative values, and y positive values. In this book, most of the graphs will use only Quadrant I because most economic data takes on only positive values.

Each point on a graph has a set of **coordinates**, a pair of numbers representing the x-value and the y-value. For example, point B on Figure 1A represents the value 2 for the x-variable and the value 4 for the y-variable. The x-value is always given first. For example, point E represents x = −3, y = 5. See if you can determine the coordinates of points G and H.

With this background, we can plot the relationship between fertilizer applied and corn output given in Table 1A. The first decision to make is which variable goes on which axis. If there is a cause-and-effect relationship, we usually put the "causing" variable on the horizontal axis and the variable being affected on the vertical axis. In mathematics, the causing variable is the **independent variable**, and the affected variable is the **dependent variable**. Since we think that fertilizer causes increased corn yields, we plot it on the horizontal axis (*x*-axis). Corn yield is plotted on the vertical axis (*y*-axis).

The next decision concerns establishing a scale for each axis. The scales can be whatever is convenient and do not need to be the same. In this case, the fertilizer units are hundreds of pounds per acre, and the corn units are bushels per acre. Once a scale is established and the axes are labeled, we can plot the coordinates of the points in Table 1A. Then we connect the plotted points with a smooth curve to produce a graph, shown in Figure 2A.

The value of a graph is that it gives you a visual picture of the mathematical relationship between the variables. In Figure 2A, you can easily see that as fertilizer is increased up to 700 pounds per acre, corn output increases. After that level, more fertilizer causes a decrease in output. The corn plants grow too rapidly and don't produce many ears, or the roots suffer fertilizer burn.

Not all relationships produce as tidy a graph as the one for fertilizer and corn yield. Sometimes researchers plot data to see if there is any visual pattern before trying to understand what, if any, is the relationship between the two variables. Such a plot of actual data is called a **scatter diagram**. Scatter diagrams are useful in searching for possible mathematical relationships between two variables.

Figure 3A plots actual data on the rate of inflation (vertical axis) and the rate of unemployment (horizontal axis) for the United States from 1975 to 1989. In this diagram, there doesn't seem to be a consistent rela-

independent variable
The variable, usually plotted on the horizontal axis, that affects or influences the other variable.

dependent variable
The variable, usually plotted on the vertical axis, that is affected or influenced by the other variable.

scatter diagram
A graph that plots actual pairs of values of two variables to determine whether there appears to be any consistent relationship between them.

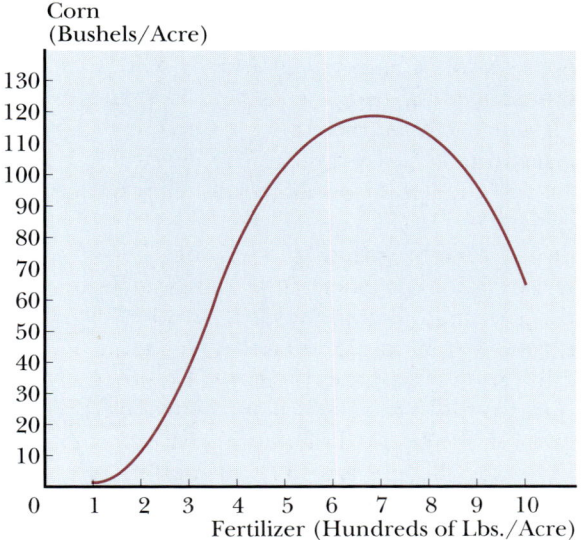

FIGURE 2A
FERTILIZER AND CORN OUTPUT
A graph is usually plotted with the dependent variable on the *y*-axis and the independent variable on the *x*-axis. Here, as the independent variable (fertilizer) increases, the dependent variable (corn output) first increases and then decreases.

FIGURE 3A
INFLATION AND UNEMPLOYMENT
A scatter diagram plots the coordinates for the values of two variables that may or may not have a consistent relationship. This diagram plots the unemployment rate and the inflation rate for the United States from 1976 to 1989. It shows no consistent relationship between these two variables.

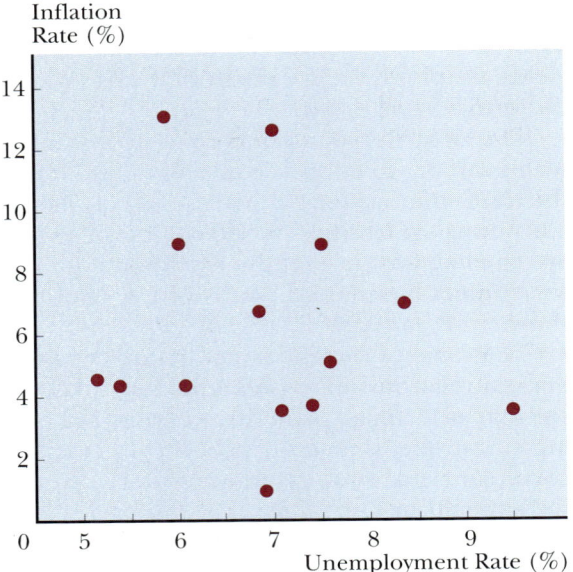

Source: Council of Economic Advisers, *Economic Report of the President* (Washington, DC: U.S. Government Printing Office, 1990).

FIGURE 4A
GNP AND MONEY SUPPLY (BILLIONS OF DOLLARS)
This scatter diagram plots the money supply and the GNP for the United States from 1976 to 1989. Unlike the diagram in Figure 3A, this one seems to show a rather consistent relationship between the two variables.

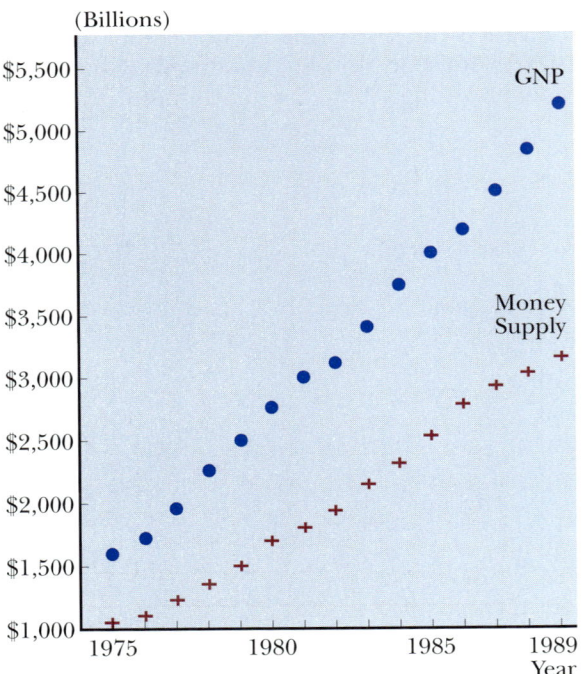

Source: Council of Economic Advisers, *Economic Report of the President* (Washington, DC: U.S. Government Printing Office, 1990).

tionship of any kind between the rate of inflation and the rate of unemployment, at least for the years plotted. Figure 4A plots the relationship between the money supply and total output, or GNP, for the United States from 1975 to 1989. As you can see, there appears to be a more consistent relationship between these two variables.

POSITIVE AND NEGATIVE RELATIONSHIPS AND SLOPES

A graph shows how two variables are related. This relationship may be positive or negative. A **positive relationship** means that an increase in the value of the *x*-variable is associated with an increase in the value of the *y*-variable, as in Figure 4A. A **negative relationship** means that an increase in the value of the *x*-variable is associated with a decrease in the value of the *y*-variable. Some relationships in economics, such as the one between fertilizer and corn output plotted in Figure 2A, are positive for some values of the *x*-variable and negative for others.

Most of the economic relationships you will encounter in this book are represented by straight lines. A straight line can have a positive slope, as in Figure 5A, or a negative slope, as in Figure 6A. The **slope** is a measure of the steepness of the line. It is the ratio of the change in the dependent variable (y) to the change in the independent variable (x). If the slope is designated by the letter m, then the equation of a straight line can be written as

$$y = mx + b,$$

where b is the value of y when $x = 0$. (The value b is also known as the *y*-intercept, because at this value the line crosses the *y*-axis.)

Even though both lines in Figure 5A are positively sloped, the rela-

positive relationship
A relationship between two variables in which an increase in one is associated with an increase in the other and a decrease in one is associated with a decrease in the other.

negative relationship
A relationship between two variables in which an increase in the value of one is associated with a decrease in the value of the other.

slope
The ratio of the change in the dependent variable (y) to the change in the independent variable (x).

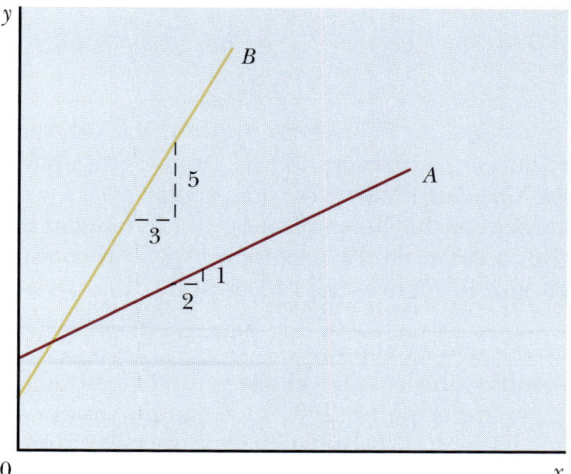

FIGURE 5A
POSITIVELY SLOPED LINES
The slope of a line is the ratio of the change in the *y*-value to the change in the *x*-value. A line sloping upward to the right has a positive slope, indicating a positive relationship between the two variables.

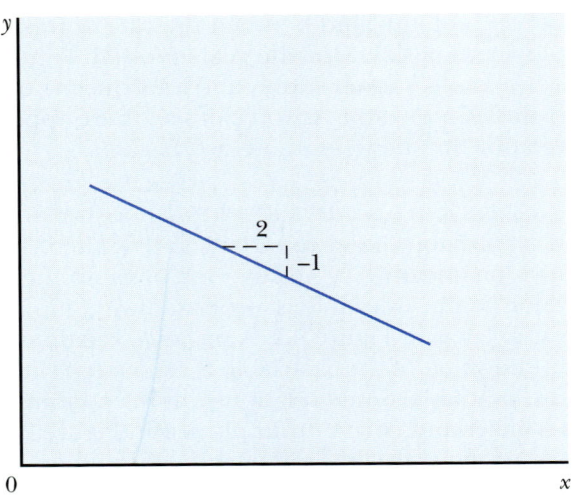

FIGURE 6A
NEGATIVELY SLOPED LINE
A negative slope represents a relationship between the variables in which an increase in the value of the independent variable is associated with a decrease in the value of the dependent variable.

tionship between the *x*-variable and the *y*-variable represented by line *A* is very different from that represented by line *B*. The same amount of change in *x* leads to a larger change in *y* along line *B* than it does along line *A*. In Figure 5A, the slope of line *A* is equal to $+\frac{1}{2}$ because the *y*-value changes by one unit for each two-unit change in the *x*-value. The slope of line *B* is $+\frac{5}{3}$, or $+1.67$. The steeper slope of line *B* indicates that a larger change in the value of *y* will result from a given change in the value of *x* than along line *A*. The sign of the slope is also very important. It indicates whether the relationship between the two variables is positive or negative. A slope with a positive sign designates a positive relationship. A slope with a negative sign, as in Figure 6A, indicates a negative relationship. The slope of the line in Figure 6A is $-\frac{1}{2}$.

NONLINEAR GRAPHS AND MAXIMA AND MINIMA

tangent line
A straight line just touching a curve (nonlinear graphic relationship) at a single point. The slope of the tangent line is equal to the slope of the curve at that point.

maximum
The point on a graph at which the *y*-variable, or dependent variable, reaches its highest value.

A straight-line graph, such as those in Figures 5A and 6A, has the same slope along the entire line. The slope of a curved line, on the other hand, varies along the curve. The slope of a curve at a particular point is the slope of the straight line tangent to the curve at that point. A **tangent line** is a straight line that touches a curve at only one point without crossing it. The slope of the curved line in Figure 7A is $+1$ at point *A* and $-\frac{3}{2}$ at point *C*.

The slope of the curve in Figure 7A at point *B* is equal to zero. A small change in the value of *x* results in no change in the value of *y* along the straight line tangent to the curve at point *B*. Point *B* is a **maximum** because the *y*-variable reaches its highest value at that point. The highest value of *y*, y_1, is associated with an *x* value of x_1. Recall that we described

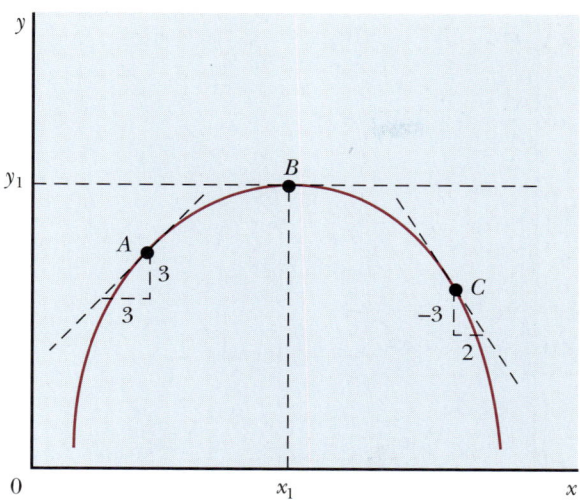

FIGURE 7A
NONLINEAR GRAPHS: SLOPE AND MAXIMUM
On a nonlinear graph, the slope changes along the curve. The slope of the curve at any point is the slope of a straight line tangent to the curved line at that point. When the slope is zero, the value of the y-variable is either at a maximum or at a minimum. At point B, y is at its maximum value, y_1, when x has the value x_1.

self-interested behavior as consumers maximizing satisfaction, resource owners maximizing income, and firms maximizing profit. Being able to find the maximum is very important in economics.

Sometimes a slope of zero is associated with a **minimum** rather than a maximum, as in Figure 8A. The y-variable assumes its lowest value, Y_1, at point B in Figure 8A. This y-value is associated with an x-value of X_1. A firm that is trying to minimize costs, or losses, may be interested in finding a minimum point. It is also important for many kinds of economic questions to determine whether a point of zero slope is a maximum or a minimum.

minimum
The point on the graph at which the y-variable, or dependent variable, reaches its lowest value.

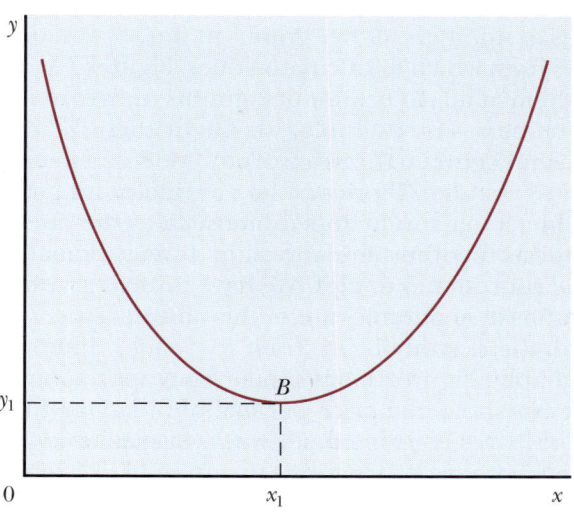

FIGURE 8A
NONLINEAR GRAPHS: MINIMUM
This nonlinear graph also has a slope of zero at point B. In this case, point B represents the minimum value of y, y_1, which is associated with an x-value of x_1.

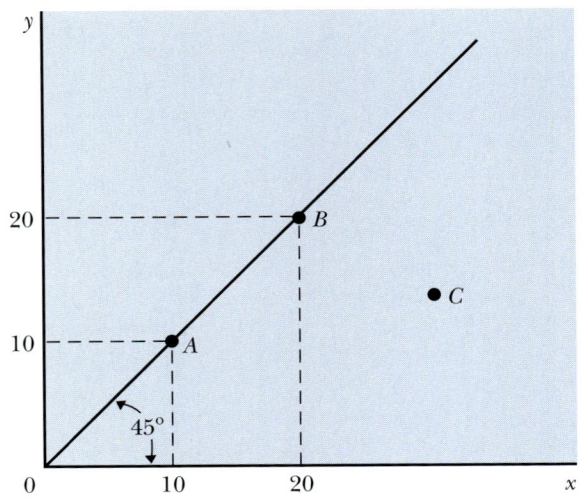

FIGURE 9A
THE 45° LINE
A 45° line drawn in the first quadrant has a slope of +1. If both axes are measured in the same units, the 45° line shows all points where the *x*-value and the *y*-value are equal.

45° line
A line in the first quadrant, passing through the origin, with a slope of +1, which divides the quadrant in half. If the scales on the axes are the same, the value of the *x*-variable is equal to the value of the *y*-variable along the 45° line.

THE 45° LINE

A geometric construction that proves very useful in economic analysis is a **45° line**. This is a straight line through the origin that divides Quadrant I into two equal sections. If both axes are measured in the same units, the values of the *x*-variable and the *y*-variable will be equal at any point on the line, and the slope will be +1. A 45° line is shown in Figure 9A. Suppose, for example, you want to know whether the value of *x* is less than, equal to, or greater than the value of *y* at point *C*. A 45° line gives you a quick answer to that question. The value of *x* is greater than the value of *y* at point *C* because point *C* lies below the 45° line.

GRAPHS WITHOUT NUMBERS

The graph in Figure 2A and the scatter diagrams in Figures 3A and 4A were constructed from sets of numbers. Other graphs in this section only give a few numerical values from which to calculate slopes. Figures 7A and 8A have no numbers on them at all. In economics, graphs of theoretical concepts often use no numbers. For example, we might theorize that there is a negative relationship between the price of any good that people consume and the quantity demanded. If price is the *y*-variable and quantity demanded the *x*-variable, a negatively sloped line such as the one in Figure 5A could represent this theoretical relationship. It doesn't matter that we don't have specific coordinates to plot. We have instead graphed an abstract idea. Many graphs in economics are of this abstract type.

On graphs without numbers, symbols are used for values, line segments, and areas. For example, Figure 10A is similar to graphs you will study in Chapter 3. The *y*-axis shows the price per loaf of bread, and the *x*-axis shows the quantity of loaves consumed per week. Particular prices are represented by symbols such as P_1. Quantities consumed are represented by symbols such as Q_1, Q_2, and Q_3. If you have studied geometry,

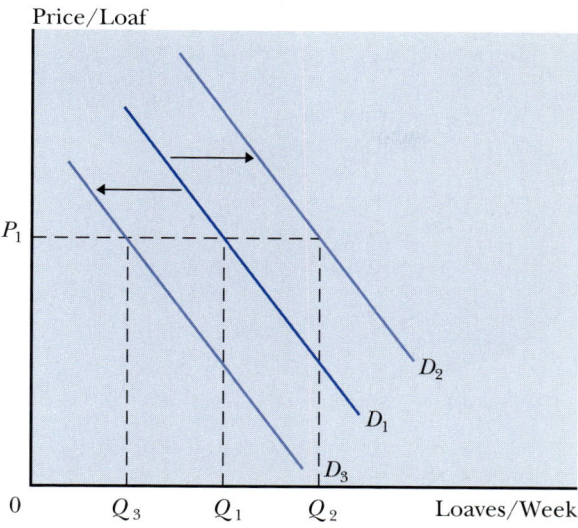

**FIGURE 10A
EFFECTS OF CHANGES IN TASTES ON THE DEMAND FOR BREAD**
Many graphs in economics use symbols rather than numbers on the axes. The symbol P_1 represents a hypothetical price, and Q_1, Q_2, and Q_3 represent hypothetical quantities.

you will note that it would be technically correct to refer to quantity Q_1 as quantity $\overline{0Q_1}$. We will, however, use the shorthand Q_1 to minimize clutter.

In addition to using symbols to represent quantities, we will also make frequent use of the symbol delta, Δ, to represent changes in a variable. For example, the symbol ΔQ is a shorthand expression for the change from Q_1 to Q_2 in Figure 10A.

PIE CHARTS AND BAR CHARTS

All of the graphs considered so far, except for the scatter diagrams, represent theoretical relationships of one kind or another. Economists also use graphs to describe the real world. Such graphs display descriptive statistics. These include the allocation of government funds between types of programs, the growth of output or the money supply over time, and the different growth rates of imports and exports.

Two common types of descriptive graphs encountered in economics are pie charts and bar charts. **Pie charts** are used to show the division of some whole into parts, usually designated by percentages. Figure 11A is a pie chart depicting the sources of household income in 1989. Pie charts have become very popular because they are easy to create on a personal computer. This visual representation often conveys a clearer sense of the relative sizes of various components than you could obtain from reading a table of numbers.

Another popular type of descriptive graph is a **bar chart**, such as Figure 12A. This diagram describes the behavior of two variables, federal government revenue and expenditures, in a series of "snapshots" from 1970 to 1989. This graph gives a much more vivid impression of how much expenditures have grown relative to revenues than you could derive from a set of numbers.

pie chart
A graphic representation in the shape of a pie that expresses actual economic data as parts of a whole. The sizes of the slices of the pie correspond to the percentage shares of the components.

bar chart
A graphic representation that expresses data using columns of different heights.

FIGURE 11A
PIE CHART OF HOUSEHOLD INCOME FOR THE UNITED STATES, 1989
A pie chart depicts the division of a whole into parts (percentages). This pie chart shows that the largest component of household income is wages and salaries. Transfer payments and interest are much smaller components.

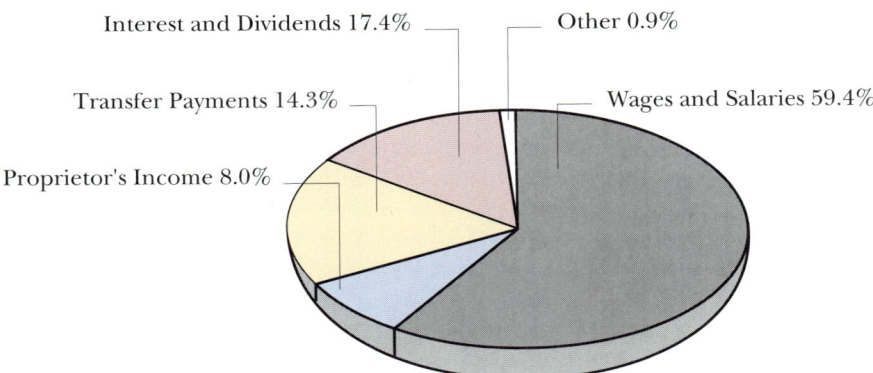

Source: Council of Economic Advisers, *Economic Report of the President* (Washington, DC: U.S. Government Printing Office, 1990).

FIGURE 12A
BAR CHART OF FEDERAL REVENUES AND EXPENDITURES, 1980–1989
A bar chart can be used in a variety of ways to present economic data in a visual fashion. This bar chart compares federal revenues and expenditures for various years.

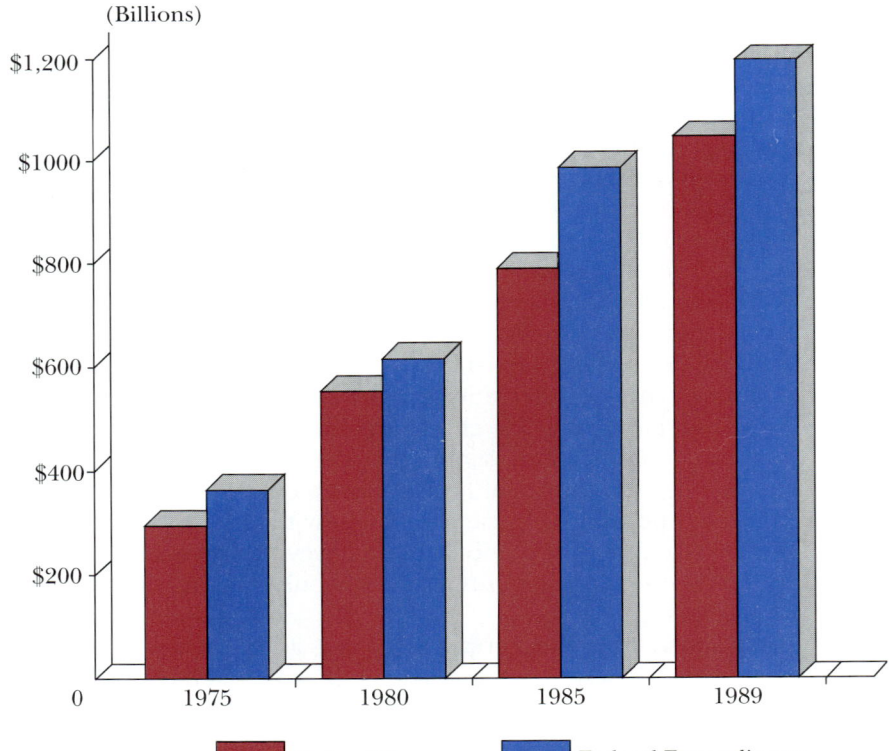

Source: Council of Economic Advisers, *Economic Report of the President* (Washington, DC: U.S. Government Printing Office, 1990).

Theoretical graphs, such as those in Figures 5A through 10A, and descriptive graphs, such as Figures 11A and 12A, are spread throughout this book. Both types are also common in textbooks in social sciences and business and in popular magazines such as *Newsweek, Time,* and *Business Week.* Economics is a very visual subject. Be sure that you feel secure with reading and interpreting graphs before proceeding further.

CAUTION: GRAPHS AND NUMBERS CAN MISLEAD AS WELL AS INFORM!
Graphs and statistics can be very informative. They put some concrete, real-world content into abstract models and economic relationships. However, it is very easy to present data in a misleading way. The choice of a scale along an axis can make changes look bigger than they really are. The use of averages conceals a great deal of information about variation. For example, three families with incomes of $24,000, $25,000, and $26,000 have an average income of $25,000. The same average could be the result of three incomes of $5,000, $5,000, and $65,000. The same average income describes two very different distributions of income.

A classic guide to the use and abuse of numbers and graphs is *How to Lie with Statistics,* by Darrell Huff and Irving Geis. This book has been through numerous paperback editions since it was first published in 1954. It should be required reading for anyone taking courses in the social sciences. It is a useful guide through the pitfalls of the means, medians, averages, bar charts, surveys, samples, and growth rates that are the daily news of the economic and political worlds.

Always be very cautious in accepting someone's graphs or numbers. Consider carefully what that person may be trying to persuade you to think or do and how the statistics could be manipulated to put that position in a more favorable light.

> **AFTER STUDYING THIS CHAPTER, YOU SHOULD BE ABLE TO:**

1. Identify the factors of production.
2. List the three basic economic questions that must be addressed by every economic system.
3. Use a circular flow model to show the relationships between firms and households in product markets and in factor markets in a market economy.
4. Describe how traditional, command, and market economies answer the three basic economic questions.
5. Explain and give examples of the basic economic functions of government.
6. Describe and calculate the benefits of specialization and exchange based on comparative advantage.

CHAPTER 2
MARKETS, GOVERNMENTS, AND NATIONS: THE ORGANIZATION OF ECONOMIC ACTIVITY

INTRODUCTION

Chapter 1 introduced the basic economic problem of scarcity and choice that every economy must address, regardless of its level of development or form of government. In this chapter, we explore some of the common problems and choices faced by people in all societies in using their scarce resources to satisfy their wants. We will also examine the different ways in which choices are made in different kinds of societies. Throughout this book, a series of international perspectives will remind you that the way economic problems are addressed in American society is not necessarily the way they are addressed in other countries.

In the last two decades, economists have become more aware of the importance of interactions between national economies. These interactions include trade in goods and services and movements of labor and capital. They affect the growth rate, production, employment, price level, and other important macroeconomic variables in both countries. Competition from foreign producers, foreign markets for products, and the use of foreign inputs also have important effects on prices and quantities in individual markets. Thus, another issue we introduce in this chapter is the difference between an isolated, or closed, economy and an open economy. An open economy is one that trades goods, services, and productive resources with other nations.

LIMITED RESOURCES: THE FACTORS OF PRODUCTION

To examine the process of choice, we can begin by identifying the scarce resources that exist. Scarce resources used to produce goods and services are called **factors of production**. The factors of production are divided into four broad categories: labor, land, capital, and enterprise. All resources used to produce goods and services fit into one of these four categories.

LABOR

Labor is the factor of production with which you are probably most familiar. **Labor** is the physical and mental exertion of human beings. The

factors of production
The inputs of land, labor, capital, and enterprise that a firm uses to produce outputs.

labor
The physical and mental exertion that human beings put into production activities.

41

efforts of a factory worker, a professional basketball player, a university professor, and a carpenter are all labor.

Wages are the payments labor receives for its productive services. Some labor is valued (and paid) more than other labor. Why? One reason is that some labor is more productive. Workers are born with different talents and abilities. Some are more intelligent. Others are physically stronger or better coordinated. Still others have artistic or musical ability. It is also possible to make labor more productive by devoting money and time to improving skills. Individuals invest in their labor skills by going to college, serving as apprentices, or practicing. Economists refer to this development of labor skills as an investment in human capital. **Human capital** consists of labor-enhancing abilities that increase labor's productivity. A large part of wage differences can be explained by differences in human capital.

wages
The return to labor, one of the factors of production.

human capital
The investment made to improve the quality of people's labor skills through education, training, health care, and so on.

LAND

The second factor of production is land. **Land**, to an economist, is not just rocks and soil, but all natural resources that can be used as inputs to production. By this definition, land includes minerals, water, air, forests, oil, and even rainfall, temperature, and soil quality. The income payment to this factor of production is called **rent**.

A key distinction between land and other productive resources is that land consists of natural resources or conditions, unimproved by any human activity. For example, acreage in Arizona that has been irrigated represents more than land. It also represents capital, the third factor of production. Thus, part of the payment that is called rent is a return to land, but part of it may be a return to capital.

land
Natural resources that can be used as inputs to production.

rent
The return to land, one of the factors of production.

CAPITAL

The third factor of production, **capital**, is defined as all aids to production that are human creations rather than resources found in nature. Capital includes tools, factories, warehouses, and inventories. You have also seen that capital can become attached to land or to labor (human capital) when investment is made in improvements or in skills and training. In common usage, real capital is often confused with financial capital. Financial capital is money lent to purchase real, physical capital. Economists reserve the term *capital* for real inputs to production, not for financial assets.

Capital, like land, receives a flow of income. The payments to capital are called **interest**. Interest is a reward for giving up present consumption in order to make resources available for the creation of more capital for future production. **Investment** is the act of adding to capital. Although the term *investment* is used by noneconomists for such activities as buying stocks and bonds, to an economist the term means the creation of real, tangible assets, such as machines, factories, or inventories that can be used to produce other goods and services.

capital
The durable inputs into the production process created by people. Machines, tools, and buildings are examples of capital.

interest
The return to capital, one of the factors of production.

investment
Purchases of real, tangible assets, such as machines, factories, or inventories, that are used to produce goods and services.

ENTERPRISE

The last factor of production is **enterprise**, which consists of the activities of combining the factors of production to produce goods and services, taking risks, and introducing new methods and new products (innovation). Entrepreneurs combine other factors of production by buying or

enterprise
The input to the production process that involves organizing, innovation, and risk taking.

renting them to produce a saleable product. The reward for innovation, risk taking, and organization is **profit**.

Profit is the most difficult of the four factor returns to measure in practice because it is whatever is left over after paying for land, capital, and labor. Noneconomists frequently count profit as what is left after the bills are paid. However, this measure is likely to overlook such opportunity costs as the value of the owner's labor (wages) or the return to the owner's capital (interest).

> **profit**
> The return to enterprise, one of the factors of production. Profit is whatever remains after all other factors have been paid.

THE BASIC ECONOMIC QUESTIONS

The process of choosing how to allocate scarce resources can be broken down into three broad economic questions.

- *What* goods and services will be produced and in what quantities?
- *How* will they be produced? (That is, what methods of production and combinations of inputs will be used?)
- *For whom* will they be produced? (That is, who gets what share of the goods and services produced?)

Different kinds of economic systems answer these three questions in different ways. However, people in all economic systems are faced with the problem of how to allocate scarce resources among an unlimited number of wants.

The market provides at least a partial answer to these three questions in many societies. A **market** is any setting in which buyers and sellers meet to exchange goods, services, or productive resources. A market system is an economic system that relies primarily on market transactions to answer the three basic economic questions.

> **market**
> A place where buyers and sellers meet to exchange goods, services, and productive resources.

The production possibilities curve introduced in Chapter 1 showed attainable levels and combinations of outputs, or the choices available. The production possibilities curve, however, does not explain how to choose among these combinations. What determines if an economy is at one particular point on the production possibilities curve instead of another, and who makes that choice?

WHAT, HOW, AND FOR WHOM

The *what* question asks exactly what mix of goods and services is to be produced—how many tons of wheat, thousands of textbooks, yards of fabric, pairs of jeans, and gallons of milk will make up the total national output. It is a difficult enough question in the simple two-product world of the production possibilities curve. With thousands and thousands of possible combinations of outputs, the *what* question is extremely complex. In a market system, the answer to the *what* question is determined by consumers, who "vote" in the marketplace by using their dollars to obtain particular goods and services. In other economic systems, other methods are used to determine what kinds of goods and services are produced and in what amounts.

A market economy may result in choices about the output mix that some economists or policy makers find peculiar or distasteful. Many policy makers may not share the public's taste for rock videos, gambling palaces, country music, or skateboards. However, unless people's consumption of these items can be shown to be harmful to others, a market society does not pass normative judgment on tastes. Markets produce what people want to buy.

The *how* question asks what input combination will be used to produce the chosen goods and services. Should missiles be produced by combining many workers with a few units of capital or by a more capital-intensive method? Is it better to produce soybeans using lots of tractors and machinery intensely cultivating a few acres of land or using more land and workers and relatively little capital? Should college students be taught in large classes by professors (highly skilled labor) or in small sections by teaching assistants (substituting less skilled labor)? Such questions must be answered in a systematic way. In a market system, prices guide suppliers and buyers of inputs to decisions that maximize profits or minimize costs.

The *for whom* question asks who will get the goods and services produced and how much each person will receive. This is a way of asking which of many possible distributions of income will be chosen. Should the distribution be equal or unequal? Should an individual's share be based on contributions to production, on need, or on some combination of the two? A pure market system answers this question directly: a person's rewards depend on contributions to production. Other systems, including a mixed market system, use a mixture of guidelines to determine the distribution of income.

The answers to the three questions are not independent of one another. The distribution of income will determine whether there is more demand for bread and milk or luxury yachts. The production process chosen may determine the amount of each kind of output that can be produced.

Tradition, Command, and the Market

Every society has to find a way to answer the three basic economic questions. The study of the different ways of organizing economic activity, or answering these questions, is called comparative economic systems. There are many ways of classifying economic systems, such as by who owns the productive resources or by the form of government. One useful way of classifying economic systems is by the method used to answer the three basic economic questions. This classification identifies three broad types of economies: the traditional economy, the command (planned) economy, and the market economy. Of course, no economy fits neatly into any one of these categories. All economies are mixed in that they contain elements of traditional, command, and market processes.

traditional economy
An economy in which the three basic questions are answered by custom, or how things have been done in the past.

THE TRADITIONAL ECONOMY. The **traditional economy** answers the basic economic questions by appeals to tradition, or custom. That is, the answers are determined by how the questions have been answered in the past. What is produced is whatever parents have taught their children to produce on the basis of customs developed in the past. A heavily traditional society is usually not highly sophisticated. Most of people's efforts are devoted to simple production of food, clothing, and shelter. Tradition determines what kinds of food are grown, what kinds of clothing are made, and what kinds of houses are built. It also determines what combination of these three is produced in any given period.

In a traditional economy, the techniques of production (how to produce) are also passed on, with little change, from one generation to the next. In many parts of Asia and Africa, the methods of building houses and of farming have been the same for many generations. These methods use simple materials, much labor, and very little capital equipment.

Traditional societies also have established answers to the distribution question (for whom). If you have studied cultural anthropology, you know that traditional societies often have rules on how to divide the spoils of the hunt or the fruits of the harvest. Medieval Europe was a highly traditional society, with shares of crops assigned to various claimants. There were also customary duties of military service or payments to the lord of the manor. In such a traditional society, a person's claim on society's resources is determined primarily by status in the hierarchy from peasant to king.

You may recognize elements of tradition that persist even in modern industrial societies. For example, there are still many small, rural communities almost untouched by modern farming techniques. Some ethnic groups have strong traditions of sons following their fathers' occupations. Women's roles and responsibilities continue to follow tradition in many respects. For the most part, however, tradition plays a limited role in the decision-making process in modern industrial economies.

THE COMMAND ECONOMY. The **command economy**, or planned economy, answers the basic economic questions through central command and control. A central planning authority makes all decisions regarding what and how to produce. Individual production units receive detailed plans and orders that carry the weight of law. The question concerning income distribution is answered in the process of determining what and how to produce. The central planners also set wage rates and levels of production. This planning process was the primary method of organization in the Soviet Union and other countries in Eastern Europe, before the recent rapid movement toward market economies. The major goal of perestroika was to decentralize decision making and reduce the amount of central control in the Soviet Union. The nations of Eastern Europe have made an even more rapid journey toward decentralization and the use of markets.

In any economy, people plan. That is, they think about the future and prepare for it. In a traditional society, people plan for a future that will be much like the past. In a command economy, the government plays the primary role in planning how to answer the production and consumption questions for society. This kind of planning is very different from the individual planning that goes on in a market economy. Decision making is highly decentralized in a market system.

THE MARKET ECONOMY. The third type of economic system is the market economy. The **market economy** relies on incentives and the self-interested behavior of individuals to direct production and consumption through

command economy
An economy in which the three basic questions are answered through central planning and control (also called a planned economy).

market economy
An economy in which the three basic questions are answered through the market, by relying on self-interested behavior and incentives.

market exchanges. Consumers, "voting" with their dollars, determine what is produced. The result of this market process determines what goods and services are available.

Suppliers determine how to produce. Since suppliers are self-interested and seek to maximize their profits, they tend to combine inputs so as to produce a good or service at the lowest possible cost. The answer to the *how* question depends on the prices of productive resources. Suppliers will use more of abundant resources because they are relatively cheap.

The goods and services are distributed to consumers who have the purchasing power to buy them. Households that have more purchasing power (because they own more valuable productive resources) receive more goods and services. The quantity and quality of the labor skills the individual sells are the most important determinants of individual income. About 75 percent of the income in the United States is wages and salaries. Those with high-quality, scarce skills that are in great demand receive high salaries and have more influence on the output mix. People with higher earnings have more "votes" in the form of dollars spent in the marketplace.

One essential condition for undirected markets to answer the basic economic questions is the institution of **property rights**. In a command economy, most property belongs to the state. There is very limited private ownership. In fact, the process of restoring private ownership and private property rights has been slow in Eastern Europe, requiring changes in the constitutions in many cases. In a market economy, however, private property and property rights play an essential role. Markets will function only if individual buyers and sellers possess the property rights to the goods and services they want to exchange.

In a market economy, productive resources are owned by individuals. Owners of capital will not invest unless they are certain that they can claim the ownership of that capital and the products that it produces. They also need to be assured that their capital and its interest will not be taken away by the state or by force or violence. Workers will not offer their labor for hire if their rights to be paid cannot be enforced or if they know their earnings are likely to be stolen. Agreements to use productive resources and to make payments for them have to be protected from violence or breach of contract. What a market system needs, then, is a legal system that defines property rights and enforces them against any violations. Defining and enforcing property rights is an important function of government even in a pure market economy.

Beyond enforcing property rights, governments undertake some amount of central planning in all economies, including that of the United States. Federal and state governments play a substantial role in determining what is produced and how it is produced. Government policy makers make decisions about highways, schools, public parks, national defense, and other goods and services produced in the public sector. Their actions also change the distribution of income through taxes and social welfare programs. However, politicians and public policy makers are not the primary decision makers in the U.S. economy or in most other modern industrial economies, such as those of Japan, Canada, Australia, and the nations of the European Community. In these countries, most decisions are made by individuals through markets.

---

property rights
The legal rights to a specific piece of property, including the rights to own, buy, sell, or use in specific ways. Markets can exist and exchanges can occur only if individuals have property rights to goods, services, and productive resources.

RESPONDING TO CHANGE. One way to compare the workings of these three types of economic systems is to consider how each responds to change. Suppose an earthquake closes some copper mines, and the supply of copper is suddenly cut in half. A traditional economy would probably have rules to ensure a fair distribution of the reduced supply. It would not, however, be very flexible in adjusting production processes or the output mix. In a command economy, government officials would determine the possible effects of the copper shortage and estimate how long it was likely to last. They would then decide which uses of copper had the highest priority and make sure that the available copper was distributed so that those uses could occur. For example, orders might be sent to firms producing electric generators to substitute some other metal for copper, in order to conserve it for uses such as house wiring.

Contrast these processes with what occurs in a market economy. When the mines close and less copper is available, copper prices rise. Consumers of copper know immediately that the price has gone up. The high price leads consumers to search for cheaper substitutes. It also attracts a sudden flow of imported copper or scrap copper to the market. The allocation of copper might not meet the traditional economy's criterion of fairness or the command economy's priorities. However, the market response is much faster. Substitution and increased supplies occur very quickly with no need for the government to process and send information. Acquiring relevant information for decisions requires the use of scarce resources. The market system economizes on the amount of costly information needed to make production and consumption decisions.

Clearly, a market system has advantages over command and traditional economies in flexibility and capacity for dealing with change. However, the market system also has some drawbacks. Many observers criticize the distribution of income that results from the workings of the market, which can create extremes of wealth and poverty. Market systems have also been criticized for encouraging self-centered behavior at the expense of community interests.

MIXED ECONOMIES

Because of the advantages of the market system, even primarily traditional or command economies incorporate some elements of markets. Conversely, the pure market system is often modified to soften some of the harshness of pure capitalism.

The blend of tradition, command, and market-decision methods varies, but most modern industrial countries such as Canada, Japan, the United States, Australia, and some of the nations of Western Europe have mixed economies. In a **mixed economy**, the basic decision method is the market, but some economic choices are made by government. These choices are designed to modify the answers to the basic economic questions reached in the course of unregulated market activity while keeping most of the benefits of markets intact. The goal is to leave economic decisions to the market when it works well, but to intervene in the economy when the market outcome is not acceptable. On a macroeconomic level, a high rate of unemployment is an example of an unacceptable market outcome. On a microeconomic level, air pollution caused by coal-fired power plants is an example of an undesirable market outcome. In both

mixed economy
An economy in which the three basic questions are answered partly by market forces and partly through government.

instances, some people argue that the government should step in to correct the performance of the market and alter its results.

All noncommunist industrial nations are properly classed as mixed economies. Increasingly, the formerly communist nations of Eastern Europe are moving in that direction as well. The mix varies significantly from country to country. Governments are much more heavily involved in the economy in Poland, Sweden, and France than in the United States and Germany. The differences in the degree of governmental involvement in economic decisions reflect variety in political systems, national values, and historical experiences. Even within economies, the division of labor between the market and the public sector changes from time to time. The movement to privatize certain activities (to shift them from the public sector to the private sector) was very strong in the 1980s in several industrial countries, including the United States and Britain. That movement has taken hold in the formerly communist nations of Eastern Europe as their governments sell off state-owned land and enterprises to private individuals.

Most of this book presents economic theory in the context of a mixed, but primarily market, economy. When we want to cite examples of how things work in reality, we will draw mostly on the experiences of the U.S. economy. The international perspectives will offer some illustrations of how things work in other countries. Despite the emphasis on the mixed economy as the model and the United States as the chief example, the economic theory we will develop is universally applicable. What differs is how often and for what purpose different governments choose to intervene in the market.

THE CIRCULAR FLOW OF ECONOMIC ACTIVITY

circular flow model
A visual representation of the relationships between the factor market (in which income is obtained) and the product market (in which income is used to purchase goods and services).

factor market
Set of markets in which owners of the factors of production sell these to producers.

product market
Set of markets in which goods and services produced by firms are sold.

Chapter 1 discussed the use of models by economists in developing simple descriptions from which wider conclusions and inferences can be made. One model that is often used to describe a mixed economy in which the market is the primary source of decisions is the **circular flow model**. This model provides an overview of the central concerns of both macroeconomics and microeconomics. The circular flow model is a visual picture of the relationships between the **factor market**, in which income is earned, and the **product market**, in which income is used to purchase goods and services.

The first economist to describe a circular flow model was François Quesnay (1694–1774), the leader of a group of French economists known as the Physiocrats. The name *Physiocrats* comes from a French word that means "rule of nature." Physiocrats believed that the economy was a part of the natural order and that there were natural laws governing the causes of wealth. Quesnay, who was also a physician, was inspired by William Harvey's discovery that blood circulated in the human body. This led him to develop the circular flow model of the macro economy. His model was based on the view that the circulation of resources and products in the

Chapter 2   Markets, Governments, and Nations   49

economy was similar to the circulation of blood in the human body. And, like a loss of blood, any reduction in this flow was a cause for concern.

THE TWO-SECTOR CIRCULAR FLOW MODEL

In a pure market economy, there are only two kinds of actors: households and business firms.[1] Firms and households interact in two types of markets: the factor and product markets. As shown in Figure 1, households purchase goods and services produced by firms, creating a flow of dollars to firms in payment for these goods and services. The individual markets in which these exchanges take place, shown in the upper part of Figure 1, make up the product market. Firms buy factors of production (inputs or resources) from households (who own all the productive resources) in order to produce the goods and services they sell to the households. The total of the individual markets in which these transactions take place, shown

**FIGURE 1
CIRCULAR FLOW OF INCOME**
Households purchase goods and services in the product market and supply land, labor, capital, and enterprise in the factor market. Firms buy the services of these inputs in the factor market and supply goods and services in the product market.

---

1. Sometimes firms and households are one and the same. A family-owned grocery store, a home-based accounting service, or a day-care facility may operate from within a household. For simplicity, we treat them as though they can be separated. That is, we assume that households own all factors of production and firms produce all goods and services.

in the lower part of Figure 1, is the factor market. The flow of productive resources to firms generates a reverse flow of dollar payments (wages, rent, interest, and profits). Quesnay saw such a system as a closed one, in which the flow would be continuous, like the flow of blood in the human body.

As you saw in Chapter 1, models are an important part of economic analysis because they permit more orderly thinking about the world. The circular flow in Figure 1 is a very simple model of the way a market economy operates. This model is a broad overview of the economy that you need to keep in mind as we proceed to look at its various specific components. We will add a few simple refinements to the model in this chapter.

Most of macroeconomics is concerned with measuring and changing the sizes of the flows of output and income, represented by the sizes of the shaded arrows. Most of microeconomics is devoted to a closer look at the operation of the individual markets that make up the circular flow and at the behavior of individual actors (households, firms, and governments).

THE CIRCULAR FLOW MODEL WITH SAVING, GOVERNMENT, AND INTERNATIONAL TRADE

We can make the simple circular flow model more realistic in several important ways. To keep things as simple as possible, however, we will limit the model to just one flow in each market instead of two. The diagrams will show the flow of income payments through the factor market to households and the flow of purchases through the product market to the business sector.

The first adjustment to the model is to relax the assumption that the flow of income from firms to households (the lower half of Figure 1) and the flow of payments from households to firms (the upper half of Figure 1) are equal. If firms pay out all of their revenues to households and households spend every dollar they receive on purchases of goods and services, then the flows will be equal. But if households save part of their incomes, there is a leakage out of the circular flow. If firms invest (buy new capital equipment), there is an injection into the circular flow. Either an injection or a leakage can change the size of the flow. Figure 2 shows a flow of savings out of the income stream and an injection of investment spending into the income stream.

A second adjustment of the simple model is to add a government sector. You know that local, state, and federal governments produce, or cause the production of, goods ranging from schools and libraries to missiles and post offices. Governments take part of household incomes in taxes—a leakage out of the spending stream. They also purchase productive inputs from households—an injection, just like investment. Government plays an important microeconomic role because its actions affect the mix of goods and services produced and the distribution of output. At the macroeconomic level, government actions affect the amount of total production, as well as unemployment and economic growth. Figure 3 on page 52 shows a circular flow diagram with a government that collects taxes from households and purchases goods and services from business firms.

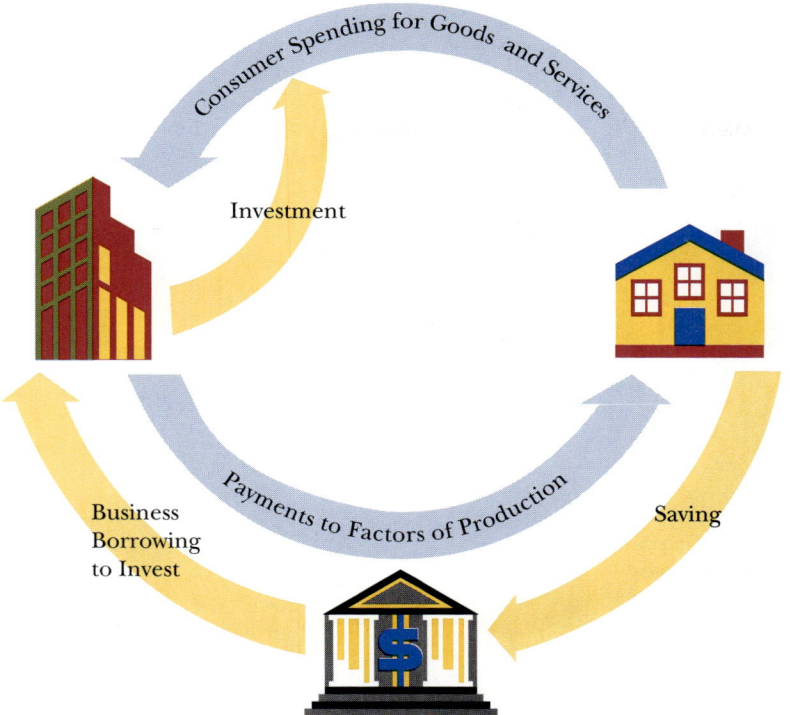

**FIGURE 2
CIRCULAR FLOW WITH SAVING AND INVESTMENT**
If households do not spend all their income, some of it will leak out of the circular flow in the form of savings. If business firms borrow in order to invest, their investment will be an injection into the circular flow.

Even this model ignores some important government transactions such as taxes on business, transfer payments to households, purchases of labor from households, and borrowing.

Finally, the simple circular flow model describes a closed economy (one that has no interaction with the rest of the world). Except for Albania, which has chosen to minimize its interactions with the rest of the world, most nations are affected by transactions with other countries. Figure 4 on page 53, therefore, adds one final change. Households purchase imports from the foreign sector (other nations). Business firms sell exports to that sector. Imports are a leakage out of the spending stream. Income earned is not directly spent on purchases of consumer goods from the domestic business sectors. Exports represent an injection of spending into the flow. Exports often represent a large part of sales and income, especially in small countries. Imports may provide a large share of total consumption. In the United States, the ratio of exports to total output is only 12 percent. In some smaller countries, this ratio is much higher. Mexico, for example, exports about 16 percent of its output, and the Netherlands exports 49 percent of what it produces.

The government sector and the foreign sector are two very important additions to the circular flow model. The government is what makes the economy a mixed economy, one in which some decisions are made outside the market. The foreign sector makes the economy an open rather

FIGURE 3
CIRCULAR FLOW WITH GOVERNMENT
Government is a third actor in the circular flow model. It interacts with households and firms in collecting taxes from households and purchasing goods and services from firms. Here households have two leakages not spent on consumption. Business firms have three customers for output: households (consumption), other business firms (investment), and government.

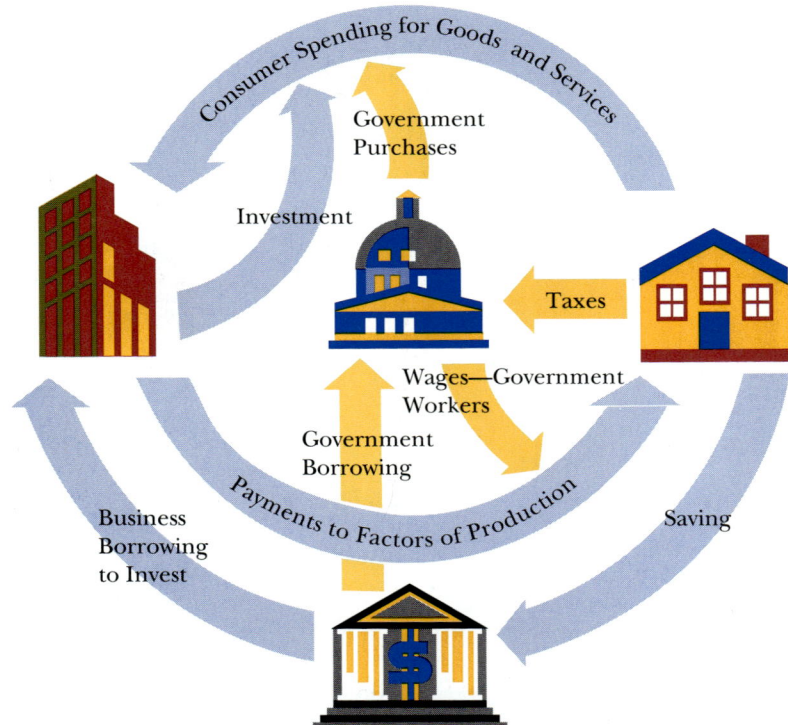

than a closed one. Actions by the three "inside" actors (households, businesses, and government) will have very different effects from what would occur in a closed economy. We will consider each of these sectors in turn.

THE ECONOMIC ROLE OF GOVERNMENT

The next chapter will introduce you to the workings of a market. All markets work in basically the same way in any economy. Supply and demand determine prices and quantities. In some economies or for some kinds of exchanges, however, the market may not be allowed to perform this function. Then some other decision-making process must be used to answer the three basic economic questions.

The most common method other than the market is to allow choices concerning the use of resources to be made by politicians or other agents of government. The kinds of decisions made through governments and the kinds made through the private sector vary among nations. In the United States, health care is private. In Canada, it is publicly financed but privately provided. In most European countries, health care is both paid

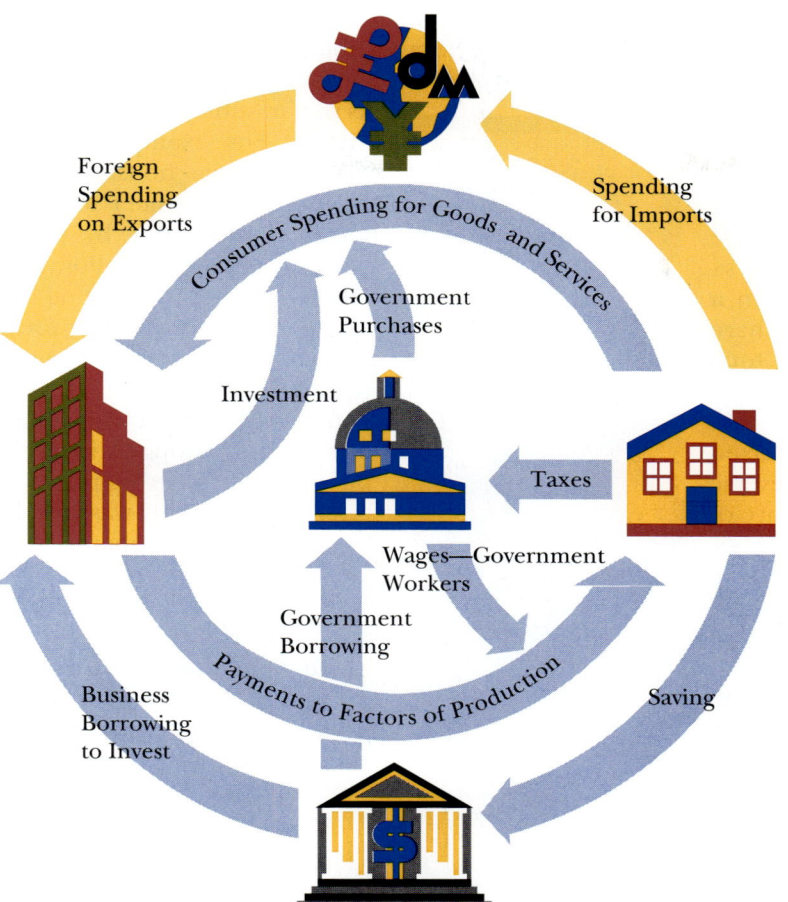

**FIGURE 4
CIRCULAR FLOW WITH A FOREIGN SECTOR**
Still another source of production and buyer of output is the rest of the world, or the foreign sector. Sales to foreign buyers are exports, and purchases from foreign suppliers are imports.

for and provided by government. Some governments (such as Sweden's) use taxes and social welfare programs to greatly modify the market distribution of income. Others (such as Japan's) do very little to change the distribution of income that results from market decisions.

In the United States, the preference is to make most decisions through the market. However, there are some things that the market cannot do or cannot do well. Many economists argue that the market does not do a very good job of addressing such problems as poverty, pollution, inflation, unemployment, and the market power of large firms. It is also difficult for private markets to provide enough of such collective goods and services as defense, education, and sewer systems.

Recall that a market system requires clearly defined property rights. That is, someone has to decide who owns what goods and services and to define their rights to use and trade those goods and services. The market cannot define and enforce property rights very well, so this role is usually assigned to governments. Citizens in most modern mixed economies cannot legally drive a car without a license, park in a handicapped space without a sticker,

International Perspective

Privatization in Britain

The division of economic activity between public and private spheres in a mixed economy is not fixed. In wartime, the share of economic activity commanded by government increases. When there are changes in citizens' preferences or political philosophy, government's share of total dollars spent may rise or fall in response. For most Western economies, there has been a gradual upward trend in the share of government spending to total GNP and the share of personal income paid in taxes. In the last decade, however, several mixed economies have tried to reverse that trend and reduce the share of economic activity controlled by government. In particular, there has been a move to spin off some allocation activities of government to the private sector. This change is called privatization. In Eastern Europe, a large part of the transition away from communism has consisted of shifting activities from government to the private sector.

Privatization has been strongly advocated in a number of countries. Nowhere was it pushed as far as in Britain under Prime Minister Margaret Thatcher. There the public sector was cut 40 percent in the 1980s. This privatization effort in Britain was stronger than in the United States in part because there had been more public sector involvement in economic activity in Britain.

Privatization can mean a variety of things. It may mean that the government continues to provide a service—for example, garbage collection—but is no longer the producer of that service. Instead, the government collects taxes to pay for the service but contracts with a private firm to actually perform it. Alternatively, the government may get out of the business of providing a service. It will either leave provision completely to the private market or limit its role to subsidizing buyers or producers. For example, instead of owning public housing, the government could meet the housing needs of the poor by providing housing vouchers to allow them to pay for housing and letting the private market respond by producing and managing the housing units. In Britain, a large amount of housing, called council housing, was owned and managed by the local public sector. One big privatization effort in the 1980s was to sell that housing to its occupants. As owners, these people have a stronger vested interest in the maintenance and upkeep of their property.

Much of what was first privatized in Britain is traditionally in the private sector in other market economies. Companies made private included British Steel, British Airways, Rolls-Royce, and Jaguar. (Jaguar was later purchased by Ford Motor Company.) When these companies were privatized, the government issued shares of stock sold to the public, creating private ownership while raising revenue for the public treasury. It was hoped that private, profit-minded managers would be more efficient, lowering costs and prices and increasing output and exports. In the last few years, however, the British government met resistance in trying to privatize such traditionally public services as water, electricity, and roads. The privatization movement has been an important episode in the continuing search for balance between the public and private sectors.

or build a fast-food restaurant in a neighborhood zoned residential. These rules represent restrictions on property rights. An unrestricted market would allow people to do all of these things, whether or not they were considered desirable by the majority. Even in a pure market economy, government is needed to establish and protect property rights.

The activities of government are grouped into three categories: allocation, redistribution, and stabilization. Stabilization and redistribution are conducted primarily through governments in all economic systems. Allocation is a microeconomic activity that is shared by the government and the market to different extents in different systems. Much of the dispute over what government should or should not do relates to its allocation activities. Also, much of the difference between market and command economies involves how allocation is divided between the market and the agencies of government.

THE ALLOCATION FUNCTION

Allocation refers to any activity of government that affects the quantity and quality of goods and services produced (that is, anything that affects the answer to the *what* question). Allocation activities in a market-based mixed economy may include producing public education, subsidizing higher education, taxing cigarettes, regulating factory and automobile emissions, setting safety standards for cars, placing quotas on steel imports, building highways, and setting prices for electric power produced by private firms.[2] In a command economy, the array of government allocation activities is much broader. Some, maybe even most, allocation activities also affect the answer to the *for whom* question because they increase the incomes of some firms and individuals at the expense of others.

PUBLIC GOODS AND POSITIVE EXTERNALITIES. In mixed economies, allocation activities are usually assigned to the public sector only when the good or service is considered a public good or when its production or consumption creates substantial external effects. We will explore each of these criteria in turn.

Economists define **public goods** as those goods that are nonrival in consumption and not subject to exclusion. What do these technical phrases mean? Sunsets and lighthouses are both nonrival in consumption. *Nonrival* means that a good or service is not used up in consumption. The fact that you are watching a sunset leaves no less sunset for someone else to enjoy. Sunsets and lighthouses are also hard to subject to exclusion. *Exclusion* means that nonpayers, or free riders, can be kept from consuming the good. **Free riders** are people or business firms who consume collective goods without contributing to the cost of their production. In addition to sunsets and lighthouses, national defense and mosquito spraying are examples of services for which it is very difficult, or at least expensive, to exclude nonpayers. Because nonpayers cannot easily be excluded, there is not much incentive for a self-interested private firm to produce such goods.

allocation
Any activities by government or its agents that affect the distribution of resources and the combination of goods and services produced.

public goods
Goods that are nonrival in consumption and not subject to exclusion.

free riders
People or business firms who consume collective goods without contributing to the cost of their production.

---

2. Some government allocation activities (for example, setting prices for electric power) relate to the regulation of monopoly.

Some economists extend the term *public good* to include goods with weak rivalry or high costs of exclusion. Examples of such nearly public goods include fire fighting, education, and highways. In all these cases, benefits spill over to nonpayers. These spillover benefits to third parties are called **positive externalities**. Where there are such positive effects, the private market may not produce enough of the good or service because some who benefit can free-ride. Note that this broader group of nearly public goods can imply an expanded role for government. In fact, all of the services mentioned have at some point been produced in the private sector. Volunteer fire departments in some rural areas still will not put out fires in nonsubscribers' homes. Education through the twelfth grade is produced in both the public and the private sector. Private toll roads were the earliest form of highways in New England.

> **positive externalities**
> Spillover benefits to third parties (free riders) that result from production or consumption of certain goods.

NEGATIVE EXTERNALITIES. When people or firms consume certain goods or engage in certain activities, they pass some of the costs of production or consumption along to others. These are **negative externalities**. Those who create noise, litter, hazards, and pollution do not bear the full cost. If the negative externalities are strong enough and widespread enough, they may constitute **public bads**. These are negative effects that impact on everyone to some degree. Public bads are the polar opposite of public goods and include such broad negative effects as global warming, depleting of the ozone layer, and extinction of endangered species. Too many negative externalities and public bads are produced if all decisions are left to private markets and individuals. Many of the regulatory activities first undertaken in the 1960s and 1970s in the United States were intended to reduce such effects.

> **negative externalities**
> Harmful spillovers to third parties that result from production or consumption of certain goods.
>
> **public bads**
> Negative external effects of production or consumption that impact a large number of individuals—for example, acid rain.

THE SCOPE OF ALLOCATION BY GOVERNMENT. Most economists agree that the government does have some responsibility to produce public goods, to encourage the production of goods with positive externalities, and to discourage the production of negative externalities and public bads. But the lines are drawn differently by different individuals within any nation. They are certainly drawn very differently in different countries. How big do spillovers have to be before government gets involved? Does the government itself have to produce public goods, or can their production be contracted out to the private sector or encouraged through subsidies? Do negative externalities have to be addressed by prohibitions or standards, or can taxes and fines do the job? An individual's, or a nation's, answers to these questions will reflect certain underlying values, ideas about the relative importance of efficiency, equity, and freedom.

Figure 5 shows a spectrum from public bads through goods with negative externalities to private goods and then to goods with positive externalities, ending with public goods. In almost all economies, it is agreed that the two ends of the spectrum call for government intervention to promote public goods and deter public bads. It is also fairly generally agreed that the market works best in the middle of the spectrum, producing and distributing private goods and nearly private goods. Nations disagree on

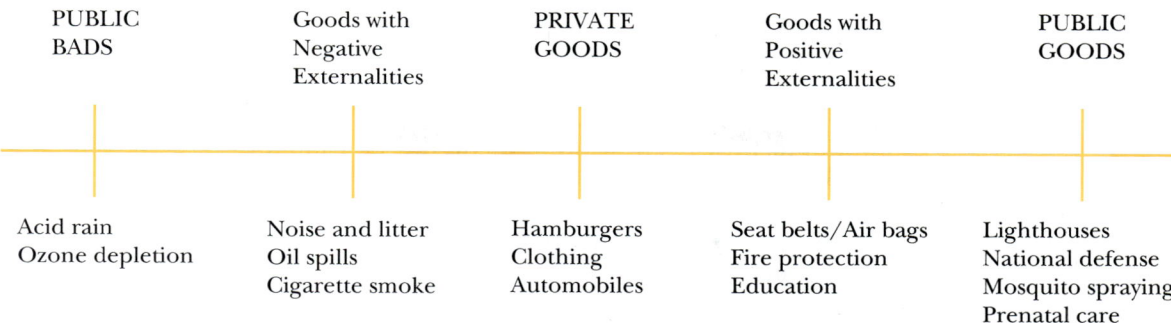

FIGURE 5
PUBLIC GOODS, PRIVATE GOODS, AND PUBLIC BADS
Goods and services fit on a spectrum from pure public goods such as defense through weak public goods, to private goods, and then to goods that cause negative external effects to some parties. At the far end of the spectrum are activities that cause widespread harm, public bads.

where to draw the lines on either side of the middle, dividing the private from the public sphere.

In the United States, there is another division of responsibility, because the United States has a federal system of government. A federal system has another layer of government (besides the national level) with independent responsibility. In the United States, a large part of allocation by government occurs at the state and local levels. Some public goods are provided on a national scale—defense, for example. But many are provided at the community level. Different cities and towns choose different combinations of public services. One city may choose more street lights and snow removal. Another may vote for public parks and better roads. Allowing this kind of variety in local choices makes governments more responsive to the values and desires of the people who are paying the bills. This diversity is an attractive feature of fiscal federalism, a system in which the economic responsibilities of government are not concentrated at a single level but dispersed among several levels. The United States, Canada, Germany, and Australia are examples of countries in which governments at the state or province level have notable power and responsibility. Economists find a federal system attractive because the autonomous lower levels of governments are in competition for residents and business firms. This competition creates diversity and choice, and perhaps greater efficiency.

THE REDISTRIBUTION FUNCTION

The distribution of income in a market economy is based on each person's contributions to production. There is no denying that the distribution of income determined by the market is quite unequal. Some people are very wealthy, and others are very poor. One way in which economies differ greatly is the extent to which the political process is involved in redistribution. **Redistribution** means taking income from one group and giving it to another through taxes and transfer payments.

In any economy, when the government taxes individuals with high incomes, they have less incentive to work, save, and invest to increase output in future years. On the other hand, some individuals cannot earn an income through the market. They may be too old, too young, too sick, or too handicapped. Others work as hard as they can with the skills and resources at their disposal but still cannot earn enough to get by. There is some private redistribution, but private charity is subject to a free rider problem. (Many people will not participate because they know others

redistribution
Actions by government that transfer income from one group to another.

will.) Such free-riding behavior makes income redistribution more or less a public good that falls within the domain of government.

How much income should be redistributed? To whom should it go? How can redistribution be managed to minimize the negative effects on work incentives? These are difficult questions to answer. As a result, the answers are very different in different countries. In general, there is more redistribution and greater equality of income in countries at the middle of the mixed economy spectrum than in countries at either the command or the market extreme.

An obvious way to redistribute income is to use taxes and transfer payments. In the United States, transfer payments take the form of Social Security benefits, food stamps, and welfare payments. Taxes that collect relatively more from the rich than the poor, such as the U.S. federal income tax, mean that the rich pay more than the poor do for the same level of public services. This difference is a form of redistribution. In the United States, transfer payments are primarily financed by the federal government rather than state governments. The states do administer the programs and pay part of the cost. Redistributing income at the federal level makes it possible to reduce inequality between rich and poor states, as well as between rich and poor individuals within states.

Transfer payments are the most visible form of income redistribution. However, there is a redistributive side to almost everything the government does. If increased funds are spent on public education, families with school-aged children benefit more than childless households. Increased spending on health care benefits those who are sick. Quotas on steel imports benefit steelworkers but not steel users. Expanded student loan programs help college-aged people who qualify at the expense of all other taxpayers and would-be borrowers. Since it is virtually impossible for the government to spend money on anything without redistributing income, it is difficult to measure how much redistribution takes place.

Indirect kinds of income redistribution often benefit those who are not poor, that is, the middle class or the rich. Income redistribution through taxes and transfer payments is often criticized because of its effect on incentives. However, other government programs are equally vulnerable to criticism as "welfare for the rich." Examples are subsidies for large farms, tax loopholes for real estate owners and developers and oil and gas producers, bailouts for savings and loan institutions, and cost overruns by large defense contractors. This kind of redistribution is a consequence of democracy, where the rich and the middle class have more political clout than the poor. In any economy, however, how much redistribution is enough, from whom it should come, and to whom it should go are very difficult questions.

THE STABILIZATION FUNCTION

The last and most recently developed task of government is stabilization. **Stabilization** refers to government actions to reduce changes in output, employment, and prices. Until recently, many people believed that stabilization problems were unique to market economies, which tended to go through severe ups and downs in output, employment, and prices. It is now clear, however, that unemployment and inflation were problems for the command economies of Eastern Europe as well.

stabilization
Actions by government to reduce changes in output, employment, and prices.

Stabilization is mainly a macroeconomic function. However, the ways in which stabilization policies are carried out also affect the mix of goods produced (allocation) and the distribution of costs and benefits (redistribution). Government attempts to stabilize the economy consist of increasing spending or cutting taxes to increase output and employment or cutting spending and increasing taxes to control inflation. In addition, changes in the money supply are used to expand or contract economic activity.

Economists disagree about how stable a market economy would be if it were left alone. Historically, in the U.S. economy (and most market economies), there have been periods of high unemployment combined with low inflation, or occasionally even deflation (falling prices). These downturns have alternated with periods of more rapid inflation (increasing prices) and lower unemployment in a cyclical pattern. Even though such cycles have been less severe since World War II, it cannot be concluded that the U.S. economy has been more stable with government intervention than it was when the government played a much smaller role.

When spending and taxes are used to try to stabilize the economy, budget deficits or surpluses are likely to result. The rationale for deficits is that price stability and full employment should dictate whether or not the budget is balanced. However, the U.S. government has run deficits that cannot be justified on the basis of stabilization activity. The central governments of both the United States and the Soviet Union had substantial budget deficits throughout the 1980s. Since 1958, the U.S. federal budget has been in deficit in all but two years.

ECONOMIC ROLES OF GOVERNMENT

FUNCTION	EXAMPLE
• Allocation	
Public goods	Defense, courts
Goods with positive external effects	Education, seat belts
Negative external effects	Pollution controls
• Redistribution	Social Security
• Stabilization	Cutting taxes to end recession

THE ROLE OF THE FOREIGN SECTOR

The last of the four sectors is the foreign sector. All nations engage in trade with other nations to some extent, because there are goods and services they cannot produce for themselves or can produce only at a very high cost. In most nations, there is also some inflow and outflow of the factors of production—labor, capital, land, and enterprise. Some nations, including the United States, allow goods and factors to flow relatively freely. Others, especially China, Japan, and the Soviet Union, restrict the movement of one or both with tariffs, quotas, immigration restrictions, capital controls, and exchange controls.

In the circular flow diagram, the sizes of the arrows labeled "imports" and "exports" indicate the size of the foreign sector, or the importance of markets and suppliers in other countries. If the foreign sector is small, the economy is more like a closed economy. In a closed economy, activities of governments or private individuals have all or most of their impact within the economy and do not spill over to the rest of the world. Also, actions in the rest of the world have little or no impact on this kind of economy. With a large foreign sector, however, an economy is more likely to affect and be affected by the rest of the world. It is more vulnerable to the effects of inflation or recession in other countries. When its export sales fall, since exports are a large share of total output, the impact is felt throughout the economy.

The larger its land area, population, and total output or income, the less dependent an economy is likely to be on trade. Trade averages 20 to 40 percent of GNP across the broad range of all countries, but there is tremendous variety within this range. The ratio of exports to total output, or GNP, in 1986 was relatively low for such large countries as India (9 percent) and China (11 percent). Countries that are geographically isolated, such as Australia (17 percent), also tend to have a lower ratio of trade to GNP because the cost of shipping is so high. At the other extreme, small countries that produce primary products (agricultural or mineral) often have very high ratios of trade to GNP. The small oil-producing nation of Bahrein exports 92 percent of its total output. The tiny duchy of Luxembourg exports 72 percent of what it produces. The Caribbean nation of Jamaica, whose revenues derive from tourism, exports 62 percent of its GNP.

INTERNATIONAL PERSPECTIVE

THE SIZE OF THE FOREIGN SECTOR

The importance of trade can be measured by comparing either exports or imports to GNP. For many nations, the two measures will be about the same, but some countries are very unbalanced. Japan, for example, exports 12 percent of what it produces but imports less than 8 percent of what it consumes. Imports greatly exceeded exports for the United States for most of the 1980s. By 1990, however, the two were close to equal, with exports being about 11 percent of GNP and imports about 12 percent. One of the largest gaps between exports and imports occurs in the small, developing nation of Guinea-Bissau. Its ratio of trade to GNP is only 10 percent for exports but 53 percent for imports.

By either measure, the share of trade in the GNP is a good indicator of how dependent on other nations a nation is. The higher the trade ratio, the more sensitive a country is to events in foreign markets and the more dependent it is on foreign sources of supply. The benefits of trade are substantial, but one of the prices nations pay for those benefits is less control over their own economic destiny.

BENEFITS AND COSTS OF INTERNATIONAL TRADE

In general, a nation benefits from trade in both goods and factors. Trade enables households to consume goods that are not produced at home or would be much more costly to produce there. Trade enables firms to produce for larger markets, often lowering their costs of production. Trade also forces firms to respond to competitors in other countries that are producing products that are cheaper, more appealing, or safer. A flow of labor or capital may help a country overcome its shortages in certain factors of production.

Those who work for or own firms whose products compete with imports as well as workers who compete directly with immigrant workers may not have a positive attitude toward such trade. These groups are likely to lobby for tariffs and other forms of protection in order to shield themselves from the effects of foreign competition. In addition, an economy that depends on international trade to market its products or supply needed goods and services will be affected by the actions of other countries. Interdependence with other countries reduces the amount of control that the government can exert over domestic economic activities.

For a nation as a whole, however, there are substantial gains from trade with other nations. Let's explore one of the main benefits of such trade, the gains that result from specializing on the basis of comparative advantage.

SPECIALIZATION AND COMPARATIVE ADVANTAGE

A major benefit of international trade is that it permits a nation to go beyond its production possibilities curve without acquiring more resources or improving technology. A nation can attain better combinations of output through specialization and exchange. **Specialization**, or the division of labor, means that individuals will produce more than they intend to consume of one or only a few items and will trade the excess for other things they want.

specialization Limiting production activities to one or a few goods and services that one produces best in order to exchange for other goods.

Specialization allows individuals to take the fullest advantage of their unique talents and skills. Some people who are strong and agile can become professional athletes. Some people who are intelligent and gifted talkers can become lawyers. Specialization allows individuals to concentrate on what they do best and to produce more than they could if they tried to engage in a variety of production activities. For people with very valuable specialized skills, such as basketball stars or brain surgeons, the opportunity cost of using their time for other purposes is very high. Think about the value of the time an NBA star spends in cooking his own dinner or mowing his lawn!

Nations, states, and regions also specialize. The phrase *banana republic* used to refer to small Latin American countries that were heavily specialized in producing bananas for export. These countries used the earnings from bananas to import and consume a wide variety of products that they did not produce. Other small countries are highly specialized in oil, coffee, cocoa, sugar, and other agricultural products and raw materials. Within the United States, pineapples come from Hawaii, oranges from Florida and California, wheat from the midwest and plains states, and peaches from Georgia and South Carolina. Nations, states, and regions also specialize in certain types of goods and services. Japan is famous for small cars and electronic products, Switzerland for watches and banking, and France and Italy for wines.

By specializing, individuals, regions, and nations can produce more total output with no increase in resources or breakthroughs in technology. Thus, specialization improves a nation's standard of living and lets it move outside the production possibilities curve. Small countries especially can consume more goods and enjoy a wider range of goods and services through specialization and trade than if they were limited to what they produced. This point was strongly emphasized by the founder of modern economics, Adam Smith. In his 1776 classic *The Wealth of Nations*, he saw specialization and trade as the engine of growth.

SPECIALIZATION AND EXCHANGE. The benefits of specializing require that people or nations engage in exchange. If you choose to specialize, you will have to engage in trade because you will give up producing all the other goods and services you need. If you are concentrating on what you do well, you don't have time to spend cutting your own hair, growing your own vegetables, or repairing your own car. You certainly don't have time to build your house or manufacture your car! One thing that distinguishes modern industrial societies from less developed countries is the extent of specialization and exchange. The average American produces very little of what he or she consumes. Instead, individuals specialize in one or two products or services and purchase everything else in the market.

COMPARATIVE ADVANTAGE. How do individuals, regions, or nations decide what products to produce for exchange? How do they answer the question "In what should we specialize?" Sometimes the answer is obvious, determined by climate or other resources. In general, the answer lies in the **principle of comparative advantage**. This principle states that each person, group, or country should specialize in that product or service for which the opportunity cost of production is lowest. If that principle is followed, the total output of a group of people, an entire economy, or, for that matter, the entire world will be maximized. Higher total output will result, with no increase in resources or improvement in technology.

Figure 6 illustrates comparative advantage using two straight-line production possibilities curves. Both George and Karen can produce various combinations of cookies and hamburgers with their available resources, as the curves illustrate. Before specializing, Karen is producing 30 hamburgers and 10 dozen cookies a month for her own consumption (point *A* in Figure 6). George is producing 10 hamburgers a month and 40 dozen cookies for himself (point *R* in Figure 6). Karen, who has had some experience working in a fast-food restaurant, is better at making hamburgers. Each hamburger she makes requires that she give up production of only ½ dozen cookies. George's hamburgers cost him 2 dozen cookies per hamburger produced. Karen has a lower opportunity cost for hamburgers, which means that George must have a lower opportunity cost for cookies. Clearly, they should specialize.

If they decide to specialize, Karen will produce 50 hamburgers (point *B* in Figure 6). George will turn out 60 dozen cookies (point *S*). Total out-

principle of comparative advantage The idea that output will be maximized if people specialize in producing those goods or services for which their opportunity costs are lowest and engage in exchange to obtain other things they want.

Adam Smith is regarded as the founder of modern economics. He was born in Kirkcaldy, Scotland. He was educated at the University of Glasgow and at Oxford University in England and eventually became a professor at Glasgow. *The Wealth of Nations*, published in 1776, marked a break with previous economic thought. Smith stressed the role of individual self-interest in promoting overall welfare. In his view, the "invisible hand" of self-interest leads people to act in socially desirable ways. For example, you know when you arrive at a hotel in a strange city in the evening that you can count on being able to buy breakfast in the morning. People who hope to make a profit will have restaurants and coffee shops open for your business.

Before Smith, people who wrote on economic issues emphasized what government could and should do to run the economy in the national interest. Smith, however, argued that the role of government should be minimal. It should provide for national defense, produce and regulate the money supply, and support a system of laws with swift, efficient justice in the courts. Beyond these activities, private individuals pursuing their own self-interest would provide direction for economic activity. There was no need for government to intervene. For more than a century, Adam Smith's ideas led economists to view the best economic role of government as minimal.

Smith was not naive about the risks of relying on self-interest. He argued that whenever producers of the same product get together, their thoughts rapidly turn to conspiring to raise prices and increase profits. He was opposed to this type of monopoly behavior and thought that government should do nothing to encourage such practices. But as long as the government does not promote monopoly, market forces and competition will limit the ability of firms to take advantage of their customers.

Opportunity cost is another useful concept developed from the work of Adam Smith. He used the example of a village where people could hunt deer or beaver. As he pointed out, the opportunity cost of bagging one deer was the number of beaver that could have been trapped with the same time and trouble. Smith recognized that the only true cost in economics is opportunity cost.

ECONOMIC PROFILE

ADAM SMITH

1723–1790

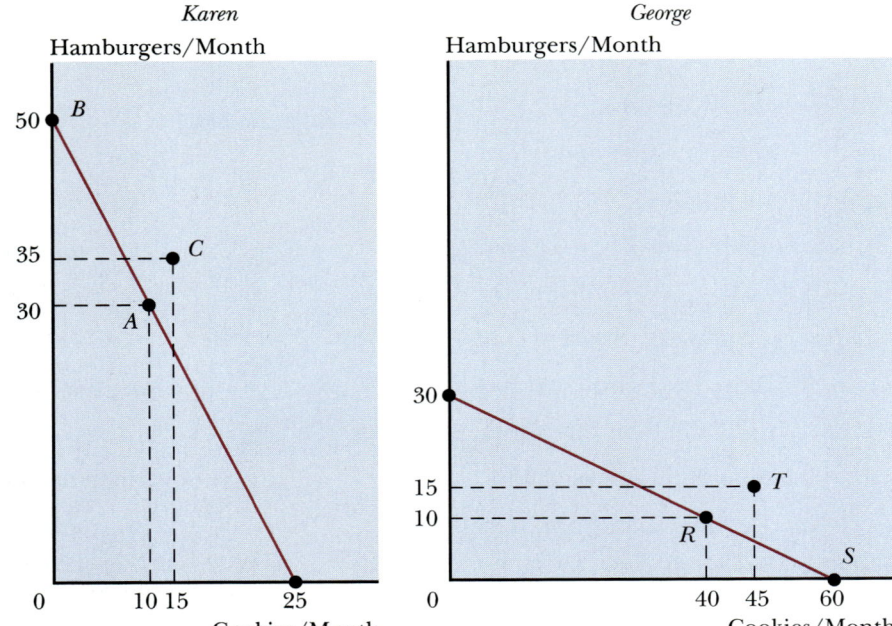

**FIGURE 6
SPECIALIZATION AND EXCHANGE**
When Karen and George specialize, total output increases from 40 hamburgers (Karen 30, George 10) and 50 dozen cookies (Karen 10, George 40) to 50 hamburgers (Karen) and 60 dozen cookies (George). After exchange, both can consume more than before. Karen is at point C instead of A and George is at point T instead of R.

put increases by 10 hamburgers and 10 dozen cookies. All that remains is to divide up the gains. One combination that makes both better off is to split the increase equally. Thus, Karen consumes at point C in Figure 6 and enjoys 35 hamburgers and 15 dozen cookies. George consumes at point T, with 15 hamburgers and 45 dozen cookies. Both have gained because they are consuming more than before. There is more total output with no new resources and no improvement in technology.

The principle of comparative advantage means that both trading partners gain when individuals and nations specialize in the products for which their opportunity cost is lower and trade for what others produce more efficiently. Comparative advantage is the basis of all trade, not just international trade. We will return to comparative advantage in great detail in the chapter on international trade.

Chapter 2 Markets, Governments, and Nations

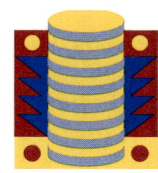

Summary

1. The factors of production consist of labor, land, capital, and enterprise. Labor receives wages, land receives rent, capital receives interest, and enterprise receives profit.

2. Every economy must address three basic economic questions: what to produce, how to produce it, and for whom to produce. Processes for answering these questions are tradition, command, and the market.

3. In different degrees, industrial nations have tried to answer the basic economic questions by using a mixed economy, where the market is the primary method, but government officials often intervene in the marketplace in an attempt to improve economic performance.

4. The circular flow model is a useful overview of the relations among sectors in a market economy. The basic model shows the interactions of households and businesses in the factor and product markets. More realistic versions add saving and investment, government, and a foreign sector.

5. There are some necessary functions that the market cannot perform or cannot perform well. These include defining and protecting property rights, providing public goods and correcting for external effects, bringing about a "fair" distribution of income, and stabilization.

6. Allocation by government includes not only the production of public goods and the reduction of public bads, but also any activities that affect private decisions about production and consumption. These activities include taxes, subsidies, and regulation. Different societies make different choices about how much allocation is carried out by government.

7. Redistribution changes the unequal distribution of income that results from the market. Redistribution occurs mainly through taxes and transfer payments, but any action of government will have redistributive effects.

8. Stabilization refers to the activities of government aimed at creating full employment, stable prices, and a satisfactory rate of economic growth. These actions include changes in taxes, transfer payments, and spending as well as changes in the money supply.

9. International trade in goods, services, and factors of production benefits both trading partners. Some workers and firms in a nation experience losses because of foreign competition. The gains usually exceed the losses, but the losers may succeed in persuading the government to restrict trade for their protection.

10. Individuals and nations can gain a higher standard of living with the same resources and technology if they engage in specialization and exchange. Total output will be larger if individuals, regions, and nations produce those goods for which their opportunity costs are lowest and trade for other things. This is the principle of comparative advantage.

New Terms

factors of production
labor
wages
human capital
land
rent
capital
interest
investment
enterprise
profit
market
traditional economy
command economy
market economy
property rights
mixed economy
circular flow model
factor market
product market
allocation
public goods
free riders
positive externalities
negative externalities
public bads
redistribution
stabilization
specialization
principle of comparative advantage

QUESTIONS FOR DISCUSSION

1. Is your college degree an investment in human capital? What is the opportunity cost of your degree?

2. Suppose you own a farm with buildings and machinery, all five members of your family work on the farm, and you take the risks and manage the production. Identify all the factors of production involved and classify them correctly.

3. How are macroeconomic problems handled in a mixed economy?

4. In what ways are factor markets and product markets similar? In what ways are they different?

5. List all the leakages and all the injections you have observed in circular flow diagrams.

6. Which of the following institutions or actions represent tradition, command, or market processes?
   a. the military draft
   b. the volunteer army
   c. encouraging daughters to be teachers and nurses
   d. requiring women to be teachers and nurses
   e. offering financial incentives to anyone who becomes a teacher or nurse
   f. five generations of farmers tilling the same land
   g. prohibiting the sale of marijuana
   h. taxing the sale of alcoholic beverages

7. What should be the role of government in providing education? Should it produce, subsidize, or get out of education altogether? Why do you suppose that education through the twelfth grade is "free" (actually, paid for through taxes) but only subsidized beyond that level? Does it have anything to do with who gets the benefits?

8. Can you find examples of services produced in the public sector in your area that are produced in the private sector elsewhere, or vice versa? Can you explain why the choice might not be the same in different sections of the country or in communities of different sizes?

9. Classify each of the following government actions as primarily allocation, redistribution, or stabilization.
   a. cutting taxes to end a recession
   b. making Social Security payments to the elderly
   c. paying farmers not to produce corn
   d. putting restrictions on the amount of sulphur dioxide factories are allowed to emit into the air
   e. buying paper shredders for government offices

10. Where would you put each of the following items on the spectrum in Figure 5?
   a. hospital wastes that wash up on beaches
   b. noise from a student apartment complex that bothers the neighbors
   c. highways
   d. Christmas decorations that make a house more attractive
   e. flu shots

11. Why is specialization necessary for exchange, and vice versa?

12. Angela and Arthur have been assigned the tasks of filing folders and grading papers. Angela can file 50 folders an hour and grade 20 papers. Arthur can file 25 folders per hour and grade 25 papers. The total output for these two work-study students is to grade 100 papers and file 200 folders. How long will it take if they divide the task equally? How long will it take if they specialize based on the principle of comparative advantage? How much time do they gain?

13. In Question 12, what is Angela's opportunity cost for filing in terms of grading not done? What is Arthur's? How does this information help you to determine comparative advantage?

14. Use the following information on the production of bushels of peaches and tomatoes in two countries, Upland and Downland. Plot a pair of production possibilities curves like those in Figure 6. Before trade, each country is producing 20 bushels of peaches and 30 bushels of tomatoes. Locate their initial production

UPLAND		DOWNLAND	
PEACHES	TOMATOES	PEACHES	TOMATOES
40	0	50	0
30	15	40	10
20	30	30	20
10	45	20	30
0	60	10	40
		0	50

combinations on the graphs. Determine who should specialize in what, locate the production points after specialization, and determine how much the total output will increase.

15. Individuals as well as nations have comparative advantages, which can change. How will going to college and getting a degree change your comparative advantage?

SUGGESTIONS FOR FURTHER READING

Carson, Robert B. *Economic Issues Today: Alternative Approaches*, 5th ed. New York: St. Martin's, 1991. The introduction gives an overview of alternative values and approaches underlying different economic systems.

Hoover, Kenneth, and Raymond Plant. *Conservative Capitalism in Britain and the United States: A Critical Appraisal.* London and New York: Routledge, Chapman and Hall, 1989. Offers a good discussion of the division of responsibilities between the state and the market and the ideological foundations for that choice.

Radford, R. A. "The Economic Organization of a P.O.W. Camp." *Economica* (November 1945): 189–201. This classic article demonstrates how a market economy quickly established itself in a P.O.W. camp during World War II and highlights the gains from exchange.

Wolf, Charles. *Markets or Governments: Choosing Between Imperfect Alternatives.* Cambridge, MA: MIT Press, 1988. Compares market and nonmarket alternatives for various kinds of productive activities.

AFTER STUDYING THIS CHAPTER, YOU SHOULD BE ABLE TO:

1. Define supply and demand and list the factors influencing each.
2. Demonstrate the concepts of supply and demand using:
   a. words,
   b. numbers or functions,
   c. graphs.
3. Identify on a graph the differences between:
   a. changes in demand and changes in the quantity demanded, and
   b. changes in supply and changes in the quantity supplied.
4. Show how changes in the *ceteris paribus* conditions affect demand and supply.
5. Explain how equilibrium is reached, and what disequilibrium and equilibrium mean.
6. Use the supply and demand model to illustrate the concepts of
   a. marginal analysis,
   b. equilibrium,
   c. comparative statics,
   d. endogenous and exogenous variables,
   e. primary and secondary effects.
7. Discuss the functions of prices in a free market.
8. Explain how interference with the market distorts its allocative mechanism.

CHAPTER 3

SUPPLY AND DEMAND: THE BASICS OF ECONOMIC ANALYSIS

INTRODUCTION

Markets are places where buyers and sellers meet to engage in exchange. In the process of exchanging, they determine prices and quantities produced. The supply and demand model explains how buyers and sellers interact to determine prices and quantities. It is the most basic and most widely used model in economics.

Economists view **demand** as the desire and ability to consume certain quantities at various prices over a certain time period. Demand is not seen as needs or wants that can be measured in some social or biological way. The concept of need is reserved for policy makers and political decision making. For needs and wants to be demands, they must be viewed not as wishes or dreams but as what people will actually do when confronted with different sets of prices. Similarly, **supply** refers to what firms are actually willing and able to produce and offer for sale at various prices over a period of time.

demand
The desire and ability to consume certain quantities of a good at various prices over a certain period of time.

supply
The quantity of a good offered for sale at various prices during a certain time period.

DEMAND

Many things affect the demand for a good or service. There is much evidence that price is a very important determinant of demand. Thus, we focus first on what happens when the price of a good or service changes relative to the prices of other goods and services. In looking at the relationship between price and quantity, economists hold constant everything else that affects demand.

69

law of demand
The quantity demanded of a good or service is negatively related to its price, *ceteris paribus*.

The **law of demand** states that the *quantity demanded* of a good or service is negatively related to its price, *ceteris paribus*. In other words, if everything else is held constant, consumers will purchase more of a good or service at a lower price than at a higher price. As price rises, *ceteris paribus*, consumers will purchase less of a good or service, because its opportunity cost in terms of other goods is higher. Note that we are saying quantity demanded—not demand—is a function of price. This distinction is critical. Demand refers to a whole set of price-quantity combinations. Quantity demanded is the amount consumers want to buy at a particular price.

demand schedule
A table that shows quantities demanded at various prices during a specific time period.

A **demand schedule** shows the various quantities demanded at various prices during a specified period of time. How can we generate a demand schedule for an individual? We could develop Mary's demand schedule for potato chips since she knows all of the *ceteris paribus* conditions that apply (tastes, income, prices of substitutes, and so on). We might suggest various prices and ask her how many bags of potato chips she would buy at each price. Actual experiments with a variety of subjects support the validity of the law of demand.

The demand schedule in Table 1 shows Fred's demand for bread. As price falls, Fred chooses to consume larger quantities of bread per week as he substitutes bread for other items he might purchase. Table 1 is consistent with the law of demand because Fred demands larger quantities of bread at lower prices. Note that there is a time dimension—a week. We cannot determine how many loaves Fred will buy without specifying a time frame—per day, per week, per month, per year, or per lifetime.

demand curve
A graph representing a demand schedule and showing the quantity demanded at various prices in a certain time period.

We can represent the demand schedule of Table 1 on a graph called a demand curve, as shown in Figure 1. A **demand curve** is a graph representing a demand schedule. When we draw a demand curve, the vertical axis shows the price per unit and the horizontal axis shows the quantity per time period.[1]

MARKET DEMAND

Table 1 and Figure 1 show a demand schedule and a demand curve for a single consumer. Sellers, however, are more interested in the market demand curve for a brand of bread or even the market demand curve for all

TABLE 1
FRED'S DEMAND FOR BREAD

PRICE PER LOAF (CENTS)	QUANTITY DEMANDED PER WEEK
50	1
40	7
30	13
20	19
10	25
5	28

1. If graphing the schedule is confusing, review the appendix to Chapter 1. We usually draw linear curves for convenience.

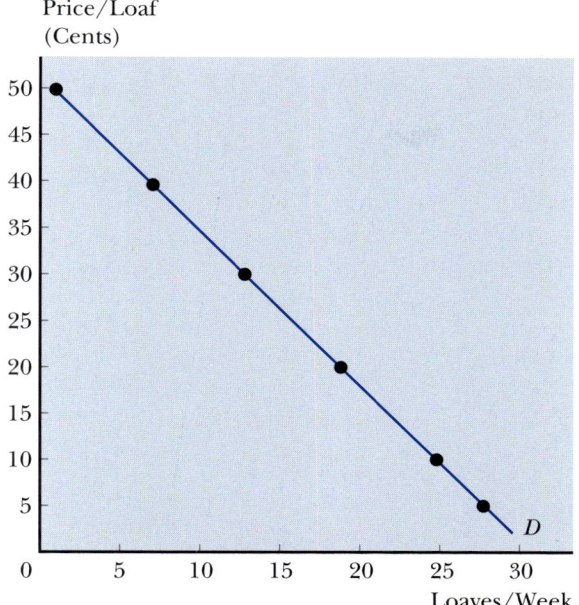

FIGURE 1
FRED'S DEMAND FOR BREAD
An individual's demand curve shows the quantity that he or she will purchase during a specific period at different prices.

bread. A **market demand curve** shows what quantities will be demanded by all consumers in a certain market at various prices. The market demand curve is the sum of all of the individual demand curves. We add the demand curves for individual consumers horizontally. For example, to determine the market quantity of bread demanded at a price of 40 cents per loaf, we add the 7 loaves demanded by Fred to 2 loaves demanded by Mary, a loaf demanded by Joanna, and so on. We find a total (market) quantity demanded of 10,000 loaves at a price of 40 cents per loaf. These two numbers represent one point on the market demand curve. We then repeat the addition of quantities demanded for every other price. The result is the downward-sloping market demand curve shown in Figure 2, showing a negative relationship between price and quantity. At higher prices, buyers want fewer loaves. At lower prices, they want more.

As price changes in the market, the quantity demanded changes in the opposite direction, just as it did for Fred. Figure 2 shows that 13,000 loaves of bread are purchased at a price of 35 cents per loaf. If the price falls to 20 cents per loaf, the quantity demanded increases to 25,000 loaves. If the price rises to 45 cents per loaf, the quantity demanded decreases to 5,000 loaves.

market demand curve The sum of all of the individual demand curves. A market demand curve shows what quantities will be demanded by all consumers in a specific time frame in a certain market at various prices.

CETERIS PARIBUS CONDITIONS AND SHIFTS IN DEMAND

Many things can affect the demand for a good or service. Economists generally focus on a few, separated into two important categories: price, and everything else. Because price is so important, economists express demand as a function of price. The price of a good affects the quantity demanded. Everything else affects demand. We held the nonprice determinants of demand constant while we focused on price. Now we want to look at the nonprice determinants and how they affect the demand curve.

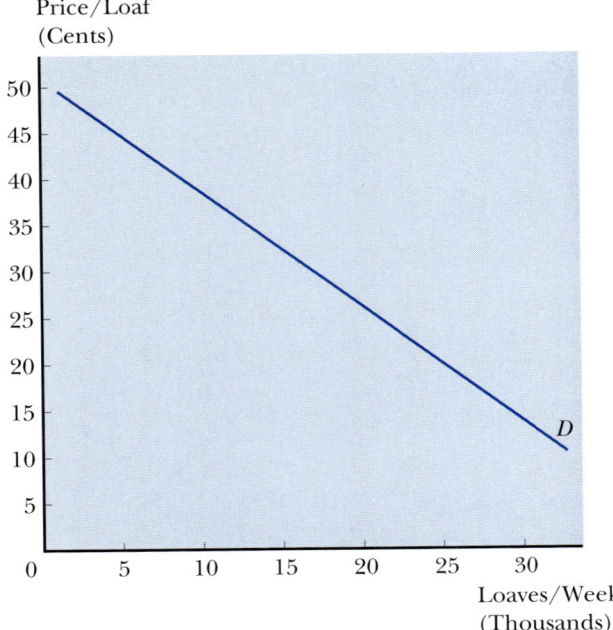

**FIGURE 2
MARKET DEMAND FOR BREAD**
A market demand curve is a graph depicting how much will be purchased in the market at various prices. It is the sum of all of the individual demand curves.

The nonprice determinants of demand are as follows:

1. tastes of the group demanding the good or service,
2. size of the group demanding the good or service,
3. income and wealth of the group demanding the good or service,
4. prices of other goods and services,
5. expectations about future prices or income.

Nearly everything that affects demand does so by working through one of these determinants. Weather, for example, may affect demand for bread by changing tastes. People may eat more cold sandwiches instead of hot meals in warmer weather. Economists study demand by holding all but one of these determinants constant and determining what happens when that one changes. Nonprice determinants of demand are the *ceteris paribus* conditions discussed in Chapter 1.

Changes in the *ceteris paribus* conditions change the demand for the good or service. On the graph, a change in demand is seen as a shift of the curve. Economists are careful to distinguish clearly between movements along a demand curve and changes (or shifts) of the curve itself. Movements along the curve are *changes in quantity demanded*, caused solely by a change in the *price* of the good. When the price of bread goes up, fewer loaves are demanded—a change in quantity demanded. Changes (or shifts) of the curve are *changes in demand* caused by changes in any of the *ceteris paribus* conditions. When the weather gets hot or population increases, more loaves are demanded at every possible price—a change in demand.

TASTES. How do changes in the *ceteris paribus* conditions affect the market demand for a good? Suppose people's tastes change in favor of bread because the weather is hot or a fad develops for high-fiber diets. As shown in Figure 3, this change in demand shifts the entire demand curve to the right, from D_0 to D_1. An **increase in demand** means that at every price, consumers demand a larger amount than before. The opposite would occur if tastes changed away from bread. Such a change in tastes would cause a decrease in demand, represented by a shift from D_0 to D_2. A **decrease in demand** means that at every price, consumers demand a smaller quantity than before.

increase in demand
A shift in the demand curve indicating that at every price, consumers demand a larger amount than before.

decrease in demand
A shift in the demand curve indicating that at every price, consumers demand a smaller amount than before.

SIZE OF THE GROUP. The market demand curve, as you saw earlier, is found by adding the individual demand curves. Thus, if the number of individuals in the group of potential consumers changes, market demand will also change. Suppose demand curve D_0 in Figure 3 represents the demand for automobiles in a state with a minimum driving age of 16 years. If the law is changed to allow 15-year-olds to drive, the group of potential consumers increases. Some of them, or their families, will want an extra car for the extra driver. The demand curve will shift from D_0 to D_1. The size of the group has increased. Therefore, there has been an increase in the demand for the good, or a larger quantity demanded at every price.

On the other hand, if the size of the group decreases, there will be a decrease in demand, a shift from D_0 to D_2 in Figure 3. The big drop in the birth rate in the late 1960s and early 1970s decreased demand first for baby food and diapers and then for public school teachers. In the 1990s, it is affecting demand for automobiles and college teachers.

INCOME AND WEALTH. Income changes can also shift the demand curve. You might expect that demand for all goods would increase as income increases. However, this is not always true. Whether demand increases in this case depends on whether the good is a normal good or an inferior

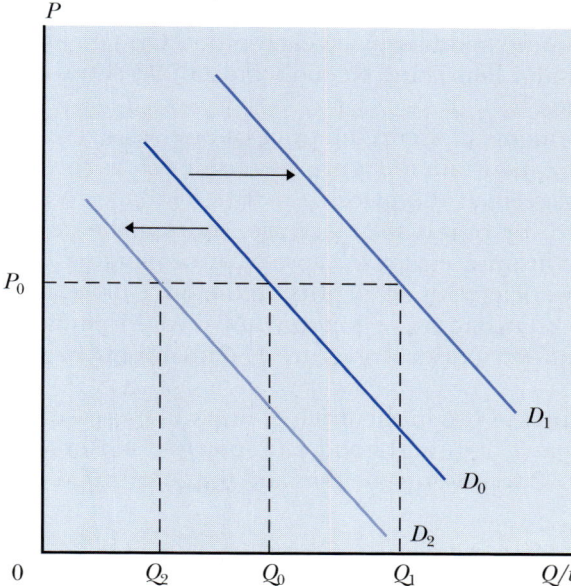

FIGURE 3
EFFECTS OF CHANGES IN THE *CETERIS PARIBUS* CONDITIONS ON DEMAND
If a change causes more of a good to be demanded at every price, the demand curve will shift to the right, as from D_0 to D_1. A change that causes less to be demanded at every price causes a shift to the left, as from D_0 to D_2.

normal good
A good for which demand increases as income increases.

inferior good
A good for which demand decreases as income increases.

good. A **normal good** is a good for which demand increases as income increases, *ceteris paribus*. If demand falls when income rises, the good is an **inferior good**. Most goods are normal goods. However, there are a few inferior goods.

Consider, for example, the difference between steak and hamburger. If, as an individual's income increases, the individual consumes less hamburger and more steak, then hamburger is an inferior good and steak is a normal good. However, meat or beef in general is still considered a normal good.[2] Likewise, a trailer might be considered inferior to a house, but housing in general is a normal good.

For a normal good, an increase in income would cause demand in Figure 3 to shift from D_0 to D_1. For an inferior good, an increase in income would shift demand from D_0 to D_2, as buyers could afford the more expensive substitute. For a normal good, a decrease in income would shift demand from D_0 to D_2 in Figure 3. For an inferior good, a decrease in income would increase demand from D_0 to D_1 as buyers were forced to economize with less appealing goods.

Changes in wealth have the same effect as changes in income. If the value of assets falls, leaving people less wealthy, demand for normal goods will decline. When the stock market crashed in October 1987, many analysts predicted a recession. They expected the decline in wealth to cause consumer spending to decrease. Though there was a decline in wealth, it was not large enough to spark a recession. It did, however, affect the demand for some goods and services.

PRICES OF OTHER GOODS. The fourth nonprice determinant of demand is the prices of other goods and services. There are two classes of other goods: complements and substitutes. **Complementary goods** are goods that are jointly consumed. If consuming two goods together enhances the enjoyment of both, the goods are called complements. Examples are bacon and eggs, lamps and light bulbs, or hamburgers and ketchup. Substitute goods have the opposite relationship. Rather than enhancing each other's consumption, **substitute goods** replace each other. Orange juice and grapefruit juice, Coke and Pepsi, and Reebok and Adidas shoes are examples of substitute goods.

complementary goods
Goods that are jointly consumed. The consumption of one enhances the consumption of the other.

substitute goods
Goods that can be interchanged. The consumption of one replaces the consumption of the other.

If two goods are complements, a rise in the price of one will decrease demand for the other. Referring again to Figure 3, consider D_0 as the demand curve for good x (bagels). If the price of complementary good y (lox) goes up, the demand for bagels will decrease, shifting the curve from D_0 to D_2. Buyers will consume less lox because its price is higher and will thus would demand fewer bagels at every price. If the price of lox fell, consumers would want to consume more lox and thus would demand more bagels to go with it at every price. In Figure 3, demand for bagels would shift from D_0 to D_1.

If two goods are substitutes, a rise in the price of one will increase demand for the other. Good x (Coke) and good y (Pepsi) are substitutes. Suppose curve D_0 in Figure 3 represents the demand for good x (Coke).

---

2. A good example of an inferior good is an outhouse. As a community's income rises, the demand for outhouses decreases. In the United States, outhouses have almost become extinct.

The price of good y (Pepsi) increases relative to the price of Coke. Since this makes the opportunity cost of Coke lower, consumers will demand more Coke at every price. The demand for Coke shifts from D_0 to D_1 in Figure 3. If the price of Pepsi decreased relative to the price of Coke, the opposite would happen. The opportunity cost of Coke would be higher, and consumers would demand less of it at every price as they shifted consumption to Pepsi. The decrease in demand for Coke is shown by a shift from D_0 to D_2 in Figure 3. The shift to substitutes as price rises means that the quantity demanded of the good falls, exactly as predicted by the law of demand.

In a broad sense, all goods are substitutes for each other because they are all alternatives on which people can spend income. Some goods are closer substitutes than others, however. The more easily that good A can be substituted for good B, the more a change in the price of one will affect the demand curve for the other. A rise in the price of watches, for example, would have much less impact on the demand for hot dogs than on the demand for clocks, bracelets, or other substitutes.

People often make the error of assuming a good has no satisfactory substitutes. How often have you heard someone say, "There is no substitute for victory (or success, steak, a new car...)." In fact, there are substitutes for anything. If the price rises sharply enough, consumers will start searching harder for acceptable substitutes.[3]

REASONS FOR A CHANGE IN THE QUANTITY DEMANDED

- The quantity demanded will *increase* if the price of the good or service *decreases*.
- The quantity will *decrease* if the price of the good or service *increases*.

REASONS FOR A CHANGE IN DEMAND

- The demand for a normal good or service will *increase* if:
  buyers' tastes change to favor that good or service,
  the number of buyers in the market increases,
  the income or wealth of buyers increases,
  the prices of complementary goods fall,
  the prices of substitute goods increase, or
  buyers' expectations for the future cause them to purchase more now.
- The demand for a normal good or service will *decrease* if:
  buyers' tastes change against that good or service,
  the number of buyers in the market decreases,
  the income or wealth of buyers decreases,
  the prices of complementary goods increase,
  the prices of substitute goods decrease, or
  buyers' expectations of the future cause them to delay purchases.

---

3. This point often makes economists seem cynical. Does honesty have a substitute? Yes. If the price becomes too high, many people (but not all) will become dishonest.

expectations
Feelings that individuals have about future conditions.

EXPECTATIONS. The last *ceteris paribus* condition that affects demand is **expectations**. If individuals expect anything important to change in the future, they may take action now that they would otherwise postpone. For example, if you expect that the demand for automobiles will be so high next year that their prices will rise, you may decide to buy a car now to avoid paying a higher price. If you expect your income to be higher in the future, you may demand more goods and borrow to pay for them so that you do not have to delay consumption until your income actually rises.

SUPPLY

supply schedule
A table that shows quantities offered for sale at various prices over a particular time period.

A **supply schedule** shows the quantities offered for sale at various prices during a specific period of time. Price is the primary determinant of quantity supplied.

THE (NOT QUITE) LAW OF SUPPLY

(not quite) law of supply
The quantity supplied of a good or service is usually a positive function of price, *ceteris paribus*.

Assume everything else is held constant but the price of the good or service. We can then state the **(not quite) law of supply** as follows: the *quantity supplied* of a good or service is *usually* a positive function of price, *ceteris paribus*.

With all else held constant, suppliers usually will supply less of a good or service at lower prices. As prices rise, the quantity supplied will increase, because it becomes more profitable to produce and sell the good. It is important to note that quantity supplied is a function of price. Note also the word *usually*. This is not quite a law because of two exceptions to this relationship. The first is when there is no time to produce more units (for example, theater seats at a sold-out performance) or when a unique supplier no longer exists (for example, paintings by Picasso). In these unusual cases, quantity supplied does not respond to price at all. The second exception occurs for certain products for which increased volume allows costs per unit to fall. For example, as a utility company increases its output of electricity, its costs per unit typically fall. These lower costs may be passed on to customers in the form of lower prices.

Table 2 shows a hypothetical supply schedule for an individual supplier—Susan's Lemonade Stand. A supply schedule shows the quantities supplied during a period of time at various prices. Like a demand schedule, a supply schedule includes a time frame—in this case, a day. Table 2 is consistent with the law of supply because Susan supplies larger quanti-

**TABLE 2
SUSAN'S SUPPLY
OF LEMONADE**

PRICE PER GLASS (CENTS)	QUANTITY SUPPLIED PER DAY
5	0
10	5
15	10
20	15
25	20
30	25

ties of lemonade at higher prices. The supply schedule of Table 2 can be drawn on a graph as shown in Figure 4. This **supply curve** is a diagram showing the quantity supplied in a particular time and at various prices. It shows a positive relationship—more will be offered for sale at higher prices. Price per unit is on the y-axis, and quantity per time period is on the x-axis, just as it was for the demand curve. Supply curves usually have a positive y-intercept, indicating that at some low price, suppliers may offer none of the good.

supply curve
A graph representing a supply schedule and showing the quantities supplied at various prices in a certain time period.

MARKET SUPPLY

The **market supply curve** is the sum of all of the individual supply schedules. Figure 5 is a market supply curve for lemonade, showing the total quantity supplied over a period of time at various prices. As price changes in the market, quantity supplied changes in the same direction. Figure 5 shows that 5,000 glasses of lemonade are supplied at a price of 10 cents per glass. If price falls to 5 cents per glass, quantity supplied decreases to zero glasses. If price rises to 20 cents per glass, quantity supplied increases to 15,000 glasses. These changes occur because most producers are willing to sell more units if the price rises enough to cover the added costs of production.

market supply curve
The sum of all of the individual supply curves. A market supply curve shows what quantities will be supplied by all firms at various prices during a specific time period.

CHANGES IN SUPPLY AND THE *CETERIS PARIBUS* CONDITIONS

A supply curve is drawn to show a relationship between price and quantity supplied, with everything else held constant. A change in one of the *ceteris paribus* conditions will cause the entire supply curve to shift. The most important of these are as follows:

1. the state of technology,
2. prices of the factors of production,
3. the number of suppliers,
4. expectations about the future,
5. prices of related goods.

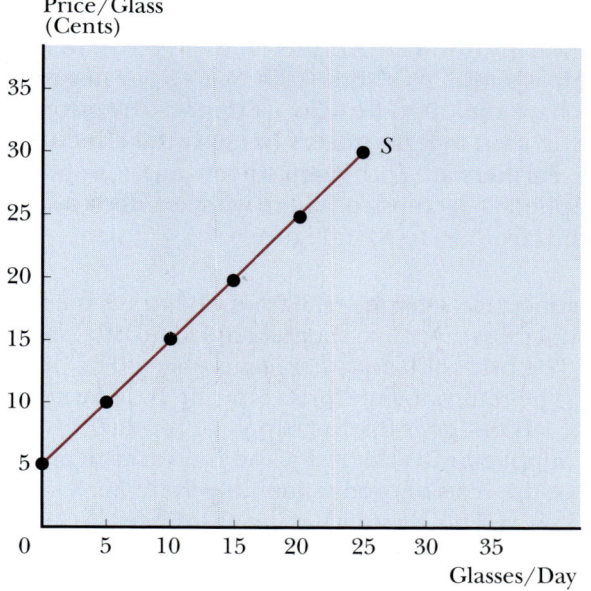

FIGURE 4
SUSAN'S SUPPLY OF LEMONADE
A supply curve for an individual (or firm) shows how much of a good will be offered for sale at various prices.

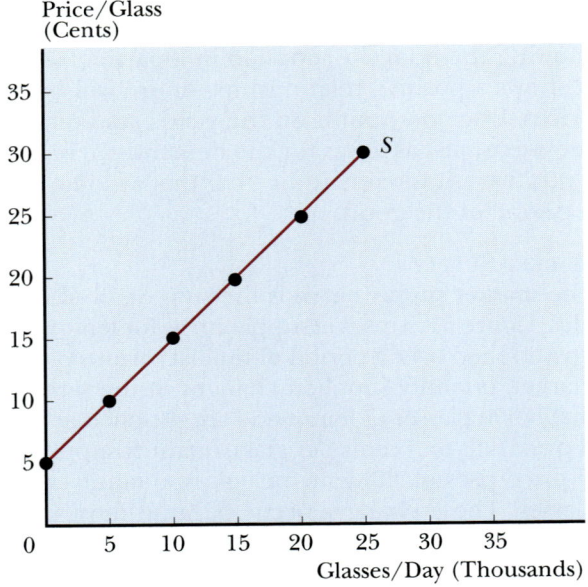

**FIGURE 5
MARKET SUPPLY OF LEMONADE**
A market supply curve shows how much of a good will be offered for sale at various prices. It is the sum of all of the individual supply curves.

Everything that affects supply works through one of these determinants. For example, if a natural disaster destroys large amounts of capital, it will affect supply by increasing the price of that factor of production. If the price of corn rises relative to wheat, a farmer might decide to grow corn instead of wheat.

TECHNOLOGY. Suppose technology improves. For instance, agricultural researchers develop a low-cost drug that causes a young steer to double in weight rapidly. This advance in technology means that more beef will be supplied at each price. There is an **increase in supply**, or a shift in the supply curve such that a larger quantity will be provided at every price. In Figure 6, an increase in supply is shown as a shift from S_0 to S_1. A negative change in technology will have the opposite effect. Suppose the government discovers that the drug used to fatten steers has harmful effects on humans who eat the beef. Farmers are forbidden to continue using the drug. Less beef will be supplied at each price. There will be a **decrease in supply**, represented as a shift from S_0 to S_2 in Figure 6.

PRICES OF THE FACTORS OF PRODUCTION. As you recall from Chapter 2, the factors of production are land, labor, capital, and enterprise. The price paid for the use of land is rent. The price of labor's services is wages. The price for using capital is interest. The return to enterprise is profit. If the price of a factor—such as wages for labor—goes up, the supply of products using that factor will be affected. Suppliers will offer less of the good at each price. Supply will decrease because the costs of production have gone up.

Suppose S_0 in Figure 6 represents the market supply of beef. Assume that the wage rate of meat cutters increases. This will mean less beef will

increase in supply
A shift in the supply curve indicating that at every price, a larger quantity will be offered for sale than before.

decrease in supply
A shift in the supply curve indicating that at every price, a smaller quantity will be offered for sale than before.

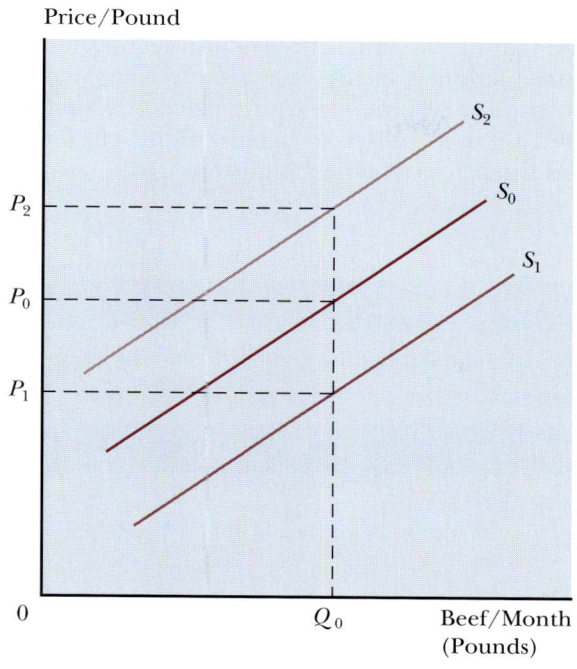

FIGURE 6
CHANGES IN THE *CETERIS PARIBUS* CONDITIONS AND SUPPLY
Changes in a *ceteris paribus* condition can cause the supply curve to shift. A change that would cause more to be supplied at each price is an increase in supply and is represented by the shift from S_0 to S_1. A change that causes the supply to decrease is represented by a shift from S_0 to S_2.

be supplied at each price. Supply will decrease from S_0 to S_2. After the increase in wages, suppliers will supply the old amount (Q_0) only at a higher price (P_2). A rise in the price of a factor of production, *ceteris paribus*, causes a decrease in supply. The cost of supplying any particular quantity has increased. Thus, less will be supplied at the old price, or the same amount will be supplied at a higher price. The opposite is also true. A decrease in the price of a factor of production will cause an increase in supply, shifting the curve from S_0 to S_1 in Figure 6.

NUMBER OF SUPPLIERS. A change in the number of suppliers will also shift the supply curve. If the number of beef ranchers declines, the supply curve will shift from S_0 to S_2 in Figure 6—a decrease in supply. In contrast, an increase in the number of beef ranchers will shift the supply curve from S_0 to S_1 in Figure 6—an increase in supply.

EXPECTATIONS. Expectations about any of the *ceteris paribus* conditions or about market price can have an effect on supply. Assume that beef ranchers expect that the price of beef will fall next year because they anticipate a poor grain harvest. (A poor grain harvest would make it more expensive to keep cattle on feedlots.) What would this expectation cause ranchers to do? They would bring more cattle to market now, before the price falls. If enough ranchers share this expectation, the supply curve for this year will increase from S_0 to S_1, as shown in Figure 6. The price of beef will fall from P_0 to P_1 because ranchers will be slaughtering more cattle. Next year, with fewer cattle available, the supply curve will shift back to the left.

PRICES OF RELATED GOODS. Changes in the prices of other goods can affect supply. If the price of a good that uses a similar production technique increases, a firm may switch production. A farmer may switch from corn to wheat when the price of corn increases relative to the price of wheat. A sewing factory might switch from men's shirts to babies' nightwear if the price of men's shirts fell and the price of babies' nightwear rose.

REASONS FOR A CHANGE IN THE QUANTITY SUPPLIED

- The quantity supplied will *increase* if the price of the good or service *increases*.
- The quantity supplied will *decrease* if the price of the good or service *decreases*.

REASONS FOR A CHANGE IN SUPPLY

- The supply of a good or service will *increase* if:
  new technology allows the good or service to be produced at lower cost,
  the prices of the factors of production decrease,
  the number of suppliers increases,
  the prices of other goods or services that can be produced with the same resources decrease, or
  suppliers' expectations for the future cause them to produce more now.
- The supply of a good or service will *decrease* if:
  the prices of the factors of production increase,
  the number of suppliers decreases,
  the prices of other goods or services that can be produced with the same resources increase, or
  suppliers' expectations for the future cause them to produce less now.

MARKET EQUILIBRIUM

We can combine market supply and market demand schedules to determine the market equilibrium. **Market equilibrium** occurs at that price for which quantity demanded by consumers is equal to quantity supplied by producers. This equilibrium price is also called the **market-clearing price**.

EQUILIBRIUM AND DISEQUILIBRIUM

In Table 3, at a price of $2, suppliers *want* to supply 4 million pounds of coffee, and consumers *want* to purchase 8 million pounds. A price of $2 is not an equilibrium price because quantity demanded exceeds quantity supplied by 4 million pounds at that price. This situation is one of **disequilibrium**, in which variables are moving toward equilibrium but are not yet there. This is an unstable position. Some consumers will not be able to purchase the amount they desire at a price of $2. As they shop for coffee, they will offer a higher price. As the price rises, quantity supplied will rise, and quantity demanded will fall. This process will continue until the price reaches $3. At $3, the amount consumers wish to purchase is exactly equal to the amount suppliers wish to sell. This quantity is the equilibrium quan-

---

market equilibrium
A point at which quantity demanded by consumers is equal to quantity supplied by producers. The price at which this occurs is the equilibrium price, or market-clearing price.

market-clearing price
The equilibrium price, which clears the market because there are no frustrated consumers or suppliers.

disequilibrium
An unstable situation in which variables are moving toward equilibrium but are not yet at equilibrium.

The number of suppliers and the number of buyers can shift the supply and demand curves, respectively. Sometimes the suppliers are offering imported goods, and sometimes the buyers live in foreign countries.

In an open economy, the market demand curve faced by producers is the sum of the domestic demand for the product and the foreign demand for the product. Consider the market demand for American corn. If there were no foreign demand, the market price would settle at P_d, and corn producers would sell Q tons of corn. (See the graph titled "Foreign Demand for Corn.") When foreign demand, D_f, is added, the price rises to P_{d+f}, and the amount sold rises to Q_{d+f}. The price of corn and the amount of corn sold have both increased. Consumers in the domestic market are paying a higher price because they now pay P_{d+f}. Since the domestic demand curve has not shifted and the price has increased, the quantity of corn demanded by domestic consumers will fall. In this example, domestic consumption falls to Q_d.

It appears that domestic corn producers have gained at the expense of domestic corn consumers. After all, consumers now pay a higher price for less corn. This conclusion is correct, but it ignores the other side of the coin. Foreign consumers can only buy the corn if they sell something that earns the currency necessary to pay for the corn. The domestic supply of the product that foreigners sell to pay for the corn will have an effect in other markets.

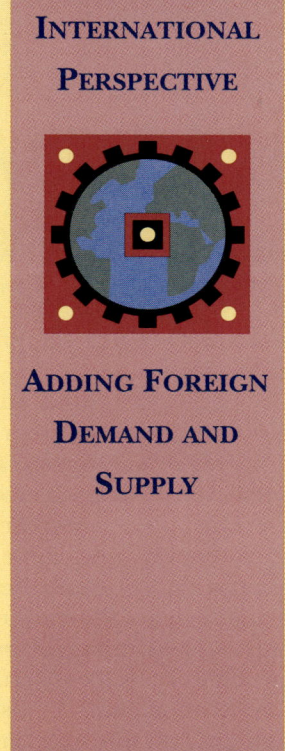

INTERNATIONAL PERSPECTIVE

ADDING FOREIGN DEMAND AND SUPPLY

The graph titled "Foreign Supply of Automobiles" shows the U.S. market for automobiles. Without a foreign supply, the domestic price and quantity would be P_d and Q_d. Adding foreign supply, S_f, changes the equilibrium. There is a decline in price to P_{d+f} and an increase in quantity demanded to Q_{d+f}. In this case, the domestic consumption of automobiles increased by $Q_{d+f} - Q_d$. Domestic consumers can purchase more automobiles at a lower price.

There is an important lesson in this example of supply and demand in an open economy. Relative to a no-trading situation, the opening of foreign trade will result in higher prices and less consumption of exported items and lower prices and more consumption of imported items. So there are winners and losers as a result of international trade. But, as you learned in Chapter 2, the principle of comparative advantage shows that the net effect of trade is an expansion of choices and an increase in total consumption for consumers in the domestic market.

FOREIGN DEMAND FOR CORN

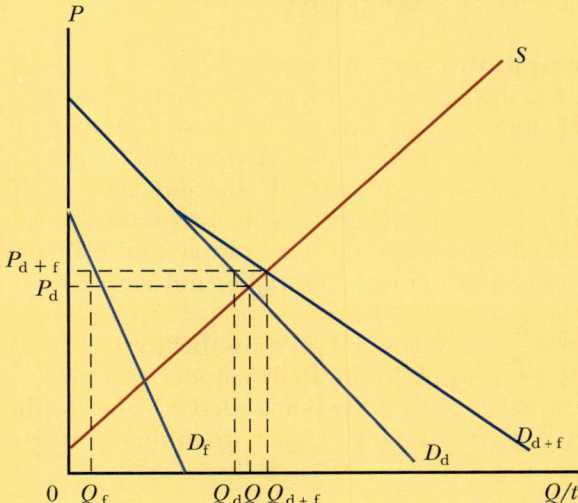

FOREIGN SUPPLY OF AUTOMOBILES

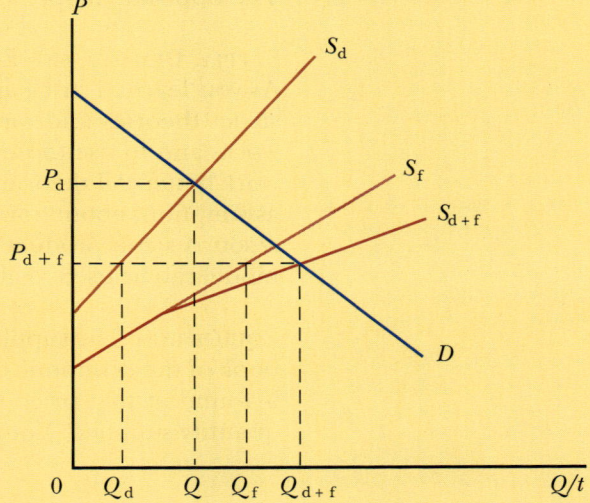

TABLE 3
SUPPLY OF AND DEMAND FOR COFFEE

PRICE PER POUND (DOLLARS)	POUNDS SUPPLIED PER MONTH	POUNDS DEMANDED PER MONTH	DIFFERENCE
1	2 million	10 million	8 million excess quantity demanded
2	4 million	8 million	4 million excess quantity demanded
3	6 million	6 million	equilibrium
4	8 million	4 million	4 million excess quantity supplied
5	10 million	2 million	8 million excess quantity supplied

tity, and $3 is the market-clearing price, because there is no tendency for price or quantity to change.

If the price was $4 per pound, suppliers would offer 8 million pounds of coffee per month, but consumers would only wish to purchase 4 million pounds. At this price, there is an excess quantity supplied of 4 million pounds per month. Suppliers with unsold coffee will accept a lower price. As price falls, some suppliers reduce their output (a movement along the supply curve), and some consumers buy more (a movement along the demand curve) until the equilibrium price of $3 is reached. This $3 price again clears the market.

Note that the equilibrium price and quantity do not simply represent the point where the amount sold equals the amount bought. Quantities bought and sold are *always* equal, even in disequilibrium. Four million pounds per month were bought and sold at $2 and at $4. Equilibrium occurs at a price for which the quantity supplied and the quantity demanded are equal.

Figure 7 shows market supply and market demand curves for coffee, based on the supply and demand schedules in Table 3. The equilibrium price is $3, and 6 million pounds per month are sold at equilibrium. At $4, there is an excess quantity supplied, and price will fall. This causes the quantity demanded to increase and the quantity supplied to decrease. The opposite happens at a price of $2 per pound.

SUPPLY, DEMAND, AND ECONOMIC MODELS
As you learned in Chapter 1, the primary work of economists is to construct theories and models that explain and predict how the economy works and to use those theories and models to devise policies to make it work better. All theories and models share certain techniques and certain assumptions about how households and firms make decisions about using resources for production and consumption. The supply and demand model can be used to illustrate some of these techniques and assumptions.

EQUILIBRIUM. The supply and demand model represents the first use in this book of the economic concept of equilibrium. In this model, equilibrium is found at that price for which the quantity demanded is equal to the quantity supplied. Equilibrium (and its counterpart, disequilibrium) is a

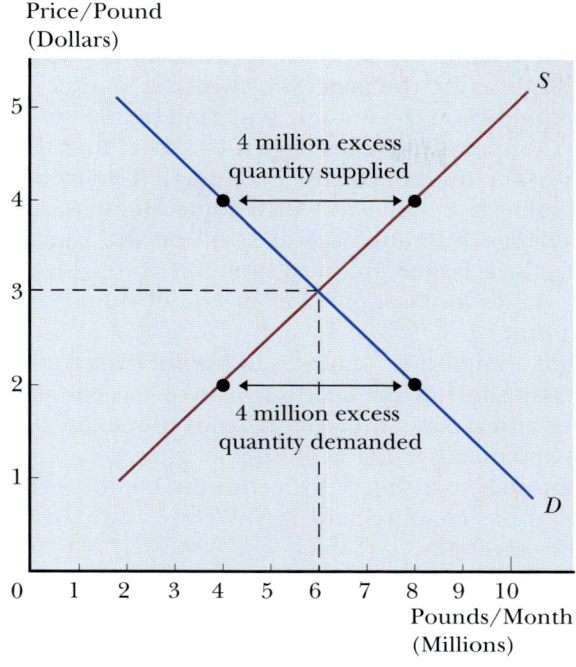

FIGURE 7
SUPPLY OF AND DEMAND FOR COFFEE
At equilibrium, the amount consumers wish to purchase is equal to the amount suppliers wish to sell. The price established at equilibrium is called the market-clearing price. At prices above the market-clearing price, quantity supplied exceeds quantity demanded. At prices below the market-clearing price, quantity demanded exceeds quantity supplied.

term that you will encounter often. This book will discuss equilibrium prices, equilibrium quantities, equilibrium levels of employment, equilibrium levels of gross national product (GNP), and so forth. Almost every economic model includes a definition of equilibrium. If the model has an equilibrium position, it will have a set of forces that can change that position. In the supply and demand model, these forces are called supply shifters and demand shifters. There are also forces that move an economy toward a new equilibrium position. In the supply and demand model, sellers' and buyers' responses to price changes will move the economy toward a new equilibrium.

Economists' notion of equilibrium is borrowed from the physical sciences. A system is in equilibrium when it is at rest or when it is moving at a constant rate in the same direction. That is, all the forces acting on the system are in balance, and there is no tendency to change. Equilibrium carries no sense of being good or bad, desirable or undesirable. In economics (as in physics or chemistry), if a system is left alone, equilibrium is where it will come to rest. Disequilibrium is a state in which the variables are moving away from old equilibrium values and toward new equilibrium values but have not yet arrived there. If the supply curve has shifted to the right but the demand curve is unchanged, there is a surplus at the old price. This situation is a disequilibrium. A surplus means that the quantity supplied is greater than the quantity demanded at the current price. Market forces are putting downward pressure on the price in order to move to a new equilibrium. If the price was too low for equilibrium to exist, there would be a shortage. Quantity demanded would exceed quantity supplied, and there would be upward pressure on the price.

COMPARATIVE STATICS. When a supply curve or a demand curve shifts, the diagram always identifies the original equilibrium and the new equilibrium. Economists are able to describe the process by which a market or economy moves from one equilibrium to another. This kind of analysis is called **comparative statics**. Comparative statics begins by describing the initial equilibrium position of the market (or the economy). This initial state is then compared to some later state in which some element has changed. For example, a change in technology has shifted the supply curve to the right, resulting in a larger quantity supplied and a lower price. That is, comparative statics looks at changes in equilibrium positions between two different times.

Another way of looking at comparative statics is to see such an analysis as a comparison of two snapshots of the economy (or of a particular market). We take a snapshot and analyze the relationships that exist. We then change one variable, which causes the economy to move to a new equilibrium. Next, we take another snapshot of the economy. We compare the two snapshots to see what has changed and why. We are comparing static (frozen) pictures of the economy.

MARGINAL ANALYSIS. Supply and demand is just one of many economic models that involve **marginal analysis**, a technique for analyzing problems by examining the results of small changes.

Marginal refers to the extra, additional, or next unit of output, consumption, or any other measurable quantity that can be increased or decreased by incremental amounts. The concept of the margin is central to economic analysis, although it is probably new to you. Most economic decisions are made at the margin: Should I consume the extra slice of pizza or work the extra hour? Should we produce the extra unit or take on a new client at our accounting firm? These kinds of daily decisions made by households and firms determine prices, output, and other important economic quantities. In the supply and demand model, the supply curve reflects the decisions of suppliers to offer extra or additional (marginal) units for sale at higher prices. The demand curve reflects the decisions of buyers to purchase extra or additional (marginal) units at lower prices. When the price of a good falls, consumers decide at the margin whether to substitute a little more of that good for other goods whose prices have not changed.

ENDOGENOUS AND EXOGENOUS VARIABLES. All economic models contain variables. Variables that a model attempts to explain or determine are called **endogenous variables**. Variables that have an impact on the endogenous variables but are themselves determined outside the model are called **exogenous variables**. In mathematics (and sometimes in economics), these are referred to as dependent and independent variables, respectively.

In the supply and demand model, both price and quantity are endogenous variables that affect one another and are determined by the model. For example, the price of oranges is endogenous to this model. Some of the other variables in a supply and demand model are exogenous. For example, in the market for oranges, the weather in Florida is an exogenous variable. The weather affects the price of oranges, but the price of oranges does not affect the weather.

---

comparative statics
A technique of comparing two equilibrium positions to determine the changing relationships between variables.

marginal analysis
A technique for analyzing problems by examining the results of small changes.

endogenous variables
Variables that are explained or determined within a model.

exogenous variables
Variables that are determined outside of a model and affect endogenous variables.

In the supply and demand model, the exogenous variables are the nonprice determinants that cause the position of the supply or demand curve to change. These determinants are technology, tastes, number of suppliers, income, prices of related goods, and so forth. Most economic models concentrate on just one or two endogenous (or dependent) variables and explain them by the behavior of a larger number of exogenous (or independent) variables.

PRIMARY AND SECONDARY EFFECTS. Economists often analyze the effect of a change in one variable on other related variables. The **primary effect** is the dominant effect they seek to analyze. For instance, the demand curve shows how doubling the price of oranges would affect the quantity of oranges consumed. But there are also **secondary effects** in related markets. These effects may not be immediately apparent and may take time to work through the economy. For example, if the price of oranges doubled, the sales of cranberry juice might increase, or the consumption of bacon and eggs might decrease. These are related goods whose demand depends on the price of oranges (or orange juice). Such changes would not be as obvious or as immediately apparent as the primary effect.

primary effect
The dominant or immediate effect of a change in an economic variable.

secondary effects
Effects indirectly related to the immediate effect, often smaller and felt after some time.

A THEORY OF PRICE FORMATION

The law of demand and the (not quite) law of supply support a very powerful theory of how markets work to set and change prices. That theory is based on two propositions. The first is that quantity demanded is negatively related to price. The second is that quantity supplied is positively related to price. When these two propositions are combined, they imply several things:

1. When the quantity demanded exceeds the quantity supplied, ($Q_d > Q_s$), price will rise.
2. When the quantity demanded is less than the quantity supplied, ($Q_d < Q_s$), price will fall.
3. When the quantity demanded equals the quantity supplied, ($Q_d = Q_s$), price is at equilibrium.

This theory, combined with the possible shifts in *ceteris paribus* conditions, produces all of the basic elements of a model of how prices (and quantities) are determined in a market system.

CHANGES IN DEMAND AND SUPPLY

When changes occur in any of the *ceteris paribus* conditions that affect demand, the model can be used to trace the effect on market equilibrium. Assume first that there is an increase in demand, that is, an outward shift of the entire curve. This increase in demand could be a result of a change in any of the *ceteris paribus* conditions. It could result from an increase in income (for a normal good), a change in tastes in favor of the good, an increase in the price of a substitute or a decrease in the price of a complement, an increase in the size of the consuming group, or a change in expectations. The increase in demand is shown as an outward shift in the demand curve from D_0 to D_1 in Figure 8. The equilibrium price rises from

P_e to P_1, and the price increase causes quantity supplied to increase to Q_1. Consumers demand a larger quantity of the good at every price than before the shift of the curve.

Now consider a decrease in demand. A decrease in demand means that consumers will demand less of a good at every price. This decrease could result from a fall in income, a change in tastes away from the good, a decrease in the price of a substitute or an increase in the price of a complement, a decrease in group size, or a change in expectations. The decrease in demand is shown as an inward shift in the demand curve from D_0 to D_2 in Figure 8. The decrease in demand causes equilibrium price to fall from P_0 to P_2, and quantity supplied responds by falling from Q_0 to Q_2.

Changes in any condition that affects supply will shift the supply curve. An increase in supply could result from an advance in technology, a decrease in the price of a factor of production, an increase in the number of suppliers, or a change in expectations. The increase in supply appears on a graph as a rightward shift of the supply curve, from S_0 to S_1 in Figure 9. This increase in supply would cause the equilibrium price to fall from P_0 to P_1, leading to an increase in the quantity demanded from Q_0 to Q_1.

A decrease in supply could result from an increase in the price of a factor of production, a decrease in the number of suppliers, or a change in expectations. A decrease in supply is shown as a leftward shift from S_0 to S_2 in Figure 9. This decrease in supply causes the equilibrium price to rise from P_0 to P_2, causing quantity demanded to decrease from Q_0 to Q_2.

The supply and demand model is very useful in analyzing a variety of economic problems and issues. As you apply this model, keep in mind the difference between changes in demand and supply (that is, shifts in the positions of the curves) and changes in the quantity demanded and quan-

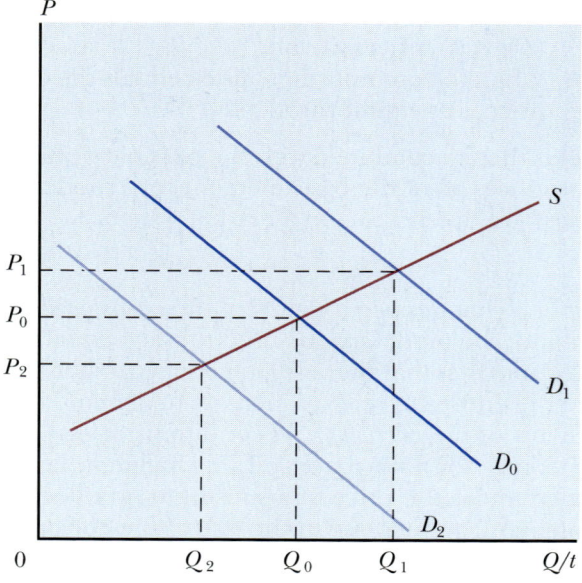

FIGURE 8

CHANGES IN DEMAND

An increase in demand from D_0 to D_1 causes the equilibrium price to rise from P_0 to P_1 and the quantity supplied to increase from Q_0 to Q_1. A decrease in demand from D_0 to D_2 causes the equilibrium price to fall from P_0 to P_2 and the quantity supplied to fall from Q_0 to Q_2.

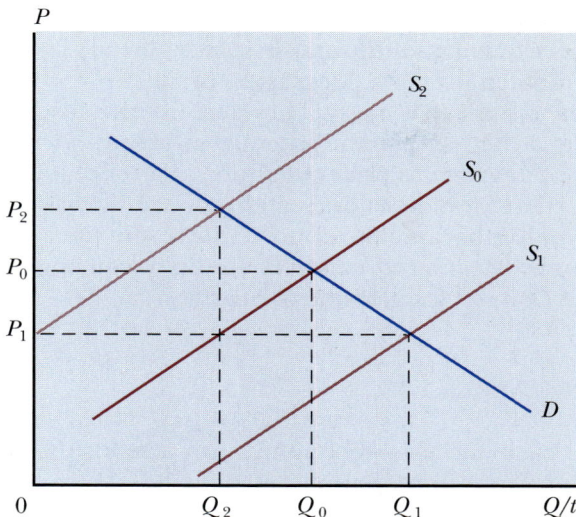

FIGURE 9
CHANGES IN SUPPLY
An increase in supply from S_0 to S_1 causes the equilibrium price to fall from P_0 to P_1 and the quantity demanded to increase from Q_0 to Q_1. A decrease in supply from S_0 to S_2 causes the equilibrium price to rise from P_0 to P_2 and the quantity demanded to fall from Q_0 to Q_2.

tity supplied (that is, movements along the curves). The importance of this difference will become very clear as you attempt to untangle situations that involve several changes in *ceteris paribus* conditions.[4]

ARE PRICES FAIR?

The analysis of supply and demand presented in this chapter has been positive rather than normative. No mention has been made of what constitutes a fair or just price. Nor has there been any comment as to whether certain minimal levels of consumption of certain goods are necessary for a fair society. Supply and demand theory predicts how an increase in demand for a good will affect price and quantity. A higher price may mean that some people can no longer afford the item, regardless of how "necessary" or "basic" it may appear to be. The supply and demand model offers no moral evaluation of what prices should be.

DIFFERENT PRICES FOR DIFFERENT BUYERS

A second adjustment to the supply and demand model is the observation that, in reality, people often pay different prices for the same good. In the supply and demand model, the equilibrium price is a single, unique price that is paid by all buyers and received by all sellers. There may be different prices for different buyers and sellers because of transactions costs. **Transactions costs** are costs associated with gathering information about markets (prices and quantities supplied) for consuming or producing. Organizing, negotiating, and searching take time and involve opportunity costs. Firms are organized to reduce transactions costs on the producing side. For consumers, the existence of transactions costs means that different people pay different prices for the same good or service.

transactions costs Costs associated with gathering information about markets (prices and quantities supplied) for consuming or producing.

---

4. To test yourself, work through these shifts. Determine the effect that changes in supply and demand have on price and quantity. For example, ask yourself: What is the effect on equilibrium of an increase in demand coupled with a decrease in supply?

A familiar example of such price differences is that gas stations next to expressways charge higher prices for gasoline than do stations farther away from expressways. Why? Transactions costs. Most users of an expressway are unfamiliar with the area and are in a hurry. They perceive the cost of searching for a lower price to be higher than the potential saving produced by such searching. Think about what gas prices might be in a retirement community. Do you think there would be lower and more uniform gas prices in a retirement community because the opportunity cost of the customers' time is lower? If you live near a retirement community, you might want to check on the prices charged for gasoline in nearby areas.

EVALUATING THE MARKET PROCESS

In Chapter 2, you saw that each and every economy must address three basic questions: what, how and for whom? Supply and demand—the market process—provide important signals to inform, direct, and motivate economic agents in answering these questions.

FUNCTIONS OF PRICES

Prices play a central role in a market system in allocating scarce resources and answering the basic economic questions. The primary functions of prices are to inform, direct, and motivate consumers and business firms.

INFORMING. Market prices condense a great deal of complex information into a simple form. This condensed information is useful to consumers and producers in making decisions. An increase in demand causes a market price to rise. The supplier of a product does not have to know what caused demand to change. All suppliers need to know is that the price has risen. They will respond by increasing the quantity supplied. Likewise, consumers do not need to understand anything about the production process or the associated costs. All they need to know is the market price. If the price rises, consumers decrease the quantity demanded. The market price, then, provides all participants in the market with up-to-the-minute information on the relative scarcity of goods.

DIRECTING. Market participants act on price information. If suppliers are bringing too much of a good to market, its price will fall. The decisions of consumers and producers will move the market to a new equilibrium. Market prices will signal for an increase in the production of those products of which consumers are demanding more. Firms will produce these goods by bringing resources together in a way directed by the market prices of those resources. All of this takes place without any individual or group of individuals telling consumers and entrepreneurs how or why to act. All of the necessary information is found in market prices.

MOTIVATING. The *for whom* question is also a reminder that price is a powerful motivator. Supply and demand establish a reward structure for owners and users of productive resources. Households and firms will seek to produce those goods or develop those skills that are highly desired by oth-

When the Berlin Wall was opened in the fall of 1989, writer Gloria Steinem observed that it was a very peaceful revolution. There was no violence, and everyone went shopping. In fact, the East Germans were hungry for markets, especially supermarkets and large department stores stocked with many kinds of goods. All of the nations of Eastern Europe are scrambling to relearn how markets work as they attempt to decentralize their economies, restore incentives, and obtain a greater variety of consumer goods for their citizens.

Some of the first foreign entrepreneurs attempting to become a part of the emerging markets in Eastern Europe have found the going rough. They were accustomed to working in a network of suppliers rather than interacting with government factories and collective farms to obtain their materials. McDonald's opened its first restaurant in Moscow after hurdling numerous obstacles in obtaining ingredients for its food products and materials for constructing the building. Finding workers, however, was not difficult. With meat always in short supply, prospective workers were attracted as much by the free meals as by the wages.

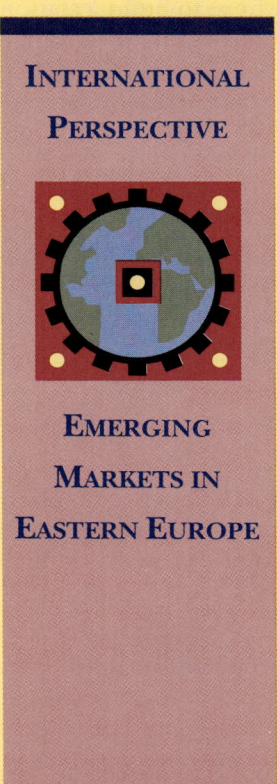

INTERNATIONAL PERSPECTIVE

EMERGING MARKETS IN EASTERN EUROPE

In spite of years of central planning, however, the market has shown a remarkable resiliency in some of the nations of Eastern Europe, where central planning has only dominated economic activity since the end of World War II. A black market—an illegal market, mostly for foreign goods and foreign currencies—has operated in these nations for the entire period. Even in the Soviet Union, some people working on collective farms were allowed to have private plots as well and to sell the output of those plots in a free market. A significant part of Soviet farm output came from those private plots, because the incentives to work hard and produce more were stronger when the workers could capture the benefits.

Private restaurants and retail shops have been quickly revived, along with farmers' markets and even one private, foreign-owned hotel in Moscow. The process of restoring the use of markets in production of manufactured goods will be slower, but the nations of Eastern Europe see markets—decentralized, efficient, with strong incentives—as their best hope for a higher standard of living in the future.

ers, in order to earn rewards in the form of higher incomes. All of this happens without any government agency or central planning bureau telling people what to do. No one has to tell a gas station owner when to be open or where to build a station, or a bright young person to invest in education. People pursue certain activities because they perceive it to be in their own self-interest. This whole process of self-interested response to incentives is what Adam Smith referred to as the **invisible hand**.[5]

invisible hand
The idea advanced by Adam Smith that individuals pursuing their own self-interest direct the market system toward socially desirable outcomes.

ALLOCATIVE EFFICIENCY

According to Adam Smith, the invisible hand informs, directs, and motivates the self-interest of market participants. Suppliers are motivated to guide resources into the production of the goods most wanted by consumers and to produce those goods with the most efficient methods and resource combinations possible. In the words of Nobel Laureate George Stigler,

. . . an economic actor on average knows better the environment in which he is acting and the probable consequences of his actions than an outsider, no matter how clever the outsider may be.[6]

allocative efficiency
The use of resources to produce the goods most desired by society. Free markets allow allocative efficiency.

Allocative efficiency is the use of resources to produce the goods most desired by society. It is the reason why most economists look to the market first for solutions to economic problems.

FREEDOM

Finally, an important result of a market system is that individuals enjoy a great deal of freedom to pursue their own self-interest. In a market system, the production and distribution of goods and services take place on a basis of voluntary cooperation in the pursuit of individual self-interest. Nobel Laureate Milton Friedman, like Stigler a champion of the market system, describes this advantage in these terms:

So long as effective freedom of exchange is maintained, the central feature of the market organization of economic activity is that it prevents one person from interfering with another in respect to most of his activities. The consumer is protected from coercion by the seller because of the presence of other sellers with whom he can deal. The seller is protected from coercion by the consumer because of other consumers to whom he can sell. The employee is protected from coercion by the employer because of other employers for whom he can work, and so on. And the market does this impersonally and without centralized authority.[7]

NONMARKET ALLOCATION AND THE SHORTCOMINGS OF MARKETS

Although the market is a highly efficient way to allocate resources, it does have some drawbacks, as we observed in Chapter 2. Some of those drawbacks include failure to provide public goods or to correct negative external effects, instability, and inequality in the distribution of income. Markets perform poorly when there is a lack of competition. The above

5. See the profile of Adam Smith in Chapter 2.
6. George J. Stigler, "Economists and Public Policy," *Regulation* (May/June 1982): 16.
7. Milton Friedman, *Capitalism and Freedom* (Chicago: University of Chicago Press, 1981): 14–15.

quotation from Friedman does not apply when monopolies interfere with freedom of choice. Often the failings of the market lead to government intervention, resulting in a mixed economy rather than a pure market economy.

Critics of the market system range from those who would replace it with central direction to those with a more middle-of-the-road approach. The latter see a variety of ways of dividing responsibilities between markets and government. If prices are not allowed to direct resources in certain situations, some other mechanism must be developed for their allocation. Government directives, waiting in line, or appeals to "good behavior" are possible allocative mechanisms. The benefits of government intervention must be weighed against the very strong advantages of markets in terms of efficiency and flexibility. The following examples suggest some areas where government intervention has reduced the efficiency of resource allocation.

TAXI FARES. One well-known example of a problem created by intervention in the market is poor taxi service in New York City. The Taxi and Limousine Commission allowed only 11,787 cabs to operate there in 1987. Because the medallions (permits) required to operate a cab were so scarce, owners paid up to $100,000 per medallion. There are a few "gypsy" cabs in New York, but the supply is limited because these drivers face severe penalties if caught operating without the required medallion. Other cities, such as Washington, D.C., allow a large number of cabs to operate and charge a relatively minimal fee for a permit. Both cities regulate the fares that cab drivers can charge, with a fixed price per mile plus a charge for standing time.

At peak traffic hours, it is difficult to get around in New York. Therefore, many cab drivers avoid working during these periods, making it even more difficult to hail a cab. Lines of well-dressed people standing forty-deep outside exclusive hotels attest to this allocation problem. In contrast, you can wave a hand at any street corner in downtown Washington, and three cabs will be immediately at your service.

What are the solutions to New York's problem? The experience in Washington suggests that visitors and residents would be better off if New York City allowed more cabs on the streets. But if you were a driver who paid $100,000 for a medallion, would you be in favor of this solution? Of course not. Another possibility would be to allow the market to set prices for taxi services. *Fortune* magazine suggested that cab drivers be allowed to change rates at peak times with "some sort of electronic display...perched atop the cab that would periodically announce new rates."[8] If cabbies could set rates and vary them by time of day, some riders would be discouraged by higher prices. Also, some cab drivers would be encouraged to put in more hours to earn higher fares. Do you think the lines outside the hotels would decrease?

ORGAN DONATIONS. Another example of markets at work occurs in the relatively new medical field of organ transplanting. Certain organs such as

---

8. "Yellow Power," *Fortune* (15 September 1986): 144.

hearts, lungs, and eyes are donated only at death, usually from accident victims. Other organs, such as kidneys, can be donated by live donors, because humans have two kidneys and can function with just one. There have also been some successful transplants of part of a liver, since this organ can regenerate itself. As organ transplants have become more popular and more successful, a shortage of organs has developed. Newspapers and television frequently carry heartrending appeals. Some hospitals even have donor seekers who contact relatives of accident victims. One explanation for the shortage of organs is that the price is being held at too low a level. In fact, the price is zero.

One writer, Barry Jacobs, proposed establishing a market for kidneys.[9] Since individuals can get along quite well with one kidney, Jacobs's proposal was to let individuals who are cash-poor and kidney-rich sell a kidney to those who are cash-rich and kidney-poor. Also, Congressional hearings were held to consider what could be done about the shortage of kidneys for transplant. Two members of Congress proposed a federal program to fund a computer organ-marketing system and a 24-hour kidney hotline. The program would, however, establish no financial incentives for donors. What do you think might happen if there were a market for kidneys?

Some idea of the possible effect of paying for kidneys comes from an experiment by two British economists, Michael Cooper and Anthony Culver. They tried to determine the supply of blood that would be offered at various prices.[10] They found that there was a moderate supply at a price of zero. At this price, blood was given by those who were motivated by charity, altruism, or other noneconomic reasons. The supply actually fell at a nominal price of about $1.00 a pint, because the payment did not compensate some potential donors for the loss of the good feeling they obtained from giving blood for free. But as the price rose, more and more donors came forward. For many years, some people in American cities have sold their blood when they needed money. The quantity supplied is positively related to price, just as our models would predict. Do you think that kidneys would be any different?

FACULTY OFFICES. A final example of market versus nonmarket allocation comes, appropriately, from an economics department trying to allocate faculty offices in a new building. The other five departments in the school of business used various methods of allocation: seniority, first come first served, and a roll of the dice. None of these methods reflected the intensity of people's preferences for corner offices, offices with windows, large offices, and so forth. There was great dissatisfaction with the outcomes. Only in the economics department was there an attempt to use the market for allocating office space. Faculty members were invited to submit sealed bids. The highest bidders got to choose first, and the proceeds went to student scholarships. A bid indicated how important the "perks" associated with a particular office were to the bidder. Those who

---

9. "Socialized Kidneys," *Fortune* (19 March 1984): 190.
10. Institute of Economic Affairs, *The Economics of Charity: Essays on the Comparative Economics and Ethics of Giving and Selling, with Applications to Blood* (Surrey, England: Gresham Press, 1973).

worked at home more or were away from campus more would presumably bid less than those who used their offices more regularly and cared more intensely about aspects of their workplace.

The experiment was quite successful. The highest bidder paid $500 for the first choice of office, and bidders down to $75 were able to secure the more desirable offices with windows. Since those who bid too low were free to recontract with others if they changed their minds, there was general satisfaction with the outcome.[11]

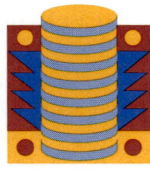

Summary

1. Demand depends on the current price of the good or service as well as nonprice determinants. These other influences on supply include the size of the group demanding the good, the tastes of the consuming group, the incomes of that group, the prices of related goods and services, and the expectations concerning the future.

2. The law of demand states that the quantity demanded of a good or service is negatively related to its price, *ceteris paribus*.

3. Changes in the price of a good affect the quantity demanded of that good. That is, a price change leads to a movement along the demand curve.

4. Changes in the *ceteris paribus* conditions that affect demand cause demand to either increase or decrease. That is, there is a shift in the position of the entire demand curve.

5. When income increases, the demand for a normal good will increase, and the demand for an inferior good will decrease.

6. Two goods are complements when a price increase in one will cause a decrease in demand for the other. Two goods are substitutes if an increase in the price of one causes an increase in demand for the other.

7. Supply depends on the price of the good or service as well as on nonprice determinants. These include the prices of the factors of production, the level of technology, the number of suppliers, and expectations.

8. The law of supply states that the quantity supplied of a good or service is usually a positive function of its price, *ceteris paribus*.

9. Changes in a good's price affect the quantity supplied of that good. Changes in factors of production that affect supply cause supply to either increase or decrease. When the prices of factors of production increase, there will be a decrease in supply. An advance in technology will usually cause supply to increase.

10. The market-clearing (equilibrium) price is the price at which the amount consumers wish to purchase is equal to the amount suppliers wish to sell. When supply or demand shifts, the market is in disequilibrium until natural forces determine a new equilibrium price and quantity. The comparison of two equilibrium positions is called comparative statics.

11. The supply and demand model has two endogenous variables that are determined within the model. These variables are price and quantity. The exogenous variables are determined outside the model but influence what goes on in the model by shifting supply and demand. These variables include prices of related goods, tastes, income, expectations, and technology.

12. The supply and demand model, like most economic models, uses marginal analysis. It focuses on decisions about the next unit purchased or sold rather than on aggregate or all-or-nothing decisions.

13. Prices play an important role in informing, directing, and motivating consumers and producers.

14. Markets maximize individual freedom by allowing individuals to pursue their own self-interest.

15. Transactions costs result from the fact that organizing, negotiating, and searching take time and involve costs. The existence of transactions costs means that different people pay different prices for the same good or service.

---

11. William J. Boyes and Stephen K. Happel, "Auctions as an Allocation Mechanism in Academia: The Case of Faculty Offices," *Journal of Economic Perspectives* (Summer 1989): 37–40.

New Terms

demand	normal good	market supply curve	endogenous variables
supply	inferior good	increase in supply	exogenous variables
law of demand	complementary goods	decrease in supply	primary effect
demand schedule	substitute goods	market equilibrium	secondary effects
demand curve	expectations	market-clearing price	transactions costs
market demand curve	supply schedule	disequilibrium	invisible hand
increase in demand	(not quite) law of supply	comparative statics	allocative efficiency
decrease in demand	supply curve	marginal analysis	

Questions for Discussion

1. Develop a simple theory to explain (predict) student grades in this course. Identify at least two exogenous variables and one endogenous variable.

2. How can expectations about economic conditions affect supply?

3. Does the fact that some people appear to buy more of some goods, such as mink coats and diamonds, as their prices go up negate the law of demand?

4. How can belief in a future change in the availability of gasoline affect the demand for automobiles?

5. Pat, a professional student, failed an economics course and decided to sell flowers on a street corner to make ends meet. A second flower seller established a business directly across the street from Pat. Pat, unconcerned, came up with the following hypothesis: "When supply increases, demand will increase. Therefore, I will be just as well off as I was before the second flower seller arrived." Did Pat deserve to fail economics? Why or why not?

6. A market-clearing price is the price at which the amount sold equals the amount purchased. Is this correct?

7. List all of the conditions that can decrease demand or supply.

8. List all of the conditions that can increase demand or supply.

9. Why is it so important to distinguish changes in demand and changes in supply from changes in quantity demanded and changes in quantity supplied?

10. Why do some people shop at convenience stores, knowing they will pay higher prices, even when a supermarket with lower prices is open in the same block?

11. The following table lists market information you gathered about landing slots at the Atlanta airport. Suppose you are asked to make a recommendation to the airport manager about pricing the slots to reduce crowding and delays. What will you recommend?

The Market for Landing Slots from 8:00 a.m. to 9:00 a.m.

Price($)	Quantity Supplied	Quantity Demanded
0	12	50
250	12	40
500	12	20
1,000	12	15
1,500	12	8
2,000	12	2

12. Draw a supply curve for personal computers that slopes upward and a demand curve for personal computers that slopes downward. They intersect at an equilibrium price of $2,000 and an equilibrium quantity of 6,000 units per month. Now experiment with each of the following.

   a. A breakthrough in the technology of making chips substantially lowers the cost of production. Which curve shifts, and which way? (Draw it on your diagram.) Find the new equilibrium price and quantity. Did they increase or decrease?

   b. The baby boom generation has bought large numbers of personal computers, and the market is saturated. The number of potential customers in the following generation is much smaller because the birth rate fell sharply during the late 1960s and early 1970s. Does this affect supply or demand? Which curve shifts, and in which direction? What is the effect on price and quantity?

   c. A foreign firm enters the market, adding a new source of supply. How does this change affect the price, quantity, and market supply curve? What is the impact on domestic firms?

13. Explain whether each of the following will shift the supply curve or the demand curve for milk and in which direction.
   a. The birth rate rises. (There are more babies.)
   b. The price of beef is very high, tempting dairy farmers to slaughter their milk cows.
   c. There is a drought, creating a shortage of feed for dairy herds.
   d. Scientists find that drinking too much milk increases the risk of heart disease.
   e. Scientists find that drinking more milk reduces the chances of developing osteoporosis.

14. If both supply and demand shift to the right, what happens to price and quantity? What happens if both supply and demand shift to the left?

15. In 1989, one of the hot gift items was the Nintendo entertainment system, which was used to play games. Only Nintendo games could be played on this system, and Nintendo games could not be played on other systems. How would a shortage of Nintendo systems affect the demand for Nintendo games?

SUGGESTIONS FOR FURTHER READING

Friedman, Milton. *Capitalism and Freedom.* Chicago: University of Chicago Press, 1981. This book presents the case for free markets by perhaps the most respected and passionate of their advocates.

Hayek, F. A. "The Use of Knowledge in Society." *American Economic Review* (September 1945): 519–528. This classic, very readable article shows the importance of markets as a source of information and coordination.

Miller, Roger LeRoy, Daniel K. Benjamin, and Douglass C. North. *The Economics of Public Issues,* 7th ed. New York: HarperCollins, 1990. An easy-to-read book that uses supply and demand to analyze issues of current interest.

DEMAND AND CONSUMER CHOICE 2

AFTER STUDYING THIS CHAPTER, YOU SHOULD BE ABLE TO:

1. Calculate the expected cost of a crime given the probability of arrest and conviction and the penalty.
2. Define:
   a. price ceiling,
   b. price floor,
   c. shortage,
   d. surplus,
   e. black market.
3. Diagram the economic effects of:
   a. rent control,
   b. the minimum wage,
   c. price supports in agriculture,
   d. regulation of the price of natural gas.
4. Discuss how markets allocate scarce resources.
5. Describe the effects of natural gas regulation and deregulation.
6. Discuss the economic aspects of the health care crisis.
7. Identify market adjustments that have occurred in the numbers and incomes of physicians.
8. Explain how disasters can be caused by humans or governments instead of being natural.

CHAPTER 4
APPLICATIONS OF SUPPLY AND DEMAND: THE BASIC MICROECONOMIC TOOLS

INTRODUCTION

This chapter makes use of some of the basic microeconomic models and theories developed in the first three chapters. These economic tools can yield profound insights into a variety of social issues. Equipped with these tools of analysis, you can understand such diverse issues as crime, rent control, the minimum wage, the energy crisis, and the effects and causes of natural disasters.

THE ECONOMICS OF CRIME: USE OF THE SELF-INTEREST ASSUMPTION

We can use one of the assumptions from Chapter 1, the self-interest assumption, to analyze crime and prevention. Assume that criminals are rational people who commit crimes when it is in their self-interest to do so. This type of simplifying assumption bothers some people who argue that some criminals are not rational. Addicts who commit crimes while on drugs are a case in point. Are they rational? Probably not in a psychological sense. Yet, as you will see, this assumption allows us to develop a model with testable implications.

The critical point for the economic model of crime is whether criminals make decisions to commit more crimes if the cost of committing crimes goes down or is perceived to be lower. The model says that a criminal calculates the costs and benefits of each crime and commits those crimes for which the benefits exceed the costs. The hypothesis is that a criminal calculates costs (C) and benefits (B) of criminal activities and commits those for which B is greater than C. According to this hypothesis, crime is an economic activity, and the criminal behaves like any entrepreneur.

The benefits are what the criminal hopes to realize by the activity. For crimes involving the theft of property, it is relatively easy to place a value on this. The anticipated benefit is the market value of the take. For other crimes such as vandalism, illegal parking, or littering, we have to impute some value to the activity. This value may not be monetary. For example, it may consist of time saved due to parking illegally rather than searching for a legal parking spot.

The cost is the penalty (P) adjusted for the probability (π) that the criminal will be caught and the penalty will be imposed. The penalty for illegal activity is not imposed every time a crime is committed. Thus, adjusting the penalty by the probability of incurring it produces an expected cost of committing the crime. The prospective criminal compares B to $P \times \pi$. For example, suppose the fine for littering is $500, but on the average one will be caught and fined only once every 500 times. The expected cost of littering is then $1 ($500 \times 1/500$). The economic model of crime thus suggests that if some people get more than $1 worth of benefit from littering, they will litter.

There are three elements to the simple model just developed. First, the model says that crime depends on the benefits from the activity so, *ceteris paribus*, as the value of those benefits goes up, so will the amount of criminal activity. Second, it says that as the penalty goes down (with no change in the probability of being caught), the criminal activity will increase. Third, it says that if the probability of being caught goes down, *ceteris paribus*, the amount of criminal activity will go up. This simple model can now be applied to crimes more serious than littering, such as armed robbery.

THE ECONOMICS OF ROBBERY

The economic model of crime can be used to advise policy makers on how to decrease the amount of armed robbery. Policy makers have three options. One possibility is to decrease the potential take, or profit. This is difficult to do, but you have probably noticed that most convenience stores and gas stations open late at night advertise that they don't keep much cash on hand. That's one way of reducing the take. Private citizens in New York City have also exercised this option by placing signs reading "no radio" in their parked cars.

The second possibility for reducing robbery is to increase the penalty. In one suburb of Washington, D.C., the local police chief recently announced that squad cars would be equipped with rifles with exploding shells (outlawed by the United Nations as being too inhumane for warfare). In addition, officers had been instructed to shoot first and ask questions later when investigating robberies. Almost immediately, the robbery rate fell in this town and increased in adjacent areas. This result is predicted by the model, which says as the potential penalty rises, criminal activity will fall. Of course, some people object to such a policy even if it does reduce crime. Remember that economic models are positive, not normative. They only indicate what the consequences of a policy will be. They don't say if it's good or bad in a moral sense.

The third option for reducing the robbery rate would be to increase the probability that robbers will be arrested and convicted. This might be accomplished by adding more police, improving the court system, putting television cameras in banks, or other similar measures.

In an economic study of crime, William Trumbull shows that the probability of punishment and the severity of the punishment both have an effect on the crime rate.[1] He shows that the certainty of punishment has a greater deterrent effect than the severity of punishment, but both have significant effects. His research also shows that when the returns to legal activity increase (the outlook for jobs improves), illegal activity declines. Illegal activity is a substitute for regular employment when jobs are scarce.

THE ECONOMICS OF THE DEATH PENALTY

The preceding analysis may have led you to conclude that economists would argue that the death penalty deters crime by increasing the expected cost. At least one economist, Isaac Ehrlich, has argued that the death penalty does act to reduce the amount of murder.[2] If you are a doubter, answer this question: Would you ever litter if the probability of getting caught was 1 in 500, and the penalty was death? To answer yes, you would have to place a high value on being able to litter or a low value on your own life. However, some people argue that murderers have such a distorted view of reality that they underestimate the probability of being caught, convicted, and sentenced to death. These people argue that the death penalty provides little deterrence. More importantly, just because positive economic theory says that the death penalty deters crime, that does not mean that you, or anyone else, has to support the death penalty if you object on moral (normative) grounds. You can still be opposed to the death penalty on humanitarian grounds even if you accept the implications of the model.

THE ECONOMICS OF ILLEGAL PARKING

Some of you may still be skeptical about this simple economic model of crime. Let's apply it to an action that you have probably committed or at least thought about committing—illegal parking on campus. On almost all college campuses, the quantity of parking spaces supplied is less than the quantity demanded at a zero price. As a result, there are benefits to parking in an illegal space. Suppose the fine for illegal parking is $10, and you find from experience that you get a ticket one out of every four times you park illegally. The expected cost of the crime is thus $2.50 ($10 × ¼). It is difficult to estimate the benefits that accrue to those who park illegally. Since there are many violators, however, it's clear that those benefits are substantial. Assume that you are appointed to a committee formed by the college president to solve the parking problem. Using the simple economic model, your committee identifies three options: (1) The college

---

1. William N. Trumbull, "Estimations of the Economic Model of Crime Using Aggregate and Individual Level Data," *Southern Economic Journal* (October 1989): 423–439.
2. Isaac Ehrlich, "The Deterrent Effect of Capital Punishment: A Question of Life and Death," *American Economic Review* (June 1975).

Gary Becker has extended the application of microeconomic theory into many areas that had been considered noneconomic. He has examined criminal behavior as the result of rational economic calculation and the selection of a spouse as an exercise in the demand for characteristics that have an economic dimension. He has also examined racial discrimination, the decision to have children, time allocation, and the pursuit of education as an investment decision.[a] His ideas about crime prevention came to him when he was rushing to a student presentation at Columbia University and couldn't find a parking place. His thoughts went to the costs, the benefits, and the probability of being caught if he parked illegally. This "intellectual flash" formed the basis for his work on crime prevention.

Becker presently teaches at the University of Chicago. He has also been on the faculty at Columbia University. He received his undergraduate education at Princeton University and his Ph.D. degree from the University of Chicago. In 1967, Becker received the John Bates Clark Award, which is awarded by the American Economic Association to an outstanding economist under forty years old. Gary Becker is a good bet to eventually win a Nobel Prize in economics.

ECONOMIC PROFILE

GARY BECKER
1930–

---

a. See Gary Becker, *The Economic Approach to Human Behavior* (Chicago: University of Chicago Press, 1976), *The Economics of Discrimination* (Chicago: University of Chicago Press, 1957), *Human Capital*, 2nd ed. (New York: Columbia University Press, 1975), *Essays in the Economics of Crime and Punishment*, with W. M. Landes (New York: Columbia University Press, 1974), and *A Treatise on the Family* (Cambridge, MA: Harvard University Press, 1981).

could lower the benefits of illegal parking by buying shuttle buses to transport students from parking areas to the classroom buildings. (2) The college could increase the likelihood of being caught by hiring more police and increasing the number of times they check the parking areas. (3) The college could raise the cost of the crime by having illegally parked cars towed away. This last solution raises the cost of the crime in two ways. Violators would have to pay towing fees in addition to the parking fine. Also, getting towed involves a great deal of time and trouble.

If you still don't think the model works, there is an empirical test you can carry out. Observe the amount of illegal parking on your campus on a nice sunny day. Then the next time it rains, observe that activity again. What does the model predict? On rainy days, the benefits of the crime go up, *ceteris paribus*; they include being closer to class plus arriving in class dry. The probability of being caught also goes down, *ceteris paribus*, because campus police don't like to get wet either. The model thus predicts that there will be more illegal parking on rainy days. Check it out—test the model!

THE ECONOMICS OF BASKETBALL "CRIME"

Economists Robert E. McCormick and Robert D. Tollison applied a similiar economic model for criminal activity to the game of basketball.[3] They picked college basketball as a subject of analysis because there is a great deal of data available and the number of referees (police) increased from two to three in 1978. Their empirical test showed that increasing the number of officials from two to three caused the number of fouls (crimes) to decline.

PRICE CEILINGS AND PRICE FLOORS

price ceilings
Upper limits on prices imposed by a governmental unit. The ceiling is a price that cannot be exceeded.

price floors
Minimum limits on prices established by a governmental unit. The floor is a price that cannot be undercut.

shortage
The amount by which the quantity consumers wish to purchase at some price exceeds the quantity suppliers wish to supply at that price. A shortage can occur on a lasting basis only when a price ceiling is in effect.

Chapter 3 described how free markets reach equilibrium. It is possible for this market process to be interfered with. Such interference is usually the result of governmental action. **Price ceilings** are upper limits on prices imposed by a governmental unit. The ceiling is a price that cannot be exceeded. **Price floors** are minimum limits on prices established by a governmental unit. The floor is a minimum price that cannot be undercut. Price ceilings and price floors disrupt the market-clearing process. Microeconomic tools make it possible to see the effects of these disruptions.

PRICE CEILINGS

A price ceiling that is set below the equilibrium price prevents the market from clearing. The amount that consumers wish to purchase at the imposed price is greater than the amount suppliers are willing to supply at that price. Figure 1 demonstrates this problem. In Figure 1, the equilibrium price is P_e and equilibrium quantity is Q_e. The government imposes a price ceiling at P_c. The amount that consumers wish to consume at price P_c is Q_d. The amount suppliers are willing to supply at that price is Q_s. The result is a shortage.

A **shortage** exists when the amount that consumers wish to purchase at

---

3. Robert E. McCormick and Robert D. Tollison, "Crime on the Court," *Journal of Political Economy* (April 1984): 223–235.

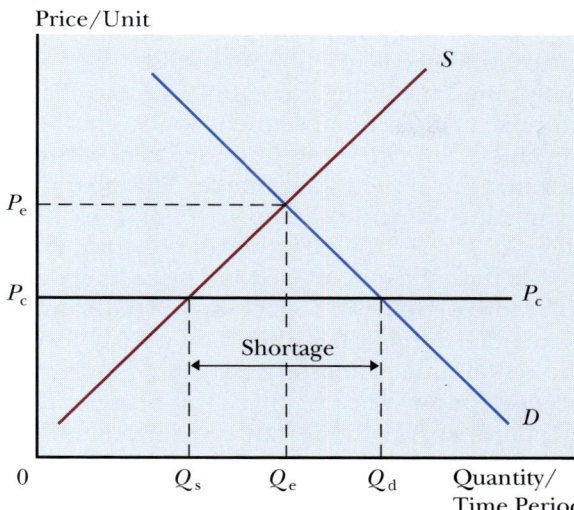

FIGURE 1
PRICE CEILING
A price ceiling that is set below the market-clearing price creates a shortage. At the price imposed by the government, consumers will demand a larger quantity of the good or service than suppliers are willing to sell.

some price exceeds the amount suppliers wish to supply. A shortage can occur on a lasting basis only when a price ceiling is in effect. It is important to realize that the shortage is caused by the ceiling. Without the ceiling, the price would rise. The quantity demanded would decrease and the quantity supplied would increase until the price reached P_e and the market cleared.

If a price ceiling is to be maintained, government officials must replace the market with some other way of allocating the good or service. Consumers will be frustrated as they try to obtain the good or service at the lower price. Some means other than price must be used to determine who will get the available supply of the good or service. The means might be ration coupons, a first-come, first-served rule, or other nonmarket allocating mechanism. Nonmarket methods of allocation waste resources in unproductive activities as consumers attempt to obtain goods in roundabout ways. People might spend hours waiting in line for goods that are priced below market-clearing prices, or they might invest resources in political activity aimed at gaining an advantage in the allocation scheme.

This allocation problem was common in the planned economies of the Soviet Union and Eastern Europe before the recent reforms. Price ceilings were maintained on many consumer goods. There were shortages of these goods and long lines of consumers waiting for a chance to purchase. Consumers would often get into any line when they saw it developing, knowing that a line meant there was some scarce product available.

In almost all cases where price ceilings are imposed, black markets spring up. **Black markets** are markets in which people illegally buy and sell goods or services at prices above government-imposed price ceilings.[4] We'll have more to say about black markets later.

black markets
Markets in which people illegally buy and sell goods and services at prices above government-imposed price ceilings.

---

4. You should be able to show why a price ceiling that is imposed *above* the equilibrium price has no noticeable effect on the market.

rent control
A price ceiling imposed by a governmental unit on housing rents.

RENT CONTROL. Price ceilings are used by various levels of government. Let's look at the effect of price ceilings on apartment rentals.

The governments of many cities, including New York City and Washington, D.C., have imposed price ceilings on apartment rents. This kind of ceiling, imposed by governmental units, is referred to as **rent control**. At first glance, the goal of rent control seems admirable. This goal is to keep rents low so that everyone, including those who are poor, can find a place to live at a reasonable price. To see the effect of rent control, refer again to Figure 1. At a price less than the market-clearing price, there will be a shortage of rental units. More people will be looking for rental units than the number of units available. Something other than market forces will determine who gets the rental units. Landlords may impose criteria for prospective tenants because, for any vacancy, there will be a number of people eager to rent the apartment. Without rent control, a landlord is more likely to rent to any prospective tenant rather than leave the apartment vacant, because the market is clearing. With rent control, the landlord can choose from the backlog of prospective tenants. The landlord can exclude those who are young (or old) or those who have pets or children. Since landlords cannot raise rents, they will instead choose tenants who seem likely to cost the least in terms of damage, noise, complaints, or hassles. Interference in the market has replaced impartial market forces with a system that encourages discrimination.

Rent control, like many other governmental intrusions into the market, has outcomes other than those intended by the well-meaning politicians who advocate them. This is certainly true of rent-controlled housing in New York. Some of the richest members of society gain from rent control, and some of the poorest are left with no housing. Donald Trump reports in his book that the actress Mia Farrow had a rent-controlled apartment for $2,000 per month that would have had a market rent of about $10,000 per month.[5] Trump thought that the most notorious example of the inequity of rent control is that Ed Koch, former mayor of New York City, has a very nice three-bedroom apartment with a terrace in a beautiful part of Greenwich Village, for $350 per month. The market rent would be close to $1,800 per month.

Rent control laws live on even though their effects are apparent. A case study of the experience in Santa Monica, California shows the political appeal of rent control. Santa Monica enacted rent control in 1979. The city rolled back rents and limited increases to about two-thirds of the increase in the Consumer Price Index. The original law was promoted by politician Tom Hayden (former husband of Jane Fonda) as a way to preserve the existing population mix, which included large numbers of blacks, Hispanics, the elderly, and low-income families. Since 1979, many apartment complexes have been abandoned by their owners, who would rather have them vacant than rent them at the controlled rents. Abandoned rent-controlled apartments sit adjacent to homes selling for more than $500,000. The problem is made worse by the fact that the owners of the abandoned apartment buildings find it very difficult to sell. Many want to

---

5. Donald J. Trump (with Tony Schwartz), *Trump: The Art of the Deal* (New York: Warner Books, 1987), pp. 255–256.

tear down the buildings and build new office or residential space. But the city passed a law to prevent such reconstruction. In order to tear down any rental unit, the owner must pay to build replacement units in the city. One apartment owner had his building spray-painted with the words "We want perestroika now."

The irony of the situation in Santa Monica is that the rent-controlled units have become a haven for rich young professionals. The parking lots outside these $350-per-month, two-bedroom apartments are filled with BMWs and Audis. The population mix that Tom Hayden wanted to preserve has not been preserved. So why isn't the law being changed? Perhaps the fact that 75 percent of the voters of Santa Monica are tenants offers a hint.[6]

These examples show the impacts of rent control on the distribution of income and the production of new housing. The short-run effects of rent control are mainly distributional. Landlords in rent-controlled areas choose to rent to richer tenants because they may cause fewer problems and "know the right people" to get in. In the long run, fewer housing units are built and the existing stock of housing units deteriorates.

BLACK MARKETS. As mentioned earlier, black markets tend to develop when price ceilings are imposed. In Santa Monica, it has been reported that "key money," up-front payments of up to $5,000, was required of some prospective tenants. This practice was one form of black market.

Assume that Figure 2 represents the market for tickets to one of the biggest college football games of the year, the Orange Bowl. The stock of tickets is completely fixed in the short run because the stadium has a seating capacity of 70,000. The athletic departments of the two colleges are selling the tickets at a price ceiling of $20 per ticket. For this game, the market-clearing price would be $30. The price ceiling creates a shortage of 30,000 tickets. At that price, there is going to be a larger quantity of tickets demanded than exist. The athletic departments have to allocate

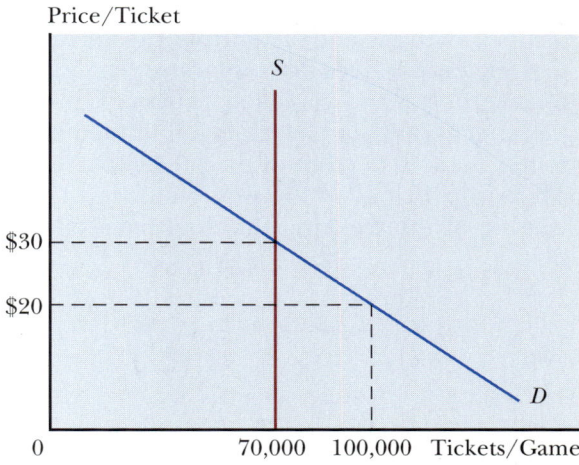

FIGURE 2
THE ORANGE BOWL
A price ceiling is often imposed by universities in selling tickets to popular events. If such a price ceiling is below the market-clearing price, it creates a black market for the underpriced tickets.

---

6. See Marc Beauchamp, "Bankrupt Landlords in Wonderland," *Forbes* (20 March 1989): 105–107.

International Perspective

Black Markets

During World War II, the U.S. government tried to control the prices of some basic commodities, such as gasoline and sugar. Ration tickets were distributed to determine who got the limited supplies. These ration tickets were sold on black markets. Since governments at all levels in the United States usually refrain from trying to set price ceilings, there has been little black market activity in the United States except for that episode. About the only direct experience you might have with a black market is the scalping of tickets to athletic events and concerts.

However, you may be aware of black markets that exist in other countries. One important black market is in currencies. Many countries attempt to control the price of their currency in terms of other currencies. Economists refer to this price as the exchange rate. Attempts to control the exchange rate always produce black markets for foreign currencies. If you went before 1990 to Eastern Europe, the Soviet Union, or some parts of Asia, you were probably approached on the street by furtive individuals who wanted to exchange their currency for dollars at a much better exchange rate than any bank provides.

Currency exchange is not the only kind of black market exchange abroad. You have probably heard stories about the black market for jeans in the Soviet Union. If you travel to the Soviet Union, pack a couple pair of extra jeans so you can finance part of your trip out of all the rubles you can get for them on the black market. But don't get caught!

Governments usually attempt to control a broad range of prices during and after wars. This effort is made more difficult by the fact that consumer goods are usually more scarce at those times. Equilibrium prices would therefore be rising rapidly while the government was trying to control them. Perhaps the extreme examples of such controls happened in Germany and Japan after World War II.

In both Germany and Japan following World War II, there were enormous national debts that were financed by monetary expansion. These large increases in the money supply led to severe inflation. At the same time, the governments of these countries imposed strict controls on food prices, even rationing the caloric intake of individuals. These strict controls led to black markets and the phenomenon of "trekking." Urban residents would leave town to go to the countryside to make black market deals with farmers. The stricter the controls, the more the trekking grew. It was reported that on one day more than 900,000 residents of Tokyo left town for the countryside. In Germany, the controls came to an end with the Erhard reforms of 1948. With the end of controls, the incentive to trek evaporated. As with most economic forces, there was a secondary effect. Railroad passenger traffic in Germany fell immediately to less than 40 percent of the prereform level. This drop in rail traffic was evidence of the volume of the trekking that had been taking place.

Sources: Jerome B. Cohen, *Japan's Economy in War and Reconstruction* (Minneapolis: University of Minnesota Press, 1949); and Lucius C. Clay, *Decision in Germany* (New York: Doubleday, Inc., 1950).

the tickets by some other means than the market. Tickets will be sold to those fans who are willing to wait in line or those who donate to the booster club. The shortage of tickets will produce a black market. Some of those who are able to get the tickets for $20 will be willing to sell them. These people will engage in black market activity by selling their tickets to those who are willing to pay more.

Black marketers dealing in tickets to sports or entertainment events are referred to as scalpers. Scalping generally has a bad connotation. But consider that a scalper is performing the service of transferring tickets from people who value other goods more highly than they value the tickets to people who value the tickets more highly than other goods. Thus, the scalper is being paid for performing a service. In most states, scalping has been outlawed. In Texas, it is legal and organized reselling of tickets takes place. In Washington, D.C., it is illegal to resell tickets—even at prices below the original price!

WHY CEILINGS? If price ceilings are so disruptive, why do they exist? One answer is that not all people are hurt by ceilings. Those who are able to purchase the good or service at the artificially low price are better off. As a result, they approve of the ceiling. For example, people who already have an apartment and don't want to move would be better off with rent control. These people would probably vote for rent control because it would make them better off. Also, those who don't mind waiting in line or those who get tickets because they are team boosters like low ticket prices.

It is important to realize that price ceilings do not generally help the poor. If there is one $20 ticket left for the big game, who do you think will get it? A poor fan who likes football more than anything else $20 would buy, or the governor who thinks it would be good politics to be seen at the game? Whenever the market is replaced, another mechanism must be substituted to allocate goods. This mechanism usually depends heavily on power and influence. Thus, the poor are not generally helped by price ceilings.

PRICE FLOORS

A price floor that is set above the equilibrium price keeps the market from clearing. The amount that suppliers offer for sale at the imposed price is greater than the amount consumers wish to purchase at that price. Figure 3 demonstrates this case. In Figure 3, the equilibrium price is P_e, and the equilibrium quantity is Q_e. The government imposes a price floor at P_f. The result is that the quantity supplied at price P_f is Q_s, and the quantity consumers demand at that price is Q_d. The higher price has attracted more suppliers into the market. At the same time, it has discouraged buyers or caused them to shift to substitutes. The result is a surplus equal to $Q_s - Q_d$.

A **surplus** exists when the amount that suppliers wish to supply at some price exceeds the amount that consumers wish to purchase. A surplus can only occur on a lasting basis when a price floor is in effect. The surplus is created by the price floor. If the floor didn't exist, the price would fall. The quantity demanded would increase and the quantity supplied would decrease until the market cleared.

surplus
The amount by which the quantity suppliers wish to supply at some price exceeds the quantity consumers wish to purchase at that price. A surplus can occur on a lasting basis only when a price floor is in effect.

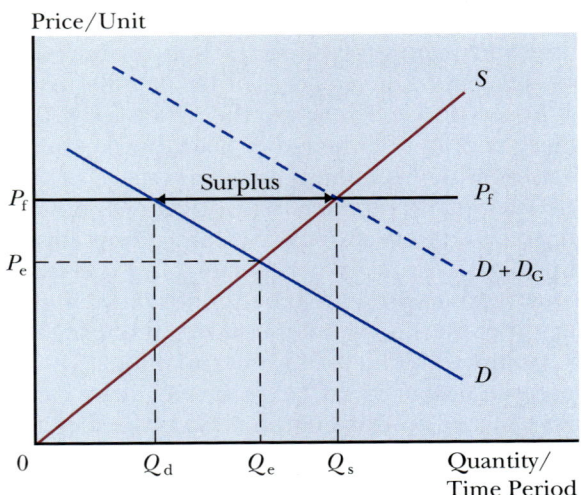

FIGURE 3
PRICE FLOOR
If the government imposes a price floor above the market-clearing price, a surplus will be created. At the price imposed by the government, suppliers will desire to sell more units than consumers will be willing to purchase. Demand would have to increase to $D + D_G$ to clear the market after the price floor was imposed.

It can be difficult for the governmental agency that imposes a price floor to keep prices from falling below the floor. Some suppliers will attempt to cut prices in order to sell the quantity they want to supply. The most effective way for the government to prevent this price cutting is to purchase the excess quantity supplied. By purchasing the surplus, the government in effect is shifting the demand curve outward to create a new equilibrium at the desired price. In Figure 3, the dashed demand curve represents the demand at the price floor (D) plus the added governmental demand (D_G). A shift to demand curve $D + D_G$ would allow the price to remain at P_f.

The best example of price floors that work in this way are the price supports operated by the Commodity Credit Corporation (CCC) for some agricultural products in the United States. The **Commodity Credit Corporation (CCC)** is a U.S. government agency that makes loans to farmers as part of federal price support programs. Suppose the federal government wants to maintain a price for grain that is above the market-clearing price. To maintain this price floor, it is necessary for the CCC to purchase some grain. The effect of this is to shift the demand curve to the right (as with $D + D_G$ in Figure 3) so that the higher price can be maintained.

Commodity Credit Corporation (CCC)
A U.S. government agency that makes loans to farmers as part of federal price support programs.

THE MINIMUM WAGE

The **minimum wage** is a price floor imposed by the federal government in the labor market. Looking again at Figure 3, a minimum wage (P_f) set above the market wage (P_e) causes a surplus of labor ($Q_s - Q_d$). If the minimum wage is set above the market-clearing wage rate, the amount of labor that workers will supply at the minimum wage will be greater than the amount of labor that firms will wish to employ, resulting in unemployment.

In 1978, Congress raised the wage floor to $2.65 an hour, up from the $2.30 an hour that was set in 1974. In addition, a formula was adopted that ensured automatic increases up to $3.35 an hour in 1981. In 1989, Congress passed legislation to raise the minimum wage to $3.80 in 1990 and $4.25 in 1991.

minimum wage
A price floor imposed by the federal government in the labor market.

Economists generally agree that minimum wage laws cause unemployment to be higher than it would be otherwise. Unemployment will especially affect young people, for whom the market-clearing wage might be much lower than the minimum wage. There is strong statistical evidence from a large number of economists that increases in the minimum wage result in higher youth unemployment. Robert Goldfarb and Edward Gramlich independently reviewed eight empirical studies by economists.[7] The studies agreed that increases in the minimum wage cause increases in unemployment among teenagers. The studies predicted that a 15 percent increase in the minimum wage would increase teenage unemployment by 3.4 to 5.3 percent.[8]

If there is agreement among economists about the harmful effects of minimum wage laws, why are they enacted? The reason is very similar to the rationale for price ceilings. Not all people are hurt by the wage floor. Some workers receive pay increases when the legislation is enacted. Those who are laid off or who seek work but are unable to find it at the new minimum wage usually don't understand the role of the higher minimum wage in causing their problems. The result is that it is politically popular with some groups—organized labor, for example—to support minimum wage increases. Remember that the economic model only predicts that such laws cause decreased employment. It does not say that minimum wage legislation is a good or bad thing in other respects. A society may decide that it is better to have fewer people employed at a higher wage rate than to have a larger number employed at a lower, market-clearing wage rate.

During the Reagan administration, the minimum wage was not increased. Thus, its impact declined as market wages rose relative to the stable minimum wage. For most workers, the equilibrium wage was already above the floor, so it did not cause much, if any, unemployment. In fact, there is some evidence that the increase to $4.25 in 1991 will have little impact, for two reasons. First, the legislation allows a subminimum wage of $3.35 per hour for training purposes. This training wage can be paid for six months. Second, it appears that for most employers in most markets the equilibrium wage is already at or above $4.25. McDonald's, for example, pays an average of $4.65 per hour. Wendy's International pays $4.25. The only region where the higher minimum wage may cause some unemployment is in the South, where both wages and skill levels of employees tend to be lower.

MARKETS AS ALLOCATION MECHANISMS

Auctions are markets in which there are seldom any barriers to letting the price allocate scarce goods. If there are enough people bidding on the items offered, the price that results should be an equilibrium price. Auc-

---

7. Robert Goldfarb, "The Policy Content of Quantitative Minimum Wage Research," *Industrial Relations Research Association Proceedings* (December 1974): 261–268; Edward M. Gramlich, "Impact of Minimum Wages on Other Wages, Employment and Family Incomes," *Brookings Papers on Economic Activity*, No. 2 (1976): 409–451.
8. These estimates were based on calculating the elasticity of supply and demand for teenaged workers.

tions are, therefore, a good way to allocate scarce resources. Yet people often object to using auctions because they think that they will do better if some mechanism other than the market is used for allocation.

A case study from Arizona State University is a good example of this phenomenon.[9] When the university built a six-story addition to its business college, whole departments had to relocate to the new facility. As in most buildings, some offices were better than others (some had windows, some didn't, some were large, some were small). The departments faced the problem of allocating a scarce resource without a market.

The chair of the management department adopted the allocation mechanism used most frequently in traditional societies—seniority (defined as the length of time spent on the faculty at Arizona State). The marketing and accounting departments followed the example of management and used a seniority system. Some of the younger assistant professors thought this to be very unfair, because they spent time in their offices doing research and preparing for classes while the full professors spent more time consulting and less in their offices. The chair of the finance department agreed that seniority allocation seemed unfair. A sign-up sheet was placed by the chair's office, and offices were allocated on a first-come, first-served basis. The result was that those professors who spent a lot of time roving the halls got the best offices. Those doing research, on sabbatical, or on a trip ended up with small offices and no windows. The chair of the statistics department decided to use a random drawing of names to allocate offices. This met with faculty approval because everyone would be treated equally. After the draw, those with seniority forced the chair to cancel the outcome and use seniority instead.

The chair of the economics department wanted to use the market to allocate the scarce resources. Being a good bureaucrat, he asked the faculty for suggestions. Surprisingly, in a department of economists, no one suggested using prices to allocate a scarce resource. Instead, the chair was advised by the most senior faculty member to use seniority as is done at "all great institutions." Other suggestions were to allocate the offices based on research productivity, teaching effectiveness, height, race, sex, and religion. One member suggested office "wrestlemania"—a brawl. The chair decided on a sealed bid auction with the proceeds going to a scholarship fund. After three weeks, the twenty-four bids were opened. The highest bid was $500 and the second highest was $250. All twenty-four bids totaled $3,200. Offices were allocated in order of the sizes of the bids. The only complaint was from the person who bid $500, who overestimated the equilibrium price, bidding twice as much as the next highest bidder and almost four times the average bid.

Trouble was brewing. A professor used the experiment as an example in a principles of economics course. The students thought it was a good idea. They even understood that it was only important that the price had to be paid. It didn't matter where the money went. One student, who happened to be a reporter for the campus newspaper, thought that the

---

9. This case is drawn from William J. Boyes and Stephen K. Happel, "Auctions as an Allocation Mechanism in Academia: The Case of Faculty Offices," *Journal of Economic Perspectives* (Summer 1989): 37–40.

office auction was such a good idea that it was reported on the front page. The story was then picked up by the Phoenix media and went out on the AP wire. The chair faced an onslaught of criticism from university administrators and local politicians who accused the chair of selling state property. Eventually, the publicity calmed down, largely because the money had gone to fund a scholarship. But the lesson was loud and clear: Many good opportunities to use the market as an allocation device are overlooked.

A LESSON FROM THE ENERGY CRISIS

You may have been a preschooler when your parents had to wait in line for gasoline at the height of the energy crisis in the mid-1970s. Times change, and some gas stations have even returned to the old practice of giving away road maps to their customers. Policy makers in the United States should not forget that crisis, however. There is an old saying: "What goes around, comes around." Policy makers should prepare for future rounds of energy policy by asking what can be learned from past mistakes. Indeed, some policy makers are predicting a second energy crisis. Secretary of the Interior Donald Hodel warned in 1987 that people would be sitting in gas lines by 1992.

In 1978, President Jimmy Carter gave a speech to the U.S. public about the energy crisis wearing a sweater and sitting next to a fire. He declared that the energy crisis was the moral equivalent of war. President Carter ultimately ordered the deregulation of natural gas prices and a windfall profits tax on large oil companies. President Reagan continued the phased deregulation but eliminated the windfall profits tax in his 1981 tax reform. Problems continue to confront the natural gas market. The tools developed in other chapters can be used to analyze many aspects of the energy "crisis." The natural gas shortage provides a good case study for that purpose.

THE CREATION OF A CRISIS: REGULATION OF NATURAL GAS

In 1938 Congress passed the Natural Gas Act, and in 1954 the Supreme Court placed all firms selling natural gas in more than one state under the regulation of the Federal Power Commission (FPC).[10] The law was intended to keep prices "just and reasonable" for consumers by allowing suppliers only a "fair" rate of return. After the Supreme Court ruling, the FPC attempted to regulate the price received by each individual producer engaged in the interstate sale of natural gas. The system broke down in 1960 because a giant backlog of cases had developed as a result of attempting to regulate more than 4,000 firms.[11] Thus, the FPC ruled in 1965 (affirmed by the Supreme Court in 1968) that it would set prices sepa-

---

10. The brief discussion that follows does not do justice to the complexity of natural gas regulation. For more information and other references, see Edward J. Mitchell, *U.S. Energy Policy: A Primer* (Washington, DC: American Enterprise Institute for Public Policy Research, June 1974).
11. Edward J. Mitchell called this "the outstanding example of the federal government in the breakdown of the administrative process" (*U.S. Energy Policy: A Primer*, p. 7).

rately for each geographical area and each individual petroleum commodity. This decision took eight years to be implemented, and during this entire period, prices were kept at 1960 levels. This individual commodity approach to pricing was next to impossible to implement because natural gas is jointly produced with crude oil. The method requires that certain costs be allocated to the production of natural gas, even though it is produced in a joint process. What were the effects of this regulation?

Paul W. MacAvoy, a member of President Ford's Council of Economic Advisers, has extensively examined the economics of the natural gas industry. In a series of books and articles in professional journals, he has studied the market for natural gas to determine the effects of regulation. MacAvoy concluded that regulation has held prices below the equilibrium level. Between 1964 and 1967, prices would have been about twice as high without regulation. The result of the artificially low prices was that 40 percent fewer new reserves were added to production than would have been added in the free-market context. The effect of the lower new reserves was painfully obvious. In the absence of the price-rationing function of the market system, there was a shortage. Existing supplies then had to be rationed, and consumers (including industry) had to substitute more expensive fuels for the cheaper natural gas that was not available. The government, in order to keep the price of natural gas low, produced a shortage that required consumers to buy more expensive gasified coal, imported liquid natural gas, or some other substitute.

This shortage of natural gas is shown graphically in Figure 4. Assume that the price originally set by the FPC was near or at equilibrium. That

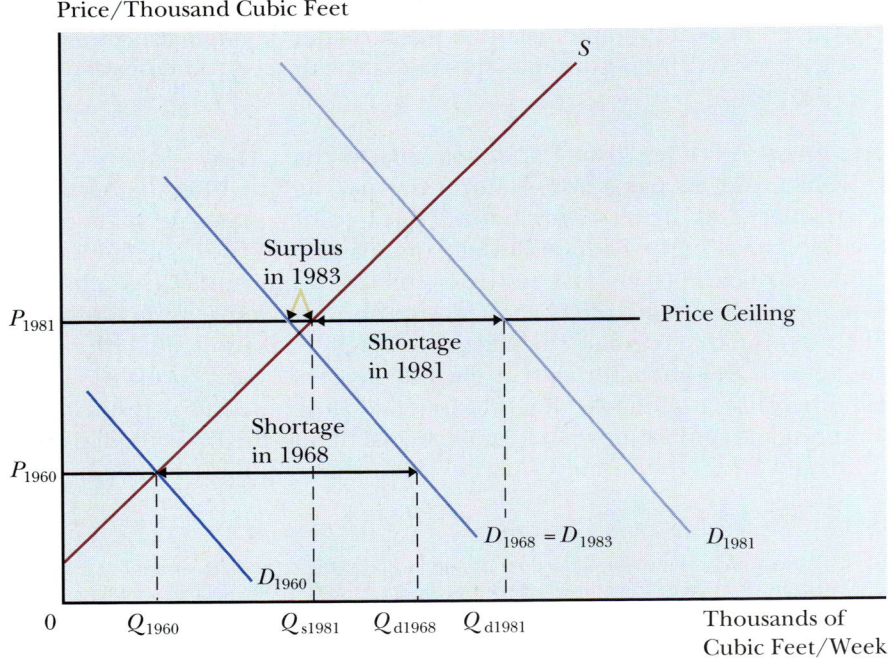

**FIGURE 4
THE MARKET
FOR NATURAL GAS**
In 1960, P_{1960} was an equilibrium price. The amount consumers *wished* to purchase was exactly the amount suppliers *wished* to sell. A shortage was created because the price was frozen at P_{1960} and demand increased to D_{1968} or D_{1981}. Allowing the price to rise to P_{1981} reduced the shortage. Some shortage remained as long as the price was controlled at a level below equilibrium.

The Japanese motorist pays double the world market price for gasoline and three times what the U.S. motorist pays. Yet the Japanese oil industry is sick. There is excess capacity, a strange pricing structure, gas stations in the wrong places, and very low profit margins. The responsibility for this situation can be placed on Japan's powerful Ministry of International Trade and Industry (MITI).

For years, MITI has tightly regulated and controlled the Japanese oil industry. Japan is almost totally dependent on imported oil. An attempt to gain control of a source of oil was one of Japan's motivations for invading Southeast Asia during World War II. After the war, foreign oil producers quickly set up business in Japan. In 1962, the Japanese government passed a law strengthening MITI's power to control the market and to protect domestic refiners against foreign competition.

MITI intervened with a vengeance. It allocated crude oil to refiners, set production quotas, limited imports of refined products, and regulated gas station openings. In order to keep oil prices low for industry and farmers, the government forced gasoline users to pay more than their proportionate share of refining costs. In many years, the refiners lose money on all products except gasoline, and gasoline accounts for only about 20 percent of the refining volume.

INTERNATIONAL PERSPECTIVE

GOVERNMENT INTERVENTION, JAPANESE STYLE

MITI also controls the distribution of oil and gas. Many Japanese gas stations are owned by local businessmen with political clout. Under the MITI licensing scheme, a new gas station can be opened only if an old one is closed. Old inefficient stations are maintained in rural areas. The average station in Japan pumps less than one-third as much gas as the average station in the United States.

In 1987, MITI admitted that it had a problem. MITI announced a five-year plan to deregulate the Japanese oil refining industry. In April 1989, MITI phased out the quota system for gasoline production. In 1990, the restrictions on opening new gas stations were lifted. In 1992, MITI will stop allocating crude oil to refineries. However, there is no plan to reform the pricing of refined products. Unfortunately for Japanese motorists, they will continue to subsidize industrial and agricultural users of oil. This anti-consumer policy is typical of Japan's business-government partnership.

Source: Andrew Tanzer, "World's Worst Oil Policy?" *Forbes* (24 July 1989): 245–248.

price is represented by P_{1960} and the equilibrium quantity by Q_{1960}. The price ceiling was not changed for eight years. During this period, there were tremendous changes in the *ceteris paribus* conditions affecting demand. For example, household income increased greatly during this period. Thus, by 1968, the demand curve had shifted from D_{1960} to D_{1968}, resulting in a shortage. At P_{1960}, the quantity supplied was still Q_{1960}, but the quantity demanded had become Q_{d1968}. There was 40 percent less production than there would have been with a free market. In 1981, the problem was still present. Demand had increased to D_{1981}. Although the FPC allowed the price to rise to P_{1981}, that rise lagged behind the demand increase. There was still a government-induced shortage because at P_{1981}, the quantity supplied is Q_{s1981} and the quantity demanded is Q_{d1981}.

It is important to realize that the shortage was caused by the price ceiling. Natural gas is scarce, but scarcity and shortage are different concepts. Scarcity simply means that an item is not as plentiful as people would like it to be. With scarcity, rising prices ensure equilibrium. A shortage means that at the prevailing price, the quantity demanded exceeds the quantity supplied. This distinction is important because much of the debate about the energy crisis confuses these two concepts.

The energy crisis and the oil industry are subjects of hot debate between politicians and analysts. These debates often center on predictions of dire consequences because the price of oil is too high (as in 1975) or too low (as in 1988). Such predictions are nothing new. As early as the beginning of the nineteenth century, some commentators were predicting the first energy crisis. At the time, houses were lit by oil-burning lamps. Demand for these lamps was increasing rapidly because of income and population growth. The lamps were fueled by oil from sperm whales. Many people predicted that the whale population would soon be depleted and, therefore, houses would be dark. In other words, they were predicting greater scarcity of whale oil. What happened? Prices rose rapidly, from about 40 cents per gallon to about $2.50 per gallon in thirty years. The higher prices caused the quantity demanded to decrease, as users found substitutes for whale oil. A shortage did not occur because prices rose in the face of greater scarcity. Shortages can only occur with artificially imposed low prices. It is disturbing that the shortage of natural gas occurred in a market where there was a potentially large quantity supplied.

THE POLITICAL DILEMMA OF DEREGULATION

Another disturbing fact is that, even after economists recognized that government regulation was creating havoc in the natural gas market, it was politically very difficult to remove the controls. Why? Those individuals who were lucky enough, or had enough political power, could purchase natural gas at below-market prices. In 1977, the regulated price of natural gas was $1.34 per thousand cubic feet. At that time, it was estimated that markets would have cleared at $3.00 per thousand cubic feet. People bought gas furnaces, and firms installed gas-driven equipment because of the low cost. The dilemma for politicians who advocate deregulation is clear. It appears to consumers as if the deregulator, not the market forces, produces the sharp rise in price. Voters might turn against a member of Congress who votes to deregulate. It is important to realize that if Con-

Chapter 4 Applications of Supply and Demand   115

gress had not interfered with the market mechanism in the first place, voters probably would not hold Congress responsible for the higher gas prices after deregulation!

THE SHORTAGE TURNS INTO SURPLUS—AND PRICES RISE?

It was a major goal of the Carter administration to lift the price ceiling. The necessary legislation was approved by Congress as the Natural Gas Policy Act of 1978. The Carter deregulation came after a hard-fought legislative battle. It immediately raised prices 25 percent and allowed for a 10 percent increase per year until 1985, when all ceilings on newly found natural gas were scheduled to be removed. The story of the legislated deregulation didn't end with the planned removal of all ceilings. Different problems began to surface in late 1982.

The recession of 1981–1982 (and warm weather) decreased the demand for natural gas, shifting the demand curve to D_{1983} in Figure 4 (shown as the same curve as D_{1968} to keep the diagram simple). In fact, in 1983, only about 85 percent of the natural gas produced was consumed, creating a surplus in 1983, as shown in Figure 4. In a deregulated market, a surplus should cause prices to decrease. Unfortunately, the Natural Gas Policy Act of 1978 didn't deregulate all natural gas. Instead, it freed prices on new gas and kept old gas prices at low levels. The immediate effect was that the price of the new gas rose dramatically and a (sort of) equilibrium was reached.

As demand for natural gas fell, supply and demand analysis predicted that the surplus would push prices downward. However, some consumers (utilities) were locked into long-term "take or pay" contracts. These contracts stemmed from the days of regulation. Utilities would enter into twenty-year contracts with gas suppliers to share the risk of price fluctuations. The gas suppliers, faced with a surplus, expanded output of the more expensive gas (the new gas) and reduced production of the cheap gas (the old gas). As a result, the price of natural gas rose.

The regulatory distinction of old gas and new gas thus had the effect of raising natural gas prices to consumers. Its intent had been to keep prices from rising as much by controlling the price of already discovered gas.

THE MARKET FINALLY CLEARS

The natural gas story didn't even end with the complete decontrol of prices in 1985. By 1987, natural gas prices were at very low levels, in part because of deregulation, but largely due to the collapse of the oil cartel and the large decline in the worldwide price of oil and related products. In August 1989, President George Bush signed legislation ending all wellhead price controls on natural gas. This end came thirty-five years after the Supreme Court placed natural gas under the regulation of the FPC. As one industry analyst put it, "Supply and demand will come into balance in 1990."[12] After thirty-five years, the market will finally be allowed to clear.

This brief review of natural gas regulation is only one example of the effect that price regulation can have on market forces. Similar kinds of ef-

---

12. Kenneth R. Sheets, "The Wonder Fuel for the 1990s," *U.S. News & World Report* (31 July 1989): 38.

fects can be found throughout the U.S. economy. One need only scan the headlines for this month's crisis—the meat shortage, the cement shortage, or the capital shortage. The problem is likely to have been caused by well-intentioned interference with market forces.

THE HEALTH CARE INDUSTRY

The rapidly rising price of health care has been receiving much attention from journalists and politicians in recent years. This increased interest is also due to the fact that health care has become one of the fastest growing industries in the United States. Between 1950 and 1980, total spending on health care increased from $11 billion annually to more than $200 billion annually. Then this figure tripled again between 1985 and 1990 (adjusted for inflation). In 1950, health care expenditures represented 4.5 percent of total national income. In 1990, they represented more than 13 percent of national income. It is possible to analyze the potential problems of the health care industry using the basic economic tools of supply and demand.

Figure 5 illustrates what has happened in the health care industry. The market in 1950 is represented by supply curve S_{1950} and demand curve D_{1950}. Equilibrium is at P_1 and Q_1. Between 1950 and 1990, there were some changes in the *ceteris paribus* conditions in the health care market. On the supply side, the sophistication of the care supplied by hospitals and doctors greatly increased. There has been a virtual explosion of technological advances in the industries that make diagnostic, surgical, and therapeutic equipment. This equipment is expensive and increases the cost of supplying health care (even as it improves that care). The effect of this more expensive care has been to shift the supply curve from S_{1950} to S_{1990} in Figure 5.

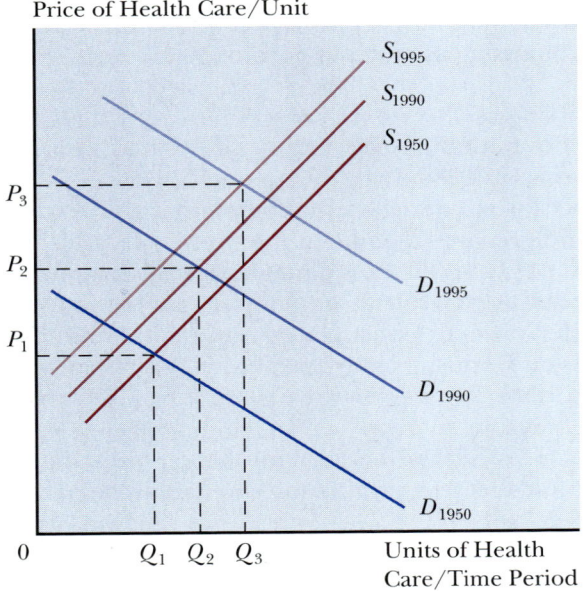

FIGURE 5
THE MARKET FOR HEALTH CARE
The health care market is characterized by decreasing supply due to increasing costs and increasing demand due to rising incomes and the aging of the population. As a result, the equilibrium price of health care has been rising rapidly.

On the demand side, the changes have been equally significant. First and foremost, the income of U.S. citizens rose over this period. The demand for health care increased rapidly as incomes increased. Second, there has been an increase in Medicare, Medicaid, and employer-provided health insurance. Since payment would be made by a third party, many individuals demanded more health care. Third, the age distribution of the U.S. population has shifted. This will become an even greater problem for health care as baby boomers age. Fourth, the very success of health care delivery creates more demand for health care in the future. As health care improves, the population lives longer. More health care is then demanded because the population is now older, and older people have more health problems. Fifty years ago, many of these people would have died of measles, polio, or tuberculosis before they would have been old enough to develop the maladies now associated with older age. The increased demand for health care is represented by the shift from D_{1950} to D_{1990} in Figure 5.

The result of these changes in supply and demand has been for the price of health care to rise to P_2 and a new level of consumption to be established at Q_2. The magnitude of the shift from P_1 to P_2 can be understood by comparing the price index for medical services to the consumer price index. Between 1950 and 1990, the price index for medical services rose 978 percent. This increase was 2.2 times the change in the consumer price index (CPI).

THE COMING CRISIS IN HEALTH CARE

What about the future? It is likely that the supply curve for health care will continue to shift leftward, representing an increase in the price of the factors of production used to produce that service. It is also likely that demand will continue to increase as incomes rise and the population ages. Thus, in response to a shift in demand from D_{1990} to D_{1995} and a shift in supply from S_{1990} to S_{1995} in Figure 5, there should be an increase in price to P_3 and an increase in the equilibrium quantity to Q_3. But this prediction supposes that the government does not intervene in this market. A quick review of Congressional interest in the health care industry would be enough to convince you that this is not a realistic assumption. The most likely governmental solution to the rapidly rising prices of health care is twofold: some form of national health insurance and/or price controls.

Senator Edward Kennedy and others have made national health insurance a major political issue. His bill, "Minimum Health Benefits for All Workers Act," would require all employers to provide health care insurance for workers and their dependents. President Reagan supported catastrophic health insurance for older Americans. The economic effects of such programs are easy to predict. Since national health insurance would make health care affordable to more citizens by shifting a large part of the cost to taxpayers in general, it would increase the demand curve even beyond D_{1995} in Figure 5. National health insurance would put even greater upward pressure on prices.

There is also increasing pressure to intervene in the health care market with price controls. Congress is talking about the "immorality" of the high price of health care. Price controls have been suggested as a solution. The effect can be predicted by examining Figure 5. At a ceiling price of P_2, the effect would be a shortage. The severity of the shortage would depend on the magnitudes of the increase in demand and the decrease in supply. There would be the same type of crisis as affected the natural gas market. Even though Congress demonstrated in the 1980s that it understood how controls implemented in the 1950s helped create the energy crisis, it is flirting with similar controls for the health care industry in the 1990s.

Does this conclusion mean that politicians can't justify supporting a national health program that would ensure health care to all citizens? Not at all! All that economics says is that such a program would increase demand and put upward pressure on prices of health care. You may decide that this upward pressure on prices is an acceptable cost and that you would support such a program. The contribution of economics is to point out that these pressures are there and they can't be ignored when deciding on policy.

PHYSICIANS AND THE MARKETPLACE

Before the mid-1950s, doctors in the United States often made house calls, drove Buicks, and were viewed as upper middle-class pillars of the community.[13] In 1955, doctors' incomes averaged $16,017. All that has changed: doctors have moved to clinics and hospitals, drive Porsches and Mercedes, and are viewed by most of us as the privileged rich. Their average pretax income jumped to $28,960 in 1965, to $58,440 in 1975, and to $108,400 in 1985. That represents an increase of 677 percent over a thirty-year period, or an average annual increase of 22.5 percent, far more than the increase in the general price level.

Until 1965, the ranks of physicians were increasing at about 2 percent per year, and spending on medical care was increasing at 10 percent per year. That goes a long way toward explaining the 22.5 percent annual increases in pretax income. But, as you have learned, supply curves slope upward. The increases in income created incentives for the number of physicians to increase. In 1965, there were 277,600 doctors in the United States, 1 for every 697 Americans. In 1986, there were 506,000, or 1 for every 471 Americans.

What has happened? First, the rate of increase in physicians' income has slowed dramatically. From 1983 to 1985, their real pretax mean income rose 2 percent per year.[14] That's drastically below the thirty-year average but a result the supply and demand model would predict. Medical school applications have declined. In 1975, there were 42,624 applications for 14,579 slots. In 1985, there were 32,893 applications for 16,268 slots. In 1990, there were 26,915 applications for 16,983 slots. As *Forbes* magazine put it, "Hippocrates Meets Adam Smith." These adjustments in price and quantity suggest that the health care "crisis" may have market

---

13. Facts and quotes in this section are from "Hippocrates Meets Adam Smith," *Forbes* (10 February 1986): 63–66.
14. The fact that physicians' incomes are slowing in growth may seem in conflict with the fact that the costs of health care are rising. Because doctors' charges are only a small part of health costs, it is possible for their income to be falling at the same time that total health care costs are rising.

Chapter 4 Applications of Supply and Demand

solutions. Government intervention through national health insurance or setting prices may not be needed.

A few other adjustments are worth noting. Many doctors have begun to advertise. In 1965, medical advertising was considered unprofessional and illegal. Other doctors now have television sets in their waiting rooms instead of year-old magazines. One doctor in a Beverly Hills mall gives her patients beepers that summon them from shopping when she is ready to see them so they don't have to languish in her waiting room. More of these adjustments can be expected as doctors face the facts of the market.

MICROECONOMICS AND SOCIAL POLICY: THE ECONOMICS OF NATURAL DISASTERS

One more aspect of the use of microeconomics as a policy tool can be demonstrated by looking at an area of social policy that hasn't received much attention from economists. This example will highlight the **unintended effects of policy**, those results that are unanticipated by policy makers but become evident through careful economic analysis. Policy makers might avoid the pitfall of creating institutionalized incentives by making use of microeconomic analysis.

unintended effects of policy
Results that are unanticipated by policy makers but become evident through careful economic analysis.

Economists have devoted little effort to studying the economics of natural disasters. There are some important areas in which microeconomics can be brought to bear on the analysis of how people respond to floods, earthquakes, hurricanes, and other natural disasters.

GOVERNMENT POLICY TOWARD DISASTERS

The U.S. government has provided a great deal of disaster relief in recent years. Before the mid-1960s, disaster victims received little economic aid from the federal government, although private relief for emergency needs was provided by the Red Cross. Before the 1960s, the federal government did give aid to state and local governments to rebuild schools, hospitals, and roads. However, it offered little in the way of disaster relief for individuals and businesses. In 1989, in the aftermath of Hurricane Hugo in South Carolina and the earthquake in northern California during the World Series, there was a massive outpouring of private, state, and federal assistance. The amount of federal aid was huge, even though these disasters paled in comparison to earlier ones such as the 1900 hurricane that took 6,000 lives in Galveston, Texas.

Why the large increase in aid? The increased information brought by television coverage and congressional involvement offer possible explanations. Disasters were brought to the attention of the nation, and local political leaders found they could expect relief since the cost could be spread to all taxpayers. This political cost-sharing game was easy to play. To mount opposition was to appear unsympathetic with victims. The result has been the present policy of massive federal aid to disaster victims.

Microeconomics can shed light on several other aspects of that policy. One lesson is that if you want to get other people to help you, they have to be reminded of your need. Television news is a good vehicle for such a campaign to "generate a demand for assistance."

THE CONSEQUENCES OF DISASTER RELIEF

The normative question "Should relief be given?" is moot politically because assistance can and will be given. Instead, microeconomists can ask the positive question "What are the consequences of disaster relief?"

The most obvious one is the uneconomic use of the nation's resources. Economic efficiency requires that economic decision makers bear the costs and benefits of their decisions. This implies risk taking. If policy shifts the risks from the individual to the government, different decisions will be made. Along with creating sympathy for disaster victims, television also shows the results of such social policy. Homes are rebuilt following mud slides in California with little thought given to the possibility of a recurrence of the disaster. The same holds for building in floodplains and coastal areas frequently hit by hurricanes. The risk of destruction is shifted from the owner to the public, and the taxpayer swallows the consequences.

Some economists have argued that, in the case of floods, the government should not give disaster relief but instead should mandate the purchase of private flood insurance. They argue that such insurance would ensure the efficient use of floodplains by creating the proper set of incentives. The insurance costs would reflect the risk. In the highest-risk areas, insurance would be so expensive that little building would occur. The use of the floodplains would then be determined by markets. The floodplains would probably be used for agriculture rather than for housing. What happens instead is that disaster relief distorts incentives. Housing development occurs in floodplains. In a sense, the destruction and loss of life from the inevitable floods are artificial (or government-induced) disasters.

One might argue that it would be unnecessary to mandate flood insurance if the government would simply cease to provide flood relief. The availability of disaster relief is viewed by many as a form of "free" disaster insurance. On the other hand, private individuals may choose not to purchase disaster insurance, even if they have no expectation of government relief, because of the huge cost of insurance in disaster-prone areas.

The conclusion from such analysis and from the generous disaster relief approved by Congress in recent years is clear. Public policy is encouraging uneconomic use of land and, in fact, is contributing to larger disaster losses by subsidizing economic activity in potential disaster areas.

BEHAVIOR AFTER DISASTERS

Yet another interesting issue in "disaster economics" is the behavior of disaster victims. The self-interest assumption (discussed in Chapter 1) would seem to predict selfish behavior by disaster victims and their neighbors—such actions as hoarding, price gouging by suppliers, and looting of disaster sites. In fact, after Hurricane Hugo, the city of Charleston passed a law to prevent price gouging, because prices of some critical items such as ice and chain saws were far above normal. Yet many observers have reported helpful, cooperative, and generous behavior immediately after disasters. This behavior can be explained in terms of self-interest as informal insurance and alliance activity. In other words, in a crisis situation, people do unto others as they would have others do unto them.

An alternative explanation of the behavior of disaster victims is the cost of not cooperating. Individuals may choose not to loot or hoard, especially in small communities, because their behavior will be observed and they will be subject to future sanctions. Similarly, business firms may choose not to "gouge" consumers because the disaster will be short-lived, and they dare not incur the bad feelings that would result. Both the positive informal insurance theory and the negative social sanctions theory explain behavior in terms of a calculation of costs and benefits.

RECOVERY FROM DISASTERS

The long-term economic effects of disaster on communities have been carefully analyzed by economists. The results of such studies are consistent. The long-term economic effects of a disaster are not profound, and there are few lingering economic effects on the local community. Indeed, the speed of recovery is often astonishing. The devastation from Hurricane Hugo in South Carolina was followed by recovery to normal economic activity in a short time.

Such rapid recovery is not surprising because modern history has shown that nations quickly repair from the destruction caused by wars. The economy of the Soviet Union recovered very rapidly from the great devastation caused by the Bolshevik Revolution of 1917. The New Economic Policy restored the economy to its prerevolution level of output in just two years. The post–World War II experience in Western Europe and in Japan was similar. In fact, new, modern capital was put into place, and economic growth resumed at faster rates than before. It will be interesting to observe the speed of recovery in Iraq and Kuwait now that the hostilities in the Gulf have ended.

THE ROAD AHEAD

Microeconomics is concerned with how incentives influence decision making and the ways in which institutions and changes in institutions influence incentives and, in turn, the behavior of individuals. This method of looking at markets gives economists powerful insights into the impact that policies have. That impact is often very different from what was intended. In order to address more complex microeconomic issues, you will need tools beyond the supply and demand model. The next few chapters develop some of these tools.

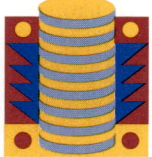

SUMMARY

1. The basic tools of microeconomics are useful in analyzing a wide range of social policy issues.
2. Crime can be modeled and analyzed as an economic activity resulting from a rational decision by the criminal. To decrease criminal activity, it is necessary to decrease the benefits the criminal receives or increase the costs the criminal must pay, or both. This holds for the entire range of crime, from illegal parking to armed robbery or murder.
3. Price ceilings are attempts to keep prices from

rising to their equilibrium level. Price ceilings cause shortages, and black markets often develop in response to the shortages. Rent control is an example of a price ceiling.

4. Price floors are attempts to keep prices from falling to their equilibrium level. Price floors cause surpluses that must be absorbed to prevent the price from falling. Agricultural price supports and minimum wages are examples of price floors.

5. Prices and markets allocate goods and services efficiently. Other methods of allocation may be viewed by participants as "fairer," but often result in problems.

6. The regulation of natural gas is a good example of how price ceilings disrupt markets. The lesson is that price ceilings are very difficult to remove even after the damage they cause is well understood. Even after partial deregulation is achieved politically, the effect of past disruptions to the market persist.

7. The health care industry in the United States is one of the fastest-growing industries. Prices have risen because of increasing demand and increasing costs. There have been political calls for regulation, but the lesson of natural gas regulation is relevant.

8. Many governmental policies have unintended effects that can be determined by applying microeconomic tools of analysis. For example, analysis of disaster relief shows that present public policy may in a sense "create" new disasters.

New Terms

price ceilings
price floors
shortage
black markets
rent control
surplus
Commodity Credit Corporation (CCC)
minimum wage
unintended effects of policy

Questions for Discussion

1. Why does a price ceiling that is set above the equilibrium price have no immediate effect on the market?

2. Can you formulate models like the simple economic model of crime for other decisions, such as having children, getting married, or getting a divorce?

3. How is the minimum wage maintained at higher than market-clearing rates? Why don't the unemployed workers agree to work for lower wages and thereby circumvent the imposed price floor?

4. Many price controls were used in the United States during World War II. Using the models developed in this chapter, how well do you think they worked?

5. Suppose you have an 8:00 a.m. economics class that is far away from the student parking lot. You learn over time that if you park in a faculty spot but move your car by 9:15 a.m., you are ticketed every fourth time. The ticket cost is $15. What value are you implicitly placing on that illegal parking space? If the university raised the ticket price to $30, would you still park illegally? What effect would a towing policy have on your behavior?

6. The price, total demand, and total supply of winter wheat on the Chicago grain market in March 1989 are as follows:

Price per Bushel (Dollars)	Bushels Demanded (Thousands)	Bushels Supplied (Thousands)
4.65	90	77
4.85	85	78
5.05	80	80
5.25	75	82
5.45	65	86

What is the equilibrium price? What is the equilibrium quantity? Why is this the equilibrium? Explain the forces that bring the market to this equilibrium, starting at a price of $5.25.

7. Draw the demand and supply curve for winter wheat using the data in Question 6.

8. What would happen if the federal government set a price floor (a support) for winter wheat of $5.45 per bushel? Draw this price floor on the diagram you produced in Question 7.

9. What would happen if the federal government set a price ceiling for winter wheat of $5.45 per bushel? Draw this price ceiling on the diagram from Question 7.

10. Usury laws are laws that set maximum interest rates.

Chapter 4 Applications of Supply and Demand

These laws are price ceilings in the market for loanable funds. What will happen in states that have usury laws when the equilibrium interest rate exceeds the established ceiling? Why then are usury laws politically popular?

11. Even when many people know the negative impacts of rent control, rent control laws are hard to repeal. Why?

12. How might the Federal Savings and Loan Insurance Corporation (FSLIC) have contributed to the savings and loan crisis?

13. What is causing the demand for health care to increase? What is causing the supply of health care to decrease? If supply decreases and demand increases, what will happen to the equilibrium price of health care?

14. In 1991, the minimum wage in the United States increased to $4.25. This increase was not met with predictions by economists of dire consequences, as previous increases in the minimum wage were. Why?

15. Why do bureaucracies seldom make use of markets to allocate scarce resources?

SUGGESTIONS FOR FURTHER READING

Benjamin, Daniel, Douglass C. North, and Roger LeRoy Miller. *The Economics of Public Issues*, 8th ed. New York: Harper & Row, 1990. A highly readable description of some innovative applications of the basic tools of microeconomics.

Butler, Stuart M., and Edmund F. Haislmair (eds.). *Critical Issues: A National Health System for America*. Washington: Heritage Foundation, 1989. Chapter 1 presents a detailed history of the health care system in the United States.

Maccaro, James A. "The Folly of Rent Control," *The Freeman* (January 1990): 18–21. A very readable essay that lays out the simple economics of rent control.

Scully, Gerald. *The Business of Major League Baseball*. Chicago: University of Chicago Press, 1989. A book that uses basic economic analysis to explain the economics of baseball.

AFTER STUDYING THIS CHAPTER, YOU SHOULD BE ABLE TO:

1. Define elasticity.
2. Calculate the coefficient of elasticity for each of the following measures:
   a. price elasticity of demand,
   b. income elasticity of demand,
   c. cross elasticity of demand,
   d. price elasticity of supply.
3. Identify the range of values for the coefficient of price elasticity of demand when demand is:
   a. elastic,
   b. inelastic,
   c. unit elastic.
4. Identify the range of values for the coefficient of the income elasticity of demand when a good is:
   a. inferior,
   b. normal.
5. Identify the range of values for the coefficient of cross elasticity of demand when two goods are:
   a. substitutes,
   b. complements,
   c. independent.
6. Use the concept of elasticity to determine the incidence of an excise tax.

CHAPTER 5

ELASTICITY: THE MEASURE OF RESPONSIVENESS

INTRODUCTION

This chapter extends the concepts of supply and demand by developing another tool of the microeconomist—the elasticity measurement. **Elasticity** is the measure of the sensitivity, or responsiveness, of quantity demanded or quantity supplied to changes in price (or other conditions). We will develop several elasticity measures and then demonstrate their usefulness in the analysis of public policy.

elasticity
The measure of the sensitivity or responsiveness of quantity demanded or quantity supplied to changes in price (or other factors).

SUPPLY AND DEMAND REVISITED

Supply and demand are basic to economic analysis. It is worth reviewing them before beginning to expand your kit of economic tools.

When developing the concept of demand, we stressed the distinction between shifts in demand curves and movement along demand curves. Any movement along a demand curve occurs in response to a change in price and is referred to as a *change in quantity demanded*. Any shift of the demand curve is called a *change in demand*. Changes in demand occur in response to changes in one or more of the *ceteris paribus* conditions that underlie the demand curve: the tastes of the group demanding the good or service, the size of that group, the income and wealth of that group, the prices of other goods and services, or expectations about any of these conditions.

Similarly, there is an important difference between changes in supply and changes in quantity supplied. The phrase *change in quantity supplied* indicates to the economist that the change that occurred was in response to a change in price. The phrase *change in supply* means that the change occurred in response to a change in one or more of the *ceteris paribus* conditions affecting supply: the prices of the factors of production, the number of sellers, the technology used to produce the good, or expectations about any of these conditions.

These principles and terms are useful in explaining economic events. Figure 1 is a diagram of supply and demand in the market for automobiles. Stable *ceteris paribus* conditions have been assumed, and differences in autos' quality, size, and gas mileage have been ignored (so that a demand curve for like units can be drawn). The market determines an equilibrium price of P_1 and quantity of Q_1. Now suppose the price of gasoline increases. Since gasoline and automobiles are complements, you know that the increase in the price of gasoline is going to cause the demand for automobiles to shift from D_1 to D_2 in Figure 1. That is, with gasoline being more expensive, people drive less, reducing the demand for automobiles. This decrease in demand for autos causes the price to fall to P_2 and the quantity supplied to decrease to Q_2. Remember that quality and other factors are held constant. Thus, the decrease in the demand for automobiles could represent a switch to smaller cars or less frequent trade-ins for newer models.

ELASTICITY AS A GENERAL CONCEPT

Elasticity measures the way one variable responds to changes in other variables. The dependent variable is the variable that changes in response to some other variable, called the independent variable. The de-

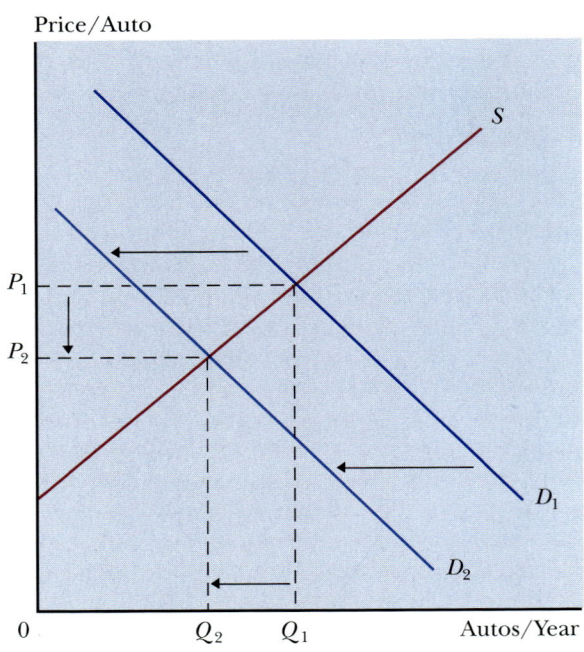

FIGURE 1
THE MARKET FOR AUTOMOBILES
Gasoline is a complementary good to automobiles. If the price of gasoline rises, there will be a decrease in the demand for automobiles. The price of autos will fall from P_1 to P_2, and the equilibrium quantity will decrease from Q_1 to Q_2. There has been a decrease in the quantity supplied.

pendent variable (y) is written as a function of one or more independent variables (x_i):

(1) $y = f(x_1, x_2, x_3, \ldots, x_n)$.

Elasticity measures how the dependent variable responds to changes in any of the different independent variables. The formula to determine this responsiveness can be expressed as follows:

(2) $E_1 = \dfrac{\%\Delta y}{\%\Delta x_1}$, $E_2 = \dfrac{\%\Delta y}{\%\Delta x_2}$, $\ldots$, $E_n = \dfrac{\%\Delta y}{\%\Delta x_n}$.

This formula says that elasticity (E) is the percent change (the symbol Δ represents change) in the dependent variable (y) divided by the percent change in the particular independent variable (x) being examined.

In examining demand, economists are interested in how the quantity demanded responds to changes in price and to changes in certain other *ceteris paribus* conditions that affect demand. The quantity demanded of good A (Q_A^d) is thus the dependent variable, and the independent variables are the price of good A (P_A), income (I), tastes (T), the price of complements (P_c), and the price of substitutes (P_s). We can thus rewrite equation (1) as

$Q_A^d = f(P_A, I, T, P_c, P_s)$.

It is now possible to determine how Q_A^d responds to change in any of the independent variables by holding all but one of them constant and calculating the elasticity coefficient using equation (2). For example, to see how quantity demanded responds to price, we use

$E_d = \dfrac{\%\Delta Q_A^d}{\%\Delta P_A}$,

where E_d is the coefficient of price elasticity of demand. This formula gives us the price elasticity of demand. **Price elasticity of demand** is the measure of the relative responsiveness of the quantity demanded to changes in price.

price elasticity of demand The measure of the responsiveness of the quantity demanded to changes in price.

PRICE ELASTICITY OF DEMAND

In the late nineteenth century, the famous English economist Alfred Marshall developed the concept of elasticity to compare the demands for various products. When comparisons are made, it is necessary to concentrate on the *relative* responsiveness of the quantity demanded to price changes rather than the absolute responsiveness. Relative comparisons make it possible to measure and then describe the sensitivity of the demand relationship. For example, in Figure 2, two demand curves are drawn. One is the demand curve for coffee, the other is the demand curve for orange juice. Although the price increases by the same amount for each curve, there are different changes in the quantity demanded. The two goods have different sensitivities to the price change. That is, they have different relative elasticities.

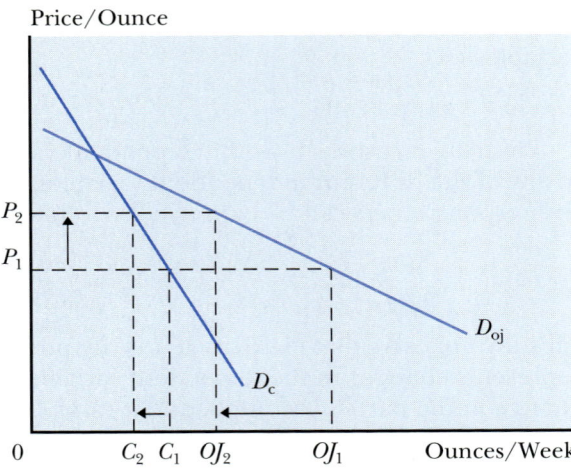

FIGURE 2
DEMAND CURVES WITH DIFFERENT ELASTICITIES
Demand curves may have different relative elasticities. For example, these demand curves are for orange juice (D_{oj}) and coffee (D_c). The same price change has a much greater impact on the quantity of orange juice demanded. Therefore, the demand for orange juice is more elastic than the demand for coffee between every pair of prices.

coefficient of price elasticity of demand (E_d) The numerical measure of price elasticity of demand, equal to the percent change in quantity demanded of a good divided by the percent change in its price.

The **coefficient of price elasticity of demand (E_d)** is the numerical measure of price elasticity of demand. It is the percent change in quantity demanded of a good divided by the percent change in price. That is, as you have seen, for good A,

$$E_d = \frac{\%\Delta Q_A^d}{\%\Delta P_A}.$$

Since percent change is the change in the variable divided by the base amount of the variable, this can be rewritten as

$$(3)\ E_d = \frac{\frac{\Delta Q_A^d}{Q_A^d}}{\frac{\Delta P_A}{P_A}}.$$

With most demand curves, the elasticity coefficient varies along the curve. However, some demand curves have a *constant* price elasticity of demand. We will examine three special cases before looking at more typical demand curves.

Figure 3 shows a vertical demand curve. With this curve, quantity demanded is totally unresponsive to changes in price. As price changes from P_1 to P_2, there is no change in the quantity demanded. The elasticity coefficient is

perfectly inelastic demand Demand represented by a vertical demand curve with a coefficient of price elasticity of demand that is equal to zero. There is no response in quantity demanded to changes in price.

$$E_d = \frac{\frac{\Delta Q^d}{Q_1}}{\frac{\Delta P}{P_1}} = 0.$$

This vertical demand curve is a limiting case that violates the law of demand and is not known to exist in the real world. This curve is called a perfectly inelastic demand curve. **Perfectly inelastic demand** occurs when

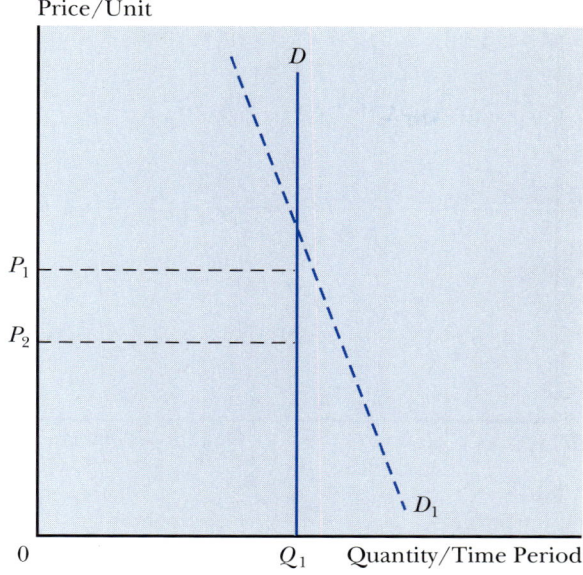

FIGURE 3
PERFECTLY INELASTIC DEMAND CURVE
On a perfectly inelastic demand curve, such as D, the quantity demanded has no responsiveness to changes in price. With a relatively inelastic demand curve, such as D_1, the quantity demanded is not very responsive to changes in price.

the coefficient of price elasticity of demand is zero. There is no response of quantity demanded to changes in price.

Although the vertical demand curve doesn't exist in the real world, there may be curves that are close to it, such as D_1, the dashed line in Figure 3. This curve is a *relatively* inelastic demand curve. A highly inelastic demand exists for goods such as medicine for a heart condition. Individuals who purchase such medicine probably do not respond very much to changes in price, especially if they are wealthy or have ample health insurance.

Figure 4 shows a horizontal demand curve, another limiting case. At P_1 or at any price below P_1, an infinite quantity of the good is demanded. If the price rises above P_1, the quantity demanded drops to zero. Calculating the elasticity coefficient for a price change from P_1 to P_2 yields

$$E_d = \frac{\frac{\Delta Q}{Q_1}}{\frac{\Delta P}{P_1}} = \infty.$$

A horizontal demand curve is called a perfectly elastic demand curve because the response to changes in price is infinite. **Perfectly elastic demand** occurs when the coefficient of price elasticity of demand is infinite.

A demand curve such as D_1, the dashed line in Figure 4, is a *relatively* elastic demand curve. A highly elastic demand exists for the wheat production of an individual farmer in the United States. The price of a bushel of wheat is determined by the market. At that price (or any lower price), buyers will demand all of the farmer's wheat that is available. But if a farmer raises the price even slightly, the quantity demanded from that farmer will go to zero.

A third kind of demand curve is shown in Figure 5. The mathematical term for this curve is a rectangular hyperbola. Any percent decrease or

perfectly elastic demand Demand represented by a horizontal demand curve with a coefficient of price elasticity of demand that is equal to infinity. The quantity demanded responds in an infinite way to a change in price.

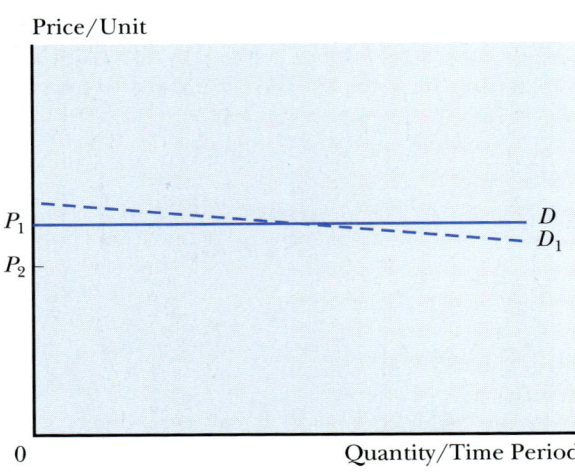

**FIGURE 4
PERFECTLY ELASTIC
DEMAND CURVE**
On a perfectly elastic demand curve, such as D, the quantity demanded has an infinite response to changes in price. If price rises above P_1, no amount of the good will be purchased. If price falls to P_2, all that is available will be purchased. With a relatively elastic demand curve, such as D_1, quantity demanded is very responsive to changes in price.

increase in price causes the same percent increase or decrease in the quantity demanded. This means that the elasticity coefficient at any point along this demand curve is equal to 1. For example, if you calculated the elasticity coefficient for a price change from P_1 to P_2, you would find that

unit elastic demand
Demand represented by a demand curve that is a rectangular hyperbola with a coefficient of price elasticity of demand equal to one. The quantity demanded responds at the same rate as any change in price.

$$E_d = \frac{\frac{\Delta Q}{Q_1}}{\frac{\Delta P}{P_1}} = 1.$$

Such a demand curve is referred to as a unit elastic demand curve. **Unit elastic demand** occurs when the coefficient of price elasticity of demand is unitary (equal to 1).

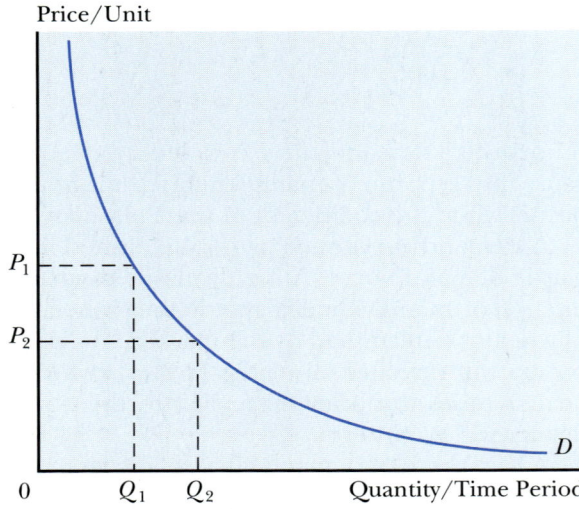

**FIGURE 5
UNITARY ELASTIC DEMAND
CURVE**
With a unitary elastic demand curve, a change in price brings about the same percentage change in quantity demanded.

Chapter 5 Elasticity: The Measure of Responsiveness

A GUIDE TO ELASTICITY COEFFICIENTS		
NUMERICAL VALUE OF COEFFICIENTS	**RESPONSIVENESS OF QUANTITY DEMANDED TO A CHANGE IN PRICE**	**TERMINOLOGY**
• $E_d = 0$	No response	Perfectly inelastic
• $0 < E_d < 1$	Quantity demanded changes by a smaller percentage than the price changes	Inelastic
• $E_d = 1$	Quantity demanded changes by the same percentage as the price changes	Unit elastic
• $1 < E_d < \infty$	Quantity demanded changes by a larger percentage than the price changes	Elastic
• $E_d = \infty$	Quantity demanded becomes infinite, or all that is available is demanded	Perfectly elastic

Most demand curves are not shaped like those in Figures 3, 4, and 5. Most straight line demand curves look like the one in Figure 6. Demand curve D has a *range* of elasticity coefficients from infinity (at the intersection with the vertical axis) to zero (at the intersection with the horizontal axis). When the coefficient is *less* than 1, demand is *inelastic* because the percent change in quantity demanded is less than the percent change in

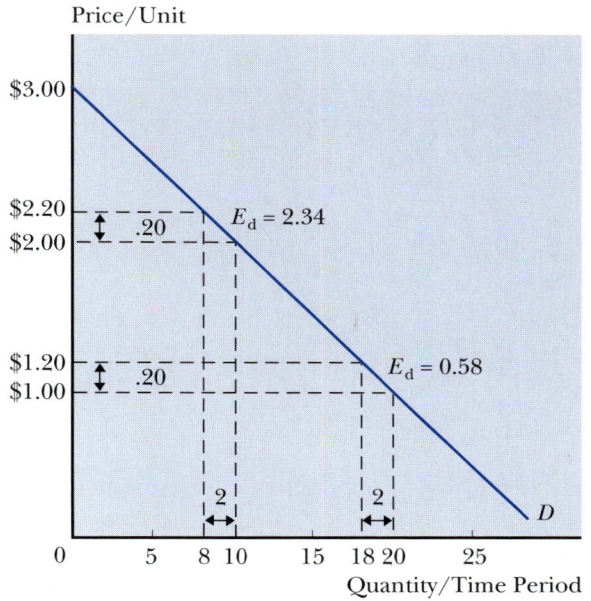

FIGURE 6
STRAIGHT-LINE DEMAND CURVE WITH VARYING ELASTICITY COEFFICIENTS
A straight-line demand curve has elasticity coefficients that vary from zero at the horizontal-axis intercept to infinity at the vertical-axis intercept.

price. When the coefficient is *greater* than 1, demand is *elastic* because the quantity demanded changes relatively more than the price. Of course, there are degrees of responsiveness. The larger the coefficient, the greater the responsiveness.

The best way to understand elasticity is to calculate and interpret some elasticity coefficients. Before we do this, we need to clarify two points.

Before an elasticity coefficient can be calculated, it is necessary to decide whether elasticity is to be calculated at a single point or between two points. The elasticity between two points is the value of the coefficient at the midpoint between the points. This value is called **arc elasticity**. Many economists use a different, but related, measure called **point elasticity**, which uses calculus to evaluate the responsiveness of quantity demanded to price at a particular point on a demand curve.[1] Basically, the elasticity is measured at a point by assuming tiny changes in price and quantity demanded. However, we will use arithmetic to calculate particular coefficients and will be working with sizable changes. The numbers we will compute will be values of arc elasticity.

The second important point is that the formula for an elasticity coefficient will always produce a negative number because demand curves are negatively sloped. In practice, economists ignore the minus signs on coefficients of price elasticity of demand. An E_d value of -5 is considered to be larger than an E_d value of -4, for example. That is, these coefficients are treated as absolute values. It will be important later when considering other measures of elasticity to keep track of their signs, but the sign is not important for price elasticity of demand.

The demand schedule of Table 1 can be used to calculate some coefficients of price elasticity of demand. Again, the formula is

$$E_d = \frac{\text{percent change in quantity demanded}}{\text{percent change in price}}.$$

arc elasticity
The elasticity at the midpoint between two points on a demand curve.

point elasticity
The elasticity at a particular point on a demand curve.

TABLE 1
DEMAND SCHEDULE FOR STRAIGHT-LINE DEMAND CURVE IN FIGURE 6

PRICE	QUANTITY DEMANDED
$0.50	25
1.00	20
1.20	18
1.40	16
1.60	14
1.80	12
2.00	10
2.20	8
2.40	6
2.60	4
2.80	2
3.00	0

1. This concept relies on differential calculus. For those who have had calculus, elasticity at a particular point can be measured using the formula $E_d = dQ/dP \times P/Q$, where dQ/dP is the first derivative of the demand function $Q = f(P)$.

For our purposes, this reduces to

$$E_d = \frac{\frac{\Delta Q}{\frac{Q_1+Q_2}{2}}}{\frac{\Delta P}{\frac{P_1+P_2}{2}}}.$$

Since we are calculating arc elasticity, we use averages. That is, we divide both the sum of the beginning price and the ending price and the sum of the beginning quantity and the ending quantity by two. If, instead of average values, we used the beginning or ending price and quantity as the bases, the formula would produce different elasticity measures between the same two points.

We can now compute the elasticity coefficients for two different price changes on the demand curve in Figure 6. First, the elasticity coefficient for the increase in price from $1.00 to $1.20:

$$E_d = \frac{\frac{20-18}{\frac{20+18}{2}}}{\frac{\$1.00-\$1.20}{\frac{\$1.00+\$1.20}{2}}} = \frac{\frac{2}{19}}{\frac{-\$0.20}{\$1.10}} = \frac{0.105}{-0.182} = 0.58$$

Recall that economists ignore the minus sign and just look at the absolute value of price elasticities of demand.

Now for the elasticity coefficient for the increase in price from $2.00 to $2.20:

$$E_d = \frac{\frac{10-8}{\frac{10+8}{2}}}{\frac{\$2.00-\$2.20}{\frac{\$2.00+\$2.20}{2}}} = \frac{\frac{2}{9}}{\frac{-\$0.20}{\$2.10}} = \frac{0.222}{-0.095} = 2.34$$

Note that the elasticity is different at different points along this demand curve, which has a constant slope. In fact, all linear demand curves except those that are vertical or horizontal have elasticity coefficients that range from zero through infinity. On a demand curve such as the one shown in Figure 7, all points above price P_1 (which corresponds to the midpoint on a straight-line demand curve) have an elasticity coefficient greater than 1. At those points, demand is elastic. At price P_1, the elasticity coefficient is equal to 1. At that point, demand is unit elastic. All points below P_1 have an elasticity coefficient less than 1. In this region, demand is inelastic.

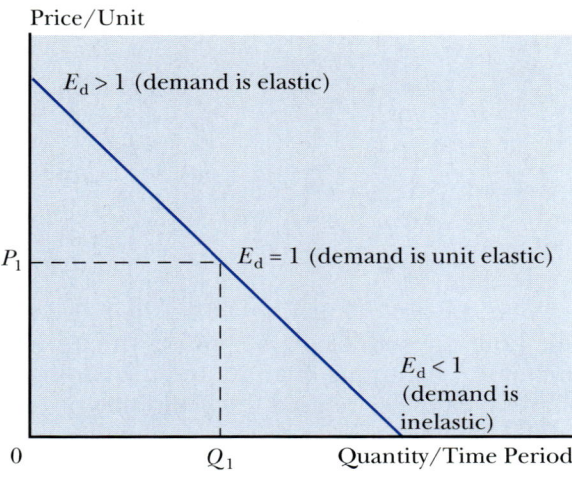

FIGURE 7
THE UNIT ELASTIC PRICE AND THE DEMAND CURVE
The point on the demand curve where $E_d = 1$ represents the unit elastic price (P_1) and divides the curve into two regions. At all prices above the unit elastic price, demand is elastic. At all prices below the unit elastic price, demand is inelastic.

To see how important it is to average the quantity demanded and the price for the bases, you can calculate the effect of an increase in price from $1.00 to $1.20 and then of a decrease in price from $1.20 to $1.00 using equation (3), which does not use averaging. If you do this, you will get two different elasticity coefficients, depending on whether the price is decreasing or increasing. The average, or arc, elasticity between two points is found by employing averaging and gives the same measure in either direction.

This example clearly demonstrates that elasticity is an entirely different concept from the geometric concept of slope. Because the demand is a straight line, the demand curve in Figure 6 has a constant slope. However, the elasticity coefficients vary along this straight-line demand curve.

ELASTICITY AND SUBSTITUTABILITY

Price elasticity of demand depends, in large part, on the number of substitutes a good or service has. If a product, such as table salt, has relatively few substitutes, it will tend to have a relatively inelastic demand. This is just another way of saying that the quantity demanded of a good like table salt isn't very responsive to changes in price over a wide range of prices. The elasticity of demand for a broad category of goods will be lower than that for a specific good. For example, the elasticity of demand for salt in general will be lower than the elasticity of demand for Morton's salt.

Another determinant of the elasticity of demand is time. The longer the period of time consumers have to adjust, the more elastic the demand becomes. The reason for this is that a longer time period allows more opportunities to modify behavior and substitute different products. A good example is the elasticity of demand for natural gas. In the short run, the demand is likely to be very inelastic. Over time, however, as industry and homes convert to other sources of energy, the elasticity will increase. Table 2 lists estimated elasticities for some commonly purchased items in the range of their typical prices.

ITEM	E_d
Fresh tomatoes	4.60
Medical care	3.60
Canned tomatoes	2.50
Airline travel	2.40
Radios and televisions	1.25
Automobiles	0.80

TABLE 2
SOME ESTIMATED ELASTICITIES

Source: Adapted from Dean A. Worcester, Jr., "On Monopoly Losses: Comment," *American Economic Review* (December 1975): 1016.

PRICE ELASTICITY OF DEMAND AND TOTAL REVENUE

Demand curves illustrate price and quantity relationships. Quantity, or the number of items sold, multiplied by price equals the **total revenue** generated. The relationship between total revenue and price elasticity of demand explains how firms set and change prices. This relationship was first considered by French mathematician and economist Antoine Augustin Cournot (1801–1877). He wondered what the owner of a hypothetical mineral spring should charge for the spring's water, which was desired for its healing powers. Cournot made three assumptions: that the spring cost nothing to operate, that it produced an unlimited quantity of output, and that the owner wanted as much income as possible.

total revenue
The amount of money a firm takes in, equal to the quantity of the good or service sold multiplied by its price.

To determine the correct price, Cournot first recognized that a price change has two (opposite) effects on total revenue. The first effect is that a price decrease, by itself, will decrease total revenue. The other effect is that a price decrease causes quantity demanded to increase, thus increasing total revenue. The net effect of these two changes on total revenue depends on whether the relative price decrease exceeds the relative increase in quantity demanded, or vice versa. This is exactly the information that the price elasticity of demand provides.

For a concrete application of this principle, look again at Figure 6 and Table 1. At a price of $2.00, the total revenue (*TR*) is $20.00. An increase in price from $2.00 to $2.20 causes *TR* to fall from $20.00 to $17.60. *TR* drops because the 10 percent increase in price caused an even greater percent decrease in quantity demanded. The elasticity coefficient at that point was greater than 1. Conversely, if the price rises from $1.00 to $1.20, *TR* increases from $20.00 to $21.60 because the percent increase in price is greater than the percent decrease in quantity demanded. The elasticity coefficient at that point is less than 1.

Figure 8 illustrates the same principle. On both demand curves, the price falls from P_1 to P_2, and quantity demanded increases from Q_1 to Q_2. This price change causes the total revenue to change. Some revenue is lost and some revenue is gained. In Figure 8, the red area represents revenue that has been lost and the gold area represents revenue that has been gained. With the relatively inelastic demand curve in part (*a*), the decrease in price brings about a decrease in total revenue. With the relatively elastic demand curve in part (*b*), the decrease in price brings about an increase in total revenue.

When a country runs a surplus or deficit in its balance of trade, adjustment in the value of its currency is one way to restore equilibrium in trade. In the early 1980s, the value of the U.S. dollar had risen a great deal in terms of other currencies, especially those of U.S. trading partners in Europe. As Americans began importing more foreign goods, however, the supply of dollars rose. Since the value of the dollar is determined in money markets, the large supply of dollars caused the value of the dollar to decline relative to the European currencies. Between 1985 and 1988, the value of the dollar fell by about 50 percent.

The decline in the value of the dollar should have reduced the trade deficit, which is the difference between the value of exports and the value of imports. The decline in the trade deficit should have come about because imports became more expensive to Americans, causing the quantity of imports demanded to decrease. Imports were more expensive because it took more dollars to buy a given amount of foreign currency. At the same time, U.S. exports to foreigners became cheaper, causing the quantity of exports demanded to increase. The experience, however, at least in the short run, was that the deficit remained high. The explanation is to be found in the differences between short-run and long-run elasticities.

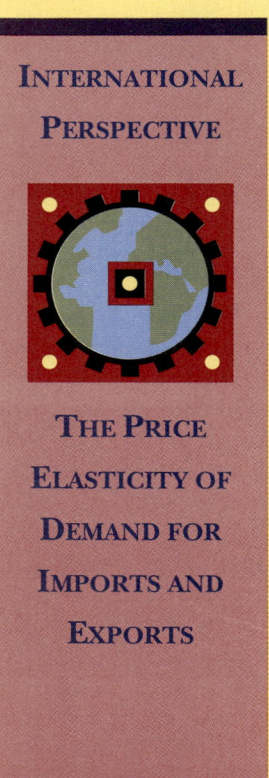

INTERNATIONAL PERSPECTIVE

THE PRICE ELASTICITY OF DEMAND FOR IMPORTS AND EXPORTS

In the short run, the demand for imports is very price-inelastic. So, when the value of the dollar falls, making imports more expensive, the quantity demanded falls, but not very much. Similarly, foreign demand for exports is inelastic. When price falls, the quantity demanded increases, but not very much. As time passes, importers in the United States have more time to adjust to the increased prices of foreign goods, and foreigners have more time to adjust to the lower prices of U.S. exports. Gradually the trade balance will come back into equilibrium.

In the short run, a cheaper dollar may actually make the trade deficit worse before it gets better. This curious result is due to the fact that short-run elasticities are much lower than long-run elasticities. Economists have come to call this worsening of the balance of trade in the face of a cheaper currency the "J-curve effect." The curve is shaped like a J because the trade deficit initially gets worse before it turns around and improves. Although this is a technical economic concept, the term has been widely adopted into the jargon of newswriters. You are quite likely to see the term "J-curve" if you read the *Wall Street Journal* or other business publications.

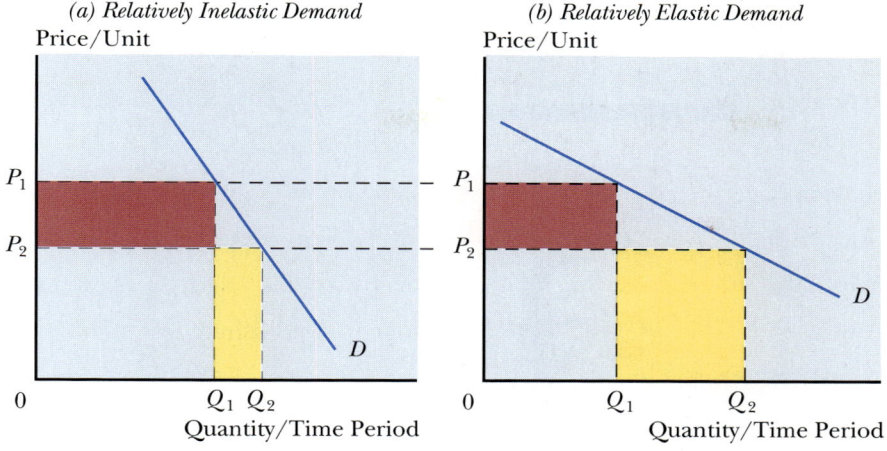

**FIGURE 8
CHANGES IN TOTAL REVENUE**
Equal price changes bring about different changes in total revenue, depending on the elasticity of the demand curve. (*a*) If the demand curve is relatively inelastic, a decrease in price will bring about a decrease in total revenue. (*b*) If the demand curve is relatively elastic, the same decrease in price will bring about an increase in total revenue.

In other words, you can determine what will happen to total revenue when price changes if you know the elasticity of demand. A reduction in price will always cause an increase in quantity demanded, but total revenue will decrease with inelastic demand and increase with elastic demand. Similarly, a rise in price will cause total revenue to fall when demand is elastic and to rise when demand is inelastic.

The answer to Cournot's question is that the owner of the mineral spring should not try to charge the highest possible price or sell the largest possible amount. The owner should set the price where the elasticity coefficient is 1. To see why, imagine that the price is where the elasticity coefficient is 0.5. (Demand is inelastic.) If the owner raises the price, quantity demanded will decrease, but by only half the rate of the price increase. Therefore, total revenue will rise. On the other hand, if the elasticity coefficient is 2 (or demand is elastic), the owner should decrease the price. If the price is lowered, the quantity demanded increases at twice the rate of the price. The owner will maximize total revenue when the demand coefficient is 1, or demand is unit elastic. So the mineral spring owner should set the price at P_1 in Figure 7. At price P_1, the area $P_1 \times Q_1$ represents maximum possible total revenue.

A good example of the importance of the elasticity of demand to setting prices occurred in the U.S. airline industry. The airline industry, believing that the demand for air travel was inelastic, had historically been against deregulation. The reason was that increased competition would result in lower fares. When deregulation occurred, the revenues of the airline companies increased dramatically despite the lower fares. The experience indicated that the demand for air travel was relatively elastic, or at least much more elastic than the airlines had thought. The airlines had set their prices based on incorrect estimates of the elasticity of demand.

Perhaps the best example of the effect of price elasticity on total revenue is that of Henry Ford's Model T. When Ford entered the scene, automobiles were a curiosity for the rich. Ford's strategy was to make autos for the average person through mass production—but he had to sell

Antoine Augustin Cournot was one of the first economists to view economic theory as a set of tools that could be used to analyze economic and social problems. Cournot showed that both supply and demand determine price and that, in time, price influences both supply and demand. Cournot used two-dimensional diagrams to demonstrate these relationships.

Cournot is now recognized as a great economist, but this was not the case when he was alive. He did some of the most original thinking in economic theory, but his life was a tragic one. Cournot studied mathematics at the Ecole Normale in Paris. He read constantly, despite very poor eyesight that eventually developed into blindness. While a student, Cournot worked as a secretary to one of Napoleon's generals. In 1834, with the support of the famous statistician Poisson, Cournot became a professor of mathematics at Lyons. In 1838, Cournot published his great work in mathematical microeconomics, *Researches into the Mathematical Principles of the Theory of Wealth*. This book did not have much impact and was hardly noticed. Some sources indicate that not a single copy was sold! In later years, as his sight was failing, Cournot published less mathematical versions of this work, which were more widely read. When Cournot died in 1877, his highly innovative work in economic theory was largely unnoticed.

The irony of Cournot's life is that, although he was not well known during his own lifetime, his vision of economics as a set of highly mathematical tools that could be used to examine a large number of social problems is very close to the thinking of most present-day economists. If Cournot were around today, he would be surprised to see how his radical vision has come to reflect the accepted role of the economist.

ECONOMIC PROFILE

ANTOINE AUGUSTIN COURNOT

1801–1877

them. He found that by reducing prices, he sold more autos and increased profits. In the process, Ford Motor Company revolutionized production. In the early years of the Model T, Henry Ford said: "Every time I reduce the charge for our car by one dollar, I get a thousand new buyers."[2]

ELASTICITY AND TOTAL REVENUE

PRICE CHANGE	CHANGE IN QUANTITY DEMANDED	COEFFICIENT OF ELASTICITY	CHANGE IN TOTAL REVENUE
• Rise	Decrease	$E_d > 1$	Decrease
• Rise	Decrease	$E_d = 1$	Unchanged
• Rise	Decrease	$E_d < 1$	Increase
• Fall	Increase	$E_d > 1$	Increase
• Fall	Increase	$E_d = 1$	Unchanged
• Fall	Increase	$E_d < 1$	Decrease

PRICE ELASTICITY OF DEMAND AND POLICY CHOICES: SMOKING

For many years, the U.S. government, primarily through the office of the Surgeon General, has pursued a policy of trying to discourage cigarette smoking.[3] It may not be appropriate for government to try to intervene in personal decisions such as smoking, but various levels of government are doing so. Many state and some local governments have required public places, such as restaurants, to set up no-smoking sections and have prohibited smoking in hospitals, doctors' offices, and public buildings.

In the 1980s Surgeon General C. Everett Koop made it his goal to create a "smoke-free society" by the year 2000. But in a report issued before he left office, he painted a picture that indicated that this goal would have to be much longer-term. In his report, he noted that in recent years the decline in cigarette smoking has been about 1.5 percent per year. At that rate, U.S. consumers will still be consuming 470 billion cigarettes annually in the year 2000. That's a pack a day for 64 million people.

Koop's report showed that cigarette smoking is less prevalent at higher socioeconomic and income levels. The ethnic group with the heaviest smoking rate is Alaska natives at 56 percent. That group is followed by Mexican-American men at 43 percent, Puerto Rican men at 40 percent, all blacks at 34 percent, all whites at 29 percent, and college graduates at 16 percent. Cigar and pipe smokers follow a different pattern. Among men with a family income over $40,000, there is a 5 percent rate of cigar smoking.

In commenting on Koop's report in *Fortune* magazine, Daniel Seligman was critical of the Surgeon General's suggestions for reducing cigarette smoking.[4] Koop's report called for more education, more regulation

---

2. *Forbes* (12 January 1987): p26.
3. Evidently the Surgeon General feels that smoking is only a problem for U.S. citizens. The warning about smoking being hazardous to health is printed only on cigarettes manufactured for domestic consumption. Cigarettes manufactured for export do not contain the warning unless it is required by the government of the importing country.
4. *Fortune* (13 February 1989): 123. Additional data on smoking and elasticity studies can be found in *Business Week* (18 June 1990): 20–21.

of smokers' behavior, and more restrictions on advertising. Seligman suggested that raising excise taxes on cigarettes was a solution brushed off too quickly in the report.

Koop's report reviewed studies of the price elasticity of demand for cigarettes. One study showed that the elasticity coefficient for smokers aged twelve to seventeen was 1.4. The elasticity coefficient for smokers as a whole was 0.7. This figure and the concept of price elasticity of demand can be used to make a policy recommendation.

Suppose the President decides to declare an all-out "war" on cigarette smoking. Assume that the President calls in the Secretary of Health and Human Services and tells the Secretary that cigarette smoking should be cut by 25 percent in the next year. The Secretary asks you, a recently hired economist at the Department of Health and Human Services, to write a memo outlining a plan to accomplish this goal.

You return to your office to begin work. Based on your study of microeconomics, you do not think that prohibitions and warnings will work. You have studied enough economics to be convinced that the only way to proceed is to unleash market forces to create the incentives that will accomplish the desired policy goal. (Remember, as an economist, you apply positive theory, without any normative considerations of whether or not the policy should be carried out.) You decide that the best way to bring about the desired reduction in smoking is to let the market do it. The best way to accomplish this is to raise price by putting an additional federal excise tax on cigarettes. Your job is now relatively simple: determine the appropriate tax.

You need data on cigarette consumption and how it responds to changes in cigarette prices. The data are not that difficult to find. You decide to use $E_d = 0.7$ from the study cited in the Koop report. It is now a simple matter to compute the tax necessary to have the desired impact on consumption. You know that the President wants to cut consumption by 25 percent and that the present average price of a pack of cigarettes is $1.42. You simply substitute into the formula to determine the tax:

$$E_d = \frac{\%\Delta Q}{\%\Delta P}$$

$$0.70 = \frac{0.25}{\%\Delta P}$$

$$\%\Delta P = \frac{0.25}{0.70} = 0.36 = 36 \text{ percent.}$$

You can now write your memo. In order to attain a 25 percent decrease in quantity demanded, it is necessary to have a 36 percent increase in price. The required additional excise tax would, therefore, be 51 cents per pack ($1.42 × 0.36), making the price of a pack of cigarettes $1.93. This price increase will reduce smoking even more among those aged twelve to seventeen, because the elasticity of demand is higher among that group.

You have used a simple economic tool in the same way that economists giving policy advice would use it. Although the example was made up, the data were real and the estimates were based on sound theory.

POLICY APPLICATION: RECRUITING STUDENTS

For many years, colleges didn't pay too much attention to the problem of recruiting students because the post–World War II baby boom produced a seemingly endless supply of new students. Many schools greatly expanded their facilities during this boom period, especially state-supported institutions. This "bubble" in the population is now past college age, and demographic data show that the college-aged population will continue to decline until 1997. This smaller pool of prospective students presents serious problems to both private and state-supported institutions of higher learning. Private institutions must attract students because tuition is often their main source of revenue. Public institutions also need students because their state funding is tied to the number of students they have enrolled.

It is a little easier to view this problem from the standpoint of the student as a demander of college services. (Since the number of students who "buy" becomes the supply of students to colleges, it is also possible to view the problem as a problem of supply.) The demand curve is like most other demand curves. It has a negative slope. If colleges raise the price, students will decrease the quantity of educational services they demand, and the number of students will be lower than before the price increase.

The situation is a supply and demand problem with elasticity considerations. To attract enough students in a competitive world, colleges have to lower their prices. But if they lower their prices to everyone, they "give back" revenue to some students who aren't the best and the brightest while significantly lowering their operating revenues. Can you think of a solution? Colleges lower the price to some selected students—those whose demand is more elastic because they have good alternatives—by giving them scholarships and other types of financial aid.

OTHER DEMAND ELASTICITIES

Price elasticity of demand is not the only microeconomic measure of responsiveness. It is possible to calculate the elasticity of almost anything because what an elasticity coefficient measures is the responsiveness of one measurable quantity to another. Two other demand elasticities are quite common in economics.

The first of these other concepts is the **income elasticity of demand**. This measures the way in which quantity demanded responds to changes in income, assuming all other things, including price, are held constant. The formula is expressed as

$$E_i = \frac{\text{percent change in quantity demanded}}{\text{percent change in income}}.$$

income elasticity of demand The measure of the responsiveness of quantity demanded to changes in income.

The sign of the coefficient of the income elasticity of demand is important. If the sign is negative, indicating an inverse relationship between income and quality demanded, the good is said to be an inferior good. If the sign is positive, the good is a normal good.

For normal goods, if $E_i > 1$, demand for the good is income elastic. If $E_i < 1$, demand for the good is income inelastic. Goods that have high and positive income elasticities are classed as luxury goods. In fact, the concept of income elasticity of demand is used as a definition of what a luxury good is. Necessities, such as food, have a low but positive income elasticity. Luxuries, such as sports cars and foreign travel, have a high positive income elasticity.

Income elasticity is useful to producers in forecasting sales. If producers can forecast changes in consumer income and know the income elasticity of demand for their product, they can estimate how much more to produce. This is one of the reasons why firms are interested in economic forecasts.

The other common demand elasticity concept is the **cross elasticity of demand**. Cross elasticity measures the responsiveness of changes in the quantity demanded of one good to changes in the price of another. The formula for the coefficient of the cross elasticity of demand is

cross elasticity of demand The measure of the responsiveness of changes in the quantity demanded of one good to changes in the price of another.

$$E_{AB} = \frac{\text{percent change in quantity demanded of good } A}{\text{percent change in price of good } B}$$

If the cross elasticity is equal to anything but zero, the two goods are related. They are either complements or substitutes. Two goods that are completely unrelated (independent of one another) have a zero cross elasticity of demand. If the sign of the coefficient is negative, the relationship is an inverse one. An increase in the price of good B will bring about a decrease in the quantity demanded of good A. A negative cross elasticity coefficient thus indicates that good A and good B are complements. Complements are goods that are used together, such as coffee and cream or pens and paper. A positive cross elasticity coefficient indicates a substitute relationship between good A and good B. An increase in the price of good B will lead to an increase in the quantity demanded of good A. Substitute goods can be used in place of each other. Examples are coffee and tea, and beef and chicken. The size of the coefficient tells how strong the complementary or substitute relationship is between the two goods. As we will see in later chapters, cross elasticity is useful in defining markets and industries because it is a measure of how closely goods are related.

PRICE ELASTICITY OF SUPPLY

The concept of elasticity of demand is also applicable to supply schedules and supply curves. **Price elasticity of supply** is the measure of the responsiveness of the quantity supplied to changes in the price. The **coefficient of price elasticity of supply (E_s)** is the numerical measure of price elasticity of supply. The equation for the coefficient of price elasticity of supply is

price elasticity of supply The measure of the responsiveness of the quantity supplied to changes in the price.

coefficient of price elasticity of supply (E_s) The numerical measure of price elasticity of supply, equal to the percent change in the quantity supplied of a good divided by the percent change in its price.

$$E_s = \frac{\text{percent change in quantity supplied}}{\text{percent change in price}},$$

or, in a more workable form,

$$E_s = \frac{\frac{\Delta Q^s}{Q^s}}{\frac{\Delta P}{P}}.$$

Chapter 5 Elasticity: The Measure of Responsiveness

As with the price elasticity of demand, when $E_s = 1$, supply is unit elastic. If $E_s > 1$, supply is elastic. If $E_s < 1$, supply is inelastic. The analogy to price elasticity of demand stops there. The coefficient of price elasticity of supply is usually positive because supply curves normally have positive slopes. Since supply curves are positively sloped, the relationship between elasticity and total revenue established for price elasticity of demand doesn't hold. Higher prices result in higher total revenue, regardless of whether supply is elastic or inelastic.

Special cases of supply curves are classified as perfectly inelastic, unit elastic, or perfectly elastic. With the vertical supply curve in Figure 9, the quantity supplied is totally unresponsive to changes in price. It is perfectly inelastic. Examples of perfectly inelastic supply curves are rare. In the short run, however, it is often impossible to produce more of a good regardless of what happens to price. This inability to produce more will affect the supply curve, which shows the amount people are willing to supply at various prices. Consider the supply of Rembrandt paintings, for example, or of Rose Bowl tickets. A rise in the price of Rembrandt paintings (even in the long run) or Rose Bowl tickets (in the short run) does not cause the quantity supplied to increase.[5] These supply curves are perfectly inelastic.

Figure 10 shows both a perfectly elastic supply curve and a unit elastic supply curve. S_1, a horizontal line, is a perfectly elastic supply curve. Any straight-line supply curve that is drawn through the origin, as is S_2 in Figure 10, is unit elastic over its entire range. Along such a curve, the percent changes of the two variables will always be equal to each other. Other linear supply curves are elastic at every price if they intersect the price (vertical) axis above the origin and inelastic at every price if they intersect the quantity (horizontal) axis to the right of the origin. This is true even though elasticity changes along both curves. Two such curves are shown in Figure 11.

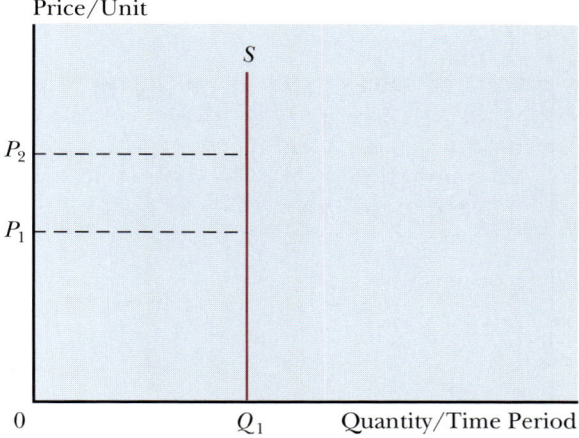

**FIGURE 9
PERFECTLY INELASTIC
SUPPLY CURVE**
A perfectly inelastic supply curve is a vertical line. It would exist if suppliers offered a fixed amount of a good, regardless of any changes in its price.

---

5. This isn't quite correct because some individuals who own Rembrandt paintings will become suppliers if the price gets high enough.

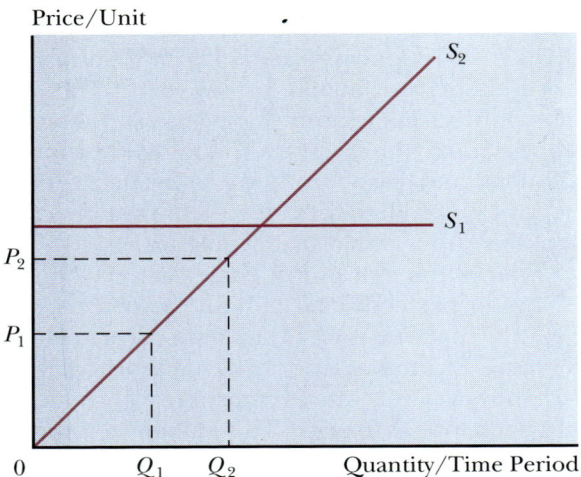

FIGURE 10
UNIT ELASTIC SUPPLY CURVE AND PERFECTLY ELASTIC SUPPLY CURVE
A perfectly elastic supply (S_1) curve is a horizontal line. With such a curve, a change in price produces an infinite response in the quantity supplied. A straight-line supply curve drawn through the origin has a unitary coefficient of elasticity along the entire curve.

PRODUCTION COSTS

Price elasticity of supply depends on the costs of production and how these costs change as the output of a good or service is increased. If costs rise rapidly as output is expanded, the quantity supplied will not be very responsive to changes in price. The supply curve is inelastic. On the other hand, if costs don't increase very much as output is increased, a rise in price will increase the profits of supplying firms and the output response could be substantial. The supply curve is elastic. Price elasticity of supply and the costs of production are so intertwined that we will discuss them in more depth in later chapters.

RESOURCE AVAILABILITY AND TIME

Elasticity of supply is the measure of responsiveness of quantity supplied to changes in price. The major factor affecting this responsiveness is the

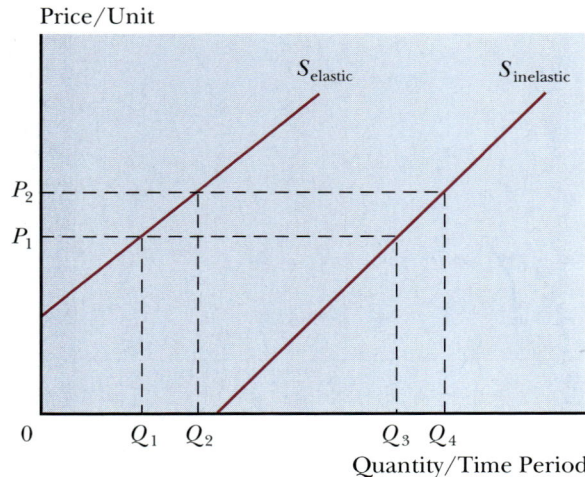

FIGURE 11
INELASTIC AND ELASTIC SUPPLY CURVES
A straight-line supply curve that intersects the price (vertical) axis will be elastic over its entire length. A straight-line supply curve that intersects the quantity (horizontal) axis will be inelastic over its entire length.

availability of resources that can be attracted away from other uses. Another factor is the time period under consideration. As the time period increases, the possibility of obtaining new and different inputs to increase the supply increases. For the two earlier examples of fixed supply, you will recognize that in the long run the stadium could be expanded and the quantity of Rose Bowl tickets increased. Rembrandts, however, have a perfectly inelastic supply because additional inputs don't exist.

These two factors—availability of inputs and time—affect elasticity of supply. Normally the elasticity of supply coefficient becomes larger with time and is larger for products that use relatively unspecialized or abundant inputs.

WHO PAYS THE EXCISE TAX: AN EXERCISE IN THE ELASTICITY OF SUPPLY AND DEMAND

Debates over tax policy can be quite confusing. Consumers are often convinced that they ultimately pay all taxes, yet business firms often fight hard to prevent tax increases on their products. If consumers pay all taxes, why should a business firm care if its product is taxed or not? The answer is not simple. The correct answer to the question of who ultimately pays such a tax is "It depends on supply and demand in the relevant market." This problem is an exercise that involves elasticity of both supply and demand.

An **excise tax** is a tax on the purchase of a particular good, such as liquor, cigarettes, or electricity, or a broad class of goods, such as food.

Let's look at an example with normally sloped supply and demand curves. Figure 12 illustrates the market for beer. Beer is a good example because excise taxes are often placed on items such as alcohol and cigarettes. These taxes are sometimes called "sin taxes." Assume that the market settles on a price of $3.00 per six-pack, with X_e representing the equilibrium quantity of six-packs per week. Now suppose the government

excise tax
A tax on the purchase of a particular good, such as liquor, cigarettes, or electricity, or a broad class of goods, such as food.

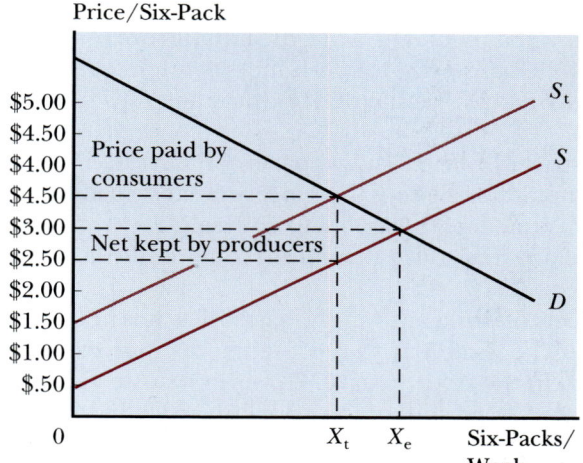

FIGURE 12
AN EXCISE TAX ON BEER
An excise tax on beer causes its supply curve to shift upward by the amount of the tax (from S to S_t). Less of the commodity is purchased at the higher price. Part of the tax is borne by consumers, and part of the tax is borne by producers.

places an excise tax of $1.00 per six-pack on beer and collects this tax from producers. The costs of production have been increased by $1.00 per six-pack. This means that the supply curve will shift up by the amount of the tax. One way to view the tax is that the producer must pay $1.00 per six-pack for the permission to produce beer. In terms of Figure 12, the supply curve shifts up at all points by $1.00. The post-tax supply curve is S_t. The equilibrium price will rise to $3.50 per six-pack, and the new equilibrium quantity is X_t.

Note that the new price is less than the sum of the old price and the tax. If the entire tax had been shifted onto consumers, the consumer would end up paying the old price of $3.00 plus the tax of $1.00, or $4.00 per six-pack. It is also clear that the amount of money the producer actually receives has fallen. Before the tax, the producer received $3.00 per six-pack, but now the producer receives $2.50 per six-pack ($3.50 price minus the $1.00 tax). The tax caused prices to rise, which caused the quantity demanded to fall. Because supply is relatively inelastic in this case, beer producers did not pass along the full amount of the tax in order to try to maintain sales. As a result, the producers sell a smaller quantity at a lower price than before. In this example, then, part of the tax was paid by consumers and part was paid by producers. Each paid half of the excise tax.

The amount of a tax paid by consumers or producers depends on the supply and demand elasticities for the goods being taxed. Figure 13 shows clearly how the elasticity of supply and the elasticity of demand affect the tax incidence. Tax incidence is the economist's term for who really pays the tax. **Tax incidence** is the place where the burden of a tax actually falls. It identifies those who pay the tax after all shifting has occurred.

Part (*a*) of Figure 13 shows a normally sloped supply curve and a perfectly inelastic demand curve. When the excise tax is placed on the good, the supply curve facing consumers shifts from S to S_t. The result is that price rises from P_e to P_t. Price has risen by the full amount of the tax, and the equilibrium quantity is unchanged. In this case, the incidence of the excise tax falls fully on the consumers of this good. The tax has been shifted forward to consumers by the full amount of the tax.

Part (*b*) of Figure 13 shows a normally sloped supply curve and a perfectly elastic demand curve. The post-tax supply curve is again S_t. After the tax is imposed, price is unchanged at P_e, but the equilibrium quantity has fallen from Q_e to Q_t. Since the price to consumers is unchanged, the producer is paying the entire tax. The incidence of the tax falls fully on the suppliers of this good.

The principle demonstrated by the first two parts of Figure 13 is clear: The more inelastic the demand for a good, the more any excise tax placed on the good will fall on consumers of that good. Conversely, the more elastic the demand, the more any excise tax placed on the good will fall on the producers.

In order to see the effects of different supply elasticities, it is necessary to refer to another graph. The usual way to represent a tax increase on a graph is by an upward shift in the supply curve. However, we can also represent a tax increase by a downward shift of the demand curve. In the case of perfectly inelastic supply, it is necessary to shift the demand curve because it is impossible to shift the supply curve.

tax incidence
The place where the burden of a tax actually falls after all shifting has occurred.

Chapter 5 Elasticity: The Measure of Responsiveness   147

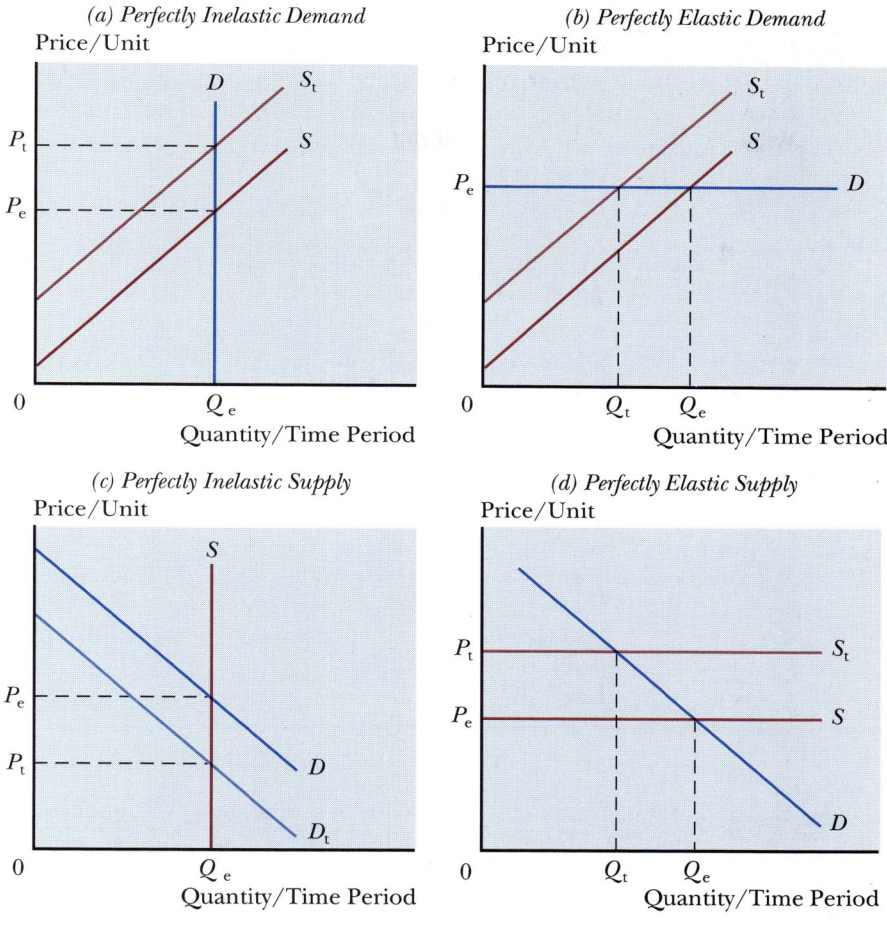

FIGURE 13
ELASTICITY AND TAX INCIDENCE
Tax incidence, or where the tax burden falls, depends on the elasticity of demand or supply. (*a*) With perfectly inelastic demand, the consumer pays the entire tax. (*b*) With perfectly elastic demand, the producer pays the entire tax. (*c*) With perfectly inelastic supply, the producer pays the entire tax. (*d*) With perfectly elastic supply, the consumer pays the entire tax.

In part (*c*) of Figure 13, *D* still shows what consumers are willing to pay for various quantities, including the tax. However, D_t is the demand curve as the producer sees it, after the tax has been subtracted. The tax does not affect the quantity, which is determined by the perfectly inelastic supply curve. The industry views the demand curve as the curve with the amount of the tax subtracted from the price. The equilibrium quantity is unchanged by the shift. The price the firm receives falls from P_e to P_t. In other words, the entire amount of the tax has been paid by the suppliers of the good.

Part (*d*) of Figure 13 shows a perfectly elastic supply curve. An excise tax shifts the supply curve from S to S_t to account for the higher price at each output. After the shift, the price of the item has increased from P_e to P_t, by the exact amount of the tax. In this case, consumers are paying the entire tax. Less is being sold, so some producers may be worse off in that sense. However, consumers are paying more for Q_t, and this increased amount is exactly equal to the amount of the tax.

The complete answer to the question of who pays the excise tax should now be clear. The answer is "It depends on the relative elasticities of sup-

> ### INCIDENCE OF AN EXCISE TAX
>
> - The more inelastic the demand, the more price rises. The tax falls more heavily on consumers.
> - The more elastic the demand, the less price rises. The tax falls more heavily on producers.
> - The more inelastic the supply, the more the tax is paid by producers.
> - The more elastic the supply, the more price rises. The tax is paid mostly by consumers.

ply and demand for the good on which the tax is placed." These elasticities depend on whether substitutes are available and are how consumers choose among competing goods when prices change. The next chapter will develop a theory of consumer choice that explains this process of adjustment.

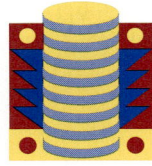

Summary

1. Elasticity is the measure of the sensitivity or responsiveness of quantity demanded or quantity supplied to changes in price (and to changes in other *ceteris paribus* conditions).

2. Straight-line demand curves, except for those that are perfectly vertical or horizontal, have points on them that range from elastic to inelastic and one point that is unit elastic.

3. Price elasticity of demand is a measure of how many substitutes a good or service has. The more substitutes an item has, the more elastic demand for it will be. Consumers will have more options and respond more readily to changes in price.

4. Elasticity of demand is greater when the time period is longer because consumers have more opportunity to substitute between goods.

5. Total revenue is closely related to elasticity because a demand curve is a price-quantity relationship, and total revenue is price times quantity. When price changes, the quantity demanded changes. This change affects total revenue. The amount of the change in total revenue will depend on the responsiveness of consumers to changes in price, or elasticity.

6. Income elasticity of demand measures the responsiveness of changes in quantity demanded to changes in income.

7. Cross elasticity of demand measures the responsiveness of changes in the quantity demanded of one good to changes in the price of another good.

8. Price elasticity of supply is the measure of the responsiveness of changes in quantity supplied to changes in price.

9. As time passes, the elasticity of supply increases. The longer the time period, the more chance there is for adjustments to take place.

10. The concepts of supply, demand, and elasticity can be used to determine tax incidence. The more inelastic the demand for a good or service and the more elastic the supply, the greater is the amount of an excise tax on the good or service paid by consumers. The more elastic the demand and the more inelastic the supply, the greater is the amount of the tax paid by producers.

Chapter 5 Elasticity: The Measure of Responsiveness

New Terms

elasticity
price elasticity of demand
coefficient of price elasticity of demand (E_d)
perfectly inelastic demand
perfectly elastic demand
unit elastic demand
arc elasticity
point elasticity
total revenue
income elasticity of demand
cross elasticity of demand
price elasticity of supply
coefficient of price elasticity of supply (E_s)
excise tax
tax incidence

Questions for Discussion

1. Several years ago the *Wall Street Journal* ran an article entitled "Chicago's Troubled Transit System Takes Unorthodox Steps to Attract Commuters." The main "unorthodox" step was to reduce fares. What does this decision indicate about what the head of the Illinois State Department of Transportation thinks about the price elasticity of demand for the services of the transit system?

2. To demonstrate the importance of using average price and quantity changes when determining elasticity, use the correct formula for calculating the coefficient of price elasticity of demand for a change in price from $2.20 to $2.40 in Table 1. Then calculate the coefficient again for a price increase from $2.20 and a price decrease from $2.40, without using averaging. Explain the difference in your answers.

3. Would the elasticity of demand for Pepsi be higher or lower than that for soft drinks in general? Why?

4. Why is public policy aimed at decreasing oil imports frustrated by the fact that demand for gasoline is income elastic and price inelastic?

5. During the energy crisis, the *Wall Street Journal* ran a headline, "Europe's Drivers Don't Reduce Gasoline Use Despite Soaring Prices." Data from the article showed that gas prices were up 120 percent in Europe, and the general price level rose 140 percent during the same period. What was wrong with the headline?

6. If the government wants to place a tax on some good for the purpose of generating revenue, should it look for a good that has a relatively inelastic demand curve or a relatively elastic one?

7. For the demand schedule below, calculate the values for the total revenue column by multiplying price times quantity demanded. Then use the formula to calculate the coefficients of price elasticity of demand based on the changes in price and total revenue.

Price	Quantity Demanded	Total Revenue (TR)	Coefficient of Price Elasticity of Demand (E_d)
$0.50	25	12.5	-.33
1.00	20	20.00	-.55
1.20	18	21.60	-.21
1.40	16	22.40	
1.60	14		
1.80	12		
2.00	10		
2.20	8		
2.40	6		
2.60	4		
2.80	2		
3.00	0		

8. Suppose one firm is the only seller of the product represented by the demand schedule in Question 7. What would you do if the price were $2.00 when you took over that firm's marketing department?

9. The price of good X increases from $1.10 to $1.15, and the quantity of good Y consumed increases from 1,100 units to 1,750 units. What is the cross elasticity of demand? What does this imply about goods X and Y?

10. If the coefficient of the cross elasticity of demand for good A and good B is infinite, what kind of goods are A and B?

11. In the discussion concerning an excise tax on cigarettes, we calculated that a 36 percent increase in price was needed to cut cigarette consumption for all consumers by 25 percent. If the 36 percent increase in price occurred, how much would the consumption of cigarettes by those aged twelve to seventeen change?

12. Why is the coefficient of the price elasticity of demand higher for those aged twelve to seventeen than for all smokers?

13. Which of the following pairs of products are complements and which are substitutes?
    a. men's suits and ties
    b. butter and margarine
    c. Pepsi and Coke
    d. gasoline and Cadillacs
    e. women's swimsuits and jackhammers

14. For each of the pairs in Question 13, is the coefficient of the cross elasticity of demand negative or positive? Do you expect the coefficient to be a large or small number? Why?

15. Why is the value of the price elasticity of demand negative? Why do we ignore the negative sign?

SUGGESTIONS FOR FURTHER READING

Browning, Edgar K., and Jacquelene M. Browning. *Microeconomic Theory and Applications*, 3rd ed. Boston: Little, Brown, 1989. This book contains a good treatment of elasticity, with problems to solve.

Lindsay, Cotton Mather. *Applied Price Theory*. New York: Dryden Press, 1984. A well-written, intermediate textbook on price theory with many elasticity applications.

AFTER STUDYING THIS CHAPTER, YOU SHOULD BE ABLE TO:

1. Define:
   a. utility,
   b. income effects,
   c. substitution effects,
   d. consumer surplus.
2. Use marginal utility to calculate total utility, and derive a marginal utility curve from a total utility curve.
3. Use the equation for maximizing total utility to determine an individual's consumption pattern.
4. Derive an individual demand curve for a good based on:
   a. the equation for maximizing total utility,
   b. the principle of diminishing marginal utility.
5. Explain the solution to the diamond-water paradox based on:
   a. marginal utility and total utility,
   b. value in exchange and value in use.
6. Discuss the argument over a progressive income tax in terms of:
   a. the marginal utility of income,
   b. interpersonal utility comparisons.

CHAPTER 6
DEMAND AND CONSUMER CHOICE

INTRODUCTION

We have used demand and supply curves to develop a variety of predictions about the outcome of different market processes. Most of our analysis made use of market demand curves, which we derived by aggregating individual demand curves. Since individual demand curves form the bedrock of microeconomic analysis, we need to consider the factors that underlie them.

The first approach economists took in examining consumer demand—the classical approach—involved the concept of measurable utility. We will use this approach to examine some problems and suggest some applications for demand analysis. The second approach to consumer demand—indifference curve analysis—is discussed in an appendix to this chapter.

CHOICE, VALUE, AND UTILITY THEORY

The idea that households and firms must make choices because of scarcity is the fundamental notion of economic analysis. We now want to expand on that analysis to determine why consumers react in the way they do. Why does a person demand a certain good or service? An obvious answer is that the good or service is expected to satisfy some need or desire of the consumer. Economists, unlike other social scientists, are content with this simple answer.

There may be moral or ethical dimensions to the desires people have. Why do people want to buy guns, pornography, narcotics, sports cars, liquor, or cigarettes? These are questions to which psychologists, moralists, and many others devote a great deal of attention. But economists generally are not interested in why desires exist or why people should buy some goods and not others. It is not because they think such questions are unimportant. In fact, such questions may be more important than the questions economists try to answer: What would happen to the sales of Porsches if their price increased by $1,000? What would happen to the sales of potatoes if the price of wheat went up $1 per bushel? Economists accept the fact that people have a certain psychological or ethical makeup. Without approving or disapproving of it or asking where it came from, economists start their analysis from there.

Economists' view of consumer choice is based on five assumptions about the psychology of consumer behavior:

1. Individuals (or households) must make choices because they have limited income and are forced to choose which of their many wants to satisfy.
2. Individuals make rational choices when they make these consumption decisions. That is, they weigh costs and benefits and make the decision that gives them the most satisfaction.
3. Individuals make these choices with imperfect information. In other words, they don't know (with certainty) all the attributes of the goods they are choosing to consume.
4. As increasing amounts of a good are consumed, the additional satisfaction gained from an additional unit becomes smaller.
5. Many goods have qualities that make them satisfactory substitutes for other goods.

All of these statements may seem simple and obvious, but they will enable us to make some powerful conclusions about the nature of demand.

THE HISTORY OF UTILITY THEORY: THE DIAMOND-WATER PARADOX

In the early development of economic theory, economists often posed questions that they then debated. One of the popular debate topics was what determined value. Adam Smith wrote that value could mean either "value in use" or "value in exchange." He posed (in 1776) what became known as the diamond-water paradox:

The things that have the greatest value in use have frequently little or no value in exchange; and on the contrary, those which have the greatest value in exchange have frequently little value in use. Nothing is more valuable than water: but it will purchase scarce anything; scarce anything can be had in exchange for it. A diamond, on the contrary, has scarce any value in use; but a very great quantity of other goods may frequently be had in exchange for it.[1]

diamond-water paradox
The fact that diamonds, although less useful than water, are more expensive than water. That is, things with the greatest value in exchange (price) often have little value in use.

The **diamond-water paradox** was the problem that classical economists used when they argued that value in use could not determine price (value in exchange). Diamonds, although less useful than water, are more expensive than water. The discussion about the diamond-water paradox

---

1. Mark Blaug, *Economic Theory in Retrospect* (Homewood, IL: Richard D. Irwin, 1968), writes that Smith, in what may be the greatest understatement in the history of economic thought, conceded that his explanation of value was obscure.

William Stanley Jevons had one of the greatest minds in the history of economic thought. Jevons combined utility theory with marginal analysis and applied it to consumer choice. He thus constructed the theory that underlies the theory of demand.

Jevons was both a theoretical and a practical economist. He was born in Liverpool and studied chemistry and mathematics at University College, London. Financial problems caused him to move to Australia to accept a job with the Sydney Mint. He spent five years in Australia. During that time, he became interested in political economy. In 1859, he returned to the University of London and studied political economy until 1865. In 1865, he published a book, *The Coal Question*, which thrust him into prominence in economic circles. His most famous book, *Theory of Political Economy*, was published in 1871.

Jevons accepted a professorship at Owens College, Manchester, in 1866. There he worked on a wide range of intellectual pursuits, from statistical analysis of commodity prices to very abstract economic theory. He even developed a sunspot theory to explain business cycles. His work generated a great deal of interest in political circles, but Jevons himself had little contact with those who made economic policy. This was largely because of his personal habits. He was, perhaps, the original "strange professor." He once wrote to his sister that he had never attended a party "without impressing upon all friends the fact that it is no use inviting me." He didn't regret his solitude. In fact, he argued that reserve and loneliness are necessary to develop ideas. He felt that social intercourse ensured that thoughts would "never rise above the ordinary level of the others." A colleague of Jevons wrote: "There never was a worse lecturer, the men would not go to his classes, he worked in flashes and could not finish anything thoroughly, the only point about Jevons was that he was a genius."

Unfortunately for economics, Jevons died at the age of forty-seven. At the time of his death, he was working on a massive book entitled *Principles of Economics*, which of course was never completed.

ECONOMIC PROFILE

WILLIAM STANLEY JEVONS

1835–1882

went on for a long time. Many famous mathematicians, economists, and philosophers took part in the debate. The confusion over the diamond-water paradox arose because of a lack of distinction between total units and marginal units and arguments over what the term *useful* meant.

In the 1870s, William Stanley Jevons, Carl Menger, and Leon Walras, all writing separately, solved the paradox by developing a theory of value in which demand and utility came to the forefront. Their solution played a major role in developing the theory of consumer demand.

Part of the debate underlying the diamond-water paradox was an argument over whether value (or price) was determined by supply or demand. In a famous analogy, Alfred Marshall, the great British economist, said that you could no more say whether supply or demand determined value than you could say which blade of a pair of scissors did the cutting. That is, value (or price) is determined by the interaction of supply and demand.

We'll consider the influence of demand on value first and leave supply for later chapters. Demand theorists used the notion of utility. In economics, if an individual wants a good or service, then that good or service has utility for that person. **Utility** is the satisfaction an individual expects to receive from consuming a good or service. The same good may have a great deal of utility for one person and none or very little for some other person. Like beauty, utility is in the eye (or mind) of the beholder.

Utility is strictly a before-the-fact concept. That is, utility measures the way an individual feels about a good *before* buying or consuming it. You may see a cake in a bakery window and have great desire for it—that's utility. If you buy and eat the cake, you may get sick and receive no satisfaction from its consumption—that's irrelevant economically. Utility is the satisfaction you *expect* to get, not what you actually get. The reason for this distinction is that utility is used in the development of the demand curve, and the demand curve shows the amounts that people will buy based on anticipated satisfaction. It does not consider the amounts of satisfaction actually received after having made the purchase.

TOTAL UTILITY AND MARGINAL UTILITY

A good unit for the measurement of utility, like the pound or gallon or mile, does not exist. Since utility is unique to the individual, however, an arbitrary (and imaginary) unit called the **util** can be employed. As long as no attempt is made to compare the number of utils of different people, this is a satisfactory measuring device. Such comparisons between people are inappropriate because the number of utils is a subjective measure of a certain individual's satisfaction and as such is not subject to meaningful comparisons. Imagine—some people prefer the beach to the mountains!

A relationship expressing a consumer's desire to consume differing amounts of a good is called a **utility function**. For example, suppose you try to construct your utility function for a certain brand of soft drink. First, choose a convenient time period, such as a day. Then, for 1 unit (1 can) of Coke per day, assign a number of utils, say 20. (You can choose any number at all: 1, or 1,000, or 47½.) Ask yourself, if I get 20 utils from 1 can, how many would I get if I consumed 2 cans per day? Suppose, after much

---

utility
The satisfaction that an individual expects to receive from consuming a good or service.

util
An arbitrary unit used to measure individual utility.

utility function
A relationship expressing a consumer's desire to consume differing amounts of a good.

reflection, you say 38. Ask yourself the same question about 3 cans per day, 4, 5, 6, and so on. You use these figures to construct a utility schedule, as shown in Table 1.

Marginal utility (*MU*) is the amount of utility that one more or less unit consumed adds to or subtracts from total utility. It is the change in satisfaction provided by one more or one less unit of consumption. The formula for marginal utility is

$$MU = \frac{\text{change in total utility}}{\text{change in quantity consumed}}.$$

marginal utility (*MU*) The amount of utility that one more or one less unit of consumption adds to or subtracts from total utility.

In Table 1, the marginal utility is determined by calculating how much each additional can of Coke adds to total utility. For example, the first can of Coke adds 20 utils to total utility. The fourth can of Coke adds 13 utils to total utility (67−54 = 13). Marginal utility is found by subtracting the total utility of consuming three Cokes from the total utility of consuming that number plus one.

Principle of Diminishing Marginal Utility

The important feature of the schedule shown in Table 1 is that, although the total utility becomes larger the more you consume per day (up to a point), the additions to total utility from each additional unit consumed become smaller. The fact that additional, or marginal, utility declines as consumption increases is called diminishing marginal utility.

The **principle of diminishing marginal utility** states that the greater the level of consumption of a particular good in a given time period, the lower the marginal utility of an additional unit. For some goods there may be increasing marginal utility in a short range. The advertisement for potato chips that says "Bet you can't eat just one" implies that the satisfaction from the second is greater than that from the first. Such examples of increasing marginal utility are exceptions that exist for only the first few units. In most cases, as you consume more units of a good, the later units yield less of an addition to total utility than the preceding units did. For instance, the seventh Coke is expected to provide less additional pleasure than the sixth

principle of diminishing marginal utility The fact that the additional utility declines as quantity consumed increases. Less satisfaction is obtained per additional unit as more units are consumed.

Table 1
Utility Schedule for Coke

Cans of Coke per Day	Total Utility (utils)	Marginal Utility (utils)
0	0	0
1	20	20
2	38	18
3	54	16
4	67	13
5	77	10
6	84	7
7	88	4
8	89	1
9	87	−2
10	82	−5

Coke. This principle is reflected in Table 1. Marginal utility falls from 7 utils for the sixth Coke to 4 utils for the seventh.

Figure 1 (*a*) shows the total utility curve plotted from Table 1. Figure 1(*b*) shows the marginal utility curve that corresponds to the table. Note that when the total utility curve reaches its maximum, marginal utility is zero. This makes sense because marginal utility must become negative for total utility to decline. In Table 1, total utility reaches a maximum at 8 Cokes per day because the ninth Coke has a negative marginal utility. The only way a total of anything can decline is for changes in that total to be negative.

UTILITY AND CONSUMER BEHAVIOR

The concepts of utility and price can be combined to show how consumers make choices in the marketplace. Consumers are confronted with a range of items and also a range of prices. A consumer may not neces-

FIGURE 1
TOTAL AND MARGINAL UTILITY
Total utility increases as consumption increases to a certain level, in this case 8 Cokes per day, and then it declines. When total utility is increasing, marginal utility is declining, illustrating the principle of diminishing marginal utility. At the point where total utility begins to decline, marginal utility becomes negative.

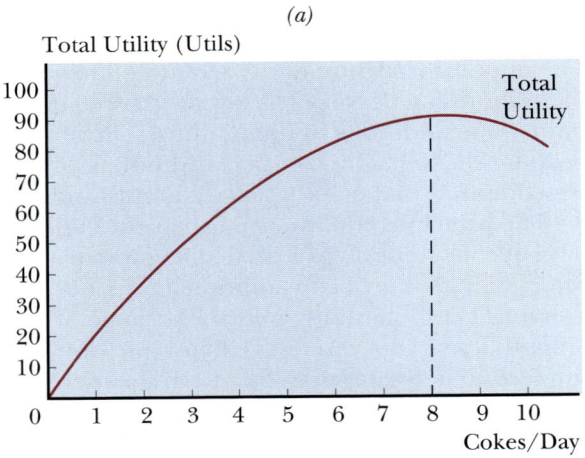

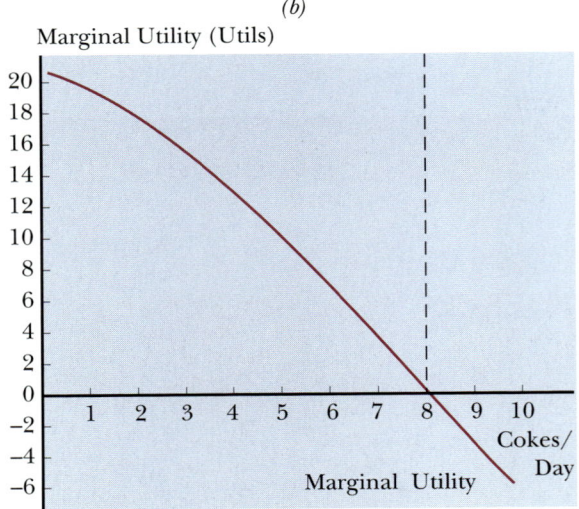

Chapter 6 Demand and Consumer Choice

sarily choose the item that has the greatest utility because its price and the consumer's income are also important factors. In other words, consumers don't always buy their first choice. You may prefer a Porsche to a Chevrolet, but you may purchase the Chevrolet. The explanation for this behavior lies in the relationship between price and utility.

Suppose, for example, you are considering purchasing a six-pack of soft drinks. You are presented with the three possibilities shown in Table 2. Coke is your first choice because it yields the most utility. But the relevant question is not which soft drink has the most utility, but which has the most utility *per dollar*. Therefore, you choose to buy a six-pack of Pepsi. This choice implies that the extra satisfaction of Coke over Pepsi is not worth $.75, but the extra satisfaction of Pepsi over 7-Up is worth $.25. There are other things you can do with the extra $.75. You are saying that $.75 spent on something other than Coke will yield more additional utils than the difference between the utility of Coke and the utility of Pepsi, but that $.25 spent on other goods will not yield more utils than spending it on Pepsi instead of 7-Up.

Thus, in deciding how to spend your money, you look at marginal utility per dollar rather than marginal utility alone. You do this because money is the common measure of what you have to give up. Dollars can be used to buy any available good. So for each dollar you spend, you want to choose the item with the highest utility per dollar. In doing so, you economize by getting the most satisfaction per dollar.

MAXIMIZING TOTAL UTILITY

The self-interest assumption implies that individuals will act to maximize their total utility. To see how marginal utility and price influence how a consumer maximizes total utility, consider an example with only two goods, Coke and pizza. A unit of Coke costs $.50 and a unit of pizza costs $1. The consumer's utility schedules for the two goods are presented in Table 3. The consumer has a given amount of income, called a budget constraint. A **budget constraint** is a given level of income that determines the maximum amount of goods that may be purchased by an individual. Let's allow this consumer a budget constraint of $13, and see how that amount will be allocated between the two goods to achieve maximum utility.

The first dollar will be allocated to pizza because a dollar's worth of pizza (1 piece) yields 32 utils of satisfaction compared with 29 utils for a dollar's worth of Coke (2 cans). The next dollar will also be spent on pizza because it yields 31 utils, which is still greater than the first dollar's worth of Coke, the alternative purchase. In other words, the consumer buys 2

budget constraint
A given level of income that determines the maximum amount of goods that may be purchased by an individual.

TABLE 2
HYPOTHETICAL UTILITY-PER-DOLLAR COMPARISONS

CHOICE	MARGINAL UTILITY (UTILS)	PRICE (DOLLARS)	MARGINAL UTILITY PER DOLLAR (UTILS)
Coke	30.0	3.00	10
Pepsi	27.0	2.25	12
7-Up	20.0	2.00	10

Coke				Pizza			
Quantity per Week (Cans)	Marginal Utility, MU (utils)	MU/P (P = $.50)	Total Utility, TU (utils)	Quantity per Week (Pieces)	Marginal Utility, MU (utils)	MU/P (P = $1.00)	Total Utility, TU (utils)
1	15	30	15	1	32	32	32
2	14	28	29	2	31	31	63
3	13	26	42	3	28	28	91
4	12	24	54	4	$24\tfrac{3}{4}$	$24\tfrac{3}{4}$	$115\tfrac{3}{4}$
5	11	22	65	5	$20\tfrac{3}{4}$	$20\tfrac{1}{4}$	136
6	$10\tfrac{3}{4}$	$21\tfrac{1}{2}$	$75\tfrac{3}{4}$	6	18	18	154
7	$10\tfrac{1}{4}$	$20\tfrac{1}{2}$	86	7	17	17	171
8	10	20	96	8	16	16	187
9	9	18	105	9	14	14	201
10	8	16	113	10	12	12	213
11	7	14	120	11	11	11	224
12	$6\tfrac{1}{2}$	13	$126\tfrac{1}{2}$	12	9	9	233

**TABLE 3
UTILITY SCHEDULES
FOR A CONSUMER
OF TWO GOODS**

pieces of pizza before buying any Coke. The third dollar is spent on Coke because the 29 utils of satisfaction gained from purchasing 2 cans are greater than the 28 utils that are yielded by a third piece of pizza. The process continues until the entire income of $13 is spent. In maximizing total utility, the consumer will spend $5 on 10 cans of Coke and $8 on 8 pieces of pizza. This allocation produces 300 utils of satisfaction—the maximum total utility that can be purchased with $13 of income. You cannot find a consumption pattern that will produce more satisfaction (try reducing Coke consumption by 2 cans and increasing pizza consumption by 1 piece, or vice versa).

The consumer's choices are based on a maximization rule that says that total utility is maximized when the last dollar spent on good A yields the same utility as the last dollar spent on good B. In algebraic form, total utility is maximized when

$$\frac{MU_A}{P_A} = \frac{MU_B}{P_B}.$$

The marginal utility of a can of Coke, when 10 cans per week are consumed, is 8 utils, and the price of a can is $.50. Thus,

$$\frac{MU_{\text{cola}}}{P_{\text{cola}}} = \frac{8}{\$.50} = 16 \text{ utils per dollar.}$$

For pizza, at the optimum consumption rate, the marginal utility is 16, and the price is $1. Thus,

$$\frac{MU_{\text{pizza}}}{P_{\text{pizza}}} = \frac{16}{\$1.00} = 16 \text{ utils per dollar.}$$

This can be generalized to include all goods by saying an individual maximizes utility when

$$\frac{MU_x}{P_x} = \frac{MU_y}{P_y} = \cdots = \frac{MU_n}{P_n}.$$

Of course, individuals don't spend all their income on goods. Sometimes individuals hold money as they do any other commodity. Including money (symbolized by $), the equation for maximization of utility is

$$\frac{MU_A}{P_A} = \frac{MU_B}{P_B} = \frac{MU_\$}{P_\$}.$$

Since the price of a dollar is $1, $MU_\$/P_\$$ can be written simply as $MU_\$$. Thus, total utility is maximized when

(1) $$\frac{MU_x}{P_x} = \frac{MU_y}{P_y} = \cdots = \frac{MU_n}{P_n} = MU_\$.$$

Utility maximization is the process by which a consumer adjusts consumption, given a budget constraint and a set of prices, in order to attain the highest total amount of satisfaction. Equation (1) is a very complete expression for utility maximization. It includes all commodities, even money. This equation says that in order to maximize total utility, the marginal utilities per dollar of all goods consumed have to be equal and also have to equal the marginal utility of money. If this is not the case, a change in the consumption pattern can produce more satisfaction for a given budget constraint. This equation is just a formal way of saying that people allocate their income so as to yield the most satisfaction possible. When utility is being maximized, the additional satisfaction from any use of a dollar will equal the additional satisfaction from any other use of that dollar. When this is not the case, the individual can reallocate personal income from one good to another and gain more satisfaction.

To see how a given consumption pattern can be adjusted to achieve maximum utility, look again at Table 3. Let's give Susan an income of $9 and say that she uses it to buy $3 worth of cola and $6 worth of pizza. The expression $MU_{cola}/P_{cola} = MU_{pizza}/P_{pizza}$ doesn't hold because

$$\frac{10\,3/4}{.50} > \frac{18}{1}.$$

Susan isn't maximizing her utility because the last dollar she spent on cola yielded more utils than the last dollar she spent on pizza. Susan should reallocate her consumption outlays. By giving up a dollar's worth of pizza, she will lose 18 utils. But she will gain 20 utils by spending that dollar on more cola. Her total utility will thus rise by 2 (rounded off), and

$$\frac{10}{.50} \approx \frac{20\,1/4}{1}.$$

By purchasing 8 cans of cola and 5 pieces of pizza, Susan is maximizing utility with a $9 budget constraint.

MARGINAL UTILITY AND THE LAW OF DEMAND

Utility theory makes it possible to derive an individual's demand curve for a good (good *x*). Suppose there are only two goods, *x* and *y*. Remember, demand curves are drawn using the *ceteris paribus* assumption. That is, income, tastes, and the prices of all other goods (good *y*) are held constant. The consumer is initially in equilibrium, maximizing utility when

$$\frac{MU_x}{P_x} = \frac{MU_y}{P_y}.$$

utility maximization The process by which a consumer adjusts consumption, given a budget constraint and a set of prices, in order to attain the highest total amount of satisfaction.

At this equilibrium, MU_{x_1} corresponds to the consumption of x_1 units of good x in Figure 2. The price of x_1 units is represented by P_1 in Figure 2. The equation should now be written

$$\frac{MU_{x_1}}{P_1} = \frac{MU_y}{P_y}.$$

Now suppose the price of good x falls to P_2. This change throws the expression out of equilibrium because the denominator on the left side is now smaller, making the left side of the expression larger:

$$\frac{MU_{x_1}}{P_2} > \frac{MU_y}{P_y}.$$

To get back into equilibrium, the individual has to lower the value of the left side of the expression and/or raise the value of the right side. How can this be done? If the individual consumes more of x, MU_x will decline because of the principle of diminishing marginal utility. As consumption moves to x_2 on Figure 2, the marginal utility of good x falls. Furthermore, consuming more of x will mean some reduction in the consumption of y. As consumption of y falls, MU_y rises. When this happens, the expression will move toward

$$\frac{MU_x}{P_x} = \frac{MU_y}{P_y}.$$

Utility-maximizing behavior requires that when the price of good x falls (as from P_1 to P_2 in Figure 2), the consumer will increase consumption of x. Since this is necessary for utility maximization, it demonstrates that the demand curves of individuals must have a negative slope. That is, the lower the price of a good, the greater the quantity demanded.

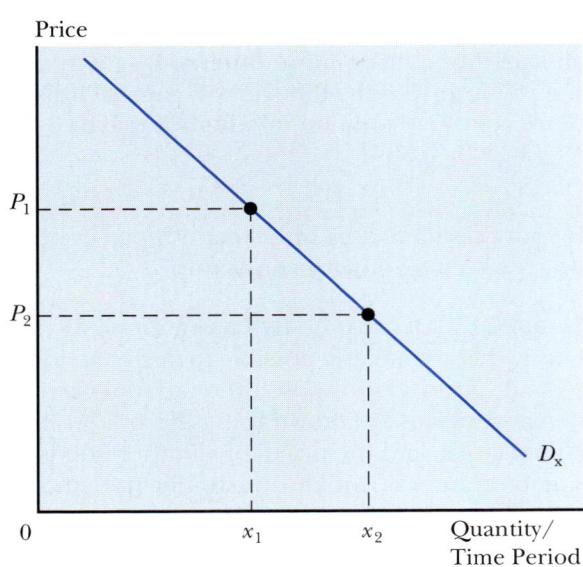

FIGURE 2
DEMAND CURVE FOR GOOD X
When price falls from P_1 to P_2, the consumer's utility maximization is thrown out of equilibrium. Equilibrium will be restored if the consumer increases consumption to x_2.

Problems with Utility Theory

There are two major problems with a demand theory based on utility. The first problem is that some goods are not divisible. The second, more serious problem is that utility cannot be measured.

The theory works well enough to describe the consumption of certain kinds of goods, such as soft drinks or pizzas. When the good being consumed is an automobile or a home, however, it is difficult to talk about additional units because the purchase is what economists call "lumpy." It is very difficult to consume a part of a house or a part of a car, but it is common to consume part of a six-pack of cola. The theory is somewhat weakened, then, by the fact that the consumer can't always make continuous decisions about successive amounts of consumption.[2]

A greater problem with utility theory is that it is impossible to measure utility. We have proceeded as if there were a way we could strap a meter to a consumer and exactly measure the utility expected from consuming one more unit, somewhat like measuring temperature or blood pressure. This is, of course, not possible. Psychology has not developed such sophisticated technology. But before you reject utility theory as useless, remember that it is a theoretical tool. It really isn't that important for the theory of demand to be able to measure utility. The purpose of utility theory is to develop a better understanding of why and how quantity demanded will change when prices change.

SOME APPLICATIONS OF UTILITY THEORY

You have practiced and observed utility maximization even though you may not have thought of it in the formal language of economics. Suppose, for example, you are organizing the beer concession for a fund-raising event. There are two ways to run the concession. You can charge an admission fee to the event and then allow unlimited consumption, or you can charge a set price for each beer, say $.50 per glass. Utility theory predicts different levels of consumption for these two alternatives and thus different requirements for planning the supply. In the first case, beer drinkers will consume beer until the marginal utility per glass is zero because the price per additional glass is zero. In the second case, beer drinkers will consume beer until the marginal utility per glass equals the marginal utility of $.50. You can predict, then, that there will be more drunken, rowdy behavior if the party is financed by an admission charge.

If you don't agree with this analysis, reflect back on parties you have observed. Were the most rowdy ones the pay-as-you-go type or the admission type? With the growing awareness of alcohol abuse on campus, student organizations on some campuses have outlawed keg beer parties

---

2. This problem with utility theory is really not a major flaw. Consumers can still make adjustments with most lumpy purchases. Consider a house as an example. Suppose the individual decides after the purchase that the house is too large and that other purchases would yield more marginal utility. Over time, expenditures on the house can be lowered by a lessening of routine maintenance so that more can be spent on the other goods that yield a higher marginal utility. Buying a smaller house, buying one at a less desirable location, and renting are also available alternatives.

("all you can drink") and required that they be replaced with can-only beer parties (pay by the can). These campus rule-setters understand diminishing marginal utility whether they know it or not.

This example may seem insignificant because the consumption of beer isn't a very earth-shaking issue. Let's change the good from beer to medical services. If the government decides to provide free national health care, what do you predict will happen to the consumption of these services?[3] Of course, people will consume them until the marginal utility of the last unit is zero. This is exactly what tends to happen with a prepaid or tax-financed health care system. If you have ever participated in such a program in the military, at a university, or under a health maintenance plan, you probably have consumed more medical services than before. Since there is no charge per visit, more services are consumed. You may also have noticed that with the free system, the waiting time is usually longer, the waiting rooms are less comfortable, and the workers are less congenial than with a fee-for-service system.

THE DIAMOND-WATER PARADOX EXPLAINED

Adam Smith (and others) argued that utility (and thus demand) could not be a determinant of price because diamonds, while less useful than water, are more expensive than water. The paradox disappears if we distinguish between total utility and marginal utility. The total utility of water is high. However, since there is a great deal in existence and large quantities are consumed, its marginal utility is low. The total utility of diamonds, on the other hand, is relatively low. However, since diamonds are rare, their marginal utility is high. Price, then, is determined by marginal utility, not total utility. Economists say that marginal utility determines value in exchange (price) and that total utility determines value in use. Price, then, is related to scarcity through utility. If something has a low marginal utility at all quantities consumed, it will have a low price, regardless of how scarce it is. If something is relatively scarce and has a high marginal utility, it will be valuable and thus expensive.

INCOME AND SUBSTITUTION EFFECTS

The law of demand, which you studied in Chapter 3, states that as the price of a good or service declines, the quantity demanded increases, *ceteris paribus*. This law is true because of two effects that result from the price decline.

The first effect is called the **substitution effect**. When the price of a good (or service) falls, the good becomes less expensive relative to all other goods. As a result, consumers purchase more of it because it has become a better substitute for other goods as it has become cheaper. Steaks and ground beef provide a good example. As the price of steak falls, more people will switch from ground beef to steaks.

The second effect of a price decline is called the **income effect**. When the price of a good or service falls, *ceteris paribus*, the individual consumer's real income, or purchasing power, rises. That is, after buying the same amount as before (of the good for which price has fallen), the consumer has more income left over. With this higher real income, more of

substitution effect
An increase in the quantity demanded of a good (or service) because its price has fallen and it becomes a better substitute for all other goods.

income effect
An increase in demand for a good (or service) when its price falls, *ceteris paribus*, because the household's real income rises, and the consumer buys more of all normal goods.

---

3. By "free" we mean there is no monetary cost to the patient. That is, price is zero.

Chapter 6   Demand and Consumer Choice

all normal goods will be consumed. Thus, the consumption of the good that experienced the price decline also will increase (if it is a normal good). These income and substitution effects are important forces, which will become clearer in this chapter.

UTILITY THEORY AND THE PROGRESSIVE INCOME TAX

Many noneconomists believe that money and income are subject to diminishing marginal utility. This idea is one of the main arguments (but not the only one) for a progressive income tax.[4] A progressive tax takes a larger percentage of dollars from the rich because for them the dollars' marginal utility is thought to be low. A smaller percentage of dollars is taken from poorer taxpayers because for them a dollar's marginal utility is thought to be much higher. This argument assumes that it is possible to measure utility *and* to make **interpersonal utility comparisons**. Such comparisons are attempts to compare the utility of one individual with that of another. One way to avoid directly comparing utilities for different people is to assume that individuals all have the same utility schedule for given levels of income. With these two assumptions, proponents of the progressive income tax argue that society can maximize total utility by taking income away from high-income individuals who have lower marginal utilities of income and transferring it to low-income individuals who have higher marginal utilities of income.

interpersonal utility comparisons Attempts to compare the utility of one individual with that of another (or others).

Those who apply principles of individual utility maximization to a society as a whole are on very shaky ground, however. First, economists generally believe that interpersonal utility comparisons are not feasible. People are different. There is no way you can prove that an additional $100 of income gives less satisfaction to actress Linda Evans than to an unemployed auto worker. In fact, Ms. Evans may get more satisfaction because she is such an expert consumer. It is impossible to prove that one individual gets more or less satisfaction from an increment to income than any other individual does.

A second and more fundamental problem with this analysis is that it assumes a diminishing marginal utility for income, or goods and services in general. This proposition cannot be verified. The principle of diminishing marginal utility, you will remember, states that the marginal utility of a *particular good* declines as consumption is increased. Increased income, however, represents an increase in the consumption of all goods. If wants are insatiable, there is no reason to believe that the principle of diminishing marginal utility holds for money or income. Even so, it is probably the case that most people think that income has diminishing marginal utility. What about you? Do you think a $100 bill would give your "rich" economics instructor more or less satisfaction than it would give you?

SHOPPING FOR BARGAINS

Economists have used the concept of utility-maximizing behavior to analyze shopping behavior. The idea is that a buyer will search for bargains until the expected savings in value or utility equals the cost of continued searching.

---

4. For a comprehensive treatment of this subject, see Walter J. Blum and Harry Kalven, Jr., *The Uneasy Case for Progressive Taxation* (Chicago: University of Chicago Press, 1970).

Several predictions can be made from this theory. The first is that the larger the amount individuals expect to save, the longer they will continue to search. In other words, the bigger the item in terms of your budget, the more you will shop around. You will search longer for a good price on a car than for a good price on a loaf of bread. You might even buy bread at a convenience store, where you know the price is higher, to save some shopping time. The second prediction is that, in percentage terms, the variation in prices for bigger budget items should be smaller than the variation in prices for smaller budget items. The search process will drive high-price sellers of large items out of business or force them to reduce their prices. The third prediction is that where search costs are higher, price differences between sellers could be higher without driving the high-priced sellers out of business. Have you ever noticed that prices of gasoline are higher near freeways than in towns? Utility-maximizing theory can explain this phenomenon. Users of freeways are going somewhere, often in a hurry. Their search costs are high. They therefore do less shopping around and as a result pay higher prices.

CONSUMER SURPLUS AND UTILITY

consumer surplus
The extra utility derived from a purchase that has a value to the consumer greater than the market price.

Consumers often benefit in a market economy because they are able to purchase a good or service by sacrificing something that is worth less to them than the value of what they receive. **Consumer surplus** is the extra utility derived from a purchase that has a value to the consumer greater than the market price. Utility theory provides a measure of consumer surplus.

Consider the demand curve for a single consumer (or group of homogeneous consumers) in Figure 3. At price P_1, the individual will consume Q_1 units of the good. According to the theory of utility-maximizing

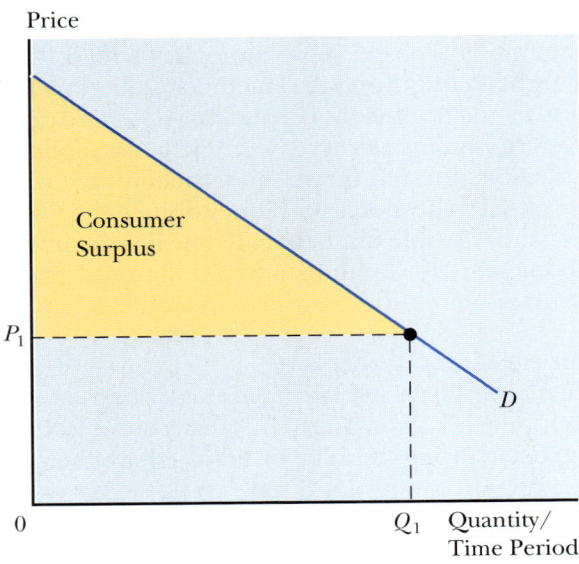

FIGURE 3
CONSUMER SURPLUS
The consumer surplus is the shaded area above the price P_1 and below the demand curve.

INTERNATIONAL PERSPECTIVE

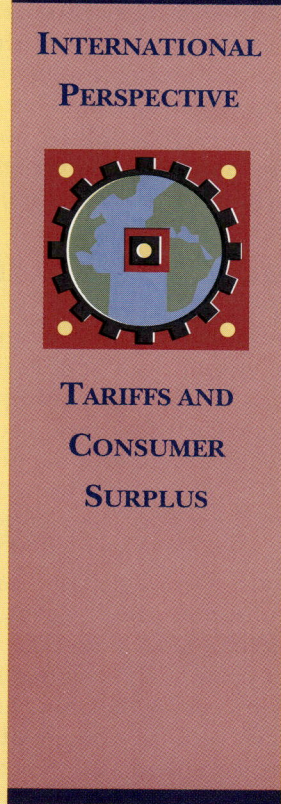

TARIFFS AND CONSUMER SURPLUS

Tariffs have many effects. They reduce the efficiency of resource allocation. They redistribute income between countries and between producers and consumers within countries. They raise revenue for the countries that impose them. All of the economic effects of tariffs are important and will be discussed in the chapter on international trade. It is possible, however, to use the concept of consumer surplus developed in this chapter to see how tariffs affect consumer well-being.

In the graph below, S_d is the domestic supply curve and S_w is the world supply curve. World supply is perfectly elastic at the world price P_f. Consumers are demanding quantity Q, of which quantity A is sold by domestic producers and quantity $Q - A$ is imported. The triangle formed by S_w, D, and the vertical axis represents consumer surplus. What happens if the government imposes a tariff equal to t? The price rises by the amount of the tariff to P_t, creating a new supply curve, S'_w. Consumers now purchase quantity B from domestic producers and $C - B$ from foreign producers. Consumer surplus is now represented by the triangle formed by S'_w, D, and the vertical axis. There has been a reduction in consumer surplus equal to the difference between the two triangles, or the shaded area. What this example demonstrates is that a tariff permits domestic producers to sell more of a product at a higher price and that government revenues rise by the amount of the tariff times the imported quantity. However, consumers experience a decline in consumer surplus.

TARIFFS AND CONSUMER SURPLUS

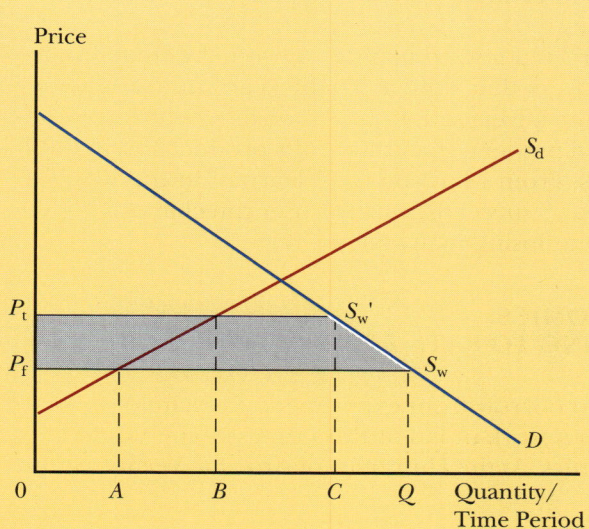

behavior, the marginal utility of the last unit purchased is equal to the price of the unit. This means that the marginal utility of each previous unit purchased was greater than price P_1. The consumer would have been willing to pay higher prices for those previous units, so at the market price of P_1, the consumer receives a bonus in terms of utility on all units but the last one. The total purchase is worth more to the consumer than the total amount (price times quantity) that is paid. This extra utility gained is called consumer surplus and is represented by the shaded area in Figure 3. Consumer surplus will be an important concept when we study monopoly. The International Perspective describes an application of consumer surplus in international trade.

ADVERTISING, MARKETING, AND DEMAND

The theory developed in this chapter explains a great deal about demand and consumer equilibrium. It does not say anything about the role of advertising and marketing. Advertising and marketing are difficult topics for economists to deal with because economic analysis usually assumes that consumers are informed, rational utility maximizers who know their own tastes and preferences. Advertising and marketing are not, however, inconsistent with those basic assumptions.

Advertisers spend a great deal of time trying to alter consumers' tastes and perceptions. If enough tastes and perceptions can be changed that the average consumer's utility from the firm's product can be increased, more will be demanded. Changes in tastes do not mean that the consumer is not rational. Even without advertising, tastes would change over time with changes in age, education, and other factors. Some tastes even change regularly with the change of season.

Advertisers also spend a great deal of time generating information for consumers about prices. This behavior of advertisers fits with the description of consumers' search behavior. If the cost of getting information falls, the cost of the search falls and consumers will do more searching. As a consequence, they may alter their purchasing patterns and buy from sellers offering lower prices.

Much advertising is directed toward making consumer demand more inelastic by convincing buyers that similar products are not satisfactory substitutes for the one being advertised. In other words, the advertiser attempts to widen the spread between the utility of its product and the utility of potential substitutes. From what you have learned in this chapter, you can see that if this strategy succeeds, an advertiser can charge a higher price for its product without losing many sales.

EXPERIMENTAL ECONOMICS: ECONOMICS ACCORDING TO RATS

Economics is beginning to borrow from experimental psychology. Some economists are carrying out work in lab settings to test some fundamental propositions in economics. At the University of Arizona, Vernon Smith has conducted research on market behavior using human subjects, usually students. At Texas A&M, economists Ray Battalio and John Kagel have experimented with human and animal subjects. These economists did experiments in mental hospitals with token economies. Patients were paid tokens for tasks and were free to spend these tokens on personal items. Some of the results of these investigations were fascinating. They found that the distribution of income earned was closely parallel to that in the U.S. economy. Perhaps even more startling was the fact that earning differences between male and female patients were similar to those between men and women in the U.S. economy.

This result led the two economists to experiment with rats. They found that rats trained to do "work for pay" (hit a bar for food) reduced their work effort after some point, choosing more leisure over additional income. They also found that among low-income rats (those that had to work hard for a little food), such work reduction patterns were more common. These experimental results are consistent with behavior patterns of individuals in real-life situations based on diminishing marginal utility.

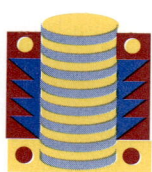

Summary

1. Total utility is the total amount of satisfaction expected from consuming an item.
2. Marginal utility is the change in total utility from consuming one more or one less unit of a good.
3. Consumers, in deciding among items, choose those items with the highest marginal utility per dollar.
4. An individual maximizes total utility by consuming all items so that their marginal utilities per dollar spent are equal.
5. When the price of a good or service falls, the quantity demanded increases because of income effects and substitution effects.
6. Utility theory is useful in explaining how much effort people will make to search for bargains.
7. Utility theory has been criticized on the grounds that utility is not measurable. Another criticism is that some items consumed are not perfectly divisible, as the theory of utility maximization requires. Despite these criticisms, utility theory is a useful tool for analyzing consumer behavior.
8. Consumer surplus is a measure of the extra benefit derived from a purchase in excess of the price that is paid.
9. Marketing and advertising can be viewed as attempts to reduce search costs and change tastes. Attempts to alter tastes are not in conflict with utility theory.
10. Experimental results have supported some of the basic propositions of marginal utility theory.

New Terms

diamond-water paradox
utility
util
utility function
marginal utility (*MU*)
principle of diminishing marginal utility
budget constraint
utility maximization
substitution effect
income effect
interpersonal utility comparisons
consumer surplus

Questions for Discussion

1. Does something have to be useful to have utility? What does it mean for a good or service to be useful?
2. What is happening when the price of a good such as petroleum is increasing without a decrease in consumption?
3. Does the fact that water is inexpensive and diamonds are expensive conflict with the theory developed in this chapter? Explain.
4. If the marginal utility of one good is 4 and its price is $2 and the marginal utility of another good is 5 and its price is $1, is the individual consumer maximizing total utility? If not, how could more utility be obtained?
5. Does advertising increase or decrease the utility you get from consuming certain goods? Is this good or bad?
6. What would you expect to happen to a normal consumer's total utility for bacon if the Surgeon General established a link between bacon and cancer? How would this announcement affect the individual's demand curve for bacon?
7. The following table shows the marginal utility that Roger gets from buying various amounts of cola, pretzels, nuts, and pizza and from holding dollars. Assume that Roger has an income of $106.
    What quantities of cola, nuts, pretzels, and pizza will Roger purchase? How many dollars will he hold?
8. The material in this chapter discusses rational consumer behavior. Is it ever rational to be irrational?
9. Observers of the wealthy often comment on the fact that they waste a lot of things, such as food, but are very careful in their use of time. Is this irrational behavior?
10. Use a graph to explain how a demand curve can be derived from indifference analysis.
11. Given an indifference map, a set of indifference curves, and a budget line, where does the consumer maximize satisfaction?
12. Suppose Kim Hagen's demand for escargot is represented by the following schedule. Assume that the market price of escargot is $6 per ounce.

Price of Escargot/Ounce	Ounces of Escargot/Month
$10	1
8	2
7	4
6	6
5	9
4	11
3	13

What is the maximum amount that Kim would pay for the first ounce of escargot per month? By how much

Units of Cola (P = $18)	MU	Units of Pretzels (P = $4)	MU	Units of Nuts (P = $6)	MU	Units of Pizza (P = $24)	MU	Dollars Held	MU
1	72	1	15	1	24	1	36	1	5
2	54	2	12	2	15	2	30	2	4
3	45	3	8	3	12	3	24	3	3
4	36	4	7	4	9	4	18	4	2
5	27	5	5	5	7	5	13	5	1
6	18	6	4	6	5	6	7	6	½
7	15	7	3½	7	2	7	4	7	¼
8	12	8	3	8	1	8	2	8	⅛

does this exceed the actual price? How much would Kim pay for the second ounce of escargot per month? By how much does this exceed the actual price? How much would Kim be willing to pay for the third and fourth ounces of escargot per month? By how much does this exceed the actual price? How much would Kim be willing to pay for the fifth and sixth ounces of escargot per month? By how much does this exceed the actual price?

13. According to the schedule in Question 12, how many ounces of escargot will Kim Hagen purchase per month? How large is Kim's consumer surplus?

14. Geno Hagen, Kim's husband, learns that the price of caviar has fallen significantly. If Kim's demand curve is their family demand curve, what will happen to their demand for escargot? What is the substitution effect? Do you think that it will be positive or negative? What is the income effect? Will it be significant in this example?

15. Some restaurants in Maryland advertise "all you can eat" crab feasts. How is this offer related to the theory in this chapter? Can you think of any restrictions a restaurant might make on the behavior of customers who buy this meal?

SUGGESTIONS FOR FURTHER READING

Browning, Edgar K., and Jacquelene M. Browning. *Microeconomic Theory and Applications*, 2nd ed. Boston: Little, Brown, 1986. A very well-written intermediate textbook on microeconomic theory.

Easterlin, Richard A. "Does Money Buy Happiness?" *Public Interest* (Winter 1973): 3–10. A short essay that challenges the notion that more goods mean more utility (happiness).

APPENDIX: INDIFFERENCE ANALYSIS, AN ALTERNATIVE APPROACH TO CONSUMER CHOICE

The marginal utility theory discussed in this chapter has the drawback that it requires precise numerical values to be assigned to alternatives (cardinal utility). A later innovation in the economic theory of choice was based on ordinal utility. Ordinal utility requires only that the utility of the choices can be ranked. Instead of saying "The next slice of pizza has 30 units of utility" or "The next Coke has 25 units of utility," the consumer needs only to be able to say "I prefer another slice of pizza to another Coke."

In the late 1800s, Italian economist Vilfredo Pareto and British economist F. Y. Edgeworth, working separately, developed an approach to analyzing consumer behavior based on ordinal utility—**indifference analysis**. It wasn't until 1939, when Nobel Prize winning British economist Sir John Hicks published his classic book *Value and Capital*, that this technique became popular with economic theorists and teachers. The theory swept the economics profession, and for a while, marginal utility analysis fell into disrepute.

Pareto, Edgeworth, Hicks, and others were not trying to discredit utility theory but rather were proposing an alternative way of viewing consumer behavior. The major improvement of their theory is that it does not require the measurement of units of utility. All that is necessary is that consumers be able to rank bundles of goods in the order, from low to high, in which they prefer them.

indifference analysis
An approach to analyzing consumer behavior based on ranking the utility of choices relative to one another.

INDIFFERENCE OR PREFERENCE

Indifference and preference seem better than marginal utility for describing the way consumers actually make decisions. Individuals make choices between bundles, or collections, of goods. For example, you might choose between four tickets to a football game and two tickets to a concert. In indifference analysis, the consumer is viewed as making choices between collections of goods and services. The only assumption is that the individual is able to state preferences for different collections or to profess indifference between some of them. In other words, confronted with a choice between going to a movie and going to a football game, the individual might rank the football game as the preferred choice. Or the individual might say, "I don't have a preference. I'm indifferent between the two choices."

Suppose Mary is considering different combinations of cans of Coke and slices of pizza, as indicated in Table 1A. Combination *A* consists of 16 cans of Coke and 3 slices of pizza, and combination *B* consists of 12 cans and 4 slices. When these two combinations are offered to Mary, she states that neither combination *A* nor combination *B* is preferred over the other. They are equal in the amount of satisfaction she expects to derive. Therefore, she is indifferent between the two. Offering Mary the choice among combinations *C*, *D*, and *E* yields the same response—indifference. Mary has indicated that all five combinations of pizza and Coke yield the same amount of satisfaction. These five combinations comprise an **indifference set** for her.

indifference set
Any number of combinations of goods among which the individual consumer is indifferent (has no preference).

Chapter 6 Demand and Consumer Choice

TABLE 1A
MARY'S INDIFFERENCE SET

COMBINATION	GOOD X (CANS OF COKE)	GOOD Y (SLICES OF PIZZA)
A	16	3
B	12	4
C	0	5
D	8	7
E	6	9

An indifference set can be represented graphically by an indifference curve. An indifference curve corresponding to the indifference set in Table 1A is shown in Figure 1A. An **indifference curve** shows all combinations of two goods (or services) among which a consumer is indifferent.

Indifference curves are negatively sloped because for a consumer to be indifferent, all points on the curve must represent equal amounts of utility. If more of one good is added to the combination, some of the other must be removed. Each combination represents a trade-off. In Mary's case, if combination B has more pizza than combination A, it must have less Coke, since the combinations yield the same level of satisfaction. If one combination had more pizza and more Coke than any other, or if it had more of one without having less of the other, it would be preferred. The consumer would no longer be indifferent. This is yet another way of saying that more is preferred to less.

The indifference set represented by a higher indifference curve is preferred to that represented by a lower indifference curve. As Mary moves from I_1 to I_2 to I_3 to I_4 in Figure 2A, she receives more satisfaction. Such a series of indifference curves is called an **indifference map**. Every individual consumer has such a map, and movement to a higher curve on the map represents a gain in utility.

indifference curve
A plot of all combinations of goods that the consumer is indifferent among.

indifference map
A set of indifference curves. Higher curves represent higher levels of utility.

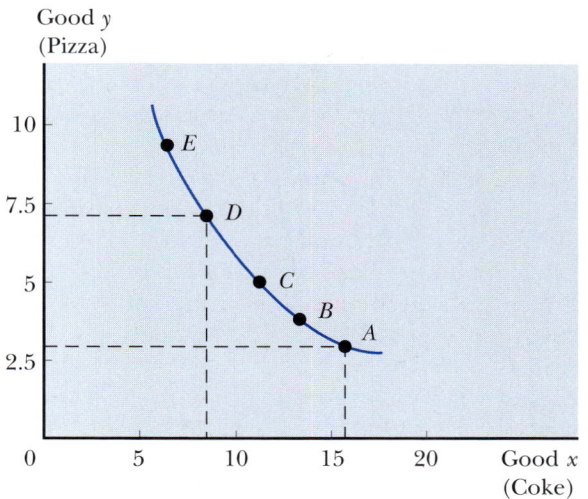

FIGURE 1A
INDIFFERENCE CURVE
An indifference curve represents combinations of two goods among which the consumer is indifferent. All combinations on the same indifference curve give the same level of satisfaction.

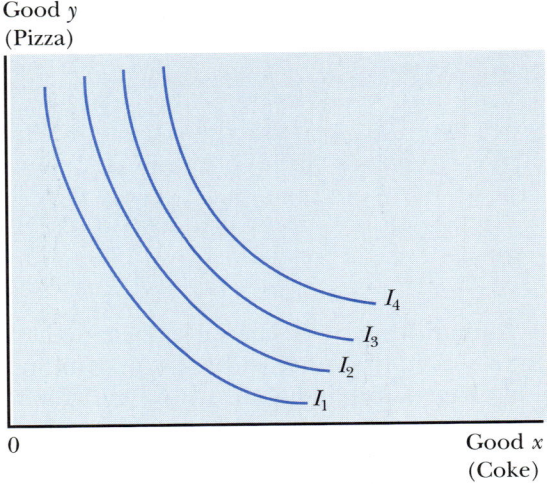

FIGURE 2A
INDIFFERENCE MAP
An indifference map is a set of indifference curves, each corresponding to a different level of satisfaction. Higher curves on the map represent higher levels of satisfaction.

The shape of the typical indifference curve for two goods will be somewhat convex with respect to the origin. The convexity means that as a consumer gets more units of one good and fewer units of the other, it takes more and more units of the more abundant good to compensate for the loss of one unit of the good that is becoming more scarce. For example, at point A in Figure 3A, the individual is consuming relatively large amounts of good y and small amounts of good x. In order to compensate for a reduction in consumption of 1 unit of y, the person would only require 2 units of x in order to be satisfied with such a trade. At point B, however, since less of y and more of x are being consumed compared to point A, it will take a larger quantity of x (5 units) to compensate for the loss of

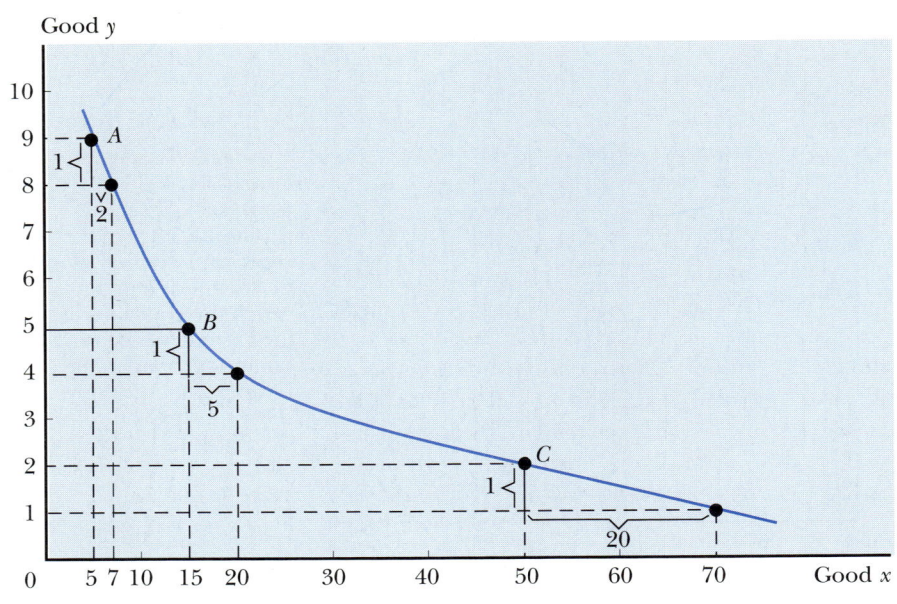

FIGURE 3A
CONVEXITY FEATURE OF INDIFFERENCE CURVES
A typical indifference curve is convex to the origin. This convexity means that it takes increasingly larger amounts of the abundant good to compensate for losses of the good that is becoming more scarce.

1 unit of y. At point C, the person is consuming a large amount of x and very little y. To give up 1 unit of y, 20 more units of x would be needed to have the same utility as before.

Why do economists expect such preference relations to hold? First, most of us would agree that this is the way we would behave in such a trade-off situation. Second, the opposite conclusion seems highly unlikely. It would say that the less you had of a good, the less you would want of it relative to other goods, and the more you had of a good, the more valuable additional units of it would become. Indifference curves reflect the concept of diminishing marginal utility for two goods without assigning numerical values to utility.

DIMINISHING MARGINAL RATES OF SUBSTITUTION

The trade-off ratio along an indifference curve is called the **marginal rate of substitution (MRS)**. The marginal rate of substitution of x for y, MRS_{xy}, shows the willingness of the consumer to substitute between goods x and y:

$$MRS_{xy} = \frac{\text{number of units of } y \text{ given up}}{\text{number of units of } x \text{ gained}}.$$

In Figure 3A, the MRS_{xy} at point A is ½. That is, 1 unit of y must be sacrificed to gain 2 units of x. At point B, the MRS_{xy} is ⅕, and at point C, it is 1/20. The declining value of MRS_{xy} is a reflection of the **principle of diminishing marginal rates of substitution**. That is, as more of one good (x) is substituted for the other good (y), the value of good x in terms of good y declines.

BUDGET CONSTRAINTS

An indifference map makes it possible to compare points representing combinations of two goods to determine whether the individual prefers one such combination or feels indifferent among several. All points on any single indifference curve are equivalent to each other in utility, even if utility cannot be measured numerically. Points on indifference curves located to the right and above other indifference curves are preferred combinations.

Which combinations are actually attainable for the individual? The answer depends on the income available and on the prices of the goods. Keep in mind that the consumer faces prices that are determined in markets and cannot influence them. Income constrains the consumer from buying all that might be desired. The income is the budget constraint and, when drawn on the indifference map, is called the budget line.

We limit the analysis to two goods (you could think of one of them as "all other goods"). Again assume that Mary can consume either slices of pizza or cans of Coke. Suppose she has a disposable income (DI) of $10.00 and pizza (good y) and Coke (good x) sell for $1.00 and $.50, respectively, per unit. The construction of the budget line is illustrated in Figure 4A. If she spends her entire income (DI) on pizza, she can buy 10 slices. This number is determined by dividing income by the price of the good:

$$\frac{DI}{P_y} = \frac{\$10.00}{\$1.00} = 10 \text{ slices of pizza.}$$

marginal rate of substitution (MRS)
The trade-off ratio along an indifference curve.

principle of diminishing marginal rates of substitution
The fact that as more of one good is consumed, more and more of the other must be given up to maintain indifference between the two.

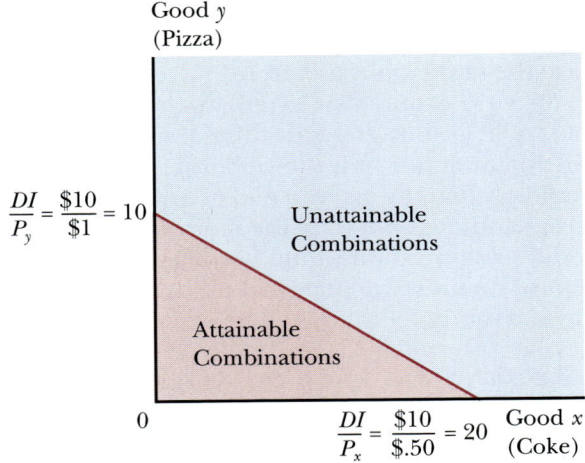

FIGURE 4A
BUDGET LINE
A budget line graphically depicts the consumption combinations that are attainable with a given level of income. Any combination above the line is unattainable.

Thus, 10 is the *y*-intercept. The *x*-intercept is calculated in the same manner:

$$\frac{DI}{P_x} = \frac{\$10.00}{\$.50} = 20 \text{ cans of Coke.}$$

A straight line connecting the two points that represent buying all good *y* (pizza) or all good *x* (Coke) shows all possible combinations that Mary can purchase with a given income level of $10. For example, $10 will buy 5 slices of pizza and 10 Cokes or 6 slices of pizza and 8 Cokes. Any combination outside (above) the line is unattainable at that income level. It is outside her budget constraint. In other words, the budget line is the dividing line between those combinations that are attainable and those that are unattainable at a given level of prices and a given level of income.

CHANGES IN INCOME AND CHANGES IN PRICES

The budget line is developed holding prices and income constant. How do changes in income and prices affect the budget line? An increase in income means that more of both goods can be purchased, if prices stay the same. A doubling of income means that twice as much of both goods can be purchased, if prices remain constant. An increase in income is represented by a parallel outward shift of the budget line. A decrease in income is represented by a parallel inward shift of the budget line. Such shifts are shown in Figure 5A.

A change in the price of one good affects the maximum amount of that good that can be purchased, but does not affect the maximum amount of the other good that can be purchased. If the price of cola rises and Mary spends all her income on pizza, the price rise has no effect on the amount of pizza purchased. A price rise, then, will only affect the intercept of the budget line with the axis for the good that has experienced the price rise. Such a change is shown in Figure 6A. A price rise for good *x* from P_{x_1} to P_{x_2} causes the *x*-intercept of the budget line to move closer to the origin, reflecting the fact that less of good *x* can now be purchased with constant in-

Chapter 6 Demand and Consumer Choice

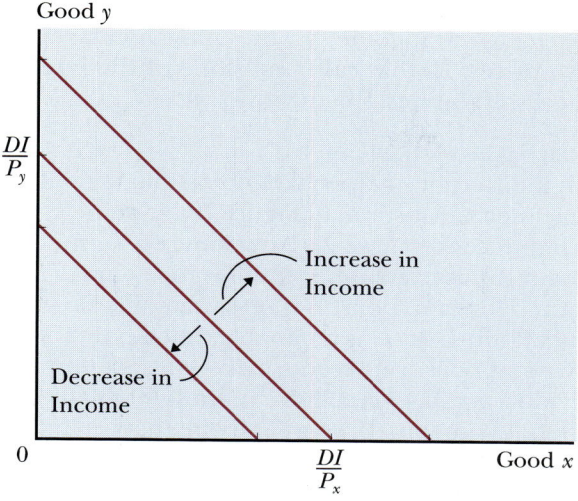

**FIGURE 5A
THE EFFECT OF INCOME CHANGES ON BUDGET LINES**
An increase in income is represented by an outward parallel shift of the budget line. A decrease in income is represented by an inward parallel shift of the budget line.

come. A decrease in the price of good x from P_{x_1} to P_{x_3} means more of good x can be purchased. The x-intercept of the budget line moves away from the origin, reflecting increases in the potential consumption of good x.

Price changes cause the slope of the budget line to change. The slope of the budget line is $\Delta y / \Delta x$. Note that the slope is the negative of the ratio of the y-intercept to the x-intercept, or

$$-\frac{\frac{DI}{P_y}}{\frac{DI}{P_x}}$$

which is equal to

$$\frac{P_x}{P_y}.$$

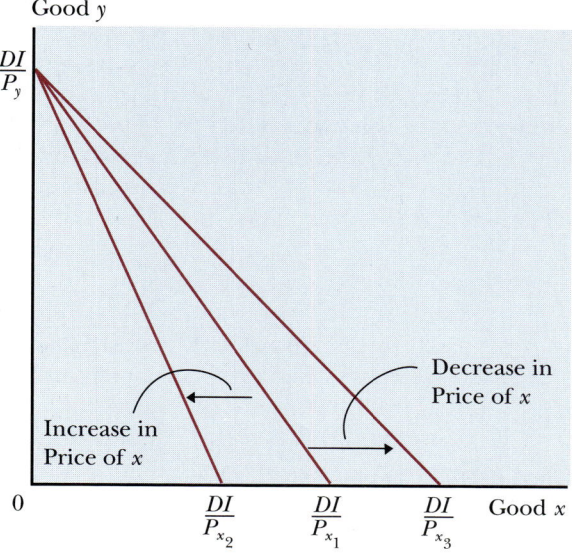

**FIGURE 6A
THE EFFECT OF PRICE CHANGES ON BUDGET LINES**
An increase in the price of one good changes the slope of the budget line because if all disposable income is spent on that good, less of it can be purchased. As a result, the intercept of the budget line will shift closer to the origin. The opposite holds for a decrease in price.

Maximization of Consumer Satisfaction

Adding a budget line to an indifference map makes it possible to demonstrate maximization of consumer satisfaction. In Figure 7A, at point A, the budget line is tangent to indifference curve I_2. Any point on I_3, such as point B, is preferred to point A because higher indifference curves represent higher levels of utility. However, point B is not attainable because it is outside the budget line. Point C on I_1 is attainable, but a point on I_2 is also attainable, and any point on I_2 represents more satisfaction than any point on I_1. The individual wants to reach the highest attainable indifference curve. The highest attainable curve will be one that is tangent to the budget line because no higher curve can be reached with the given income and prices. In this example, the consumer is maximizing utility, or is in equilibrium, at point A on indifference curve I_2.

You should remember from geometry that two curves that are tangent have equal slopes at the point of tangency. At the point of tangency between the indifference curve and the budget line, the marginal rate of substitution is equal to the ratio of the price of x to the price of y.[a] That is,

$$MRS_{xy} = \frac{P_x}{P_y}.$$

This expression means that the marginal rate of substitution expresses the willingness of the consumer to trade a certain amount of x for a certain amount of y, and the slope of the budget line reflects the market's will-

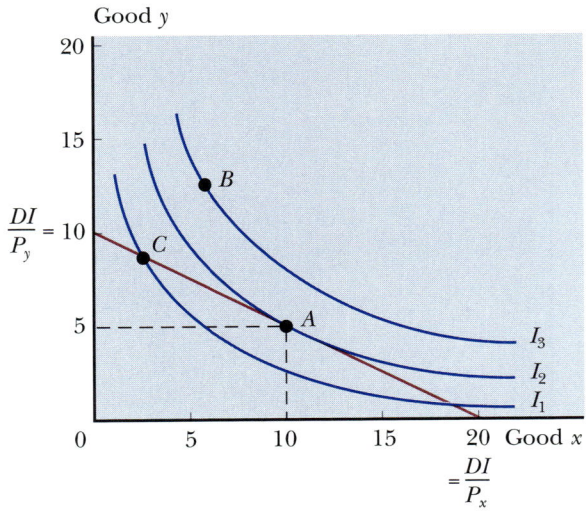

**FIGURE 7A
MAXIMIZATION OF CONSUMER SATISFACTION**
An individual maximizes consumer satisfaction at the point where the budget line is tangent to the highest attainable indifference curve.

---

a. Technically, MRS_{xy} is equal to the negative of the slope of the indifference curve. The price ratio, as we have seen, is the negative of the slope of the budget line. Therefore, at the (equilibrium) point of tangency between the indifference curve and the budget line, $MRS_{xy} = P_x/P_y$.

ingness to trade a certain amount of *x* for a certain amount of *y*. The impersonal forces of the market impose the relative prices on the consumer, so the consumer adjusts consumption amounts in such a way that his or her trade-off is the same as the trade-off in the market.

Suppose you are consuming 15 units of *y* and 5 units of *x* (you are at point *A* in Figure 8A). According to your indifference curve (I_1), you would be willing to give up 5 units of *y* if you received 2 additional units of *x*. The market, however, is willing to give you 5 units of *x* in exchange for 5 units of *y* (note point *B*). You would probably consume less *y* and more *x*. In fact, you would be able to increase your utility by moving in the direction of the tangency of some higher indifference curve with the budget line.

CONSUMER REACTION TO INCOME CHANGES. The best feature of indifference curve analysis is that it allows us to analyze the reaction of consumers to price and income changes. Using the indifference map and the budget line, we can trace the adjustment process that takes place when a household experiences a change in income. In Figure 9A, for example, if the household's income is represented by the budget line DI_1, and *x* and *y* sell for P_x and P_y, respectively, the optimum utility is at point *A*. A decrease in income is represented by budget line DI_0, and two increases in income are represented by budget lines DI_2 and DI_3. The respective optimum positions representing tangencies of these budget lines with an indifference curve are points *B*, *C*, and *D*. Connecting points *A*, *B*, *C*, and *D* generates an **income-consumption curve**. This curve shows how consumption of the two goods changes as income changes. Recall the discussion of the income elasticity of demand in the preceding chapter. The income elasticities of both good *x* and good *y* in Figure 9A are positive because consumption of both goods increases as income increases. (Remember that a positive income elasticity indicates that a good is a normal good. An inferior good has a negative income elasticity since, in that case, as income increases, consumption of the good decreases.)

income-consumption curve
A curve that uses parallel budget lines to show changes in consumer equilibrium when income changes.

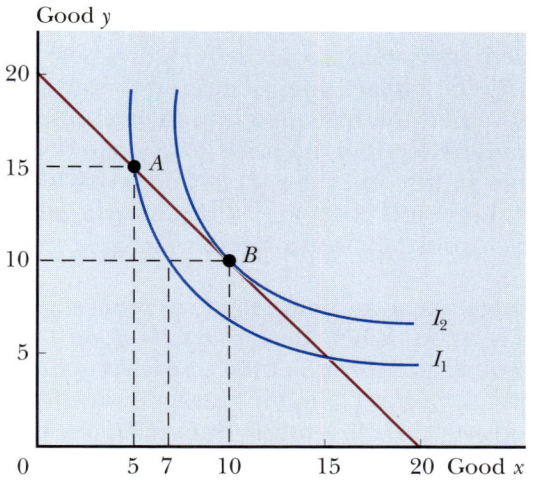

FIGURE 8A
TANGENCY ONCE AGAIN
Lower indifference curves that are within the budget constraint represent lower levels of utility than the highest, but still attainable, indifference curve.

FIGURE 9A
INCOME CHANGES AND THE INCOME-CONSUMPTION CURVE
An income-consumption curve traces the response of consumption combinations to changes in income.

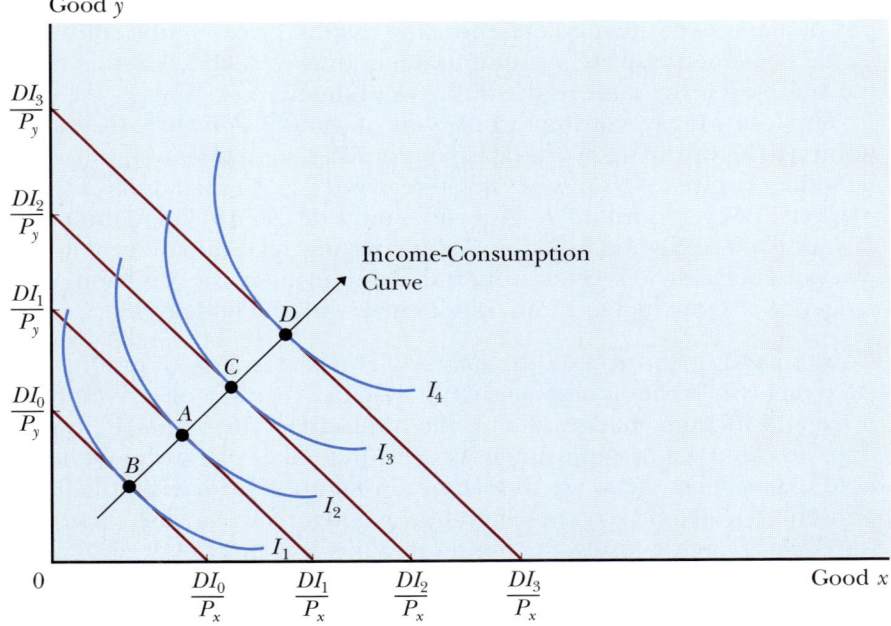

Figure 10A shows a case where one commodity, good x, is a normal good for a household until its income reaches DI_3. When income increases above DI_3, the household buys less of x. So x is a normal good up to point A and then becomes an inferior good as the income-consumption curve bends backward. There is nothing derogatory about the term *inferior*. A daily newspaper might be considered an inferior good for some buyers. As income falls, a person may buy the paper more often because it is a less expensive form of entertainment and also because it offers job listings. Remember, also, that a normal good to some people may be an inferior good to others.

CONSUMER REACTION TO PRICE CHANGES. Let's look at how the optimum consumption combination will be affected by price changes. Initially the consumer is at the point of maximum utility (point A in Figure 11A). As the price of x falls from P_{x_1} to P_{x_2}, the budget line rotates out to intersect the x-axis at DI/P_{x_2}, and the consumer now has a new optimum at point B on indifference curve I_2. Another decrease in price to P_{x_3} allows the consumer to reach a still higher indifference curve, I_3, and a new optimum at point C. Connecting the points A, B, and C produces a **price-consumption curve**. This curve shows how consumption changes when relative prices change.

The theory behind this change in consumption patterns relies on the income and substitution effects again. When the price of a good falls, there are two forces at work to cause the consumer to increase purchases of that good. First, when the price of a good falls, the market trade-off between this good and other goods (or the substitution rate) changes. This part of the response to a price change is the substitution effect. Second,

price-consumption curve
A curve that shows changes in consumer equilibrium when the price of one good on an indifference curve changes.

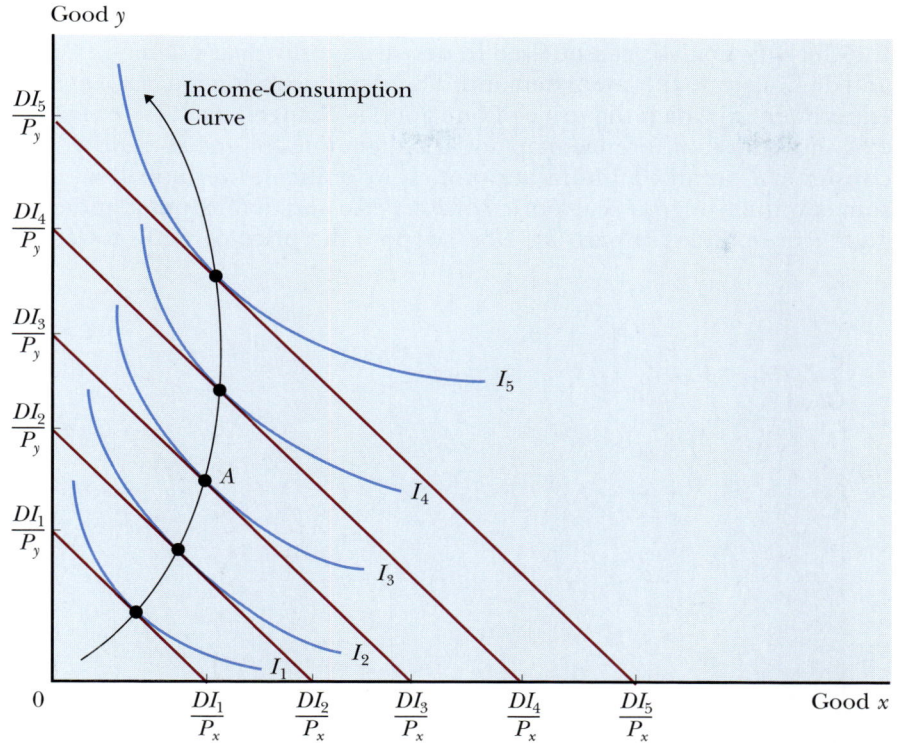

**FIGURE 10A
INCOME-CONSUMPTION CURVE FOR AN INFERIOR GOOD**
The income-consumption curve for an inferior good bends backward, indicating that less of the good is consumed as income increases beyond a certain level.

the individual has a larger real income, meaning that with the same nominal income, more of both (or all) goods can be purchased (and will be purchased as long as the good is not an inferior good). This part of the response to a price change is the income effect.

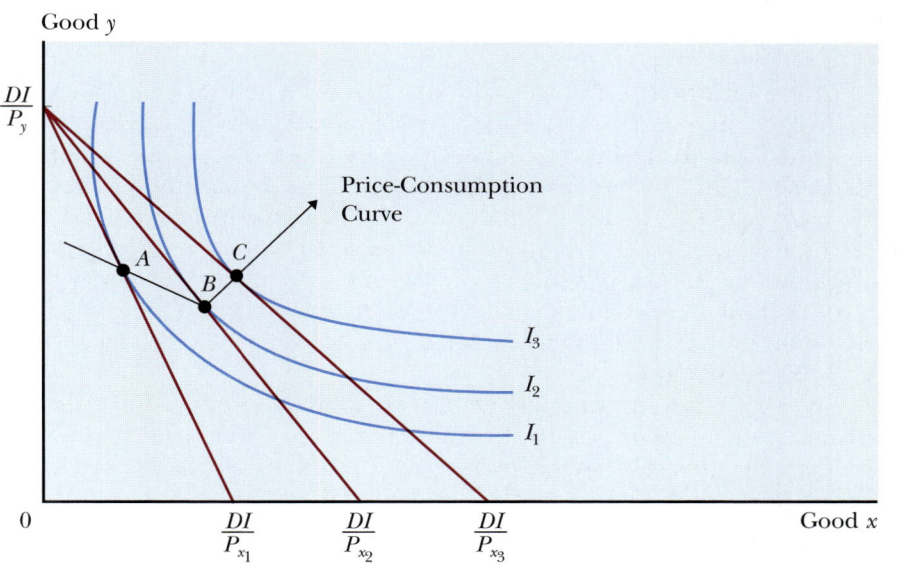

**FIGURE 11A
PRICE-CONSUMPTION CURVE**
A price-consumption curve depicts how consumption changes when relative prices change.

INDIFFERENCE ANALYSIS AND THE LAW OF DEMAND

Indifference analysis can be used to derive an individual's demand curve and demonstrate the law of demand. This demonstration is a *ceteris paribus* experiment in which the price of one good is changed. Part (*a*) of Figure 12A shows an indifference map and a budget line for goods *x* and *y*. The consumer is at an optimum at point *A*. At point *A*, the individual consumes x_1 units of good *x* at a price of P_{x_1}. Price and quantity demanded of good *x* are plotted in part (*b*). Now suppose the price of *x* falls to P_{x_2}. As

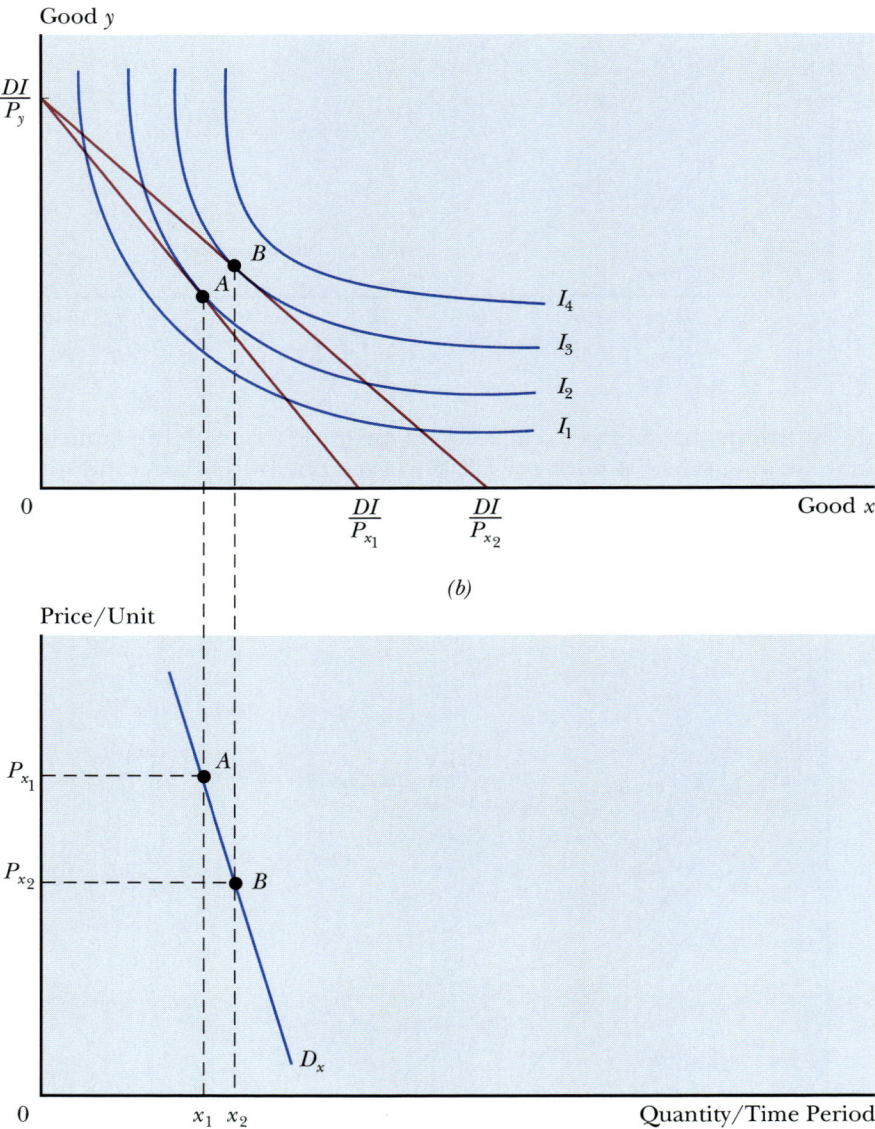

FIGURE 12A
DERIVING A DEMAND CURVE
When the price of good *x* decreases, the consumer can reach a higher indifference curve. This increased consumption of good *x* at a lower price means that the demand curve must have a negative slope.

before, this decline in price causes the budget line to rotate outward. A new optimum is reached at point B, where the new budget line is tangent to indifference curve I_3. The change in price has caused the quantity demanded to increase from x_1 to x_2, as shown in part (b). The line connecting two price-quantity points in part (b) is a demand curve for good x, and it has the usual negative slope.

Product Markets

3

> **AFTER STUDYING THIS CHAPTER, YOU SHOULD BE ABLE TO:**
>
> 1. Define the various types of firms, including profit-seeking firms, nonprofit private sector firms, and nonprofit governmental firms.
> 2. List the advantages and disadvantages of the various forms of business organization.
> 3. Calculate the least-cost method of production to determine economic efficiency.
> 4. Use a production function to explain increasing and diminishing returns.
> 5. Diagram total, average, and marginal product.
> 6. Show how a firm chooses its mix of inputs to maximize output.

CHAPTER 7
FIRMS AND PRODUCTION

production
The process of transforming inputs into marketable outputs.

INTRODUCTION

The next two chapters set the stage for examining the behavior of firms. Before we can analyze firms as sellers of products in different types of markets, we must look at how firms organize the process of production. The firm buys factors of production (also known as inputs) and attempts to transform them into marketable outputs. Remember that the factors of production are land, labor, capital, and enterprise. This chapter examines the process of transforming inputs into marketable outputs, which economists call **production**.

THE FIRM IN THEORY

It is easy to take the existence of firms for granted because we have all had dealings with many types of firms. We need to stop, however, to ask why firms exist. Economic theory recognizes that firms exist to accomplish certain economic objectives and are organized in different ways to meet those objectives.

HOUSEHOLDS AS FIRMS

In many ways, households compete with firms. Firms exist to organize production, and households also organize some production. Thus, there are aspects of household activities that are similar to the activities of firms. Firms put "things" together to make other "things" that have economic value. Households clearly do, too. Households cook meals, and so do restaurants. Households make clothes, and so do tailors. Households organize entertainment, and so do movie theaters.

An interesting economic question is why households don't do everything for themselves. Why don't they make their own cars, for example? That's an easy one. They don't make their own cars because it is more efficient for them to buy cars from firms that produce cars. It gets more difficult when we ask why households don't make their own granola or build their own homes. The answer is that some do. As the price of granola and homes produced by firms increases, more households may compete with organized business firms to produce their own products for consumption.

In fact, as relative market prices change, the kinds of production carried out by households change. In recent years, many households have

184

started to grow their own vegetables in response to rising food prices and the lifestyle changes that emphasize gourmet cooking with high-quality, organically grown vegetables. This home production, in turn, affected the demand for products of firms that produced canning equipment and related products.

WHAT BUSINESS FIRMS DO

Firms are organizations that plan production. They assign tasks, monitor those tasks, and generate incentives that reward individuals for completing assigned tasks. An important point is that there are many different sizes of firms. At one extreme, households behave like very small firms. At the other, governments can be seen as extremely large, multipurpose firms. In the Soviet Union, the government has historically acted as a single firm in that it plans, organizes, and provides incentives. As market reforms proceed in the Soviet Union, it will be interesting to watch how the relationship between firms and the government evolves. The Soviet Union has had central planning for so long that there are very few experienced entrepreneurs to take on the organizing function of business firms. This problem of reform in previously centrally planned economies will be discussed in detail in a later chapter.

Within the category of business firms, there is great diversity. Many firms in the U.S. economy are **vertically integrated firms**, which means they perform many steps in a production process. For example, a firm may grow cotton, weave cloth, dye the cloth, and finally sew it into garments. Firms that are not vertically integrated may simply weave cloth or make garments. Still others are **horizontally integrated firms**, which means that they perform many similar production operations in the same industry. For example, a firm may produce men's, women's and children's shoes. Some firms are **conglomerates**, which means that they engage in many, often quite unrelated, activities.

Economic theory should help to explain why these different organizations can all coexist in a market economy. Part of the answer to this question can be found in the incentives that bring about such organizations. Ronald Coase, in a now famous article, showed that transaction costs create firms.[1] He argued that buying and selling imposes costs. **Transaction costs** are costs associated with the conduct of a business. For example, organizing and negotiating involve costs. These transaction costs are minimized by the formation of firms. What Coase was talking about was the effort that a buyer and seller in a market economy must make in continually exploring options. Buyers must search for quality and price. Sellers must monitor the changing demands of buyers.

The transaction costs of these activities can often be reduced by carrying out more research and exploration within a firm. Workers agree to join a firm that provides a workplace, incentives, and guidelines. The firm exists because it economizes on the transaction costs. But the firm also faces constraints. Costs may rise as the size and complexity of the firm increase. Thus, smaller firms (maybe even households) will become potential competitors. In other words, firms exist in many organizational forms

vertically integrated firms
Firms that perform many sequential steps in a production process.

horizontally integrated firms
Firms that perform many similar production operations in the same industry.

conglomerates
Firms that perform many unrelated operations or produce many unrelated products or services.

transaction costs
Costs associated with the conduct of a business.

---

1. Ronald Coase, "The Nature of the Firm," *Economica* (November 1937): 286–405.

and sizes because various forms and sizes make the most efficient use of information and reduce transaction costs for different kinds of production activities.

Further developments in this theory of organization added other elements to the reasons why firms exist. Armen Alchian and Harold Demsetz added two important elements to this analysis.[2] First, firms exist because the production of many types of products is more efficiently carried out by teams than by individuals. **Teams** are groups of employees that work together to produce something. Firms exist to organize teams to produce goods or services efficiently. Second, when team production is not organized in a firm (as with volunteer activities), it is difficult to measure the contribution of the individual. There are incentives to **shirk**, to put forth less than the agreed-on effort.

The firm exists, then, to reward individuals for team effort and to monitor shirking behavior. Management is primarily responsible for developing organizational forms that use both negative and positive incentives in order to limit shirking.

teams
Groups of employees that work together to produce something.

shirk
To put forth less effort than agreed on.

THE BUSINESS FIRM IN PRACTICE

A **business firm** is organized by an entrepreneur (or group of entrepreneurs) to combine inputs of raw materials, capital, labor services, and technology in order to produce marketable outputs of goods and services. Firms are parts of industries. There are many ways to define an industry. In general, what economists mean by an **industry** is a group of firms producing similar or related products. For example, the automobile industry might include just the big three—General Motors, Ford, and Chrysler. Or the industry might also include all foreign auto makers selling in the U.S. market and all small domestic producers. It might also include firms that supply parts, materials, and services to automobile producers or automobile consumers. There are no absolute rules on how to define a specific industry. The definition usually depends on the purpose or the particular problem or issue being studied.

business firm
An organization formed by an entrepreneur to combine inputs in order to produce marketable outputs.

industry
A group of firms producing similar or related products.

FORMS OF ORGANIZATION

In the United States, firms are organized primarily in three ways. These categories are legal, not economic, and they differ mainly in the legal liability of the owners. Some interesting economic questions arise because of the different types of ownership and the different treatment under the law. These issues will become clearer as we proceed through the next six chapters.

SOLE PROPRIETORSHIPS. A **sole proprietorship** is a form of enterprise in which no legal distinction is made between the owner and the firm. The financial resources of the firm are limited to those of the individual owner and what can be borrowed from friends or financial institutions. Thus, the

sole proprietorship
A form of enterprise in which no legal distinction is made between the firm and its owner.

---

2. Armen A. Alchian and Harold Demsetz, "Production, Information Costs and Economic Organization," *American Economic Review* (December 1972): 777–795.

Chapter 7 Firms and Production   187

profits and losses accrue solely to that individual. The owner also bears unlimited liability for any and all debts of the firm. Success of the firm is success of the owner; bankruptcy of the firm is bankruptcy of the owner. This close relationship usually means a constant involvement of the owner with the affairs of the firm. There are obviously great incentives for hard work and diligence in a sole proprietorship.

Compared to other forms of business enterprise, a sole proprietorship can be established or go out of business very easily. In certain lines of business, government approval is required, because licenses or permits are needed. Typically, however, the sole proprietor starts or ends a business by simply doing so. The IRS reported that, in 1990, 69 percent of the business firms in the United States were sole proprietorships. Most farmers and many small firms, especially in retailing and services, are sole proprietorships. Although dominant in numbers, sole proprietorships account for only 10 percent of annual business sales.

PARTNERSHIPS. Partnerships are similar to sole proprietorships except they have more than one owner. The firm does not have a legal existence separate from the owners (the partners). Like sole proprietorships, firms organized as partnerships tend to be quite small. They are typically found in professional services: medicine, law, consulting, and financial services.

partnership
A form of enterprise in which there is more than one owner, and the firm does not have a legal existence separate from the owners.

There are more personal and financial resources available to a partnership than if only one person formed the firm. Besides funds, each partner may also bring special skills, knowledge, energy, or decision-making powers. Offsetting these advantages are the frictions that usually arise in operating the firm. Partners have to agree on the proportions of ownership owned by each partner, which may be dictated by the amounts of funds contributed, the amounts of work, or the amounts of other kinds of value contributed (such as ideas or patents). Partners also have to agree on joint rights and responsibilities. The partners share in any profits, but each partner bears unlimited liability for any debts incurred by the firm.

The disadvantages of a partnership arrangement apparently outweigh the advantages. The IRS reports that, in 1990, only 10 percent of the business firms and only 5 percent of annual business sales in the United States were accounted for by partnerships.

CORPORATIONS. The dominant form of business organization in the United States, measured in any way except absolute numbers, is the corporate form. A corporation is more formal and complex than the other types of business organization. A **corporation** is a form of enterprise in which persons who own shares of stock are the owners of the firm. Owners of a corporation are called **stockholders**. The legal liability of stockholders is limited. The IRS reports that, in 1990, corporations accounted for 21 percent of business firms and about 85 percent of annual business sales.

corporation
A form of enterprise in which stockholders are the owners of the firm but have limited liability.

stockholders
The owners of a corporation.

The number of stockholders may run into the hundreds of thousands, although some corporations have only a few stockholders. The stockholders vote, according to the number of shares they hold, for a board of directors. The board, in turn, appoints officers of the corporation to manage it along the guidelines set by the charter of incorporation and the di-

International Perspective

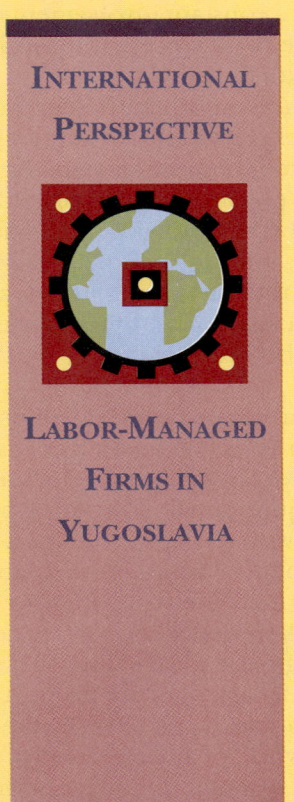

Labor-Managed Firms in Yugoslavia

In the United States, there have been few experiments with labor-managed firms. In contrast, almost all firms in Yugoslavia are owned and managed by the workers. This type of firm might become more popular as the nations of Eastern Europe struggle with reform in the 1990s. This hybrid form of organization may appeal to reformers in countries such as Poland and Romania because it has a somewhat Marxist flavor to it.

In the United States, worker management exists in a few craft industries and has been attempted in a few instances when manufacturing plants were about to close, mostly in the steel industry. The closest parallel to a labor-managed firm in the United States is profit sharing by labor in some industries. In Yugoslavia, however, the workers actually own the plant and decide how it will be managed through councils. The ownership rights end when a worker leaves the firm, so these ownership rights are different from stockholder rights in U.S. corporations. The labor-managed firm is an interesting concept for a socialist country because such worker democracy is closer to Marxist philosophy than the state-owned and -managed firms that exist in most communist countries. The question for economists is how such organization and control by workers affects incentives and ultimately the economic development of the country.

Entrepreneurs maximize profits. If the firm is owned by workers, will something other than profit be maximized? Worker self-management means that workers may seek to maximize wages and other benefits that they can capture while they are with the firm. Since workers have no ownership rights that they can sell, they may opt for a management policy that increases the short-term income of the firm over policies that would increase the firm's value over time. This bias would tend to reduce the firm's investments, which in turn (in the aggregate) would reduce the long-term economic growth of the country.

rectors. A **board of directors** consists of individuals elected by the stockholders of a corporation to select the managers and oversee the management of the corporation.

One of the strengths of the corporate form of business organization is the relative ease of acquiring capital. Capital is often acquired by issuing shares of **stock**, which are certificates of ownership in a corporation. A corporation can borrow funds by issuing **bonds**, which are interest-bearing certificates issued by governments or corporations. A corporation can also borrow directly by taking out loans from banks or other financial agencies. (Only the third option for obtaining outside funding is available to partnerships and sole proprietorships.)

The attractiveness of the corporation as a form of organization stems from the fact that the stockholders are the legal owners and have rights to the profits, but their legal liability is very limited. **Limited liability** means that the stockholders of a corporation cannot be sued for failure of the corporation to pay its debts. Only the corporation itself can be sued. This limited liability is the critical advantage of the corporate form of business. In many countries, corporations are referred to as limited liability companies, and the letters Ltd. appear after the name of the firm. The letters Inc. (Incorporated) after the name of a firm in the United States mean the same thing. Thus, a corporation, defined in law as a legal person in its own right, can go bankrupt without the owners going bankrupt. Of course, individuals who have most of their wealth in the stock of one corporation might go bankrupt because the stock would no longer have any value.

A second important advantage of corporate organization is the ease of transferring ownership. Ownership rights can be transferred through the sale of stocks, and markets (stock exchanges) have evolved to handle such transfers. The costs of transfer of ownership are for this reason significantly lower for corporations than for partnerships or sole proprietorships. The major drawback of corporate organization is double taxation. Corporate income is subject to corporate income taxes, and then part of that income is taxed again when it is distributed to stockholders as dividends.

In the late 1980s, a hybrid type of corporation evolved very rapidly in the United States. The **S corporation** enjoys some of the advantages of a corporation, most notably limited liability, but is not subject to double taxation. The income of an S corporation is simply passed to the owners and only taxed once as personal income. Most S corporations tend to be relatively small. The S corporation is replacing sole proprietorships and partnerships as a form of business organization in many industries.

Different types of ownership cause managers of firms to behave in different ways. For instance, an owner-manager of a sole proprietorship may make decisions that are different from those of the hired manager of a large corporation, because the owner-manager benefits more directly from higher profits. For now, we will ignore such differences. We'll assume that business firms, however they are organized, exist for only one purpose—to increase the wealth of their owners. To do this, firms try to maximize profits. This assumption of profit maximization makes it possible to develop a powerful theory to predict the economic effects of different market structures.

board of directors
The individuals elected by the stockholders of a corporation to select the managers and oversee the management of the corporation.

stocks
Certificates of ownership in a corporation.

bonds
Interest-earning certificates issued by governments or corporations in exchange for borrowed funds.

limited liability
The fact that the stockholders of a corporation cannot be sued for failure of the corporation to meet its obligations.

S corporation
A hybrid type of corporation that passes income directly to the owners, avoiding the double taxation of corporate profits.

FORMS OF ORGANIZATION	
• Sole proprietorship	No legal distinction between owner and firm Financial resources limited to those of owner Profits accrue solely to owner Owner is liable for debts
• Partnership	More than one owner Partners bring different skills and greater financial resources Partners share profits and legal liability
• Corporation	The legal liability of stockholders is limited Board of directors oversees management Ownership is transferred with ease Face double taxation, except S corporations

ENTERPRISE, ENTREPRENEURS, AND THE FIRM

Enterprise is the factor of production provided by an entrepreneur. The entrepreneur is the founder and often the guiding spirit of a business firm. Many business schools now offer courses in entrepreneurship. But what is it that entrepreneurs do? They identify consumer demands, organize production, allocate resources, and acquire assets. In the process, they take risks. Entrepreneurs are rewarded with profits if they have good hunches or go bankrupt if they are wrong. Many more go bankrupt than succeed, yet we read in the newspapers about the most successful. A *Fortune* survey about getting rich in America concluded that "most successful entrepreneurs didn't start out as fortune seekers; they were pursuing visions, not the almighty buck."[3]

More than 4 million men and women operate small businesses in the United States, employing about 10 percent of all workers. Two economists who have looked at the characteristics of entrepreneurs found that age and labor market experience have no bearing on the likelihood of becoming an entrepreneur.[4] They also found that men who have been unemployed and changed jobs frequently have a higher probability of becoming self-employed. This finding is consistent with the view of sociologists that entrepreneurs are "misfits." Also, individuals who score high on a psychological test known as the Rotter Scale have a higher propensity to start a new business. This test measures the belief that personal success depends largely on one's internal locus of control.

THE NONPROFIT FIRM

Although economic models assume that business firms exist to maximize profits or wealth, an increasingly large number of firms are organized as nonprofit organizations. These firms differ from for-profit firms mainly

---

3. Monci Jo Williams, "How the Wealthy Get That Way," *Fortune* (13 April 1987): 38.
4. David S. Evans and Linda Leighton, "Some Empirical Aspects of Entrepreneurship," *American Economic Review* (June 1989): 519–535.

in that they do not have a residual claimant. A **residual claimant** is an individual, or group of individuals, who shares in the profits (if any) of an enterprise. Thus, it is difficult to determine who owns a nonprofit organization. We can separate nonprofits into two categories: those in the private sector and those in the government sector.

residual claimant
Individual, or group of individuals, who shares in the profits of an enterprise.

NONPROFITS IN THE PRIVATE SECTOR

Nonprofit firms in the private sector are not part of, or sponsored directly by, a governmental unit. They exist for many reasons. Many of them (for example, health clinics and soup kitchens) are engaged in private transfers. Some provide collective goods that cannot conveniently be provided through government.

The manager (organizer) of a private nonprofit firm usually receives a salary for managing the firm. Economists expect more shirking behavior to occur in these firms because the manager cannot convert increased efficiencies into profits that affect his or her salary. Such shirking behavior has been documented by economist Kenneth Clarkson.[5] He found that nonprofit hospitals had higher budgeted expenses for supervisory positions than for-profit hospitals did. The chief manager of a nonprofit hospital was also much less concerned with the price and productivity of equipment. Automatic, across-the-board pay increases were more frequent in nonprofit hospitals. This method of giving raises is a type of shirking behavior. It would require more effort to separate good employees from bad employees.

Most economists would argue that nonprofit firms have significant organizational disadvantages that introduce inefficiencies. Yet nonprofits have increased rapidly in recent years. Why have they become such a popular form of organization? Earl Thompson has suggested an answer.[6] He points out that most nonprofit firms are associated with charitable organizations. Contributors to these charitable organizations are usually remote from the production or use of the product or service they are supporting. These contributors would have a difficult time monitoring the managers of these firms. They wouldn't be able to determine easily whether a manager was using their gift to produce the charitable product or was simply "taking it home" in the form of higher wages. However, tolerating the inefficiencies caused by managers who are not profit seekers is less costly to contributors than is monitoring manager behavior. As a result, charitable donors accept some inefficiency in preference to supporting the provision of the products or services through the for-profit or governmental sector. Thompson argues that one way to lessen the problem is to specify certain salaries for the managers.

It is also true that tax laws play a role in encouraging the formation of nonprofit organizations. In some cases, individuals can create nonprofit firms that produce output for their own consumption. They can then support this production through tax-deductible "charitable" contributions. You might, for example, create a nonprofit organization to support the

---

5. Kenneth W. Clarkson, "Some Implications of Property Rights in Hospital Management," *Journal of Law and Economics* (October 1972): 363–384.
6. Earl Thompson, "Charity and Nonprofit Organizations," in *The Economics of Nonproprietary Organizations*, eds. K. W. Clarkson and D. C. Martin (Greenwich, CT: JAI Press, 1980): 125–128.

local theatre in which you act and make tax-deductible gifts to this nonprofit organization.

NONPROFITS IN THE GOVERNMENT SECTOR

Everyone does business with some nonprofit governmental firms. Often these firms compete directly with private, business firms. The U.S. Postal Service competes with United Parcel Service and Federal Express. City and county hospitals compete with private hospitals. Municipal golf and tennis clubs compete with private country clubs. City bus lines compete with private cab companies. Public and private colleges and universities compete for students. The list goes on and on.

What characterizes these governmental firms? To begin, like a private nonprofit firm, a governmental nonprofit has no profit and no residual claimant to that profit. Second, the manager of a governmental nonprofit usually has little control over price. If a price is charged, it is usually set by a board or some political entity. The price is often below the operating costs of the firm. In addition, the customers often cannot influence the behavior of the organization. Customers can express frustration with a private firm by switching to a competing firm. This is not always possible when dealing with a governmental firm.

The tendency to shirk is prevalent in governmental firms for the same reasons as in private nonprofits. In addition, a bureaucratic manager can get promoted by being "better" than other bureaucratic managers. In many instances, causing the agency to grow is taken as a sign of success and a cause for advancement. We will discuss this bureaucratic incentive in the chapter on market and government failure.

Some economists argue that the quality of products produced by governmental nonprofit firms is likely to be poorer than that of similar private, for-profit firms. This poorer quality results from the fact that prices charged by the governmental organization are usually lower. Customers will often choose the low-priced product or service, even though it is of lower quality. Research on Veterans Administration hospitals in comparison to private, for-profit hospitals supports this observation.[7]

WHAT ABOUT THE PROFITS OF NONPROFIT FIRMS?

In recent years, many private and governmental nonprofit organizations have entered into profit-making activities. The profits from these activities are often referred to instead as "excess of revenues over expenses." Hospitals are selling health-related equipment, universities are selling in-company training programs, university presses are producing best sellers, alumni groups are selling tours, and religious organizations are selling condos at theme parks. Profits from such activities are not taxed because they are intertwined with the nonprofit firms' noncommercial activities.

In addition, nonprofit firms may have the advantages of access to referrals and free space for doing business. They can also use bulk mail instead of paying first-class rates, as the private sector must. These factors give a cost advantage to these firms over private-sector firms in the same business.

---

7. See C. M. Lindsay, "A Theory of Government Enterprise," *Journal of Political Economy* (October 1976): 1061–1077.

Delegates to the 1990 White House Conference on Small Business voted that the second biggest problem facing small businesses was nonprofit organizations using their tax-exempt status to compete with the private sector. (This problem ranked after government-mandated employee benefits and before liability insurance.) This subsidized competition from nonprofit organizations has led private-sector firms to pressure the U.S. Congress to change the law as it relates to profit-making activities of tax-exempt nonprofit organizations. In the late 1980s, the House Ways and Means Committee held hearings on the tax status of nonprofit organizations. As one witness from New Jersey put it, "I'm not opposed to the Girl Scouts having an annual cookie sale, but if the Girl Scouts want to open a cookie store next door to a Mrs. Fields cookie store, they should have to pay the same taxes."[8]

ECONOMIC EFFICIENCY

The firms that produce most of the U.S. output are private, profit-maximizing firms. An entrepreneur must combine resources efficiently if the firm is to maximize profits.[9] To do this, entrepreneurs must decide among competing ways of producing a given product. Suppose, for example, that the printer producing this textbook was faced with the alternatives listed in Table 1. The production engineer told the production manager that 100,000 copies could be produced in any of these four ways. The production manager informs the president and CEO of the firm, the entrepreneur, who must decide how to actually produce the textbooks. The entrepreneur must have a decision rule in order to select a production alternative. This is where profit maximization comes into play. Without profit maximization as a goal, the entrepreneur might choose on some other basis, such as a consideration of physical units of input or output.

**TABLE 1
ALTERNATIVE WAYS TO PRODUCE 100,000 COPIES OF THIS TEXTBOOK**

METHOD	CAPITAL (MACHINES)	PRICE OF CAPITAL SERVICES (PER MACHINE)	LABOR (WORKER-YEARS)	PRICE OF LABOR SERVICES (PER WORKER-YEAR)	LAND (ACRES)	PRICE OF LAND SERVICES (PER ACRE)	TOTAL COST
A	5	$30,000	5	$4,000	1	$10,000	$150,000 + $ 20,000 + $10,000 = $180,000
B	4	30,000	10	4,000	1	10,000	$120,000 + $ 40,000 + $10,000 = $170,000
C	3	30,000	15	4,000	1	10,000	$ 90,000 + $ 60,000 + $10,000 = $160,000
D	2	30,000	25	4,000	1	10,000	$ 60,000 + $100,000 + $10,000 = $170,000

8. "Profits? Who, Me?" *Forbes* (23 March 1987): 108.
9. Entrepreneurs combine factors of production, inputs, or resources. Economists use all three of these terms synonymously. Historically, factors of production was most commonly used. In this book, we use all three, but when we want to be precise, we usually fall back on factors of production.

technical efficiency
The basis for minimizing the physical inputs to a production method according to some specific rule (an engineering concept).

The method that would minimize the inputs in a physical sense would be method A, which uses the fewest inputs. The basis for choosing this method is technical efficiency. **Technical efficiency** refers to the minimizing of the physical inputs to a production method according to some specific rule. It is an engineering concept with little economic relevance. The drawback of this decision rule is that it requires the decision maker to compare physical units of such diverse inputs as machines, acres of land, and worker-years of labor.

Technical efficiency has been widely used in command economies, such as that of the Soviet Union. The reforms in the Soviet Union and Eastern Europe have put this type of decision rule in question. In the 1990s, these countries will be struggling to replace such calculations with more appropriate decision rules.

A market system puts the inputs into dollar terms and lets the entrepreneur choose the least-cost method of producing. The least-cost method, or the economically efficient method, is chosen by the entrepreneur because of the assumption of attempted profit maximization. **Economic efficiency** is therefore defined as the least-cost method of production. In Table 1, the entrepreneur would choose method C to produce the textbooks. Regardless of the price of the textbooks, method C maximizes profits (or minimizes losses) because costs are minimized. However, the entrepreneur must know the prices of the various inputs in order to make this choice. This price information is not usually available in a command economy. Lack of market price information is one of the major problems facing the command economies of Eastern Europe as they try to implement reforms.

economic efficiency
The least-cost method of production.

PRODUCTION FUNCTIONS IN THE SHORT AND LONG RUN

production function
A description of the amounts of output expected from various combinations of inputs.

A **production function** is a description of the amounts of output expected from various combinations of inputs. It is usually expressed in the form of a table or graph, but it also can be shown by a mathematical formula. The production function describes a technical or technological relationship. The input combinations and the corresponding output quantities are determined by engineers, agronomists, chemists, or other technical experts.

Only the technically efficient input combinations are included. For example, it might be that an output of 100 units could be produced by 5 units of capital, 20 units of labor, and 2 units of land or by 6 units of capital, 30 units of labor, and 3 units of land. The second combination is inferior to the first because it takes more of all inputs to produce the same output. That method of production would be ignored. The production function reflects the most efficient technology available to produce a given level of output.

fixed factors
The factors of production that cannot be varied in the short run.

Usually entrepreneurs are interested in only a portion of the production function. For instance, it is often convenient to ask what would happen to total production if all but one of the inputs were at a given level. When considering a production function, it is possible to distinguish between fixed factors and variable factors. **Fixed factors** are the factors of

Economists view a firm, whether a sole proprietorship or a corporation, as existing to make profits for the owners. Some economists argue that it is improper for a corporation to be involved in philanthropy (charity) because it is giving away the profits of its stockholders. They argue that the profits should be distributed to the stockholders, who can give it to charity themselves if they wish. However, corporations have been giving money to various causes for decades. For many years, this corporate giving was at the whim of the CEO, or whoever had the ear of the CEO. In recent years, the pattern has changed dramatically. Corporate giving is more likely to be based on self-interest, accountability, and cause-related marketing.

Corporate philanthropy is big business. More than $5 billion was given away in 1990. American Express started cause-related marketing with its promise to earmark a portion of its revenue to the Statue of Liberty restoration program. That identified American Express with patriotism. Ben Cohen (of Ben & Jerry's Ice Cream) has set up a company that will give 40 percent of the revenue from the flavor Rainforest Crunch to protect the Amazon rainforest. Such gifts serve worthy causes while creating a good image and potential future customers. An investment in philanthropy may make a corporation even more profitable in the long run.

The biggest givers in corporate America are some of the biggest corporations. The table lists seven of these and the main beneficiaries of their corporate largesse. You will notice from the table that corporations tend to support universities. Often these gifts are to universities in the corporation's geographic area or universities that do research of immediate benefit to the corporation. Other corporate gifts are made to promote affirmative action goals or community development in the region in which the corporation is located. In some cases, the tie between the company and the recipient is clearly business-related. Time Warner, Inc. combats illiteracy by selling its Time to Read Program to other corporate sponsors.

ECONOMIC INSIGHT

CORPORATE PHILANTHROPY

CORPORATION	RECIPIENTS
IBM	Recipients not made public!
General Motors	University of Michigan, GM Cancer Research Foundation
Exxon	New Jersey Science-Technology Center, Community Summer Jobs Program
Hewlett-Packard	MIT, Stanford University Hospital
RJR/Nabisco	University of Delaware, West End Neighborhood House
AT&T	Stanford University, National Urban League

Source: "What's in It for Me?" *Business Month* (November 1989).

variable factors
The factors of production that can be increased or decreased in the short run.

production that cannot be varied in the short run, such as the size of the plant. **Variable factors** are the factors of production that can be increased or decreased in the short run. Which factors are fixed and which are variable usually depends on the problem under consideration. In many cases, however, the land and the buildings of a firm (the physical plant) are considered fixed factors and labor the variable factor.

When economists distinguish between fixed and variable factors, they are referring to a time period called the short run. In this context, the **short run** is the period of time that is too short to vary all the factors of production. The **long run** is the period of time in which all inputs, including plant and equipment, can be varied. Short-run decisions are those concerning the profit-maximizing use of the existing (fixed) plant and equipment. The plant is used more intensively by increasing the amount of variable factors, such as labor or new machines. Long-run decisions are those concerning the selection of a plant size that will maximize profits.

short run
The period of time that is too short to vary all the factors of production.

long run
The period of time in which all inputs, including plant and equipment, can be varied.

These time horizons cannot be defined in the calendar sense, because they are different in different industries. In some industries, firms may be able to increase in size very rapidly. In some cases, contractions can occur more quickly, depending on whether the plant and equipment are adaptable for other uses. It is primarily for convenience of analysis that decisions are classed as being either short-run or long-run. Keep in mind that such decisions are inherently interrelated. Once a long-run decision to build a plant of a certain size is made, a whole series of short-run decisions are affected because they must deal with that size of plant.

Increasing and Decreasing Returns

As more and more units of a variable factor are added to a set of fixed factors, the resulting additions to output will eventually become smaller. This economic conclusion is referred to as the **principle of diminishing returns**. It is easy to see that returns must eventually diminish. Otherwise, all the wheat needed to feed the world could be produced on one acre of land by simply adding more seed, more fertilizer, more water, and more labor.

principle of diminishing returns
The fact that as more and more units of a variable factor are added to a set of fixed factors, the resulting additions to output eventually become smaller.

The principle of diminishing returns is a fascinating and pervasive phenomenon. The principle is almost never contradicted by real-world observations. A tree grows more slowly as it grows larger. Little pigs put on more weight from a given amount of corn than big ones do. It is more costly to add a floor to a twenty-story building than to a ten-story building. Adding water to parched soil yields remarkable crop improvement, but adding the same amount of water to already moist soil has very little effect. If a firm adds a worker when its labor force is already large, the increase in output is less than if a worker is added at a time when the labor force is small. These are only a few examples of the principle of diminishing returns.

Note that the principle of diminishing returns applies to the short run and says nothing about the long-run production function. It only says that if more and more variable input is added to a fixed factor, after a while the return will decline. Think of your own experience in studying for exams. The output is your test score, and the variable factor is the time you spend studying. Assume that you could get a score of 55 percent without studying. One hour of studying would boost your score to 66 percent, two hours to 75 percent, three hours to 80 percent, four hours to 84 percent, five hours to 86 percent, and so on. Each additional unit of variable input (hour spent studying) produces a smaller increment in output (improvement in test score). The first hour of studying produces an improvement of 11 percentage points, the second hour yields 9 points, the third hour 5 points, and so on. There is a diminishing return to studying. It is up to you to decide when the return for an additional hour of studying is not worth the opportunity cost of that hour in terms of the other things you could be doing. So you see, even deciding how much to study is an exercise in rational economic choice.

AVERAGE AND MARGINAL RELATIONSHIPS

There is a very important relationship between average values and marginal values. Think of your grade point average. If your grade in this course (the marginal grade) is below your grade point average for all courses you have taken, your average will fall. If your grade in this course is above your grade point average, your average will rise. If a basketball player's lifetime shooting percentage (average) is higher this week than last week, you know that in the intervening games, the player has shot higher-than-average (marginal) percentages. If a marginal value is above average, it will pull the average up. If the average value is falling, the marginal value must be below the average.

In production, the important relationship of marginal and average values is between marginal physical product and average physical product. In order to describe more precisely the relationship between inputs and outputs, economists use the concept of the marginal physical product. **Marginal physical product (*MPP*)** is the change in total output that is produced by a unit change in a factor of production. The marginal physical product of labor, for example, is the change in total output per unit change in the use of labor service. That is,

$$MPP_L = \frac{\Delta TPP}{\Delta L},$$

where MPP_L is the marginal physical product of labor, ΔTPP is the change in the total physical product, and ΔL is the change in the number of units of labor employed. The **total physical product (*TPP*)** is the amount of output that a firm produces in physical units. The **average physical product (*APP*)** of a factor of production is simply the total physical product divided by the number of units of the factor employed. For example, the average physical product of capital (APP_K) is

$$APP_K = \frac{TPP}{K},$$

where K is the number of units of capital used.

Table 2 illustrates these relationships for a short-run production function. All the factors of production are fixed except labor. Labor, the variable input, can vary between 1 and 10 units. In Table 2, as more variable input is added to the fixed inputs, output goes through three distinct

marginal physical product (*MPP*)
The change in total output that is produced by a unit change in a factor of production.

total physical product (*TPP*)
The amount of output that a firm produces in physical units.

average physical product (*APP*)
The total physical product (output) divided by the number of units of a factor used.

TABLE 2
A SHORT-RUN PRODUCTION FUNCTION

VARIABLE INPUT (UNITS OF LABOR)	TOTAL PHYSICAL PRODUCT (UNITS OF OUTPUT)	MARGINAL PHYSICAL PRODUCT OF LABOR	AVERAGE PHYSCIAL PRODUCT OF LABOR
1	6	6	6.0
2	14	8	7.0
3	24	10	8.0
4	32	8	8.0
5	38	6	7.6
6	42	4	7.0
7	44	2	6.3
8	44	0	5.5
9	42	−2	4.7
10	36	−6	3.6

stages. When the first three units of labor are added, output increases at an increasing rate. That is, the marginal physical product of labor is increasing. Adding the fourth unit of labor causes output to increase but by a smaller amount than for the third unit of labor. The marginal physical product of labor is now declining. The eighth unit of labor produces no increase in output, and the ninth and tenth units of labor actually cause total output to fall.

Figure 1 shows the relationships of Table 2 in graphical form. From zero to L_1 units of labor, the total physical product is increasing at an increasing rate. This means that marginal physical product and average physical product of labor are also increasing. At L_1, the marginal physical product of labor reaches its maximum. From L_1 to L_3, total physical product is increasing at a decreasing rate. This is the region of diminishing returns. The marginal physical product of labor is declining throughout this range. At L_2, the average physical product of labor is at its maximum. At L_3, the total physical product reaches its maximum. Adding further units of labor produces no more output. The marginal physical product of labor is equal to zero at L_3.

THE CHOICE OF INPUTS

We can use the concepts of production function and diminishing returns to consider the choice of a production method. Earlier in this chapter, we demonstrated the concept of economic efficiency by showing how a printer might choose to produce this textbook. We can now add complexity and realism to this example.

Assume that we are again looking at the production of textbooks by a firm that is of a given size. This means that the firm is in the short run and, as a result, its size cannot be altered. Let's also assume that there are only two variable inputs: labor and printing presses. Table 3 shows the possible quantities of labor and printing presses and their corresponding marginal physical products. You can see from those values that this firm is in the range of diminishing returns. This corresponds to the range between L_1 and L_3 in Figure 1.

Chapter 7   Firms and Production   199

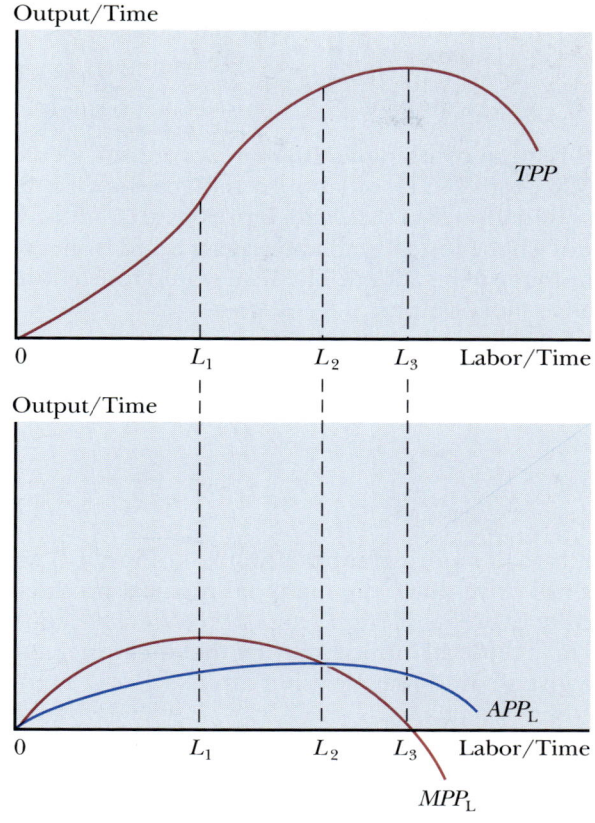

FIGURE 1
PRODUCT CURVES
When *TPP* is increasing at an increasing rate, *MPP* is increasing. When *TPP* is increasing at a decreasing rate, *MPP* is diminishing. When *TPP* is at a maximum, *MPP* is equal to zero.

The question facing the firm is to determine which combination of labor and presses will produce the largest amount of textbooks for a given expenditure of dollars. Let's say that presses cost $2 per unit per day, labor costs $1 per unit per day, and the firm has a budget of $26 per day.

The firm will maximize output by using labor and presses to the extent that will make their marginal physical products per dollar spent equal. This is written as follows:

$$\frac{MPP_L}{P_L} = \frac{MPP_P}{P_P}.$$

VARIABLE INPUT— LABOR (UNITS)	MARGINAL PHYSICAL PRODUCT OF LABOR (MPP_L)	VARIABLE INPUT— PRESSES (UNITS)	MARGINAL PHYSICAL PRODUCT OF PRESSES (MPP_P)
7	6	5	10
8	5	6	9
9	4	7	8
10	3	8	6
11	1	9	3
12	0	10	0

TABLE 3
FACTOR INPUTS FOR PRINTING THIS TEXTBOOK AND THEIR MARGINAL PHYSICAL PRODUCTS

The firm would use 10 units of labor and 8 presses per day because

$$\frac{3}{\$1} = \frac{6}{\$2}.$$

You can easily see why this input combination maximizes output, given a spending constraint of $26. Add 2 units of labor to replace the eighth press, for example. This combination also costs $26. If presses are reduced from 8 to 7, 2 units of output will be lost, and if labor is increased from 10 to 12 units, only 1 unit of output will be added. The firm would lose a unit of output with this alternative mix of inputs.

We now can see that a firm maximizes output by choosing its mix of inputs so that the marginal physical product of a dollar's worth of each input is equal to the marginal physical product of a dollar's worth of every other input. If

$$\frac{MPP_a}{P_a} > \frac{MPP_b}{P_b},$$

the firm reallocates its inputs to use more of input a and less of input b. As the firm uses more of a, it will drive down the marginal physical product of a and bring about equality between MPP_a/P_a and MPP_b/P_b. This conclusion can be generalized to include all inputs by saying that the firm maximizes its production for a given cost outlay by using inputs ($a, b, \ldots, n$) so that

$$\frac{MPP_a}{P_a} = \frac{MPP_b}{P_b} = \cdots = \frac{MPP_n}{P_n}.$$

You will note that the principles developed here are very similar to those developed for utility analysis. According to utility theory, the consumer maximizes utility for a given income, or budget constraint. Here the firm maximizes output given a cost constraint. The principles of maximization are the same.

ON TO COSTS

The principles of production are a foundation for analyzing costs. In the next chapter, we will see how production functions and the principle of diminishing returns relate to the cost functions firms face.

PRODUCTION FUNCTIONS AND INPUTS

- At least one input is fixed in the short run.
- All inputs are variable in the long run.
- The marginal physical product of an input is the change in output produced by a one-unit change in that input.
- Diminishing returns is a short-run phenomenon.
- If the marginal physical product is negative, total physical product is declining.

Chapter 7 Firms and Production

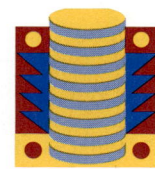

Summary

1. Firms are organized by entrepreneurs to produce outputs by combining inputs. The entrepreneur does this in such a way as to maximize profits.
2. Nonprofit firms, both private and governmental, face different incentives than for-profit firms do because nonprofit firms have no residual claimants.
3. Sole proprietorships are the dominant form of business organization by number. Corporations account for about 85 percent of annual business sales in the United States. S corporations have become popular because they are not subject to double taxation of corporate profits.
4. Economic efficiency is the basis for selecting that combination of resources that minimizes the cost of producing a certain level of output.
5. A production function is the technical relationship between factors of production and outputs.
6. In the short run, some factors are fixed. In the long run, all factors are variable.
7. In the short run, as variable factors are added to fixed factors, the firm may experience increasing returns at low levels of output but eventually will incur diminishing returns at some higher levels of output.
8. Firms choose their input mix from the production function to maximize output subject to cost constraints.

New Terms

production
vertically integrated firms
horizontally integrated firms
conglomerates
transaction costs
teams
shirk

business firm
industry
sole proprietorship
partnership
corporation
stockholders
board of directors
stocks
bonds

limited liability
S corporation
residual claimant
technical efficiency
economic efficiency
production function
fixed factors
variable factors
short run

long run
principle of diminishing returns
marginal physical product (*MPP*)
total physical product (*TPP*)
average physical product (*APP*)

Questions for Discussion

1. How does the short run differ from the long run? What would the short run be for farming, for a lemonade stand, and for electricity generation?
2. Is there a parallel between diminishing marginal utility in consumption and diminishing returns in production? Describe any similarities you see.
3. List some of the differences you have observed between private for-profit firms and nonprofit firms that produce the same good.
4. In professional sports, there are very few player-coaches. Yet many players become coaches immediately after their playing days end. Can you think of any reasons why this may be the case, based on economic theories of why firms are formed and what managers do in these firms?
5. Suppose the following production function describes three ways to produce 1,000 shirts in a sewing factory.

Method	Units of Capital (Sewing Machines)	Units of Labor (Sewer Weeks)	Units of Land (Acres)	Units Output (Shirts)
A	4	60	$\frac{1}{5}$	1,000
B	10	10	$\frac{1}{5}$	1,000
C	30	5	$\frac{1}{5}$	1,000

If you were the plant manager of this sewing factory, which method of production would you choose?

6. If the cost basis of the capital services of sewing machines in Question 5 is $3,000 per 1,000 shirts and the wage rate is $6.25 per hour (forty-hour week), which method of production would you choose?

7. What would happen to your choice of inputs if the sewing factory in Question 5 were successfully unionized and the union contract specified a wage rate of $10.65 per hour?

8. The price of land was irrelevant to your decision in Questions 5–7 because the plant uses $\frac{1}{5}$ of an acre of land for all three methods of production. What would your reaction be (as plant manager) if the governor in a neighboring state offered you free land in an industrial park and forgave all property taxes on that land for 10 years?

9. Classify the firm resulting from each of the following mergers as vertically integrated, horizontally integrated, or a conglomerate.
   a. An oil company buys a chain of gas stations.
   b. A cosmetics company buys a financial institution.
   c. An airline buys a travel agency.
   d. An airline buys an interstate bus line.
   e. A movie company buys a television studio.
   f. A supermarket chain buys a rental car company.

10. Deming management, quality circles, and similar techniques that increase worker involvement in the manufacturing process have become popular. These techniques are sometimes referred to as the Japanese style of management. How does such a style of management address the problem of shirking behavior?

11. Should corporate philanthropy be applauded or condemned from the standpoint of economic efficiency?

12. What is the advantage of an S corporation?

13. Why must the marginal physical product of labor be equal to zero at the point where the total physical product is at its peak?

14. Your grades on weekly quizzes are 90, 85, 75, 65, 90, and 95. What was your average grade after three weeks, four weeks, and five weeks? When your average fell, was the marginal grade below or above the average? What about when your average rose?

15. The typical isoquant curve is curved and convex to the origin. What does this shape imply?

SUGGESTIONS FOR FURTHER READING

Eckert, Ross D. *The Price System and Resource Allocation*, 10th ed. Hinsdale, IL: Dryden Press, 1988. An intermediate text that goes into greater detail on some of the topics discussed in this chapter.

Lindsay, Cotton M. *Applied Price Theory*. Hinsdale, IL: Dryden Press, 1984. An intermediate price theory text that develops the material found in this chapter in much greater detail.

Moore, John H. *Growth With Self-Management*. Stanford, CA: Hoover Institution Press, 1980. A very readable account of the economics of labor-managed firms.

White, Michelle J., ed. *Nonprofit Firms in a Three Sector Economy*. Washington, DC: Urban Institute Press, 1981. A collection of articles looking at the behavior of private nonprofit firms.

Chapter 7 Firms and Production

APPENDIX: PRODUCER CHOICE

If you have not already done so, you should study the preceding chapter's appendix, which describes indifference analysis and consumer choice. A similar approach can be used to analyze producer choice.

ISOQUANT CURVES

An **isoquant** (called a producer indifference curve by some economists) is a curve that shows all combinations of quantities of two inputs that can be used to produce a given quantity of output. ("Isoquant" means equal quantity.) Along an isoquant, the amount of output produced remains the same, but the combinations of inputs vary. There is a separate isoquant for each level of output.

Suppose Eric, an entrepreneur, is considering the use of the different combinations of capital and labor shown in Table 1A. Combination A consists of 16 units of labor (measured in person-years) and 3 units of capital (measured in number of machines used per year). Combination B is 12 units of labor and 4 units of capital. Eric states that neither combination A nor combination B is preferred. They are equal with respect to the amount of output he expects to produce, and therefore, in the absence of prices, he is indifferent between these input combinations. When Eric considers input combinations C, D, and E, he has the same response because they all produce the same output, 1,000 dozen shirts. Such production choices can be plotted as an isoquant curve. An isoquant curve corresponding to the production choices in Table 1A is shown in Figure 1A. The isoquant curve shows all combinations of two inputs that produce a given output.

Input combinations lying on a higher isoquant curve are associated with larger quantities of output. As Eric moves from I_1 to I_2 to I_3 to I_4 in Figure 2A, he is producing more output. Figure 2A is an isoquant map. An isoquant map makes it possible to compare points representing combinations of inputs x and y so as to determine whether the producer prefers one such combination. All points on any single isoquant curve represent the same level of output. Points on isoquant curves located to the right of and above a particular curve are combinations that produce greater levels of output.

The typical isoquant curve has a negative slope, which means that in order to produce the constant output, some extra amount of one input is necessary to compensate for the loss of some amount of the other. In other words, each combination of two inputs on the same isoquant curve

isoquant
A curve that shows all combinations of two inputs that can be used to produce a given output.

TABLE 1A
INPUT COMBINATIONS FOR PRODUCING 1,000 DOZEN SHIRTS

COMBINATION	INPUT X (LABOR)	INPUT Y (CAPITAL)
A	16	3
B	12	4
C	10	5
D	8	7
E	6	9

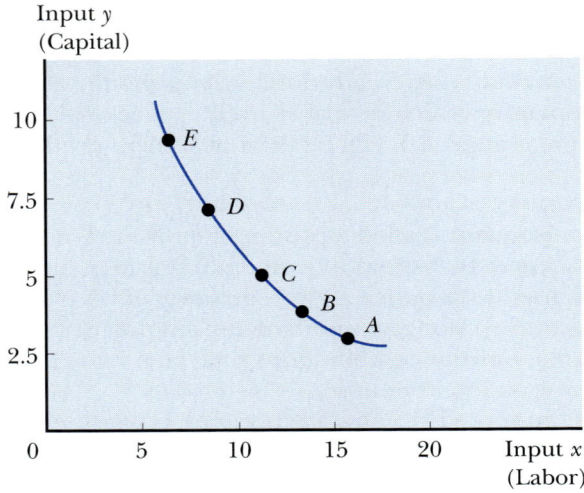

FIGURE 1A
ISOQUANT CURVE
Isoquants are curves representing combinations of two inputs that produce the same output. All combinations on the same isoquant represent the same level of output.

has more of one of the inputs but less of the other compared to other combinations on that same isoquant curve.

DIMINISHING MARGINAL RATES OF SUBSTITUTION

The curvature of the isoquant is convex to the origin. The convexity means that as a producer uses more units of one input and fewer units of the other input, it takes more and more units of the more abundant input to compensate for the loss of one unit of the input that is becoming more scarce. Just as with indifference curves, the convexity of the isoquant reflects the principle of diminishing marginal rates of substitution.

The trade-off ratio along the isoquant curve is called (as before with indifference curves) the marginal rate of substitution. The marginal rate

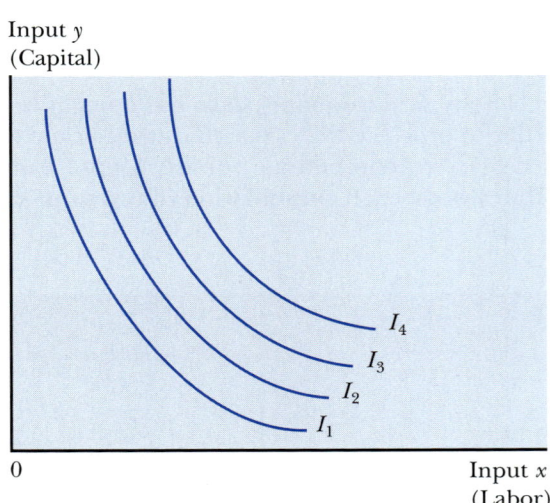

FIGURE 2A
ISOQUANT MAP
An isoquant map is a set of isoquant curves, each corresponding to a different level of output. Higher curves on the map represent higher levels of output.

of substitution of input x for input y, MRS_{xy}, shows the willingness of the producer to substitute between the inputs:

$$MRS_{xy} = \frac{\text{number of units of } y \text{ released}}{\text{number of units of } x \text{ substituted}}.$$

As more of one input (x) is substituted for the other input (y), the value of input x in terms of input y declines.

COST CONSTRAINTS

Which combination of inputs should a producer choose? The answer depends on the budget of that producer and on the prices of the inputs. Keep in mind that the producer faces input prices that are determined in markets. The typical producer cannot influence these prices. Total costs constrain the producer from buying all the inputs that might be desired. For every possible value of total costs, there is an **isocost line**. ("Isocost" means equal cost.) This line identifies all combinations of inputs the firm can purchase for a given total cost. This concept is analogous to the budget line in indifference analysis.

A straight line connecting the two points that represent buying only input y or only input x will show all possible combinations that can be attained with a given cost outlay. Any combination outside (above) the line is unattainable at that cost outlay. It is outside the budget constraint. In other words, the isocost line is the dividing line between those input combinations that are attainable and those that are unattainable at a given level of prices and a given cost outlay. An isocost line is shown in Figure 3A. The intercept on the axis representing each input is determined by dividing the total cost outlay (TC) by the price of that input (P_x or P_y). The slope of the isocost curve is therefore the ratio of the per-unit costs of the two inputs.

isocost line
A line that shows the amounts of two inputs that can be purchased with a fixed sum of money (a firm's budget line).

CHANGES IN COST OUTLAY OR PRICES OF INPUTS

The isocost line is developed by holding prices of inputs and total cost out-

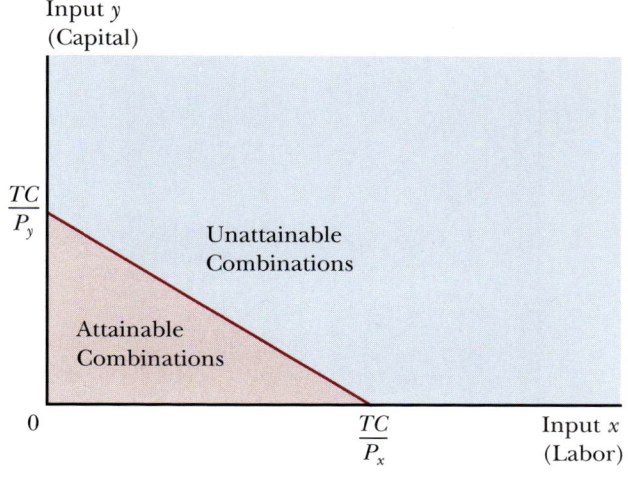

FIGURE 3A
ISOCOST LINE
An isocost line shows the input combinations that are possible at a given level of total cost outlay. Any combination outside (above) the line is unattainable.

lay constant. How do changes in total cost outlay or prices affect the isocost line?

An increase in total cost outlay (or the firm's budget) means that more of both inputs can be purchased, if input prices stay the same. A doubling of cost outlay means that twice as much of both inputs can be purchased. Increases in cost outlay are represented by a parallel outward shift of the isocost line. Decreases in cost outlay are represented by a parallel inward shift of the isocost line. Such shifts are shown in Figure 4A.

A change in the price of one input only affects the amount of that input that can be employed, not the amount of the other input. A price rise, then, will affect only the intercept of the isocost line with the axis for the input that has experienced the price rise. The effect of such a change is shown in Figure 5A. A price rise for input x from P_{x_1} to P_{x_2} causes the x-axis intercept of the isocost line to move closer to the origin. This shift reflects the fact that less x can now be purchased with the same cost outlay. A decrease in the price of input x from P_{x_1} to P_{x_3} would mean that more of x could be purchased. The x-intercept moves away from the origin, reflecting increases in the potential employment of input x.

Price changes cause the slope of the isocost line to change. Note that the slope is the negative of the ratio of the prices of the two inputs, or $-(P_x/P_y)$. The slope of the isocost line changes when the ratio of the input prices changes. A change in total cost outlay, on the other hand, represents no change in relative prices. The slope of the isocost line remains the same in that case, shifting in a parallel fashion as described above.

Choosing the Optimum Combination of Inputs

Drawing the isocost line on an isoquant map makes it possible to demonstrate the choice of input combination. In Figure 6A, at point A on isoquant I_2, the isocost line and isoquant I_2 are tangent. Any point on I_3, such as point B, is preferred to point A because higher isoquant curves

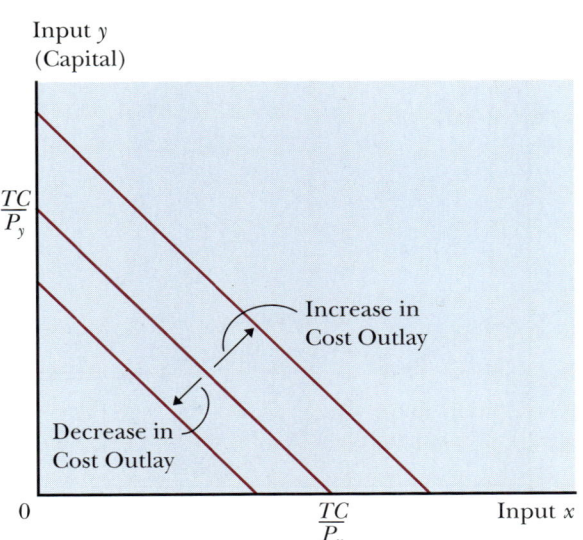

FIGURE 4A
THE EFFECT OF CHANGES IN TOTAL COST OUTLAY ON THE ISOCOST LINE
An increase in total cost outlay is represented by a parallel outward shift of the isocost line. A decrease in total cost outlay is represented by an inward parallel shift of the isocost line.

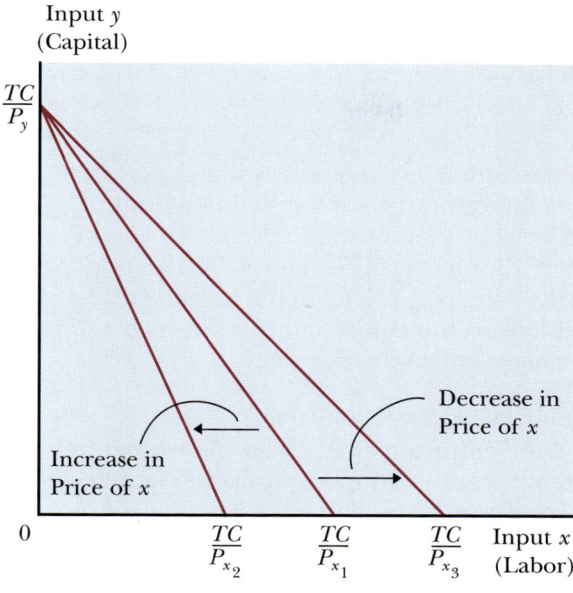

**FIGURE 5A
THE EFFECT OF INPUT PRICE CHANGES ON THE ISOCOST LINE**
An increase in the price of one input changes the slope of the isocost line. An increase in the price of an input means that if all of the firm's cost outlay is spent on that input, less of it can be purchased. As a result, the intercept of the isocost line with the axis for that input will shift closer to the origin. The opposite holds for a decrease in the price of an input.

represent higher levels of output. However, point B is not attainable because it is outside the isocost line. Point C on I_1 is attainable. Point A on I_2 is also attainable, however, and any point on I_2 represents more output than any point on I_1. The producer wants to reach the highest attainable isoquant. The highest attainable curve will be one that is tangent to the isocost line because no higher isoquant can be reached with the given cost outlay and prices.

You should remember from geometry that two curves that are tangent have equal slopes at the point of tangency. At the point of tangency be-

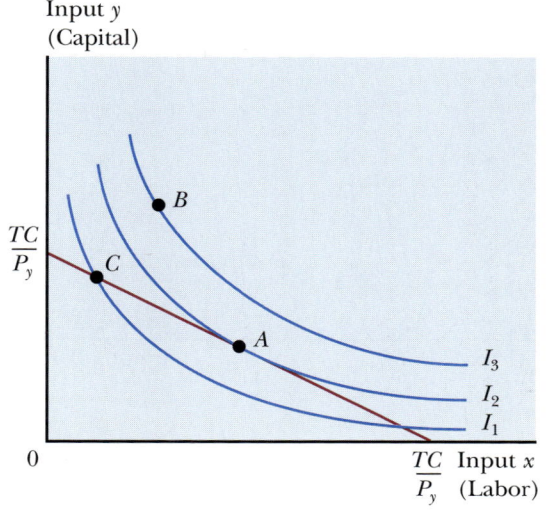

**FIGURE 6A
THE CHOICE OF INPUT COMBINATIONS**
A producer maximizes output for a given cost outlay at the input combination where the isocost line is tangent to the highest attainable isoquant curve.

tween the isoquant curve and the isocost line, the marginal rate of substitution is equal to the ratio of the price of x to the price of y:[a]

$$MRS_{xy} = \frac{P_x}{P_y}.$$

The marginal rate of substitution expresses the willingness of the producer to substitute a certain amount of x for a certain amount of y. The slope of the isocost line reflects the market's willingness in terms of prices to trade a certain amount of x for a certain amount of y. The impersonal forces of the market impose the relative prices on the producer. The equation says that the producer adjusts the choice of inputs in such a way that his or her trade-off is the same as that of the market.

THE FIRM'S REACTION TO PRICE CHANGES

Figure 5A shows how changes in input prices affect the isocost line. We can now see how the optimum combination of inputs will be affected by price changes. Suppose a producer is initially at a point of maximum output at point A on isoquant I_1 in Figure 7A. As the price of output x falls from P_{x_1} to P_{x_2}, the isocost line rotates out to intersect the x-axis at TC/P_{x_2}, and the producer now has a new optimum at point B on isoquant I_2. Another decrease in price to P_{x_3} allows the producer to reach a still higher isoquant, I_3, and a new optimum at point C. Connecting points A, B, and C produces an expansion path, which shows how the input combination changes when relative input prices change.

FIGURE 7A
THE FIRM'S EXPANSION PATH
An expansion path depicts how the firm's choice of inputs changes when relative prices change.

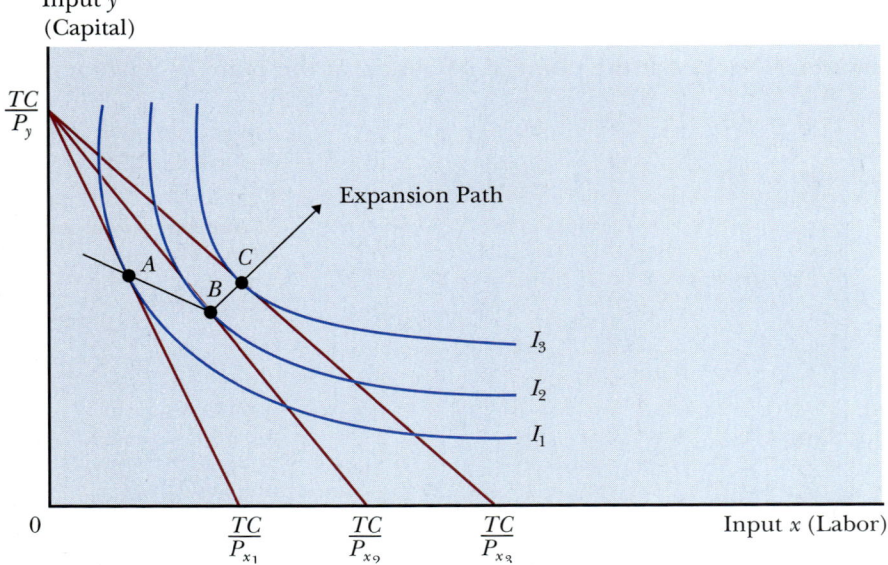

a. Technically, MRS_{xy} is equal to the negative of the slope of the isoquant curve. The price ratio, as we have seen, is the negative of the slope of the isocost line. Therefore, at the (equilibrium) point of tangency between the isoquant curve and the isocost line, $MRS_{xy} = P_x/P_y$.

AFTER STUDYING THIS CHAPTER, YOU SHOULD BE ABLE TO:

1. Define:
   a. explicit cost,
   b. implicit cost,
   c. accounting cost,
   d. accounting profit,
   e. economic profit,
   f. normal profit.
2. Use a total cost schedule to calculate:
   a. average total cost (AC),
   b. average fixed cost (AFC),
   c. average variable cost (AVC),
   d. marginal cost (MC).
3. Graph total cost (TC), total variable costs (TVC), total fixed costs (TFC), average cost (AC), average variable cost (AVC), average fixed cost (AFC), long-run average cost ($LRAC$), and marginal cost (MC).
4. List the reasons for economies and diseconomies of scale.
5. Determine the profit-maximizing level of production using:
   a. total revenue and total cost,
   b. marginal revenue and marginal cost.
6. Calculate the present value of a future stream of income using a table.

CHAPTER 8
COSTS AND PROFITS

INTRODUCTION

In the preceding chapter, we examined firms and how they carry out production. We developed the concept of a production function and the idea that a firm chooses its mix of inputs using a production function. Such choices translate into costs and cost functions. This chapter focuses on the cost relationships that result from production decisions.

We also explained in the preceding chapter how an entrepreneur attempts to minimize costs to achieve economic efficiency. But we need to be careful how we define cost. Costs of inputs should be expressed in terms of their opportunity cost. You were introduced to opportunity cost earlier, and now you need to apply it with a vengeance. Measuring costs of inputs in this way can be a problem if you are not used to thinking in terms of opportunity cost and are more used to thinking in terms of explicit cost. **Explicit costs** are accounting costs or money outlays. **Implicit costs** are those additional costs implied by the alternatives given up. When economists talk of costs, they include opportunity costs—explicit and implicit.

Some examples can make this clearer. Suppose you have the option of working two hours of overtime at $10 an hour or going to a concert that costs $5. The cost of attending the concert is the $5 ticket charge *plus* the $20 you could have earned working overtime. Attending the concert will cost you $25. The explicit cost is $5. The implicit cost is $20. Or suppose your rich aunt in Great Britain sends you her "old" Rolls Royce that is worth $100,000. She doesn't care what you do with it. You are excited because now you can drive a classic car at very low cost. You need only pay for gas, oil, insurance, and repairs. Right? No! You have forgotten to in-

explicit costs
Accounting costs or money outlays.

implicit costs
Costs measured by the value of alternatives given up.

clude a calculation of the implicit cost. If you sold the car, you could invest the $100,000. You could put the money in a high-yield account that earns 10 percent per year. In other words, you are giving up $10,000 per year if you choose to drive the Rolls. The total cost is the implicit cost of that $10,000 plus the explicit costs of gas, oil, insurance, and repairs. Do you still want to drive the Rolls?

ACCOUNTING PROFIT AND ECONOMIC PROFIT

In Chapter 3, Susan's lemonade stand was used as an example of a firm as a supplier. Now suppose we can obtain Susan's account books in order to calculate her profits. Let's say she had total sales of $15,000 for the summer. Her books say that she has accounting (explicit) costs of $11,500. Her **accounting profit** is $3,500, determined by subtracting her explicit costs from her total sales. These are the profits reported for tax purposes. But economists think that profits figured in this way give a misleading view of a firm's health because implicit costs are ignored. If Susan's skills and talents are worth $2,000, then her opportunity cost, which is her implicit costs plus her explicit costs, is $13,500. She will be earning an economic profit of $1,500. **Economic profit** is the difference between total revenue and the total of explicit and implicit costs of production. An entrepreneur who does not earn a profit that is at least equal to his or her opportunity cost will quit the endeavor.

accounting profit
The difference between total sales and explicit costs.

economic profit
The difference between total sales and the total of explicit and implicit costs of production.

OPPORTUNITY COST AND NORMAL PROFIT

The opportunity cost of capital and enterprise is referred to as **normal profit**. A normal profit represents the rate of return that is necessary to keep capital and enterprise in an industry. Say, for example, the normal profit is 8 percent. Then a firm earning an 8 percent rate of return is earning zero economic profit because its capital and enterprise could earn 8 percent elsewhere. The concept of normal profit is used by regulators in setting prices for public utilities (such as electric and telephone companies). If an electric utility is not granted a price increase and the rate of return on its capital falls below the normal profit, capital will leave that industry to try to earn its opportunity cost elsewhere.

normal profit
The opportunity cost of capital and enterprise, or the rate of return that is necessary for a firm to remain in a competitive industry.

In other words, normal profit is part of the implicit cost structure of firms. Just like the "free" Rolls Royce, a firm's capital, even if it is paid for, represents wealth that could be sold and invested elsewhere. The calculation is, in principle, exactly the same as in the Rolls Royce example.

Figure 1 shows the relationships of the concepts of accounting profit, economic profit, and normal profit. Total revenue is the same in both bars, but the difference between economic profit and accounting profit is the implicit costs, including normal profit.

A correct definition of costs is important because economists use costs and profits to predict behavior. When economic profits are positive, economists predict that new firms will enter an industry. When economic profits are negative, firms will leave the industry. When economic profits are zero, existing firms will remain and earn normal profits, but no new ones will enter. Economic profit serves as a signal, calling forth entry into

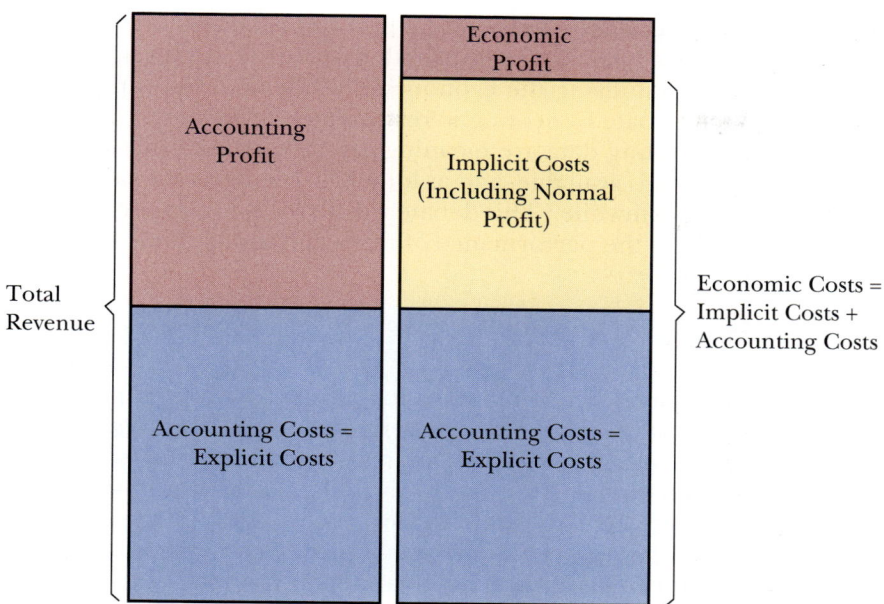

FIGURE 1
ECONOMIC PROFIT AND ACCOUNTING PROFIT
Economic profit differs from accounting profit by the amount of implicit costs.

or exit out of an industry. If a firm isn't earning a normal profit in its present industry, its resources will flow to an industry where a higher rate of return can be earned. If more than a normal profit is being earned in an industry, resources will be attracted to it.

THE USE OF ACCOUNTING PROFITS IN ECONOMIC ANALYSIS

Economic theory is based on the concepts of economic costs and economic profit, but these data aren't usually available for real-world analyses. Economists are suspicious of accounting costs and accounting profits for at least two reasons. The first has to do with the way in which accounting costs are gathered. The second has to do with the discrepancy between accounting costs and economic costs.

Since federal income tax is paid on accounting profits, firms have incentives to make profits look as small as possible for the IRS and as large as possible for potential investors. There are many things that can be done to manipulate accounting profits. Some flexibility in measuring profits comes from the very different ways in which firms can account for items whose value is estimated subjectively. Several years ago, *Fortune* magazine asked experts at several "Big Eight" accounting firms how they could "pump up" the profits of a mythical $10-billion-a-year company. These experts reported a number of accounting techniques that could boost reported profits as much as 15 percent.[1] These techniques fall into three categories: altering approved accounting methods, manipulating managers' estimates of costs, and changing the time periods in which costs are paid and revenues are received.

---

1. Ford S. Worthy, "Manipulating Profits: How It's Done," *Fortune* (25 June 1984): 49–54. For an interesting article that shows how Hollywood movie makers manipulate accounting profits, see Danna Wechsler, "Profits? What Profits?" *Forbes* (19 February 1990): 38–40.

Even though economists argue that accounting data do not reflect economic reality and can be manipulated, that data is all that is available for them to use in studying the economy. The use of accounting data is subject to much debate by economic researchers. Some argue that studies that use accounting data are meaningless. Others hold that accounting data are all that is available, and as long as economists are careful, using such data is worthwhile.[2] This debate will go on as long as economists attempt to measure the performance of firms and industries.

COSTS IN THE SHORT RUN

The production function relates inputs to outputs. The inputs in the production function have prices and represent costs to the firm. These input prices, which are determined in factor markets, may or may not be affected by the actions of the firm itself. Given the prices of inputs and the production function, it is possible to derive cost data for the firm. Although the derivation can be done formally, we will show the relationship on a graph and then derive the costs in a simpler fashion.

DEFINING COSTS

An example of a cost profile for a firm is given in Table 1. **Total cost (TC)** is simply the sum of all the costs of production for a given level of output. Total cost is made up of two components: total fixed costs (TFC) and total variable costs (TVC). That is, $TFC + TVC = TC$. **Total fixed costs (TFC)** are the costs of the fixed factors of production. Therefore, they can't be avoided or changed in the short run. These costs will be the same re-

total cost (TC)
The sum of all the costs of production for a given level of output.

total fixed costs (TFC)
The costs of the fixed factors of production, which can't be avoided in the short run.

TABLE 1
COST PROFILE FOR A FIRM

OUTPUT PER WEEK (Q)	TOTAL FIXED COSTS (TFC)	TOTAL VARIABLE COSTS (TVC)	TOTAL COST (TC)	AVERAGE FIXED COST (AFC)	AVERAGE VARIABLE COST (AVC)	AVERAGE TOTAL COST (AC)	MARGINAL COST (MC)
0	$60	$ 0	$ 60	$—	$ 0	$—	$ 0
1	60	40	100	60	40	100	40
2	60	76	136	30	38	68	36
3	60	108	168	20	36	56	32
4	60	140	200	15	35	50	32
5	60	175	235	12	35	47	35
6	60	216	276	10	36	46	41
7	60	262	322	$8^4/_7$	$37^3/_7$	46	46
8	60	312	372	$7^1/_2$	39	$46^1/_2$	50
9	60	369	429	$6^2/_3$	41	$47^2/_3$	57
10	60	430	490	6	43	49	61

2. The most recent exchange in this debate was kicked off by George J. Benston, "The Validity of Profits-Structure Studies With Particular Reference to the FTC's Line of Business Data," *American Economic Review* (March 1985): 36–67. Thirteen economists responded to Benston's article in the March 1987 issue of the *American Economic Review*. See also Franklin M. Fisher and John J. McGowan, "On the Misuse of Accounting Rates of Return to Infer Monopoly Profits," *American Economic Review* (March 1983): 82–97. A series of comments in opposition to their position can be found in the June 1984 issue of the *American Economic Review*.

gardless of how many units of output the firm produces. **Total variable costs (*TVC*)** vary directly with output. Variable costs increase as more output is produced because more of the variable factors of production have to be purchased if more output is to be produced. Total fixed costs and total variable costs are shown in the second and third columns in Table 1. In this cost schedule, we assume that the firm has already identified that combination of inputs that minimizes the total variable costs for every level of output. These figures represent the cost of the economically efficient input combinations. Why should the firm pay a higher total variable cost than it has to?

Given the information in the first four columns of Table 1, the rest of the columns are computed as follows: **Average fixed cost (*AFC*)** is total fixed costs of production divided by the number of units of output. **Average variable cost (*AVC*)** is total variable costs divided by the number of units of output. That is,

$$AFC = \frac{TFC}{Q} \quad \text{and} \quad AVC = \frac{TVC}{Q}.$$

Average total cost (*AC*) is equal to the total costs of producing a level of output divided by that level of output. That is,

$$AC = \frac{TC}{Q}.$$

Marginal cost (*MC*) is the change in total cost as a result of producing one more (or one less) unit of output. That is,

$$MC = \frac{\Delta TC}{\Delta Q} = \frac{\Delta TVC}{\Delta Q}.$$

Marginal costs are really marginal *variable* costs because there are no marginal fixed costs. When output changes, the change in fixed costs is zero.

COST CURVES

We can draw a series of cost curves from the data given in Table 1. The curves are drawn smoothly to better emphasize their relationships.[3]

The total fixed costs, total variable costs, and total cost curves are shown in Figure 2. The shape of the production function determines the shapes of the total cost curve and the total variable costs curve. As the amount of the variable factor of production increases, both output and total costs increase. If output increases more rapidly than factor cost, total cost (as well as total variable costs) increases at a decreasing rate, and returns increase. In Figure 2, the production function shows decreasing costs, or increasing returns to the variable factor, as output increases from zero to Q_1. From Q_1 to higher levels of output, output increases less rapidly than the factor cost increases. Then total cost (along with total variable costs) increases at an increasing rate. The principle of diminishing returns operates beyond output level Q_1.

---

3. Drawing the curves smoothly assumes that the gaps between the discrete points in Table 1 can be filled in with a continuous curve.

---

total variable costs (*TVC*)
The costs of the factors of production that vary directly with output, increasing as more output is produced.

average fixed cost (*AFC*)
Total fixed costs of production divided by number of units of the output.

average variable cost (*AVC*)
Total variable costs of production divided by the number of units of output.

average total cost (*AC*)
Total costs of producing a level of output divided by the number of units of output.

marginal cost
The change in total cost from producing one more (or one less) unit of output.

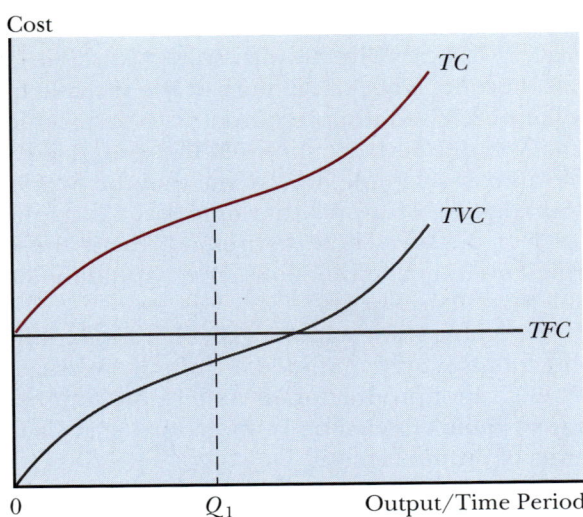

FIGURE 2
TOTAL COST CURVES
The shapes of the total cost (TC) curve and total variable costs (TVC) curve are a reflection of the production function. From zero output to an output level of Q_1, total cost and total variable cost increase at a decreasing rate. Beyond output level Q_1, diminishing returns set in. Then costs increase at an increasing rate.

Consider this simple example. Suppose a firm hires 1 additional worker and output increases by 10 units. The variable cost increases by the wage of that worker (for a given time period). Now, if it takes 2 more workers to increase output by 10 more units, total variable costs would increase by the wage rate times 2. Clearly the cost would be increasing at an increasing rate.

Now let's look at average and marginal costs. Figure 3 shows the average fixed costs (AFC), average variable costs (AVC), average cost (AC), and marginal cost (MC) curves for a firm. The AFC curve declines continuously, getting closer and closer to the horizontal axis of the graph.

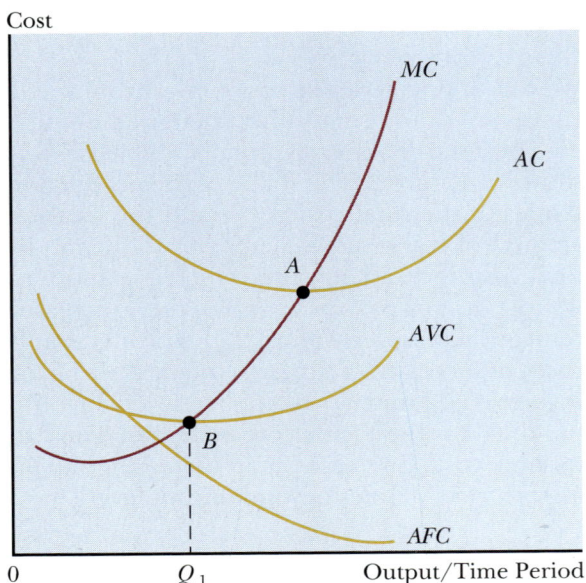

FIGURE 3
MARGINAL AND AVERAGE COST CURVES
The average fixed costs (AFC) curve declines continuously. The average variable costs (AVC) and average cost (AC) curves decline, reach a minimum, and then increase, resulting in a U shape. The marginal cost (MC) curve intersects the AVC and AC curves at their minimum points.

This decline occurs because fixed costs are constant, since average fixed costs are calculated by dividing that constant amount by an ever increasing quantity (levels of output). Thus, the average fixed costs become smaller and smaller as output increases.

Average variable costs first decline and then increase, as does average cost. The U-shaped *AVC* curve represents returns to the variable inputs that at first increase and then diminish. The variable inputs are being added to a given quantity of fixed factor, such as a fixed-size plant. Increasing returns occur for output levels up to Q_1 in Figure 3.

At output levels above Q_1, returns to the variable factors decline. That is, returns are diminishing. Increasing returns mean decreasing average costs, and diminishing returns mean increasing average costs. The *AVC* and *AC* curves are U-shaped because of decreasing costs (increasing returns) for small levels of output and then increasing costs (diminishing returns) for higher levels of output. Average cost declines sharply at first because average fixed costs drop rapidly and then more slowly.

Note that the *MC* curve intersects the *AC* and *AVC* curves at their lowest points—points *A* and *B* in Figure 3. These points illustrate the relationship between average and marginal values, discussed in the preceding chapter. For the *AC* and *AVC* curves to be declining, the marginal cost must be below the average cost. For the *AC* and *AVC* curves to be rising, the marginal cost must be above the average cost. Thus, marginal cost and average cost must be equal where the *AC* curve is at its minimum point. Think about how your grade point average goes up or down depending on your grade in an added (marginal) course. Also, note that when the *MC* curve starts to rise as output is increased, it is still below the *AVC* curve. Thus, average variable costs are still falling. An average value falls as long as the marginal value is below it, regardless of whether the marginal value is falling or rising.

THE RELATIONSHIP BETWEEN PRODUCT CURVES AND COST CURVES

We have said that cost curves could be derived from production functions. This derivation is an advanced topic in economics, but you can see the relationship between a production function (represented by product curves) and cost curves in Figure 4.

Part (*a*) of Figure 4 shows the marginal physical product (*MPP*) and average physical product (*APP*) curves discussed in the preceding chapter. In this case, the variable factor is labor. Part (*b*) represents the cost curves that are derived from the production function that produced the product curves. The marginal cost (*MC*) curve is a mirror image of the MPP_L curve. At those output levels where marginal physical product is increasing, reflecting increasing returns, marginal cost is decreasing. When the MPP_L curve is at its maximum, the *MC* curve is at its minimum point. When marginal physical product is declining, reflecting diminishing returns, marginal cost is rising.

Similar relationships hold for the *APP* and *AVC* curves. When average physical product is increasing, average variable costs are decreasing, and when average physical product is decreasing, average variable costs are increasing. The maximum and minimum points of the two curves also coincide.

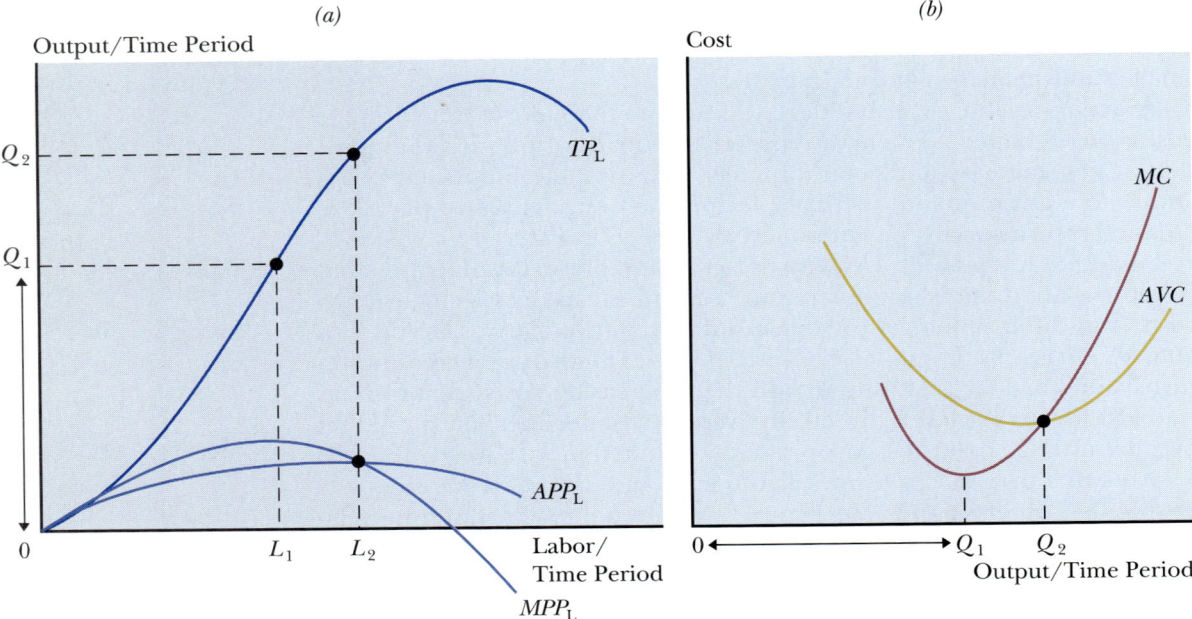

FIGURE 4
THE RELATIONSHIP BETWEEN PRODUCT CURVES AND COST CURVES
The cost curves are mirror images of the respective product curves. When the product curve is increasing, the cost curve is decreasing, and vice versa. Q_1 on the vertical axis of part (a) is the same as Q_1 on the horizontal axis of part (b). L_1 in part (a) represents the units of labor required to produce Q_1 units of output.

This relationship is based on simple logic. The cost curves are simply monetary measures of inputs needed to produce a given output, and the production function measures outputs for a given amount of inputs. Given prices of resources, increasing returns have to mean decreasing costs and diminishing returns have to mean increasing costs.

COSTS IN THE LONG RUN

In the long run, all factors of production are variable. Therefore, there are no fixed factors of production. As a result, there are no fixed costs in the long run. All costs are variable in the long run. In fact, the long run is defined as the period long enough to vary all inputs.

The most important long-run decision is what size plant to build. Each possible size is represented by a short-run average cost (AC) curve. The long-run decision is based on the selection of the desired short-run average cost curve. That choice will be based on the output the firm expects to produce. Figure 5 illustrates this decision. Suppose the technological factors (given by the production function) are such that only three plant sizes are feasible. These plants are represented by curves AC_1, AC_2, and AC_3 in Figure 5. The long-run decision of which short-run curve to operate on will depend on the planned output of the firm. If output is to be less than Q_1, then the plant represented by AC_1 should be built because its size will produce any output level between zero and Q_1 at a per-unit cost that is lower than it would be for any other size. If an output level between Q_1 and Q_2 is planned, the plant represented by AC_2 should be built. If output is to be greater than Q_2, the plant represented by AC_3 should be built.

Chapter 8 Costs and Profits

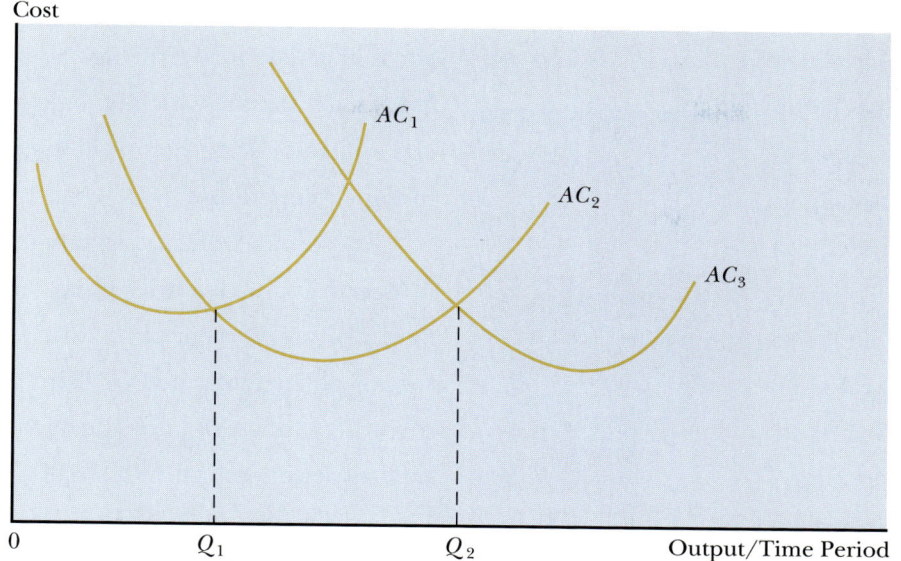

FIGURE 5
ALTERNATIVE PLANT SIZES
The determination of which size plant to build is a long-run decision of a firm. This decision is based on selection of the short-run cost curve that is optimal for the expected output level.

It is likely that more than three alternative plant sizes would be feasible. They would all be examined in the planning stage. Assume the firm faces all the short-run average cost curves depicted in Figure 6. All these possible short-run curves are tangent to a curve that is sometimes referred to as a planning curve. A **planning curve** is the long-run average cost curve. It is called a planning curve because any point on the curve could be chosen in the planning stage by deciding to build a certain size of plant. Such a planning curve, more commonly called the long-run average cost curve, is shown in Figure 6. The **long-run average cost (LRAC) curve** rep-

planning curve
The long-run average cost curve used in the planning stage.

long-run average cost (LRAC) curve
A curve tangent to all the possible short-run cost curves and representing the lowest attainable average cost of producing any given output.

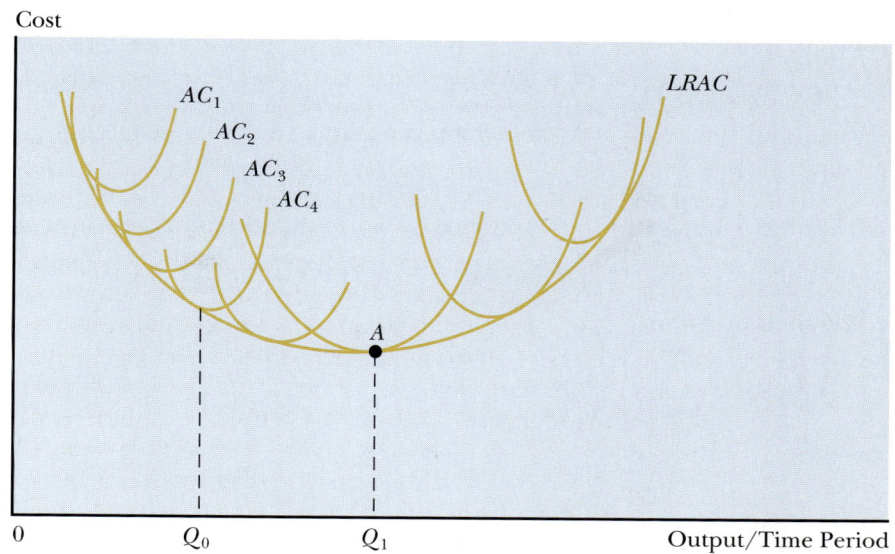

FIGURE 6
LONG-RUN AVERAGE COST CURVE
All the possible short-run cost curves are tangent to the planning curve. This planning curve is the long-run average cost (LRAC) curve and represents the lowest attainable average cost of producing any level of output. The optimal plant size is represented by point A, where the minimum point on a short-run average cost curve is tangent to the long-run average cost curve at its minimum point.

International Perspective

Economic Development and Economies of Scale

Manufacturing is quite often subject to economies of scale over a relatively large output range. As a result of these large-scale economies, policy makers have argued that manufacturing in less developed countries needs to be protected from foreign competition in order to get a toehold in domestic markets and someday be able to compete with industry in developed countries. This position, called the infant industry argument by economists, was strongly advocated by Alexander Hamilton (1755–1804), who served as the first Secretary of the U.S. Treasury in George Washington's cabinet. Hamilton was a promoter of economic growth and a strong federal government.

Hamilton argued that it would be very difficult for the U.S. economy to develop in a system of free trade because Great Britain had entrenched manufacturers with established trade networks. He argued that the only way U.S. firms could compete with developed foreign firms was with the "interference and aid" of the federal government. These infant industries could stand on their own after a "nursing period." An important element of this argument is that the new firm needs to grow to a size at which it enjoys economies of scale before it faces foreign competition.

The infant industry argument is used by many countries today. In fact, many observers point to the sort of policy advocated by Hamilton when they examine the Japanese experience with industrialization in the postwar period. The Japanese government and business leaders defined a few key industrial sectors. They nurtured these key industries with subsidies and high-tariff barriers until the industries attained economies of scale and low enough long-run average costs to be competitive in world markets.

The problems with the infant industry argument should be obvious. How can policy makers recognize promising industries in advance? Also, unless the infant industries have a domestic market that is large enough to attain economies of scale that make them cost-competitive on world markets, the government may have to protect the industries into old age.

resents the lowest attainable average cost of producing any given output. It is a curve tangent to all the possible short-run average cost curves. For example, if you knew you were going to produce exactly Q_0 units of output, the plant size represented by AC_4 would have the lowest average cost.

Only at point A in Figure 6, which corresponds to an output of Q_1 units, is there tangency between the minimum point on a short-run AC curve and the minimum point on the $LRAC$ curve. This point indicates the optimal-size plant. The **optimal-size plant** is represented by the short-run average cost curve with the lowest attainable per-unit costs.

ECONOMIES AND DISECONOMIES OF SCALE

The $LRAC$ curve in Figure 6 is U-shaped. This shape means that, at first, as plant size and firm output increase, long-run average costs fall. After a certain point (point A on Figure 6), however, bigness becomes costly. As the plant continues to increase in size, average cost begins to rise. Economists refer to these changes in long-run average cost due to increased plant size as economies and diseconomies of scale. **Economies of scale** are declines in long-run average cost that are due to increased plant size. **Diseconomies of scale** are increases in long-run average cost that are due to increased plant size. As scale (plant size) increases, economies (cost savings) result. After a while, further growth results in diseconomies (higher costs).

Economies and diseconomies of scale are distinct from increasing and decreasing returns. Increasing and decreasing returns are the result of using a given size plant more or less intensively in the short run. Economies and diseconomies of scale result from changes in the size of a plant in the long run.

It is easy to see how economies of scale result from an increase in plant size. As a firm increases its scale of operations, it usually can employ more specialized machinery. Also, jobs can be more specialized. Equipment can be used more efficiently. By-products of the operation that might be uneconomical to recover or exploit in a small-scale plant may become economical for a large operation. A large firm is often able to obtain quantity discounts on intermediate products from other firms. Political influence that has economic value is also more likely to accrue to a large, rather than a small, firm. These are just a few of the reasons for the negative slope of the $LRAC$ curve as the scale of operations increases.

Diseconomies of scale are slightly harder to grasp. However, anyone who has dealt with giant bureaucracies, public or private, will have seen evidence of them. Diseconomies result from the fact that as an organization becomes very large, communication and coordination become more difficult and time consuming, and control from the top diminishes. After a firm has taken advantage of the gains to be achieved by growing larger, managerial inefficiencies set in. With further growth, the $LRAC$ curve turns upward.

OPTIMAL-SIZE PLANTS IN THE REAL WORLD

If you look at real-world industries, you see many different sized firms operating side by side in the same industry. Steel, for example, is produced by both very large and very small firms. If there is a single, optimal size plant

optimal-size plant
The plant represented by the short-run average cost curve with the lowest attainable per-unit costs.

economies of scale
Declines in long-run average cost that are due to increased plant size.

diseconomies of scale
Increases in long-run average cost that are due to increased plant size.

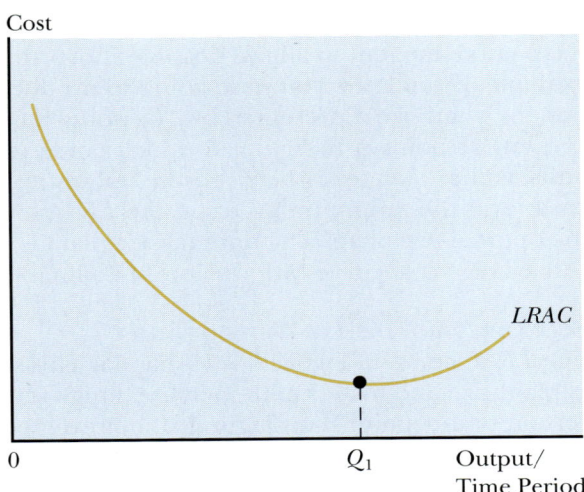

FIGURE 7
ECONOMIES OF SCALE AND A FEW VERY LARGE PLANTS
When economies of scale exist over large ranges of output, one large plant or a few large plants are most efficient.

for each industry, why do firms of so many different sizes exist? Economists have spent much time investigating real economies of scale. Several different types of *LRAC* curves are represented in Figures 7, 8, and 9.

Figure 7 shows economies of scale over a large range of output. This situation occurs in the auto industry, where there are a few very large firms. The optimal-size plant in Figure 7 is that producing output level Q_1, which conceivably might represent the normal sales of the entire industry. In such industries, a natural monopoly can occur. A **natural monopoly** is a monopoly that emerges because of economies of scale. The size of the market is such that there is room for only one optimal-size firm. Many public utilities (gas and electric), for example, need to have all the sales in a market in order to become large enough to be of optimal size.

In Figure 8, a large number of plants of different sizes can be of optimal size. Firms in a range of sizes can all produce efficiently in the same

natural monopoly
A monopoly that emerges because economies of scale mean that there is room for only one firm in the market.

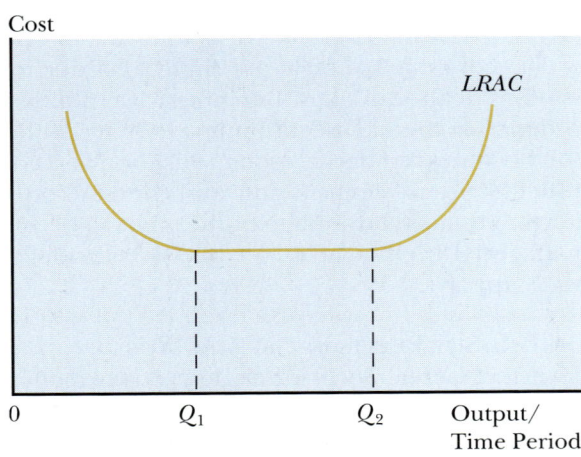

FIGURE 8
MANY OPTIMAL-SIZE PLANTS OF DIFFERENT SIZES
A range of outputs for the optimal-size plant can exist. When this situation exists, plants of distinctly different sizes can all produce efficiently in the same industry.

Chapter 8 Costs and Profits

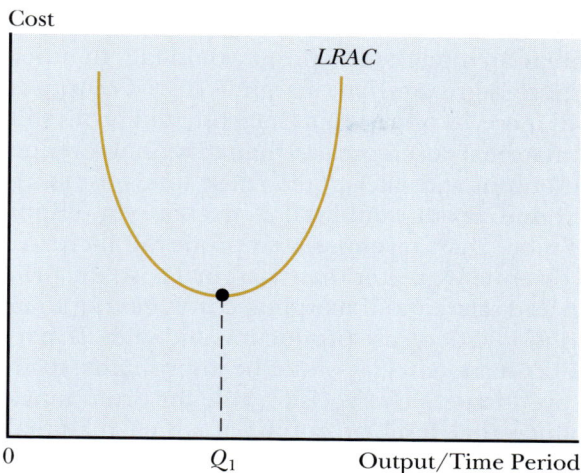

FIGURE 9
MANY OPTIMAL-SIZE PLANTS OF SIMILAR SIZES
If there is a unique minimum point on the long-run average cost curve, all the plants in an industry will be similar in size.

industry at the same per-unit (or average) cost. In Figure 8, any firm producing an output between Q_1 and Q_2 would be efficient. If the demand for the product is large enough to support many firms in this size range, a very competitive situation exists. This situation prevails in many industries, such as textiles, publishing, and packaged food products.

Figure 9 illustrates an industry in which there are rapidly achievable economies of scale and diseconomies of scale. This kind of *LRAC* curve occurs when all the firms in an industry are of a similar size. The optimal-size plant in Figure 9 is the one whose short-run average cost curve hits a minimum point at Q_1.

The benefit of economies of scale may not be passed along to consumers. Economies of scale mean that it is efficient to have production carried out by large firms. However, these large-scale firms may exert monopoly pricing power so that lower costs are not passed on to consumers. We will return to this problem in the chapter on monopoly.

PROFIT MAXIMIZATION

The choice of plant size is one of several decisions that determine a firm's profits. The firms examined here and in the next three chapters are all profit-maximizing firms. What does profit maximization mean in terms of production decisions? It means that, in the short run, the firm will attempt to choose the output that maximizes the difference between total revenue and total cost. **Total revenue (TR)** is the price an item sells for multiplied by the number of units sold. **Marginal revenue (MR)** is the change in total revenue from selling one more (or one less) unit.

Profit will be maximized at the level of output at which marginal revenue equals marginal cost, or $MR = MC$. For any output level where marginal revenue is greater than marginal cost ($MR > MC$), total revenue is increasing faster than total cost when output and sales increase. This means that profit is increasing (or losses are decreasing). If output were

total revenue (TR)
The price an item sells for multiplied by the number of units sold.

marginal revenue (MR)
The change in total revenue from selling one more (or one less) unit.

reduced when marginal revenue was greater than marginal cost, total revenue would decline by more than total cost, so profit would fall. In other words, when marginal revenue is greater than marginal cost, if output is increased, total revenue will increase more than total cost, and profit will rise. On the other hand, if marginal cost is greater than marginal revenue ($MC > MR$), an increase in output and sales would cause total cost to increase more than total revenue. Profit would fall. A decrease in output and sales will reduce costs more than revenues, and profit will increase.

Therefore, if marginal revenue is greater than marginal cost, the firm should expand production and sales, and if marginal cost is greater than marginal revenue, the firm should decrease production and sales. If marginal revenue and marginal cost are equal, it would be unprofitable to either increase or decrease production. The decision rule for profit maximization, then, is to produce that level of output at which marginal revenue equals marginal cost ($MR = MC$). This rule is just another way of saying "Produce where total profit is at its maximum" or "Produce where total revenue exceeds total cost by the largest amount." Generally, the $MR = MC$ rule is the most convenient to work with.

It's easy to see this relationship on a graph. In Figure 10, the firm is a price taker, which means that the price is given as far as this firm is concerned. Thus, the total revenue (TR) curve in Figure 10(a) is a straight line from the origin. The marginal revenue (MR) curve in part (b) is a horizontal line at the level of the price of the product. The total cost (TC) curve is consistent with the law of diminishing returns beyond output level Q_2. (From zero output to Q_2, the TC curve represents increasing returns and decreasing average costs.) The vertical distance between TR and TC is greatest at output level Q_2. At that point the slopes of TR and TC are equal. The slope of TR is MR, and the slope of TC is MC. Thus, it is clear that $MR = MC$ at output level Q_2. This can be seen in part (b). Note that if output were decreased below Q_2, MC would fall below MR, and TR would fall by more than TC. Thus, profit would fall. If output were increased above Q_2, TC would increase more than TR, and MC would be above MR. Again, profit would fall. Profit is at a maximum at Q_2.

The decision to produce that output where marginal revenue equals marginal cost will come up again and again, so it is important to make sure you understand it. It will always be true that maximum profit will be obtained by operating at the point where $MR = MC$.

RULES FOR PROFIT MAXIMIZATION

- $MR > MC$ Expand output
- $MR = MC$ Profits maximized, output unchanged
- $MR < MC$ Reduce output

PRESENT VALUE

The discussion of costs and the movement from the short run to the long run has ignored both uncertainty and differences between present and

Chapter 8 Costs and Profits 223

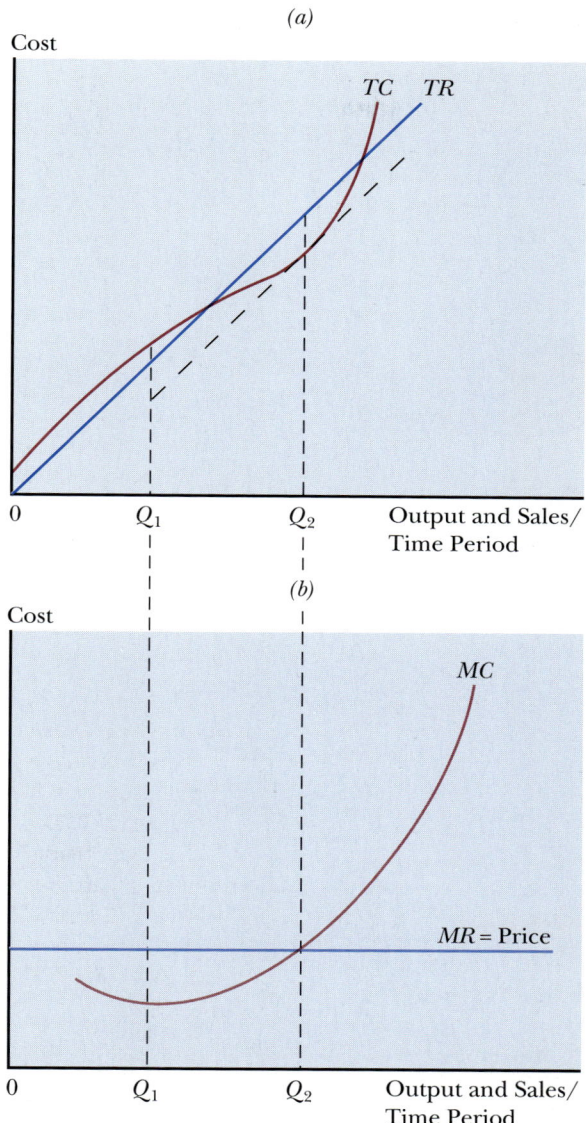

FIGURE 10
PROFIT MAXIMIZATION
Profit is maximized where marginal cost is equal to marginal revenue. The vertical distance between total revenue (*TR*) and total cost (*TC*) is greatest in part (*a*) at Q_2, the same level of output where marginal cost (*MC*) equals marginal revenue (*MR*) in part (*b*).

future income. It is important to keep in mind that when an entrepreneur makes the decision of which plant to build, based on forecasted production, much uncertainty surrounds that decision. To make production forecasts, a great deal of information must be gathered and many factors must be considered. Production decisions (in fact, most economic decisions) affect costs and revenues over a number of periods of time. The decision maker needs a way of comparing revenues and costs in different time periods because a dollar cost or a dollar revenue today is not the same as a dollar cost or a dollar revenue next year or ten years from now.

To compare future dollars (costs or revenues) for different periods with present dollars, firms calculate the present value of the future dol-

Economic Insight: Present Value and Lottery Jackpots

Many state governments use legalized gambling to generate revenue for public projects. The most common form of this sanctioned gambling is a state-run lottery. It has even been suggested that the federal government run a lottery and use the profits to retire the federal deficit. State governments usually earmark the proceeds from a lottery for some special purpose. The most common use is to support education.

Some people feel that lotteries are a very regressive form of tax because the poor spend a higher percentage of their income in buying lottery tickets. Others who support the lottery concept argue that a lottery ticket is a voluntary purchase. Thus, a lottery cannot be viewed as a tax because people purchase the tickets of their own free will. These advocates point out that people are going to gamble and the state might as well get involved and make some profit to do "good things," such as spending more on education.

In many states, the newspapers on Sunday morning now carry a headline about the latest millionaire created by the lucky drawing on Saturday night. These drawings are usually done on television to add to the drama. In early January 1990, it was reported in the *Rocky Mountain News* that a Denver carpenter, Don Wittman, Jr., was the co-winner of $4 million.[a] "It hasn't hit me yet," he said, smiling broadly under the brim of a new Colorado Lottery baseball cap. "But I wouldn't know what to do if I quit my job. I like to work."

Let's look at the present value of Wittman's jackpot using a 10 percent interest rate and assuming that he will be paid in one lump sum on December 31 of each year. The *Rocky Mountain News* reported the amount to be received each year, after deductions for state and federal taxes: $1.583 million of the $2 million will actually be paid out, after $417,000 or about 21 percent is withheld in taxes. We have rounded off these payments to simplify the arithmetic. The table below shows what the reported $2 million is really worth. The present value of the $1.583 million at 10 percent is only $526,516. This low present value results from the fact that the payout is made over a long period of time and larger payouts are made in the most distant years.

In all, Wittman's payout adjusted for taxes and present value was only 26.3 percent of what the headlines reported. This is still a very nice prize. Most of us would be happy to be in his shoes. But perhaps it is a good thing that Wittman "likes to work." A critic of lotteries referred to state-run lotteries as a "weekly tax on stupidity." This critic understood present value.

	Year	Payout in Dollars	Present Value in Dollars		Year	Payout in Dollars	Present Value in Dollars
		$ 38,000	$ 38,000				
1.	1990	40,000	36,306	14.	2003	66,000	17,358
2.	1991	41,000	35,137	15.	2004	68,000	16,252
3.	1992	43,000	32,293	16.	2005	72,000	15,624
4.	1993	45,000	30,735	17.	2006	74,000	14,578
5.	1994	46,000	28,520	18.	2007	77,000	13,783
6.	1995	48,000	27,072	19.	2008	80,000	13,040
7.	1996	50,000	25,650	20.	2009	83,000	12,284
8.	1997	52,000	24,232	21.	2010	87,000	11,745
9.	1998	54,000	22,896	22.	2011	90,000	11,070
10.	1999	56,000	21,560	23.	2012	94,000	10,528
11.	2000	58,000	20,300	24.	2013	97,000	9,894
12.	2001	61,000	19,398	Total:		$1,583,000	$526,000
13.	2002	63,000	18,207				

a. "Carpenter Claims Half of Lotto Jackpot," *Rocky Mountain News* (3 January 1990): 7.

lars. **Present value (PV)** is the capitalized value of an item to be paid for or sold in the future. It is a future value discounted to the present. **Discounting** is the technique of calculating present values by adjusting for interest that would be earned between now and some specified future time. It works simply and has many important uses in daily life.

Present value is based on the fact that you can choose to save (refrain from consumption) and receive interest as a reward for your saving. As a result, you are always better off delaying a payment of a fixed sum that you must make and speeding up a payment of a fixed sum you are to receive. For example, suppose you owe a friend $100, and your friend doesn't care when you pay off the debt within the next year. If the interest rate is 10 percent, you could take $90.90, put it in the bank now, and in one year receive from the bank $100 to pay your friend—the $90.90 you deposited *plus* interest of $9.10. In other words, the present value of $100 to be paid in one year at 10 percent interest is only $90.90. Another way of saying this is that the $90.90 you put in the bank today will be equivalent to the $100 you pay to your friend a year from now. On the other hand, if you were owed $100, you would want the money now so you could put $100 in the bank and have $110 at the end of a year. Two principles emerge from this example of discounting:

1. The higher the interest rate, the lower the present value.
2. The longer the time period, the lower the present value.

The formula for calculating present value is

$$\frac{V_t}{(1+r)^t},$$

where V_t is the value in year t, r is the interest rate, and t is the number of years. Table 2 shows the present value of $1 received in various future years (up to fifty years) at different interest rates. You can use the table to see that the present value of $100 for one year at a 10 percent interest rate is $90.90 (0.909 × $100).

Applications of present value surround you in your day-to-day life. Let's look at an example. Suppose that on your job as project manager, you are given the task of planning a new phase of operations. The engineer tells you the necessary equipment can be built in any of three ways over a period of three years. In each case, the firm's cash outlay will be spread out differently over the years. The alternatives are listed in Table 3. All alternatives are equal in the sense that each costs $600, all have the same date of completion, and all payments are made at the end of the year. Which should you choose? The only way to determine which alternative will maximize profit is to use present value analysis and discount the future dollar amounts. Using Table 2, we calculated the present value of each amount in Table 3, at a 10 percent interest rate. We totaled the present value amounts to find the least-cost method of production, which turns out to be alternative *C*. The present value of the outlay for alternative *C* is 5 percent less than that of alternative *A* and 9 percent less than that of alternative *B*. Choosing *C* means a substantial savings for the firm.

A profit-making firm that expects to be in business for a while will try to maximize profits. However, it will maximize the present value of profits

present value (PV) The value of a future payment or series of future payments discounted to the present.

discounting The technique of calculating present values by adjusting for interest that would be earned between now and some specified future time.

TABLE 2
PRESENT VALUE OF $1.00

YEAR	3%	4%	5%	6%	7%	8%	10%	12%	15%	20%	YEAR
1	0.971	0.962	0.952	0.943	0.935	0.926	0.909	0.893	0.870	0.833	1
2	0.943	0.925	0.907	0.890	0.873	0.857	0.826	0.797	0.756	0.694	2
3	0.915	0.890	0.864	0.839	0.816	0.794	0.751	0.711	0.658	0.578	3
4	0.889	0.855	0.823	0.792	0.763	0.735	0.683	0.636	0.572	0.472	4
5	0.863	0.823	0.784	0.747	0.713	0.681	0.620	0.567	0.497	0.402	5
6	0.838	0.790	0.746	0.705	0.666	0.630	0.564	0.507	0.432	0.335	6
7	0.813	0.760	0.711	0.665	0.623	0.583	0.513	0.452	0.376	0.279	7
8	0.789	0.731	0.677	0.627	0.582	0.540	0.466	0.404	0.326	0.233	8
9	0.766	0.703	0.645	0.591	0.544	0.500	0.424	0.360	0.284	0.194	9
10	0.744	0.676	0.614	0.558	0.508	0.463	0.385	0.322	0.247	0.162	10
11	0.722	0.650	0.585	0.526	0.475	0.429	0.350	0.287	0.215	0.134	11
12	0.701	0.625	0.557	0.497	0.444	0.397	0.318	0.257	0.187	0.112	12
13	0.681	0.601	0.530	0.468	0.415	0.368	0.289	0.229	0.162	0.093	13
14	0.661	0.577	0.505	0.442	0.388	0.340	0.263	0.204	0.141	0.078	14
15	0.642	0.555	0.481	0.417	0.362	0.315	0.239	0.183	0.122	0.065	15
16	0.623	0.534	0.458	0.393	0.339	0.292	0.217	0.163	0.107	0.054	16
17	0.605	0.513	0.436	0.371	0.317	0.270	0.197	0.146	0.093	0.045	17
18	0.587	0.494	0.416	0.350	0.296	0.250	0.179	0.130	0.081	0.037	18
19	0.570	0.475	0.396	0.330	0.277	0.232	0.163	0.116	0.070	0.031	19
20	0.554	0.456	0.377	0.311	0.258	0.215	0.148	0.104	0.061	0.026	20
25	0.478	0.375	0.295	0.232	0.184	0.146	0.092	0.059	0.030	0.0105	25
30	0.412	0.308	0.231	0.174	0.131	0.0994	0.057	0.033	0.015	0.0042	30
40	0.307	0.208	0.142	0.0972	0.067	0.0460	0.022	0.011	0.0037	0.0006	40
50	0.228	0.141	0.087	0.0543	0.034	0.0213	0.008	0.003	0.0009	0.0001	50

over a period of several years, not just the current period. The concept of present value is very important in business decisions but is *not* understood by many decision makers. It is often joked that the first year of an MBA program should be devoted solely to getting students to understand and make use of present value.

TABLE 3
PRESENT VALUE OF THREE ALTERNATIVES AT A 10 PERCENT INTEREST RATE

ALTERNATIVE	COST IN YEAR 1	COST IN YEAR 2	COST IN YEAR 3	TOTAL COST
A	$200.00 (PV = 181.80)	$200.00 (PV = 165.20)	$200.00 (PV = 150.20)	$600.00 (PV = 497.20)
B	$400.00 (PV = 363.60)	$100.00 (PV = 82.60)	$100.00 (PV = 75.10)	$600.00 (PV = 521.30)
C	$100.00 (PV = 90.90)	$100.00 (PV = 82.60)	$400.00 (PV = 300.40)	$600.00 (PV = 473.90)

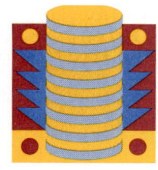

Summary

1. Economists calculate both implicit and explicit costs of production. Implicit costs are those costs implied by alternatives given up. Explicit costs are money expenditures, or accounting costs.
2. When total cost (both implicit and explicit costs) is equal to total revenue, economists say there is zero economic profit. This means the firm is covering all economic costs, including a normal profit. When costs exceed revenues, firms and resources will leave an industry in order to earn the opportunity cost associated with those resources.
3. In the short run, as variable factors of production are added to the fixed factors, the firm may experience increasing returns at low levels of output. Eventually the firm will incur diminishing returns at some higher levels of output.
4. Increasing and diminishing returns account for the U shape of the short-run average cost curve.
5. The U shape of the long-run average cost ($LRAC$) curve is due to economies and diseconomies of large-scale production.
6. Profit maximization means that an entrepreneur will produce that level of output that equates marginal cost and marginal revenue. This choice ensures that total revenue exceeds total cost by the largest possible amount.
7. Present value calculations are used to make dollar amounts to be received or paid in the future comparable with dollar amounts in the present.

New Terms

explicit cost
implicit cost
accounting profit
economic profit
normal profit
total cost (TC)
total fixed costs (TFC)
total variable costs (TVC)
average fixed cost (AFC)
average variable cost (AVC)
average total cost (AC)
marginal cost (MC)
planning curve
long-run average cost ($LRAC$) curve
optimal-size plant
economies of scale
diseconomies of scale
natural monopoly
total revenue (TR)
marginal revenue (MR)
present value (PV)
discounting

Questions for Discussion

1. Why are cost curves normally U-shaped both in the long run and in the short run?
2. What is a normal profit? Why is it necessary for a firm to earn at least a normal profit?
3. The famous epigram of the Chicago School of Economics is "There is no such thing as a free lunch." What does this mean?
4. At what size do universities start experiencing diseconomies of scale? What does the existence of many different sizes of universities indicate about the optimal-size university?
5. Does a university have to reach a certain size to have an efficient (winning) sports program? How would you gather empirical evidence on this?
6. What is the difference between diminishing returns and diseconomies of scale?
7. Would you rather win $6 million in a lump sum or $1 million a year for 10 years? Use a present value table to find an answer. What interest rate did you use? Why?
8. Give an example of an explicit cost and an implicit cost of your college education. Why does enrollment in colleges and graduate schools increase when economic times are bad and unemployment rates are high?
9. Complete the table on the following page. (You will

Total Output per Day (Q)	Total Fixed Costs (TFC)	Total Variable Costs (TVC)	Total Cost (TC)	Average Fixed Cost (AFC)	Average Variable Cost (AVC)	Average Total Cost (AC)	Marginal Cost (MC)
0	$10.00	$ 0	$10.00	$ —	$ —	$ —	$ —
1	10	5.00	15.00	10	5.00	15	5.00
2	10	8.00	18.00	5	4.00	9.00	3.00
3	10	9.99	19.99	3.33	3.33	6.66	1.99
4	10	11.00	21.00	2.50	2.75	5.25	1.01
5	10	13.00	23.00	2.00	2.60	4.60	2.00
6	10	16.00	26.00	1.66	2.66	4.33	3.00
7	10	20.00	30.00	1.42	2.85	4.28	4.00
8	10	25.04	35.04	1.25	3.13	4.38	5.04
9	10	31.00	41.00	1.11	3.44	4.55	6.04
10	10	38.00	48.00	1.00	3.80	4.80	7.00
11	10	46.00	56.00	.90	4.18	5.09	8.00

be referring back to this table when you answer questions at the end of the next two chapters.)

10. Graph the values of *AFC*, *AVC*, *AC*, and *MC* from the table in Question 9. Why does *MC* cut *AVC* and *AC* at their low points?

11. In 1990, major league baseball salaries exploded. The large increases were the result of the end of salary collusion by the owners and greatly enhanced revenues. Each day a record salary was reported in the newspapers. Mark Langston, a pitcher with the California Angels, signed for a reported $16 million over five years. With the table below, calculate the present value of Langston's salary at the time of the contract (1989), using an 8 percent interest rate. (For ease of calculation assume the salary is paid in one lump sum on December 31 of each year.)

12. You are running a lottery and the current interest rate is 7 percent. Assume that you sell $10 million worth of tickets and that it costs you $40,000 for printing and other related expenses. If you make one payment of $10 million to the winner at the end of ten years, how much profit will you make?   4,160,000

13. In this chapter a distinction was drawn between short-run and long-run costs. What is the length of time that distinguishes between short-run and long-run costs? Can it be different in different industries?

14. What is the infant industry argument? How is it related to economies of scale?

15. Why are profits maximized when $MC = MR$?

Year	Salary (Millions of Dollars)	Present Value (Millions of Dollars)
1. 1990	3.2	2.96
2. 1991	3.2	2.74
3. 1992	3.2	2.54
4. 1993	3.2	2.35
5. 1994	3.2	2.17
Total	16.0	12.76 = 3.24 savings

Suggestions for Further Reading

Davis, John S., and J. J. Kanet. "Net Present Value Made User-Friendly," *Bobbin* (September 1989): 23–26. A business article that shows how present value can be used by decision makers in the garment industry.

Dung, Tran Hu, and Robert Premus. "Do Socioeconomic Regulations Discriminate against Small Firms?" *Southern Economic Journal* (January 1990): 686–697. This article shows how federal regulations to hire the handicapped impact more significantly on smaller firms. The cost of complying with regulations is another element that impacts on the long-run average cost curves in an industry.

Eckert, Ross D. *The Price System and Resource Allocation*, 10th ed. Hinsdale, IL: Dryden Press, 1988. An intermediate price theory text that develops the material found in this chapter in much greater detail.

AFTER STUDYING THIS CHAPTER, YOU SHOULD BE ABLE TO:

1. List the assumptions of perfect competition.
2. Diagram the relationship between a representative firm and the total market.
3. Identify the profit-maximizing level of output.
4. Calculate profits, given information on quantity, marginal revenue, marginal cost, average cost, and price.
5. Define the shutdown point in terms of:
   a. price and average variable costs,
   b. total fixed costs and losses.
6. List the characteristics of each of three kinds of industries:
   a. constant cost industry,
   b. increasing cost industry,
   c. decreasing cost industry.
7. Describe the short-run and long-run equilibrium for the firm and the industry under perfect competition.
8. Explain how economic rent can exist in perfect competition, even in long-run equilibrium.

CHAPTER 9
PERFECT COMPETITION

INTRODUCTION

The last two chapters developed the principles of production and the general cost relationships derived from the production process. Any firm that makes production decisions will relate potential, or forecasted, revenues to costs in order to determine output levels. However, the forecasted revenues will depend on the market conditions faced by the firm.

This and the next two chapters look at four different models, referred to as market structures. The model discussed in this chapter is perfect competition. **Perfect competition** is the market structure in which there are many sellers and buyers, firms produce a homogeneous product, and there is free entry into and exit out of the industry. It is important to keep in mind that this is a theoretical model and does not precisely describe reality. The model is useful, however, because it allows the development of tools that indicate what determines price and quantity when conditions are close to those of perfect competition. The perfectly competitive market is the abstract ideal to which we will compare other market structures. This model underlies the basic supply and demand model developed earlier.

perfect competition
The market structure in which there are many sellers and buyers, firms produce a homogeneous product, and there is free entry into and exit out of the industry.

CHARACTERISTICS OF PERFECT COMPETITION

There are six basic assumptions for the model of perfect competition. In developing the theory, we assume that six characteristics exist in the market in which a firm is selling its product.

The first assumption is that there is a large number of sellers (producers) in the market. No specific number is indicated. A large number means there are so many sellers of the product that no single seller's decisions can affect price. For example, no single wheat farmer can influence the price of wheat. A farmer could sell the entire crop or none of the crop. The farmer's decision wouldn't affect the price of wheat one bit because the market for wheat is so large relative to any single producer.

The second assumption is that there is a large number of buyers (consumers) in the market. Again, a large number means that no one buyer can affect the price in any perceptible way. In other words, no single purchaser has any **market power**.

market power
The ability of buyers or sellers to affect price.

The third assumption is that perfectly competitive firms produce a homogeneous product. The product of one firm is no different from that of other firms in the industry. Since this is the case, purchasers have no preference for one producer over another. If you are a miller and want to purchase wheat, you don't care if it was produced by Farmer Jones or Farmer Smith—a bushel of number 1 winter wheat is a bushel of number 1 winter wheat!

The fourth, and very important, assumption is that there is free entry into and free exit out of the market. This means that if one firm wishes to go into business or if another firm wishes to cease production, it can do so without any kind of constraint. This assumption is crucial in distinguishing perfect competition from monopoly, which we will examine in the next chapter.

The last two assumptions are that there is perfect knowledge and perfect mobility of resources. These assumptions are even more unrealistic than the others because information is costly to acquire and resources are usually costly to move. The effect of these two assumptions is that when economic profits exist, firms will find out about these profits and enter the industry. Even though these assumptions are unrealistic, the resulting model is valuable because it shows what adjustments would take place in an ideal setting.

If these six assumptions are met, a market will be perfectly competitive. These assumptions create a model market in which no firm or individual has the power to exert control over the market. This means that neither buyer nor seller has any influence over price.

The six assumptions were first stated more than two centuries ago by Adam Smith in a general outline of the perfectly competitive model in his book *The Wealth of Nations*. In the nineteenth century, the model of perfect competition was the main way of looking at how firms and markets determine price and output levels. The study of other market structures arose later.

COMPETITIVE ADJUSTMENT IN THE SHORT RUN

Since the perfectly competitive firm is small relative to the market and its product is the same as that of other firms, this firm views itself as having no influence on market price. If the perfectly competitive firm wants to sell any of its output, it must sell at the market price. A firm in perfect competition is referred to as a **price taker** because it has no influence on price. It can sell any amount at the market-clearing price. The firm takes that price as its selling price. If it sets a higher price, none of its output will be sold because buyers will be able to purchase an identical product at the lower market price elsewhere. On the other hand, it makes no sense

price taker
A seller (or buyer) in perfect competition that has no influence on price and can sell any amount at the market-clearing price.

to sell below the market price because the firm can sell all it produces at that market price.

The market demand and supply curves and the firm's resultant demand curve are shown in Figure 1. (The graphs in this chapter are based on models first developed by Alfred Marshall.) Market demand (D) and supply (S) curves are such that the market equilibrium price is P_1. If the market is in equilibrium, the perfectly competitive firm can sell as much of its product as it wishes at price P_1. From the firm's viewpoint, the demand curve is perfectly elastic at price P_1.

The demand schedule a firm faces is also its average revenue schedule. If, for example, the price consumers pay in the market is $15, the average revenue a seller receives per unit sold is also $15. As price changes along a market demand curve, the average revenue that sellers receive will also change. Total revenue of a firm is the price times the quantity sold ($TR = P \times Q$). **Average revenue (AR)** is total revenue divided by the quantity sold. It is the revenue per unit sold, or the price of the product. A demand curve is an average revenue curve. With perfect competition, price does not vary with output. Thus, $AR = (P \times Q)/Q = P$ is a constant. The firm's perfectly elastic demand curve in Figure 1 is also a perfectly elastic average revenue curve.

average revenue (AR)
Total revenue divided by the quantity sold, or the revenue per unit sold (the price).

Recall that a profit-maximizing firm always produces that quantity for which marginal revenue is equal to marginal cost. Thus, we need to determine what the competitive firm's marginal revenue curve looks like. Marginal revenue is the change in total revenue from selling one more (or one fewer) unit:

$$MR_n = TR_n - TR_{n-1}.$$

In Figure 1, the change in total revenue if sales increase from x_1 to x_2 (where x_2 is one unit more than x_1) is $P_1(x_2 - x_1)$. If sales increase from x_2 to x_3, the change in total revenue is $P_1(x_3 - x_2)$. In other words, in the case of a perfectly elastic demand curve, such as the firm's demand curve in Figure 1, $D = P = AR = MR$. The marginal revenue curve associated with

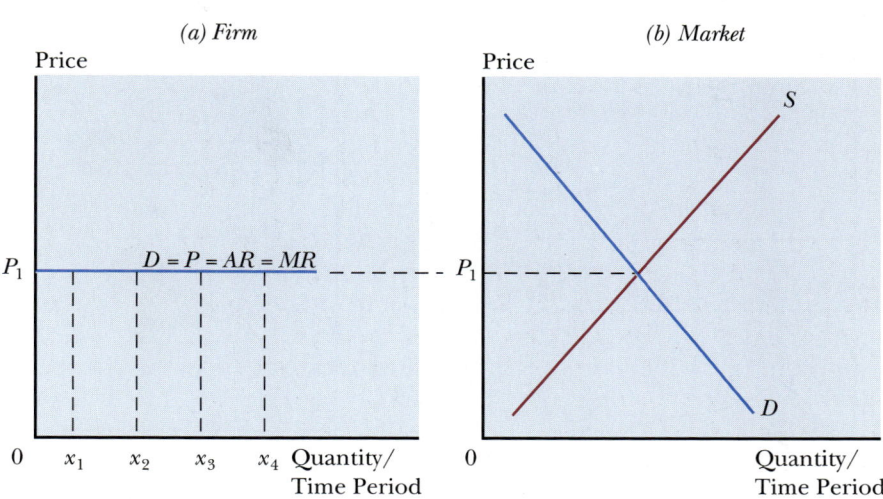

FIGURE 1
ELASTIC DEMAND AT MARKET EQUILIBRIUM
In perfect competition, a firm's demand curve is perfectly elastic at the market equilibrium price.

representative firm
A typical firm in perfect competition, one of the many identical firms in the market.

short-run supply curve
The supply curve for the period in which the size of the plant cannot be varied (in perfect competition, the same as the short-run marginal cost curve).

a perfectly elastic demand curve is the same as the demand curve. The demand curve is always the average revenue curve for any market structure. The demand curve is equal to the marginal revenue curve only in perfect competition. Remember the relationship between average and marginal values—if the average value doesn't change, the marginal value must be the same as the average.

Using marginal cost and marginal revenue, we now can determine how a perfectly competitive firm will adjust its output to changed prices in the short run. The demand curves for the market and a representative firm are depicted in Figure 2. A **representative firm** is a typical firm in perfect competition, one of the many similar firms in this market. In Figure 2, the representative firm's marginal cost curve is also shown. This firm maximizes profit by producing quantity x_1 when the price per unit is P_1 because at that output level, $MR = MC$. Now assume the market demand increases to D_1. The market price rises to P_2. The firm's demand curve, average revenue curve, and marginal revenue curve change to $D_1 = AR_1 = MR_1$. The firm responds by increasing its output level to x_2, where $MR_1 = MC$.

In Figure 2, the firm's short-run marginal cost curve is the same as its short-run supply curve. A **short-run supply curve** is a supply curve for the period in which the size of the plant cannot be varied (the short run). In perfect competition, the short-run marginal cost curve is the short-run supply curve. As market price rose, the firm in Figure 2 increased its output along its marginal cost curve. Further increases or decreases in price would cause further movements along the marginal cost curve, or the short-run supply curve. We will soon see how these short-run supply curves relate to the market (or industry) supply curve.

PROFITS, LOSSES, AND SHUTTING DOWN

We have just seen how a representative firm adjusts in the short run to changes in market demand. We don't yet know whether the firm has a profit or a loss, or how large this profit or loss is. To find out, we need to add the average cost curve to the graph. Also, in order to decide if the

FIGURE 2
PROFIT MAXIMIZATION
An increase in market demand causes the equilibrium price to rise. The demand curve the firm faces adjusts by the amount of the increase in price, and the firm increases its output to equate MC and MR. The adjustment process is such that the firm's marginal cost curve is its short-run supply curve.

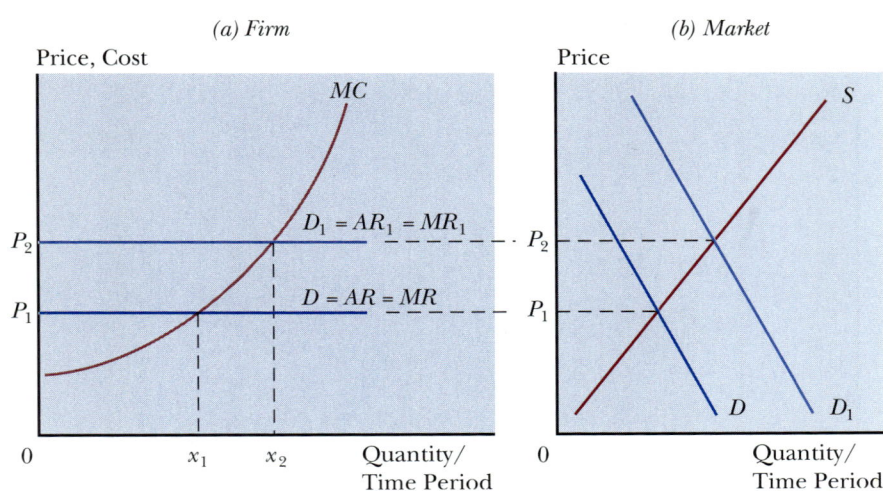

firm should continue to produce if losses are encountered, we need to add the average variable cost curve.

In Figure 3, the firm is maximizing profit by producing output x_1 at price P_1, where $P = MR = MC$. The average cost of producing x_1 is measured by distance x_1C in Figure 3. The total cost of producing x_1 is represented by the area of the rectangle $0P_1Cx_1$. Total revenue in Figure 3 is also the area of $0P_1Cx_1$, so $TR = TC$. This firm is therefore making zero economic profit, although it is meeting its opportunity costs. Remember that total cost includes normal profit, which is the return on capital and enterprise necessary to keep firms in an industry.

If the firm's average cost (AC) curve is the one drawn in Figure 4, the average cost of producing x_1 is the distance x_1A. Total revenue (TR) is still $P_1 \times x_1$, or the area of $0P_1Bx_1$. Total cost is now the area of $0CAx_1$. Since $TR > TC$, there is an economic profit equal to the area of CP_1BA in Figure 4. On the other hand, if the firm's average cost curve is the one drawn in Figure 5, the average cost of producing x_1 is the distance x_1A. Total revenue is the area of $0P_1Bx_1$, and total cost is the area of $0CAx_1$. In this case, $TC > TR$, so losses are being incurred. The loss is equal to the area of P_1CAB in Figure 5.

Should the firm of Figure 5 continue to produce and, if so, for how long? It is suffering a loss, which means the factors of production employed by this firm could earn more in some other use. Revenues are less than opportunity costs. But keep in mind that this diagram shows the short run, which means that some factor is fixed. This fixed factor means that there are fixed costs that cannot be eliminated. Fixed costs must be paid in the short run even if production ceases. We need to include the average variable cost (AVC) curve to determine the conditions under which the firm should cease production, because variable costs are the only ones under the firm's control in the short run.

The short-run cost curves of a firm are depicted with several equilibrium points in Figure 6. At a price of P_1, which represents a marginal revenue of MR_1, the firm maximizes profits by producing x_1. At P_1, the firm is making an economic profit because total revenue (area of $0P_1Ax_1$) is greater than total cost (area of $0C_1Dx_1$). At price $P_2 = MR_2$, the firm would

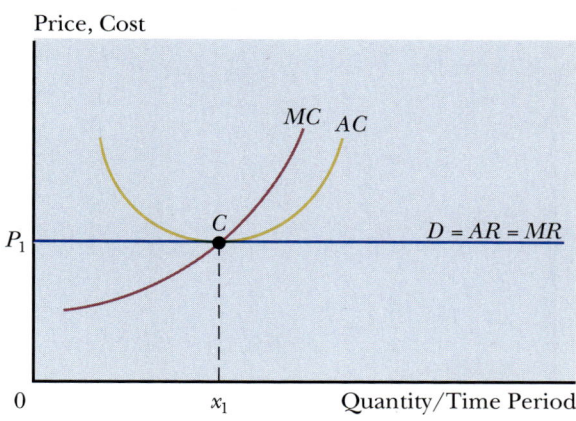

FIGURE 3
A FIRM EARNING ZERO ECONOMIC PROFIT
The average cost (AC) curve is used to determine if a firm is making an economic profit. If average revenue (price) is equal to average cost, the firm is making zero economic profit.

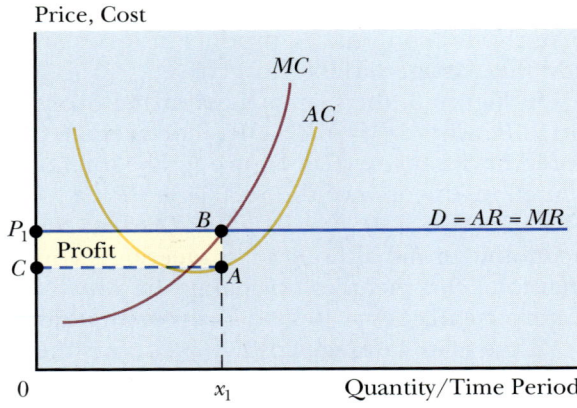

FIGURE 4
A FIRM EARNING AN ECONOMIC PROFIT
If the firm's average revenue is greater than its average cost at the level of output being produced, the firm is making an economic profit.

produce x_2 and make zero economic profit because total revenue (area of $0P_2Bx_2$) is equal to total cost (area of $0C_2Bx_2$).

Examine carefully what happens when price falls to P_3 and marginal revenue falls to MR_3. The profit-maximizing or loss-minimizing output is now x_3. At output level x_3, losses are incurred because total revenue is the area of $0P_3Sx_3$, and total cost is the area of $0C_3Ex_3$. Losses are thus represented by the rectangle P_3CES. The firm needs to answer this question: Should it produce and incur this loss or should it cease production? Remember, if production is halted, fixed costs must still be paid. In Figure 6, if the market price is P_3, the firm is earning a total revenue equal to the area of $0P_3Sx_3$, and its total variable costs ($TVC = AVC \times Q$) are $0P_3Sx_3$. In other words, the firm is covering (exactly) its total variable costs and losing an amount equal to its total fixed costs. It must pay the fixed costs even if it shuts down, so at price P_3 the firm is indifferent about shutting down or continuing to produce. If the price falls below P_3, the firm will shut down in order to minimize losses. By shutting down, it will lose only total fixed costs, instead of total fixed costs plus some portion of variable costs if it continues to produce. The minimum or low point on the AVC curve (S in Figure 6) is called the **shutdown point** because if price (P or MR) falls below that point, the firm loses less by ceasing production.

shutdown point
The minimum point on the average variable cost (AVC) curve, or the level of output at which a perfectly competitive firm minimizes its losses by ceasing operation.

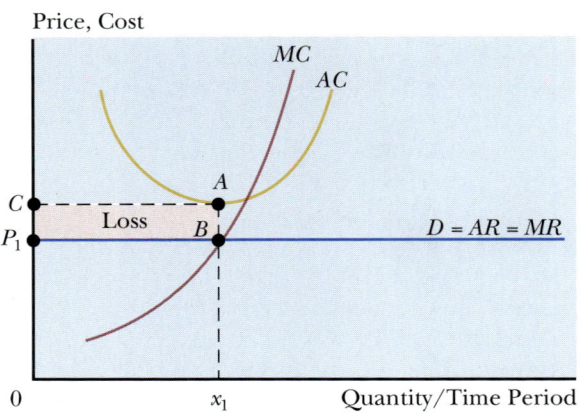

FIGURE 5
A FIRM SUFFERING A LOSS
If the firm's average cost is greater than its average revenue at the level of output being produced, the firm is incurring a loss.

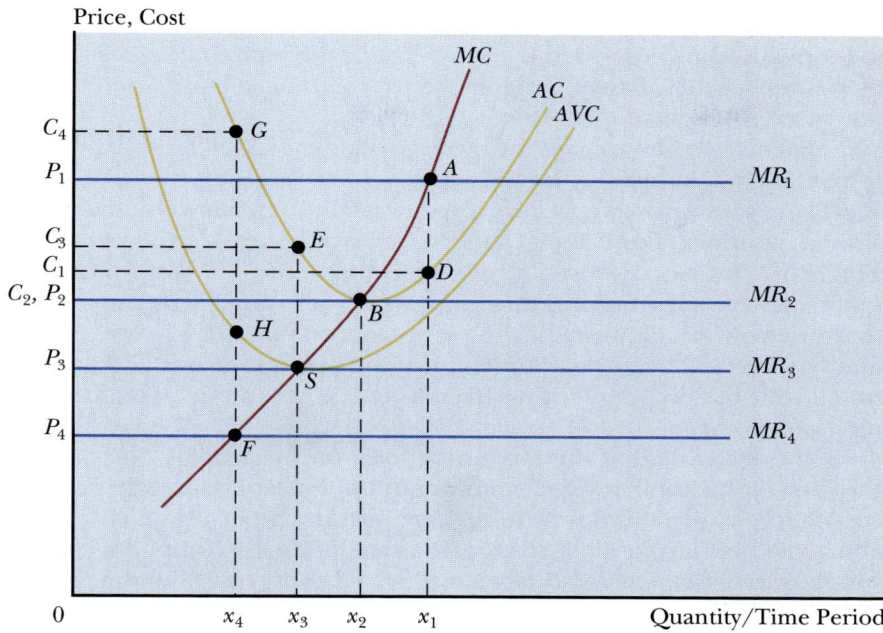

FIGURE 6
THE SHUTDOWN POINT
If a firm's average revenue is greater than its average variable cost, the firm will be able to cover total variable costs and make a payment toward total fixed costs. If price falls below average variable costs, the firm will lose less money if it shuts down than if it continues to produce. The shutdown point in this case is point S at a price of P_3.

Consider price P_4 (or MR_4) in Figure 6. The $MR = MC$ rule tells the firm that at P_4 it should produce output level x_4. However, at x_4 the firm is losing P_4C_4GF ($0P_4Fx_4 - 0C_4Gx_4$). Total revenue of $0P_4Fx_0$ does not cover the total variable costs of producing x_4, which are x_4H times x_4. In other words, the firm is losing more than its total fixed costs. It is making variable cost outlays that it wouldn't have to make if it stopped production entirely. The firm would be better off to shut down and only incur its fixed costs.

Because the firm shuts down, we need to modify the earlier statement that the firm's marginal cost curve represents its short-run supply curve. That statement is not completely correct. A firm's short-run supply curve is represented by its marginal cost curve only *above* the shutdown point (point S in Figure 6). Below the shutdown point, the firm will produce no output, so only the part of the marginal cost curve above the minimum point on the average variable costs curve is the firm's supply curve.

The model has just told us that in the short run, the firm will shut down when price falls below average variable cost. It says nothing about the real-world timing of such a shutdown. The decision to shut down is more difficult in reality than in theory. It depends on many factors, including time and anticipated changes. A few examples may illustrate such problems.

First, imagine yourself the owner of a sporting goods store in a ski area or a beach resort. Shutdown may be a seasonal decision. If revenues fall below average variable costs (clerks' wages, electricity, and so on) in the off-season, you may close up, bearing only your fixed costs (such as rent on the store) until crowds return and your revenues increase. In this case, shutdown does not mean you are moving your investments in plant and equipment into other businesses. It simply means that you lose money in certain seasons and you lose less money if you shut down. You fully intend to reopen for business when the snow flies or the temperature sends people to the beaches. Past experience helps you to determine when to shut down and when to reopen.

Second, imagine yourself the owner-manager of a steel mill. The price of steel has fallen below your average variable costs of production. In the short run, you shut down (if laws and union contracts allow you to do so—a union contract might change labor from a variable to a fixed resource). The short run is too short a time period for you to vary your plant size (which is one way of saying that you can't move your fixed resources in this time period). However, if you are convinced that this low price is permanent, you will begin to liquidate. You will sell equipment and attempt to sell your buildings and other fixed assets. As you do this, you are moving to the long run.

To review, note that the minimum point on the average cost curve is the least-cost combination. The minimum point on the average variable costs curve is the shutdown point. The part of the marginal cost curve above the average variable cost curve is the perfectly competitive firm's supply curve. Keep in mind that these are all short-run phenomena. We will trace the long-run adjustment later.

AN EXAMPLE OF PRODUCTION DECISIONS

The short-run output decisions and profit determination for a perfectly competitive firm can be illustrated with a simple example. Table 1 presents some production cost data for a firm. Assuming that different market prices are the result of different market equilibrium situations, it is possible to determine the firm's response to different prices. In Table 2, six different market prices corresponding to different market conditions are assumed. When the market price is $61, the demand and marginal revenue curves the firm faces are perfectly elastic at $61. The firm produces 10 units (where $MR = MC = \$61$) and earns an economic profit of $120. This situation corresponds to the graph in Figure 4. At a market price of $46, the firm maximizes profit where $MR = MC = \$46$, which is at an output of 7 units. Since $TR = TC$ at 7 units, there is zero economic profit. This situa-

TABLE 1 PRODUCTION COSTS FOR A FIRM

OUTPUT	AVERAGE VARIABLE COSTS (AVC)	AVERAGE COST (AC)	MARGINAL COST (MC)	TOTAL COST (TC)
1	$40	$100	$40	$100
2	38	68	36	136
3	36	56	32	168
4	35	50	32	200
5	35	47	35	235
6	36	46	41	276
7	37 3/7	46	46	322
8	39	46 1/2	50	372
9	41	47 2/3	57	429
10	43	49	61	490

Chapter 9 Perfect Competition

TABLE 2
PRODUCTION DECISIONS AT VARIOUS MARKET PRICES

MARKET PRICE (MR)	FIRM'S OUTPUT	TOTAL REVENUE (TR)	TOTAL COST (TC)	FIRM'S PROFITS
$61	10	$610	$490	$120
50	8	400	372	28
46	7	322	322	0
41	6	246	276	−30
35	5	175	235	−60
32	4	128	200	−72

tion corresponds to Figure 3. When market price falls to $41, the firm reacts by decreasing its output to 6 units (where $MR = MC = \$41$). At 6 units of output, it incurs a loss of $30. This economic loss corresponds to that shown in Figure 5.

The firm will continue to produce in the short run unless price falls below $35 because the minimum value of average variable costs (minimum point on the AVC curve) is at $35. To see why, look at how the firm responds when market price falls to $32. At $32, the firm produces 4 units. However, it loses $72 ($TR = 4 \times \$32 = \$128$, $TC = 4 \times \$50 = \$200$, and $\$128 - \$200 = -\$72$). If it shuts down, the firm loses only $60 in total fixed costs. The total variable cost (TVC) would have been $140 if production had taken place ($TVC = 4 \times \$35 = \$140$ and $TFC = \$200 - \$140 = \$60$). So the firm loses less if it ceases production. At any price less than $35, the firm will shut down.

A MARKET SUPPLY CURVE

We can now look at the relationship between the firm's supply (marginal cost) curve and the market supply curve. The firm's supply curve represents its output response to increased market prices. If we were to add (horizontally) the short-run supply curves for all firms, we would construct the short-run market (or industry) supply curve. The market supply curve is simply the aggregate of all the firms' supply curves. The short-run market supply curve, then, is the aggregate of the portions of all firms' marginal cost curves that lie above their average variable cost curves. In the long run, more firms can enter an industry as a response to economic profits. The market supply curve will shift to the right because it is made up of more individual supply curves. On the other hand, as firms leave an industry due to losses, the market supply curve will shift to the left, representing a decrease in supply. This decrease is due to the fact that there are fewer individual supply curves to be summed.

THE LONG RUN: CONSTANT, INCREASING, OR DECREASING COSTS

The process of determining price and output when firms have time to alter their fixed inputs and when new firms can enter the industry is illustrated in Figure 7. The D_1 and S_1 curves are the equilibrium demand and supply curves for the industry. The industry is in long-run equilibrium

International Perspective

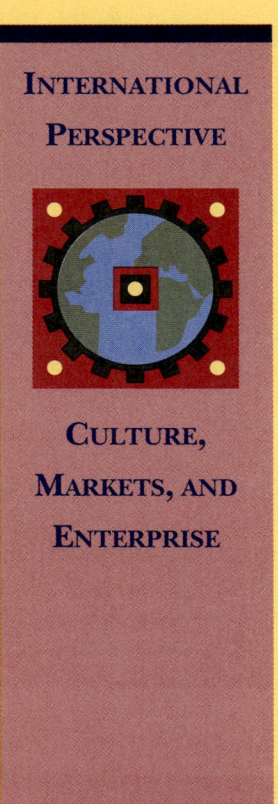

Culture, Markets, and Enterprise

In many countries, markets are not as well developed as they are in the United States. In these countries, many nonmarket institutions have strong holds on culture in ways that affect production, distribution, and consumption. The laws of supply and demand still hold, but customs, systems of land tenure, village and family organization, religious practices, and corruption all have an impact on the functioning of markets.

Cultural differences affect the emergence of entrepreneurs and the profit motive. In poor countries, entrepreneurs may lack the help of markets to bring together materials, labor, and capital. If individuals are not inherently risk takers, their reaction may be to say "no" to new business opportunities. In fact, in some cultures, risk taking is viewed as unacceptable behavior, and minorities become the entrepreneurs. Jews played this role in medieval Europe, the Chinese in some countries in South America, and Indians in Africa. This kind of cultural bias is a serious obstacle to economic development in many less developed countries, because development requires a strong entrepreneurial class. Also, if the ruling structure of a society does not encourage entrepreneurial development but supports the stability of a traditional society, the effect is to slow economic growth. In such traditional societies, a trauma often produces a spurt of economic growth. The trauma of World War II and its shakeup of the power structure in Japan is a case in point.

Another difference between the markets of less developed and industrialized countries is that retail markets are often less organized and products are less standardized. As a consequence, neither buyers nor sellers are price takers. Much time and effort is expended in negotiating prices. This time does not go into producing goods and services. Also, the market information widely available in industrialized countries is absent. The absence of this information adds to the cost of doing business in a traditional society and offers another cultural barrier to exchange, enterprise, and economic growth. It is easy for people in developed, industrialized countries to take markets and entrepreneurs for granted and overlook the role they play in creating and sustaining a high standard of living.

when no economic forces are working to cause it to expand or contract (or to cause the price to change). In part (*a*) of the figure, the firm is making zero economic profit at price P_1 and output x_1. Let's assume this firm is representative of 1,000 identical firms. Thus, the market supply curve (S_1) in part (*b*) is the summation of 1,000 MC curves (above the AVC curves). Since these firms are making zero economic profits at P_1, the industry is in equilibrium with an industry output of Q_1. Since each firm is producing x_1, $1{,}000 \times x_1 = Q_1$. Now suppose there is an increase in market demand to D_2, brought about by an increase in consumers' real income, and assume that the good under consideration is a normal good. When market demand shifts to D_2, market price rises to P_2. The demand curve for the firm rises to D_2 and is perfectly elastic at price P_2.

The firm's initial (short-run) response is to increase its output to x_2 because $MR_2 = MC$ at output level x_2. Thus, the increase in market demand from Q_1 to Q_2 is met by an increase in output by each of the 1,000 firms, from x_1 to x_2. Note, however, that each firm will then make an economic profit equal to the shaded area in Figure 7(*a*). Economic profit, you recall, means that factors of production are earning more than their opportunity cost. This profit means that the industry is out of equilibrium. Other firms are going to attempt to get some of this profit. The existence of profit is the signal for new firms to enter this industry.

Since free entry and perfect knowledge are assumed to be characteristics of perfect competition, entrepreneurs will be aware of this profit and will enter the industry. As firms enter the industry, the market supply curve will shift because it now is the summation of the 1,000 original MC curves plus the MC curves of the new entrant firms. In fact, firms will keep entering the industry until equilibrium (zero economic profit) is restored. This is illustrated in Figure 7. If all firms have the same costs (that is, all firms are exactly like the representative firm) and if nothing happens to change these costs, equilibrium will be restored when the price has been reduced to P_1, the original equilibrium price. If the new equilibrium price is P_1 and industry output is Q_3, each firm is producing x_1 units.

FIGURE 7
LONG-RUN ADJUSTMENT TO AN INCREASE IN MARKET DEMAND
An increase in market demand will cause the price to rise. The demand curve the representative firm faces will shift upward. Economic profit will result, and new firms will enter the industry in response to this profit. As new firms enter, the market supply curve shifts to the right, causing price to fall to the point at which the representative firm is again earning zero economic profit.

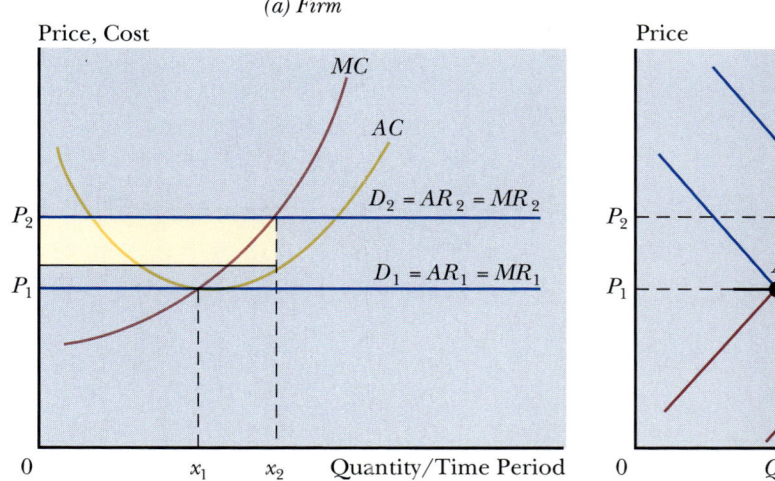
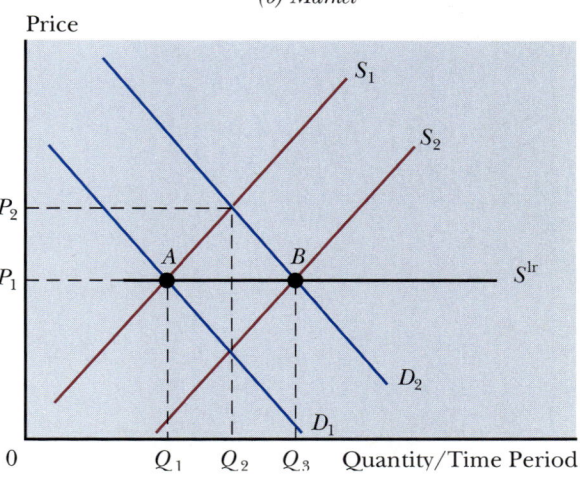

The summation of the firms' output (1,000 plus the number of new firms times x_1) is equal to the industry output (Q_3). Connecting the market equilibrium points, points A and B in Figure 7(b), gives the industry's long-run supply curve, S^{lr}. This curve represents what firms will supply after all adjustments have taken place.

You can check your understanding of this process by tracing the response to a decrease in demand. In Figure 8, the industry is initially in equilibrium at price P_1 and output Q_1. Firms are making zero economic profits and producing x_1 units of output each. Now suppose medical researchers discover that the product is dangerous to people's health. This news causes market demand to decrease to D_2. Market price falls to P_2, and industry output falls to Q_2. In the short run, each firm adjusts its output to x_2 (where $MC = MR_2$). At x_2, however, each firm is incurring losses represented by the shaded area in part (a). The industry is now out of equilibrium.

Just as profits are the signal for firms to enter an industry, losses are the signal for firms to exit an industry. Entrepreneurs move their factors of production to other uses, seeking to earn their opportunity cost elsewhere. Perfect knowledge is assumed, so entrepreneurs will know where they can earn at least normal profit. As firms leave the industry, the short-run market supply curve will shift to the left because it is now derived by adding up the short-run supply curves of fewer firms. Firms will leave the industry until the remaining firms have zero economic profits. Equilibrium is restored when the market supply curve shifts to S_2 in Figure 8(b) and restores a price of P_1. Industry output is now at Q_3, with each of the remaining firms producing x_1 units of output. As before, the long-run supply curve (S^{lr}) can be found by connecting the industry's equilibrium points, which are represented by points A and B in Figure 8(b).

CONSTANT-COST INDUSTRIES

The adjustments traced in Figures 7 and 8 assumed that factor prices, and thus costs, were unaffected by the quantity of output the industry pro-

FIGURE 8
LONG-RUN ADJUSTMENT TO A DECREASE IN MARKET DEMAND
A decrease in market demand will cause the price to fall. The demand curve the representative firm faces will shift downward. Losses will be incurred, and some firms will leave the industry. As firms leave, the market supply curve shifts to the left, causing price to rise until a remaining representative firm is earning zero economic profit.

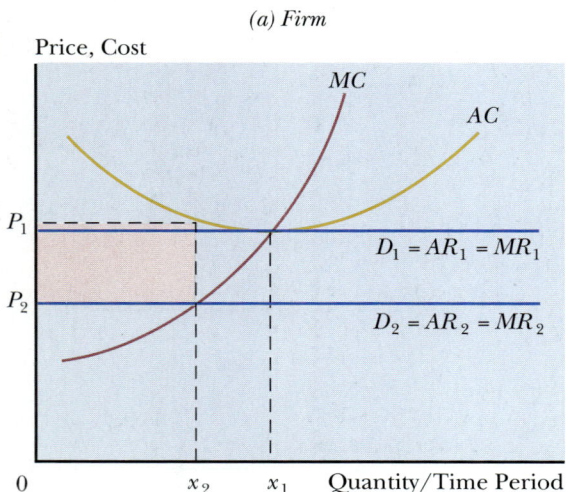
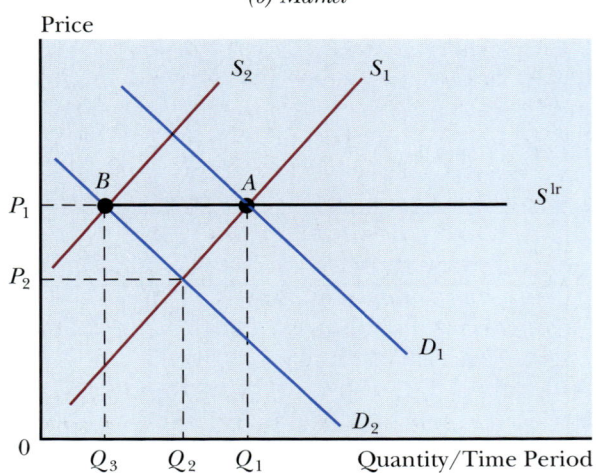

duced. As firms entered the industry (Figure 7) or exited the industry (Figure 8), the price of the factors of production did not change. As a result, the average and marginal cost curves didn't change. When cost curves don't change as an industry expands or contracts, the industry is referred to as a constant cost industry. A **constant cost industry** is an industry in which expansion of output does not cause average costs to rise in the long run. In a constant cost industry, as more steel, labor, electricity, and other inputs are purchased, the cost of those inputs does not increase. Constant costs are most likely to occur when the industry's purchase of inputs is small relative to the market supply of those inputs. If the industry's use of inputs is small relative to the market supply, increased demand for those inputs would not increase their prices. For example, consider the home computer industry. If profits exist and firms enter, these firms will demand more inputs. They will demand more plastic, more labor, and more microchips. If all the computer-producing firms use a small fraction of the total supply of these inputs, the increase in demand will not cause the price of plastic, labor, and microchips to rise.

Figures 7 and 8, then, represent long-run contractions and expansions in constant cost industries. The short-run response to a contraction in demand is a decrease in price. An expansion in demand produces a short-run increase in price. The market adjustment, however, will return price to its original level, with fewer firms in the case of the contraction or more firms in the case of the expansion. The long-run supply curve in a constant cost industry is perfectly elastic, even though the short-run supply curve has a positive slope.

constant cost industry
An industry in which expansion of output does not cause average cost to rise in the long run.

INCREASING COST INDUSTRIES

Sometimes an expansion in industry output will cause costs to increase in the long run. In this case, as an industry expands output and demands more inputs, the increased demand causes prices of inputs to rise. For example, an increase in demand for chicken causes new firms to enter the packing industry and to demand more chicken coops, chicken pluckers, land, and plastic bags. If the increased demand causes the price of chicken coops, chicken pluckers, land, or plastic bags to rise, the average production costs of the representative firm will increase as a result of the increased demand for chicken. Also, less efficient factors and firms may be drawn into the industry. These conditions describe an increasing cost industry. An **increasing cost industry** is an industry in which expansion of output causes average costs to rise in the long run.

Figure 9 illustrates the long-run adjustment process in an increasing cost industry. The industry is originally in equilibrium at price P_1 and output level Q_1. Each firm is producing x_1 units of output. Market demand increases to D_2. As a result, market price rises to P_2. The firm's demand is now represented by $D_2 = AR_2 = MR_2$. The firm's short-run response is to increase output to x_2, where $MC_1 = MR_2$. The industry's output is now at Q_2. At this increased output, two things will happen. First, new firms will enter the industry because of the economic profits that now exist. Second, costs will rise as a result of the increased demand for inputs. This rise in cost is represented by the upward shift in the marginal and average cost curves to MC_2 and AC_2 in Figure 9(a).

increasing cost industry
An industry in which expansion of output causes average cost to rise in the long run.

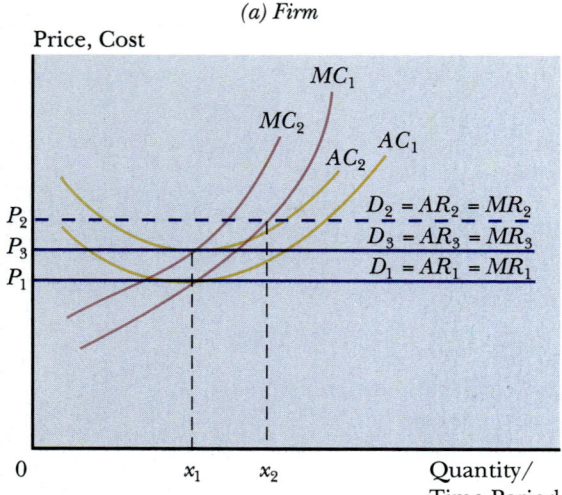 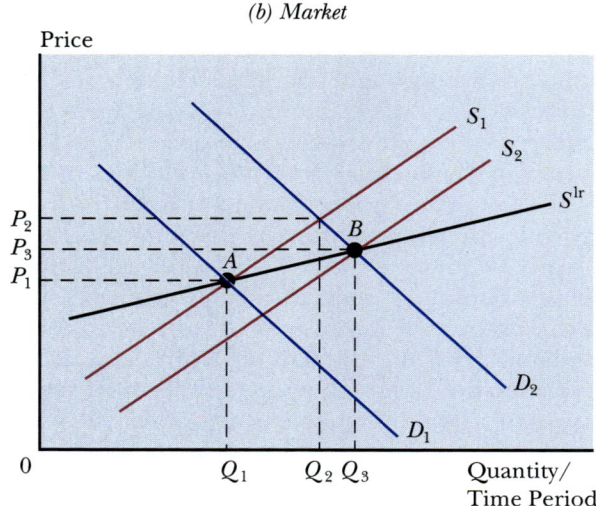

**FIGURE 9
LONG-RUN ADJUSTMENT TO INCREASING DEMAND IN AN INCREASING COST INDUSTRY**
When demand increases in an increasing cost industry, the firms that enter the industry bid up the prices of the factors of production for all firms in the industry. As a result, price does not return to the old equilibrium. Instead, a new equilibrium with the representative firm earning zero economic profit is established at a price above the old equilibrium price.

The upward shift of the marginal and average cost curves is based on the assumption that all costs increase at the same rate. In most cases, this would not be true, since the prices of some inputs (the scarcer ones) would rise faster. However, the example is clearer if we assume that all factor prices rise proportionally, and this assumption does not seriously affect the analysis. Firms, as purchasers of inputs, are likely to have much influence in some input markets and little influence in others. In the chicken-packaging example, as the demand for chicken increases and firms enter the industry, there may be no effect on the price of land but a large effect on the price of machines used to pluck chickens. This kind of cost increase is most likely when specific, rather than general, factors are used in the production process. It is also possible that the new firms attracted to an industry will be less efficient at producing the good in question. In this case, the representative firm will have higher costs, indicating less efficient production.

The net result of an increased number of firms and increased costs is a rightward shift in the short-run market supply curve. The supply curve shifts to the right because it is the sum of the supply curves of more firms. However, it will not shift as far to the right as it did in the constant cost industry because costs have risen for every firm. The new short-run market supply curve will be S_2 in Figure 9(b). Equilibrium is reached at price P_3, where firms are no longer making profits. Industry output is now Q_3, and each firm is producing x_1 units, where $MR_3 = MC_2$.

As before, the long-run market supply curve connects the industry's equilibrium points on all of the short-run supply curves. Connecting points A and B in Figure 9(b) produces a long-run supply curve (S^{lr}) with a positive slope, indicating an increasing cost industry.

Diagraming the adjustment process to a decrease in demand for an increasing cost industry is left as an exercise for the reader.

DECREASING COST INDUSTRIES

To complete the analysis, we must consider a decreasing cost industry. A **decreasing cost industry** is an industry in which an expansion of output

decreasing cost industry
An industry in which expansion of output causes average cost to fall in the long run

Economic Profile

David Ricardo
1772–1823

David Ricardo may have been the most influential of all the classical economists. Ricardo was born into a wealthy family and was sent from London to Amsterdam for an education. He returned to enter his father's business at age fourteen. The group of businessmen he joined was the prosperous community of Jewish merchants and stockbrokers in London. To his family's horror, he fell in love with a Quaker. He was disowned and expelled from the family business. He had no alternative but to go into business for himself. Ricardo quickly became very successful and then grew bored. In 1814, Ricardo retired from business to devote his time to political economy. He became a leading intellectual. His experience contrasts with that of almost all the other classical economists, who pursued rigorous programs of formal education in philosophy. In 1819, Ricardo became a member of Parliament and, with the help of James Mill (father of the great economist John Stuart Mill), founded the Political Economy Club of London. This club became the forum in which the classical economists discussed their ideas.

Ricardo was a prolific writer of letters and pamphlets intended to influence policy discussions on economic matters. His chief formal work, *On the Principles of Political Economy and Taxation*, was published in 1817. He is best remembered for his statements on the principles of comparative advantage and his support of free trade. These ideas are only a part of his comprehensive work. In fact, much of his early interest in economics was generated by his interest in international trade and in showing the benefits of such trade. Ricardo also developed a labor theory of value that greatly impressed Karl Marx, who extended and radicalized it.

causes average costs to fall in the long run. In a decreasing cost industry, as more firms enter the industry, causing the demand for inputs to increase, input prices fall. Falling input prices imply that there are economies of scale in an industry that is supplying an input to the decreasing cost industry. For example, as more electricity is demanded, more efficient generators are built and the price of this input falls.

Figure 10 derives a long-run supply curve for a decreasing cost industry. The initial market equilibrium price, P_1, is determined by the intersection of the market demand and supply curves, D_1 and S_1. The representative firm is in equilibrium producing x_1 units at price P_1. Now suppose there is an increase in the price of a substitute good, so that demand for the product of this industry increases to D_2. The short-run response is that price rises to P_2, shifting the firm's demand curve to $D_2 = AR_2 = MR_2$. The representative firm responds by increasing its output to x_2, where $MR_2 = MC_1$. Profits now exist and new firms will enter this industry. As new firms enter, two things happen. First, the market supply curve will shift to the right because it is now composed of individual supply curves. Second, as industry output increases, costs fall. In Figure 10(a), the decrease in costs is assumed to be a proportional decrease in the cost of all inputs.[1] The decrease in costs for the representative firm is shown in Figure 10(a) as a shift from AC_1 to AC_2 and from MC_1 to MC_2.

The industry's decrease in costs and increase in supply cause the market price to fall. A new equilibrium at a price such as P_3 will be reached. At P_3, the representative firm faces demand curve D_3. Equilibrium is reached at output x_1, where $MR_3 = MC_2$. No economic profits exist.

As before, the long-run supply curve connects the equilibrium points in the market. These points are represented by points A and B in Figure

FIGURE 10
LONG-RUN ADJUSTMENT TO DECREASING DEMAND IN A DECREASING COST INDUSTRY
When demand increases in a decreasing cost industry, the firms that enter the industry cause the prices of the factors of production to fall for all firms in the industry. As a result, a new equilibrium price is established that is below the old equilibrium price.

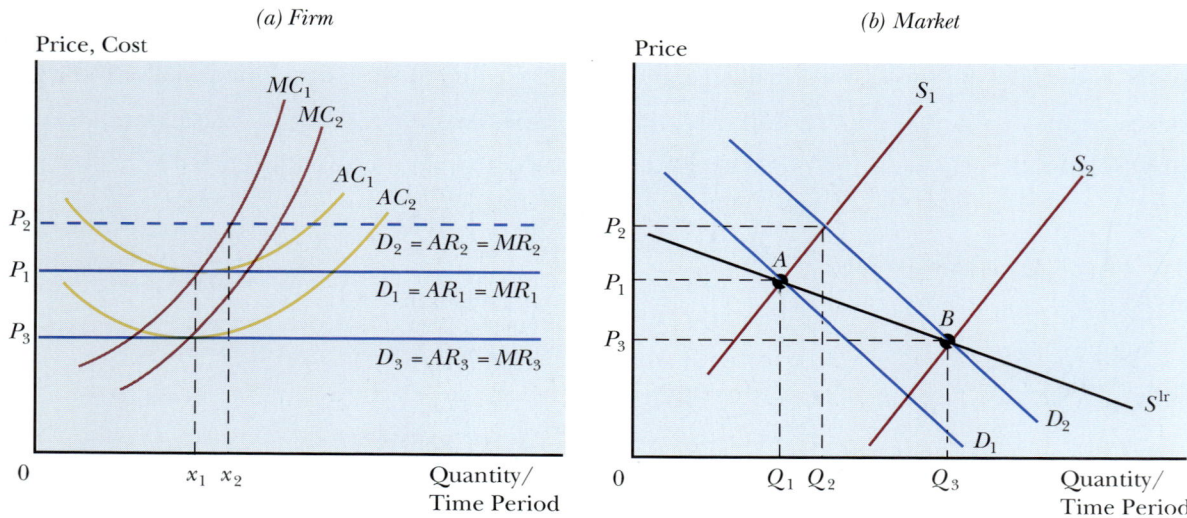

1. Again, this assumption is not essential, but it is convenient because it simplifies the graph. If costs decrease with industry expansion, it is more likely that the decrease results from a decline in the price of a major input rather than a proportional decline in the price of all inputs.

10(b). The long-run market supply curve is represented by S^{lr}. This curve has a negative slope, meaning that an increase in market demand would eventually lead to a new equilibrium at a lower price for the industry's product. Decreasing cost industries thus have negatively sloped long-run supply curves. (The short-run market supply curves are still positively sloped, since they are the aggregate of individual firms' short-run marginal cost curves.)

Diagraming the effects of a decrease in demand in a decreasing cost industry is left as an exercise for the reader.

COMPETITIVE EQUILIBRIUM: WHAT'S SO GREAT ABOUT PERFECT COMPETITION?

The nature of perfect competition is such that the firm and industry are driven to equilibrium at zero economic profit. This equilibrium is the appeal of perfect competition as a standard against which to judge other market structures. Economists view this equilibrium as an ideal, or a social optimum. In equilibrium, resources are optimally allocated among competing uses. Figure 11 shows a perfectly competitive firm in equilibrium. At equilibrium, price (P) is equal to average cost (AC) and also is equal to marginal cost (MC).

First, consider $P = MC$. This means that allocative efficiency is being achieved and that the resources of the firm are being allocated exactly as consumers wish. It means that firms are expanding production exactly to the level desired by consumers. If P were greater than MC, it would mean that not enough resources were going into the production of the good in question. Consumers would be willing to pay a higher price (P) than it costs to produce another unit of the good (MC). If P were less than MC, too many resources would be devoted to the production of the good. Con-

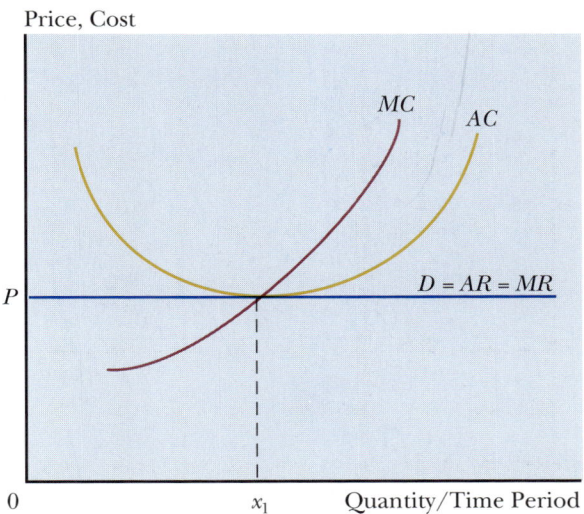

FIGURE 11
THE EQUILIBRIUM CONDITION FOR A PERFECTLY COMPETITIVE FIRM
In short-run equilibrium with perfect competition, allocative efficiency is met. This means that the resources of the firm are being allocated as consumers wish.

sumers would not be willing to pay as much as it costs to produce another unit of the good. In other words, where $P = MC$, the correct amount of resources is being devoted to producing the good.

Second, consider $P = AC$. This means that firms are earning only normal profits. There is no incentive for firms to enter or leave the industry. It is important to note the role of profits in the perfectly competitive model. Economic profits serve as the signal for firms to move in or out of an industry. When profits exist, entrepreneurs rush in to attempt to capture them. The industry is forced to a new equilibrium. When losses are present, entrepreneurs leave to seek higher returns elsewhere. Equilibrium is attained because of the profit-seeking nature of firms. In equilibrium, there is efficiency. It is not because of some altruistic behavior on the part of entrepreneurs that firms are efficient. Entrepreneurs are assumed to be profit maximizers motivated by individual self-interest, and their response to changing profits brings about efficiency. In the competitive model, self-interest and the quest for profits produce the efficiency that benefits consumers. The firm is striving not for efficiency but for profits. When economic profits have served their signaling function, they disappear.

Third, consider $MC = AC$. This means that average cost AC is at a minimum. Therefore, the representative firm in this industry is using the least-cost combination of inputs. The variable resources are being combined as efficiently as possible.

In long-run equilibrium, the short-run average cost (AC) curve also will be tangent to the long-run average cost ($LRAC$) curve at its minimum point, where $AC = LRAC$, as in Figure 12. This means that all firms are at the most efficient size and are also combining the variable resources efficiently. The firms are using the least-cost combination of inputs and the optimal plant size. All firms must be efficient, or they will be driven from the market by losses. If any one firm is more efficient than normal (more efficient than the representative firm), it will be able to make an economic profit even though the other firms don't. At long-run equilib-

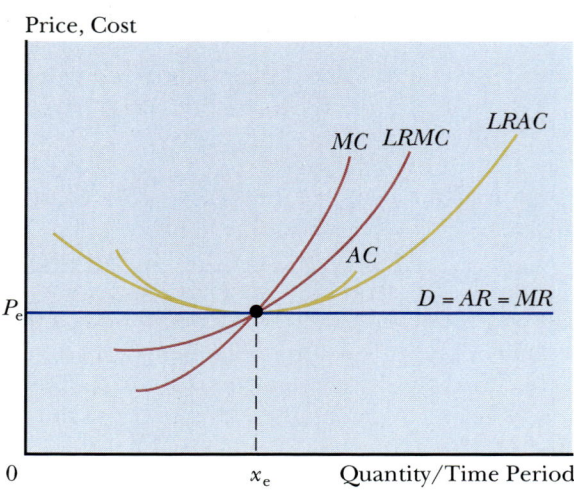

**FIGURE 12
LONG-RUN
EQUILIBRIUM WITH
PERFECT COMPETITION**
In long-run equilibrium with perfect competition, average cost is equal to long-run average cost. This means that all firms are at the optimal size and are also combining variable resources efficiently. This is the ideal of efficiency to which other market structures are compared.

Chapter 9   Perfect Competition   247

> ### WHAT EQUILIBRIUM IN PERFECT COMPETITION MEANS
>
> - $P = MC$ Production is at the level consumers indicate (through the market) they want.
> - $P = AC$ Firms are earning normal profits. There is no movement into or out of the industry.
> - $AC = MC$ Firms are using the least-cost method of production.

rium, then, $P = AC = MC = LRAC = LRMC$, since the long-run marginal cost curve ($LRMC$) crosses $LRAC$ at its minimum point.

The model of perfect competition is not meant to be a precise description of reality. Nor is it, in every case, the ideal state that society should be striving to reach. In certain industries, it may be too costly to bring about the necessary conditions for perfect competition. In that case, society can accept less than the ideal. The model of perfect competition is a tool for the economist. The economist can compare the real-world situation to the hypothetical world of perfect competition to determine what would be the case if perfect competition existed. In this sense, perfect competition is a benchmark, or yardstick, by which economists can measure the performance of other market structures.

AN EXAMPLE OF PERFECT COMPETITION

In recent years, the financial services industry has become close to the model of a perfectly competitive industry. The services that this industry offers are very homogeneous. A checking account at a financial institution in a given city is pretty much the same as a checking account anywhere else. In addition, the Depository Institutions Deregulation and Monetary Control Act (DIDMCA) of 1980 opened up entry into this industry. As a result, insurance companies, stockbrokers, and savings and loan institutions all began to compete with commercial banks for checking account business. One of the results is that consumers now earn interest on their checking accounts. This interest is equivalent to a lower price for bank services. This market entry was beneficial to consumers and drove bank profits down to normal levels.

LARGE NUMBERS OF BUYERS: COMPETITION ON THE BUYER'S SIDE

We have concentrated on developing a theory of firms in perfect competition, or competition on the sellers' side of the market. The assumption of many sellers means that all sellers perceive the demand curve they face to be perfectly elastic at the market price. Keep in mind, however, that we also assumed large numbers of buyers, so many that none possessed market power.

Concentrating on the firm should not obscure the importance of competition on the buyers' side of the market. In order for markets to be competitive, there must be enough buyers that none can affect the price by withholding purchases or increasing purchases. A competitive market cannot be "cornered" by buyers with market power or wealth. A competitive market is too big and too impersonal to be influenced by single buyers. In most of your transactions as a buyer, you will find that you are a perfect competitor—too small to influence the price.

ECONOMIC RENT IN PERFECT COMPETITION

According to the model of perfect competition, in industries in which free entry exists, profits will be driven to normal rates of return. Yet we all know of individuals who have become rich in industries that are very competitive and that have relatively free entry. How can this happen without totally invalidating this model? To explain how returns in excess of normal profits can exist in the long run, even under perfect competition, we must introduce some new concepts.

ECONOMIC RENT

Rent is a familiar term. You pay rent on your apartment. But economists have a special (and very different) meaning for this term. **Economic rent** is a payment to a factor of production in excess of the opportunity cost of that factor of production. Let's say, for example, you are trained as a teacher and could earn $20,000 per year in that profession. However, you also have beautiful teeth and can do toothpaste commercials, for which you earn $50,000 per year. Economists would say that $30,000 of your income is economic rent because it is the amount by which your earnings exceed your opportunity cost. They would predict that you would do the commercials for $20,001 per year since you would then be earning more than your opportunity cost.

Economic rent, then, is more general than economic profit. Since economic profit is defined as revenue in excess of all the implicit costs (including normal profit) and explicit costs of production, economic profit is rent to entrepreneurs. Entrepreneurs will earn only normal profits in perfect competition because new entry will drive out higher rates of return. But it is possible that economic rents to other factors of production will exist. Thus, we need to relate the concept of economic rent to the model of perfect competition.

REPRESENTATIVE FIRMS AND ECONOMIC RENTS

The theory of perfect competition uses a representative firm that is one of many firms with cost structures that are identical. This assumption is not always realistic. Consider agriculture as an example. Some farmland is far superior to other farmland. It is more fertile, gets more rainfall, or is located where the weather is warmer. The quality of the land will affect the farmer's costs of production. Economic rent will always be earned on the better land, and entry of new firms will not eliminate such rent. In other competitive industries, location, family connections, or talent will make firms' cost structures different, creating economic rents.

---

economic rent
A payment to a factor of production in excess of its opportunity cost.

Differential Rent Theory

Economic rent does not weaken the theory of perfect competition. In 1817, classical economist David Ricardo reconciled the existence of economic rents with perfect competition by developing differential rent theory. He was interested in explaining the fact that fertile farmland earned a higher rent than poor farmland.

Consider, for example, the cost and revenue functions of two farms, shown in parts (*a*) and (*b*) of Figure 13. The market is represented in part (*c*). Supply and demand are such that market price for the farms' product is P. Farm A is earning zero economic profit ($P = AC_A$). Farm B is earning an economic profit equal to the shaded area. This economic profit comes from the fact that the land used to produce the farm product is much more fertile for farm B. As a result, the costs of production are lower.

Farmers would be willing to pay the owner of the land owned by farm B a higher price for being able to farm that land. This higher price becomes a cost of production to farm B because economic rent for the more fertile land will rise as farmers seek to either purchase or lease this land. Even if the owner of the land is also the farmer, economic rent is still an opportunity cost of production because the owner could lease the land to other farmers.

The result of differential rent to factors of production is that rents rise on more productive factors. This rise equalizes the average cost of production among firms. In other words, the economic profit for farm B is a result of a superior factor of production, more fertile land. The user of the factor (it could be the owner of the farm or someone else) will receive this rent. When the rent is paid, AC_B will, in fact, rise until the shaded area for farm B disappears.

The point is that competitive firms may appear to earn economic profits (more than a normal rate of return), but these returns are economic rents to unique factors of production, not economic profits. In many cases, the firm's entrepreneur is the owner of the factors. As a result, the rent looks like an economic profit. In fact, many times the en-

FIGURE 13
DIFFERENTIAL RENTS IN PERFECT COMPETITION
Farms A and B both face perfectly elastic demand curves at price P, determined in the market for their product, part (*c*). Because its land is more fertile, farm B has lower average costs and earns a profit shown by the shaded area in part (*b*). That profit will be converted to economic rent as competition for the fertile land bids up its price.

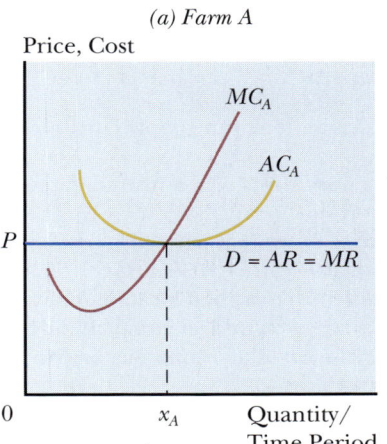

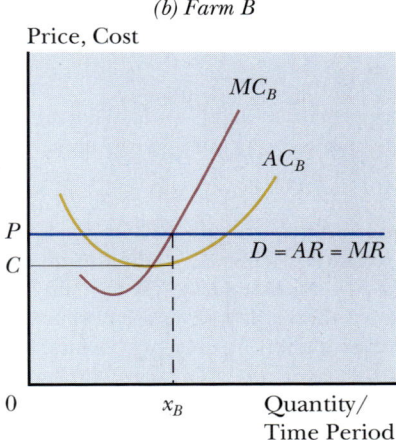

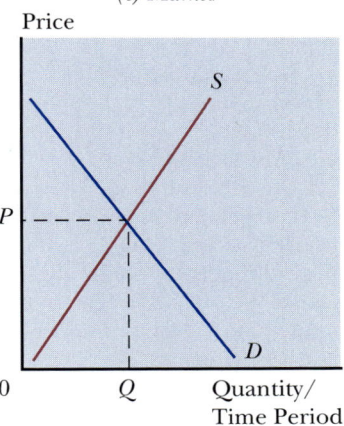

trepreneur has special skills that form the basis for the firm. The return to these skills is an economic rent to the factor of production enterprise. It is not an economic profit. The concept of economic rent is an important one and will be discussed in more detail in several upcoming chapters.

SUMMARY

1. Perfect competition is characterized by large numbers of buyers and sellers, homogeneous products, ease of entry into and exit out of the industry, perfect knowledge, and mobility of resources.

2. A firm in a perfectly competitive market faces a perfectly elastic demand curve at the price determined by equilibrium in the market.

3. The firm's short-run supply curve is the same as its short-run marginal cost (MC) curve above the minimum point on the average variable cost (AVC) curve, known as the shutdown point.

4. Long-run adjustments to changes in market demand are dependent on the cost characteristics for the industry. Since entry is easy, additional firms will enter an industry as long as economic profits are present. Thus, economic profits, brought about by an increase in demand, will lead to new entry.

5. An industry can be characterized by constant, increasing, or decreasing costs. The slope of the long-run market supply curve will depend on which of these cost situations prevails.

6. At perfectly competitive equilibrium, $P = AC = MC = LRAC = LRMC$. This condition describes the ideal efficiency of perfect competition, to which other market structures are compared.

7. Profits are the force that drives the perfectly competitive model to efficiency. The firm is seeking not efficiency but profits. This search for profits produces the efficiency that characterizes the model of perfect competition.

8. Large numbers of buyers in a perfectly competitive market ensure that no single buyer can influence price.

9. Economic rent is a payment (return) to a factor of production over the opportunity cost of that factor.

10. Competitive firms may appear to be earning long-run economic profits, but these returns are actually economic rents to specific factors of production in the firms.

NEW TERMS

perfect competition
market power
price taker
average revenue (AR)
representative firm
short-run supply curve
shutdown point
constant cost industry
increasing cost industry
decreasing cost industry
economic rent

QUESTIONS FOR DISCUSSION

1. Show how the long-run market supply curve will be determined by short-run supply adjustments in an increasing cost industry.

2. Draw the graphs for a decreasing cost industry in perfect competition, showing a market equilibrium and a representative firm. Then for a decrease in market demand, trace through the short-run and long-run adjustments.

3. "If the price of wheat doesn't rise, farmers will lose money and the long-run price will be even higher." Analyze this statement.

4. Why does profit maximization bring about efficiency?

5. What situations cause long-run supply curves to be positively sloped?

6. Explain in your own words why a firm might keep producing in the short run even if it were incurring a loss.

7. What does it mean to say that perfectly competitive equilibrium means that $P = AC = MC = LRAC = LRMC$?

8. Explain how the return to a good location for a firm (for instance, a gas station) in perfect competition does not violate the conclusion that economic profits are driven to zero by new entry.

9. Assume that the data from the table in Question 9 in the last chapter represent the unit-cost data for a perfectly

competitive firm in a constant cost industry. What will the firm produce in the short run if the market price is $7.00? Why? What is the economic profit or loss? If this is a representative firm, where is the market price going to settle?

10. What would happen to the firm in Question 9 if the market price fell to $2.50? Why?

11. What would happen to the price, output level, and profit for a firm in a perfectly competitive industry if the price of capital increased? Distinguish between short-run and long-run changes.

12. The assumptions of perfect competition include both large numbers of sellers and large numbers of buyers. Why is it important that there be large numbers of buyers?

13. Why do economists use the term *price taker* when discussing a firm in perfect competition?

14. Why do some restaurants stay open all year and others are open only during certain times and/or certain seasons?

15. Why is it that entrepreneurs in perfectly competitive firms can't earn economic rent in the long run, but other factors can?

SUGGESTIONS FOR FURTHER READING

Eckert, Ross D. *The Price System and Resource Allocation*, 10th ed. Hinsdale, IL: Dryden Press, 1988. Develops the graphical analysis in this chapter in great detail.

Stigler, George J. "Perfect Competition, Historically Contemplated," *Journal of Political Economy* (1957). Reprinted in Edwin Mansfield. *Microeconomics: Selected Readings*. New York: W. W. Norton, 1975, 167–187. A classic article that reviews the historical development of the theory of perfect competition.

Stigler, George J. *The Theory of Price*, 4th ed. New York: Macmillan, 1987, Chapter 10. A classic introductory price theory text by a Nobel Prize-winning economist.

AFTER STUDYING THIS CHAPTER, YOU SHOULD BE ABLE TO:

1. Define monopoly.
2. Calculate and diagram average revenue and marginal revenue, given data on price and output.
3. Label sections of a downward-sloping demand curve with the price elasticity, given information on marginal revenue.
4. Diagram average revenue, marginal revenue, marginal cost, and average cost curves for a monopolistic firm making:
   a. an economic profit,
   b. a loss,
   c. a normal profit.
5. List natural and artificial barriers to entry into an industry.
6. Discuss how a monopolist misallocates resources in terms of price and costs.
7. Explain why a monopolist does not have a supply curve.
8. Describe two types of price discrimination.
9. Discuss the alternatives to profit maximization.
10. Define:
    a. dumping,
    b. local monopoly,
    c. natural monopoly.

CHAPTER 10
MONOPOLY

INTRODUCTION

Monopoly is at the other end of the market continuum from perfect competition in the sense that perfect competition involves many firms and monopoly involves just one. The word *monopoly* is derived from the Greek words *mono* for "one" and *polein* for "seller." **Monopoly** is the market structure in which there is a single seller of a product that has no close substitutes.

Monopoly is a theoretical model. As with perfect competition, real-world examples of monopoly are almost nonexistent. The theory is still useful, however, as a tool to examine real-world situations. Although there are no pure monopolies, there are many firms that have some degree of monopoly power. **Monopoly power** is the ability to exercise power over market price and output. As you learned in the last chapter, firms in perfect competition are price takers. In this chapter, you will see that, because it has some control over price, a monopoly is a price searcher. A **price searcher** is a firm that sets price in order to maximize profits. A price-searching firm has monopoly power. It searches for the price-quantity combination that will maximize its profit.

One of the best examples of monopoly in U.S. history is the Aluminum Company of America (Alcoa). Before World War II, Alcoa was the only aluminum producer in the United States. But even this example falls short of absolute monopoly because aluminum does have some close substitutes. For example, soft drinks can be put into glass bottles, steel cans, or plastic containers instead of aluminum cans. Because everything has substitutes in some uses, it is difficult to find a real monopoly. Let's analyze market adjustments under monopoly and then compare the allocation of resources under monopoly to that under perfect competition.

monopoly
The market structure in which there is a single seller of a product that has no close substitutes.

monopoly power
The ability to exercise some of the conomic effects predicted in the model of monopoly by restricting output.

price searcher
A firm that sets price in order to maximize profits and thus has monopoly power.

DEMAND AND MARGINAL REVENUE

A perfectly competitive firm faces a perfectly elastic demand curve. As a result, price (or average revenue) and marginal revenue are equal. However, a monopolistic firm faces the *market* demand curve because the firm is the single seller and is, therefore, the industry. This distinction is very important because market demand curves have negative slopes. Since the monopolist's demand curve has a negative slope, its marginal revenue curve will lie below that curve, which is also the average revenue curve. The common sense reason why the marginal revenue curve lies below the average revenue curve is that the monopolist must lower price in order to sell more units of output. The price reduction applies to *all* units of output that the monopolist sells, not just the last, or marginal, unit. Each additional unit sold adds to total revenue by the amount it sells for (its price) but takes away from total revenue by the reduction in price on each unit sold. Thus, the change in revenue (the marginal revenue) must be less than the change in price.

Some data illustrating the relationship among average, total, and marginal revenue for a monopoly firm are presented in Table 1. When 3 units are sold, the total revenue is $186 (3 × $62). In order to sell 4 units, the monopolist must reduce the price from $62 to $60. Total revenue will then increase by $60 because an additional unit is being sold for $60. At the same time, it will decrease by $6 because the other 3 units now sell for $2 less each (for $60 each rather than for $62). The net result is that the monopolist has added $54 ($60 − $6) to total revenue by reducing the price from $62 to $60. Note that marginal revenue is $54 and price (average revenue) is $60 for 4 units. Marginal revenue has to be smaller than average revenue whenever units other than the marginal one suffer a price reduction.

This relationship is graphed in Figure 1. When demand is inelastic, decreases in price will cause total revenue to decline. If total revenue is declining, additions to total revenue must be negative. That is, marginal revenue is negative. In Figure 1, a reduction in price below P_1 will decrease total revenue because marginal revenue will be negative. This corre-

TABLE 1
AVERAGE, TOTAL, AND MARGINAL REVENUE FOR A MONOPOLIST

UNITS SOLD	PRICE (AVERAGE REVENUE)	TOTAL REVENUE	MARGINAL REVENUE
1	$64	$ 64	$ 64
2	63	126	62
3	62	186	60
4	60	240	54
5	58	290	50
6	56½	339	49
7	55	385	46
8	52	416	31
9	47	423	7
10	40	400	−23

Chapter 10 Monopoly

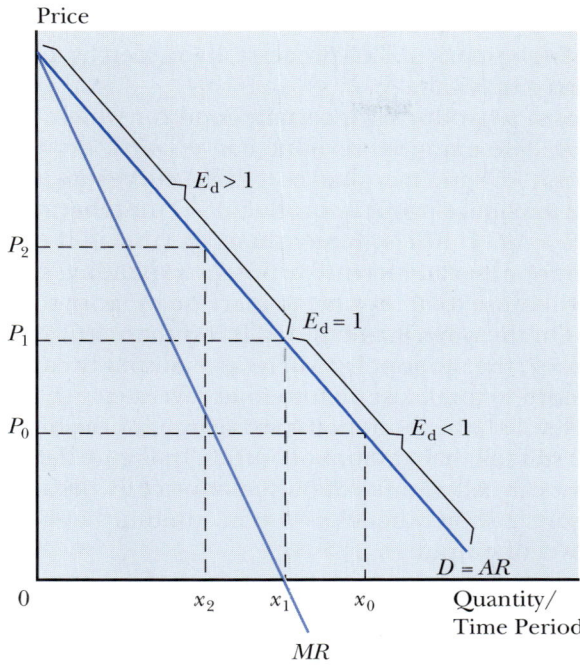

FIGURE 1
DEMAND AND MARGINAL REVENUE
The marginal revenue curve lies below the average revenue curve when there is a negatively sloped demand curve. In showing the relationship between average and marginal revenue, the marginal revenue curve will intersect the x-axis exactly halfway between the origin and the point where the average revenue curve intersects the x-axis. Demand is elastic above P_1 and inelastic below P_1.

sponds to the inelastic portion of the demand curve. However, a reduction in price from P_2 to P_1 would increase total revenue because the demand curve is elastic in this range.

Think back to the discussion of demand elasticity and Cournot's analysis of the mineral spring owner's situation. In that problem, the monopoly owner of a mineral spring with no production costs maximized profits by setting price where the price elasticity of demand was unitary. We can now apply the profit maximization rule $MR = MC$ to this case. If costs were zero, the MC curve would lie along the horizontal axis. In Figure 1, the monopolist would maximize profits by producing x_1 units (where $MR = MC = 0$) and selling them at price P_1. Since monopolists are profit maximizers, they produce the quantity where $MR = MC$ and sell the product for whatever the market will pay. The demand curve shows what price buyers will pay for any quantity of output. The mineral spring monopolist will increase sales of water as long as marginal revenue is positive, since it costs nothing more to produce another unit. You should note that this does *not* mean the mineral spring monopolist sells as much as possible. The monopolist sells the quantity that maximizes profit. In this case, it happens that the quantity at which profit is maximized is at a marginal revenue of zero, since costs are zero.

PRICE AND OUTPUT DECISIONS UNDER MONOPOLY

In the more general case, where costs are positive, the monopolist finds the profit-maximizing level of output by equating marginal cost and marginal revenue. The perfectly competitive firm is a price taker. The monopoly firm is a price searcher. A monopolist searches for the profit-maximizing price, not the highest price. This process can be seen by looking at the cost relationships graphically.

In Figure 2, a monopolist is producing a certain good for which the market demand curve is D. The marginal revenue curve (MR), derived from D, and the average cost (AC) and marginal cost (MC) curves are also given. The monopolist will maximize profit by producing x_1 units because at that level of output, $MR = MC$. If MR is greater than MC (that is, if output is less than x_1), the monopolist can increase profits by expanding output. Additions to output will cause total revenue to increase by more than the increase in total cost. On the other hand, if MR is less than MC (that is, if output is greater than x_1), the monopolist will reduce output because additions to output add more to total cost than to total revenue.

After choosing output level x_1, the monopolist will search for the highest price it can charge and still sell that amount of output. In Figure 2, this price is P_1. The monopolist can sell x_1 units of output at price P_1 because the demand curve in Figure 2 shows that P_1 is the maximum that consumers will pay for that level of output.

At P_1 and x_1, the monopolist is making an economic profit. The average revenue (price) is P_1, and average cost is C_1. Since P_1 is larger than C_1, the monopolist is making a profit of $P_1 - C_1$ on each unit for a total profit of $(P_1 - C_1) \times x_1$. In Figure 2, total cost is represented by rectangle $0C_1Bx_1$, and total revenue is represented by rectangle $0P_1Ax_1$. Total revenue minus total cost equals economic profit, or rectangle C_1P_1AB. Since the cost curves include both explicit and implicit costs, the monopoly firm is making more than its opportunity cost. That is, the firm is earning more than is necessary to keep its resources employed in this industry—it is making an economic profit.

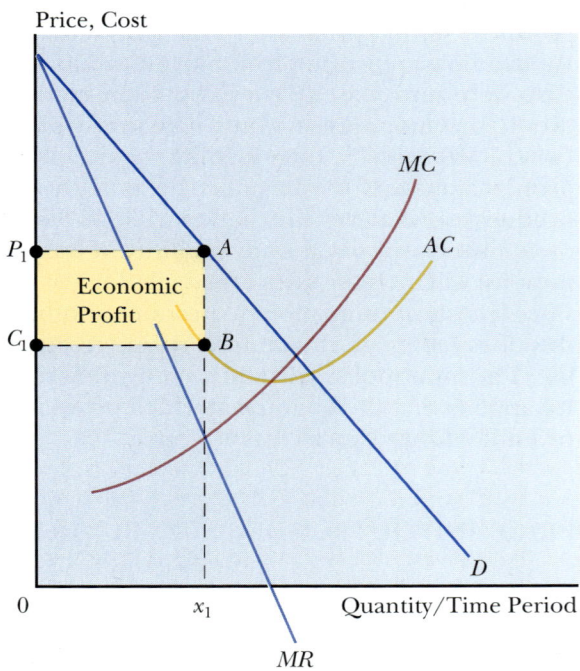

FIGURE 2
THE PROFIT-MAXIMIZING POSITION OF A MONOPOLIST
The profit-maximizing monopolist will produce x_1 units of output, where $MC = MR$. Since average cost (C_1) is less than average revenue (P_1) for output level x_1, this monopolist is making an economic profit.

Chapter 10 Monopoly   257

OUTPUT AND SALES	TOTAL COST (TC)	AVERAGE COST (AC)	MARGINAL COST (MC)	AVERAGE REVENUE (AR)	TOTAL REVENUE (TR)	MARGINAL REVENUE (MR)
0	$ 60	$ —	$ —	$ —	$ 0	$ —
1	100	100	40	58	58	58
2	136	68	36	57	114	56
3	168	56	32	56	168	54
4	200	50	32	55	220	52
5	235	47	35	54	270	50
6	276	46	41	53	318	48
7	322	46	46	52	364	46
8	372	46½	50	51	408	44
9	429	47⅔	57	50	450	42
10	490	49	61	49	490	40

TABLE 2
COST AND REVENUE DATA FOR A MONOPOLIST

Table 2 combines the revenue data of Table 1 with cost data for the same monopolist. The monopolist would maximize profits at an output level of 7 units, where $MC = MR = \$46$. Price should be set at $52 because the demand curve (AR) indicates that 7 units will sell for $52 each. At a price of $52, total revenue is $364 ($7 \times \$52$) and total cost is $322 ($\$46 \times 7$), which means that the monopolist is making a profit of $42 ($364 − 322). If you don't believe this is maximum profit, calculate the profit at each level of output from 1 to 10 units. You will see profit is maximized at 7 units because at that level, $MR = MC$.[1]

THE MONOPOLIST'S SUPPLY CURVE
A supply curve shows how much output will be offered for sale at various prices. In order to determine a supply curve, it is necessary to show that a firm will supply a unique quantity of output at any given price. This supply is by definition independent of demand. A monopoly firm does not have a supply curve in this sense. A monopolist sets the price at the profit-maximizing level of output, so it doesn't make sense to ask how much will be supplied at various prices. For a monopoly, the profit-maximizing output, where $MC = MR$, will depend on the location and shape of the demand curve. A monopoly firm therefore doesn't have a supply curve that is independent of demand.

To convince yourself that the monopolist does not have a supply curve, examine Figure 3. In part (a), two different prices, P_1 and P_2, are consistent with output x_1, depending on where the market demand curve is located (D_1 or D_2). The marginal revenue curves that are derived from the demand curves D_1 and D_2 both intersect the monopolist's marginal cost curve at the same level of output. In part (b), two different output levels,

---

1. If you do the calculation, you will find that profit is $42 at an output of 6 units and at an output of 7 units. This result is due to the fact that this numerical example uses whole-number data. The principle of profit maximization implies producing where $MR = MC$, but a unique point exists only when dealing with functions and using calculus. In this example, the actual profit-maximizing output would be somewhere between 6 and 7 units of output.

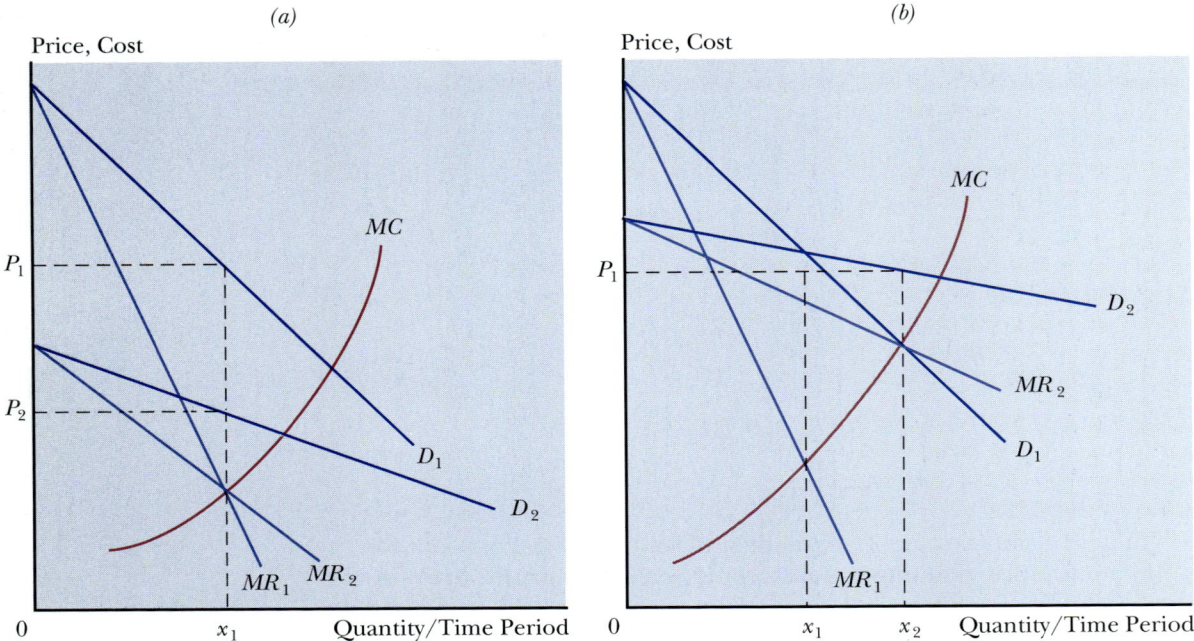

FIGURE 3
ONE OUTPUT WITH TWO PRICES OR ONE PRICE FOR TWO OUTPUTS
It is possible to trace out a supply curve only if a unique price is associated with a certain output. (a) Here there are at least two prices, P_1 and P_2, consistent with output x_1. (b) Here there are at least two outputs, x_1 and x_2, consistent with price P_1.

barriers to entry
Natural or artificial obstacles that keep new firms from entering an industry.

x_1 and x_2, can be produced at price P_1, depending on whether market demand is represented by D_1 or D_2.

Figure 3 shows that it is impossible to identify a supply curve for a monopolist. There is no way to predict what the monopolist will do without knowing the demand curve. In this sense, then, the monopolist has no supply curve. The predictive powers of economists are, therefore, more limited in an analysis of monopoly. In this case, economists cannot say that an increase in demand will cause price to rise, *ceteris paribus*.

PROFITS AND BARRIERS TO ENTRY

If a monopolist is earning profits, other entrepreneurs will want some of those profits. As a result, there will be pressure from new firms entering the industry. But wait! A monopoly is a *single* seller producing a product for which there are no close substitutes. If there is new entry, there is no longer a monopoly. If a monopoly is to persist, there must be some forces at work to keep new firms from entering. **Barriers to entry** are natural or artificial obstacles that keep new firms from entering an industry. Without such barriers, monopoly cannot continue.

Economies of scale provide a natural barrier to entry. If the long-run cost curves are such that the optimal-size plant is very large relative to the size of the market, there may be room for only one cost-efficient firm in the industry. If there are great economies of scale, one firm that is bigger than any of the others will be able to undersell the rest. In such a case, the bigger firm will cut its price below that of its rivals and capture their customers. Eventually the large firm will become the only firm in the industry. When just one firm emerges in this way, the firm is called a natural monopoly. This happens in very few industries.

Public utilities such as telephone companies, electric companies, and cable television companies fit this category. The government recognizes that these are natural monopolies and therefore regulates their prices and output levels. Problems associated with such regulation will be discussed in a later chapter. Some economists argue that even public utilities are not really natural monopolies. Since the occurrence of a natural monopoly is rare, most of the monopoly power that exists in our economy is due to artificial barriers.

An artificial barrier to entry is one that is contrived by the firm (or someone else) to keep others out. It doesn't take much imagination to come up with a list of such barriers. The least sophisticated, but perhaps the most effective, would be the use of violence. Suppose you have a monopoly on the illegal numbers racket in South Chicago. If new entrepreneurs move in to reap some of these profits, you simply "do away" with them—very effective! This sort of tactic may sound barbaric, but business history contains many examples of the use of violence to keep out competitors. The early history of oil exploration and drilling is one example—private armies were often a must.

On a more civilized level, it may be possible to erect artificial barriers that are legal, or at least quasi-legal. If exclusive ownership of all the raw materials in an industry could be captured, entry could be controlled by refusing to sell to potential new entrants. Alcoa enjoyed a monopoly before World War II because it controlled almost all the known sources of bauxite, the essential ore for the production of aluminum.

A current example of the use of artificial barriers occurs in the sale of diamonds. The de Beers Company of South Africa controls most of the world's diamond supply. This firm effectively controls the mining and marketing of new diamonds and has a great influence on price. In this case, there is still competition because all diamonds produced in the past are potential competitors. If de Beers manipulated production to drive price "too high," individuals might enter the market as suppliers, selling diamonds they presently own.

Another way to create artificial barriers is to own the patent on a process or machine that is vital in production. Patent rights give sole authority to use the process or machine to the holder of the patent. The problem with a patent, however, is twofold. First, it expires after seventeen years in the United States, and then everyone is entitled to use the idea. Second, to get a patent, detailed plans on how the item is produced must be provided, and these plans are available to potential competitors at the Library of Congress. So it appears a patent is not a very effective entry barrier to anyone who is willing to risk a lawsuit brought by the patent holder (and patent holders don't always win their cases). A good alternative to patents is secrecy. If a firm can keep its vital process or machine secret, it can keep new firms out of its industry. Now you know why there is barbed wire around some research and development offices, why you aren't told the formula for Pepsi Cola, and why corporate spying is big business.

GOVERNMENT AND BARRIERS TO ENTRY

It is very difficult to be a monopolist because it is very hard to keep new entrants out of an industry—unless you can get the government to help you. Let's look briefly at two industries where firms have significant market power: the steel industry and the taxicab industry.

Suppose firms in the U.S. steel industry are earning economic profits. Firms that are producing steel in other countries see profits being earned and gear up to export steel to the United States to earn some of these profits. In effect, the foreign steel firms are entering the U.S. industry. The domestic firms then appeal to Congress and/or the President to keep the foreign firms out (to block their entry). Tariffs or quotas may be put into effect. These tariffs or quotas serve as artificial barriers to entry for foreign firms by raising the price of foreign goods or prohibiting their sale in the United States.

Next, consider the taxicab industry. You probably consider this to be a competitive industry since in any large city there are cabs from many companies on the street every day. But, if you decide to start a cab business, you might be in for some trouble. Suppose you already own a car, so the entry costs are relatively small. All you need to do is to mark your car so that it can be recognized as a cab, and perhaps install a meter. However, you will need a permit, which in some cities will be very difficult and expensive to obtain. If you operate as a "gypsy," an underground cab that avoids city regulations, you will make the existing cab owners very unhappy. In many cities, cabs are a monopoly enterprise, and it is government that protects the monopoly.

In these examples, government supplied the artificial barriers to entry. Federal, state, and local governments all restrict entry and thereby ensure protected market positions. It should not be too surprising that many instances of corruption in government have centered on the granting of monopoly privileges. A government official or agency protects a monopoly by keeping competitors out. The monopolist is often willing to pay for this with campaign contributions, favors, or outright bribes, such as direct cash payments, free vacations, or jobs for relatives.

If monopoly power persists for a long period of time, there is very likely to be some explicit or implicit government role in creating barriers to entry. Monopoly profits are a very powerful and attractive force, and new entry is very difficult for the monopolist alone to block. As a result, monopolies usually try to enlist governmental support of one kind or another.

IS MONOPOLY BAD?

Any entrepreneur would prefer to sell in a monopoly rather than a perfectly competitive industry, because economic profit always tends to zero. A firm that can create a successful monopoly will be rewarded with continuing profits. (This ability to use power in markets is stressed in marketing and management courses—thus, there are no marketing courses for wheat farmers!) Monopoly is obviously good for the monopolist, but monopoly can be bad for society.

How Monopoly Compares to Perfect Competition

To see what's so bad about monopoly, look at Figure 4. First, assume that Figure 4 represents a perfectly competitive industry. The market demand

International Perspective

Multinational Corporations as Monopolies in Foreign Countries

Many multinational corporations are very large relative to the countries in which they operate. It is conceivable that some companies may have worldwide net sales that are larger than the GNP of the country in which they are operating. Thus, multinationals have a large amount of monopoly power in small host countries.

The political and economic dilemmas faced by multinational corporations and host governments have even come to the United States. For decades, U.S. policy makers were confronted with only one side of the problem, that of U.S. corporations in foreign countries. Recently, however, the United States has become a host country for foreign, primarily Japanese and European, investment.

Small less developed countries face a political dilemma in bargaining with large multinational companies. At the onset, such a country may have very little bargaining power with the multinational because the company can "shop around" for hospitable governments. If the country's policy makers want to pursue economic growth, they may have to agree initially to the multinational's terms. As time passes and the company invests more fixed capital assets in the country, the host government can increase taxes and capture more of the monopoly profits. However, a delicate balance must be maintained. Taxes and government controls diminish the profitability of investment and future investment for the multinational. Other multinationals may be driven away by changes in a host country's business climate.

Host country controls on multinationals can take several forms. Some countries impose foreign exchange regulations that require the foreign firm to convert earnings at exchange rates that are different from market exchange rates. Another control is a rule requiring the foreign firms to use their earnings to buy local products and export them to countries with freely exchangeable currencies. Some countries (such as India) require foreign companies to divest their assets over time by selling them to native investors. This policy is a form of expropriation with compensation. Still other countries force foreign firms to purchase a certain percent of the components in a manufacturing process from domestic sources. Finally, although it may be illegal (or if not illegal, at least hushed), politicians in some countries may require bribes as a condition for doing business. This is not uncommon in countries with dictators.

In a small country, multinational companies not only exert monopoly power but also must confront monopoly power exerted by the host government. In this situation, with one monopoly confronting another, it is not always clear who wins.

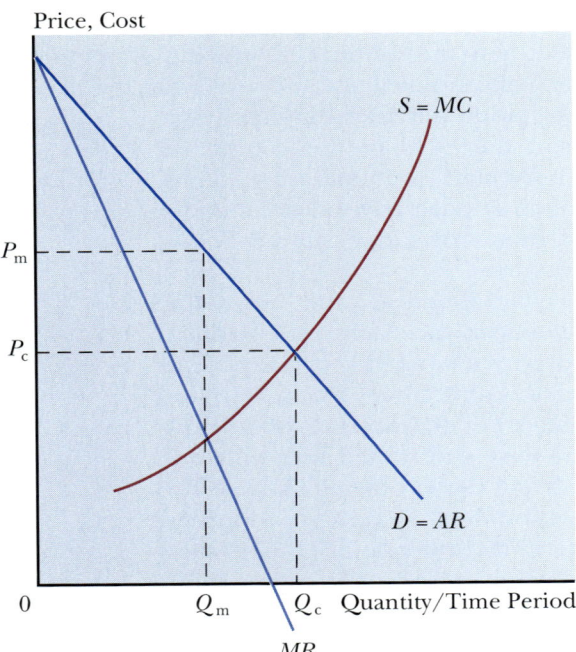

**FIGURE 4
PRICE AND OUTPUT DETERMINATION UNDER MONOPOLY AND PERFECT COMPETITION**
The monopolist, equating marginal cost and marginal revenue, produces output Q_m and sells it at price P_m. If this same firm were perfectly competitive, the price would be P_c and output would be Q_c.

curve ($D = AR$) is that faced by the numerous sellers, and the marginal cost (MC) curve is the summation of all the individual firms' marginal cost curves. The competitive price and output are P_c and Q_c. Now suppose the industry is monopolized by one firm that has bought up all the competitive firms but still has the same cost curves. The monopoly firm, then, will face the same cost conditions that the aggregate of competitive firms faced. The *market* supply curve becomes the monopolist's marginal cost curve because it is the summation of the purchased firms' marginal cost curves. The monopoly firm also faces the *market* demand curve and its corresponding marginal revenue curve. The monopoly firm will produce at Q_m and P_m. In this case, it is a very simple matter to contrast monopoly with perfect competition. The monopolist produces a smaller output ($Q_m < Q_c$) and charges a higher price ($P_m > P_c$) than the perfectly competitive firms did. This is possible because entry into the industry is blocked. Since new firms cannot enter, consumers are not getting the optimal amount of the good produced by the monopolist. Monopolies restrict output. This is the principal economic argument against monopoly.

The monopolistic output and price, then, represent misallocation of resources if the monopoly has the same cost conditions as the aggregate of the competitive firms. Note that the misallocation under monopoly could be even worse if, in buying up the individual firms, the monopoly introduced some inefficiencies of large-scale management. Such inefficiencies would cause an upward shift of the cost curves in Figure 4.

The misallocation of resources in a monopoly is illustrated in Figure 5. The monopoly is in equilibrium producing x_1 units at a price of P_1. The monopolist's profits, which are total revenue minus total cost, are represented by rectangle CP_1AB. Let's examine closely what is going on at this

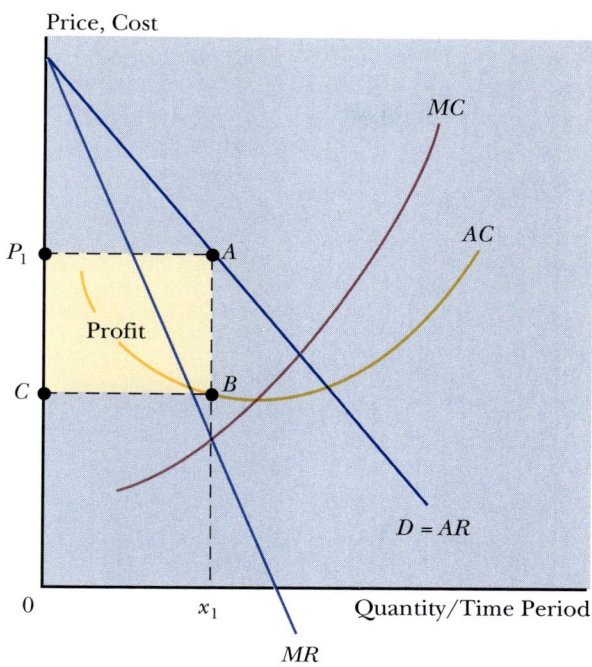

**FIGURE 5
MISALLOCATION OF
RESOURCES IN A
MONOPOLY**
A monopoly misallocates resources because price is greater than marginal cost. This means the value consumers place on the item exceeds the opportunity cost of producing it.

equilibrium. First, price P_1 is greater than average cost (which is x_1B per unit). That is, $P_1 > AC$, and economic profits are being earned. Second, price is greater than marginal cost ($P_1 > MC$), which means the value consumers place on the last unit (P_1) exceeds the opportunity cost of producing it (MC). From the consumer's point of view, more should be produced. The monopolist prevents that from happening by restricting entry. Third, average cost at output x_1 is greater than marginal cost at x_1. That is, $AC > MC$. This means that x_1 units are not being produced using the least-cost combination of factors. The monopolist is not forced to be fully efficient. You can easily see, therefore, what economists mean when they say that monopoly misallocates resources.

MONOPOLY PROFITS AND LOSSES

There is a common misconception that a monopoly situation guarantees profits. A monopoly is not a license to make profits. If the U.S. government granted you an absolute monopoly in the sale and manufacture of Conestoga wagons, you might lose money. High costs or insufficient demand may cause a monopolist to lose money.

Figure 6 shows a monopoly suffering a loss. The monopoly is producing x_1 units and charging the profit-maximizing price, P_1. Average costs of producing are x_1A per unit. As a result, the monopolist is incurring losses equal to rectangle P_1CAB. Since the demand curve is below the average cost curve, there is no way to avoid losses. Will the monopolist continue to produce? If price is above average variable costs, as is the case in Figure 6, the monopolist will be better off in the short run if it continues producing. In the long run, if demand does not increase, the monopoly

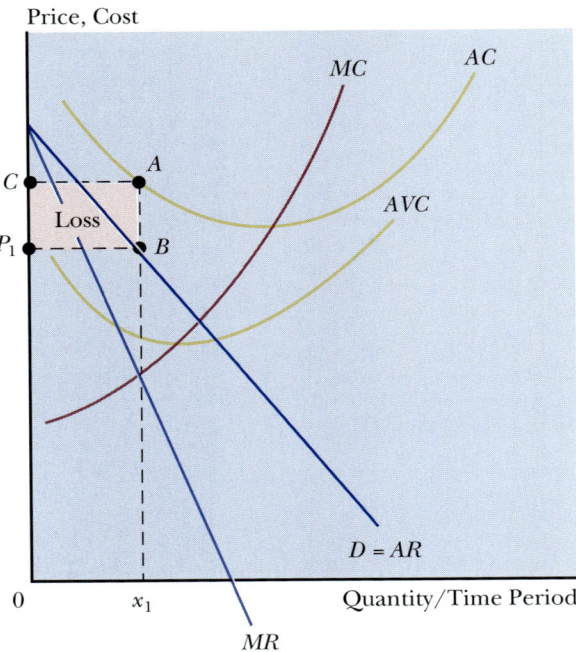

**FIGURE 6
A MONOPOLY
SUFFERING LOSSES**
The monopolist might suffer losses in the short run. If average cost is greater than average revenue, the monopolist is suffering a loss.

will go out of business. The presence of losses indicates that the factors of production are not earning their opportunity cost. Those factors will move to more productive uses.

A monopolist can also earn only normal profits. Figure 7 illustrates this case. The monopoly is producing x_1 units and charges price P_1. Total revenue is equal to rectangle $0P_1Ax_1$. In this instance, the monopoly is earning its opportunity cost. There will be no incentive for other firms to try to enter this industry or for this firm to leave the industry. Price is equal to average cost, which means that producers are not earning economic profits. However, price is still greater than marginal cost, indicating that more units should be produced.

You can see, then, that monopolies don't always make profits. In fact, they often incur losses and go out of business. Also, monopolists do not charge the highest price possible. Remember the mineral spring example? Monopolists charge the profit-maximizing price, and this price will depend on the demand conditions and costs in the industry.

MONOPOLY IN THE LONG RUN
The monopolist, unlike the perfectly competitive firm, can continue to earn economic profits in the long run. As long as the barriers to entry remain, economic profits can be maintained. Sustaining these barriers in the long run is very difficult, however, because the economic profits will attract new firms, substitute products, and new processes. In principle, then, even with government help, the power of any single monopoly is likely to decline in the very long run.

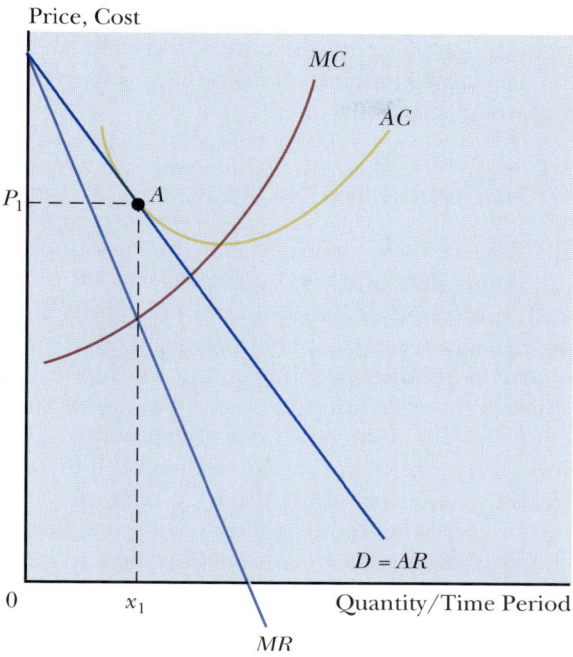

FIGURE 7
A MONOPOLY EARNING NORMAL PROFITS
It is possible that a monopoly might earn only normal profits. In this case, there is no incentive for other firms to enter the industry and no need for barriers to entry.

REAL-WORLD MONOPOLIES

We have pointed out that there are no examples of true monopoly in the real world. A complete monopoly cannot exist, because all products or services have some substitutes with which they compete. There are, however, firms with some monopoly power. The model of monopoly is useful in explaining the behavior of these firms. Public utilities, for example, are considered natural monopolies and are regulated as a result. Monopolies that are set up by some nations to engage in international trade are also monopolistic.

Local monopolies are another form of real-world monopoly. A **local monopoly** is a firm that has monopoly power in a geographic region. Even though close substitutes for the firm's product exist, the distance to other sources of supply creates a virtual monopoly. If you grew up in a small, remote town, there may have been only one movie theater or perhaps only

local monopoly
A firm that has monopoly power in a geographic region because of the large distance from other suppliers of its product (or substitutes).

COMPARISON OF MONOPOLY AND PERFECT COMPETITION	
MONOPOLY	**PERFECT COMPETITION**
• One firm	• Many firms
• Barriers to entry	• Free entry
• $P \neq AC$, so economic profits exist	• $P \neq AC$, only normal profit earned
• $MC \neq AC$, not producing at least-cost combination	• $MC = AC$, producing at least-cost combination

one grocery store. A firm in such a situation is a local monopoly because the substitutes are costly in the sense that you must travel to reach them. Economists use the model of monopoly to examine the effects of monopoly power in such real-world situations.

MONOPOLY POWER AND PRICE DISCRIMINATION

In analyzing monopoly behavior, we have assumed that the monopolist charges the same price to all consumers and the same price for all units sold to a specific consumer. If, on the other hand, the monopolist is able to charge different consumers different prices or charge a given consumer different prices depending on the quantity purchased, the monopolist is practicing **price discrimination**. Price discrimination is a way to expand monopoly profits by extracting consumer surplus from consumers.

To see how price discrimination works, you need to recall the discussion of consumer surplus in the chapter on utility theory. Consumer surplus is the extra utility gained by consumers who end up paying less for an item than they would be willing to pay for it. Consumers purchase an item until the marginal utility of the last dollar spent on the item is equal to the marginal utility of spending the dollar on any other good or of holding the dollar. The marginal utility of previously purchased units was greater than the price paid for those units because they were all purchased at the price of the last unit. The consumer would have been willing to pay higher prices for those units. Figure 8 illustrates this concept. At price P_1 in Figure 8, the consumer was receiving a "bonus" in terms of utility. This extra utility is called consumer surplus, represented by the shaded area in Figure 9.

A monopoly producer might be able to deal separately with consumers depending on the number of units purchased. In terms of Figure 9, the

price discrimination
The practice of charging different prices to different consumers or to a single consumer for different quantities purchased.

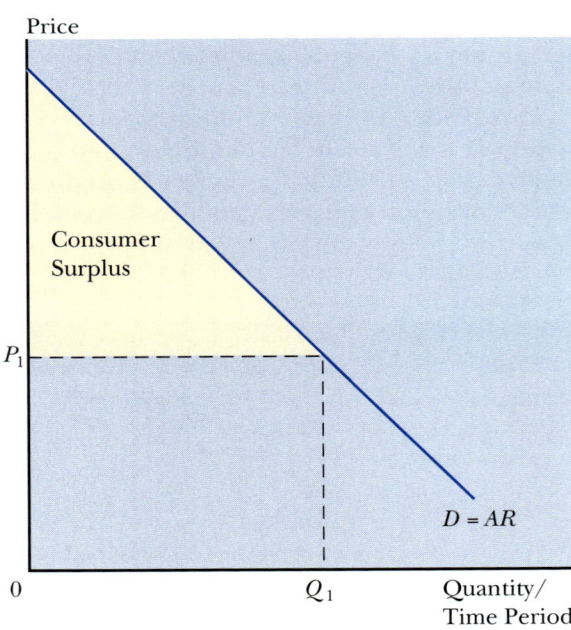

FIGURE 8
CONSUMER SURPLUS
Consumer surplus is the difference between the total utility received from the purchase of a product and the total revenue generated by the product. It exists because the marginal utility of each previous unit purchased was greater than price P_1.

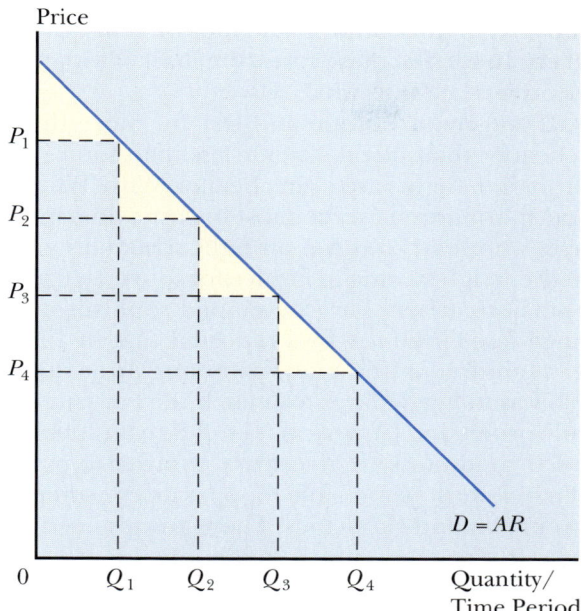

**FIGURE 9
A PRICE-DISCRIMINATING MONOPOLIST**
A price-discriminating monopolist can capture most of the consumer surplus by charging different prices for different amounts of consumption.

monopolist could say, "You may buy up to Q_1 units for P_1, from Q_1 to Q_2 units for P_2, from Q_2 to Q_3 units for P_3, and from Q_3 to Q_4 units for P_4." By doing this, the monopolist extracts most of the consumer surplus and converts it into revenue for the firm. Compare the shaded areas in Figure 9 to the shaded area in Figure 8. Both represent consumer surplus. In Figure 9, by charging different prices for different amounts of consumption, the monopolist has expropriated much of the consumer surplus. It is theoretically possible for the monopolist to capture all of the consumer surplus by charging different prices for each number of units.

The second type of price discrimination occurs when a monopolist can separate markets and charge different prices to different groups of consumers. If the monopolist can separate the markets and prevent resale, it can price discriminate by adjusting output for the different demand elasticities in the two markets.

PRICE DISCRIMINATION IN PRACTICE

In practice, the first type of price discrimination is common. It requires that the seller have the power to separate sales on a unit-by-unit basis. This form of price discrimination is what is being practiced when multiples of a product can be purchased for a total that is less than the per-unit price times the number purchased. "Artichokes 40¢, two for 65¢" and "Coffee 50¢ a cup, refills a quarter" are examples of this type of price discrimination.

The second type of price discrimination requires that the seller be able to separate markets according to different elasticities of demand. Bookstores offer lower prices to professors than to students. Airlines charge lower fares to students and vacationers than to businesspeople. University athletic departments offer lower-priced tickets to sports events to students and faculty. Medical doctors charge different patients different fees for the same service. Senior citizens get discounts on all kinds of items, from prescriptions to theater tickets. In each of these cases, the market with the greater elasticity gets lower prices. Let's see why.

Consider plane tickets. If you fly to Europe and stay for more than fourteen days, the fare is cheaper than if you stay for less than fourteen days. If you stay a month or longer, flights are even cheaper. Why? Which class of consumers of air transportation have the most inelastic demand? Business travelers, of course, who tend to travel on tight schedules and have bosses who don't want them sight-seeing in France for fourteen days! With airline deregulation, major carriers have developed sophisticated techniques to set and change fares. *Business Week* reported that in 1985 American Airlines had over a hundred traffic analysts working three shifts seven days a week. Their job was to juggle fares to "match the bargain offerings of low-cost rivals while protecting [American's] full-fare business."[2]

It should be clear that two conditions are necessary in order to practice price discrimination. First, it must be possible to separate consumers into groups that have different demand elasticities. These groups need to be economically identifiable. If it costs too much to identify the groups, discrimination might not pay. When economists talk about price discrimination, they're not talking about discriminating on the basis of race, sex, or national origin, unless different races, sexes, or nationalities have different demand elasticities for certain products. Many times, age is used to identify groups with different demand elasticities. Senior citizens and students have more elastic demand curves because they typically have a tighter budget and more time to shop around than middle-aged people do. In the case of airfares, the classes of consumers are separated by length of stay. Businesspeople seldom want to stay at a destination for more than a few days.

Time-of-day price discrimination includes matinee performances of cultural events and movies, bowling alley use, and lunch and dinner menus. In these cases, demand is more inelastic at night because some consumers are limited to night consumption. Magazine publishers charge higher prices for magazines purchased at newsstands than for subscriptions. Sometimes subscription prices are only a fraction of the newsstand prices. Newsstand demand is more inelastic because it is a spur-of-the-moment, unplanned purchase. Book publishers charge much higher prices for hardcover novels than for softcover versions of the same novel. They separate the markets by publishing the softcover version after the hardcover demand has been satiated. Some colleges charge in-state and out-of-state tuition because it is very easy to separate these two markets. Has your car ever broken down when you were out of town? Your demand is very inelastic in such a situation. You have little information about services available, and you are easy to identify as a one-time customer (you may have an out-of-state license plate). What do you think happens? You're right! You pay much more than a local person with car trouble would pay.

The second major requirement for price discrimination is that the monopolist *must* be able to prevent the resale of goods or the movement of

---

2. *Business Week* (2 December 1985): 34.

customers between markets. Consider charging different prices to different classes of customers for tickets for a college football game. It only works if the customers paying the lower price are prohibited from reselling their tickets. If not, the college is no longer a monopolist in the sale of the higher-priced tickets. Is it any wonder that the athletic department requires you to show your picture I.D. card *and* your ticket at the gate? The higher-priced ticket holders are only required to present their tickets. Price discrimination works well where resale is very difficult. Services are good candidates for price discrimination because it is very difficult to resell a service. Medical doctors are very successful in practicing price discrimination because they have easily recognizable submarkets with different elasticities (by income and insurance category) *and* because resale is almost always ruled out.

The seller often justifies price discrimination as helping a group. For example, doctors might claim they practice price discrimination (charging less to some groups) in order to "help" the poor. Students or senior citizens might be charged less "to help them out." In reality, price discrimination is almost always practiced because it increases profit.

GAINERS AND LOSERS FROM PRICE DISCRIMINATION
Price discrimination does have a positive side effect. It will usually cause output under monopoly to increase. Earlier in this chapter, you learned that one of the disadvantages of monopoly is that it restricts output. If a monopoly can, however, sell output one unit at a time, output will be pushed to the point where price equals marginal cost. This is common sense because the monopolist only restricts output in order to keep price from falling on all units. If price falls only on the additions to output (not other units), then price equals marginal revenue, and output will be increased to the point where price equals marginal cost. This is the same conclusion as for perfect competition. The difference, of course, is that more of the benefit accrues to the monopolist. Price discrimination converts consumer surplus into monopoly profits, making monopolists wealthier and consumers worse off.

Many people believe price discrimination is unfair because people pay different prices for the very same product. Why should an airplane ticket be cheaper because someone is a tourist rather than a business traveler? Why should professors get their books and pens for lower prices than students? Why should students pay less for a football ticket than nonstudents?

Interestingly, it is sometimes the group that benefits from price discrimination that complains. Price discrimination is common in international trade because the separation of national markets is often easy to maintain. Tariffs and transportation costs can help prevent resale. When firms in a country sell in a foreign market at a lower price than they do at home, they are engaging in price discrimination. Demand in the foreign country may be more elastic than domestic demand because there is more competition, and, therefore, more good substitutes are available. The foreign monopolist sells to foreigners at a lower price than at home. The U.S. Treasury calls this form of price discrimination **dumping**. Dumping occurs, for example, when the Japanese sell televisions in the United States at a lower price than they sell the same sets at home.

dumping
The practice of selling in foreign markets at lower prices than in domestic markets (a form of price discrimination).

State trading occurs when a government acts as a monopoly buyer or seller of a product in international markets. Although most nations engage in some state trading, especially in military goods, it has been more common in centrally planned economies. The communist countries of Eastern Europe and the Soviet Union have historically carried out all their international trade through state trading monopolies. These monopolies determined how much was to be imported or exported and the prices at which this trade would take place. In many instances, trade was carried out in a manner that economists call countertrade. If a firm wanted to do business with the Soviet Union, it would have to accept payment in Soviet goods rather than in hard currency.

Countertrade resulted in complicated arrangements that discouraged some Western firms from exporting to the Soviet Union. Some examples can show how complicated countertrade could be. If a U.S. firm wanted to sell computers to the Soviet Union, it might, for example, have to take payment in vodka. The U.S. firm would then have to find a firm that wanted to buy the vodka or set up a firm to distribute the vodka to liquor stores. A firm that wanted to sell textile equipment to East Germany might have to take payment in the cloth that this equipment produced. The firm would then have to somehow market the cloth.

INTERNATIONAL PERSPECTIVE

STATE TRADING MONOPOLIES

Another difficulty that Western firms faced in dealing with state trading companies is that the state monopoly could have an unfair advantage in the market. It was one firm dealing with competitive firms from all other countries. The power of the monopoly was even greater because it was the government. There is evidence that these state monopolies were able to get better than market deals because of their monopoly power.

All these relationships are likely to change in the next few years. The political reforms that swept Eastern Europe and the Soviet Union in the early 1990s are bound to have important economic effects. There is great potential for increased trade between firms in the West and those in the formerly communist countries. It is still too early to tell how the institutions of this trade will develop. If democratic market economies emerge, however, most state trading could be a thing of the past.

The odd thing is that dumping has a bad reputation. When the Japanese dump televisions in the United States, the U.S. government takes action against Japan. This is curious because Japanese firms are giving U.S. consumers a better deal than Japanese consumers.[3] Complaining about being offered a lower price doesn't seem to make sense. Seen from the producer's angle, however, dumping is worth complaining about. You can understand why domestic manufacturers don't particularly approve of foreign competitors selling in this country more cheaply than in their own home market.[4]

PRICE DISCRIMINATION AND MONOPOLY

We developed the concept of price discrimination in connection with the study of monopoly. Price discrimination is not limited to monopolies, however. It will never occur in perfect competition but could occur in monopolistic competition and oligopoly, which we will study in the next chapter. However, since the opportunity to use price discrimination is greater if consumers have few good substitutes, it is easiest to price discriminate under monopolistic conditions.

THE COSTS OF MONOPOLY

We have made the point that a monopoly misallocates resources by contriving shortages—producing less than the competitive output to create monopoly profits. There are, however, other costs associated with monopoly. Figure 10 depicts a monopoly firm with constant marginal costs and, thus, constant average costs. Constant marginal costs and average costs are assumed for simplicity.

The monopolist will produce output level Q_m and set price at P_m. A perfectly competitive structure would have produced an output of Q_c at price P_c. As a result of restricting output, the monopolist earns a monopoly profit equal to the shaded area in Figure 10. This shaded area represents a transfer from consumers (in terms of lost consumer surplus) to the monopolist (in terms of monopoly profit). This transfer, however, is not the only cost the monopoly creates.

DEADWEIGHT LOSS

The crosshatched triangle in Figure 10 represents lost consumer surplus that was not converted into monopoly profits. This lost consumer surplus is received by no one. Consumers have lost it because the monopoly has restricted output, but it has not been received by anyone in the economy. The lost consumer surplus is referred to as the deadweight loss of monopoly. The **deadweight loss** is the lost consumer surplus due to monopolistic restriction of output. It is a deadweight loss because nothing is received in exchange for the loss. It is equivalent to throwing a valuable resource away.

deadweight loss
The lost consumer surplus due to monopolistic restriction of output.

---
3. In fact, the dumping case concerning Japanese television sets was a rarity in that the initial complaint came from Japanese consumers.
4. There may be some other objections to dumping. The U.S. government may fear that the Japanese are selling below cost to drive U.S. firms out of business in an attempt to corner the market on televisions. Or the government may fear that Japan is transmitting macroeconomic disturbances to the United States by weakening the U.S. television industry.

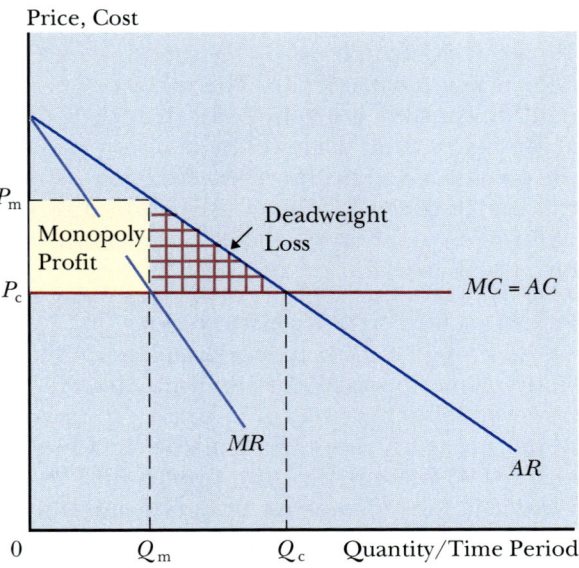

**FIGURE 10
THE DEADWEIGHT
LOSS OF MONOPOLY**
A monopoly converts some consumer surplus to monopoly profit. The crosshatched area, however, represents consumer surplus that is lost. It is the deadweight loss associated with monopoly.

Many years ago, Arnold C. Harberger attempted to measure this deadweight loss of monopoly.[5] He estimated that deadweight loss (he referred to it as the welfare loss from monopoly) was quite small. In 1954, for example, only about 1/10 of 1 percent of GNP was lost due to the deadweight loss effect. This small fraction of GNP amounted to about $1.50 for each U.S. citizen in 1954. Since Harberger's study, other economists have attempted to measure deadweight loss. Most of their estimates are also small and tend to congregate in the range of 1 percent of GNP.[6] This is still a surprisingly low figure, although it is ten times larger than Harberger's original estimate. Harberger's work implies that, if the transfer from consumers to monopolists (the captured consumer surplus) is ignored, monopoly has little effect on welfare.

MONOPOLY RENT SEEKING

Gordon Tullock believes that deadweight loss estimates are likely to underestimate the costs of monopoly. Tullock argues that since the monopoly profits (the captured consumer surplus) are potentially huge, monopolists spend a great deal of time, effort, and resources in establishing a monopoly.[7] He developed his argument by drawing an analogy to theft. If thieves steal $100 million, they transfer that $100 million from victims to themselves. This transfer is just like the transfer of consumer surplus. But thieves invest time, effort, and resources in guns and getaway cars. In addition, victims invest money in protecting themselves from

---

5. See A. C. Harberger, "The Welfare Loss from Monopoly," *American Economic Review* (May 1954): 77–87. For a recent study confirming Harberger's result and summarizing many other studies, see Micha Gisser, "Price Leadership and Welfare Losses in U.S. Manufacturing," *American Economic Review* (September 1986): 756–767.
6. For a review of these other studies, see F. M. Scherer, *Industrial Market Structure and Economic Performance*, 2nd ed. (Chicago: Rand McNally, 1980), Chapter 17.
7. G. Tullock, "The Welfare Costs of Tariffs, Monopolies and Theft," *Western Economic Journal* (June 1967): 224–232.

theft. Both of these costs are wasted from the viewpoint of society as a whole. Tullock argues that the same holds true for monopoly. Monopolists "waste" resources (from a societal viewpoint) in seeking to establish a monopoly. Society also expends resources trying to break up and prevent monopolies. The efforts and resources expended by those attempting to establish monopolies to earn monopoly profits have become known as **monopoly rent seeking**. This is a cost of monopoly because these resources are no longer available to produce goods and services. We will discuss monopoly rent seeking in greater detail in a later chapter.

monopoly rent seeking
The efforts and resources expended by those attempting to establish monopolies to earn monopoly profits.

Managerial Inefficiency

Still another cost of monopoly has been identified by Harvey Leibenstein.[8] Leibenstein argues that competitive firms are forced to be efficient by the market, but this does not hold true for monopolies. Since the monopolist is not punished by the market for slack management, it will tend to have more managerial "looseness" than a competitive firm. This looseness will manifest itself in corporate jets, limousines, expense accounts, and golden parachutes. Leibenstein coined the term ***x*-inefficiency** to describe the inefficiency associated with the "slack" management of monopoly firms. The monopolist escapes the market discipline and is therefore less conscious of management efficiencies. Leibenstein estimated this cost to be as high as 2 percent of GNP.

***x*-inefficiency**
The inefficiency associated with the "slack" management of monopoly firms because of the lack of market discipline.

WHO RUNS THE FIRM? ALTERNATIVES TO PROFIT MAXIMIZATION

We have consistently assumed that firms are profit maximizers. This assumption makes it possible to predict how a firm will adjust to changes in demand in the market structure of perfect competition. What happens in the realm of giant firms run by professional managers? Corporations account for about 85 percent of the annual business sales in the United States. Corporations are run by hired managers, not owners. Managers might operate by some principle other than profit maximization. This idea is sometimes referred to as the **separation of ownership and control**, which simply means that managers who control corporations may behave differently than owner-managers would. Different behavior will occur only if the managers have different goals *and* if owners can't control managers. It has been argued that separation is part of the reason behind some of the takeovers in the 1980s. Leveraged buyouts occurred, according to this argument, because hired managers were not running their firms as profitably as owner-managers would have.

separation of ownership and control
The idea that large firms are run (controlled) by hired managers, not the owners, and the managers might have different goals from those of the owners.

The hypothesis that managers' behavior deviates from profit maximization is based on organizational theory. (You may have studied that theory in a course on social psychology or management.) The hypothesis assumes that managers will follow standard procedures even if these procedures result in lower profits. Managers of big business firms are seen as bureaucrats who make conservative decisions to avoid mistakes and to minimize liability, like managers in the military, the federal bureaucracy,

---

8. H. Leibenstein, "Allocative Efficiency vs. x-Inefficiency," *American Economic Review* (June 1966): 392–415.

Nobel Prize winner Herbert Simon was born in Milwaukee, Wisconsin, and educated at the University of Chicago. Simon has held teaching positions at the University of California, the Illinois Institute of Technology, and the University of Pittsburgh. He is presently at Carnegie-Mellon University. Simon has never held a teaching post as an economist. Instead, he has held professorships in political science, administration, psychology, and information sciences. He is an economist in the broadest sense of the word, like the early classical economists.

In awarding the 1978 Nobel Prize in Economics to Simon, the Royal Swedish Academy noted his work concerning the development of alternatives to profit maximization. The committee made the following statement in its official announcement: "In his epoch-making book, *Administrative Behavior* (1947), and in a number of subsequent works, he (Simon) described the company as an adaptive system of physical, personal, and social components that are held together by a network of intercommunications and by the willingness of its members to cooperate and to strive towards a common goal. What is new in Simon's ideas is, most of all, that he rejects the assumption made in classic theory of the firm as an omnisciently rational, profit-maximizing entrepreneur."[a]

Simon has had an impact on more academic disciplines than any other Nobel Prize winner in economics. His work in management science and public administration is credited with bringing scientific approaches to the study of management. Herbert Simon is perhaps the best example of an economic theorist who has made a major impact on business and public administration.

ECONOMIC PROFILE

HERBERT SIMON
1916–

a. "The Nobel Memorial Prize in Economics," *The Scandinavian Journal of Economics*, 81, no. 1 (1979): 72–73.

or any large organization. Those who argue that managers do not maximize profits offer several alternatives to that standard assumption. Let's look briefly at some of these.

The **satisficing** hypothesis argues that the management of a firm does not seek maximum profits but rather looks for certain target levels of output and profits that are satisfactory to the ownership interests. Owners' goals might include size or market share, altruism or philanthropy. Unfortunately, in order to test this hypothesis and determine its validity, it would be necessary to specify a firm's target. Otherwise, any result that is found would be consistent with satisficing behavior. The proponents of the satisficing hypothesis have not as yet found a way to specify targets. As a result, the hypothesis cannot be proved or disproved.

Another goal that might be substituted in place of profit maximization is religious or racial discrimination. Firms with monopoly power and little threat of competition may sacrifice some of their profits in order to sell to, or hire, a particular group of people. A very interesting test of this hypothesis was conducted several years ago by Armen Alchian and Reuben Kessel.[9] They classified Jewish and non-Jewish graduates of the Harvard Business School according to the market structures of the industries in which they were employed. In the years examined, 36 percent of the school's graduates were Jewish. Alchian and Kessel discovered that employment of Harvard MBAs in monopolized industries was 18 percent Jewish compared with 41 percent Jewish in competitive industries. This evidence is consistent with the hypothesis that monopoly power makes discrimination against minorities easier (less costly) and points to yet another cost of monopoly power.

Thomas DiLorenzo disagrees with the satisficing hypothesis and argues that rational profit-maximizing behavior of managers of private monopolies will not be more lax than that of their counterparts in competitive firms.[10] He maintains that monopoly managers will try just as hard because they get to share in monopoly profits in the form of salary increases and added benefits.

Another hypothesis has been suggested by William Baumol. Baumol argues that given some level of profits, managers' primary goal is to increase the sales of the firm. In essence, Baumol is saying that managers are rewarded by stockholders, according to the relative size of the firm in the market, for increasing the firm's relative share of the market, say, from 15 to 20 percent. This hypothesis is called **constrained sales maximization**. The implication of this hypothesis is that monopoly might not be as bad as we concluded earlier. If sales, rather than profits, are the primary goal of a monopoly, the firm will charge lower prices and produce more output than a profit-maximizing monopolist. With lower prices and increased output, there will be less misallocation of resources than predicted with profit maximization.

A rejoinder to these competing hypotheses is the long-run profit maximization hypothesis. **Long-run profit maximization** says that even if man-

satisficing hypothesis
The argument that managers do not seek to maximize profits but rather seek target levels of output and profits that are satisfactory to the ownership interests.

constrained sales maximization
The hypothesis that managers' primary goal is to increase the sales of the firm because they will be rewarded by stockholders for increasing the firm's relative share of the market.

long-run profit maximization
The argument that even if managers seem to behave in accord with satisficing or constrained sales maximization, they only do so because it leads to higher profits in the long run.

---

9. A. Alchian and R. A. Kessel, "Competition, Monopoly, and the Pursuit of Money," in H. G. Lewis et al., *Aspects of Labor Economics* (Princeton, NJ: Princeton University Press, 1962).
10. Thomas J. DiLorenzo, "Corporate Management, Property Rights, and the x-istence of x-Inefficiency," *Southern Economic Journal* (July 1981): 116–124.

agers seem to behave in accord with satisficing or constrained sales maximization, they do so only because it leads to higher profits in the long run. According to this hypothesis, if the firm maximizes sales, it is doing so because this will lead to higher profits in the long run. Also, if a firm demonstrates a concern for social responsibility or philanthropy, it may be doing so in the interest of long-run profits. The problem with the hypothesis of long-run profit maximization is that unless a distinct time period is specified, almost any behavior could be consistent with the hypothesis. There is no way to prove or refute this hypothesis.

Competing theories of monopoly behavior highlight our earlier discussion of what theory is and what it does. Theory abstracts from the real world by concentrating on the important aspects or effects of a phenomenon. If profit maximization is a valid assumption, it will yield reasonably accurate predictions about firms' behavior. Profit maximization is a cornerstone of many hypotheses that have been empirically tested and found to be valid. Alternative assumptions have yet to be rigorously tested.

FALLACIES AND FACTS ABOUT MONOPOLY

In this chapter, we have developed a model of monopoly. Although there is no such thing as a true monopoly in the real world, there are firms that have monopoly power. The model is useful in describing their behavior. Since there are so many misconceptions about monopoly, it is worthwhile to summarize a few fallacies and facts about monopolies.

FALLACY—MONOPOLIES CHARGE THE HIGHEST POSSIBLE PRICE

The public often believes that monopolies charge the highest possible price and "rip off" consumers. This view is often supported by the press and by consumer lobby groups. As you have seen in this chapter, however, monopolies produce the profit-maximizing output and then sell that output on the market at a price that is constrained by the market demand curve.

FALLACY—MONOPOLIES ALWAYS EARN (HIGH) PROFITS

A similar, but slightly different, fallacy is that monopolies always earn profits. You have seen in this chapter that some monopolies earn profits, some earn normal profits, and others suffer losses. To be sure, monopolists try to earn profits, but if demand changes, they might lose money. The key difference between monopoly and competition is that profits of a monopoly can persist because they don't lead to new entry. In cases where monopolies suffer losses, however, the resources will flow to other industries. In some cases, the government has tried to keep unprofitable monopolies from going out of business.

FALLACY—MONOPOLISTS DON'T HAVE TO WORRY ABOUT DEMAND

It is a commonly held belief that monopolists don't have to worry about demand. Some social critics have even suggested that monopolists can manipulate demand. You have seen, however, that monopolists are constrained by the market demand for the good or service they produce.

Their search for the price that maximizes their revenue is strictly tied to that demand curve.

Fact—Monopolies Charge a Price Higher Than Marginal Cost
You have seen in this chapter that a monopoly restricts output in order to earn economic profits. This restriction of output means that the price charged is greater than marginal cost. Compared to perfect competition, monopolies are less efficient in allocating resources to match consumer preferences.

Fact—Monopolists Produce Where Demand Is Elastic
It is often mistakenly believed that a monopoly will produce where demand is inelastic. You have seen, though, that monopolies will always raise the price if demand is inelastic. Every monopoly will always be producing in an elastic portion of its demand curve.

Fact—Monopolies Do Not Have Supply Curves
As you have seen in this chapter, a monopoly is a price searcher. The monopoly establishes the profit-maximizing output and then sets the price equal to average revenue. As a result, the concept of a supply curve is meaningless. This lack of a supply curve makes the model of monopoly less useful than the model of perfect competition because it is difficult to analyze supply responses to demand shifts.

Fact—The Monopolist Ultimately Faces Competition
The model of monopoly assumes that the firm faces little or no competition because it defines a market structure consisting of a single firm producing a good with no close substitutes. In reality, however, the monopolist that earns a profit will be pursued by potential competitors, and the natural or artificial barriers to entry will be difficult to maintain. In a global economy, even if there are no domestic competitors, there is almost always a threat of competition from abroad.

As a closing note, it is appropriate to quote Alfred Marshall, the great neoclassical economist, on this subject:

> *It will in fact presently be seen that, though monopoly and free competition are really wide apart, yet in practice they shade into one another by imperceptible degrees: that there is an element of monopoly in nearly all competitive business: and that nearly all the monopolies, that are of any practical importance in the present age, hold much of their power by an uncertain tenure; so that they would lose it ere long, if they ignored the possibilities of competition, direct and indirect.*[11]

CONTESTABLE MARKETS

A number of economists have developed a new theory of industry structure called contestability theory.[12] **Contestable markets** are markets com-

contestable markets Markets composed of large firms that are nevertheless efficient because easily reversible entry into the market is possible.

---

11. Alfred Marshall, *Industry and Trade*, 4th ed. (London: Macmillan, 1923): 397.
12. William J. Baumol, John C. Panzar, and Robert D. Willig, *Contestable Markets and the Theory of Industry Structure* (New York: Harcourt, Brace, Jovanovich, 1982).

posed of large firms that are nevertheless efficient because easily reversible entry into the market is possible. This theory attempts to bring more reality to microeconomics by analyzing large multiproduct firms. The theory is very complex because it relies heavily on mathematical models, but the insights produced are essentially quite simple.

The basic idea is that the ease of entry into their market constrains the behavior of large firms and makes them efficient. Using contestability theory, economists argue that it is no longer necessary to assume that there are large numbers of firms, each a price taker, acting as if their production had no impact on the market in order to obtain efficiency. If easily reversible entry is possible, efficiency can be shown to coexist with large-scale production. In the past, this large-scale production might have been labeled monopoly.

Elizabeth Bailey, a proponent of contestability theory, was a commissioner at the Civil Aeronautics Board during the Carter administration. She suggested that contestability in the airline industry was enough to ensure efficiency because capital there consists mostly of aircraft, and capital costs can be recovered with little loss. In other words, entry into a particular air travel market is easy. She argued that even if a route were flown by only one airline, it is unlikely that monopoly prices would be charged because those prices would elicit entry by contesting airlines. According to this theory, it is the recovery of capital costs rather than economies of scale that is important.

Critics of this theory argue that it says nothing new. They argue that the model is not much different from models that show that the possibility of entry limits the pricing behavior of monopolists. Regardless of who wins the debate, it is important to note that entry conditions are important in both theories. Monopoly cannot persist in open markets, and whether one refers to this threat as competition or contestability makes little difference for public policy.

Summary

1. Monopoly is a market structure in which there is a single seller of a product with no close substitutes.

2. The monopoly firm faces a negatively sloped demand curve and a marginal revenue curve that lies below that demand curve.

3. The monopolist maximizes profits by producing the output level at which marginal revenue equals marginal cost. The price is the one on the demand curve at which exactly that amount of output can be sold. Since price is often greater than average cost for a monopoly, economic profits may exist.

4. A monopolist is sometimes able to erect barriers to entry that allow profits to persist in the long run. Such barriers are very difficult to maintain. As a result, monopolists often appeal to the government for help in maintaining entry barriers.

5. Monopolies produce a lower output at a higher price than do competitive firms. At equilibrium, the monopoly firm is producing at a level of output where price is not equal to average cost or marginal cost.

6. Monopoly power is not a guarantee of profits. Some monopolies go out of business because of persistent losses. Others make only normal profits.

7. A monopoly can increase its revenues if it practices price discrimination. For price discrimination to be successful, customers must have different demand elasticities, and they must be separated and prohibited from reselling the product or service.

8. The costs of monopoly include misallocation of resources, deadweight loss, monopoly rent seeking, and x-inefficiency.

9. The satisficing hypothesis and the constrained sales maximization hypothesis are both derived from the idea of the separation of ownership and control. These hypotheses suggest that hired managers, as opposed to owner-managers, may attempt to meet satisfactory profit targets or to maximize sales rather than to maximize profits.

10. Although no examples of pure monopoly exist, the model of monopoly is useful in analyzing monopoly power.

11. Contestability theory says that large firms are forced to efficient outcomes if there is free entry into their markets.

New Terms

monopoly
monopoly power
price searcher
barriers to entry
local monopoly
price discrimination
dumping
deadweight loss
monopoly rent seeking
x-inefficiency
separation of ownership and control
satisficing hypothesis
constrained sales maximization
long-run profit maximization
contestable markets

Questions for Discussion

1. Explain in your own words why marginal revenue is less than average revenue under conditions of monopoly.

2. Should business firms be socially responsible? Respond to the argument that they should maximize profits and leave social responsibility to elected and appointed officials.

3. List as many barriers to entry as you can. Which are the most effective?

4. Why will a monopolist never attempt to produce in the inelastic portion of its demand curve?

5. Should government subsidize monopolies that are losing money to keep them in business?

6. Is some supermarkets' practice of giving trading stamps a form of price discrimination? If so, how does it work?

7. The following table describes the demand curve faced by a monopoly firm. Complete the marginal revenue column.

Price	Quantity Demanded	Marginal Revenue (MR)
$10	0	_____
9	1	_____
8	3	_____
7	4	_____
6	5	_____
5	6	_____
4	7	_____
3	8	_____

8. Assume that the cost data you calculated in Question 9 in the chapter on costs and profits represent the cost data of the monopoly firm of Question 7. How much would the monopolist produce in the short run? Why? What price would the monopolist charge?

9. What is the monopolist's profit, using the data from Question 9 in the chapter on costs and profits?

10. What will happen in the long run, based on the data used in the preceding two questions?

11. Years ago the U.S. government banned advertising of cigarettes on television. Can you speculate on how this ban might have affected the cigarette companies?

12. If you buy a round-trip airline ticket that includes a Saturday night stay at your destination city, the ticket price is often less than half that for the same round trip without a Saturday night stay. Is this price discrimination? Why is Saturday night the important night in this pricing scheme?

13. How does a monopolist maximize profits?

14. In what ways is monopoly thought to be inefficient?

15. What is x-inefficiency?

Suggestions for Further Reading

Asch, Peter. *Industrial Organization and Antitrust Policy*, rev. ed. New York: John Wiley and Sons, 1983. The first chapter of this book contrasts monopoly and competition.

Browning, Edgar K., and Jacquelene M. Browning. *Microeconomic Theory and Applications*, 2nd ed. Boston: Little, Brown, 1986. Chapters 11 and 12 present in-depth treatment of monopoly theory.

Bulow, Jeremy, and John Roberts. "The Simple Economics of Optimal Auctions," *Journal of Political Economy* (October 1989): 1060–1090. Shows how the seller's problem in auctions is identical to the monopolist's problem of price discrimination.

AFTER STUDYING THIS CHAPTER, YOU SHOULD BE ABLE TO:

1. Define monopolistic competition.
2. List the characteristics of the model of monopolistic competition.
3. Diagram a representative firm in monopolistic competition making an economic profit, a zero economic profit, and a loss.
4. Diagram the long-run equilibrium in monopolistic competition and compare it to the long-run equilibrium in perfect competition.
5. Explain the relationships between:
   a. excess capacity and product differentiation,
   b. product differentiation and elasticity of demand.
6. Define:
   a. oligopoly,
   b. pure oligopoly,
   c. differentiated oligopoly,
   d. formalized market coordination,
   e. informal market coordination.
7. List the characteristics of a cartel and the conditions necessary to assure its success.
8. Diagram:
   a. price leadership with a dominant firm and a competitive fringe,
   b. the kinked demand curve faced by firms in an oligopoly.
9. Discuss factors that limit or aid market coordination.

CHAPTER 11
MONOPOLISTIC COMPETITION AND OLIGOPOLY

INTRODUCTION

The last two chapters have examined the two theoretical extremes of market structures. At one extreme is monopoly, and at the other is perfect competition. There are no perfect real-world examples of either extreme. For many years, however, all real-world industries were analyzed in terms of these two models. In the 1930s, theories were developed that filled out the spectrum. Market structures between the two extremes show imperfect competition. Economists divide the middle of the spectrum into monopolistic competition and oligopoly. We will study these two market structures in this chapter.

The theory of monopolistic competition is usually associated with Edward Chamberlin and Joan Robinson. Chamberlin was a Harvard professor who published a book in 1933 entitled *The Theory of Monopolistic Competition*. Joan Robinson taught at Cambridge University in England and published *The Economics of Imperfect Competition*, also in 1933. (Robinson, who died in 1983, was only thirty years old when this classic was published!)

In 1934, German economist Heinrich von Stackelberg published a book entitled *Market Structure and Equilibrium*. It discussed the idea of firms' interdependence and formed the basis of the model of oligopoly. Oligopoly is the market structure in which a few firms compete imperfectly. The scarcity of sellers is the key to firms' behavior in oligopoly. In oligopoly, firms realize that their small number produces mutual interdependence. As a result, each firm will forecast or expect a certain response from its rivals to any price or output decision that it might make. We will examine the model of oligopoly after we study monopolistic competition.

MONOPOLISTIC COMPETITION

monopolistic competition
The market structure in which a large number of firms sell differentiated products.

differentiated product
A good or service that has real or imagined characteristics that are different from those of other goods or services.

The model of **monopolistic competition** describes an industry composed of a large number of sellers. Each of these sellers offers a **differentiated product**, which is a good or service that has real or imagined characteristics that are different from those of other goods or services. This differentiation can take many forms. The salespeople may be nicer, the packaging prettier, the credit terms better, or the service faster. It could even be that a famous person is associated with the product, as Bill Cosby is with Jell-O gelatin and puddings. It is important to note that a product is differentiated if consumers perceive it as different. For example, chemists tell us that aspirin is aspirin, that there is no real difference among the various brands. Yet many consumers view the brands as different, so there is product differentiation.

In monopolistic competition, the industry consists of a large number of firms, each producing a differentiated product. A very important assumption is that entry into this industry is relatively easy. New firms can enter the industry and start selling products that are similar to those already being produced. In Chamberlin's original description of monopolistic competition, a market for a set of goods that were differentiated but had a large number of close substitutes was called a **product group**. Chamberlin characterized monopolistic competition as the large-group case where there was rivalry between many firms in a product group.

product group
A market for a set of goods that are differentiated but have a large number of close substitutes.

You may have recognized monopolistic competition as a familiar market structure, since retail firms often fit this model. Monopolistic competition is generally what most people think of when they think of competition. Perfect competition, with its homogeneous products, simply does not fit the popular idea of competition in which firms are scrambling to make their products different.

SHORT-RUN EQUILIBRIUM

Analysis of the short-run equilibrium of the monopolistically competitive firm is very similar to that for the monopolistic firm. Figure 1 shows the demand curve for a representative firm in monopolistic competition. When we depicted perfect competition, we started with the market and derived the representative firm's demand curve. In analyzing monopolistic competition, we begin with a representative firm, rather than with the market. With product differentiation, each firm faces a unique demand curve. The firm's demand curve in Figure 1 is negatively sloped, unlike the perfectly elastic demand curve faced by the perfectly competitive firm. The negative slope is a result of the differentiated nature of the firm's product. If the product's price is raised, the firm will not lose all its customers because some will continue to prefer this product to substitutes that are close but not perfect. Likewise, if the price is lowered, the firm will gain customers, but some customers will remain loyal to the products produced by other firms.

The elasticity of the demand curve is a measure of the degree of differentiation within the industry. If the products are only slightly differentiated, then they are close substitutes and each firm's demand curve will be very elastic. If the products are highly differentiated, the demand curve

Joan Robinson and Edward Chamberlin are given joint credit for developing the theory of monopolistic competition. Chamberlin published his *Theory of Monopolistic Competition* (1933) six months before Robinson published *The Economics of Imperfect Competition* (1933). Chamberlin, in later years, was preoccupied with trying to differentiate his ideas from Robinson's. Robinson is reported to have commented on Chamberlin's anguish over having to share the credit by saying at one point, "I'm sorry I ruined his life."

Chamberlin was born in the state of Washington but attended high school in Iowa, where he was a successful student and athlete. He later attended the University of Iowa and the University of Michigan, and ultimately received his Ph.D. from Harvard. He taught there until his death.

Joan Robinson developed her ideas quite independently of Chamberlin (they did not know each other) while a junior faculty member at Cambridge University in England. After the appearance of her path-breaking book, Robinson expanded her interests and research over a wide range of economic policy issues. She was an outspoken critic of the market system. Her antimarket publications include *An Essay on Marxian Economics* (1956), *Economic Philosophy* (1962), and *Freedom and Necessity* (1970).

Robinson thought that economic analysis should begin with monopoly and that perfect competition should be studied only as a special case. She was one of the first economists to draw marginal cost curves the way we do now. Her account of monopolistic competition differs from Chamberlin's and from the model in this chapter. Robinson thought it natural for profits to exist in the long run.

Both Robinson and Chamberlin have had a significant impact on economics, but their careers were strikingly different. Chamberlin's career was characterized by a single pursuit—the development of the theory of monopolistic competition. Few economists have applied themselves to so narrow a purpose and yet achieved fame. Perhaps this in part explains Chamberlin's pain at having to share his fame with Robinson. Unlike Chamberlin, Robinson had wide-ranging interests. After contributing to micro theory, she worked with Keynes and helped to develop macroeconomics. Subsequently, she became a fiery social critic.

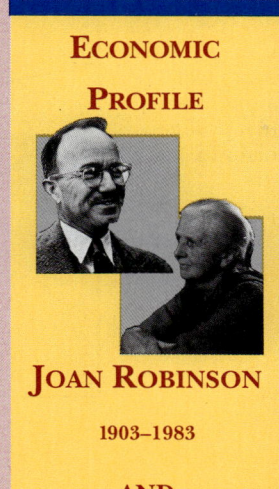

ECONOMIC PROFILE

JOAN ROBINSON
1903–1983
AND
EDWARD CHAMBERLIN
1899–1967

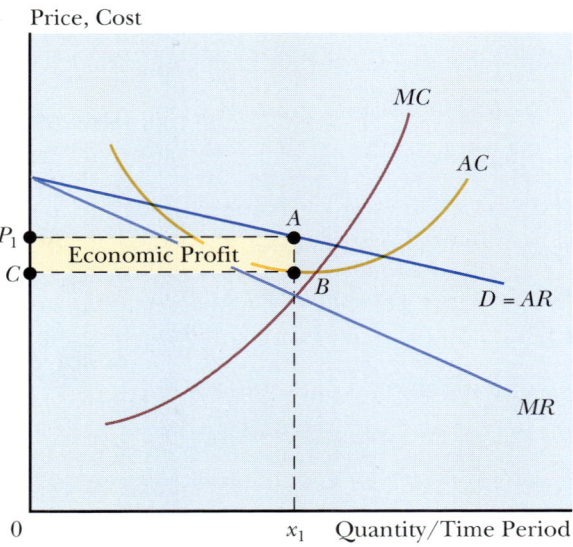

**FIGURE 1
SHORT-RUN PROFITS
IN MONOPOLISTIC
COMPETITION**
In the short run, an economic profit can exist for firms in monopolistic competition. Such profits will cause new firms to enter the industry.

will be relatively inelastic, indicating that the firm can more easily raise the price without losing many customers. Its customers are more loyal. Think of aspirin, for example. Some people are willing to pay more for Bayer than for Brand X because they think it is different. The makers of Bayer are able to charge a higher price without losing a large number of customers. Bayer will be limited in price flexibility by the amount of differentiation it is able to create. As price goes higher and higher, fewer people will be willing to pay for the differentiation. Some people may be willing to pay 10¢ more for Bayer than for a different brand, but if the price of Bayer is increased further, more and more people will shift to the other brands.

The demand curve in Figure 1 has a negative slope, indicating product differentiation. However, demand is very elastic, indicating that there are many good substitutes. Since the demand (average revenue) curve is negatively sloped, the marginal revenue curve will lie below it, for the same reasons it does in the case of monopoly. The firm will, of course, maximize profits at price P_1 and output x_1, where marginal revenue is equal to marginal cost. The firm in Figure 1 is earning an economic profit because average revenue, P_1, exceeds average cost, C. Total revenue is represented by rectangle $0P_1Ax_1$, and total cost is represented by rectangle $0CBx_1$. Economic profit is thus the area of the shaded rectangle CP_1AB.

This analysis is very similar to the one developed in the preceding chapter for monopoly in the short run. The most important difference is that the demand curve here is very elastic. The monopolistically competitive firm is, in one sense, a minimonopolist for a product with close substitutes. The key to whether it is more like a perfectly competitive firm or more like a monopoly depends on what happens in the long run in response to the economic profit.

LONG-RUN EQUILIBRIUM

What about long-run equilibrium in a monopolistically competitive industry? Figure 1 shows that a short-run equilibrium results in an economic profit. Robinson thought the analysis ended here, with the firms able to earn economic profits in the long run. We assume instead that new firms can respond to these economic profits.

Entry into monopolistically competitive industries is assumed to be relatively easy. Thus, new firms will enter the industry in response to the economic profits. As firms enter the industry, the demand curve that is faced by any representative firm will shift to the left because the new firms will be attracting customers away from firms already in the industry. This is what happens, for example, when a new grocery store opens in an area. It draws customers away from the existing stores. The existing firms' demand curves will continue to shift down and to the left as new firms enter, and new firms will enter as long as economic profits are to be made. Long-run equilibrium will occur when all firms are earning zero economic profit (or normal profit). Such an equilibrium is depicted in Figure 2. Price is P_1 and output is x_1. Total revenue and total cost are represented by rectangle $0P_1Ax_1$. There are no economic profits being earned, and no additional firms will attempt to enter this industry.

Of course, too many firms might enter an industry due to a mistaken anticipation of economic profits. If this happens, losses will be realized, and some firms will leave the industry as the long-run adjustment proceeds. Figure 3 shows a monopolistically competitive firm suffering a loss equal to rectangle P_1CBA. Firms would respond to such losses by leaving the industry. The demand curves faced by the remaining firms would shift up and to the right until the equilibrium shown in Figure 2 was restored. The long-run adjustment process under monopolistic competition produces an equilibrium with zero economic profits.

MONOPOLY AND COMPETITION

As you can see, the model of monopolistic competition borrows from the model of monopoly and the model of perfect competition. In the short run, the monopolistically competitive firm is a mini-monopolist produc-

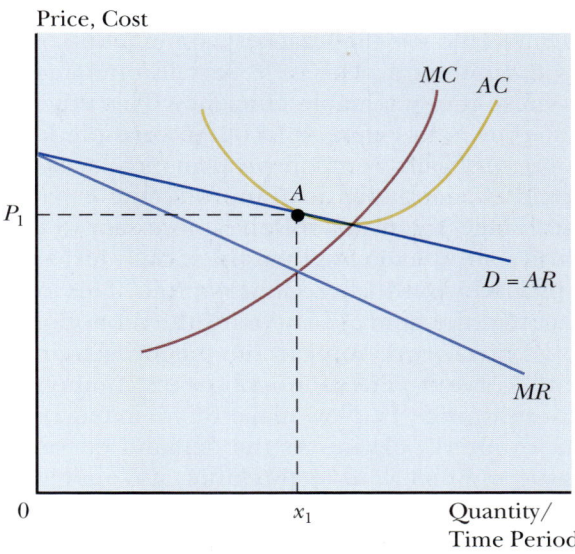

FIGURE 2
LONG-RUN EQUILIBRIUM IN MONOPOLISTIC COMPETITION
Since entry into a monopolistically competitive industry is relatively easy, there can be no long-run economic profits. Firms will enter until all firms are earning only a normal profit.

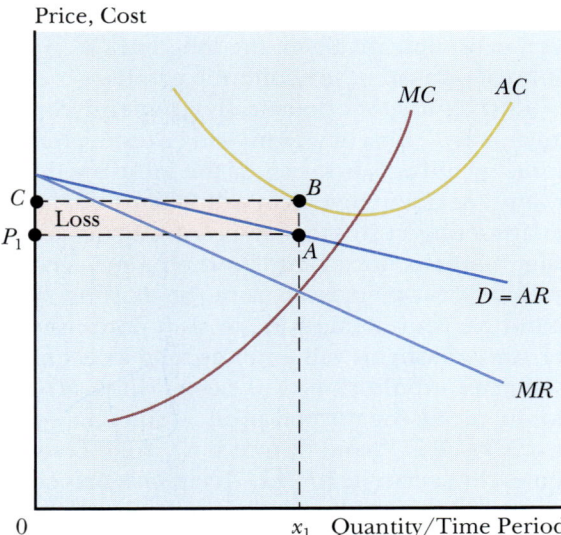

**FIGURE 3
SHORT-RUN LOSSES
IN MONOPOLISTIC
COMPETITION**
Short-run losses, indicated by the shaded area, will cause some firms to exit the industry. Firms will exit until the remaining firms are earning a normal profit, as in Figure 2.

ing the profit-maximizing output and searching for the best price that can be charged for this output. In the long run, the economic profits disappear as new firms enter the industry. The demand curve of each firm then shifts to the left because market demand is shared by more firms. This result is similar to the long-run outcome in perfect competition. The market structure of monopolistic competition is at once both monopolistic and competitive, which explains its name.

EXCESS CAPACITY

excess capacity
The unutilized part of existing production facilities by a monopolistically competitive firm.

In long-run equilibrium, the monopolistically competitive firm chooses an output that does not fully utilize existing plant size. The unutilized part of the production facilities, called **excess capacity**, is depicted in Figure 4. The profit-maximizing output is x_1, where $MR = MC$. This is not, however, the output that would have resulted under perfect competition. Under perfect competition, the firm would use the least-cost combination of inputs, where average cost is at a minimum. This is the socially optimal output because it represents maximum attainable efficiency. This efficient level of output is represented by x_2 in Figure 4. In other words, in long-run equilibrium, the monopolistically competitive firm produces less than the quantity that would efficiently use its full productive capacity.

Is excess capacity a bad thing? To answer this, it is necessary to consider what causes it. The firm is producing less than the socially ideal output because it maximizes profits by producing a lower output. This lower output results from the fact that the demand curve for the monopolistically competitive firm slopes downward. You can see this by examining Figure 4. Begin with demand curve D_1. The monopolistically competitive firm is producing quantity x_1 at price P_1. Now make the demand curve more elastic by rotating it counterclockwise. As the demand curve becomes more and more elastic and finally perfectly elastic, at D_2 in Figure 4, the output will increase toward the socially efficient output x_2. Excess capacity is a result of the negative slope in the demand curve. This nega-

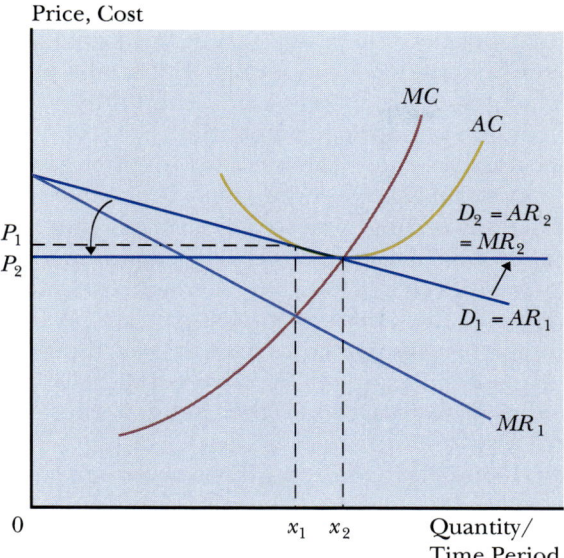

FIGURE 4
EXCESS CAPACITY
Excess capacity results from the negative slope of the demand curve. As the demand curve becomes more elastic, the excess capacity diminishes. It disappears when the curve becomes perfectly elastic.

tive slope, you recall, is a result of the product differentiation. The excess capacity, therefore, results from product differentiation.

It can be argued that this excess capacity is not necessarily a bad thing. Consumers may be willing to incur the extra cost in return for the perceived benefits of product differentiation. It would indeed be a very boring world without product differentiation. We might all be wearing khaki-colored shirts, for example.

The major problem with this argument lies in separating desired from undesired product differentiation. A consumer who is faced with a wide range of product choices but little price competition is not able to choose whether or not to pay extra to get the differentiated product. This problem isn't likely to be too important, however, when there are many firms, as in monopolistic competition. Consider aspirin. If the only products in the industry were Anacin, Bayer, Bufferin, and Excedrin, the consumer would not have a low-price choice, since these brands compete almost exclusively by advertising rather than by cutting prices. But the consumer actually does have a choice of lower-priced generic brands of aspirin. So in choosing Anacin over Brand X, the consumer voluntarily chooses product differentiation. In this case, product differentiation seems to be a good thing because the consumer making the choice is maximizing individual utility. If, on the other hand, there are no lower-priced products and the consumer must choose among products that compete only through advertising, then the consumer does not really have a choice about bearing the cost of the differentiation (unless, of course, he or she simply does without the product altogether).

PRODUCT DIFFERENTIATION AND ADVERTISING

The firm in monopolistic competition will try to differentiate its product in order to shift its demand curve to the right and to make demand more inelastic by developing consumer loyalty. The firm will advertise as well as

nonprice competition Competing with rival firms through advertising, style changes, color changes, and techniques other than lowering price.

make changes in color, style, quality, and so on. Advertising can inform consumers about higher quality or develop brand loyalty. Either of these results creates product differentiation. Competing with rival firms through advertising, style changes, color changes, and techniques other than lowering price is referred to as **nonprice competition**.

Advertising does not necessarily cause an increase in price. Even though costs rise because of advertising expenditures, it is possible that the increased output that the advertising generates will result in lower prices because of economies of scale. You can see this by examining Figure 5. In Figure 5, AC_1 represents a firm's long-run average cost before advertising. With sales of x_1 units, the price consumers pay is P_1. Advertising raises costs, shifting the firm's average cost curve to AC_2. If output increases because the firm gains sales because of the advertising, price can fall to P_2 because of economies of scale. On the other hand, if sales and output stay at x_1, average cost will rise to P_3.

If effective use of nonprice competition differentiates a firm's product enough that other firms' products do not seem to be good substitutes, the firm can earn an economic profit in the long run. Nonprice competition will often be gradual, so the firm can avoid a price war in which all firms will lose. A firm that is successful in such nonprice competition has in essence turned its share of the monopolistically competitive market into a long-run minimonopoly. The profit of such a firm could exist in the long run and not be driven to zero by new entrants.

Fast-food preparation is a monopolistically competitive industry. There are large numbers of firms, and entry is relatively easy. If a firm is able to successfully differentiate its product so that consumers don't consider the products of other firms close substitutes, the firm will be able to earn a long-run economic profit because it can keep would-be competitors out of its segment of the market. For example, McDonald's can't keep

FIGURE 5
A DECLINE IN PRICE DUE TO ADVERTISING
AC_1 represents long-run average costs without advertising. AC_2 represents costs made higher by advertising. If the firm increases output from x_1 to x_2 because of advertising, it is possible for the price charged to fall from P_1 to P_2. If sales do not increase, price will rise to P_3.

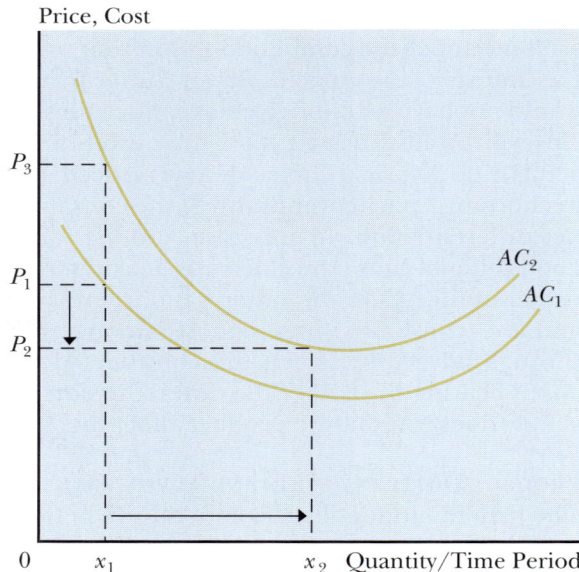

firms out of the hamburger market, but it can keep firms out of the Big Mac market. If enough people believe there's nothing like a Big Mac, this persistent brand loyalty might allow McDonald's to maintain an economic profit in the long run. Remember—Robinson thought this would be the equilibrium state.

It is easy to determine how successful a firm is at product differentiation by examining the difference between its prices and its competitors' prices. The consumer may go to McDonald's if a Big Mac costs 15¢ more than the competition, but what if it cost 55¢ more or $1.15 more? There is some price at which the other products will become good substitutes. That price is a measure of the success of product differentiation. It may be that a Big Mac is worth more to the consumer because of higher quality or because McDonald's has a very successful advertising and public relations program. The point is that it doesn't matter what causes the differentiation. The economic impact is that McDonald's may be able to earn an economic profit in the long run.

CHARACTERISTICS OF MONOPOLISTIC COMPETITION

- There are many sellers of similar but differentiated products.
- Economic profits can exist in the short run..
- Price is equal to average cost in the long run.
- Excess capacity exists in the long run (price is greater than marginal cost).
- Nonprice competition increases product differentiation.

RESOURCE ALLOCATION IN MONOPOLISTIC COMPETITION

The model of monopolistic competition has several implications for the allocation of resources. The resulting allocation will be different from the societal ideal achieved with perfect competition. First, even at the long-run equilibrium with zero economic profit, there will be excess capacity with monopolistic competition. This means that price will be greater than minimum average cost. Consumers are paying only the average cost of production, but this cost is higher than it would be with the most efficient level of production.

Second, if costs are the same under perfect competition and monopolistic competition, prices will be higher with monopolistic competition because price is greater than marginal cost (or marginal revenue). Third, firms in monopolistic competition will provide a wider variety of styles, colors, qualities, and brands. These choices are, unfortunately, related to the product differentiation and excess capacity that cause average cost to be higher.

Fourth, in monopolistic competition, there will be advertising and other forms of nonprice competition. This outcome is not necessarily bad. To the extent that advertising adds to customer satisfaction and the product is voluntarily purchased, it can be a good thing. Some social critics consider any advertising that does more than convey information to be a bad thing. Economists would argue that advertising is undesirable only if people don't have the option to consume alternative goods.[1]

OLIGOPOLY

oligopoly
The market structure in which a few firms compete imperfectly and recognize their interdependence.

The last of the four market structures is oligopoly. Oligopoly is important because there are so many real-world examples of it. **Oligopoly** is the market structure in which there are only a few firms. Since there are few firms, the actions of the firms are interdependent.

In some people's minds, oligopoly and monopoly are essentially the same. Among economists, this view is expressed by John Kenneth Galbraith. Galbraith argues, "So long as there are only a few massive firms in an industry, each must act with a view of the welfare of all."[2] This view, which is not widely shared among economists, regards oligopoly as shared monopoly. **Shared monopoly** is the model of oligopoly that says that oligopolists coordinate decisions and share markets to act as a monopoly.

shared monopoly
The model of oligopoly that says that oligopolists coordinate and share markets to act as a monopoly.

Most economists view oligopoly as more complex and difficult to analyze than monopoly. There is no single model of oligopoly, as there is for the other three market structures. The difficulty stems from the interdependence that characterizes oligopoly. Because of the complexity of oligopoly, economic analysis of it often includes heavy doses of descriptive economics rather than formal models with graphs. We will follow this tradition and describe several types of oligopoly and forms of oligopolistic behavior.

Oligopolies are sometimes categorized by the type of product they produce: homogeneous or differentiated. An oligopolistic industry that produces a homogeneous product is referred to as a **pure oligopoly**. The distinction is important because in pure oligopolies a single price is charged for the output of all the firms. An example of a pure oligopoly is the cement industry. As a consumer, you would be indifferent about which firm produced the sack of cement you purchased.

pure oligopoly
An oligopolistic industry that produces a homogeneous product.

differentiated oligopoly
An oligopoly that produces heterogeneous products that are very close substitutes.

In contrast, a **differentiated oligopoly** produces products that are different. The auto industry is a good example. In differentiated oligopolies, there are **price clusters**, which are groupings of prices for similar, but not homogeneous, products. The range of prices within a cluster will depend on the amount of product differentiation. The more differentiated the products, the greater the price divergence. Tight price clusters indicate very little product differentiation.

price clusters
Groupings of prices for similar, but not homogeneous, products.

COLLUSIVENESS AND OLIGOPOLIES

Perhaps the most useful classification tool for analyzing oligopolies is the system of definitions proposed by Fritz Machlup.[3] Machlup divided

---

1. The theory of monopolistic competition has been criticized by George Stigler as not offering any additional insights into or predictions of firms' behavior. Stigler admits that monopolistic competition is more descriptive of the real world, but he argues that the theory of perfect competition offers the same insights and predictions. See G. Chris Archibald, "Chamberlin versus Chicago," *Review of Economic Studies* (October 1961): 1–28.
2. John K. Galbraith, *American Capitalism*, 2nd ed. (Cambridge: Riverside Press, 1956), 83.
3. Fritz Machlup, *The Economics of Sellers' Competition* (Baltimore: Johns Hopkins Press, 1952).

Chapter 11 Monopolistic Competition and Oligopoly

oligopolistic behavior into three classes based on the degree of communication, coordination, and collusion among the firms in the industry. **Communication** refers to the firms' ability to signal their intentions to one another. **Coordination** refers to the firms' ability to relate their production decisions to those of the other firms in the industry. **Collusion** refers to agreements between the firms in an industry to set a certain price or to share a market in certain ways. It should be obvious that the abilities to communicate, coordinate, and collude will depend on the number of firms in an industry. As the number of firms increases, the cost of these activities will increase.

Machlup's system identifies three categories of oligopolies. The first category is characterized by formalized market coordination. The second is characterized by informal market coordination. The third category displays no market coordination.

FORMALIZED MARKET COORDINATION: CARTELS

Organized, collusive oligopolies are cartels. **Cartels** are groups of independent firms that agree not to compete but rather to determine prices and output jointly. A perfect cartel, which is able to behave as a monopoly, corresponds to Galbraith's concept of a shared monopoly.

In striving for joint profit maximization, a cartel must set prices, outputs, and marketing areas. However, the cartel can't always set these variables so that each individual firm in the cartel is maximizing its own profit. Figure 6 shows this problem clearly. In Figure 6, there are two firms, A and B, in a cartel that produces a homogeneous product. The marginal cost curves of these firms are MC_A and MC_B. MC_t is the horizontal summation (total) of MC_A and MC_B. The cartel will maximize profits, behaving exactly as a monopoly, by producing x_C where $MR = MC_t$. This output level results in a price of P_C.

Now the cartel must enforce this decision by requiring firms A and B to produce x_A and x_B, respectively. The difficulty is that neither firm would be at its individual profit-maximizing output. If each firm views one-half of the market as its own, its demand curve is represented by MR in Figure 6.[4] The firms' profit-maximizing outputs are where $MC_A = MR_A$ and where $MC_B = MR_B$. Firm A would like to produce x_a, and Firm B would like to produce x_b.

In short, profit maximization for the cartel as a whole is not necessarily consistent with profit maximization for each individual member. In the example of Figure 6, firm A would prefer to produce *more* and sell it at a *higher* price, and firm B would prefer to produce *less* at a *lower* price. This example points out the most important problem faced by cartels. Joint profit maximization and individual profit maximization are often in conflict. As a result, a cartel is very unstable.

Perhaps the greatest threat to a cartel's existence is that members find it in their own self-interest to cheat on the cartel. **Chiseling** refers to cheating on a cartel agreement by lowering prices in an attempt to capture more of the market. If, for example, a cartel agrees on a set price, such as P_C in Figure 6, individual members may attempt to give secret price cuts

communication
Firms' ability to signal their intentions to each other.

coordination
Firms' ability to relate their production decisions to those made by other firms in an industry.

collusion
Agreements between firms in an industry to set a certain price or to share a market in certain ways.

cartel
A group of independent firms that agree not to compete but rather to determine prices and output jointly.

chiseling
Cheating on a cartel agreement by lowering prices in an attempt to capture more of the market.

---

4. Remember that $MR = \frac{1}{2}D$. So if each firm views half the market as its own, the demand curve that each firm faces would be identical to the marginal revenue curve for the market.

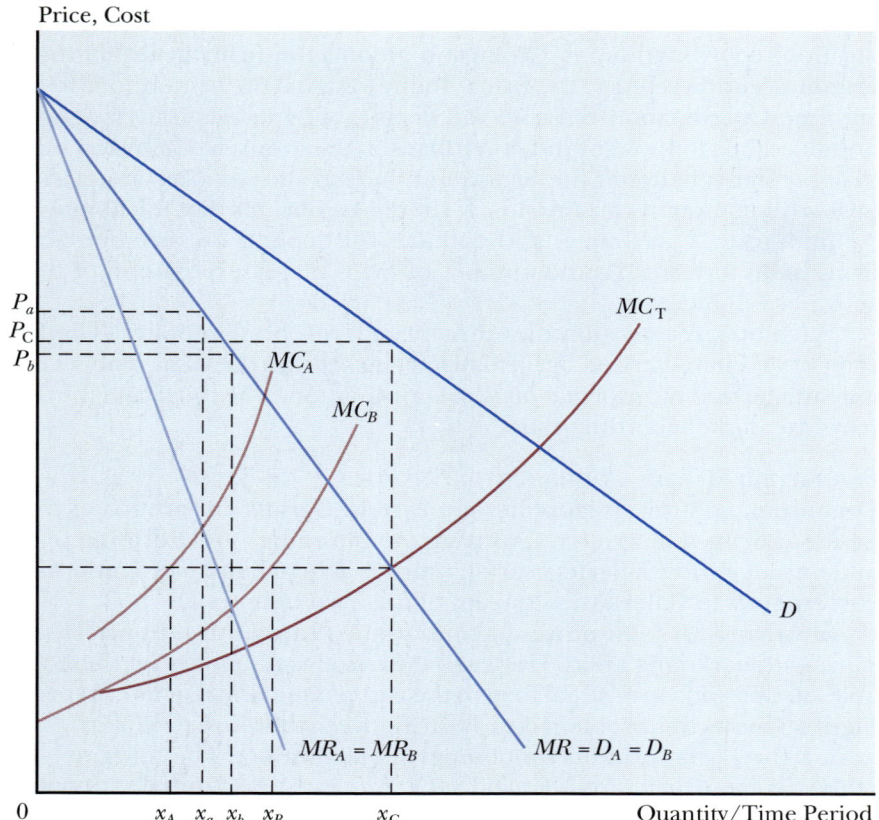

FIGURE 6
PROFIT MAXIMIZATION BY A CARTEL
Joint profit maximization by two firms occurs where $MC_t = MR$. This quantity establishes a price of P_C and output of x_C. The cartel must then force firms A and B to produce output x_A and x_B, respectively. Assuming that each firm could view one-half of the market represented by the demand curve (D) as its own, individual profit maximization would establish a price of P_a and output of x_a for firm A and a price of P_b and output of x_b for firm B. To succeed, the cartel must compel firm A to produce less and firm B to produce more than its individual profit-maximizing output.

and capture more of the market. The total demand for a cartel is inelastic, so price cuts would reduce total revenue. However, the demand facing one member is elastic if it cuts price and the others do not.

If any firm in a cartel believes the others to be untrustworthy, it will have more of an incentive to chisel. As the number of firms in a cartel increases, it becomes increasingly likely that individual firms will become suspicious of the other members. The amount of chiseling is thus closely related to the number of firms in a cartel. The fewer the firms, the more closely the cartel will be able to monitor their behavior to determine if any firm is chiseling. Other factors can help a cartel control chiseling. For example, if the number of buyers is small and if the price is widely publicized, the cartel will not worry so much about one of its members chiseling.

Another threat faced by cartels is new entry. If a cartel is successful in acting as a monopoly and earning higher than normal profits, it must create barriers to entry. Otherwise, new firms might enter the market and compete with the cartel.

Let's briefly examine a few cartel-type organizations to see what elements affected their success or failure.

CARTELS IN THE REAL WORLD. The history of cartels is not impressive. Most have held together for only short periods of time, mainly because of chis-

International Perspective

Commodity Cartels

Commodity cartels have a long history of failure. In the 1950s, commodity agreements, which are essentially cartels of commodity-producing countries, existed for tin, coffee, sugar, and wheat. The success of OPEC in 1973 reenergized some of these cartels as many commodity-exporting countries tried to emulate OPEC. The result was a flurry of activity that produced the following official organizations:

International Bauxite Association (IBA)
International Coffee Organization (ICO)
Intergovernmental Council of Copper-Exporting Countries (CIPEC)
International Sugar Association (ISA)
International Tin Council (ITC)
Organization of Banana Exporting Countries (OBEC)

In addition, there were attempts in the late 1970s and early 1980s to organize cartels in iron ore, nickel, rubber, tungsten, molybdenum, cobalt, columbium, and tantalum. Very few of these cartels, however, enjoyed the success that OPEC had in the 1970s.

Several lessons can be learned from the experience of these commodity cartels and the success of OPEC. To be successful, a commodity cartel must:

1. have few members,
2. produce a product with few substitutes (have inelastic demand),
3. have buoyant world demand (have high income elasticity),
4. pursue a moderate pricing policy,
5. have at least tacit approval of consuming nations, and
6. have effective sanctions against chiselers.

Most cartels have great difficulty with the last three requirements and, as a result, break down rather quickly.

The effects of commodity cartels are often mixed up with economic development and world politics. Members tend to be less developed countries, and the consuming nations tend to be developed countries. The reasons for the formation of the cartel are often put in terms of a "fair" price that will redistribute wealth from rich to poor countries. Cartels are anticonsumer. Although some of those consumers live in high-income countries, many are poor people in poor countries. The OPEC oil price hike caused more hardship in poor countries than it did in rich countries.

eling. In the few cases where cartels have had long-term success, there has usually been direct government support. Once a government is involved, it becomes more difficult to chisel because the government can police and penalize this behavior.

Organized, collusive activity in private industry in the United States has usually been invalidated by the courts. However, General Electric and Westinghouse engaged in a conspiracy in the late 1950s to act as a cartel. They decided on a scheme that allowed them to submit low bids alternately on government contracts. The scheme depended on the phases of the moon. At either full or new moon (every two weeks), the firm designated to be the low bidder would gain the contract because the other firm would submit an uncompetitively high bid. This plan worked well because there were only two firms dealing with one buyer, the federal government. Each firm would know if the other was cheating because the bids were made public. In this case, the government was inadvertently helping the cartel overcome the chiseling problem.

Another example, involving a large number of firms, was an attempt to form a cartel known as the National Farm Organization (NFO). The industry for milk and beef production is composed of large numbers of firms (farms), and the NFO cartel only included about 10 percent of them. In 1967 and 1968, the NFO attempted two separate actions: one to raise milk prices and the other to raise beef prices. The cartel tried to organize farmers to keep production from the market. In order to raise prices, cartel members were to destroy milk and keep cattle away from the market. If the NFO members had been successful in raising prices, the nonmembers who continued to produce and sell would have benefited. They would have reacted to the higher prices by expanding output. Also, as prices began to rise, there would have been tremendous pressure on cartel members to chisel on the withholding action. In fact, the chiselers would have benefited much more than the members who refused to chisel. The attempt to organize the cartel resulted in violence. Cattle scales were blown up. NFO farmers sat in the roads to keep others from taking their products to market. Some farmers even resorted to taking cattle to market in house trailers to avoid detection. The lesson is clear: A cartel with many members will find it very difficult to succeed.

Cartels are much more common in Europe than they are in the United States. In Europe, cartels are permitted and often encouraged by governments. In Nazi Germany, all the major industries operated as cartels. Currently in Western Europe, the Common Market Commission is actively promoting cartels in steel, textiles, and shipbuilding.

Cartels are—with one exception—illegal in the United States. The one exception, based on the Webb-Pomerene Act of 1921, allows the formation of cartels when they are necessary to participate in foreign trade. These Webb-Pomerene cartels have not been successful in raising prices, primarily because of the large number of firms participating.

OPEC—A Decade of Success. The best-known cartel of recent years is the Organization of Petroleum Exporting Countries, known as OPEC. In the 1950s, international oil companies controlled a major portion of the world's oil supply. These companies frequently engaged in price competition. In an attempt to stop price cutting, some Arab governments and a few non-Arab governments formed OPEC in 1960. At first, OPEC enjoyed little success. But this changed in 1973, as the Arab-Israeli war heated up and the Arab countries banded together. On January 1, 1973, the price of oil was $2.12 per barrel. Of this $2.12, $1.52 went to the OPEC governments. By January 1, 1974, the price was $7.61 with $7.01 going to the governments. By January 1975, the price was about $10.50. By 1982, the price had risen to $35.00.

How did this cartel, which had been in existence since 1960, come to flex its muscles in 1973? At that time, importing governments helped by posting prices and dealing with OPEC in open forums, so individual members were less likely to chisel. More important, however, Saudi Arabia was willing to cut back its production of oil to allow other members to sell all they wanted to produce at the high prices set by the cartel.[5] In 1984, after production had to be cut back by 5 million barrels a day to prevent the cartel from collapsing, Saudi Arabia's willingness to bear this cost began to weaken.

The price of oil began to fall. The January 1984, price was $29 per barrel, down from the 1982 high of $35. The slide continued. In January 1987, the price was $13 per barrel. In January 1990, it was under $12 per barrel. As prices fell, chiseling became more common. The predictions made by economists in the 1970s that the cartel would eventually weaken started to come true. Some of the Persian Gulf countries, notably Kuwait, the United Arab Emirates, and Qatar, were experiencing cash flow problems. These countries started grandiose development schemes when their oil revenues were in excess of $300 billion per year. Their revenues fell significantly because of the decreased price, but the development projects still had to be paid for. Kuwait began shipping more oil than allowed by OPEC agreements—one of the factors underlying the Gulf War. In 1986, Nobel Prize winner Milton Friedman wrote an editorial entitled "Right at Last, an Expert's Dream" reminding readers that he had predicted in 1974 that OPEC would not last very long.[6]

As we pointed out earlier, all cartels face two problems. The first is chiseling, or secret price cutting. OPEC faced this problem in the presence of oil surpluses. The second problem a cartel faces is new entry. Large amounts of oil have been coming into the market from non-OPEC sources, such as the North Sea and Alaska. In addition, other sources of energy, such as solar and nuclear energy, which were uneconomical when oil was $2 per barrel, became profitable at the much higher prices. The new entry has been slow to develop, but the future should prove even more difficult for OPEC as new firms producing oil and other competing products enter the market and challenge the cartel's cohesiveness.

The impact of new oil supplies is evident in the statistics. In 1973, OPEC's share of world oil production was 56 percent. In 1975, its share was 51 percent. In 1980, it was 45 percent, and in 1984, it was 35 percent. In 1990, OPEC's share had fallen to 28 percent. This declining share of

---

5. An interesting side issue is that much public criticism was leveled on the oil refining companies rather than the OPEC members. This is odd because the cartel profits are not going to the oil companies but to the governments of the OPEC member countries.
6. Milton Friedman, "Right at Last, an Expert's Dream," *Newsweek* (10 March 1986): 8.

production signaled the weakening of the cartel better than any other piece of data. If a cartel is going to set prices, it must control a large share of total production.

In addition to the new oil supplies, the high oil prices have also had an effect on quantity demanded. The decade of OPEC's dominance resulted in adjustments in consumer demand. Perhaps the most evident of these adjustments is the increased fuel efficiency of automobiles.

INFORMAL MARKET COORDINATION

Informally coordinated oligopolies engage in unorganized and unstated attempts to practice joint actions. Such **tacit collusion** is much weaker than the collusion among members of a cartel. It is weaker because all the incentives to chisel are still present, but organized vigilance against chiseling is not. Tacit collusion is found in U.S. industries because cartels are illegal under federal antitrust laws. Informal cooperation among oligopolistic firms can be viewed as an attempt to form cartels while avoiding antitrust laws. Such collusion usually takes the form of informal agreements to behave in certain ways. Often these agreements arise naturally, without any need for formal organization. The most common form of tacit, informal agreement is based on price leadership.

tacit collusion
Unorganized and unstated attempts by informally coordinated oligopolies to practice joint actions.

PRICE LEADERSHIP. Price leadership is a form of tacit collusion in an oligopolistic industry in which one firm, the price leader, sets the price or initiates price changes and the other firms follow that lead. The firm that is the most influential in an industry is called the **dominant firm**. It may be either the largest firm or the lowest-cost firm. Price leadership is most effective where firms are few and have clearly similar products (for example, in the auto, cigarette, and steel industries). It helps if the demand for the product is price-inelastic since this will further discourage price cutting. When the demand curve for the product is perfectly inelastic, a firm that chisels on price will gain sales only at the expense of other firms. The lower price will not bring about additional sales for the industry. Thus, the conflict between firms will be sharper when demand is not very responsive to price cuts.

price leadership
The form of tacit collusion in an oligopolistic industry in which one firm, the price leader, sets the price or initiates price changes and the other firms follow that lead.

dominant firm
The most influential firm in an industry, usually the largest firm.

THE DOMINANT FIRM. In price leadership, the dominant firm sets a profit-maximizing price, and the other firms divide up the market at that price. The other firms, known as the **competitive fringe**, act much like firms in perfect competition. This result can be seen in Figure 7. The market demand curve for the product is D. The marginal cost curve of the dominant firm is MC_d, and the summation of all the other firms' marginal cost curves is MC_f. Those firms (the fringe) will make production decisions as price takers and will always produce where price is equal to their marginal cost. MC_f can thus be viewed as their supply curve. The demand curve that the dominant firm faces can be derived by subtracting the amount supplied by the fringe firms (MC_f) from the market demand curve (D). This subtraction gives the dominant firm's demand curve, D_d, and thus its marginal revenue curve, MR_d. The dominant firm will set a profit-maximizing price and output of P_1 and x_d. Once price P_1 is determined, the fringe firms view this price much as competitive firms view the market

competitive fringe
The smaller competitors in informally coordinated markets with one large, dominant firm.

Chapter 11 Monopolistic Competition and Oligopoly

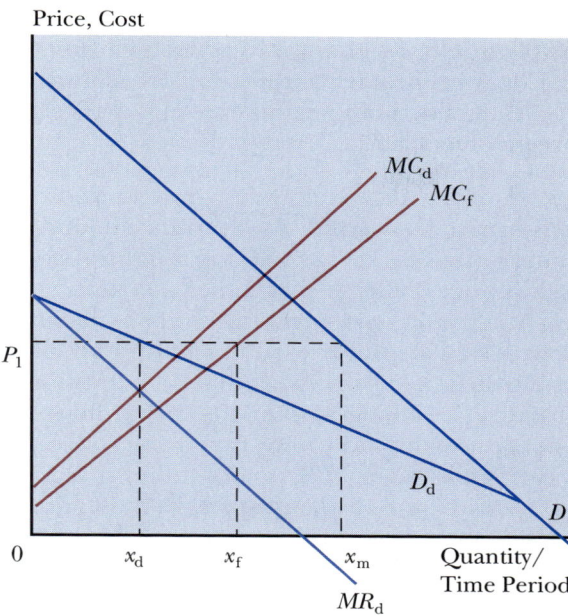

**FIGURE 7
A DOMINANT FIRM WITH A COMPETITIVE FRINGE**
The dominant firm views a part of the market, D_d, as its own. D_d is determined by subtracting the supply curve of the competitive fringe, MC_f, from the market demand, D. The dominant firm produces where $MC_d = MR_d$, setting price P_1 and producing x_d units. The fringe firms face a perfectly elastic demand curve at P_1, and produce x_f units (where $P_1 = MR = MC_f$).

price. The fringe firms will produce x_f units at the market price P_1 because for them $P_1 = MR$ and they want to produce where $MR = MC_f$. The sum of the production of the dominant firm (x_d) and the production of the fringe firms (x_f) satisfies the market demand of x_m at price P_1.

This model of price leadership is applicable to the oil refining industry in the United States. There is a small group of dominant firms and a large number of small fringe firms. Price leadership by a dominant firm also appears to have prevailed at one time or another in the aluminum, automobile, and cigarette industries in the United States.

HISTORICAL PRICE LEADERSHIP. In a few cases, especially in mature industries, it is possible for a firm to emerge as the price leader because it is convenient for the other firms in the industry to follow the leader and thus coordinate their pricing. This type of price leadership, called historical price leadership, is very similar to cartel behavior. Its intent is collusion—to achieve industrywide profit maximization. Historical price lead-

CHARACTERISTICS OF OLIGOPOLY

- There are only a few sellers of homogeneous or differentiated products.
- Interdependence leads to attempts at communication, coordination, and collusion.
- Cartels may be formed to determine industry pricing and output.
- Price leadership may be used to coordinate industry pricing.
- The price leader may be a dominant firm.
- Nonprice competition increases product differentiation.

ership, however, is unorganized and thus not illegal in the United States. It was rampant within U.S. oligopolies. General Motors was the recognized price leader in autos, U.S. Steel in steel, and DuPont in chemicals. In the last ten years, the price leadership of these domestic oligopolies has been severely limited by foreign competition.

SUCCESSFUL PRICE LEADERSHIP. In order to be successful—that is, in order to raise industry profit levels—price leadership must produce a kind of cartel but still avoid legal sanctions. This means walking a tightrope. As the tacit collusion embodied in price leadership becomes successful, the incentive to chisel increases. As a result, most successful price leadership not involving a dominant firm occurs in industries in which there are only a few firms. The record of such tacit collusion shows that such industries are characterized by rigid prices. Price changes, when they occur, are generally small. Such industries are usually those that can blame price increases on rising costs and can punish firms that do not follow the price increase. The steel and auto industries are two examples. In these industries, potential chiselers know they cannot easily get away with not following the price leader.

THE GARY DINNERS. The way in which oligopolies can coordinate markets informally is clearly demonstrated by what have come to be known as the Gary Dinners. In 1901, U.S. Steel put together mergers that made it the dominant firm, supplying 65 percent of the domestic steel market. From 1907 to 1911, Judge Elbert H. Gary, chairman of the board of U.S. Steel, held a series of dinners for executives of competing companies. Gary explained that the close communication *and contact* developed at these dinners "generated such mutual *respect and affectionate regard* among steel industry leaders that all considered the obligation to cooperate and avoid destructive competition *more binding . . . than any written or verbal contract.*"[7] Efforts to prosecute U.S. Steel's behavior as an antitrust violation were unsuccessful.

In recent years, there haven't been any reported "informal" gatherings as effective as the Gary Dinners. However, trade associations, country clubs, and other such business and social gathering places can serve as forums for developing cooperative behavior among potential competitors.[8]

NO MARKET COORDINATION

Unorganized, uncollusive oligopolies are characterized by independent action. Firms in these oligopolies practice profit maximization independently but are affected by the actions and responses of their rivals. Each firm tries to anticipate the response of its rivals and then takes that prediction into account when making decisions. Economists tried to develop a model for this behavior in the early nineteenth century. In 1838, A. Augustin Cournot (1801–1877) published a theory of duopoly (a market

---

7. F. M. Scherer, *Industrial Market Structure and Economic Performance* (Chicago: Rand McNally, 1980), 170. Italics indicate Judge Gary's actual words, taken from a government antitrust brief.
8. Adam Smith recognized the potential for such collusion. Here is his famous statement on this subject from *The Wealth of Nations*: "People of the same trade seldom meet together, even for merriment and diversion, but the conversation ends in a conspiracy against the public, or in some contrivance to raise prices."

with only two firms). His theory and those that followed (up to the post–World War II period) were unsatisfactory because they assumed that the rival firm would not react to the action of the firm being analyzed. The post–World War II developments in oligopoly theory rest heavily on game theory. Game theory is a relatively new field of mathematics that can provide insights into oligopolistic behavior.

GAME THEORY. **Game theory**, a theory of rational decision making under conditions of uncertainty, was first developed by John von Neumann (1903–1957) and Oskar Morgenstern (1902-1977) in a book entitled *The Theory of Games and Economic Behavior*.[9] Game theory says that players try to reach an optimal position through strategic behavior that takes into account the anticipated moves of other players. This model describes very accurately how oligopolists behave.

Standard microeconomic decision-making theory is based on the assumption that the outcomes of various decisions are known with certainty. Game theory suggests rational solutions when the outcomes are uncertain. Games are usually described as being either zero-sum or non-zero-sum. Zero-sum games are those in which one player's gain is another player's loss. Non-zero-sum games open the door to collusion or cooperative action because all players may gain (or all may lose) from a certain course of action. This aspect of game theory has proved very useful in the study of oligopolies in which each firm must take into account the reactions of its competitors.

One of the most famous of non-zero-sum games is called the Prisoner's Dilemma. Two prisoners are interrogated separately. Each one knows that if neither confesses, both will go free. However, if one confesses and implicates the other, the one who confesses can go free and the other will be convicted. The interrogator separately offers each prisoner the opportunity to confess and go free. The rational course of action for the self-interested prisoner is to confess and implicate the other. Since both face the same incentive and the same uncertainty about the other's action, both will confess. The outcome of the two rational decisions will make both of the prisoners worse off. They would both be better off if they could engage in collusion. This lesson holds for oligopolistic firms.

THE KINKED DEMAND CURVE. One explanation of why prices in oligopolistic industries tend to be less flexible than prices in other market structures was presented by Paul Sweezy. Sweezy hypothesized that price rigidity exists because the firms in an oligopoly face a **kinked demand curve**. The demand curve has two sections because the firms come to believe that if they cut prices, their rivals will also do so. The price cut will not produce much of an increase in sales. A price increase, on the other hand, will not be imitated and will, therefore, result in a loss of sales for the firm making the increase. As a result, once a price is reached in an oligopoly, it tends to remain in effect for long periods.

game theory
A mathematical theory about rational decision making under conditions of uncertainty that can provide insight into oligopolistic behavior.

kinked demand curve
A demand curve with a bend in it at the price settled on in an oligopolistic industry because other firms' price cuts, but not price increases, are matched.

---

9. For a detailed and highly mathematical treatment of game theory, see John von Neumann and Oskar Morgenstern, *The Theory of Games and Economic Behavior* (Princeton, NJ: Princeton University Press, 1949). For a short survey on game theory, see F. M. Scherer, *Industrial Market Structure and Economic Performance* (Chicago: Rand McNally, 1980), 160–166.

You can see the effect of a kinked demand curve by examining Figure 8. There is a kink in the demand curve D at point A (or at price P). Below point A, the other firms in the market will match any price decrease, making the demand curve relatively inelastic. A firm won't increase sales very much by decreasing price below P. Any increase in price above P will have the opposite effect. Competing firms will not match the increase. As a result, the demand curve above point A is relatively elastic. At the kink in the firm's demand curve, the corresponding marginal revenue curve, MR, is discontinuous. As you can see, MR has a break in it between B and C in Figure 8. This break allows a large variation in marginal cost with no effect on the profit-maximizing price, P, or output, x. For example, marginal cost could change from MC to MC_1 with no effect on price and output. Sweezy used this model to explain why prices were so rigid in oligopoly.

NONPRICE COMPETITION. All oligopolists, whether organized or unorganized, compete in dimensions other than just the price dimension. In formulating models, economists tend to treat goods as homogeneous and view competition as occurring mostly through price adjustments. In the real world, however, competition can take other forms. Firms can change the quality, color, texture, design, size, advertising, and a host of other attributes of a product.[10] Even an apparently homogeneous product can be differentiated by the quality of customer service.

OLIGOPOLY ADVERTISING. Casual observation leads to the conclusion that a great deal of the advertising on television is done by firms in oligopolistic

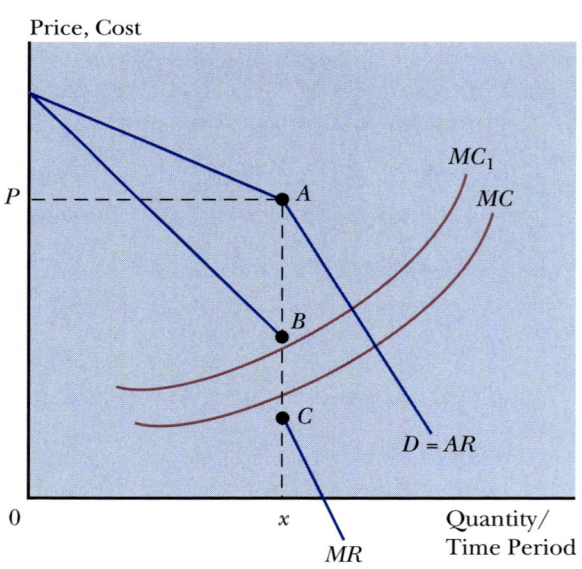

FIGURE 8
A KINKED DEMAND CURVE
In this model, the firm faces a kinked demand curve, D, because prices above P will not be matched and prices below P will be matched. The kink creates a discontinuity in the marginal revenue curve, which causes the price to be very rigid at the kink (P).

---

10. Sometimes quality changes substitute for price changes. For example, if the price of a candy bar remains at 45¢ but the amount of chocolate or nuts decreases, this change is equivalent to an increase in price. Oligopolists often engage in this kind of disguised price changing because it seems to provoke less response from rivals.

George Stigler and Paul Sweezy represent polar extremes in economic analysis. Both have written extensively in the field of industrial organization, but the similarities end there.

George Stigler is the personification of the Chicago School of free-enterprise capitalism. He received a bachelor's degree from the University of Washington, an MBA from Northwestern University, and a Ph.D. from the University of Chicago. In 1982, Stigler was awarded the Nobel Prize in economics. Paul Sweezy is an American Marxist. He has a B.A. degree and a Ph.D. in economics from Harvard University.

Both economists are coeditors of prestigious journals that are at opposite ends of the ideological spectrum. Stigler is coeditor of the *Journal of Political Economy*, and Sweezy is coeditor of the *Monthly Review*. Stigler's views are best delineated in *The Theory of Price* (1966) and *Organization of Industry* (1968). Sweezy's views can be found in *The Dynamics of U.S. Capitalism* (1972), *Introduction to Socialism* (1968), and *Modern Capitalism and Other Essays* (1972).

Stigler and Sweezy have clashed over Sweezy's use of the kinked demand curve to explain why prices in oligopolies are more stable than prices in other market structures. This model has been severely criticized by Stigler, who argues that Sweezy's theory is wrong. Stigler says that Sweezy's claim that prices in an oligopoly are more stable than in other market structures does not stand up to real-world evidence.

ECONOMIC PROFILE

GEORGE STIGLER
1911–

AND

PAUL SWEEZY
1910–

markets. Most informational advertising is done on radio or in the print media. Most of the major ads on television appear to be aimed at a goal other than informing consumers.

There may be several economic goals of this advertising. George Stigler points out that institutional advertising, saying, for example, "our firm is the oldest or largest in the industry," is meant to convey to the consumer the comfort of reliability.[11] The idea is that the firm must treat consumers well or it wouldn't be large or old. **Name brand capital** is the value that consumers place on a product because of experience, reputation, or image. This name brand capital can be very important in terms of maintaining market share in the face of price (or quality) competition from new rivals that don't have it. In the extreme, name brand capital is a barrier to entry that may allow the firm to behave in a monopolistic fashion.

Robert Wills and Willard Mueller have examined the effect of brand advertising on pricing in oligopolistic markets.[12] They were motivated in part by the fact that in some markets consumers show a preference for high-priced brands even though competing brands are physically identical. Brands of lemon juice concentrate, evaporated milk, and household bleach, for example, are exactly the same in every respect except packaging. In addition, blind taste tests of some products, such as beer and cookies, show that consumers often cannot distinguish their preferred brand from competing brands. The research by Wills and Mueller showed that monopoly power in such markets produces price premiums and higher profits. This monopoly power was created by advertising. They conclude that large firms will tend to advertise more heavily, have higher prices, *and* have higher profits than their smaller competitors.

An oligopolistic firm may resort to nonprice competition in an attempt to increase its market share. We can apply the model of oligopoly to these other types of competition. For example, a firm contemplating a new advertising program has to consider whether the program will increase its market share or prompt a rival to undertake a similar program. In the first case, the program may be worthwhile. In the second, it would probably only increase costs without creating a larger market share. Thus, even with respect to advertising, firms in an oligopoly are interdependent and need to consider the reactions of rivals.

FACTORS DETERMINING MARKET COORDINATION BY OLIGOPOLIES

As you have seen, there are benefits to be gained by oligopolists who can coordinate output and pricing, whether such coordination is formal or informal. There are strong forces pulling in opposite directions. It is worthwhile to review some variables that facilitate or limit such market coordination.

THE NUMBER OF FIRMS. The number of firms in an oligopoly has the most obvious impact on the likelihood of formal or informal market coordination. As the number of firms increases, the incentive and ability to coordinate diminish. In addition, as the number of firms increases, the cost of

---

name brand capital
The value that consumers place on a product because of experience, reputation, or image.

---

11. George Stigler, *Memoirs of an Unregulated Economist* (New York: Basic Books, 1988), 81.
12. Robert L. Wills and Willard F. Mueller, "Brand Pricing and Advertising," *Southern Economic Journal* (October 1989): 383–395.

coordinating and policing the agreement increases. It is obvious that as the size of the group increases, the probability that it will include a maverick also increases. As the number of firms increases, the likelihood of effective coordination diminishes rapidly. Some economists have suggested that after the number of firms in a market reaches ten, it is likely that they will ignore each other's actions, making coordination impossible.[13]

BARRIERS TO ENTRY. Barriers to entry play a key role in determining market coordination because they are related to the number of firms. An oligopoly will not be able to practice effective coordination if it can't limit entry. New firms will destroy market coordination and erode any economic profit created by it. The lesson is a simple one. If strong barriers to entry (including barriers created by government) exist, the possibility of coordination exists. If barriers to entry are weak, coordination is highly unlikely.

THE SIZE OF FIRMS. If the oligopolistic industry is dominated by one firm, or if several of the firms are large relative to the others, the possibility of market coordination is enhanced. In such a case, coordination would only require agreement by the dominant firm or firms.

SECRECY. Coordination requires the elimination of secrecy so that uncooperative behavior can be punished. Monitoring chiseling is easier in an environment in which secret deals don't stay secret long. Government has often aided in market coordination by requiring the full disclosure of contract details.

UNSTABLE OR FLUCTUATING DEMAND. If demand fluctuates or is otherwise unstable, a firm in an oligopoly will have difficulty determining if changes in its demand are the result of market forces or, alternatively, the competitive behavior of a rival. As a result, unstable or fluctuating demand will make market coordination more difficult.

PRODUCT DIFFERENTIATION. The more homogeneous a product is, the easier it will be to coordinate the sale of that product. As product differences increase, firms will be unable to determine whether the price concessions of rivals are attempts to chisel or are due to actual differences in product characteristics.

INDUSTRY SOCIAL STRUCTURE. As you have already seen, the maturity of an industry can affect market coordination. The social structure of an industry is also important. Do the leaders know and trust each other? Do they get together at meetings? Do they play golf or engage in other recreational pursuits? If they do, coordination might be easier. Note, however, that socializing does not mean that entrepreneurs are not competitive. What appears to be cooperation may be a subterfuge for future chiseling on a coordinated effort. Remember, if an oligopolist can get all the oth-

---

13. See F. M. Scherer, *Industrial Market Structure and Economic Performance*, 3rd ed. (Boston: Houghton Mifflin, 1990).

ers in the market to agree and then can chisel on the agreement, it can be very profitable.

ANTITRUST ACTIVITY. The U.S. antitrust laws make collusion illegal. If these laws are vigorously enforced, it will make coordination more costly. The antitrust laws will serve to limit attempts at coordination.

MARKET STRUCTURES IN REVIEW

This chapter concludes the discussion of the four theoretical market structures. Table 1 summarizes some of the important characteristics that differentiate these market structures. The key to understanding the theory of the firm is a solid understanding of monopoly and perfect competition. Oligopoly and monopolistic competition expand the models of monopoly and perfect competition and, in effect, generalize from those models to real-world situations.

TABLE 1
SUMMARY OF MARKET STRUCTURES

TYPE	NUMBER OF FIRMS	PRODUCT DIFFERENTIATION	CONTROL OVER PRICE	TYPE OF NONPRICE COMPETITION	EXAMPLES
Perfect competition	Many	Homogeneous product	None	None	Financial markets
Monopolistic competition	Many	Slightly differentiated products	Some	Advertising and product differentiation	Retail trade and service industry
Oligopoly	Few	Homogeneous *or* differentiated products	Some to considerable (it depends)	Advertising and product differentiation	Auto and steel industries
Monopoly	One	Unique product (no close substitutes)	Considerable	Public relations	Some utilities and aluminum industry before 1945

Chapter 11 Monopolistic Competition and Oligopoly

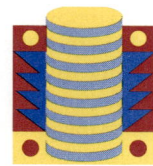

Summary

1. Monopolistic competition is a market structure characterized by many firms selling differentiated products.
2. Key assumptions in the model of monopolistic competition are a large number of producers, product differentiation, and relative ease of entry.
3. Economic profits can exist in the short run in this market structure, but entry of new firms will ensure a long-run equilibrium with zero economic profit.
4. Because of product differentiation, a monopolistically competitive firm at equilibrium produces less than the socially optimal output. The production facilities that are not used are referred to as excess capacity.
5. Monopolistically competitive firms produce a smaller output at a higher price than firms (with the same costs) engaged in perfect competition.
6. In long-run equilibrium in monopolistic competition, marginal cost is not equal to average cost.
7. Oligopoly is the market structure in which there are only a few firms competing imperfectly. Because there are so few firms in an oligopoly, they are interdependent. They take this interdependence into account in their economic decision making.
8. Oligopolies can be divided into three classes: those characterized by formalized market coordination (cartels), those characterized by informal market coordination, and those characterized by no market coordination.
9. Cartels are threatened by chiseling behavior on the part of individual members and by new entry. The larger the number of firms in a cartel, the more difficult it is for the cartel to hold together. Barriers to entry are thus important in oligopoly, just as they are in monopoly.
10. Successful cartels have often been supported by governments, which police chiseling behavior.
11. Price leadership is common in oligopolies where formalized market coordination is not possible. The price leader can be a dominant firm or, in mature industries, a historical leader.
12. Oligopolies are characterized by extensive use of nonprice competition.
13. Economic forces that work to limit coordination in oligopoly or to facilitate it pull in opposite directions.

New Terms

monopolistic competition
differentiated product
product group
excess capacity
nonprice competition

oligopoly
shared monopoly
pure oligopoly
differentiated oligopoly
price clusters
communication

coordination
collusion
cartel
chiseling
tacit collusion
price leadership

dominant firm
competitive fringe
game theory
kinked demand curve
name brand capital

Questions for Discussion

1. Firms in monopolistic competition earn only normal profit in the long run, unless they can successfully convince consumers that their product is different. List four examples of product differentiation. Do you think the differences are real, imagined, or created? Does product differentiation make any economic difference?
2. What are the differences between the model of perfect competition and the model of monopolistic competition? What assumption is different?
3. What is excess capacity? Is it a good or a bad thing?
4. Would you consider the National Collegiate Athletic Association (NCAA) a cartel? How do some universities (firms) chisel on the agreement? Why do they do this?
5. Explain how the expectation of new entry would limit cartel formation.

6. How would you expect the number of firms in a cartel to affect the probability of its success? Why?

7. In what sense is monopolistic competition like monopoly and in what sense is it like competition?

8. What does the kinked demand curve imply about the oligopolists' response to the pricing of rivals? What does the kinked demand curve say about prices in oligopolistic industries? On what grounds has this model been criticized?

9. How would you characterize the market in which the major television networks compete with each other? Are NBC, CBS, and ABC monopolists, oligopolists, or monopolistically competitive firms? How do they compete with one another?

10. Suppose advertising in an oligopolistic market does not increase the total volume of sales but only the distribution of sales among the oligopolistic firms. How does this fit with the Prisoner's Dilemma game?

11. How can changes in technology affect oligopoly? Reconsider your answer to Question 9 in light of this answer.

12. Some experts have predicted that the energy crisis will be back to haunt the United States by 1992 and that OPEC will again be an effective cartel. How would each of the following events affect the probability of OPEC becoming as powerful as it was from 1974 to 1982?

    a. Reforms in the Soviet Union permit the entry of Western oil companies to develop the vast Soviet oil reserves as joint ventures.

    b. Research on the accident at Chernobyl causes most Western governments to shut down all nuclear power plants.

    c. Environmental concerns over acid rain cause the United States to prohibit the burning of soft coal.

    d. The President authorizes an increase in California off-shore drilling.

    e. The international debts of some members of OPEC grow significantly.

13. Twenty years ago, the U.S. steel industry was a coordinated oligopoly. New technology now allows smaller steel producers to compete with the larger firms. What effect do you think this has had on labor unions in the steel industry?

14. How do oligopolies compete?

15. Figure 2 depicts the long-run equilibrium for monopolistic competition.

    a. What is the equilibrium rate of output?
    b. What is the equilibrium price?
    c. What is the average cost?
    d. What is average revenue?
    e. What is the level of profit?
    f. What output level is necessary to reach the least-cost combination?
    g. What is the level of excess capacity?

Suggestions for Further Reading

Breit, William, and Roger L. Ransom. *The Academic Scribblers: Economists in Collision*, 2nd ed. New York: Dryden Press, 1982. Covers the ideas of several of the economists discussed in this chapter.

Friedman, James W. *Oligopoly Theory*. New York: Cambridge University Press, 1984. A thorough study of oligopoly theory using numerical examples.

Scherer, F. M. *Industrial Market Structure and Economic Performance*, 3rd ed. Boston: Houghton Mifflin, 1990. A reference work on industrial organization, market structure, and antitrust that contains a good review of monopolistic competition and oligopoly theory.

AFTER STUDYING THIS CHAPTER, YOU SHOULD BE ABLE TO:

1. Explain what a code number in the Standard Industrial Classification system means.
2. Identify the characteristics of the structure of an industry.
3. Discuss the merger movements of the 1980s and 1990s.
4. Calculate a concentration ratio and a Herfindahl Index for an industry.
5. Interpret a concentration ratio as an indication of monopoly power.
6. Describe the results of studies of the relationship between concentration and prices and between concentration and profits.
7. Diagram the regulation of monopoly power through price regulation and through taxation.
8. Calculate a Lerner Index and discuss its limitations as a tool of antitrust policy.
9. Identify and discuss the major events in the history of antitrust legislation.
10. Discuss the economic consequences of antitrust activity.
11. Discuss the nature of recent antitrust actions and conglomerate mergers.
12. Describe the public policy debate concerning competitiveness.

CHAPTER 12
THEORY IN THE REAL WORLD: REGULATION, DEREGULATION, AND ANTITRUST POLICY

INTRODUCTION

The preceding chapters examined four theoretical market structures. In this chapter, we will apply these models to the real world and examine the extent of monopoly power in U.S. industry. We will look at empirical industry studies to illustrate the real-world monopoly problem. **Industry studies** are investigations of specific industries to determine the degree of competitive behavior. This subfield of economics is sometimes referred to as industrial organization.

If an industry possesses some degree of monopoly power, it may be desirable to control or mitigate the worst effects of that power. Monopoly power could be reduced through antitrust action, monopoly profits could be taxed away, or the monopoly could be regulated and thus forced to behave in some prescribed fashion. In some cases, however, the answer might be to do nothing. This chapter will examine the theory and practice of regulation and the development of antitrust laws in the United States. It concludes with an assessment of the success of regulation and antitrust policy and an examination of recent trends in merger activity in U.S. industry.

industry studies
Investigations of specific industries to determine the degree of competitive behavior.

WHAT IS AN INDUSTRY?

We have, up to this point, been using the term *industry* without carefully defining it. In general, an **industry** is a group of firms producing the same, or at least similar, products. The difficulty with this definition is that it does not specify how dissimilar products must be before they are thought

industry
A group of firms that produce the same or similar products.

of as being produced in different industries. Consider containers. Are firms producing glass bottles and aluminum cans similar enough to be included in the container industry? How about firms making paper cups or even pewter mugs? Most consumers regard pewter mugs and paper cups as quite different. If you are willing to pay substantially more for a pewter mug than for a paper cup, you regard them as being distinct products. What about a plastic Ronald McDonald glass? Is it closer to a paper cup or a pewter mug? These questions demonstrate that whatever scope is assigned to an industry will be arbitrary to some extent. Some people, even some economists, may disagree with a classification of two products as belonging to the same industry or to different industries.

Cross elasticity of demand, a concept we discussed earlier, can be useful in determining whether products belong to the same industry. If the cross elasticity of demand between two products is positive, the goods are substitutes.[1] Goods that are close substitutes have a positive and very high cross elasticity of demand. If economists could agree on a value of this cross elasticity that would define goods as belonging to the same industry—again an arbitrary decision—they could use that number to draw the boundaries between industries.

The problem of assigning firms to industries is made even more difficult by the fact that some multiproduct firms produce a variety of goods that might be included in different industries. In which industry is a firm that produces coffee in addition to soap and cake mixes? General Electric produces goods as unrelated as jet engines and toasters. Informed judgments and somewhat arbitrary definitions are necessary in order to move from the world of theory into the real world of industry studies.

There is a standard set of data available from the U.S. government in which these judgments have already been made. The Commerce Department classifies firms according to the **Standard Industrial Classification (SIC) system**.[2] The SIC system divides the economy into about 400 industries and assigns them different four-digit code numbers. These four-digit industries can be combined into three-digit or two-digit industry groups or further differentiated into five-digit (or even seven-digit) product classes. Table 1 presents an example of how a code becomes more specific as more digits are added. The purpose of the SIC system is to provide a

Standard Industrial Classification (SIC) system
A code devised by the U.S. Census Bureau for classifying industries using about 400 four-digit numbers.

TABLE 1
SAMPLE CODES FROM THE SIC SYSTEM

CODE	EXAMPLE	DESIGNATION	NAME
Two-digit	20	Major Industry Group	Food and kindred products
Three-digit	201	Industry Group	Meat products
Four-digit	2011	Industry	Meat-packing plants
Five-digit	20111	Product Class	Fresh beef

Source: U.S. Bureau of the Budget, *Standard Industrial Classification Manual* (Washington, DC: U.S. Government Printing Office, 1988).

1. E_{xy} = (percent change in quantity demanded of good x)/(percent change in price of good y).
2. See U.S. Bureau of the Census, *Standard Industrial Classification Manual* (Washington, DC: U.S. Government Printing Office, 1988).

workable, consistent classification of U.S. industries. This system is used in studies cited in the remainder of this chapter.

INDUSTRY STRUCTURE

Once an industry has been defined, it is possible to determine its market structure, or where it lies on the spectrum from perfect competition to monopoly. The structure will depend on several characteristics of the industry. The degree of concentration and conditions of entry are especially important characteristics. Entry affects concentration because high barriers to entry result in a more concentrated industry.

CONCENTRATION RATIOS

Concentration refers to the extent to which a certain number of firms dominate sales in a given market. Measures of concentration have, for many years, been a major tool of industry studies. A **concentration ratio** is used by economists to provide a measure of the distribution of economic power among firms in an oligopolistic market. To calculate a concentration ratio, the economist lists all the firms having a particular four-digit SIC code in order of decreasing size. The next step is to calculate the percentage of that industry's total sales accounted for by a certain number of the largest firms.[3] For example, a four-firm concentration ratio measures the percentage of sales accounted for by the four largest firms in an industry. Other commonly used concentration ratios are for the largest firm, the three largest firms, the eight largest firms, and so on. Most industry studies employ four-firm ratios. Table 2 gives four-firm concentration ratios for a few industries.

It could be argued that the percentage of sales accounted for by the largest firms is not the best measure of concentration in an industry. Concentration ratios might instead be calculated using percentage of assets, percentage of employees, or value of shipments. The various measures of concentration are all closely related, however, so the choice of a ratio isn't crucial.

concentration ratio A measure of the distribution of economic power among firms in an oligopolistic market.

TABLE 2
FOUR-FIRM CONCENTRATION RATIOS FOR SELECTED INDUSTRIES

PRODUCT	CONCENTRATION RATIO
Automobiles	94%
Chewing gum	93
Window glass	89
Sewing machines	82
Detergent (household)	80
Tires	71
Canned beer	66

Source: Federal Trade Commission, *Selected Statistical Series* (Washington, DC: U.S. Government Printing Office, 1990).

3. Prelaw students might anticipate a strategy for defense in antitrust cases—have the concentration ratios calculated on the basis of the most general category possible to ensure that any one firm has a small share of the sales in the industry.

The more concentrated an industry, the more likely it is that there will be a recognized interdependence and joint action of either a collusive or noncollusive nature. When the four-firm concentration ratio exceeds 50 percent, the degree of interdependence in the industry is likely to be very high.

BARRIERS TO ENTRY

Entry conditions are the second characteristic affecting market structure. If barriers to entry are high and the industry is highly concentrated, it is more likely that joint action can be undertaken to create monopoly profits. You saw earlier that cartels are very unstable and that economic profits will strongly attract new firms into the industry. If concentration is high and entry is blocked, the existing firms will be in a better position to restrict output, raise price, and maintain persistent profits.

THE HERFINDAHL INDEX

Herfindahl Index
A summed index of concentration that takes into account all the firms in an industry.

The U.S. Justice Department has been using the **Herfindahl Index,** a summed index of concentration, to replace the more traditional concentration ratios.[4] The Herfindahl Index takes into account the market shares of all of the firms in an industry, not just the market share of the few largest firms. Later in this chapter, we will look at how the Herfindahl Index was used by the Justice Department in the 1980s.

The Herfindahl Index is the sum of the squares of market shares in an industry. The formula for this sum is

$$H = (S_1)^2 + (S_2)^2 + \cdots + (S_n)^2,$$

where H is the Herfindahl Index and S_1 through S_n are the market shares of individual firms 1 through n. These market shares total 100 percent. An industry that had ten equal-sized firms each having 10 percent of the market would have a Herfindahl Index of 1000.

Table 3 shows how the Herfindahl Index is calculated for two industries and compares each index to a four-firm concentration ratio. Note

TABLE 3
SAMPLE CALCULATIONS OF THE HERFINDAHL INDEX

	INDUSTRY A			INDUSTRY B	
FIRM	MARKET SHARE (%)	SQUARE MARKET SHARE	FIRM	MARKET SHARE (%)	SQUARE MARKET SHARE
1	90	8100	1	24	576
2	2	4	2	24	576
3	2	4	3	24	576
4	2	4	4	24	576
5	1	1	5	1	1
6	1	1	6	1	1
7	1	1	7	1	1
8	1	1	8	1	1

Four-Firm Concentration Ratio = 96%.   Four-Firm Concentration Ratio = 96%.
Herfindahl Index = 8116.   Herfindahl Index = 2308.

---

4. The Herfindahl Index was developed in 1950 by Orris Clemens Herfindahl in his Ph.D. dissertation at Columbia University.

that both industries have four-firm concentration ratios of 96 percent, but industry *A* has a much higher Herfindahl Index (8116) than industry *B* (2308). These Herfindahl Index values show that industry *A* is 3.5 times more concentrated than is industry *B*. The table demonstrates that the Herfindahl Index has a much higher value for industries that have a firm or group of firms that are relatively large. This higher value is the result of squaring the individual market shares to construct the index.

THE NUMBER EQUIVALENT

M. A. Adelman has developed another way to interpret the Herfindahl Index. The **number equivalent** is the reciprocal of the Herfindahl Index (1 divided by the value of the Herfindahl Index). It shows the theoretical number of equal-sized firms that should be found in an industry. Industry *A* in Table 3 should have 1.2 equal-sized firms, and industry *B* should have 4.3. Adelman would conclude that, *ceteris paribus*, industry *B* would be more competitive than industry *A* because *A* has a higher likelihood of collusion.

number equivalent
A measure of the theoretical number of equal-sized firms that should be found in an industry (the reciprocal of the Herfindahl Index).

CONCENTRATION AND PERFORMANCE

It might seem that the number of concentrated, oligopolistic industries in the U.S. economy is high. But just how concentrated is U.S. industry? And does the concentration make any difference? In other words, would you as a consumer be better off if U.S. industry were generally less concentrated and, thus, perhaps more competitive?

STUDIES OF CONCENTRATION TRENDS

Given the difficulty of defining industries and the fact that any classification scheme requires arbitrary judgments, it is not surprising that studies have reached widely differing conclusions on the degree and trend of concentration in U.S. industry. The studies can be divided roughly into three groups.

One group of studies, which investigated trends in concentration in the first half of the twentieth century, concluded that there had been a pronounced increase in industrial concentration in the United States. This group of studies is associated with and represented by the work of Gardiner Means. Means found that the percentage of total assets controlled by the 200 largest nonfinancial corporations in the United States increased from 33.3 percent to 54.8 percent between 1909 and 1933. In contrast, a second group of studies done more recently by the Federal Trade Commission (FTC) using the same method that Means used showed that the percentage of assets controlled by the 200 largest nonfinancial corporations has not changed since 1950.[5]

---

5. Gardiner Means, National Resources Committee, *The Structure of the American Economy* (Washington, DC: U.S. Government Printing Office, 1939); Norman R. Collins and Lee E. Preston, "The Size Structure of the Largest Industrial Firms," *American Economic Review* (December 1961); Adolf A. Berle and Gardiner C. Means, *The Modern Corporation and Private Property* (New York: Macmillan, 1933); Richard Duke, "Trends in Aggregate Concentration," FTC Working Paper No. 61 (June 1982).

The studies that found increased concentration in the early part of the century were challenged in a third group of studies begun by G. Warren Nutter. Nutter argued that industrial concentration declined in the United States between 1901 and 1937. His studies were attacked on the grounds that they relied heavily on data from 1899, which he took as a starting point. Critics argued that these early numbers were suspect because of the poor quality of data for that period. Later, Nutter's study was updated and extended by Henry A. Einhorn.[6] Einhorn used Nutter's data for 1939 as a benchmark and sought to determine if concentration had changed between 1939 and 1958. Einhorn concluded that between 1939 and 1958, roughly 60 percent of national income was generated by firms producing in a competitive structure. The monopolistic sector declined slightly, and the governmental sector increased slightly. The conclusion of Nutter and Einhorn's research is that market concentration in the twentieth century has been surprisingly stable.

William Shepherd looked at a later period using a method similar to Nutter and Einhorn's.[7] Shepherd divided firms in the economy into pure monopoly, dominant firm, tight oligopoly, and effective competition. He then categorized firms according to these in 1939, 1958, and 1980. Shepherd concluded that there was a slight increase in effectively competitive firms between 1939 and 1958. He found a significant increase in competitiveness between 1958 and 1980. The share of effectively competitive firms increased from 56.3 percent in 1958 to 76.7 percent in 1980. Shepherd attributed this growth in effectively competitive firms to increased competition from imports, deregulation of U.S. industries (airlines, banking, and trucking), and government antitrust activity.

Can we draw any conclusions from these seemingly conflicting studies? At one extreme in the debate is the position that the level of monopoly power has been stable. At the other extreme is the position that concentration in U.S. industry increased dramatically in the early part of this century and then increased at a much slower pace since World War II.

Keep in mind that these measures of concentration are all aggregate measures. That is, they measure concentration at the national level. These measures may understate the degree of monopoly power in U.S. industries because they ignore or understate the power of local and regional monopolies. The food distribution industry is a good example. At the national level, there is a good deal of competition among supermarket chains. However, in some regions, the concentration ratios are much higher. In some smaller markets, there is a virtual monopoly. Thus, the national figures might lead to the conclusion that the industry is competitive, but the regional or local figures might suggest that the industry consists of a series of local monopolies.

THE MERGER WAVE OF THE LATE 1980S

Beginning in 1983, U.S. industry experienced what many observers think is the greatest reshuffling of corporate assets in its history. Between Jan-

---

6. G. Warren Nutter and Henry A. Einhorn, *Enterprise Monopoly in the United States: 1899–1958* (New York: Columbia University Press, 1969).
7. William G. Shepherd, "Causes of Increased Competition in the U.S. Economy 1939–1980," *Review of Economics and Statistics* (November 1982): 601–631.

uary 1983 and January 1987, 12,200 companies worth at least $490 billion changed hands. And this was just the beginning. In 1989, the fifty largest acquisitions, mergers, and recapitalizations set a record of $144 billion in combined value. In the 1980s, $1.3 trillion in assets of U.S. corporations were acquired, merged, or purchased.[8]

For the most part, the public and political leaders thought the merger wave was bad for the economy. In 1987, a Louis Harris poll indicated that "the American people are fed up with takeover raiders. Such types are viewed as little better than predators."[9] Most of the corporate raiders and many economists see the situation differently. They see takeovers as a catalyst that is necessary to shake up complacent managers. Often a company is completely restructured in the wake of a takeover or attempted takeover. Companies have eliminated whole levels of management after they are victims of a takeover or in order to prevent a takeover.

Business journalist Leonard Silk points out that the boards of directors of most public companies are not looking out for the stockholders because inside directors owe their careers to the CEO and the outside directors are usually close friends of the CEO.[10] Indeed, Michael Jensen has argued: "The publicly held corporation, the main engine of economic progress in the United States for a century, has outlived its usefulness."[11] Jensen believes that the merger movement of the 1980s was not a merger movement in the usual sense but, instead, an organizational revolution. He believes it is a positive step, because it will resolve the conflict inherent in a public corporation. This conflict is due to the separation of ownership and control that we discussed in the chapter on monopoly. It is the conflict over the control of corporate resources and the use of those resources.

A study by Randall Morck, Andrei Shleifer, and Robert Vishny showed that corporate boards of directors have not been the main force behind removing unresponsive managers in industries that have been performing poorly.[12] Instead, these corporate managers have been removed through hostile takeovers. This academic study confirms the anecdotal stories offered by corporate raiders.

The Merger Wave of the Early 1990s?

As the decade of the 1980s ended, the activity in leveraged buyouts (LBOs) came to an end. The end was due to problems in the junk bond market, which meant that the raiders couldn't find financing for their deals. A second difficulty was the recession that began in 1990. Stephen Schwarzman, President of the Blackstone Group, commented: "When we look back on 1989, it will be the year the LBO party ended."[13] The wave

---

8. A detailed report of the fifty largest mergers and acquisitions in 1989 is found in *Fortune* (29 January 1990): 136–145. *Fortune* publishes an annual report (in January) of the preceding year's fifty largest mergers or acquisitions. *Business Week* reports on the two largest deals in each year of the decade, (15 January 1990): 52–57. It also profiles the ten best and the ten worst deals of the 1980s.
9. *Fortune* (27 April 1987): 10.
10. Leonard Silk, "On Outside Directors," *Business Month* (November 1989): 11–13.
11. Michael C. Jensen, *Harvard Business Review* (September/October 1989); 43.
12. Randall Morck, Andrei Shleifer, and Robert W. Vishny, "Alternative Mechanisms for Corporate Control," *American Economic Review* (September 1989): 842–852.
13. Christopher Knowlton, "Deals of the Year," *Fortune* (29 January 1990): 136.

of LBOs required the confluence of a strong economy, lower interest rates, and a lower stock market.

The LBO mania of the 1980s is expected to be replaced in the 1990s by friendly mergers of big firms in related industries. The criteria for these friendly mergers are reported to be bigness and synergy. There are signs that U.S. companies are becoming more interested in foreign acquisitions. Many of these friendly mergers have been transatlantic deals between U.S. firms and European firms in the same industry. Some of these mergers may be motivated by the fears of U.S. firms about being excluded from the European market after the European Community becomes fully integrated in 1992.

THE MARKET CONCENTRATION DOCTRINE

Since the merger movement of the 1980s probably increased concentration in U.S. industry to some degree, we should examine the assumption that concentration, *per se*, is undesirable. Industrial organization economists typically see a sequence relating (1) the structure of the industry to (2) the behavior of firms in that industry (conduct) and then to (3) the performance of the industry itself. According to this line of thought, a highly concentrated structure will produce the antisocial behavior and unsatisfactory performance of a monopoly. The industrial organization economist, therefore, examines the structure of an industry to predict price and output behavior. This structure-conduct-performance chain has been termed the market concentration doctrine.

market concentration doctrine
The hypothesis that the degree of concentration in an industry is a reliable index of monopoly power and that a high concentration ratio is likely to be associated with undesirable monopoly behavior.

The **market concentration doctrine** holds that the degree of concentration in an industry is a reliable index of monopoly power and that a high concentration ratio is likely to be associated with undesirable monopoly behavior. Strict application of this doctrine might lead policy makers to suggest antitrust action or some other form of control when concentration ratios reach a certain level. Before examining policy action against monopoly, let's first look at the observations underlying this doctrine.

Those who support the market concentration doctrine base their arguments primarily on two empirical observations. The first is that prices are more rigid (less flexible) in concentrated industries. The second is that profit rates and concentration are positively correlated. Supporters of this doctrine believe that both rigid prices and higher profit rates reflect the effects of the monopoly power that is associated with high degrees of concentration.

administered prices
Prices that are relatively rigid, or changed only infrequently.

ADMINISTERED PRICES. The lack of price flexibility in concentrated industries was first noted by Gardiner Means, whose findings were published in a famous monograph.[14] Looking at data from 1926 to 1933, he argued that price movements in different industries varied in frequency. In some industries, prices changed very often. In others, prices tended to be constant for relatively long periods of time. He labeled prices that were relatively rigid, or changed only infrequently, **administered prices**. Later he

---

14. Gardiner Means, *Industrial Prices and Their Relative Inflexibility*, Senate Document 13, 74th Congress, 1st Session (17 January 1935).

International Perspective

Will Europe Become Monopolized?

In 1992, the European market becomes unified. Most observers believe that this unification will produce an economic boom for the countries in the European Community (EC). There seems to be a move on the part of U.S. firms to merge with European firms to "protect" their ability to participate in this boom. U.S. firms want to merge with European firms in case the EC becomes more protectionist toward the United States and Japan.

According to business writer Joel Kotkin, however, not all business firms in the EC have been looking forward to 1992. Some firms are worried about the increased regulation and bureaucratization the unification is likely to bring. Regulation will shift from the individual national governments to the powerful 12,000-member EC bureaucracy in Brussels. These regulators are often referred to by their critics as "Eurocrats."

Small businesses are especially concerned about their future in a unified Europe. The Eurocrats appear to be insensitive to the concerns of small and medium-sized companies. Alexander Flach is a case in point. Mr. Flach does not fear competition. His German firm, Afri-Cola Bluch Corp., produces cola and has competed with Coca-Cola and PepsiCo in Europe for generations. Looking to 1992, Mr. Flach says, "I have no fears of open markets." What he is afraid of is the political power of the Eurocrats. He has already had problems from Brussels. Recent regulations of the Eurocrats established strict standards for listing the contents of soft-drink bottles. This regulation weighed more heavily on the small regional bottlers. Yet, when Mr. Flach tried to lobby in Brussels, he couldn't even get an appointment.

Kotkin argues that what is the most disturbing to entrepreneurs in Europe is the mindset of the Eurocrat, a conviction that what Europe needs is larger, more centralized firms. This attitude worries European entrepreneurs, who believe that, in order to be competitive in a world market, they need to foster a competitive entrepreneurial economy. These entrepreneurs worry that if bigness prevails, it might promote a political move for protectionism within Europe. "Fortress Europe" would be the result, and the experiment with unification would lead to economic stagnation rather than economic growth.

Perhaps the concern is best summed up by Manfred Kotter, who owns a speciality metals shop in Mainz, Germany: "They say we are building a great market and economy. But so far it looks like we're doing it on the maps, not in our minds. We seem to be forgetting the role of competition in making this happen. A common market cannot be competitive if industries are dominated by two or three companies and by the bureaucrats. I wonder if we are capable of learning from the history of the past forty years."

Source: Adapted from Joel Kotkin, "Will Europe Blow It?" *INC.* (December 1989): 41–42.

demonstrated that administered prices were related to the degree of concentration in the industry.[15]

This early work by Means had a significant influence on discussions of public policy toward industry. As is usually the case, the data and methods used by both sides in the debate have been criticized. Competing researchers criticized Means's study because his data were gathered from reports submitted by firms to the Bureau of Labor Statistics. Since firms reported at different intervals, his reported price flexibility (or inflexibility) might simply have reflected a different frequency of reporting.[16] Other researchers claimed that the Bureau's data were composed of prices *asked* by firms and that the relevant data are prices *paid* by consumers.[17] In order to hide their price cuts from their competitors, firms in oligopolies often grant buyers secret cuts on posted prices. For this reason, there could be significant discrepancies between prices asked and prices paid.

Even though this issue of administered prices has been scrutinized by economists for some time, there hasn't been a scientific conclusion. The conventional wisdom that has become part of public policy debates is that there is a loose association between concentration and price inflexibility. The economist, however, in the capacity of scientist, would be hard put to prove this relationship.

CONCENTRATION AND PROFIT LEVELS. The second observation underlying the market concentration doctrine is that profits and concentration ratios are positively correlated. The theoretical explanation for this relationship is that a small number of firms finds it easier to behave collusively. The empirical link between concentration and profits began with the work of Joe Bain.[18] Bain found that profit rates and concentration ratios were positively correlated for a sample of forty-two manufacturing industries. Bain also found that when the concentration ratio exceeded 70 percent, there was a significant increase in average profit rates. George Stigler, on the other hand, conducted similar research and found there was no clear-cut relationship between concentration ratios and profit rates.[19] In his study, Stigler defined an industry as concentrated if the four-firm concentration ratio for the value of output exceeded 60 percent. Other studies examining this link concluded that there is a weak, but positive, relationship between concentration and profit rates.[20]

There has been debate about the tendency for profits to be higher in

---

15. National Resources Committee, *The Structure of the American Economy* (Washington, DC: U.S. Government Printing Office, 1939).
16. U.S. Congress, Joint Economic Committee, *Government Price Statistics*. Hearings before the Subcommittee on Economic Statistics of the Joint Economic Committee, 87th Congress, 1st Session (1961).
17. George J. Stigler and James K. Kindahl, *The Behavior of Industrial Prices* (New York: National Bureau of Economic Research, 1970).
18. Joe S. Bain, "Relation of Profit-Rate to Industry Concentration: American Manufacturing, 1936–1940," *Quarterly Journal of Economics* (August 1951).
19. George J. Stigler, *Capital and Rates of Return in Manufacturing* (Princeton, NJ: Princeton University Press, 1963).
20. For a review of these studies, see Harold Demsetz, *The Market Concentration Doctrine* (Washington, DC: American Enterprise Institute for Public Policy Research, 1975).

concentrated industries over the years. In 1967, President Johnson's Task Force on Antitrust Policy concluded that such a correlation exists:

The adverse effects of concentration on output and price find some confirmation in various studies that have been made of return on capital in major industries. These studies have found a close association between high levels of concentration and persistently high rates of return on capital. It is the persistence of high profits over extended time periods and over whole industries rather than in individual firms that suggests artificial restraints on output and the absence of fully effective competition. The correlation of evidence of this kind with very high levels of concentration appears to be significant.[21]

Bain's conclusion has also been challenged by Yale Brozen.[22] Brozen calculated more recent profit rates for the same industries considered in earlier studies. He found that, with the passage of time, there was a tendency for rates of profit in concentrated industries to converge with those of less concentrated industries. Rates of profit increased in the industries that previously had below-average profit levels and decreased in the industries with above-average profit levels.

DOES CONCENTRATION PREDICT PERFORMANCE? Thus, the relationship between concentration and profit levels, like the relationship betwen concentration and price rigidity, has been challenged. There appears to be some evidence to dispute the conventional wisdom that concentration ratios are a good predictor of monopoly performance, especially over time.

Why is this issue important? It is important because present policy proposals to reformulate antitrust law use market concentration as a guide. If concentration is made illegal because it is taken as an indicator of monopoly behavior and performance, many industries may be restructured by the courts simply because they are concentrated. If, instead, these industries are concentrated because there are economies of scale or because they have better, more aggressive managers or more innovation, why break them up? In such cases, antitrust activity would only serve to introduce inefficiencies into the market. In addition, many economists view the increase in concentration in the 1980s as a restructuring of corporate form rather than an increase in monopoly power.

In short, the challenges to the market concentration doctrine are significant enough to deserve closer examination. It is important that economists reach a scientific consensus on this important issue before policy makers take public action to restructure U.S. industry on the basis of a model that has not been empirically validated.

POLICIES AIMED AT REDUCING MONOPOLY POWER

In the remainder of this chapter, we will discuss policy aimed at correcting the problems associated with monopoly power. Even though there is

---

21. White House Task Force on Antitrust Policy, *Role of the Giant Corporation* (Washington, DC: U.S. Government Printing Office, 1967), 883.
22. Yale Brozen, "The Antitrust Task Force Deconcentration Recommendation," *Journal of Law and Economics* (October 1970): 279–292.

disagreement over the connection between concentration and monopoly behavior, for most policy decisions, a high level of concentration is taken as implying monopoly behavior.

THE CASE FOR MONOPOLY

In the chapter on monopoly, we examined in detail the costs associated with monopoly. The arguments in favor of policy against monopoly are based on a perceived need to reduce those costs. You should review the chapter on monopoly if you are unclear as to what those costs are. At least two arguments have been made in support of monopoly power. These arguments concern countervailing power and the promotion of technological progress.

COUNTERVAILING POWER. John Kenneth Galbraith has developed the notion of **countervailing power**. He argues that monopoly produces power on both sides of the market, and these two kinds of power countervail, or offset, each other. According to Galbraith, the U.S. economy is made up of big unions, big government, and big firms. In bargaining with each other, these big units are equally powerful. Although Galbraith did not develop the concept of countervailing power as a defense of monopoly, other economists have used it for that purpose.

countervailing power
The offsetting power possessed by both sides of the market in a monopoly.

This argument seems to make some sense. Concentrated tire manufacturers deal with concentrated automobile producers. Large retail chains purchase from concentrated industries that manufacture the products they sell, and labor unions are most successful in concentrated industries, such as steel, autos, and mining. Consumers are, however, left out of this process, as Galbraith points out. The costs associated with monopoly still hold for them. In essence, countervailing power redistributes the monopoly profit only among monopoly sellers, monopoly buyers, and monopoly unions.

INNOVATION. Some economists, most notably Austrian-born economist Joseph Schumpeter and John Kenneth Galbraith, have argued that monopoly, or at least oligopoly, is more conducive to technological innovation than competition is. They argue that the costs of monopoly power are offset by the dynamic innovation that monopolistic firms introduce into the economy. Schumpeter called his conclusion that monopoly power leads to innovation "shocking," since traditional analysis showed that monopoly would not be innovative because it did not face the pressure of competition.[23]

Years later Galbraith sounded the same theme, that monopoly power and bigness promote innovation:

In the modern industry shared by a few large firms, size and the rewards accruing to market power combine to insure that resources for research and technical development will be available. The power that enables the firm to have some influence on prices insures that the resulting gains will not be passed on to the public by imitators (who have stood none of the costs of development) before the outlay for de-

---

23. Joseph Schumpeter, *Capitalism, Socialism, and Democracy*, 2nd ed. (New York: Harper and Row, 1942), 81–82.

velopment can be recouped. In this way, market power protects the incentive to technical development.[24]

The argument that bigness allows a financial commitment to research and development seems logical. For years, General Electric advertised that progress was its most important product. But what are the facts? The facts, or more correctly the case histories, of invention and innovation are not so convincing. Researchers have found that the majority (as high as two-thirds) of important inventions are the products of individuals working independently and had no support from large research labs funded by giant corporations.[25]

MONOPOLY REGULATION

You have seen that monopoly power is present in the U.S. economy. For an optimal allocation of resources, monopoly is a bad thing. Society may decide that it is best to regulate rather than restructure a monopoly. Two common ways to do this are through price regulation and taxation.

MARGINAL COST PRICING

Consider the monopoly represented in Figure 1. The monopoly is maximizing its profits by producing output level Q_1 at price P_1. Assume that the government wants to force the firm to produce the amount that would

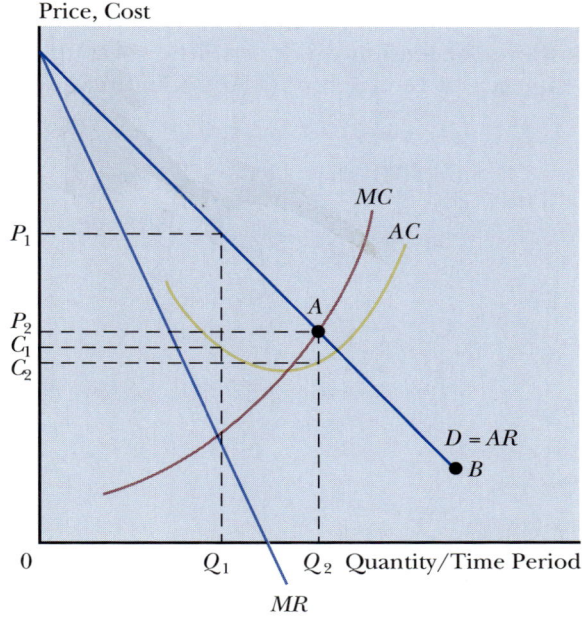

FIGURE 1
MARGINAL COST PRICING
If the regulator imposes a price of P_2, the monopoly would produce output level Q_2. Per-unit profits would decrease from $P_1 - C_1$ to $P_2 - C_2$.

---

24. John Kenneth Galbraith, *American Capitalism*, 2nd ed. (Boston: Houghton Mifflin, 1956), 86–87.
25. John Jewkes, David Sawers, and Richard Stillerman, *The Sources of Invention* (New York: St. Martin's Press, 1959).

be produced if this were a purely competitive market, that is, to produce where the marginal cost curve intersects the demand curve. If the government set a price ceiling of P_2, the monopoly would react by producing Q_2 units of output because the demand curve the monopoly would face would be represented by line P_2AD. The firm, as always, produces where $MR = MC$, and MR would be equal to line P_2A because demand is perfectly elastic for that line segment. The setting of such a price ceiling is sometimes called marginal cost pricing. **Marginal cost pricing** is a policy tool for forcing a monopoly to behave more like a competitive firm by regulating the monopoly price so that it is equal to marginal cost. Note that regulating monopoly in this way reduces per-unit profits from $P_1 - C_1$ to $P_2 - C_2$. Why not lower the price below P_2, since every decrease in price from P_1 to P_2 increases output even more? The problem is that for output levels greater than Q_2, every unit produced costs society more than it is willing to pay ($MC > P$). This larger output is just as inefficient as monopoly behavior when $MC < P$, because the cost of an extra unit is less than society is willing to pay.

Now let's look at a more realistic example, a natural monopoly. Remember, a natural monopoly is one that results from a constantly declining average cost curve. In Figure 2, the profit-maximizing monopolist produces output level Q_1 at price P_1 and receives profit of $P_1 - C_1$ per unit. Now suppose a regulated price of P_2 is imposed on the monopolist. At P_2, it appears that the monopolist would increase output to Q_2. But note that at price P_2 and output level Q_2, the monopolist would lose $P_2 - C_2$ per unit sold. Price would be below average cost, so the monopolist would leave the industry. In other words, the optimal output from society's viewpoint would be where $MR = MC$, but this output would force losses on the monopolist.

The output Q_2 could, however, be feasibly produced if the government would make up the loss, the area of rectangle P_2C_2AB in Figure 2. The

marginal cost pricing
A policy tool for forcing a monopoly to behave more like a competitive firm by regulating the monopoly price so that it is equal to marginal cost.

FIGURE 2
MARGINAL COST PRICING AND LOSSES
If the regulator sets a price of P_2, the monopolist would lose $P_2 - C_2$ per unit of output sold. The monopolist would thus only produce if the regulator subsidizes it.

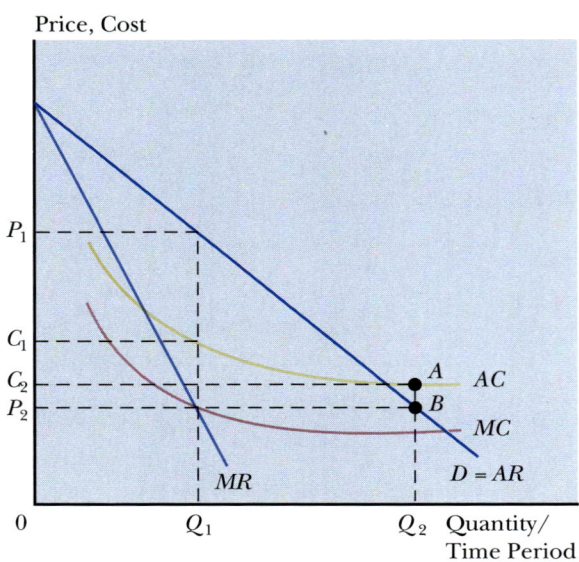

Chapter 12 Regulation, Deregulation, and Antitrust Policy

monopolist would then produce output level Q_2 at price P_2. The problem with this solution is that if the government subsidizes an industry out of general tax revenues, it is transferring income from taxpayers in general to the consumers of the good produced by the monopoly. Most people (except consumers of the good) would view such a transfer as an unfair redistribution of income. The trick, then, for the would-be price regulator is to set price equal to marginal cost at the point where the *MC* curve intersects the demand curve, but only if price is equal to or greater than average cost for that level of output. This might not be possible in the case of a natural monopoly.

TAXATION OF MONOPOLISTS

Another approach is to use a tax to regulate monopoly power. Suppose government officials impose a license fee (tax) on the monopolist. In Figure 3, before the tax, the monopolist is producing output level Q_1 at price P_1. The average cost curve is AC_1. The monopolist is earning profits of $P_1 - C_1$ per unit. If the monopolist is charged a fee for the right to do business, the fee represents an increase in its fixed cost, but no change in variable or marginal cost. The *AC* curve shifts up by the amount of the fee, to AC_2 in Figure 3. The monopolist still maximizes profits by producing output level Q_1 at price P_1, but profits have been reduced to $P_1 - C_2$ per unit. Note that it is possible to set the fee so as to capture all the monopoly profit and shift average cost to AC_3 in Figure 3. However, no increase in output would occur.

There are practical difficulties with both methods of regulating monopoly, and they have quite different effects. Price regulation can cause the monopolist to produce the competitive output at a lower price.

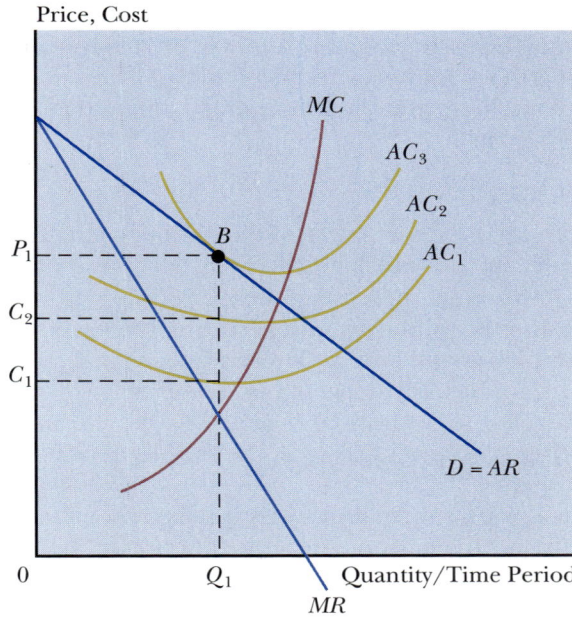

FIGURE 3
TAXING A MONOPOLIST
A license fee will be viewed by a monopolist as a fixed cost and will increase average cost but not marginal cost. The monopoly profit can be taxed away with no effect on output.

Taxation, on the other hand, leaves price and output unchanged. A tax simply captures the monopoly profit for the public coffers. It should be clear, then, that for optimal allocation of resources, price regulation is preferred because it increases output and lowers price. Taxation only corrects for the effect of monopoly on the distribution of income. The monopoly profit goes to the government instead of the monopolist and is spent on governmental projects. In this case, there is still an impact on the distribution of income because consumers will be paying "too much" for the product.

THE LERNER INDEX OF MONOPOLY POWER

The theory of regulation just discussed suggested a policy of marginal cost pricing as one way to correct for the misallocation of resources by a monopoly. That suggestion is based on the theoretical notion presented in the last two chapters that the degree of monopoly power is measured by the gap between marginal cost and price. Using this concept, Abba P. Lerner developed an index to measure monopoly power. The **Lerner Index of Monopoly Power (LMP)** evaluates the gap between price and marginal cost as a measure of monopoly power. The index is calculated as follows:

$$\text{LMP} = \frac{\text{price} - \text{marginal cost}}{\text{price}}.$$

Lerner Index of Monopoly Power (LMP) An index that evaluates the gap between price and marginal cost as a measure of monopoly power.

In a purely competitive industry, LMP would be zero because price would equal marginal cost. If monopoly power is present, LMP takes on positive values because price will exceed marginal cost. As the gap between price and marginal cost increases, the value of the index rises. Using LMP values permits a researcher to compare the monopoly power of firms.

The LMP is a valuable theoretical tool, but the difficulty of determining marginal cost limits its value in empirical work. If average cost data are used to approximate marginal cost data, the results will be misleading. Purely competitive firms might even appear to have monopoly power in the short run because price could be greater than average cost and at the same time equal to marginal cost.

REGULATION IN PRACTICE

Attempts at regulation often increase the power of oligopolies as the regulatory bodies are "captured" by the industry. The firms use the regulation to create barriers to entry, thus increasing their monopoly power. Even if regulators are pursuing the public interest in setting prices to regulate monopoly power, they may not be able to determine marginal costs. They must, in that case, turn to the alternative of regulating price on the basis of average cost information. Although it may not be the most efficient solution, such average cost pricing solves "the problem" of natural monopoly illustrated in Figure 2.

cost-plus pricing The form of price regulation that allows firms a markup that is a percentage of average costs of production.

The usual practice is to allow the firm a markup that is a percentage of average costs of production. This most common form of price regulation is referred to as **cost-plus pricing**. This type of regulation creates some distortions. If the monopolist is allowed to charge a price, say, 10 percent above its average cost, it has less incentive to minimize costs. However, consumer demand gives the firm some incentive not to let price get too high.

Perhaps the best example of this form of regulation is in the present regulatory environment for utilities—electricity, gas, water, and so forth. Since utilities are considered natural monopolies, they are regulated for the public interest. Such regulation is based on cost-plus pricing. The markup is often called a fair rate of return. A **fair rate of return** is the normal profit that a regulated industry must earn in order to stay in business. Under such a regulatory policy, utilities have less incentive to cut costs than profit-oriented firms do. For those firms, profits increase whenever costs decrease.

Some communities have debated whether utilities should be allowed to advertise their products. The argument against such advertising is that it simply raises average costs and results in higher prices to consumers. The argument in favor of such advertising is that it usually increases demand, which leads to more output at lower average cost and thus lower prices. The analysis here tends to support the first argument. Interestingly, the assumption of self-interested behavior would predict that a certain group in the community would support utility advertising. Any guesses? Of course, it would be the news media. The news media have strongly supported utility advertising, often on the grounds of free speech.

Regulation not only makes a firm less cost-conscious, but can also raise the actual cost of doing business. The costs of compliance (and noncompliance) with regulation could mean that less is produced at higher prices because costs are higher. In this case, regulation does not promote the goal of making monopolies produce a larger output. Regulation is also rarely limited to price regulation. Most often, regulatory bodies interfere in a wide range of the firm's decisions. Regulation often changes the firm into a quasi-governmental firm, rather than a firm that is responsive to market forces.

fair rate of return
The normal profit that a regulated industry must earn in order to stay in business.

ANTITRUST LAWS IN THE UNITED STATES

Toward the end of the nineteenth century, there was a substantial increase in the number of large business organizations in the United States. This period saw the establishment of legal arrangements such as **trusts**, which were organizations set up to control the stock of other companies through boards of trustees, and **holding companies**, which were firms set up for the sole purpose of owning and thus controlling other firms. Trusts and holding companies enabled robber barons, as they have been called by economic historians, to control and coordinate the activities of many previously independent firms. At first, these new types of companies were viewed as a natural outgrowth of the Industrial Revolution in the United States.

Eventually the public began to view some of these arrangements with suspicion. One of the earliest groups organized to oppose the trust movement was the National Grange. The Grange was a farm-based group or-

trusts
Organizations set up to control the stock of other companies through boards of trustees.

holding companies
Firms set up for the sole purpose of owning and thus controlling other firms.

ganized in 1867 to oppose trusts. The efforts were mainly directed at the railroad trust, because of the high monopoly prices it set and also because it was able to practice price discrimination in the hauling of agricultural products.

In response to the Grange and other political movements against trusts, several states enacted antitrust statutes that regulated businesses chartered in those states. These state laws failed because corporations were able to obtain charters in less restrictive states. Two of the more lenient states were New Jersey and Delaware. By 1888, the antitrust sentiment had become so widespread and intense that both national political parties had an antitrust plank in their platforms.

In 1890, Congress passed the **Sherman Antitrust Act**, the first federal antitrust law. This act had two major provisions. Section 1 declared every contract, combination, or conspiracy in restraint of trade to be illegal. Section 2 made it illegal to monopolize or attempt to monopolize.[26] The language of the act is strong, but it is also vague, and the courts took years to determine its scope. We will trace some of the important decisions, after identifying the other major antitrust laws.

The **Clayton Act**, passed in 1914, made illegal certain business practices that could lead to monopoly. It prohibited a company from acquiring the stock of a competing company if such an acquisition would "substantially lessen competition." The act also prohibited tying contracts and price discrimination. **Tying contracts** are agreements between producers and retailers that call for the retailer to stock certain items in return for being allowed to stock other items. In 1936, the **Robinson-Patman Act** amended the Clayton Act to make predatory pricing illegal. **Predatory pricing** is selling below cost to destroy competitors. Although the Clayton Act prohibited the acquisition of competing firms through stock purchase, firms could get around this obstacle because the law did not prohibit acquisition of physical assets. The **Celler-Kefauver Antimerger Act**, passed in 1950, made it illegal in certain circumstances for a firm to merge with another by purchasing its assets. This act strengthened the Clayton Act.

In 1914, Congress passed the **Federal Trade Commission Act**. This act set up the Federal Trade Commission (FTC) to police unfair and deceptive business practices. Initially, the FTC had many powers, but in 1919 the Supreme Court denied it the power to issue cease and desist orders without judicial review. In 1938, the FTC Act was amended by the **Wheeler-Lea Act**, which added "unfair or deceptive acts or practices in commerce" to the list of transgressions. The **Hart-Scott-Rodino Antitrust Improvement Act** further amended the FTC Act in 1970. It required firms contemplating a merger or acquisition to notify the FTC and the Department of Justice before carrying it out.[27]

Sherman Antitrust Act
The first federal antitrust law in the United States, passed in 1890. Section 1 of the act declared every contract, combination, or conspiracy in restraint of trade to be illegal. Section 2 made it illegal to monopolize or attempt to monopolize.

Clayton Act
Federal law, passed in 1914, prohibiting the acquisition of the stock of a competing company if such an acquisition would "substantially lessen competition."

tying contracts
Agreements between producers and retailers that call for the retailer to stock certain items in return for being allowed to stock other items.

Robinson-Patman Act
A federal law that amended the Clayton Act in 1936, making predatory pricing illegal.

predatory pricing
The act of selling below cost to destroy competitors.

Celler-Kefauver Antimerger Act
A federal law that strengthened the Clayton Act in 1950 by making it illegal in certain circumstances for a firm to merge with another by purchasing its assets.

---

26. "Section 1: Every contract, combination in the form of trust or otherwise, or conspiracy, in restraint of trade or commerce among the several States, or with foreign nations, is declared to be illegal. . . . Section 2: Every person who shall monopolize, or attempt to monopolize, or combine or conspire with any other person or persons, to monopolize any part of the trade or commerce among the several States, or with foreign nations, shall be deemed guilty of a misdemeanor." (Sherman Antitrust Act, Sec. 1, 26 Stat. 209, 1890).

27. For more detail on all these laws, see J. G. Van Cise, *Understanding the Antitrust Laws* (New York: Practicing Law Institute, 1973).

Antitrust activity like that in the United States is not found in most other countries. Interestingly, after World War II, the U.S. government imposed antitrust policies on the defeated powers, Japan and Germany. Occupation forces set up new governments in Germany and Japan and imposed stringent antitrust measures aimed at deconcentrating industry. There were two stated goals. The first was to punish leading industrial groups for their wartime efforts, and the second was to weaken the German and Japanese industrial base so that those countries would be less able to pursue future wars.

This second objective was inconsistent with domestic antitrust policy in the United States at the time. Domestic policy was to pursue antitrust actions to limit monopoly power and make the U.S. economy *more* efficient. At the same time, foreign policy was to break up German and Japanese trusts to make them *less* efficient. After the United States decided that Japan and Germany should be allowed to grow economically, to counter Soviet expansion in the Cold War period, the first policy changed was the antitrust policy. One might legitimately ask what caused policy makers to view concentration as good for Germany and Japan and bad for the United States.

INTERNATIONAL PERSPECTIVE

ANTITRUST ABROAD

Except for the vigorous antitrust policy imposed temporarily on Germany and Japan, there have been no antitrust laws in other countries that are concentration-based and result in divestiture. In the mid-1970s, there was vigorous debate about proposed legislation for divestiture in Japan, but it was not enacted. Japan's trading conglomerates, called *sogo shosha*, are informal associations of industrial, financial, and commercial companies. They could not exist under U.S. antitrust laws.

Much of the relevant law in Europe is based on the Treaty of Rome, which established the European Economic Community. Individual countries tend to monitor the activities of "market-dominating" firms and regulate their price-setting ability. The emphasis is not on breaking up monopolies or potential monopolies but rather on preventing the abuse of any market power. A typical remedy is a price rollback and a requirement of government approval of future price increases. European governments often monitor the prices, costs, and profit rates of large firms.

Federal Trade Commission Act
A federal law passed in 1914 that set up the Federal Trade Commission (FTC) to police unfair and deceptive business practices.

Wheeler-Lea Act
A 1938 federal law amending the FTC Act to make unfair or deceptive acts or practices in commerce illegal.

Hart-Scott-Rodino Antitrust Improvement Act
A 1970 federal law amending the FTC Act to require firms to report mergers or acquisitions to the FTC and Department of Justice before the fact.

UNITED STATES ANTITRUST LAWS

Act and Year Passed	Major Provision(s)
Sherman Antitrust Act (1890)	Makes it illegal to monopolize or attempt to monopolize. Makes contracts, combinations, or conspiracies in restraint of trade illegal.
Clayton Act (1914)	Prohibits the acquisition of the stock of another company if that action will substantially lessen competition. Prohibits tying contracts and price discrimination.
Robinson-Patman Act (1936)	Amendment to the Clayton Act that makes predatory pricing illegal.
Celler-Kefauver Antimerger Act (1950)	Amendment to the Clayton Act that makes it illegal to purchase the assets of another company if that action will substantially lessen competition.
Federal Trade Commission Act (1914)	Established the FTC to police unfair and deceptive business practices.
Wheeler-Lea Act (1938)	Amendment to the FTC Act that makes unfair or deceptive trade practices illegal.
Hart-Scott-Rodino Antitrust Improvement Act (1970)	Requires that the FTC and Justice Department be notified prior to mergers or acquisitions.

THE HISTORY OF ANTITRUST ENFORCEMENT

It took some time for the courts to determine the scope of the Sherman Act, in particular, to form a legal definition of the phrase "in restraint of trade." Under a strict economic definition, a firm with any monopoly power (that is, power to restrict output or to increase price) would be guilty of restraint of trade. In two famous cases against Standard Oil and American Tobacco in 1911, the Supreme Court interpreted the law using the rule of reason, which said that monopolies that behaved well were not illegal. In effect, the Court defined—some might say rewrote—the Sherman Antitrust Act to make only "unreasonable" restraints of trade illegal. The test of reasonableness was itself difficult to define. The Court held that the existence of competitors was sufficient to demonstrate reasonable behavior. In 1920, U.S. Steel, despite its dominance of the steel industry, was found not to be an unreasonable monopoly. The Court stated that the law did not make mere size an offense.

In 1945, after thirteen years of litigation, the rule of reason was dropped. Judge Learned Hand ruled in a case against Alcoa that size itself *was* enough to prove the exercise of monopoly power. The change was so fundamental that the ruling became known as the "new Sherman Act." The Alcoa case was based on estimates of market power and structural aspects of the industry. In such cases, the way in which an industry is defined is extremely important. In fact, to a large degree it determines defense and prosecution strategies. As you might guess, the defense would prefer the industry to be broadly defined, both geographically and by the number of products included, since that definition tends to reduce the importance of any one firm in any particular industry.[28]

The DuPont Cellophane case in 1956 gave further indication of what the courts thought about markets. The Justice Department filed suit against DuPont for monopolizing the cellophane market because the company controlled 75 percent of U.S. sales. DuPont's lawyers successfully argued that the relevant market was not that for cellophane only, but rather that for flexible wrapping materials. These included waxed paper, aluminum foil, and vegetable parchment. The court said that products that are "reasonably interchangeable" must be included in the definition of a market. DuPont controlled only 20 percent of the market for a "reasonably interchangeable" set of wrapping products.

In 1982, the Justice Department's case against IBM, initiated in 1969, was dismissed. The case began when the Justice Department accused IBM of monopolizing the "general-purpose computer and peripheral-equipment industry." In 1969, IBM controlled 70 percent of the large mainframe computer market and 40 percent of the office equipment market. When the case was dismissed, IBM still controlled 70 percent of the mainframe computer market but was experiencing strong competition in office equipment and microcomputers. This case, like the others, centered on market share and the definition of the industry or market. The trend seems to be toward defining markets in a much broader way.

Another significant change in antitrust activity took place much more recently. The Sherman Antitrust Act provides that private parties who are victims of monopoly under Sections 1 and 2 are entitled to sue for treble damages. In other words, if a firm is convicted under the Sherman Antitrust Act, individuals can recover three times the damages they have sustained. Historically, it was seldom invoked. Recently, however, consumer groups have brought many class action lawsuits under the provisions of the antitrust laws. Consumer groups bring action on behalf of the entire class of consumers, and treble damages in these cases can be very large.

Although the courts have made some significant changes in enforcement, they can only rule on cases brought before them. In general, very few antitrust cases have been brought by damaged firms or individuals. This raises an important question: Who initiates most antitrust cases? The decision on whether to bring charges or not rests largely with the Antitrust Division of the Department of Justice. This decision is made by a presidential appointee, the assistant attorney general for antitrust. Antitrust policy therefore reflects the wishes of the President. Theodore Roosevelt campaigned as the great "trust-buster." When he became President, he set up the Antitrust Division, and his administration brought the first cases.

Franklin Roosevelt's first term saw virtually no activity on the antitrust scene. On the contrary, in the early years of the Depression, the federal

---

28. For some examples of the ridiculous lengths to which defense lawyers will go in defining the relevant market, see Franklin M. Fisher, "Diagnosing Monopoly," *Quarterly Review of Economics and Business* (Summer 1979): 7–33.

National Recovery Administration (NRA)
A major New Deal program that was aimed at business recovery but was anticompetitive since it allowed and encouraged agreements between firms. It was eventually declared unconstitutional.

government actually fostered anticompetitive practices through the National Recovery Administration (NRA). The **National Recovery Administration (NRA)** was a major New Deal program aimed at business recovery. It allowed and encouraged agreements between firms. It set up cartels in virtually every industry, but they eventually were declared unconstitutional. In 1937, the Roosevelt administration changed its position and vigorously pursued antitrust cases, including the Alcoa case, which ultimately reversed the rule of reason.

Both the Eisenhower and Kennedy administrations pursued active antitrust programs. Johnson's administration retreated from vigorous antitrust policy, although the IBM case was filed at the end of his term in office. Nixon's first assistant attorney general, Richard McLaren, worked at restricting conglomerate mergers (in which a company buys a firm unrelated to its existing business). The Ford administration pursued an active antitrust policy. A major case was launched against AT&T, and many price-fixing cases were filed.

Carter appointees promised to use the antitrust laws to change the concentration of power. They also promised to attack shared monopolies (in which very few firms control an industry) and to speed up the litigation process so cases would not drag on for years. Very little was accomplished along these lines during Carter's tenure.

In 1980, Reagan's appointees made it clear that they did not equate big business with bad business practices. William Baxter, Reagan's first assistant attorney general for antitrust, believed that the purpose of antitrust activity should be to promote efficiency. To this end, Baxter argued that government should not interfere with most vertical mergers (mergers in which a company acquires other firms involved in different stages of production in the same production process). He also felt that conglomerate mergers should be allowed. Baxter argued that vertical mergers and conglomerate mergers seldom foster price fixing and do not reduce competition. On the other hand, Baxter approved of tough action against horizontal mergers (in which a firm acquires a competitor).

Baxter changed many of the practices of the Antitrust Division, dropping the Nixon administration's attack on conglomerates and the Carter administration's attack on shared monopoly. Reagan's first chair of the FTC, James C. Miller III, engineered a similar policy change there. These policy changes encouraged the merger movement of the 1980s. Most observers feel that many of those mergers would never have been permitted by previous administrations.

In 1986, the policies of the Reagan administration were supported by the Supreme Court, which ruled that antitrust laws were not meant to prevent mergers just because they create larger, more formidable competitors. The Supreme Court overturned two lower court decisions in allowing Cargill to buy Spencer Beef, combining the second and third largest beef packing companies.

When George Bush was elected President in 1988, it was believed that his administration would follow the laissez-faire policies of the Reagan administration. However, by 1990, it became clear that the policies of the Bush administration were decidedly different from those of the Reagan administration. The business news was full of reports with headlines such as "Return of the Big Stick" and "Psst! The Trustbusters Are Back in Town."[29] President Bush's chief antitrust appointees, Janet D. Steiger, chair of the FTC, and James F. Rill, assistant attorney general for antitrust, have expressed skepticism about the Reagan view that bigness means efficiency and will benefit consumers. They have been stepping up antitrust and regulatory activity.

In the Reagan era, the FTC stayed out of most merger proposals. In late 1988, executives at Winn-Dixie tried to increase their market share in Florida by buying U-Save Supermarkets. Under Reagan, this purchase would not have been challenged by the FTC, but Steiger demanded so much data from Winn-Dixie that the merger was abandoned in early 1990. Increased FTC scrutiny will surely discourage mergers in the 1990s. The FTC is also investigating U.S. subsidiaries of foreign corporations. For example, Steiger announced in early 1990 that the FTC would investigate Toyota, Nissan, and Honda to determine if they are violating antitrust laws by favoring Japanese suppliers of parts for their American-produced cars.

At the Justice Department, antitrust activity is being extended to deal with countries that exclude U.S. imports. Rill has participated in trade talks between the United States and Japan and is examining ways in which U.S. law can be used to strike at bid rigging in Japan. It is argued that this bid rigging hurts U.S. exports of semiconductors, wood products, and other goods to Japan.

THE ROLE OF ECONOMIC VARIABLES IN FILING CASES

Economists and lawyers have used statistical analysis to study case-bringing activity of the Justice Department. The first such study, by Richard Posner, found that in the first eight decades of the Sherman Act, 1,551 cases were brought by the Justice Department.[30] Antitrust activity can also be initiated by the FTC and even by private citizens. Posner found that, contrary to popular belief, the antimonopoly activity of the FTC has not increased over time. However, the number of cases brought by private citizens has increased continuously since 1949.

Antitrust enforcement by the states has also been stepped up. This change, in part, resulted from a 1976 law that allows state attorneys general to sue suspected price fixers for treble damages on behalf of citizens. Politics often influence the use of this power. State attorneys general are often campaigning for re-election or for higher office. They will bring lawsuits for publicity value but will be careful to avoid suits against powerful groups that may help them in future elections. Cases are often brought against out-of-state firms. This approach creates good publicity but doesn't damage the attorney general's support from in-state businesses.

Although many antitrust cases last as long as five and six years, the success rate of the Justice Department is very high. The success rate is much lower for FTC and private cases. However, the remedies the court imposes have been far from successful in terms of restoring competition. In civil cases, the remedy has often taken the form of regulation. The goal of anti-

---

29. "Return of the Big Stick," *U.S. News & World Report* (4 June 1990): 54; "Psst! The Trustbusters Are Back in Town," *Business Week* (25 June 1990): 64.
30. Richard A. Posner, "A Statistical Study of Antitrust Enforcement," *Journal of Law and Economics* (October 1970).

trust activity is restoring competition, but regulation is in fact an admission that competition cannot be restored. The problems that regulation introduces make it a very unsatisfactory remedy. Criminal cases have resulted in very weak penalties for those found guilty. Not until the late 1950s was an individual sentenced to jail for price fixing. In 1960, seven more executives were sentenced to jail. In the few cases in which sentences have been imposed, the terms have been very short. In addition, the fines levied have been too small to have much of a deterrent effect.

Posner's study spawned some attempts to examine the determinants of antitrust activity. Posner pointed out that the level of antitrust activity and the kinds of cases did not seem to be related to economic conditions in the country. He also found that the political party of the President does not seem to affect the number of cases initiated. This, of course, does not mean that politics does not affect the Justice Department's antitrust activity. It only means that the amount of political interference has not, on the average, been too much affected by which party holds the presidency.

William Long, Richard Schramm, and Robert Tollison analyzed case-bringing patterns of the Justice Department and found that cases were more likely to be brought in larger industries, measured by sales.[31] Other variables that may more meaningfully indicate monopoly power, such as profit rates on sales and concentration, were found to be less important in explaining Justice Department cases. John Siegfried has found that economic variables have little influence on the kinds of cases filed by the Justice Department.[32] The work of Siegfried and Peter Asch suggests that the case-bringing criteria of the Justice Department are complex and difficult to forecast using economic variables.[33] The limited role of economic considerations is probably not surprising, since the Justice Department is staffed by lawyers rather than economists.

THE ECONOMIC CONSEQUENCES OF ANTITRUST ACTIVITY

In addition to looking for an economic explanation of antitrust activity, economists have begun to examine its economic consequences. Several of these empirical studies are informative. Peter Asch and J. J. Seneca found that firms that were known to be engaged in collusion were, surprisingly, less profitable than firms that were not known to be in collusion.[34] Robert Feinberg argued that these results were actually due to the deterrent effect of antitrust cases.[35] Dosoung Choi and George Philippatos found that the filing of antitrust cases caused restraint in pricing but that this restraint decreased with the number of times the firm had been indicted.[36] This finding implies a diminishing return to bringing cases

---

31. William F. Long, Richard Schramm, and Robert Tollison, "Economic Determinants of Antitrust Activity," *Journal of Law and Economics* (October 1973).
32. John J. Siegfried, "The Determinants of Antitrust Activity," *Journal of Law and Economics* (October 1975).
33. Peter Asch, "The Determinants and Effects of Antitrust Activity," *Journal of Law and Economics* (October 1975).
34. Peter Asch and J. J. Seneca, "Is Collusion Profitable?" *The Review of Economics and Statistics* (February 1976).
35. Robert Feinberg, "Antitrust Enforcement and Subsequent Price Behavior," *The Review of Economics and Statistics* (November 1980).
36. Dosoung Choi and George Philippatos, "The Financial Consequences of Antitrust Enforcement," *The Review of Economics and Statistics* (August 1983).

against a single firm, an implication that any beginning student of economics should be able to explain. Finally, and not too surprisingly, Kenneth Garbade, William Silber, and Lawrence White have found that the announcement of an antitrust suit against a firm has a negative impact on the stock price of that firm.[37]

ANTITRUST, GOVERNMENT-SPONSORED MONOPOLY, AND DEREGULATION

In recent years, the policy discussion about monopoly has shifted to looking at the role of government in fostering monopoly. Harold Demsetz has argued that there are two systems of belief about monopoly.[38] One system views private sector monopoly as a major threat to the economy. This view is held by supporters of the market concentration doctrine, who think such monopolies should be aggressively regulated and pursued by strictly defined antitrust policy. The other system, which Demsetz calls "the new learning," views the more serious economic threat as coming from monopolies that are sponsored and protected by government. Reducing the threat from this type of monopoly calls for deregulation and less governmental control. The new learning approach is helpful in understanding antitrust activity in the 1980s because it represents the Reagan administration's view of monopoly.

THE ALPHABET SOUP OF REGULATORY AGENCIES

Regulation at the federal level has resulted in a host of regulatory agencies aimed at protecting consumer welfare. The acronyms for these agencies read like a can of alphabet soup: CAB, EEOC, EPA, FCC, FDA, FTC, ICC, NHTSA, OSHA, ITC, and SEC. The number of such agencies grew very rapidly in the 1960s and 1970s. The Reagan administration cut back their budgets and staffing. Presumably, lower budgets and fewer people meant less regulation. The Bush administration seems less intent on starving regulatory agencies, so some of them may gain increased power in the 1990s. This is especially likely for the Environmental Protection Agency (EPA).

In many cases, regulatory agencies that were formed for consumer protection actually inhibited competition and innovation. Before airline deregulation, the Civil Aeronautics Board (CAB) set fares and prohibited entry. The Food and Drug Administration (FDA) still tightly controls innovation and entry in drug markets, forcing U.S. citizens to travel to foreign countries for access to certain medical procedures and drugs. On a local level, most cities regulate taxicabs by setting minimum prices, controlling entry, or both. Ironically, in many instances, regulatory agencies set up for consumer protection are responsible for the monopoly power that exists in the regulated market. Many companies defend the regulatory status quo because they have already met the regulations, and these regulations serve as an effective barrier to new entry and new competition. These firms are the government-supported monopolies that Demsetz identified.

---

37. Kenneth Garbade, William Silber, and Lawrence White, "Market Reaction to the Filing of Antitrust Suits: An Aggregate and Cross Sectional Analysis," *The Review of Economics and Statistics* (November 1982).
38. Harold Demsetz, "Two Systems of Belief about Monopoly," in H. Goldschmid, H. M. Mann, and J. F. Weston (eds.), *Industrial Concentration: The New Learning* (Boston: Little, Brown, 1974).

A Case Study of Deregulation

In 1978, the Airline Deregulation Act took many operational decisions about running an airline away from the CAB and gave them back to the private managers.[39] In the twelve years between 1978 and 1990, the airline industry and air travel were revolutionized. But there have been calls for reregulation of the airline industry. An article in *Fortune* magazine painted the following picture of air travel:

A plane rips open like a sardine tin in mid-flight, spilling an unfortunate stewardess to her death. Just about every aircraft you board seems packed. Just about every flight seems late. The attendants are too often unsmiling, the food unspeakable. Once-mighty airlines like Eastern and Pam Am struggle to stay aloft as enraged workers and creditors pick over bare corporate bones. Something is very, very wrong here, and someone had better do something about it—fast. Is that scenario accurate? Many Americans emphatically think it is. They consider each flight a grim possibly perilous ordeal. We could add to that the complaints of business travelers. In the regulated days, they could count on a plane when they wanted it, where they wanted it, and it was on time. Best of all it wasn't crowded so they could work if they wanted to. Who cares if the prices were higher, they had expense accounts to cover the cost. Right?"[40]

We have all heard these complaints about airline deregulation. Perhaps you have made them yourself. Should the airlines be reregulated? To answer this question, we need to look at what has actually happened since deregulation in 1978. David Swierenga, who analyzes data for the Air Transport Association, says, "When you look at the really important issues, the big picture if you will, deregulation has to be considered a public policy triumph."[41]

Contrary to the popular perception, air safety has improved with deregulation. The major air carriers recorded an average of 33 fatal and nonfatal accidents per year and 1,459 fatalities in the nine years before deregulation. In the nine years following deregulation, the number of accidents fell to 20 per year and the number of fatalities declined to 1,036. Given the huge increase in passenger miles, this record is very impressive. Fatal accidents per million miles traveled fell 57 percent.

Airlines flew 85 percent more miles in 1989 than they did in 1978, before deregulation. Before deregulation, half of all Americans had never flown on a commercial aircraft. Since deregulation, three out of four Americans have done so. Passenger boardings per year have increased from 275 million in 1978 to 455 million in 1989. It's no wonder that aircraft seem more crowded. This increase in consumption has been generated by the decreased price of air travel.

The most compelling argument in favor of deregulation is that air fares, adjusted for inflation, decreased 21 percent between 1978 and 1988. The FTC estimates that this decline in prices saved passengers about $100 million. A portion of this $100 million was saved by business firms

---

39. This case study is based on Kenneth Labich, "Should the Airlines Be Reregulated?" *Fortune* (19 June 1989): 82–90.
40. Labich, "Should the Airlines Be Reregulated?" 82.
41. Labich, "Should the Airlines Be Reregulated?" 82.

that use air travel as an input and lowered their cost of producing goods and services.

However, deregulation has not done away with problems in air travel. Crowding *is* a problem in planes and terminals. Those harried business travelers are correct—it isn't as "nice" as it was before deregulation, it's just cheaper. Furthermore, it isn't cheaper in all markets. Before deregulation, higher fares on well-traveled routes were used to subsidize travel to remote cities. After deregulation, fares to remote spots were increased or service was terminated. Congestion at airports is a big problem. Landing fees and times at major airports are regulated, and at present they do not respond to market forces. Landing fees are based on a plane's weight. A corporate jet may pay $25, and an airliner carrying 400 passengers may pay $800. Yet both require the same time and the same attention from air traffic controllers. In addition, some airlines control available landing slots based on a historical basis. The ownership of the slots represents a barrier to entry for new airlines. A discussion in Congress centers on whether there should be more regulation of these slots or whether they should be auctioned to create more efficiency. The private aviation lobby makes such reform very difficult.

COMPETITIVENESS

Those who propose a national economic policy to improve competitiveness seem to draw their ideas from the success of the Japanese economy. There is a belief that that success stems from the government's working closely with private industry to ensure that private industry is successful. The idea, in part, is that government should take steps to back industrial "winners" to make them even more successful. Such proposals rest on the premise that the U.S. economy is in serious decline and that other countries (notably Japan) have had a positive experience that is a result of industrial-governmental "partnerships."

Regardless of the form that a policy fostering competitiveness may take at the federal level, it would represent an increased governmental role in making economic decisions. Proponents of such a policy are quick to point out that the United States already has a kind of industrial policy because every action of government in taxing and spending rewards some participants in the economy and penalizes others. Those individuals argue that a coordinated and intentional policy would be preferable to what exists at present. A competitiveness policy, however, would result in a more active role for government in the economy than most market-oriented economists would find acceptable.[42]

The latest argument for an industrial policy has come out of Silicon Valley in California. The high-tech manufacturers there want the United States to form a cohesive industrial policy to help them compete with what they refer to as "Japan, Inc." At the beginning of the Bush administration,

---

42. For a thorough review of the industrial policy debate, see R. D. Norton, "Industrial Policy and American Renewal," *Journal of Economic Literature* (March 1986).

**TABLE 4
INDUSTRIAL POLICY
PROPOSAL BY THE
ELECTRONICS INDUSTRY**

GOAL	SHORT-TERM ACTIONS	LONG-TERM ACTIONS
Lower-cost capital	Create a "patient" venture capital corporation with funding from government Provide federal aid for critical but very risky technologies Make R&D tax credits permanent Shorten depreciation schedules for high-tech equipment	Stimulate more savings Trim the federal deficit Reduce consumer and business debt Curtail leveraged buyouts Index the capital gains tax to zero on long-term investments End the double taxation on corporate dividends
Fair trade	Enforce existing antidumping laws	Require reciprocity with foreign nations
Antitrust reform	Exempt collaborative manufacturing under some conditions Eliminate treble damages in private suits against consortiums	Adjust rules to take account of offshore competition

Source: *Business Week* (5 February 1990): 57.

their lobbyists in Washington were hopeful that the new administration would develop a plan to help them. They soon learned that Bush's advisers were opposed to industrial policy. As his chief of staff, John H. Sununu, put it, "I assure you, our commitment is to try and create a competitive climate without falling into the trap of a competitiveness vehicle, which may itself be a vehicle for mischievous legislation."[43]

The trade associations of the electronics industry have banded together to continue to try to persuade the administration to come to their aid. However, many of their proposals are general ones aimed at encouraging investment and economic growth. A few are aimed specifically at foreign competition. Table 4 highlights what the electronics industry wants as industrial policy.

The competitiveness debate has a different focus at the state level. Policy makers at that level have become very involved in economic development activities. Almost every state has a state development board that aids the governor in recruiting new firms to the state from other states and foreign countries. Government officials use all types of tax breaks and other incentives to lure new firms to their states. In this context, fostering competitiveness can mean writing state tax laws, changing state regulatory activity, and examining state services, to make a state competitive with other states. Such competition puts constraints on state governments because if state officials create an environment that is hostile to business, firms will migrate to more friendly states.

43. "The Future of Silicon Valley," *Business Week* (5 February 1990): 59.

ALTERNATIVES FOR CONTROLLING INDUSTRY

There is a great deal of monopoly power, or at least concentration, in U.S. industry, and monopoly power is undesirable from society's point of view. Unfortunately, attempts to control monopoly or to restore competition through antitrust actions have not always produced the desired results. Antitrust cases drag on for many years. The economic analysis in these cases is very complex and often conflicting. The arguments are difficult to present, and juries, judges, and even lawyers do not always understand them. Generally, the result is government intervention in the market that can introduce new inefficiencies.

There does, however, seem to be at least one policy action that could increase competition without endangering the efficiency resulting from economies of scale. This policy is based on the benefits from the threat of new entry. If public policy could support new entry by dismantling artificial barriers to entry, competitive pressure would increase. These artificial barriers are both privately and publicly imposed. In many cases, the threat of new entry alone would be enough to alter the behavior of oligopolies.

Internationalization of the economy destroys many domestic barriers. As world markets become more integrated, the relevant market for antitrust activity becomes larger. If international trade is expanded, there may be less need to worry about domestic monopolies, from an antitrust perspective.

SUMMARY

1. Industries can be defined by SIC codes established by the Commerce Department. These groupings can be used to calculate concentration ratios, which are measures of the degree to which markets are concentrated.

2. The Herfindahl Index may be a better measure of monopoly power than a concentration ratio because it accounts for all of the firms in the industry.

3. There is no conclusive evidence on the trend of concentration in U.S. industry. Some researchers have found the concentration level to be quite stable. Others have found an increase in competitive firms.

4. The merger movement of the 1980s may have increased the concentration of some U.S. industries. This movement involved $1.3 trillion in assets. Some economists believe that the business trend of the 1980s was more a restructuring of corporate management than a traditional merger movement.

5. Mergers in the 1990s seem to be motivated by a desire to become internationalized, especially with respect to the European market.

6. The market concentration doctrine states that the structure of an industry determines its ultimate performance in terms of prices and profits. This model implies that concentrated industries should be restructured.

7. There is a good deal of debate concerning the degree to which concentration leads to higher profit rates and more rigid prices.

8. Countervailing power and innovation are sometimes considered to be positive aspects of monopoly power.

9. Regulation of monopoly leads to cost-plus pricing, which destroys the incentive to minimize costs.

10. Taxation of monopoly is an alternative to regulation. It simply captures monopoly profits without affecting price or output.

11. A Lerner Index of Monopoly Power (LMP) measures the percentage difference between price and marginal cost. It is perhaps the best measure of monopoly power, but unavailability of marginal cost data limits its use.

12. U.S. antitrust law began with the Sherman Antitrust Act in 1890. The Sherman Act and later laws have been applied with varying vigor and success.
13. The record of antitrust enforcement is not too impressive. Lawsuits take a long time and rarely restore competition. Politics plays an important role in antitrust activity.
14. Deregulation of the airline industry has increased competitiveness, lowered prices, increased the numbers of people flying, and (contrary to popular opinion) increased safety.
15. Competitiveness became a major public concern in the late 1980s. At the federal level, it is an aspect of industrial policy. At the state level, it relates to economic development.

New Terms

industry
industry studies
Standard Industrial Classification (SIC) system
concentration ratio
Herfindahl Index
number equivalent
market concentration doctrine
administered prices
countervailing power
marginal cost pricing
Lerner Index of Monopoly Power (LMP)
cost-plus pricing
fair rate of return
trusts
holding companies
Sherman Antitrust Act
Clayton Act
tying contracts
Robinson-Patman Act
predatory pricing
Celler-Kefauver Antimerger Act
Federal Trade Commission Act
Wheeler-Lea Act
Hart-Scott-Rodino Antitrust Improvement Act
National Recovery Administration (NRA)

Questions for Discussion

1. Are profits a good measure of monopoly power? Is concentration a good measure of monopoly power? Discuss the advantages of using either or both.
2. What would happen in a regulated industry if the price were set such that a representative firm could not earn a normal profit?
3. If prices charged by all firms in an industry are identical, is this evidence of an antitrust violation?
4. Do concentration ratios provide any useful information about changes in conglomerate merger activity?
5. The following data are for the soft drink industry in a certain country.

Firms	Annual Sales (in dollars)
1	$400,000,000
2	300,000,000
3	200,000,000
4	150,000,000
5–35	300,000,000

What is the four-firm concentration ratio for this industry?
6. Now assume that the entire soft drink industry is made up of the first four firms listed in Question 5. What is the four-firm concentration ratio? What is the Herfindahl Index? What is the number equivalent? What does the number equivalent tell you?
7. What would happen to the concentration ratio in Question 5 if the industry were defined as the beverage industry? As the name-brand, nationally advertised soft drink industry?
8. Why is it so difficult to regulate a natural monopoly?
9. Why do some economists favor deregulation as a way of dealing with monopoly rather than "better" or "tougher" regulation?
10. Imagine that the President has just appointed you the major national adviser on antitrust. Convince the Cabinet that the government should pursue an active antitrust policy. After you have done that, take the opposite side and argue that monopoly is not so bad and the government shouldn't worry too much about it.
11. A comprehensive study of the U.S. economy argued that it became more effectively competitive between 1958 and 1980. What are the three reasons for this increase in the number of competitive firms? How did each of these three reasons work to increase competitiveness?
12. Some economists argue that the merger movement of the 1980s was different from earlier movements because of the inherent problem of the separation of ownership and control in U.S. corporations. What do these economists have in mind?
13. Why would U.S. firms want to merge with foreign firms, especially European firms?
14. What has been the outcome of the Airline Deregulation Act of 1978?
15. The term *competitiveness* is used increasingly in political campaigns. How does the meaning of the term differ when it is used by a candidate for federal office as opposed to a candidate for state office?

Suggestions for Further Reading

Adams, Walter, and James Brock. *Dangerous Pursuits: Mergers and Acquisitions in the Age of Wall Street.* New York: Pantheon, 1989. A critique of the merger wave of the 1980s by two economists who argue that the long-run effects will be greater concentration and reduced innovation.

Asch, Peter. *Industrial Organization and Antitrust Policy.* New York: John Wiley and Sons, 1986. A textbook that gives detailed accounts of important antitrust cases.

Bauer, Paul W. "Airline Deregulation: Boon or Bust?" *Economic Commentary*, Federal Reserve Bank of Cleveland (1 May 1989). A commentary on the issues surrounding airline deregulation.

Hermaann, Werner, and G. J. Santoni. "The Cost of Restricting Corporate Takeovers: A Lesson from Switzerland." *Review, Federal Reserve Bank of St. Louis* (November/December 1989): 3–11. According to this article, the Swiss experience shows that restricting corporate takeovers has serious consequences on the wealth of stockholders.

Newcomb, Peter. "No One Is Safe." *Forbes* (13 July 1987): 121–160. An account of how the largest firms ebb and flow, keeping concentration in flux.

Reich, Robert B. *Tales of a New America.* New York: Times Books, 1986. A book on competitiveness by one of the advocates of industrial policy.

Scherer, F. M. *Industrial Market Structure and Economic Performance.* Chicago: Rand McNally, 1980. A source book with detailed references to the literature on regulation and antitrust matters.

Factor Markets

4

AFTER STUDYING THIS CHAPTER, YOU SHOULD BE ABLE TO:

1. Distinguish between product markets and factor markets and describe their relationship to each other in terms of the circular flow model.
2. Explain what makes the demand for labor different from the demand for final goods in terms of:
   a. derived demand,
   b. interdependent demand,
   c. technologically determined demand.
3. Explain how to calculate each of the following:
   a. marginal physical product of labor (MPP_L),
   b. value of the marginal physical product of labor (VMP_L),
   c. marginal revenue product of labor (MRP_L),
   d. marginal resource cost of labor (MRC_L).
4. Describe how a profit-maximizing firm decides how much labor to employ in terms of its marginal revenue product and marginal resource cost.
5. Use a factor market diagram to illustrate:
   a. pure competition versus monopoly in the product market,
   b. pure competition versus monopsony in the factor market.
6. Explain why a monopsonist has fewer workers at a lower wage.
7. Discuss the effects of investment in human capital on wages.
8. Explain how the difference between white and nonwhite income levels relates to human capital.
9. List arguments for and against comparable worth legislation.

CHAPTER 13

MARGINAL PRODUCTIVITY THEORY AND LABOR MARKETS

INTRODUCTION

Income is earned through ownership of any (or perhaps all) of the factors of production. Most individuals receive income from their labor. Many others own land or capital, or are entrepreneurs. Personal income flows to all these factors. In most discussions, much more attention is given to the equity aspects of the distribution of personal income than to the reasons for this distribution. This chapter explains how labor income is determined in a market system and why the distribution of income is what it is. In a later chapter, we will discuss actions that can be taken if society doesn't like the distribution of income that is produced by the market process.

Earlier in this book, we examined the circular flow as a starting point. It is worthwhile to return briefly to that discussion. Figure 1 reproduces the circular flow diagram from Chapter 2. It shows the firm involved in two markets: the product market and the factor market. We have studied the theory of the firm in the product market, the upper half of the circular flow diagram. We now turn our attention to the theory of the firm in the largest part of the factor market, the labor market.

The demand for labor is similiar to other types of demand we have studied. In earlier chapters, we described product markets, in which firms or individuals sell the goods and services they produce to consumers. Now we want to examine the labor market, the market in which firms buy—or

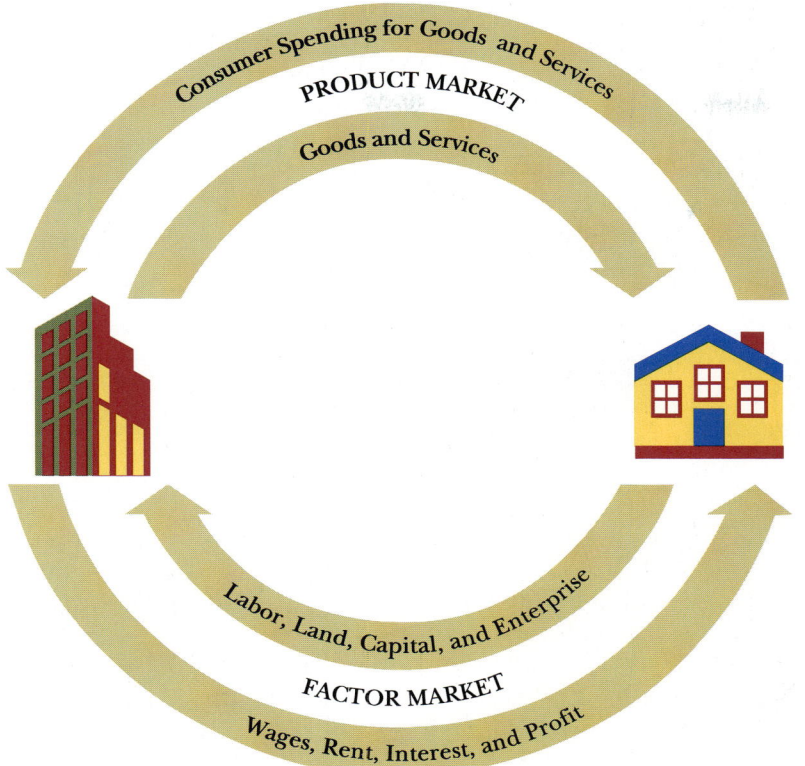

FIGURE 1
THE CIRCULAR FLOW OF INCOME
Households purchase goods and services and supply land, labor, capital, and enterprise. Firms buy these factors of production and supply goods and services. In the product market, buyers and sellers exchange goods and services. In the factor market, buyers and sellers exchange the services of factors of production (resources).

rent—the services of labor from individuals. We can adopt many of the same analytical tools we used to study product markets. There are, however, some differences between labor and product markets, and we will concentrate on these differences.

SPECIAL FEATURES OF THE DEMAND FOR LABOR

The demand for labor has three features that make it somewhat different from the demand for a product. The first is that the demand for labor is **derived demand**. A firm demands labor because the labor can be used to produce goods that consumers are demanding. The demand for labor is thus derived from the demand for the product it produces. If there were no consumer demand for wood, there would be no demand for loggers. This principle holds for all factors of production. They are only valuable to a firm if they help to produce products that consumers value.

The second feature of the demand for labor is that it is **interdependent demand**. It depends on the demand for other factors. In other words, the amount of labor demanded will depend on the amounts of other factors a firm plans to use. The amount of labor a firm demands depends on the amounts of land, capital, and enterprise that will be used in combination with the labor. It is also true that the demand for most products is interdependent with the demand for other products. As you know, almost all

derived demand
Demand for a productive resource that results from demand for a final good or service. For example, the demand for labor is derived from the demand for the product that the labor produces.

interdependent demand
Demand that depends on another type of demand. For example, a firm's demand for labor depends on the amount of other factors that the firm plans to use.

John Bates Clark was the first person born in the United States to achieve an international reputation as an economic theorist. He was a reformer and an activist who helped form the American Economic Association and later became its third president.

Clark was born and raised in Providence, Rhode Island. He graduated from Amherst College in 1872. He studied economics at the University of Heidelberg and the University of Zurich. After returning to the United States, Clark taught political economy at Carleton College and then moved to Smith College, Amherst, Johns Hopkins, and finally to Columbia, where he taught political science from 1895 to 1923. After 1911, he became very active in pacifist causes and was the first director of the Carnegie Endowment for International Peace.

The nature of Clark's theoretical interests reflected the times in which he lived. The American Industrial Revolution caused Clark to examine problems of production and distribution. In his book *The Distribution of Wealth* (1899), he developed a positive theory based on the competition of rational, self-interested people. This approach was a radical change from that in his earlier work, *The Philosophy of Wealth* (1887), in which he attacked the "hedonistic" assumptions of the classical economists. His influence on later economists stems from the analytical tools he developed.

Economic Profile

John Bates Clark

1847–1938

Clark's status in the U.S. economics profession is recognized by the John Bates Clark Prize of the American Economics Association. Every two years, this prize is awarded to an economist under the age of forty who has made a significant contribution to economic theory. The list of winners reads like a *Who's Who* of American economists.

goods have substitutes and many goods have complements. However, the interdependence of the demand for labor with the demand for other factors of production is unusual in that the other factors can be both complements and substitutes at the same time.

The third feature is that the demand for labor is in part **technologically determined demand**. That is, the demand for labor will depend on techniques of production and on technological progress, or the production function. Recall that the production function tells how much labor is needed to produce a certain level of output, given a certain production process and amounts of the other factors of production. This technological relationship can change with new inventions and new innovations. Any change resulting in a new technology or a new innovation will have an impact on the demand for factors of production, including labor.

These basic elements are combined in marginal productivity theory, which was originally developed by John Bates Clark. **Marginal productivity theory** explains how the distribution of income is determined in a market system. Each factor is paid according to its contribution, or its marginal productivity. The more productive factors will be paid more. We will follow Clark's lead by developing marginal productivity theory in terms of labor supply and demand. The theory holds for all factors of production, but most interest centers on labor and the returns to labor.

technologically determined demand Demand that depends on techniques of production and technological progress. For example, the demand for labor will be affected by the introduction of new technology in a firm or industry.

marginal productivity theory An explanation of how the distribution of income is determined in a market system. Each factor is paid according to its contribution, or its marginal productivity.

SPECIAL CHARACTERISTICS OF FACTOR MARKETS

- Demand is derived from the demand for the final product.
- Demand is interdependent with demand for other inputs.
- Demand is technologically determined.

THE MARKET FOR LABOR WITH PERFECT COMPETITION

Remember that a demand curve shows the relationship between price and quantity demanded. A demand curve for labor shows how much labor will be demanded at various wage rates. In order to develop a theory about the market demand for labor, we start by asking how much labor an individual firm will employ at various wage rates. Then we sum the results for all firms in the same way we added individual demand curves to find the market demand for a product.

Consider a firm that is selling its product in a perfectly competitive product market and buying its labor in a perfectly competitive labor market. This means that the firm will take both the price of its product *and* the price of labor as given. The firm is too small to have any effect on either product prices or wage rates.

THE DEMAND FOR LABOR

What determines the firm's demand for labor? Suppose the production function is such that, as the firm increases the amount of labor employed, *ceteris paribus*, the resulting increases in the amount of total product become smaller. This production function reflects the principle of diminishing marginal productivity, which we discussed in an earlier chapter. Holding constant the quantities of land and capital, it is possible to determine how the firm's output varies with the quantity of labor it uses. As the firm employs more labor in combination with fixed amounts of the other factors, the additional amounts of output per additional unit of labor eventually decline. If this were not the case, it would be theoretically possible to grow the entire world's supply of wheat on one acre of land just by employing more workers.

The amount of total physical product associated with various amounts of labor inputs for the firm is given in the second column of Table 1. This output depends on the technical relationship defined by the production function. Once we know the total product, we can determine how much extra product is produced when labor inputs are added. That value is the marginal physical product of that unit of labor (MPP_L). It is the marginal physical product because the output is in physical units, such as number of autos or tons of coal.

value of the marginal product of labor (VMP_L) A measure of the value of the additional output that each unit of additional labor adds to a firm's total, found by multiplying the marginal physical product by the price at which the firm can sell the product.

To put a market value on the additional output, we simply multiply the number of added units of the product by the price at which the firm can sell it. This value is called the **value of the marginal product of labor (VMP_L)**. It is listed in the sixth column of Table 1. The VMP_L, which is $P \times MPP_L$, is a measure of the value of the additional output that each additional unit of labor adds to the firm's total. The **marginal revenue product of labor (MRP_L)** is the amount that an additional unit of labor adds to the firm's total revenue. It is found in the seventh column of Table 1. It is found by multiplying MR by MPP_L. With perfect competition in the product market, $VMP_L = MRP_L$. These values are equal because the product price remains constant ($P = MR$). The firm can produce and sell as much as it wants at the market-determined price, which is $2 in this example. When the firm faces a given price, marginal revenue is exactly equal to that price in the model of perfect competition. Later in this chapter, we will

marginal revenue product of labor (MRP_L) The amount that an additional unit of labor adds to a firm's total revenue.

TABLE 1
THE DEMAND FOR LABOR IN A PERFECTLY COMPETITIVE PRODUCT MARKET

UNITS OF LABOR	TOTAL PHYSICAL PRODUCT	MARGINAL PHYSICAL PRODUCT OF LABOR (MPP_L)	PRODUCT PRICE	TOTAL REVENUE	VALUE OF MARGINAL PRODUCT OF LABOR (VMP_L)	MARGINAL REVENUE PRODUCT OF LABOR (MRP_L)
0	0		$2	$ 0		
		10			$20	$20
1	10		2	20		
		8			16	16
2	18		2	36		
		6			12	12
3	24		2	48		
		4			8	8
4	28		2	56		
		2			4	4
5	30		2	60		

look at how the value of the marginal product and the marginal revenue product differ when there is monopoly power in the product market.

The values of VMP_L and MRP_L from Table 1 are plotted on a graph in Figure 2. The MRP_L curve is the firm's demand curve for labor. It shows the value of each additional unit of labor to the firm. Thus, it shows how much labor the firm will purchase at various prices (wage rates). If you know the price of labor, you will be able to determine how much labor this firm will demand.

THE SUPPLY OF LABOR

An individual's supply curve of labor looks like the other supply curves we have considered. As wage rates rise, the quantity of labor supplied increases. This supply curve of labor, like most supply curves, is upward sloping. As wage rates rise, an individual will want to work more hours. In general, as wages rise, more people will choose to give up leisure in favor of more income. This trade-off of income for leisure is the substitution effect of a wage increase. Individuals will substitute the increased consumption of goods and services that higher wages represent for leisure. This substitution effect occurs along the upward-sloping portion of Figure 3.

There is also an income effect associated with the increased income brought about by a wage increase. Individuals want to consume more leisure at higher incomes because leisure is a normal good. The income effect of a higher wage is that individuals want to supply a lower quantity of labor. At some point, the income effect of a wage increase could dominate the substitution effect. In that case, an increase in the wage rate would bring about a decrease in the quantity of labor supplied. This is represented by the crook in the individual's supply curve in Figure 3. For this individual, an increase in the wage rate above $15 per hour causes the quantity of labor supplied to decrease. Economists refer to a supply curve with this shape as a **backward-bending supply curve**. It is important to keep in mind that this is an individual supply curve. Where the bend oc-

backward-bending supply curve
A labor supply curve that slopes back to the left at the point where the income effect dominates the substitution effect.

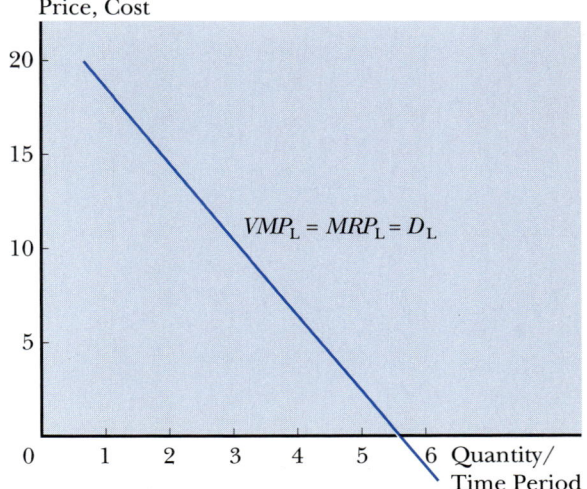

FIGURE 2
THE FIRM'S DEMAND FOR LABOR IN A PERFECTLY COMPETITIVE PRODUCT MARKET
The marginal revenue product of labor (MRP_L) curve is the firm's demand curve for labor. When the firm's product market is perfectly competitive, MRP_L and the VMP_L are identical.

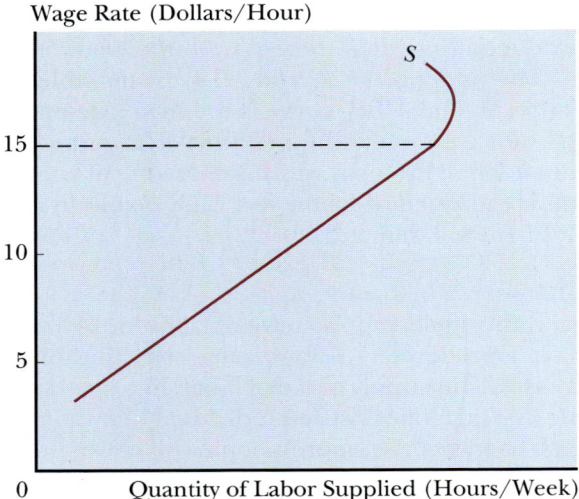

FIGURE 3
AN INDIVIDUAL'S LABOR SUPPLY CURVE
When the substitution effect of a wage increase for an individual exceeds the income effect, the quantity of labor supplied increases. Up to some wage ($15 per hour here), the income effect dominates. Above that wage, further increases in the wage rate cause the quantity of labor supplied to decrease.

curs is an individual decision. Some entertainers perform less as they get more famous. Others appear to keep increasing the quantity of labor supplied as their wage rate increases.

The market supply curve of labor (S_L) is the aggregate of all the individual supply curves. It shows how much labor is available at different wage rates, as in Figure 4. This market supply curve is not backward-bending because more workers will enter the market at higher wage rates and different individuals have different opportunity costs and will make choices resulting in different substitution effects and income effects. In other words, higher wages are needed to attract additional workers who have higher opportunity costs.

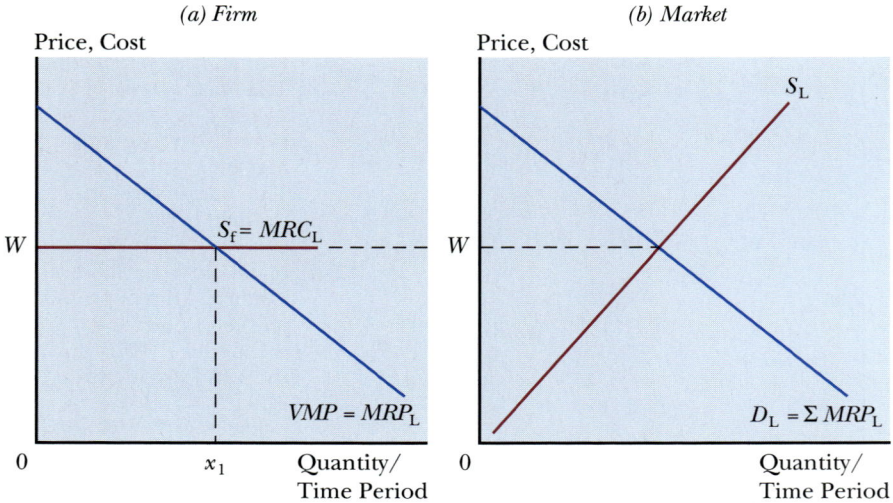

FIGURE 4
PERFECTLY COMPETITIVE LABOR MARKET
In a perfectly competitive labor market, the firm faces a perfectly elastic supply curve (S_f). If the supply curve is perfectly elastic, the marginal resource cost (MRC_L) curve is also perfectly elastic. The firm can purchase as much labor as it wants at the market-determined wage rate.

We assumed that the firm is in perfectly competitive factor markets. Perfect competition in the labor market means the firm can purchase labor at the market wage without affecting that wage. The equilibrium wage rate is W in Figure 4. The firm can purchase as much labor as it wants at the wage rate W. The supply curve the firm faces, represented by S_f in Figure 4, is thus perfectly elastic at W. If the supply curve a firm faces is perfectly elastic, the cost of each additional unit of labor is the same, or constant. The cost of each additional unit of labor is the **marginal resource cost of labor** (MRC_L). For a firm in a perfectly competitive labor market, the marginal resource cost curve of labor, MRC_L, is the same as the labor supply curve.

marginal resource cost (MRC)
The cost of each additional unit of a productive resource.

EQUILIBRIUM IN THE PERFECTLY COMPETITIVE LABOR MARKET

The MRC_L curve is the supply curve the firm faces because it shows the relationship between price and additional units of labor supplied. A profit-maximizing firm will employ or purchase labor until $MRP_L = MRC_L$. If a unit of labor adds more to revenue than to cost (if $MRP_L > MRC_L$), it will be profitable for the firm to purchase more units of labor. However, if a unit of labor adds more to cost than to revenue (if $MRP_L < MRC_L$), the firm should purchase fewer units. The firm will hire laborers until the amount they add to total cost (MRC_L) is exactly equal to the amount they add to revenue (MRP_L). In Figure 4, the firm would employ x_1 units of labor at wage rate W. In terms of the numbers in Table 1, the firm would employ 4 units of labor if the market wage was $8 per unit. If the market wage was $4 per unit, 5 units of labor would be employed.

A COMPETITIVE LABOR MARKET WITH A MONOPOLISTIC PRODUCT MARKET

We now consider a firm that sells its product under monopoly conditions. The monopolist's demand for labor is shown in Table 2. The difference be-

UNITS OF LABOR	TOTAL PHYSICAL PRODUCT	MARGINAL PHYSICAL PRODUCT OF LABOR (MPP_L)	PRODUCT PRICE	TOTAL REVENUE	VALUE OF THE MARGINAL PRODUCT OF LABOR (VMP_L)	MARGINAL REVENUE PRODUCT OF LABOR (MRP_L)
0	0	0	$0	$0		
		10			$100	$100
1	10		10	100		
		8			72	62
2	18		9	162		
		6			48	30
3	24		8	192		
		4			28	4
4	28		7	196		
		2			12	–6
5	30		6	180		

TABLE 2
THE DEMAND FOR LABOR IN A MONOPOLISTIC PRODUCT MARKET

Give me your tired, your poor,
Your huddled masses yearning to breath free,
The wretched refuse of your teeming shore,
Send these, the homeless, tempest-tossed to me:
I lift my lamp beside the golden door.
—Inscription on the Statue of Liberty

International Perspective

U.S. Immigration Policy and Wage Rates

The United States is a country of immigrants and descendants of immigrants—a "melting pot," as you learned in elementary school. In the early nineteenth century, Europeans, mostly from Western Europe, flooded into the United States. In the late nineteenth century, a wave of Chinese immigrated to California. In the early twentieth century, a huge flood of immigrants arrived from Southern and Eastern Europe. The most recent large waves of immigrants have been from Southeast Asia after the end of the Vietnam War, and from Central America. Many of those coming from Central America are illegal immigrants, making them distinct from most of the other waves of immigrants.

Each influx of immigrants caused a great debate among Americans who were already citizens. The issue was always the same—whether or not to shut the door to new immigrants. Often the answer was yes, and new restrictions were passed. There was the Chinese exclusion law in 1882, the "Gentlemen's Agreement" with Japan in 1907 (halting the immigration of Japanese), and the national-origin quotas in 1921 and 1924. These quotas were designed to freeze the ethnic composition of the United States by limiting the entrance of any one nationality to a small percentage of the number of people of that nationality who were already here. The Quota Law of 1921 limited immigration from any Eastern Hemisphere country to 3 percent of the foreign-born persons from that country living in the United States in 1910. In l924, the Immigration Origins Act set an annual quota of 2 percent of each country's U.S. residents in 1920. In l965, Congress did away with the national-origin quotas and placed a yearly limit of 290,000 on all immigrants.

Many legal restrictions on immigration are racist in origin. Many groups support immigration of those who are like themselves but are opposed to altering the racial mix of the country. This motivation was clear in the 1924 act.

There is at least one economic motive for restricting immigration. Immigration makes the supply of labor much more elastic for each skill level, putting downward pressure on wage rates. It isn't surprising that organized labor groups are often opposed to liberalizing immigration policy. In fact, some states even prohibit the transfer of certain occupational skills within the United States. For example, a CPA in Wisconsin who plans to migrate to Arizona will not be licensed until he or she passes an Arizona exam. This requirement clearly reduces the supply of accounting services in Arizona. As a result, accountants in Arizona have higher incomes than they would otherwise.

In October 1986, the U.S. Congress passed an immigration reform bill that offered citizenship to illegal aliens who could prove they entered the United States before January 1, 1982. However, the law imposed strict penalties on employers who hire illegal aliens. If effectively enforced, this law will put upward pressure on wage rates in the unskilled labor markets in the South and Southwest, where illegal aliens are a large fraction of the work force. In 1986, there was evidence that the law was deterring illegal immigration. Illegal border crossings declined, and there were numerous reports of employers firing undocumented workers. By 1988, this trend seemed to have reversed. Field observations at the busiest illegal crossing point reported an increase in illegal crossing to the level recorded before the law went into effect. Data on the apprehension of illegal aliens confirms that this law has not substantially deterred entry as long as enforcement was weak and the wage pull was strong.

tween this case and the firm of the preceding section is that product price (fourth column) declines as the firm produces and sells more of its product. VMP_L and MRP_L are calculated in the same way as before. VMP_L is the value of the labor's marginal physical product, so $VMP_L = MPP_L \times P$. MRP_L is found by calculating the change in total revenue due to additional units of labor. For example, when the third worker is added, total revenue rises from $162 to $192. Thus, MRP_L for the third worker is $192 − $162 = $30. Note that VMP_L is greater than MRP_L for all but the first unit of labor, because in a monopoly, product price is greater than marginal revenue.

Both the VMP_L curve and the MRP_L curve are graphed in Figure 5 using the data from Table 2. The MRP_L curve is the monopolist's demand curve for labor. This firm, like the perfectly competitive firm, will employ labor until $MRP_L = MRC_L$. Although this firm is selling its product in a monopolistic product market, it is purchasing labor in a competitive labor market.

The supply and demand curves for the monopolist in the competitive labor market are diagrammed in Figure 6. The market demand curve for labor is, as usual, found by summing the MRP_L curves for all firms purchasing this type of labor. The market supply curve (S_L) is the sum of individual supply curves of workers. The market-determined wage is W. This firm can purchase as much labor as it desires at W, since the supply curve it faces, S_f, is perfectly elastic at W. Since S_f is perfectly elastic, MRC_L for this firm is constant. The firm maximizes profits where $MRC_L = MRP_L$, so it hires x_1 units of labor. Note from Figure 6 that the monopolist pays W, the market wage. The fact that MRP_L is less than VMP_L does not mean that the monopolist exploits labor by paying too little. The monopolist has to pay the market wage just like any other employer in this market. Because MRP_L is less than VMP_L, the monopolist *does* employ fewer workers than similar competitive firms would employ. Recall from the chapter on

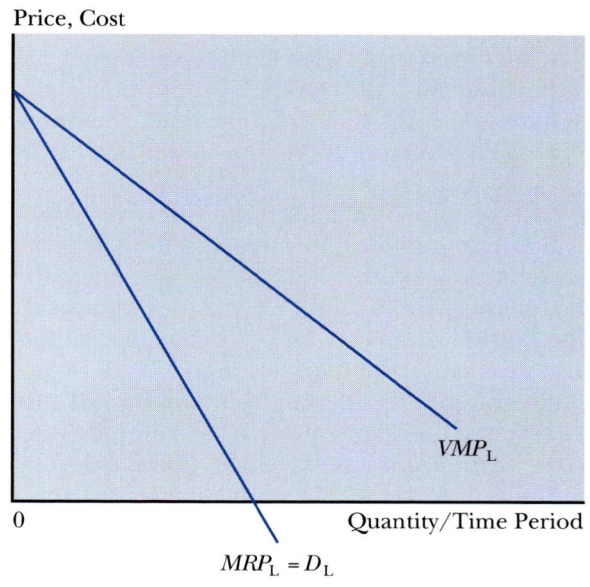

FIGURE 5
THE MONOPOLIST'S DEMAND FOR LABOR
When a firm has monopoly power in the product market, the MRP_L will lie below VMP_L. This is because product price is greater than marginal revenue under monopoly. Thus, $P \times MP_L$ is greater than $MR \times MP_L$.

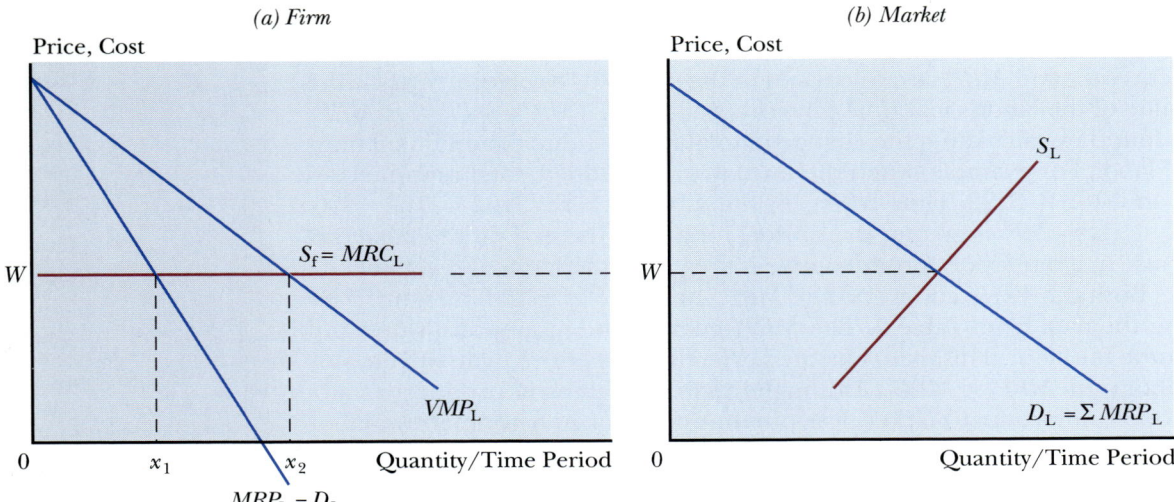

FIGURE 6
A MONOPOLISTIC FIRM FACING A PERFECTLY COMPETITIVE LABOR MARKET
A firm with monopoly power in the product market and in a perfectly competitive labor market will face a perfectly elastic supply curve. The firm will hire units of labor until the marginal revenue product of labor is equal to the marginal resource cost of labor ($MRP_L = MRC_L$).

monopsony
A market structure in which there is a single purchaser of a factor of production.

monopoly that the monopolist restricts output to keep price high. The result of this restriction of output in the factor market is that the monopolist uses fewer inputs, including labor. If this were a competitive firm rather than a monopolist, it would want to be on the VMP_L curve (which would then also be the MRP_L curve) and hire x_2 workers.

MONOPSONY

We have looked at competitive and monopolistic firms demanding labor in competitive labor markets. Now we want to consider a firm that has an influence on price in the labor market. We have assumed to this point that the purchasing firm has no effect on wage rates. But what if the firm does affect wage rates? What if the wage rate rises as the firm hires more labor? We refer to such a firm as having monopsony power. The word *monopsony* comes from a Greek word meaning "one purchaser." A monopoly is the market structure in which there is a single seller of a product. A **monopsony** is a market structure in which there is a single purchaser of a factor of production.

We begin by assuming that we know what the monopsonist's MRP_L curve is, shown in Figure 7. It doesn't matter if this firm is selling its product in a competitive market or a monopolistic market. We also know the market supply curve of labor to this firm, S_L. Table 3 provides values that correspond to Figure 7. The market supply curve, S_L, is the labor supply curve the firm faces because the firm is the market for this labor by the definition of monopsony. In a competitive market, this situation of supply and demand would have resulted in a wage rate of W_c and employment level of Q_c. However, since the firm in this case faces the upward-sloping supply curve, S_L, the MRC_L curve lies above that supply curve, as shown in Figure 7. To see why this is the case, refer to Table 3. The supply curve is, of course, the graph of the values in the first and second columns of

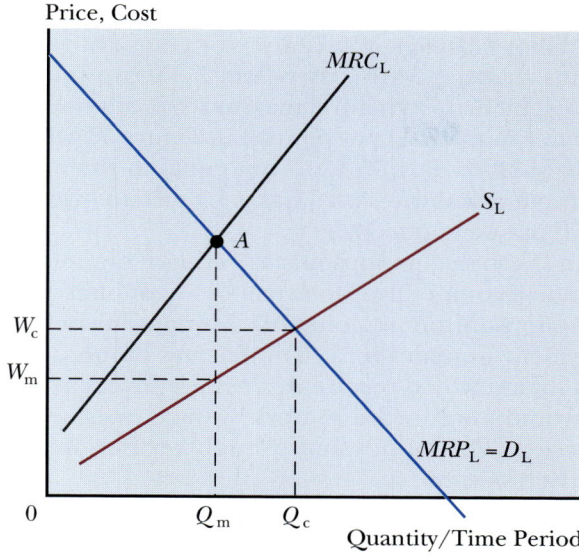

FIGURE 7
MONOPSONY
The monopsonist faces the market supply curve for labor (S_L). Since this curve has a positive slope, the marginal resource cost (MRC_L) curve lies above it. The monopsonist thus hires Q_m units of labor at a wage rate of W_m.

the table. Since the curve is upward sloping, the firm must pay a higher wage rate as it hires more labor. This result is different from that for a firm hiring in a competitive labor market. The total wage costs go up with additional workers in monopsony for two reasons. First, the wage must rise to attract more labor. Second, wage costs rise because all the other workers receive a higher wage as the firm hires more workers.

TABLE 3
THE DEMAND FOR LABOR IN A MONOPSONY

UNITS OF LABOR	WAGE RATE	WAGE COST	MARGINAL RESOURCE COST OF LABOR (MRC_L)
0		$ 0	
			$ 5
1	$ 5	5	
			7
2	6	12	
			9
3	7	21	
			11
4	8	32	
			13
5	9	45	
			15
6	10	60	
			17
7	11	77	
			19
8	12	96	
			21
9	13	117	
			23
10	14	140	

The amount that each additional worker adds to total wage cost is the marginal resource cost of labor (MRC_L). You can see by comparing the second and fourth columns that the MRC_L curve will lie above the S_L curve, as shown in Figure 7. The firm, as before, maximizes profits where $MRP_L = MRC_L$. Profit maximization occurs at point A in Figure 7, where the firm employs Q_m units of labor. But MRC_L is not equal to the wage rate. Remember, the supply curve indicates what has to be paid to hire Q_m units of labor. The firm will pay wage rate W_m.

Note that W_m is less than W_c, so the monopsonist is paying a lower wage than would have been paid in a competitive labor market. Economists refer to this situation as monopsonistic exploitation. **Monopsonistic exploitation** is the underpayment of wages by a firm that has monopsony power. Labor receives less than it would receive in a competitive market. This does not mean that workers are forced to work at wage rates below what they are willing to accept. The monopsonist simply restricts input, just as the monopolist restricts output.

monopsonistic exploitation
The difference in wages paid by a firm that has monopsony power, compared to what would be paid in a competitive market.

MONOPSONY IN THE REAL WORLD

Are there any real-world examples of pure monopsony in a labor market? No, because all labor has some other possible employment. Pure monopsony, like pure monopoly, is a theoretical extreme. There are, however, real-world examples of some degree of monopsony power. You may have heard the song about the miner who "owes his soul to the company store." This song was written about mining companies when they dominated the labor market as the major employer in certain areas. Company towns—small towns with only one major employer—were common in the early twentieth century. An example was Pullman, Illinois, where railroad sleeping cars were manufactured. A large college or university in a small town provides a more current example of monopsony power in a labor market. If you compared secretarial salaries at similar-sized schools in cities of varying size, you would find that where the college or university dominates the labor market, the salaries are lower. This lower pay may in part be due to monopsony power.

Perhaps the best example of monopsony in a labor market in the U.S. economy comes from professional sports. Congress has made sports leagues exempt from the federal antitrust laws. This exemption allows the leagues to hire as monopsonists by drafting players and maintaining control through reserve clauses.[1] Players are not free to quit one team and go to work for another unless they become a free agent. As a result, wage rates for professional athletes are lower than they would be if the teams competed for players on an open market. An early study of the economics of baseball by Gerald Scully found empirical evidence of monopsonistic exploitation in that sport.[2] Scully found that the typical MRP_L for star pitch-

---

1. Reserve clauses have been and are being challenged. Players can now lay out their options, thus reducing the monopsony power of the owners.
2. Gerald W. Scully, "Pay and Performance in Major League Baseball," *American Economic Review* (December 1974): 915–930. Thomas H. Bruggink and David R. Rose, Jr. calculated the MRP_L of 103 major league baseball players and compared them to their salaries: "Financial Restraint in the Free Agent Labor Market for Major League Baseball: Players Look at Strike Three," *Southern Economic Journal* (April 1990): 1029–1043.

ers in 1969 was $405,300, but the typical salary was only $66,800. Think about basketball player Michael Jordan. He receives a very high salary, but consider what he adds to his team's (and the league's) marginal revenue. He fills up the arena for practically every game he plays. His salary is surely less than his MRP_L.[3]

The formation of the United States Football League (USFL) in the early 1980s had a profound effect on salaries in professional football. The new league introduced competition for players and the effect was startling. Rookie salaries in 1983 jumped an average of 52 percent over 1982 salaries. Many of football's general managers called this trend an "economic disaster" and blamed it on players, agents, and other teams. If they had studied economics, they would have realized it was due to the breakdown of monopsony power. When the USFL folded, the upward pressure on football salaries declined.

Except for such special cases, where buyers are purchasing very specialized labor skills, there are few instances of real monopsony power. In general, improved transportation and communication in the United States have increased labor's mobility. With increased labor mobility, there is less monopsony power. If miners are aware of job possibilities in other areas and in other occupations, the mine will be forced to pay a competitive wage. Indeed, if even a small percentage of miners are willing to pull up stakes, the mine will be forced to pay competitive wages. Complete mobility of labor isn't necessary to reduce monopsony power. It's enough to have mobility at the margin.

MONOPSONY POWER AND MINIMUM WAGES

The minimum wage is a price floor set above the market-clearing price and, thus, generally causes a surplus of labor, or unemployment. However, if there is no monopsony power, a minimum wage can cause employment to increase. In Figure 8, the monopsonist would employ Q_m units of labor at wage rate W_m. Now suppose a minimum wage of W_1 is imposed. Part of the market supply curve is replaced by a horizontal line at W_1, the imposed minimum wage. In effect, the monopsonist is forced to accept the minimum wage. The market supply curve is now represented by the line W_1AC. The marginal resource cost labor curve is now W_1A, because the supply curve is perfectly elastic in the range W_1A. At a wage rate of W_1, Q_1 units of labor would be employed. If the minimum wage imposed is W_2 instead of W_1, the supply curve the firm faces is W_2BC. The firm will face perfectly elastic supply and MRC_L curves in the range W_2B. In this case, the firm will employ Q_m units of labor at wage rate W_2. You can see that if the minimum wage that is imposed lies between W_m and W_2, more employment at a higher wage rate will result.

What we have just considered is an exception to the usual case where minimum wages result in unemployment. Be careful, though. This result

---

3. *Sports Illustrated* reported that the Milwaukee Bucks realized an additional $700,000 profit during Kareem Abdul-Jabbar's first season. His salary was $250,000. So, for Abdul-Jabbar's team, $MRP_L > MRC_L$. Although salary figures are not available for Michael Jordan's 1986–1987 year with the Chicago Bulls, *Sports Illustrated* reported in December 1987 that Jordan brought in 276,996 more fans than had attended the previous season. At the average ticket price of $13.14, that represented $3.71 million in marginal revenue.

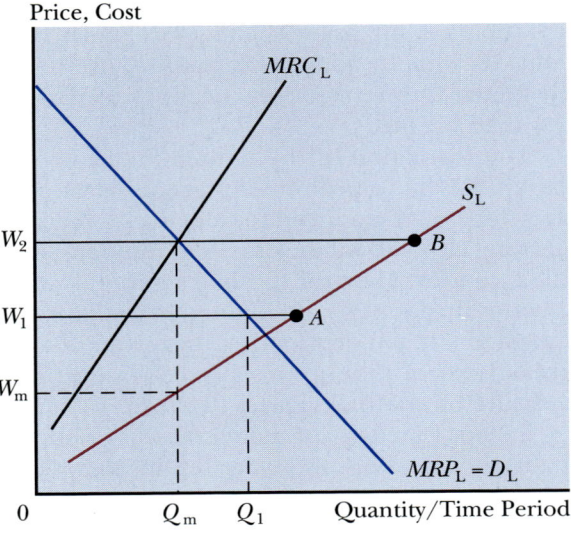

**FIGURE 8
MONOPSONY POWER AND
MINIMUM WAGES**
A minimum wage of W_2 in a monopsonistic labor market changes the market supply curve from S_L to $W_2 B$ and the part of S_L above B. The marginal resource cost curve is the same as $W_2 B$, the perfectly elastic portion of the supply curve.

only occurs when there is monopsony power in the labor market. A monopsony is relatively uncommon except in certain labor markets for specialized skills, such as the market for professional basketball players. Most empirical studies of the effects of minimum wages show that the monopsony exception to the negative effects of a minimum wage on employment is not very common.[4]

DETERMINANTS OF THE ELASTICITY OF THE DEMAND FOR LABOR

At the beginning of this chapter, you learned that the demand for labor has three features making it somewhat different from the demand for a product. These features also influence the elasticity of the demand for labor, because they determine how the quantity of labor demanded will respond to changes in the wage rate. In other words, the demand for labor has a price elasticity just as the demand for products does. This elasticity is influenced by the distinguishing features of the demand for labor.

ELASTICITY OF THE DEMAND FOR THE PRODUCT
If the wage rate falls for all of the firms in the product market, the cost of producing the product will also fall. There will, as a result, be a decline in the selling price of the product. As the price of the product declines, consumers will increase their consumption of the product. The price elasticity of the demand for a product determines how much more of the product consumers will purchase in response to a decline in its price. Thus, the price elasticity of the demand for the product affects the price elasticity of the demand for labor. If the product demand is elastic, the firm

---

4. For a review of these empirical studies, see Jack Hirshleifer, *Price Theory and Applications*, 4th ed. (Englewood Cliffs, NJ: Prentice-Hall, 1988), 336–340.

Chapter 13 Marginal Productivity Theory and Labor Markets

will hire more labor in order to increase production to respond to the increased quantity demanded by consumers. The larger the increase in quantity demanded of the product, the larger the increase in quantity demanded of labor will be. As a result, labor demand is more elastic when the demand for the final product is more elastic.

SHARE OF LABOR IN FACTOR COSTS

The second element that affects the elasticity of demand for labor is a bit more complex. First, assume that only labor is used to produce the product. Labor costs are 100 percent of product cost. If the price of labor falls 10 percent, the cost of production falls 10 percent, and price (in perfect competition) falls 10 percent. Now, more realistically, let labor costs constitute only 50 percent of product cost. Then if the price of labor falls 10 percent, the cost of production would fall only 5 percent. In other words, the larger the share of labor cost in total production cost of a product, the more a change in the wage rate will affect the cost of production and the price of the product. As a result, the larger the share of the total cost of production that wages represent, the greater the elasticity of demand for labor will be.

OPPORTUNITIES FOR FACTOR SUBSTITUTION

In actual production, a great deal of substitution among the factors of production is possible. We discussed this factor substitution in detail in the chapter on production. The choice of which combination of factors of production to use depends, as you learned earlier, on the prices of those factors. As the price of labor increases, entrepreneurs will substitute capital and land for labor to the extent that such substitution is feasible in the production function. Substitution can occur for all the factors of production. Perhaps it is most visible in the substitution that takes place among land, labor, and capital in urban versus rural areas. In urban areas, where land is expensive, labor and capital are substituted for land. High-rise structures, which use much more labor and capital, are built. In rural areas, low-rise office buildings and housing units are constructed. They use far less labor and capital than the high-rise structures of the central city.

Consider what happens when the wage rate falls. To the extent that labor can be substituted for other factors of production, more labor will be hired. The greater the degree of substitutability in production, the greater will be the price elasticity of the demand for labor.

SHIFTS IN THE DEMAND FOR LABOR

The demand curve for labor, like the demand curve for products, can shift in response to changes in underlying conditions. Two of the most important causes of such shifts are changes in demand for the product and changes in the employment of the other factors of production.

CHANGES IN THE DEMAND FOR THE PRODUCT

The demand for labor is derived from the demand for the product it is used to produce. To see this more clearly, look again at Table 1 and Table

2, which show the situations for a competitive and a monopolistic firm, respectively. Suppose there is an increase in demand in the product market. The market demand curve will shift to the right. This shift will cause the product price to increase for the competitive firm, because the value of the marginal product of labor will be larger at all levels of production. That is, the values of MRP_L in Table 1 will increase in proportion to the increase in product price. In most cases, an increase in product demand will also increase the monopolist's values of MRP_L compared to those given in Table 2.[5] The MRP_L curve shifts outward for either kind of firm, representing an increase in the demand for labor.

In a competitive labor market, each kind of firm will want to hire more labor at the existing wage rate. The market demand for labor could increase, raising both the level of employment and the wage rate. The amount by which the market wage increases will depend on how large the industry is relative to the labor market. If the industry is small, there may be only a very slight increase in wages. If it is large, however, the wage rate could rise significantly. Even in a monopsonistic labor market, the result will be an increase in wages and employment.[6]

EFFECT OF CHANGES IN OTHER INPUTS

A second important cause of shifts in the demand for labor results from the fact that the demands for different factors of production are mutually interdependent. Refer again to Table 1 and Table 2. Suppose the capital stock of the firm is doubled. If labor and capital used together are complementary in the sense that an increase in capital makes labor more productive, each unit of labor will have a larger physical product. This is a fairly general phenomenon. Consider an example. Suppose there is a great blizzard of 1993 and you and your friends have a few days off because your school has been closed. Four of you decide to make some extra cash by pulling stranded vehicles out of snowdrifts. It turns out that the effort is profitable enough that instead of relying on your jeep and a chain, your group invests the profits in a tow truck. When it snows the next time, how do you think your physical product will compare to the first experience?

If the capital stock is increased, the total physical product in Table 1 and Table 2 will increase. As a result, the values of MPP_L will increase and the values of MRP_L will also increase. The MRP_L curve will shift outward, signifying that the demand for labor has increased. This is what is meant by complementarity: an increase in usage of one factor raises the marginal revenue product of the other.

Increased productivity resulting from an increased capital stock can have several effects. Consider what happens if the capital stock expands in one firm but not the whole industry. The firm's demand curve (MRP_L) would shift to the right in Figures 4 and 6 without any (noticeable) effect on the market demand curve, because the firm is very small relative to the industry. The result would be that the firm would employ more units of labor at the market-determined price.

---

5. It is possible to think of cases in which the demand facing the monopolist increases at every price, but marginal revenue, and thus marginal product, actually falls so the demand for labor falls.
6. You should work through the geometry of such increases.

On the other hand, consider the effect of an industrywide increase in the capital stock. All firms in the industry have an increase in capital, causing their individual MRP_L curves and the industry MRP_L curve to shift outward. More labor is employed at a higher wage rate. Such a situation is depicted in Figure 9. The initial equilibrium occurs where the firm employs x_1 units of labor at the market wage of W_1. The industry is employing Q_1 units of labor. Now there is an industrywide increase in capital. The firm's MRP_L curve shifts to MRP'_L. Since all the firms in the industry experience this increase in MRP_L, the industry demand curve for labor will also shift, from D_L to D'_L in Figure 9. The market wage rises to W_2. As a result, the horizontal supply curve that the individual firm faces shifts from S_f to S'_f. The firm will now employ x_2 units of labor at wage rate W_2. Industry employment has risen from Q_1 to Q_2. The response of the firm to an increase in its capital stock was to hire more workers at higher wages because the increase in capital increased the marginal productivity of the workers. The demand for the two factors labor and capital can thus be seen to be interdependent.

Some U.S. manufacturing industries have hired more workers because of increases in the capital stock in recent years. The textile industry is a good example. The technology of weaving cloth has changed dramatically from shuttle looms to air jet and water jet shuttleless looms. Investment in this new technology has greatly increased the physical productivity of workers in the weaving sector of the textile industry.

PRODUCTIVITY AND HUMAN CAPITAL

In this chapter, we have applied marginal productivity theory to labor markets. We have shown that labor becomes more productive and wages rise when the labor is used with more capital. The notion of capital is, however,

FIGURE 9
AN INDUSTRYWIDE INCREASE IN CAPITAL
An increase in the capital stock will increase the productivity of labor if capital and labor are complementary factors. This increase in productivity will shift the marginal revenue product curve from MRP_L to MRP'_L and the market demand curve for labor from D_L to D'_L.

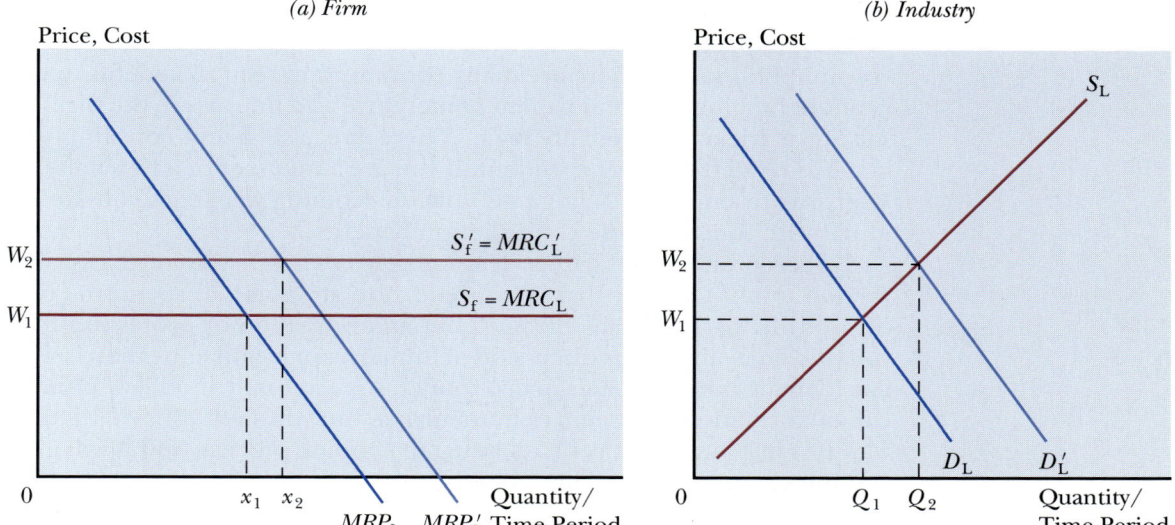

broader than simply physical tools. Capital is anything used to increase the flow of output. For example, economists define human capital as anything such as health, vigor, education, or training that (1) can be enhanced by "investment" and (2) increases the productivity of the individual.

Just as a firm can increase its investment in physical capital, an individual can invest in human capital. An individual's decision to seek additional education is similar to an entrepreneur's decision to purchase a new piece of equipment. In both cases, the investment is productive if the return (properly discounted) exceeds the cost (properly discounted).

HIGHER EDUCATION AS AN INVESTMENT

Your decision to pursue higher education is a form of investment. The costs are the direct costs (tuition, fees, books, and so on) plus the opportunity costs, primarily lost income (which you could earn instead of going to college). The return is the present value of the increased future earnings caused by the investment in education.

The anticipated future wage rate will have a profound impact on the type and amount of education that is pursued. For example, if wages of accountants rise relative to those of engineers, economists would expect more students to study accounting. Wages in professions that require long periods of study will have to be higher to attract new entrants, for three reasons. First, those in school for long periods of time (like medical doctors) incur greater current costs. Second, they sacrifice a great deal of present income. Third, their future income is a longer way off. As you know, income a long way into the future is worth a great deal less than income now. As we discussed in an earlier chapter, incomes of medical doctors have stopped rising as rapidly as they did decades ago. As a result of these declining (relative) incomes, applications to medical schools declined sharply in the 1980s.

This analysis does not deny that people attend universities and colleges for other reasons besides the return to investment in human capital. Some engage in education for its consumption value. For example, retired people returning to school are not investing in human capital, because their productive years have ended. Instead, they are acquiring education for its consumption value. There are many consumption-related benefits to education, ranging from enjoyment of literature and fine arts to the thrill of solving a tricky problem in logic. There are also many consumption benefits related to being a student. If you are a member of a fraternity or a sorority or enjoy the "big game" or homecoming weekend, you are familiar with some of these consumption benefits.

Not everyone makes career decisions on a strictly economic basis, and we don't want to imply that you should. You are going to spend the rest of your life working. Why not pick out an occupation or profession that you find enjoyable? This discussion of human capital and education is similar to many policy debates in economics. An economic model of human capital formation may seem dehumanizing, but you shouldn't view it that way. It is just another way of analyzing a complex process, and it will give you important insights. These insights can help explain why workers enjoy different income levels or why two workers in the same occupation working for the same firm may receive different salaries. Let's explore some of these insights.

HUMAN CAPITAL AND RACE

The idea that differences in human capital result in differences in wage rates is related to the issue of racial (or sexual) discrimination. The important economic question is how much of the income difference between whites and blacks in the United States is the result of discrimination and how much is a market phenomenon—the result of differences in human capital.

Many economists have examined income differences between blacks and whites from a human capital perspective. In 1955, Morton Zeman's doctoral dissertation at the University of Chicago began the debate over the cause of such differences.[7] Zeman examined the effects of schooling and on-the-job training, two elements of human capital formation, on income differences. He reported that increases in schooling and training increased the incomes of both whites and blacks, but increased the earnings of whites more. In other words, the rate of return to this investment in human capital appeared to be higher for whites. Zeman's work implied that the income differences were the result of different pay for the same skill (that is, discrimination) and that increasing the schooling of blacks would do little to change these differences.

As more data became available in the 1960s, Zeman's result appeared to be confirmed. Blacks gained access to more schooling, yet income differences seemed to become more pronounced. In 1974, Finis Welch found support for a human capital explanation of the income differences.[8] Welch showed, using newly available and more extensive data, that rates of return to education were in fact as high for blacks as for whites.

James P. Smith of the Rand Corporation studied the effects of race on human capital formation using historical records.[9] Smith found that the increase in black education after the Civil War had important implications for income differences. This human capital approach also helped to explain the differences between the findings of Welch and those of other researchers. Before the Civil War, every Southern state had laws prohibiting the schooling of slaves. As a result, 95 percent of all black Southerners were illiterate in 1860. At the end of the Civil War, the difference in average schooling of blacks and whites was enormous. Smith reported that whites of either sex (on the average) finished four to five more years of schooling than blacks did. In the first two decades after the war, blacks began to close this gap. In the next two decades (1886 to 1906), however, black schooling made little progress, and human capital formation of whites outstripped that of blacks. This difference was the result of two factors: the disenfranchisement of blacks in the South and the increase in the number of whites in the North who finished high school. Finally,

---

7. Morton Zeman, "A Comparative Analysis of White and Non-White Income Differentials" (unpublished dissertation, University of Chicago, September, 1955).
8. Finis Welch, "Education and Racial Discrimination," in Orley Ashenfelter and Albert Rees (eds.), *Discrimination in Labor Markets* (Princeton: Princeton University Press, 1974).
9. James P. Smith, "Race and Human Capital," *American Economic Review* (September 1984): 865–898.

Smith found that the differences in education between blacks and whites continually narrowed from 1906 to 1950.

Smith concluded that education, or human capital formation, profoundly affects race-related income differences, but with a great lag. Smith shows that interruptions in the progress of black schooling in the early 1900s are still influencing the income difference. The lesson of this research is that the key to further narrowing the income gap between the races (or sexes) will depend in large part on the availability of education and on-the-job training. It further shows that such changes are slow and evolutionary.

COMPARABLE WORTH

A public policy area in which issues of perceived labor market inequities and human capital are important is the debate concerning comparable worth. **Comparable worth** is a standard for determining wages on the basis of equal pay for jobs that require similar levels of training, responsibility, skills, and so on. Support for such a standard is a response to the fact that women earn an average of about 67 percent of what men earn and are heavily concentrated in nursing, teaching, retail sales, and secretarial and clerical jobs. The comparable worth standard is criticized heavily by many economists and is also politically controversial.

> **comparable worth**
> A standard for determining wages that calls for equal pay for jobs that require similar levels of training, responsibility, and skills.

THE PROS AND CONS OF COMPARABLE WORTH

Advocates of using comparable worth to adjust wages argue that the Equal Pay Act of 1963 and the Civil Rights Act of 1964, which require equal pay for equal work, do not go far enough. They claim that these laws are inadequate because average female pay is only about 67 percent of average male pay. Comparable worth advocates argue that there should be equal pay for jobs requiring similar levels of training, responsibility, and abilities.

The argument for comparable worth is based on two observations: the existence of sex discrimination and monopsony power in labor markets. If employers practice discrimination on the basis of race or sex and federal laws prohibit discrimination in pay in the same job category, then an indirect way to perpetuate discrimination is to separate jobs into categories. These categories would be predominately black or white, or male or female, and different wages would be offered for jobs with similar skills and responsibilities. Since competition would undermine such subtle discrimination, it could only persist if there is monopsony power in the labor market.

The chief difficulty with comparable worth as a way of determining wages is that it substitutes bureaucratic judgments about job classifications for the forces of the marketplace. Shifts in supply and demand for products and services, subtle differences in skills, varying attractiveness of occupations, and other market determinants of wages are difficult to identify and can change more rapidly than a bureaucratic system could handle.

Peter F. Orazem and J. Peter Mattila highlight some problems of setting wages according to any comparable worth scheme. The fundamental problem is that the valuation of different jobs is subjective. Equally in-

International Perspective

Comparable Worth, Canadian Style

In the United States, comparable worth legislation has been limited to public sector employment. In Canada, a recent law extends comparable worth adjustments into the private sector. This legislation could have an indirect impact on firms in the United States since many Canadian firms affected by the law are subsidiaries of U.S. firms.

The law was passed in the Province of Ontario in 1987 and went into effect January 1, 1990. In the first phase, every firm that employs more than 500 people must publish the results of a comparable worth study for the firm and solicit comments from employees. The pay-equity plan must reflect employees' comments and criticisms.

The law did not specify how the pay-equity plans were to be developed, but it did offer suggestions. It suggested that each job be allocated points on a scale of 1 to 100. The points should be based on the job's requirements, such as education, experience, physical exertion, mental exertion, money handling, personnel supervision, type of equipment operated, physical environment, stress, and working conditions. Employers should then identify any job classification in which more than 60 percent of the workers are female. The wages in these job classifications must then be compared to wages in male-dominated classifications with the same score. For example, if the secretarial job classification has a score of 50, the employer must compare wages in that classification with the wages for a male-dominated classification with a score of 50. If the male-dominated classification has a higher average wage than that of the female-dominated classification with the same score, the firm must raise the pay of the female-dominated group.

An interesting twist is that if the male-dominated classification is paid less than the female-dominated classification with the same score, the law says that the wages of the female-dominated group cannot be cut, *and* employers are not required to raise the pay of the male-dominated group. In essence, this plan is not comparable worth, but pay adjustment for females.

The preliminary results of this law are starting to unfold. The Canadian headquarters of Campbell Soup Co. may have to raise the average salaries of secretaries by $3 per hour to make them comparable to earnings of janitors. This adjustment may, however, take some time. The law does not require firms to increase their payroll cost by more than 1 percent per year to meet these goals.

Some U.S. advocates of comparable worth think that the Canadian law may give women leverage in U.S. lawsuits. They believe that if discrimination is identified by the subsidiary of a U.S. corporation in Canada, that fact could be used as evidence in a sex discrimination case against the parent company in the United States.

Source: Frank Swoboda, "How Many Secretaries Are Worth One Janitor?" *The Washington Post National Weekly Edition* (26 November 1989): 21.

formed, unbiased, and qualified analysts can come up with very different results. Orazem and Mattila found that the potential gains for female state employees in Iowa under a proposed scheme were greatly modified by interest groups in the bureaucratic setting. Gains were shifted away from women and toward special interest groups. "Through a series of modifications to the plan and through collective bargaining compromises, other interest groups such as unions, supervisors, and professionals were able to avoid potential losses in pay that would have accrued under the original plan. Indeed, these groups ended up with pay raises."[10]

HUMAN CAPITAL AGAIN

Discrimination is not the only explanation of male-female wage differences. Some observers claim that women bring less human capital to the market. Less human capital could be the result of less education and on-the-job training or the result of lower strength, vigor, dependability, and health of women in general. Historically, females have invested less in education and training than have males. As a result, the average market value of their skills is lower. However, like the educational gap between whites and blacks, the gap between male and female education levels is closing. Over the past thirty years, women have been enrolling in colleges and completing degrees at rates approaching those of men. The economics of this trend is simple. As human capital equalizes, wage differences between men and women should decline. We will explore this issue further in the chapter on income distribution.

MARGINAL PRODUCTIVITY AND INCOME

The analysis in this chapter leads to an important conclusion of marginal productivity theory. In a competitive labor market, the interaction of the value of the marginal product of labor and the supply of labor determines the wage rate. In turn, the productivity of labor depends on the inherent qualities of the labor, the quantity of labor employed, and the amounts of the other factors that are used. This is another way of saying that the distribution of income is determined by the relative marginal revenue products of the different factors of production. Since wages make up the incomes of laborers, more productive workers will have higher incomes. Laborers that are less productive will have lower incomes.

John Bates Clark, the creator of this theory, claimed that it presented a "morally correct" outcome of economic activity. Morality is not the province of economic theory, however. Economic theory is positive. The marginal productivity theory says nothing about whether the income distribution that results is a good one. Rather, the theory indicates that if labor markets are competitive, each worker will receive returns based on individual productivity. If people don't like the outcome, they can work to change it through political action (a topic that will be discussed in a later chapter). The theory also indicates that output will be maximized in societies in which labor is paid according to its marginal productivity.

10. Peter F. Orazem and J. Peter Mattila, "The Implementation Process of Comparable Worth: Winners and Losers," *Journal of Political Economy* (February 1990): 43.

Chapter 13 Marginal Productivity Theory and Labor Markets

SUMMARY

1. A firm is a supplier in the product market and a demander in the factor market.
2. The demand for labor differs from the demand for a product in that it is derived, interdependent, and technologically determined.
3. A firm demands labor because labor is productive. The marginal revenue product of labor (MRP_L) curve is the firm's demand curve for labor.
4. In a competitive labor market, the firm faces a perfectly elastic labor supply curve (S_L). When the labor supply curve is perfectly elastic, the marginal resource cost of labor (MRC_L) curve is the same as the labor supply curve.
5. A firm that is a monopolist in a product market uses less labor than a competitive firm would use, because the firm restricts inputs in the process of restricting output.
6. A monopsony is a market structure in which there is a single purchaser of a factor of production. Monopsony results in fewer units of labor being purchased at less than the perfectly competitive wage, because the marginal resource cost curve lies above the supply curve. The difference between the monopsonistic wage and the competitive wage is monopsonistic exploitation. Improved market information and mobility of workers greatly reduce monopsony power.
7. The elasticity of demand for labor is greater when the price elasticity of demand of the product it is used to produce is greater, when labor is an important share of the cost structure of the product, and when the opportunity for factor substitution is present.
8. The decision to pursue more education can be viewed as an investment decision that adds to one's stock of human capital. As education rates of blacks and whites converge, the human capital argument predicts that income levels will also converge.
9. The comparable worth movement calls for equal pay for jobs of equal worth.
10. Marginal productivity theory explains how the distribution of labor income in a market economy is determined. It says nothing normative about the morality of this distribution.

NEW TERMS

derived demand
interdependent demand
technologically determined demand
marginal productivity theory
value of the marginal product of labor (VMP_L)
backward-bending supply curve
marginal revenue product of labor (MRP_L)
marginal resource cost of labor (MRC_L)
monopsony
monopsonistic exploitation
comparable worth

QUESTIONS FOR DISCUSSION

1. Can you describe a situation that might involve monopsonistic exploitation? What would you recommend as a correction?
2. The demand for accountants has skyrocketed in recent years and the salaries of accountants have increased significantly. Is the demand for accountants a derived demand? If so, from what?
3. Why are professional athletes opposed to reserve clauses?
4. Discuss your decision to attend college in human capital terms. Include your opportunity costs and projected income. Will continued investment be required to keep your human capital from depreciating?
5. How could the potential of career interruptions have an impact on starting salaries and create a difference between women's and men's earnings?
6. Firms operate in both the factor market and the product market. How does the market structure in the

product market affect the market structure in the factor market? In other words, is a monopolist always a monopsonist, or vice versa?

7. Describe how an entrepreneur decides how much labor to employ.

8. How is a change in the quantity of labor demanded different from a change in the demand for labor?

9. Does the fact that undergraduate students with high grade-point averages are recruited by "Big Eight" accounting firms have any impact on the supply of accounting professors?

10. How can the elasticity of demand for the product that labor is producing affect the elasticity of demand for that labor?

11. Do you think minimum wage legislation is a good idea? Why or why not?

12. Why might janitors earn higher wages than secretaries, even though the secretaries could do the janitors' job, but the janitors could not do the secretaries'?

13. How is equilibrium in the factor market different for a competitive firm and a monopsonistic firm? How are they the same?

14. Name three factors that could cause a firm's demand for labor to increase. How would such a shift affect the relative wages of the firm's employees?

15. What if the factors that caused the increase in demand in Question 14 affected the whole industry and not just the specific firm?

SUGGESTIONS FOR FURTHER READING

Bergmann, Barbara R. *The Economic Emergence of Women.* New York: Basic Books, 1986. An argument for comparable worth made by an economist who chaired the Committee on the Status of Women in the Economics Profession of the American Economics Association for a number of years.

Hill, John K., and James E. Pearce. "The Incidence of Sanctions against Employers of Illegal Aliens," *Journal of Political Economy* (February 1990): 28-44. A well-written analysis of the effects of U.S. Immigration Bill of 1986, restricting illegal immigration.

Leftwich, Richard H., and Ross Eckert. *The Price System and Resource Allocation,* 10th ed. Homewood, IL: Dryden Press, 1988. Chapters 15 and 16 provide a standard treatment of factor markets at the intermediate level.

AFTER STUDYING THIS CHAPTER, YOU SHOULD BE ABLE TO:

1. List the economic goals of unions and the ways they can be achieved.
2. Define:
   a. exclusive union,
   b. inclusive union,
   c. featherbedding,
   d. bilateral monopoly,
   e. yellow-dog contract,
   f. secondary boycott,
   g. closed shop,
   h. union shop,
   i. right-to-work laws,
   j. mediation,
   k. arbitration.
3. Discuss the effects of unions on wages and productivity.
4. Diagram and analyze the economic effects of:
   a. an exclusive union,
   b. an inclusive union,
   c. a bilateral monopoly.
5. Trace the history of the labor movement.
6. List the economic factors that strengthen and weaken unions.

CHAPTER 14

THE LABOR MOVEMENT IN THE UNITED STATES

INTRODUCTION

Having looked at labor markets in theory, we can now examine the effect that unions have on those markets. Unions in many countries have goals that are social and political as well as economic. However, for the most part, unions in the United States have concentrated on economic goals such as higher salaries, job security, and good pensions. The most important goal has been to raise wages, so we will concentrate on the effects unions have had on the wage rate. We will begin with a theoretical look at determining how unions attempt to raise wages. We will then consider empirical evidence of the success of unions in raising wages and discuss at whose expense these increased wages have come. Finally, we will take a look at the history of the labor movement in the United States and examine some recent trends.

THE ECONOMICS OF UNION GOALS

Labor unions have been formed for all sorts of reasons, many of which are social and political. However, the most successful labor unions in the United States have concentrated on economic goals. When we speak of economic goals, the bottom line is the real income of union members. It is largely correct, though oversimplified, to think of unions as existing to increase the wages of their members. Unions do pursue goals other than increasing wages, such as shorter hours and better working conditions. These goals also have the effect, *ceteris paribus*, of increasing the well-being of union workers. If wages are unchanged and working conditions have improved, the worker has received an increase in real income. In order to increase wage rates in a competitive labor market, such as those shown in Figures 1 and 2, the union must do one of two things. It must either increase the demand for labor (from D_L to D'_L in Figure 1) or decrease the supply of labor (from S_L to S_u in Figure 2).

Increasing the demand for labor is very difficult for a union. In Figure 1, the demand curve for labor depends on both the demand for the product the labor produces and the productivity of the labor. One way for the union to increase the demand for labor is by increasing the demand for the product the firm produces. Unions have advertised in an attempt to influence people to "buy union-made." They have also lobbied to decrease imports through tariffs and quotas, in an attempt to increase the demand for domestically produced (union) products. Unions have encouraged educational training programs aimed at increasing productivity and thus increasing the demand for labor. Unions have also tried to persuade the government to help by buying union-made goods and by using macroeconomic policy to increase the demand for such goods. In some instances, unions could keep demand from falling by preventing jobs from being eliminated in declining or dying industries. All things considered, however, it is very difficult for unions to significantly increase the demand for labor.

featherbedding
The maintenance of jobs that management claims are unnecessary or redundant.

One way to maintain jobs is the practice of **featherbedding**, or keeping jobs that management claims are unnecessary or redundant. The classic example of featherbedding concerns railroad firemen. The advent of diesel and electric power made firemen obsolete, but railroad unions were successful in maintaining the job. Featherbedding is also common in the newspaper industry, where typesetters' unions have forced the hand setting of some layouts that could be prepared by computer. In the

FIGURE 1
EFFECT OF INCREASED DEMAND FOR LABOR
One way in which a union can raise its members' wages above competitive levels is to increase the demand for union labor. An increase in demand from D_L to D'_L would increase wages from P_c to P_u. This increase in demand would cause employment to increase.

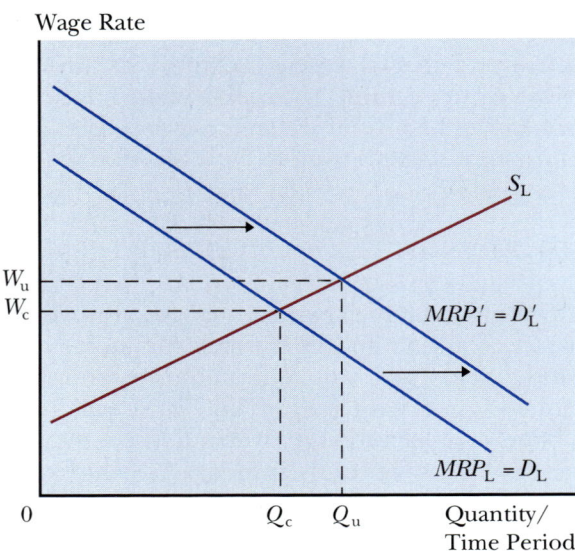

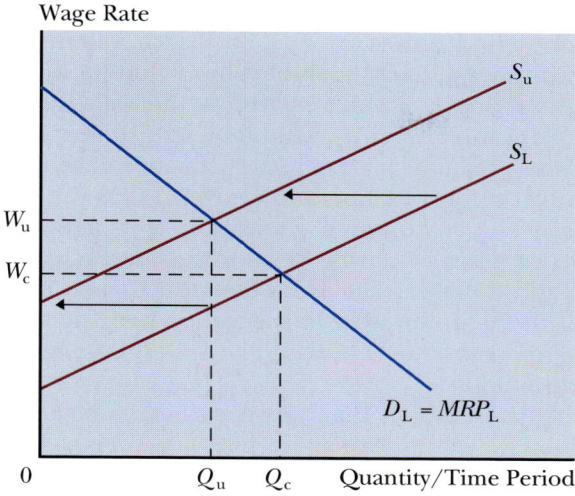

**FIGURE 2
EFFECT OF DECREASED SUPPLY OF LABOR**
Another way in which a union can raise its members' wages above competitive levels is to decrease the supply of labor. A decrease in the labor supply from S_L to S_u will cause wages to rise from W_c to W_u. This decrease in supply causes employment to decrease.

theater industry, Broadway producers are required to use a certain number of union members regardless of need. For example, a backstage crew of four union members is required no matter what kind of show is being staged. This kind of union success may be only temporary, however, because the added costs may speed the decline of an already dying industry, and the decline of the industry ultimately weakens the union.

Because of the difficulties of increasing demand, unions often focus on the supply side of the market, attempting to shift the supply curve leftward, as illustrated in Figure 2. Historically, many of the "social" goals of unions have had the effect of restricting the supply of labor. Unions have sought to reduce immigration, limit child labor, encourage compulsory and early retirement, enforce a shorter work week, and enact minimum wage legislation. Whatever else you may think of these goals, they all make economic sense for unions if the goal is to increase the wage rate of union members.

Regardless of whether unions focus on demand (Figure 1) or supply (Figure 2), their efforts have the same effect on wages. In both cases, successful union activity will cause the wage rate to rise. The effect on employment, however, is quite different. An attempt to increase demand, as shown in Figure 1, will cause employment in the industry to rise. If, however, the union tries to decrease supply, as in Figure 2, employment in the industry will decline. Since unions are much more effective at reducing supply than at increasing demand, a key economic implication of unions is that they probably reduce employment in those industries in which they are most successful at organizing.

TYPES OF UNIONS

From a theoretical point of view, we can class unions into two basic types: exclusive and inclusive.

EXCLUSIVE UNIONS

exclusive union
A union that restricts the supply of labor and maintains a higher-than-competitive wage for its members by excluding workers from a trade or occupation. Craft unions are exclusive unions.

An **exclusive union** is a union that restricts the supply of labor and maintains a higher-than-competitive wage for its members by excluding workers from a trade or occupation. Because of this exclusion, the wage rate is higher in that part of the work force than it would be in the absence of the union. Figure 3 represents the labor market with such a union. Curve S_L represents the competitive supply of labor, and D_L represents the demand for labor. In the absence of any union organization, the wage rate would be W_c, and Q_c units of labor would be employed. The exclusive union attempts to exclude additional workers from the industry and thus shift the supply curve to S_u. If the union were to succeed in keeping new entrants out, the wage rate for union workers would be W_u, and the number of those workers hired would be Q_u.

The key, then, to an exclusive union is that it restricts entry into a job or occupation. The most familiar example of an exclusive union is a **craft union**, which is composed of specific kinds of skilled laborers, such as plumbers or carpenters. These unions very often require workers to serve apprenticeships and internships in order to become members.

craft union
A union composed of specific kinds of skilled workers, such as plumbers or carpenters.

It should be obvious that a successful exclusive union is very powerful because increases in the wage rate result directly from the exclusionary tactics. The union doesn't need to bargain, coerce, or threaten to strike. Its power to exclude competing workers is sufficient to cause the market wage to increase. The power of the exclusive union is difficult to challenge once the union has been established.

It is also difficult to exclude workers from a union. When wages rise, there will be pressure from outside workers seeking employment in these trades. This natural economic force makes it necessary for the union to be able to control licensing. Many exclusive unions owe their success to getting the government to help them by requiring a worker to earn a license or permit to be a member of the trade. If the union can gain control of this licensing function, it has an automatic way of excluding labor.

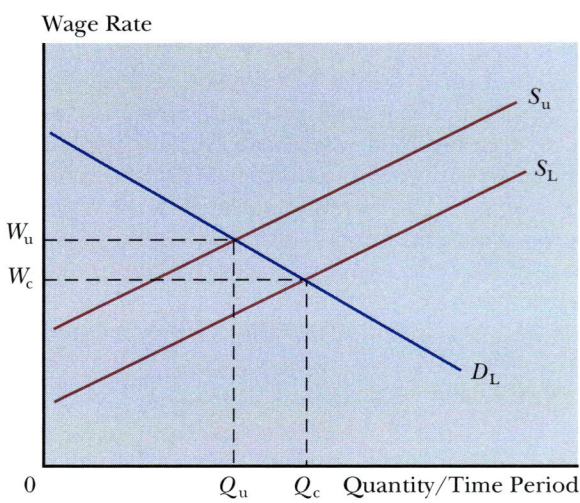

FIGURE 3
EFFECT OF AN EXCLUSIVE UNION
With an exclusive union, union membership is a precondition for employment. As a result, the union can exclude workers and decrease the supply of labor from S_L to S_u.

This is one way in which plumbers and electricians have maintained their union power. Professional associations, such as the American Medical Association or the American Bar Association, are similar to craft unions in their effects on the labor market for their members. Also, entry is restricted through licensing and control over professional schools.

INCLUSIVE UNIONS

The **inclusive union** attempts to organize all the workers in an industry and to maintain a strong bargaining position with respect to the management of firms in that industry. Inclusive unions, also referred to as **industrial unions**, include the United Steelworkers, the United Auto Workers, and the Teamsters. The goal of an inclusive union is to bring all workers in an industry into the union, resulting in a strong bargaining position. It is also important that an industrial union organize most of the firms in an industry. Otherwise, non-unionized firms will enjoy a cost advantage and be able to undersell union-organized firms. This competitive disadvantage will create an incentive for non-unionized firms to try to break the union. Inclusive union organization has been most successful in oligopolistic markets, where there are fewer firms in which the labor needs to be organized.

The labor market with an inclusive union is represented by Figure 4. The competitive wage and employment are W_c and Q_c, respectively. The union organizes the industry and bargains the wage rate, W_u. The bargained rate W_u has the same effect as a minimum wage in this industry, so employment will be Q_u. At W_u, however, the quantity of labor supplied will be Q_s. There will be a surplus of labor. Some extra workers would like to work at the bargained wage, and they may offer their services if a strike occurs. This surplus of labor is the so-called scabs you often see on television when management is trying to break a strike by hiring non-union workers.

inclusive union
A union that attempts to organize all the workers in an industry and to maintain a strong bargaining position with respect to management.

industrial union
An inclusive union that gains power by organizing all (or a large share) of the workers in an industry.

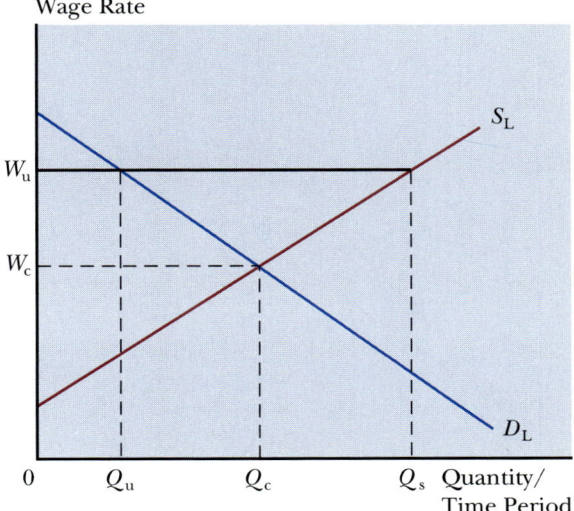

FIGURE 4
EFFECT OF AN INCLUSIVE UNION
An inclusive union attempts to organize all labor in an industry and then to bargain a wage. This bargained wage works like a price floor (or minimum wage) in this labor market.

It should be clear that the ability of an inclusive union to raise wages depends on the strength of its bargaining position, which will, of course, depend on how large a share of the employment in the particular industry is held by its members. It is important that an inclusive union have a significant membership in the industry in which it operates because its success depends on its ability to threaten the firms in that industry.

Inclusive unions have been most successful in industries that are very concentrated. The firms in these industries may possess monopsony power in labor markets, and an inclusive union can offset some of that power. **Bilateral monopolies** are market structures in which monopolies deal with each other as buyers and sellers, such as an inclusive union selling labor to a monopsonistic firm. Such bilateral monopolies may exist in the steel, auto, and farm machinery industries, where there are both big unions and big oligopolies. This situation is depicted in Figure 5. In the absence of the union, the monopsonistic firm would employ Q_f units of labor at a wage rate of W_f. The competitive wage rate and employment level would have been W_c and Q_c.

In the absence of monopsony power on the part of the purchaser, the union would want a wage of W_u because it faces a downward-sloping demand curve (D_L) for its product (labor). Since the demand curve is downward sloping, the marginal revenue curve lies below it. The union is a monopolist in the selling of its labor. The marginal revenue of the union is thus represented by MR in Figure 5. The union maximizes its gains where MR is equal to MC, at an employment level of Q_u. The result in terms of the wage rate is logically indeterminate. That is, the theoretical model will not say exactly where the resulting wage will fall. All it will say is that the wage will be between W_f and W_u. Whether it is closer to W_f or to W_u will depend on the relative bargaining strengths of the union and the monopsony firm. Note that if the wage is anywhere between W_m and W_f, unionization in a monopsonistic industry increases employment over

bilateral monopoly
Market structure in which monopolies deal with each other as buyers and sellers, such as when an inclusive union sells labor to a monopsonistic firm.

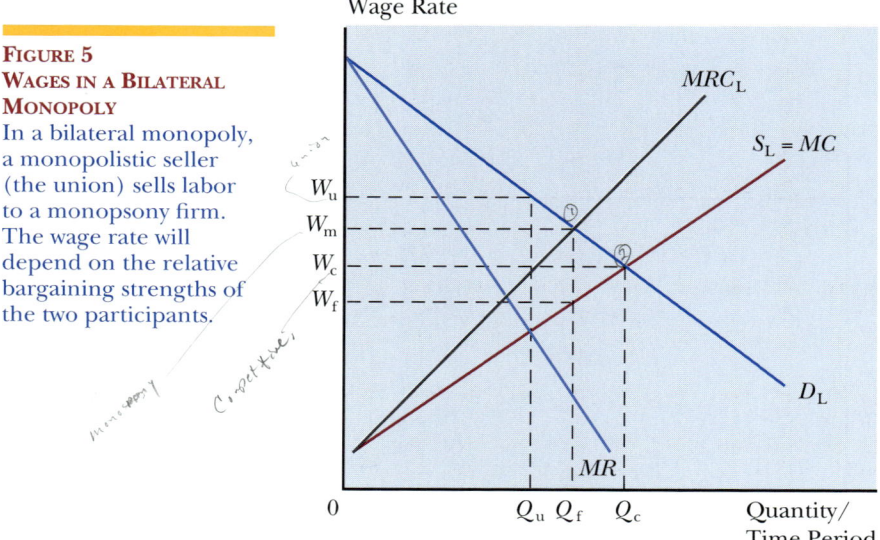

FIGURE 5
WAGES IN A BILATERAL MONOPOLY
In a bilateral monopoly, a monopolistic seller (the union) sells labor to a monopsony firm. The wage rate will depend on the relative bargaining strengths of the two participants.

the non-union level, Q_f. The monopsonist hired fewer workers than would have been the case with competition. If the union is successful in bargaining a wage rate of W_c (the competitive rate), employment will rise to Q_c. Note that this result is very similar to the effect of a minimum wage in a monopsonistic labor market, which was discussed in the last chapter.

ECONOMIC EFFECTS OF UNIONS

Much of the controversy over unions centers on their effects on wages, income distribution, productivity, stock prices, and inflation. We will examine each of these issues.

Do Unions Raise Wages?

Regardless of the power of a union, there are constraints on the degree to which it can influence wages. Competitive pressure from non-union labor and the possibility of substituting other inputs will always put limits on union demands. For example, consider a union attempting to organize migrant workers. In response to higher wages resulting from the union, the farmer may substitute machinery for labor. A second powerful restraint on unions' demands exists in the product market. If unions raise wages, costs and prices rise. Consumers will react to an increased price by shifting consumption to non-union products. The demand for union-made products, and thus for union labor, will then fall. These constraints are always present, and the union can do very little to offset them.

Given these limitations, how successful have unions been in increasing the wages of their members? The difficulty in answering this question lies in separating wage differences due to varying productivity from those based solely on union power. The path-breaking empirical study in this area was done by H. Gregg Lewis.[1] Lewis based his study on data from the 1940s and 1950s. He found that union workers received on average from 10 to 15 percent higher wages than non-union workers with similar productivity characteristics. Later studies using Lewis's techniques and more recent data indicate that union salaries are 15 to 25 percent higher for workers with similar productivity characteristics.[2] These same studies also indicate that craft unions are more successful in raising wages than industrial unions are.

In 1980, C. J. Parsley published an extensive review of empirical studies on the effects of unions on wages.[3] His survey of U.S. studies is summarized in Table 1. Parsley's review showed that wages are consistently higher in unionized sectors. The evidence seems to indicate that unions increase wages. Parsley, however, gave an important warning. He pointed out that the previous studies only showed that high wages and unioniza-

---

1. H. Gregg Lewis, *Union Relative Wage Effects: A Survey*, (Chicago: University of Chicago Press, 1986), p. 56.
2. See M. J. Boskin, "Unions and Relative Real Wages," *American Economic Review* (June 1972); and P. M. Ryscavage, "Measuring Union-Nonunion Earnings Differences," *Monthly Labor Review* (December 1974).
3. C. J. Parsley, "Labor Union Effects on Wage Gains: A Survey of Recent Literature," *Journal of Economic Literature* (October 1980).

**TABLE 1
EFFECT OF UNIONS
ON WAGES**

AUTHOR	TIME PERIOD OF DATA	INDUSTRY OR OCCUPATION	UNION/NON-UNION WAGE DIFFERENTIAL
Lewis (five studies)	1923–1958	Industrial workers	0–25%
Throop (two studies)	1950–1960	Selected industries	25–29.7%
Personick	1972	Construction	35–70%
Personick and Schwenk	1971	Shirt manufacturing	7–16%
Ashenfelter	1961–1966	Firefighters	6–16%
Schmenner	1962–1970	Public employees	12–15%
Weiss	1959	Craftsmen—operators	6–8%
Stafford	1966	Various occupations	−8–52%
Boskin	1967	Various occupations	−5.3–24.7%

Source: C. J. Parsley, "Labor Union Effects on Wage Gains: A Survey of Recent Literature," *Journal of Economic Literature* (October 1980); and H. Gregg Lewis, *Union Relative Wage Effects: A Survey, 1986* (Chicago: University of Chicago Press, 1986).

tion were correlated. A correct statistical approach would also have to show that the unionization affected wages rather than wages affecting unionization. In other words, workers may unionize after the wages are already higher. Parsley notes, however, that this argument is paradoxical if laborers join unions because they believe that unionization raises wages!

Where do union members' higher wages come from? Your first reaction may be that they come out of business profits, but can this be so? Recall the theory developed in earlier chapters. Wages are a cost of production. If markets are competitive, the increased cost of higher wages will result in higher prices because in the long run, with or without unions, the average firm will only be earning a normal profit. If the firm possesses some monopoly power, the higher labor costs might reduce monopoly profits, but part of the increased costs will be passed forward in higher prices.

In addition, in any product market structure faced by the firm, the increased costs of union-made products will cause the quantity demanded to be lower than it would have been without a union. The reduction in sales in unionized industries means a loss of jobs in those industries. As unemployed workers from unionized industries seek jobs elsewhere, wage rates will fall in the non-union sector.

This analysis implies that the higher wages of union workers are paid partly by consumers in the form of higher prices for union-made goods and partly by non-union workers in the form of lower wages. H. Gregg Lewis has also done empirical research in this area. He concluded that non-union wages are 3 to 4 percent lower because of union-increased wages in the organized labor sector.[4] There also appears to be some evidence that non-union wages are higher in some sectors because non-unionized firms raise wages as a defensive tactic to keep unions out.[5]

UNIONS, WAGES, AND PRODUCTIVITY

As you saw earlier in this chapter, if unions could raise the marginal revenue product of labor, the demand for labor would increase and wage rates would rise. Increasing the demand for labor is difficult to do. In fact,

---

4. Lewis, *Union Relative Wage Effects.*, p. 78.
5. See Barry Hirsch and John Addison, *The Economic Analysis of Unions* (Boston: Allen and Unwin, 1986).

some critics argue that unions are not only unsuccessful at raising worker productivity but, in fact, may introduce inefficiencies that decrease the marginal revenue product of labor.

Examples of these inefficiencies are well known. There are work rules requiring that certain jobs be performed by certain workers. A light bulb can't be changed by a custodian because the work rules require that the job be performed by an electrician, or a display for a convention must be unloaded by a teamster. Featherbedding, which we mentioned earlier, is another form of inefficiency. Unions can also introduce inefficiency into the production process through disruptive strikes. Strikes cause production to fall, and strikes in major industries can even cause production to be disrupted in related industries. The third way unions can introduce inefficiency is through the effects of wage increases. If unions raise wages in an industry above competitive levels, they must restrict entry into the jobs in that industry, and output is reduced.

Labor in a unionized industry might be more productive because of success in raising wages. If unions raise wages, there will be an incentive for firms to substitute capital for labor. As you learned in the last chapter, if more capital is employed in an industry, the labor in that industry will be more productive.

In a recently published book, economists Richard Freeman and James Medoff argue that unions can increase productivity because of their effect on worker turnover. They argue that unions give workers a "voice/response mechanism" that enables management and workers to iron out problems. This mechanism, they argue, "changes the employment relationship from a casual dating game, in which people look elsewhere at the first serious problem, to a more permanent 'marriage,' in which they seek to resolve disputes through discussion and negotiation."[6] Freeman and Medoff go on to argue that unionization produces loyal employees who are more skilled and have higher levels of productivity. In fact, they argue, productivity is between 20 and 25 percent higher in the unionized sector of U.S. manufacturing.

STOCK PRICES OF UNIONIZED FIRMS

Another area where unions may have an economic impact is the stock prices of firms. Economists have increasingly looked to the stock market to analyze the effect that economic events have on the value of a firm. The price of a firm's stock gives a measure of what an economic event has done to the value of the company.

A study by John M. Abowd examined the effect of union contracts on the value of the stock of the company that signs the contract. Abowd shows that shareholders' wealth moves in the opposite direction from union members' wealth.[7] There was a dollar-for-dollar trade-off between the two variables. This finding suggests that the union can negotiate a contract that extracts economic profit from a firm that has market power. This union contract then takes wealth away from the stockholders. This suggests that if unions are successful in raising wages, the increased wages

---

6. Richard B. Freeman and James L. Medoff, *What Do Unions Do?* (New York: Basic Books, 1984), p. 38.
7. John M. Abowd, "The Effects of Wage Bargains on the Stock Market Value of the Firm," *American Economic Review* (September 1989): 774–800.

A great deal of personnel managers' attention is focused on dealing with problem employees. If you are a business major, you will spend time studying psychology in your personnel course in order to better understand such problems. If you go to work in business and end up managing workers, your firm is likely to enroll you in a special course to help you better handle employees who seem to be constantly complaining and causing trouble.

Management has paid considerable attention to this problem in recent years. Entire jobs have been overhauled to make them more "interesting" and "meaningful." Pay and benefits packages have been improved to help keep employees happy. However, a study at the University of Minnesota suggests that the problem is much more basic. It may be in the genes. The study suggests that job satisfaction is related to stable personality characteristics. Or as *U.S. News & World Report* puts it, "some people may be born to whistle while they work."

The study grew out of the famous twin research at the University of Minnesota. A team at the Minnesota Center for Twin and Adoption Research studied thirty-four pairs of identical twins who were separated at birth and raised apart. Since identical twins are genetic equals, any behavioral similarities may be based on characteristics that are inherited rather than learned.

Economic Insight

If You Like Your Job, Thank Your Parents

The twins were asked questions that related to pay, the chance to work independently, the amount of praise received, and general job satisfaction. The results surprised the researchers. Some twins' questionnaires were so similar that the same person might have filled them out. Twins tended to choose jobs with the same level of complexity, motor skills, and physical requirements. A research chemist's twin was a systems analyst. A coal miner's twin was a machinist. One set of twins even chose the same occupation—firefighting. Clearly, although human capital is acquired, the decisions about where to employ it and how much to invest in it are heavily influenced by heredity. From a management perspective, choosing the right worker for the job may be more important than supervising the worker or dealing with problems later.

Source: *U.S. News & World Report* (24 October 1988): 61.

come at the expense of owners of capital. The study also suggests that unions will only be successful in raising wages in industries where the firms have some degree of monopoly power. Interestingly, Abowd's results are inconsistent with Freeman and Medoff's conclusion that unions enhance productivity. A dollar-for-dollar loss of stockholders' wealth would mean that the stockholders could not expect to recoup any of the additional wage cost through productivity increases.

DO UNIONS CAUSE INFLATION?

You have just seen that unions cause wages and prices to be higher in unionized industries than in non-unionized ones. But do unions cause inflation? The answer is no! Unions are only affecting relative prices across industries—not the absolute level of prices. Of course, unions bargain for higher wages and businesses raise prices in inflationary times, but these are responses to inflation, not causes of it. In fact, the empirical evidence indicates that union wages rise less rapidly during the early stage of an inflationary period than do non-union wages.[8] This is partly because unions are unaware in the beginning how high the inflation will be. Even if unions anticipate that inflation will occur, they may already have committed their members to long-term contracts with wage increases less than the inflation rate. When these contracts expire, the unions try to make up for the inflation in their wage demands. It sometimes appears as if unions are responsible for the inflation, rather than victims who are trying to catch up.

There are some indirect ways in which union activity can be inflationary. If unions are successful in raising wages above competitive levels in one sector of the economy, employment in that sector will fall. If the unemployed workers from that sector of the economy are unable to find employment in other sectors, unemployment rates will rise. Then, if policy makers pursue expansionary monetary and fiscal policy to reduce the unemployment rate in response to union pressures, inflation might result. In this sense, then, unions may encourage an inflationary bias in macro policy.

A second way that unions might have an inflationary effect is through a successful effort to raise wages faster than productivity increases. Again, unemployment could result, putting pressure on policy makers to pursue expansionary policies. Keep in mind, though, that unions and businesses do not cause inflation. Government policy makers cause inflation through expansionary monetary and fiscal policy.

A SHORT HISTORY OF THE LABOR MOVEMENT

Around the turn of the century, the U.S. economy shifted from a largely agrarian base to an industrial one. By 1910, employment in industry exceeded employment in agriculture. The industrial labor force grew rapidly, and labor organizers became more successful. In 1914, about 7 percent of the work force was unionized. Growth in the labor force and

---

8. See Albert Rees, "Do Unions Cause Inflation?" *The Journal of Law and Economics* (October 1959).

growth in unionization were accompanied by a rapidly rising real wage rate. That rise in wages was largely due to rapid advances in technology and in the human capital of wage earners. Both union and non-union labor received substantial wage increases during this period.

The Early Unsuccessful Years

The best way to understand the labor movement in the United States is to view it in historical perspective. In the early nineteenth century, the labor movement was unsuccessful in organizing large numbers of workers, and its operations were mostly limited to cities in the eastern United States. During this period, the workday changed from sunup to sundown to ten hours. Workers still spent twelve hours on the job but received two one-hour (mid-morning and mid-afternoon) breaks.

It became apparent by the middle of the century that a coordinated national effort to organize labor was necessary if unions were to be effective. Even if labor did successfully raise wages above the free market equilibrium wage in a certain area, the gains were short-lived. Labor from other regions of the country produced cheaper goods that could be shipped via the rapidly growing, low-cost transportation network. The U.S. Constitution forbids any interference with interstate commerce, so regions or states could not place tariffs on goods from other regions or states. Thus, all or most of the labor in the firms of an industry had to be organized if unionization was to be successful.

The first successful national union was organized by William H. Sylvis. Sylvis had been treasurer of the short-lived Iron Molders International Union. In 1867, he founded the National Labor Union. The **National Labor Union** was involved in political action and favored the eight-hour day, arbitration, and cooperatives (firms owned by the union members who worked there). The union published a journal, *The Workingman's Advocate*, to voice its political aims. The union grew rapidly to a membership of 600,000 but quickly fell apart after Sylvis's death in 1869.

In 1869, the **Knights of Labor** was organized by Uriah Stevens as a secret society. The secrecy was to protect members from reprisals by management, but it also led to suspicion of the union and bad public relations. As a result, the policy of secrecy was dropped in 1879. The Knights' greatest accomplishment was to win the first major strike in U.S. history. This strike was one against the Wabash, Missouri-Kansas-Texas, and Missouri Pacific railroads, which were owned by Jay Gould, one of the most famous of the robber barons. By the turn of the century, however, the Knights of Labor had become unimportant as a force for labor reform. The reasons for its decline were important for future labor organizations. The Knights' philosophical goal for labor reform was to abolish the wage system and replace it with worker cooperatives. It thus had a reformist political agenda rather than "bread and butter" economic goals. The focus on reformist political goals, coupled with some unsuccessful large strikes and some violent acts of sabotage, contributed to the union's failure.[9]

National Labor Union
The first successful national union in the United States, founded in 1867 by William Sylvis.

Knights of Labor
Organized as a secret organization by Uriah Stevens in 1869, it won the first major strike in the United States against the railroad industry but had political reformist goals that led to its demise.

---

9. The Knights of Labor was linked to the infamous Haymarket bomb-throwing incident in Chicago in which seven policemen were killed. Eight anarchists were arrested. One was a Knight and the local union refused to expel him because of his involvement. This incident caused many people to identify the Knights with the most radical elements of the labor movement, which was politically costly to the labor movement in general.

The **American Federation of Labor (AFL)** was founded in 1886 by Samuel Gompers.[10] The AFL was an association of exclusive unions primarily made up of skilled workers. It was the first business union, which allowed it to overcome many of the problems earlier national unions had faced. A **business union** was defined by Samuel Gompers as a union that worked for economic goals without wanting to change or destroy the business organization or the political environment in which it worked. Gompers was, above all, pragmatic. He set a single goal of economic gains for the union's members, with no political reformist goals. Gompers thought that national labor leaders had to have the sole authority to call strikes and control membership dues. This principle has remained important in the U.S. labor movement to the present.

Gompers was elected the first president of the AFL. By 1904, membership had grown to nearly 2 million. Much of the union's success was due to Gompers's abilities. Although Gompers had been a radical in his younger days, he realized that the labor movement had to shed its radical-socialist image in order to succeed in the United States. He worked hard to overcome organized labor's negative image, which was generated by the management of large corporations and fed by the activities and tactics of radical unions. Gompers joined the National Civic Federation, an association of wealthy Eastern capitalists, editors, professional people, and corporation officers. This organization emphasized that labor unions' strength did not undermine U.S. business and that strong business was good for labor.

Perhaps the best evidence of Gompers's success was his acceptance by the political establishment. During World War I, President Wilson appointed Gompers to the advisory commission to the Council of National Defense. In 1919, at the Versailles Peace Conference, Gompers served as chairperson of the Commission of International Labor Legislation. He proved that labor leaders were respectable citizens, not communist radicals seeking to overthrow U.S. capitalism.

The early struggles of organized labor were understandable, since it was easy to break strikes and weaken labor organizations because there was a steady supply of eager workers pouring in from Europe. World War I brought prosperity and high labor demand and marked the beginning of success for American unions. Membership increased steadily during this period, and the image of unions started to improve. Much credit for this is due to Gompers. Unions flexed their muscles during the war period, and there were many strikes in 1917. These strikes were caused by the war-generated inflation and booming labor demand and the effect this inflation had on long-term union contracts. In 1918, labor was successful in negotiating an eight-hour day and collective bargaining rights in exchange for a no-strike agreement. As a result, labor emerged from World War I stronger than it had ever been.

The postwar period brought increased inflation and more strikes aimed at increasing wages. The **Industrial Workers of the World (IWW)** was an international union that organized steelworkers after World War I.

> **American Federation of Labor (AFL)**
> An exclusive union for skilled workers founded by Samuel Gompers in 1886 as the first business union.
>
> **business union**
> According to Samuel Gompers, a union that works for economic goals without wanting to change or destroy the business organization or the political environment in which it functions.
>
> **Industrial Workers of the World (IWW)**
> An international union that organized U.S. steelworkers after World War I and was viewed as a socialistic organization, which contributed to its demise.

---

10. In 1881, Gompers founded the Federation of Organized Trades and Labor Unions, which is regarded as the precursor of the AFL.

International Perspective

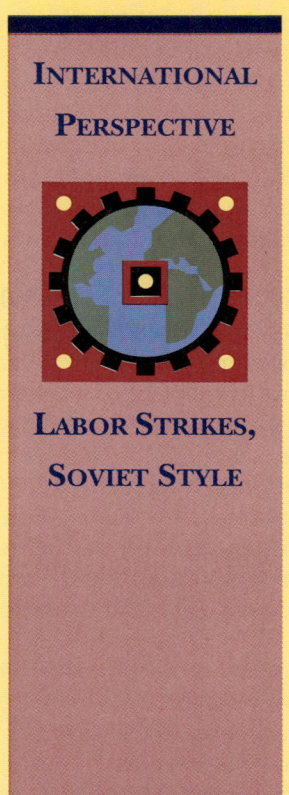

Labor Strikes, Soviet Style

Marxism was to be the workers' revolution. "Workers of the world unite!" Yet workers and independent labor unions have not fared too well in the Soviet Union.

As in the United States, some of the most aggressive union actions in the Soviet Union have been in the mining industry. In 1989, Gorbachev faced a wave of strikes by Soviet coal miners. These miners' strikes have been truly a mass movement. Unlike other movements in the Soviet Union, the miners' unrest crosses ethnic, religious, and geographic boundaries. The miners' grievances are longstanding, and their activism is representative of the real challenge that Gorbachev's reform faces.

In the 1970s, a small group of coal miners (Russians and Ukrainians) began to organize a free trade union outside the control of the state and the KGB. The organizer was Vladimir Klebanov, and the union was called the Association of Free Trade Unions of Workers in the Soviet Union. The primary aim was to protest violations of labor rights guaranteed under the Soviet constitution. The union had reformist political goals like some of the early U.S. unions.

In the early 1980s, Alexei Nikitin, a mine-safety engineer, was arrested for his activity with these union groups and was confined to a psychiatric hospital for the criminally insane. When a psychiatrist, Anatoli Koryagin, diagnosed Nikitin and several other union activists as sane, he was arrested and convicted of crimes against the state. In 1983, the Soviet Union withdrew from the World Psychiatric Association rather than face censure for this episode.

Soviet governments have used two different tactics for dealing with labor unrest in the mining industry. The first is the type of repression just discussed. The second is temporary appeasement. Brezhnev would buy time by filling empty stores with food and promising changes in the mining communities. For the latest protest by the miners, Gorbachev used the same tactic, but the Ukrainian miners held out for more. They got what they wanted—a series of political and economic concessions. Ultimate success of Gorbachev's reforms will put goods in the stores where the miners shop. Getting to that point is the challenge facing perestroika.

Source: Kevin Klose, "Behind the Strikes: An Oppressed and Neglected Proletariat," *The Washington Post National Weekly Edition* (6 August 1989): 7–8.

These workers were unskilled laborers and thus not members of the AFL. The IWW had been associated with several prominent socialists and was regarded as a radical movement. At this time, after the Russian Revolution, the fear of a worldwide Bolshevik revolution gripped the United States. The IWW went on strike against U.S. Steel in 1920 and lost. The breaking of the strike was a major victory for steel companies, who successfully branded the union leaders as socialists who were attempting to overthrow capitalism. The IWW's failure, coupled with the recession of 1920 to 1922, halted what had been a steady rise in union prestige and membership.

The 1920s proved to be a difficult time for the labor movement. The Republican Presidents Harding, Coolidge, and Hoover were pro-business, and business at that time was aggressively opposed to organized labor. The federal government sanctioned **yellow-dog contracts**, which required the employee to agree to refrain from union activity as a precondition of employment and which allowed the firm to discharge a worker for violation of that agreement. In addition, the courts were hostile to union activity. This hostility was apparent in the ease with which management was able to get court injunctions. An **injunction** is a court order to cease some action. In labor-management disputes, it was often used to order labor back to work. A section of the Clayton Act (1914), which had been hailed by Samuel Gompers as the Magna Carta of labor because it limited the use of injunctions against labor, was declared unconstitutional in 1926.

SUCCESS AND POWER

Bad times for unions ended with the election of Franklin D. Roosevelt in 1932. Roosevelt campaigned as the friend of the worker. The legislation that was proposed and passed during Roosevelt's terms established a bond between organized labor and the Democratic party that still exists today. The two key pieces of legislation were the Norris-La Guardia Act (1932) and the Wagner Act (1935). These acts vastly strengthened the power of labor unions and set the stage for their rapid development. They gave workers the right to organize and made it illegal to interfere with this right.

Under the **Norris-La Guardia Act**, yellow-dog contracts were outlawed. Injunctions against unions and their activities were limited to unlawful acts, and businesses were required to engage in collective bargaining and to bargain in good faith. Thus, the most common union-bashing tactic of employers was thwarted by the Norris-La Guardia Act. Court-issued injunctions had been used to stop strikes, boycotts, and other union activities. The intent of this act was to make the federal government neutral with respect to labor policy. Compared to past practices, this was a strong stimulus to union activity.

The **Wagner Act** made it federal policy that every worker should "have full freedom of association, self-organization, and designation of representatives of his own choosing, to negotiate terms and conditions of his employment." The act also established the **National Labor Relations Board (NLRB)**. The NLRB was empowered to investigate unfair labor practices by employers and to determine the legitimate bargaining agent for labor when there are competing unions. The Wagner Act was challenged in the courts and declared to be constitutional by the Supreme Court in 1937. Under this act, private sector workers were given the right

yellow-dog contracts
Contracts that require employees to agree to refrain from union activity as a precondition for employment and that allow firms to discharge workers who violate that agreement.

injunctions
Court orders to cease some activity, such as ordering labor to stop a strike or walkout.

Norris-La Guardia Act
A law passed in 1932 that vastly strengthened the power of labor unions by limiting the court's use of injunctions in labor-management disputes.

Wagner Act
A law passed in 1935 that gave employees the right to organize and bargain collectively and outlawed certain unfair labor practices by employers.

National Labor Relations Board (NLRB)
A board established by the Wagner Act in 1935 and empowered to investigate employer unfair labor practices and to determine the legitimate bargaining agent for labor when there are competing unions.

Congress of Industrial Organizations (CIO)
An affiliation of industrial unions that was organized when the AFL decided not to move into mass-production industries.

Taft-Hartley Act
Act passed in 1947 to reverse some of the Wagner Act's favoring of labor by shifting some legal rights back to employers.

closed shops
Firms where workers must be union members before being employed.

union shops
Firms where union membership is necessary for a worker to remain employed.

right-to-work laws
State laws that allow people to hold jobs without belonging to unions.

secondary boycotts
Union actions to stop an employer from doing business with other firms.

mediation
Third-party intervention in a dispute consisting of attempts to keep the parties together and talking by offering suggestions and clarifying issues.

arbitration
Third party intervention in a dispute consisting of hearing the arguments of both sides, studying their positions, and rendering a decision. In binding arbitration, both sides must abide by the decision.

to organize without interference from management. In practice, if organizers can get 30 percent of the work force in a place of employment to sign authorization cards, the NLRB steps in and conducts a vote. If the majority of the workers support the union in the vote, the management of the company must recognize the union and bargain with it.

During the early 1930s, a debate was going on within the AFL concerning whether it should organize unions in mass-production industries such as steelworking, automobile manufacturing, and mining. The AFL, primarily an organization of craft unions, decided not to organize in these industries. As a result, a number of its affiliated unions broke away from the AFL in 1935 and formed the Committee for Industrial Organization. The name was soon changed to the **Congress of Industrial Organizations (CIO)**. John L. Lewis, the colorful, forceful head of the United Mine Workers, became its first president.

WORLD WAR II AND THE 1950S

The boom economy of the World War II years brought a number of serious strikes. The Wagner Act had given unions more legal power, and the coffers of union treasuries were full. Unions flexed their muscles through a wave of work stoppages. Although the unions were successful in achieving sizable settlements, public sympathy began to shift away from organized labor. As a result, Congress passed the **Taft-Hartley Act** in 1947, which was designed to offset some of the labor gains created by the Wagner Act. President Truman vetoed the act, but Congress overrode the veto, an indication of the anti-union political atmosphere.

The Taft-Hartley Act shifted some legal rights back to employers. **Closed shops,** in which workers were required to become union members before employment, were made illegal. **Union shops,** in which union membership was necessary for a worker to remain employed, remained legal under the act. However, states were given the right to pass **right-to-work laws**, which allowed people to hold jobs without belonging to unions. These laws obviously undermined union power. As you saw earlier in this chapter, an inclusive union must present a united front if it is to be successful in bargaining with management. Right-to-work laws greatly undermined the ability of inclusive unions to present this united front.

The Taft-Hartley Act also required unions to bargain in good faith and outlawed featherbedding and secondary boycotts. **Secondary boycotts** are union actions to stop an employer from doing business with other firms. In other words, a union not only boycotts the firm it has a grievance against, which would be a primary boycott, but it also boycotts firms (and their products) who do business with that firm. A secondary boycott is more powerful than a picket line because it involves actions against and pressures on third parties. In certain instances, the Taft-Hartley Act empowers the President to call an eighty-day cooling-off period before a strike. During this period, mediation is attempted by a government-appointed fact-finding board.

Mediation is third-party intervention into a dispute. The mediator attempts to keep the parties together and talking by offering suggestions and clarifying issues. This process is different from arbitration. In **arbitration**, a third party hears the arguments of both sides in a dispute, studies their positions, and renders a decision. If the dispute has been submitted to binding arbitration, both parties must abide by that decision.

Union leaders fought the Taft-Hartley Act as a "slave labor law" every step of the way. They continue to campaign to reverse some of its provisions. Despite the Taft-Hartley Act, however, unions have continued to show great strength, which has been enhanced by careful and well-organized political activity.

Business and labor are not always at odds. Unions and management have often worked together to lobby for reduced pollution controls, to curb imports, and even to urge tax cuts for business. In some cases, union organization brings stability to an industry. An oligopolistic industry may even use labor power to help monopolize the industry. Before the days of the United Mine Workers, mine operators had a very difficult time with labor because miners were (and are) a very independent lot. The **United Mine Workers (UMW)** is the industrial union for mine workers founded in 1890. Under the leadership of John L. Lewis, it brought organization *and* discipline to mine labor. When Lewis ordered the miners back to work, they went back to work! In later years, however, the leadership of the UMW has not been able to exercise such strong control, and **wildcat strikes**, which are local strikes unauthorized by the national union, have been frequent.

In 1955, the American Federation of Labor and the Congress of Industrial Organizations merged to form the **AFL-CIO**. This merger unified the labor movement under the leadership of Walter Reuther and George Meany. The **Landrum-Griffin Act**, passed in 1959, was a response to public concern over union power and certain questionable practices. The act made unions more democratic, prohibited Communist Party members and convicted felons from union leadership, and strengthened the Taft-Hartley Act by making picketing illegal under certain circumstances.

RECENT LABOR HISTORY

The real world of labor-management relations does not always run the way a review of the law would indicate. The NLRB is often slow to act and sometimes slow to rule in cases of unfair labor practices. The battleground of labor-management relations has shifted to the South, where much of recent industrial growth in the United States has taken place. It is also mainly in the South that right-to-work laws are found. Some economists attribute at least part of the growth of industry in the South to those laws.

The 1960s and 1970s saw a decline in the share of the labor force that was unionized. This trend was partly a result of the fact that the economy was becoming more service-oriented and less manufacturing-oriented. Thirty-five years ago, almost 40 percent of the U.S. labor force was unionized. Today, less than 20 percent is unionized. Some observers predict that by 1995 relative union membership will be at the same level as before the wave of unionization in the mid-1930s.

One exception to this trend was a dramatic increase in the membership of public employee unions. The **American Federation of State, County, and Municipal Employees (AFSCME)** was one of the few unions

United Mine Workers (UMW)
The industrial union for mine workers.

wildcat strikes
Local strikes that are unauthorized by the national union.

AFL-CIO
Organization formed by the merger of the American Federation of Labor and the Congress of Industrial Organizations in 1955, which gave labor a more unified political front.

Landrum-Griffin Act
An act passed in 1959 and aimed at curbing union power by making unions more democratic, restricting Communist Party members and convicted felons from union leadership, and making picketing illegal under certain circumstances.

American Federation of State, County, and Municipal Employees (AFSCME)
A union of public employees that was one of the few unions that grew in the 1970s.

that grew in the 1970s. In the early 1970s, under the leadership of Jerry Wurf, AFSCME was politically active. However, in 1977 the union lost its first major battle in a confrontation with Mayor Maynard Jackson of Atlanta. Garbage workers affiliated with the union struck the city of Atlanta. Mayor Jackson refused to bargain with the local AFSCME chapter and hired strike breakers. A high level of unemployment in the city aided the strike breaking, and the jobs were quickly filled. In August 1981, President Reagan dealt the public sector union movement another blow when, in response to an unauthorized strike, he disbanded the Professional Air Traffic Controllers Organization (PATCO).[11]

In late 1978, President Carter signed the Humphrey-Hawkins Act. The **Humphrey-Hawkins Act** was an amendment to the Employment Act of 1946 that set specific targets for output, employment, and prices. The original bill included increases in public sector jobs and was strongly supported by organized labor. The version that finally passed Congress was viewed by many labor leaders as meaningless. The act set national goals to reduce unemployment to 4 percent in 1983, and to cut inflation to 3 percent in 1983 and to zero by 1988. Full employment was defined as the right to full opportunity for useful employment at fair rates of compensation for all individuals able and willing to work. The bill was regarded by labor as merely symbolic. It did not include any means to reach the goals specified, such as more public sector jobs, but left that to future legislation.

There has been little labor legislation since the Landrum-Griffin Act, except for an increase in the minimum wage approved in 1989, the first since 1981. Labor has campaigned vigorously to repeal some aspects of the Taft-Hartley Act. The two most important pieces of legislation that organized labor currently favors are the repeal of right-to-work laws and the common situs picketing bill. The latter bill grants any union the right to picket an entire construction job even when the union represents only a small part of the labor used on the project.

In the 1980s, the situation of organized labor was affected by President Reagan's policies toward the union movement. In his first term, the administration was antagonistic toward unions, an attitude perhaps best exemplified by the dismantling of PATCO in 1981. Reagan's appointees to the NLRB reversed earlier NLRB decisions that were favorable to organized labor. These reversals began in December 1983, when Reagan appointees gained a majority on the board. The effect of these reversals was to make it more difficult for labor to receive favorable rulings. For example, the board ruled that all grievance procedures must be exhausted before an appeal to the NLRB is allowed and that the NLRB cannot force a company to bargain with a union unless the union proves it represents a majority of the workers.

The 1980s was a decade of decreased influence for labor unions. NLRB data show that unions won 60 percent of the certification elections they held in 1965. In 1989, they won less than 20 percent. This decline is the result of active policy on the part of many business firms to fight unionization. Also, firms have increasingly used sophisticated labor con-

---

Humphrey-Hawkins Act A 1978 amendment to the Employment Act of 1946 that set specific targets for output, employment, and prices.

---

11. For a review of the public sector union movement, see Richard B. Freeman, "Unionism Comes to the Public Sector," *Journal of Economic Literature* (March 1986).

Summary of Major Labor Laws

Statute (Year)	Major Provisions
• Norris-La Guardia Act (1932)	Outlawed yellow-dog contracts and made picket lines and secondary boycotts legal. Limited injunctions against labor to illegal acts and required management to bargain in good faith with unions.
• Wagner Act (1935)	Established right to form unions and set up NLRB.
• Taft-Hartley Act (1947)	Made closed shops illegal. Permitted union shops but also allowed states to pass right-to-work laws.
• Landrum-Griffin Act (1959)	Strengthened Taft-Hartley Act and made unions more democratic.
• Humphrey-Hawkins Act (1978)	Set employment targets, but did not provide any implementation.

sultants who advise them on how to prevent union-forming activity. In 1990, the Bureau of Labor Statistics reported that union membership had declined by more than 3 million members between 1980 and 1990. This figure represented a drop in the unionized part of the labor force from 23 percent to 17.7 percent. During Reagan's terms, total union membership declined by 16 percent. This period also saw a decline in union strike activity. Strike activity put 454,000 workers on the picket line in 1990, compared to 432,000 workers in 1982.

Nowhere is the weakness of the labor movement more obvious than in wage settlements in the 1980s. Because of increased pressure from imports and because of deregulation in some sectors, companies have sought lower wage contracts with unions in attempts to be more competitive. What evolved was a system of two-tier labor contracts. In these contracts, which were very popular in the mid-1980s, the union agreed to accept lower wages for future employees as a way of maintaining the higher wages of existing members. These contracts created significant pay differences. A new pilot for TWA was paid $22,000, while a pilot with seniority on foreign routes was paid $110,000. The Giant Foods contract called for $6.96 per hour for "old hires" and $5.00 per hour for "new hires." The same type contract at Briggs & Stratton produced a wage of $5.50 per hour for new workers and $8.00 per hour for old workers. The strategy started to backfire on union leaders in 1987. New union members eventually become old union members. They form powerful voting blocs. They pay the same union dues and resent being treated differently.

Finally, the structure of the U.S. economy has been changing in such a way that there are fewer jobs in the industries that have traditionally been unionized. Union leaders were slow to grasp the implications of the changing structure and internationalization of the economy. At the beginning of the 1980s, many labor leaders argued that recruits from the expanding service sector of the economy would offset losses in the manufacturing industries. This has failed to happen, partly because firms in the service sector are usually smaller than firms in manufacturing and therefore harder to organize. Service workers accounted for 70 percent of the U.S. work force in 1990, but only 10 percent of them were unionized. In

International Perspective

The Foreign Policy of the AFL-CIO

During the Reagan administration, it seemed that the AFL-CIO and the President should be the bitterest of enemies. After all, Reagan cut the budget of the U.S. Department of Labor and destroyed the union of the air traffic controllers by firing more than 11,000 controllers when they went out on strike. In foreign policy, however, the AFL-CIO and the President were strange bedfellows. In fact, in 1985 alone, the AFL-CIO spent $43 million in eighty-three foreign countries, much of it on anti-communist projects. Many of these sound as though they come from a spy novel. A union in El Salvador complained that it was undermined by the AFL-CIO because it criticized José Napoleòn Duarte, who was supported by Reagan. In another instance, Prodemca, a private group supported by AFL-CIO officials, sponsored tours of the United States by Contra leaders.

Spending by the AFL-CIO in foreign countries is done through four operating groups: The American Institute for Free Labor Department, The African-American Labor Center, The Asian-American Free Labor Institute, and The Free Trade Union. These four make up the AFL-CIO's International Affairs Department. Their 1985 expenditure of $43 million was almost equivalent to the AFL-CIO's domestic U.S. budget of $45 million for that year. The $43 million was financed partly from union dues ($5 million) but mainly from U.S. government funds ($38 million). Most of the government funds were transfers from the U.S. Agency for International Development.

In 1984, $20,000 of government funds channeled through the AFL-CIO went to fund a union in Panama. The Panamanian union used the money to hold an election rally that featured the candidates supported by the military. The U.S. Ambassador to Panama, Everett Briggs, sent a cable to the U.S. State Department accusing the AFL-CIO of meddling in Panama's election. He wired that "the embassy requests that this harebrained project be abandoned before it hits the fan."[a]

Although you might expect pro-business *Forbes* magazine to argue that foreign policy should be left to the U.S. government, in 1990 *Forbes* congratulated the AFL-CIO on its foreign policy success in Poland. When Solidarity was persecuted by the Polish government, the AFL-CIO gave money to the underground and smuggled printing presses and electronic equipment to them. As M. S. Forbes, Jr. put it, "by acting upon their principles, Kirkland (President of the AFL-CIO) and American labor played a vital part in the most dramatic expansion of human freedom this century has seen."[b]

a. *Business Week* (4 November 1985): 92–96.
b. "Fact and Comment II," *Forbes* (22 January 1990): 27.

1990, only 26 percent of manufacturing workers were unionized, compared to 38.7 percent of transportation, communication, and public utility workers and 35.7 percent of government employees. In the private sector, only 15.3 percent of the work force was unionized.

THE FUTURE OF UNIONS

Despite recent trends, many union leaders still think in terms of "old-style" unions. This attitude is revealed in an article by labor economist Audrey Freedman reporting on an AFL-CIO gathering she attended. The chairperson broke the attendees into two groups by saying: "The real unions—steelworkers, boilermakers, etc.—go into the room next door. Pantywaist unions—communications workers, teachers—stay here."[12] However, the "pantywaist" unions have been growing, and the "real" unions have shrunk. This trend is exemplified by the autoworkers. In 1978, the UAW won a hard-fought battle with General Motors and Ford. The settlement called for more than $3 billion in wage increases. Despite this success at the bargaining table, UAW membership shrank by 270,000 members by 1990. Many labor leaders are unaware of or unwilling to accept the fact that any growth in union membership will have to come in the white collar and service trades.

The late 1980s witnessed a battle over labor legislation related to plant closings. In 1987, labor supporters in Congress proposed a bill that would require all U.S. firms with more than 100 employees to give sixty-days' notice before shutting down or making large-scale layoffs. The bill was called the **Worker Adjustment and Retraining Notification Act (WARN)**. The political lines were clearly drawn over WARN. Republicans in Congress warned that if the bill were passed it would choke off economic growth. Democrats countered that WARN was only fair to workers and would have little negative impact. Michael Dukakis, who was the Democratic candidate for President, campaigned with a banner that read: "60 days is only fair." Organized labor launched a major radio campaign supporting the bill and Dukakis. In late 1988, Congress passed WARN for the second time. This time President Reagan, who had vetoed the first bill, signed it into law—even though he had earlier called it a "ticking time bomb." Dukakis was robbed of an issue, and candidate Bush did not have to explain away a Reagan veto.

What is the impact of this hotly debated labor legislation? In theory, it gives workers more search time to find a new job. It is in effect a type of severance pay. There is some evidence that workers receiving advance notification are able to find new jobs more quickly than workers who receive no notice.[13] However, the out-of-work employees covered by the law hardly regard it as a major victory for the working class. As the mayor of Sanford, N.C., Rex McLeod, put it, when a company citing WARN notified its employees in that town that it would shut down: "The only notification WARN gave me was that I was notified I had a bigger problem."[14]

Worker Adjustment and Retraining Notification Act (WARN)
An act passed in 1988 that required all firms with more than 100 employees to give sixty-days' notice before shutting down or laying off workers.

---

12. Audrey Freedman, "What Has Happened to Unions?," *Bell Atlantic Quarterly* (Autumn 1985): 11.
13. See Paul Swaim and Michael Podgursky, "Advance Notice and Job Search," *Journal of Human Resources* (Spring 1990): 147–178.
14. Matthew Cooper and Allen Homes, "The Disaster That Never Happened," *U.S. News & World Report* (26 February 1990): 47.

THE BROAD PICTURE

As the union movement developed in the United States, several motives for unionization were evident. These different motives are reflected in union goals. Some unions were welfare unions (the Knights of Labor, for example), which had lofty ideals of social welfare and sought these goals by advocating an end to the wage system and the establishment of worker cooperatives. Other unions were revolutionary unions (the International Workers of the World), which sought changes in the social order. Still others were business unions (the American Federation of Labor), which ignored social and political goals and sought only to better the economic status of their members. History indicates that only this third type has been successful and able to survive in the U.S. economic system.

The development of unions in the United States can be divided into several periods. The early period from the late eighteenth century until 1930 might be called the repression phase because of the hostility of the government and the courts. This was a difficult time for union organization and one in which the successes of unions were few and far between. The period from 1930 to 1947 might be termed the encouragement phase. Government support and key labor legislation greatly increased the power and prestige of unions. Unions reached their peak of influence during this period. The period from the passage of the Taft-Hartley Act in 1947 to 1980 could be labeled the intervention phase. Government intervened in labor disputes, took away some of labor's earlier gains, and attempted to put big business and big labor on a more equal footing. The current period, since 1980, should perhaps be labeled the decline phase. The basic underpinnings of the labor movement are in a state of flux, the membership mix is changing, and unions are being challenged by government and business firms at all levels.

FORCES THAT STRENGTHEN UNIONS

After more than a century of organized labor, the future of unions depends on the economic forces that work to make unions stronger, as well as those that weaken unions. Monopoly power and inelastic demand strengthen unions.

MONOPOLY POWER

Market power in the product market means that the firm has some degree of control over the price of its product. As a result, the firm has less incentive to fight attempts at unionization. Therefore, unions should be more successful in monopolistic or oligopolistic industries.

ELASTICITY OF FACTOR DEMAND

The preceding chapter discussed the determinants of the elasticity of factor demand. The elasticity of demand for labor directly affects the strength of unions. The more inelastic the product demand, the more inelastic the demand for labor will be and the stronger the union can be.

The share of total cost that is labor cost is the second determinant of the elasticity of the demand for labor. The smaller the share of labor cost, the more inelastic the demand for labor will be and, as a result, the stronger the union will be.

The substitutability of factors also affects elasticity of factor demand. The fewer opportunities the firm has to substitute other factors of production for labor, the more inelastic the demand for labor will be and, again, as a result, the stronger the union will be.

FORCES THAT WEAKEN UNIONS

Any factor that increases the competitiveness in the economy (decreases monopoly power) or increases the elasticity of demand for labor will work to weaken union power. Such factors are simply the opposites of the factors that strengthen unions. However, there are a few additional forces that have weakened unions in recent years and deserve special mention.

CHANGING STRUCTURE OF U.S. INDUSTRY

The changing structure of U.S. industry has weakened the labor movement. More than 70 percent of the work force is now employed in service sector jobs. Fewer than 10 percent of these workers are unionized. As the economy becomes more service-oriented and less industrial, organized labor will suffer erosion of its membership.

RIGHT-TO-WORK LAWS

Twenty states, mostly Southern and Southwestern, have right-to-work laws. Table 2 lists these states. Right-to-work laws, coupled with favorable tax laws, abundant labor supply, and nice weather, attracted industry from the "Rust Belt" to the "Sun Belt" during the 1970s and 1980s. This movement presents a challenge to unions and undermines their strength. The products that these largely non-unionized workers produce compete with union-made products and weaken unionized firms. The unions have responded by attempting to unionize workers in right-to-work states but firms there have successfully resisted these attempts. A study of organizing activity in right-to-work states concluded that union organizing is reduced by 50 percent in the first five years after passage of right-to-work legislation and that union membership is reduced by 5 to 10 percent.[15]

DEREGULATION

The increased deregulation of certain industries undermines the strength of unions in those industries. This trend is most obvious in the transportation industry, which underwent widespread deregulation in the early 1980s. Deregulation makes a previously regulated monopoly subject to competition, and firms may find it hard to compete if labor has previously bargained for higher-than-competitive wage rates. For example, before deregulation of the airline industry, salaries over $100,000 were common for airline captains. Post-deregulation airlines were offering much lower salaries. Continental Airlines, for example, declared bankruptcy,

---

15. David Ellwood and Glenn Fine, "The Impact of Right-to-Work Laws on Union Organizing," *Journal of Political Economy* (April 1987): 250–273.

TABLE 2
RIGHT-TO-WORK STATES

STATE	YEAR OF LEGISLATION
Alabama	1953
Arizona	1946
Arkansas	1944
Florida	1944
Georgia	1947
Iowa	1947
Kansas	1958
Louisiana	1976
Mississippi	1954
Nebraska	1946
Nevada	1951
North Carolina	1947
North Dakota	1947
South Carolina	1954
South Dakota	1946
Tennessee	1947
Texas	1947
Utah	1955
Virginia	1947
Wyoming	1963

reorganized, tore up pilots' contracts, and offered starting salaries of $43,000. In addition, airlines increased work weeks for pilots to forty-hour, five-day weeks, and required them to do administrative work when not flying. American West Airlines, one of the new carriers that entered the industry in the competitive environment, offered pilots $32,500 and received 4,000 applicants for twenty-nine positions.

The lesson is an important one. Regulation protects not only businesses in regulated industries, but also unions. Don't be surprised to see unions fighting deregulation.

IMPORTS

Imports, like deregulation, undermine monopoly power and union power in some industries. The steel and auto industries are examples. The United Auto Workers (UAW) was successful over the years in negotiating wage contracts significantly above competitive wage rates. These high wages made the U.S. auto industry less competitive on world markets. Foreign autos have been a threat to union strength because they represent competition. As auto imports increased and auto profits fell in the early 1980s, the UAW found wage negotiations increasingly difficult. The unions and the automakers joined ranks and went to Washington to plead, successfully, for import restraints.

Chapter 14 The Labor Movement in the United States

Summary

1. Exclusive unions are more likely to be successful at raising wages than inclusive unions.
2. Evidence indicates that unions have been successful in raising wages and that these increases have been partly at the expense of consumers and non-union labor and partly at the expense of business profits.
3. Unions may add to productivity if they reduce employee turnover.
4. Union wage increases tend to reduce the stock value of unionized firms.
5. Early unions in the United States had reformist political goals and were largely unsuccessful. When Samuel Gompers turned the American Federation of Labor toward strictly economic goals, he was successful.
6. Beginning in 1932, with the election of Franklin Roosevelt, unions received active encouragement from government. The Norris-La Guardia Act (1932) and the Wagner Act (1935) greatly enhanced the power of unions.
7. The Taft-Hartley Act (1947) and the Landrum-Griffin Act (1959) diminished the power and put unions and management on a more equal footing. Reagan appointees to the NLRB reversed several rulings favorable to unions.
8. In recent years, union membership has declined as a percentage of the U.S. labor force, except among public employees.
9. Factors that enhance monopoly power and make the demand for labor more inelastic increase the strength of unions.
10. Factors that make the economy more competitive weaken union strength. Right-to-work laws, imports, and deregulation all fit in this category.

New Terms

featherbedding
exclusive union
craft unions
inclusive union
industrial unions
bilateral monopoly
National Labor Union
Knights of Labor
American Federation of Labor (AFL)
business union
United Mine Workers (UMW)
wildcat strikes
Industrial Workers of the World (IWW)
yellow-dog contracts
injunctions
Norris-La Guardia Act
Wagner Act
secondary boycotts
National Labor Relations Board (NLRB)
Congress of Industrial Organizations (CIO)
Taft-Hartley Act
closed shop
union shop
right-to-work laws
mediation
arbitration
AFL-CIO
Landrum-Griffin Act
American Federation of State, County, and Municipal Employees (AFSCME)
Humphrey-Hawkins Act
Worker Adjustment and Retaining Notification Act (WARN)

Questions for Discussion

1. Do unions raise wages? If so, at whose expense?
2. Is there a difference in the way inclusive unions and exclusive unions organize an industry? Which is more difficult?
3. Explain how closed shops and union shops differ. What are right-to-work laws?
4. Suppose César Chavez was successful in organizing the grape pickers in California. What would have been the likely effect on the price of California wine? What would have been the likely effect in the number of grape pickers employed? Would the fact that the border with Mexico is relatively easy to cross and that the supply of undocumented workers is relatively elastic have any impact on Chavez's organizing costs?
5. Has union strength in the North had any impact on business activity in the South?
6. Public employee unions have increased in strength, yet many states and the federal government forbid these

unions from going on strike. Can you think of any reasons why this should be so? Is a police officer in Los Angeles any different from a bank guard there?

7. Is the American Medical Association (AMA) a union?

8. Unions are often viewed as existing simply to bargain for higher wages for their members. What other things do unions do?

9. In the fall of 1987, the Players Association of the National Football League went on strike. The strike lasted four weeks and was unsuccessful from the players' point of view. Why?

10. How do unions affect the distribution of labor income?

11. How do unions affect the distribution of income?

12. Why has union strength (measured as the percentage of the work force that is unionized) declined in the past twenty-five years?

13. What do labor unions maximize?

14. Public employees who are union members should have (should not have) the right to strike. Which of these positions do you support? Defend it.

15. Why might labor union leaders and business leaders be in Washington lobbying for the same legislation? Can you think of any areas on which such legislation might focus?

Suggestions for Further Reading

Blair, Roger D., David L. Kaserman, and Richard E. Romano. "A Pedagogical Treatment of Bilateral Monopoly," *Southern Economic Journal* (April 1989): 831–841. An article showing that many intermediate economic texts incorrectly present the case of bilateral monopoly.

Freeman, Richard B., and James Medoff. *What Do Unions Do?* New York: Basic Books, 1984. A study that claims unions are good for America because they increase productivity.

Hirsch, Barry T., and John T. Addison. *The Economic Analysis of Unions: New Approaches and Evidence.* Boston: Allen and Unwin, 1986. An evaluation of the literature on the economics of labor unions, with over thirty pages of bibliography.

Hughes, Jonathan. *American Economic History.* Glenview, IL: Scott, Foresman, 1990. A well-written economic history of the United States with a good chapter (21) on the early years of the labor movement.

Neff, James. *Mobbed Up: Jackie Presser's High-Wire Life in the Teamsters, the Mafia, and the FBI.* New York: Atlantic Monthly Press, 1990. An interesting account of Presser's activities as president of the Teamsters Union. According to one reviewer, the book "oozes with the sleaze of Teamster activity."

Wendland, Michael F. "The Calumet Tragedy." *American Heritage* (April/May 1986): 38–48. A vivid account of union busting in northern Michigan in 1913, which resulted in deaths and ultimately the making of a ghost town.

> **AFTER STUDYING THIS CHAPTER, YOU SHOULD BE ABLE TO:**

1. Define:
    a. economic rent,
    b. single tax,
    c. capitalized value,
    d. crowding out,
    e. roundabout production,
    f. functional distribution of income.
2. Discuss the sources of profit and the role that profit plays in a market economy.
3. List the influences that help determine the distribution of income.

INTRODUCTION

CHAPTER 15
RENT, INTEREST, AND PROFIT

In an earlier chapter, labor markets were used to illustrate the marginal productivity theory of factor pricing. As you know, there are other factors of production that generate income for their owners. Most of the theory that describes labor markets holds for these other factors. Firms demand the services of land and capital because land and capital are productive. Like the demand for labor, the demand for land and capital is derived from the demand for the products they help produce. The price that firms are willing to pay for the services of land and capital depends on their marginal productivity. Rather than repeating the discussion of the marginal productivity model, this chapter discusses the important differences between the other factor markets and labor markets. We will examine rent and interest, the payments to the owners of land and capital. We will conclude with a discussion of profits, the payment to enterprise.

LAND AND RENT

The property income that has generated the most political interest in the United States is rent. To begin, we must define the concepts of land and rent. To the British economists of the eighteenth and nineteenth centuries, land was the input to the productive process that was fixed by nature. Such assets as arable acreage, water, oil, and coal all qualified as land. Recall that if something is fixed in supply, its supply curve is perfectly inelastic. If the supply of land is perfectly inelastic, as in Figure 1, its price is determined solely by changes in demand. Such a price is known as a **demand-determined price**. In Figure 1, if the demand curve is D_0, the price is zero. As the demand curve shifts to D_1, D_2, and D_3, the price rises to P_1, P_2, and P_3, respectively. These prices are not actually rent, but they are related to rent. *Rent* is the payment for the productive services of land, not the price of the land itself. The price of the land would be the present value of the expected future flow of rent payments for future years' productive services.[1]

demand-determined price
A price that is determined solely by changes in demand because supply is perfectly inelastic.

---
1. To review the concept of present value, refer to the earlier chapter on costs and profits.

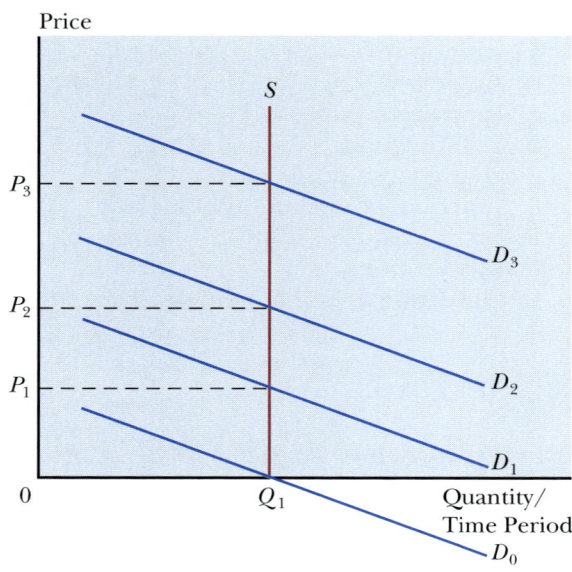

FIGURE 1
THE SUPPLY OF LAND
If the supply of land were perfectly inelastic, the price of land would be determined solely by the position of the demand curve.

ECONOMIC RENT

The idea of rent can be generalized to apply to any factor of production. Economic rent is technically a payment greater than the amount necessary to bring a factor into productive use. In other words, in Figure 1, all the payments to land are rent because the amount Q_1 is fixed, and the payments don't bring any more land into existence. This supply curve is different from the labor supply curves described earlier. In the labor market, higher wage rates increase the quantity of labor supplied, and marginal workers enter the market only at the higher wage rate. One essential difference between labor and land is that people have alternatives to work, such as leisure, which have utility.

Economic rent is a surplus paid to the owner of the factor of production. Because it is a surplus, this rent could be taken away with no effect on economic activity. For example, suppose actor Harrison Ford's skills are such that he has only two work alternatives: being a carpenter and earning $35,000 per year or being an actor and earning $2,500,000 per year. Assume that all other aspects of the two alternatives are equal. Under such circumstances, Ford is earning economic rent as an actor. If the two occupations are equally attractive to him, he could be paid $35,001 for being an actor, and he would continue to act.[2] The government could tax away $2,464,999 of his earnings as an actor, and he would not change his behavior. An idea similar to this was suggested by Henry George as a method of raising money to conduct governmental activity.

THE SINGLE TAX

single tax
A tax proposed by Henry George to capture the economic rent on land.

In 1879, Henry George (1839–1897) wrote a book entitled *Progress and Poverty*, which suggested a single tax on land. A **single tax** is a tax on land to capture its economic rent. George argued that the return to land was

---

2. Competition among movie studios and producers for stars has kept Ford's earnings above $35,001.

a surplus of unearned income and should be taxed away by the government. A social reformer, George felt that this land tax should be the only tax that government collects. His followers became known as the single taxers, and some are still active today.

George's proposal rested on two basic ideas. First, the rent was unearned, and landowners were receiving the return simply because they held good land. If you think about this, it has political appeal. Why should someone get rich just because his or her grandfather happened to stake a claim on a piece of land that was located in a future population center? Second, taking this rent from landowners would not affect economic activity because the supply was perfectly inelastic. In other words, the tax wouldn't cause less land to be supplied, as an income tax causes less labor to be supplied.

ECONOMIC FUNCTIONS OF RENT

The single tax movement died because of political reasons (landowners are a strong political force) as well as some serious theoretical flaws. The first weakness is the idea that the quantity of land is fixed. Remember, when economists draw a demand or supply curve, they hold quality constant. It is possible to make improvements in the quality of land, thus increasing the quantity of land of a given quality. Anyone who has seen agriculture in the Arizona or California deserts can attest to this fact. Increasing payments for land cause more land to be irrigated, increasing the quantity of arable land supplied. If the return to land were taxed away, this incentive to improve land would be gone. Similarly, swamps can be drained, and land can be reclaimed from the sea with dikes, as in the Netherlands. For example, several years ago, there was a proposal to build a new airport near downtown Chicago. The idea was to build a dike in Lake Michigan, pump out the water, and build an airport at the bottom of the lake. Such projects would not even be considered if the single tax were in effect.

The second problem with George's idea is that rents do serve a very important function, even if they have no influence on the quantity of land in existence. George argued that the rent the landowners receive plays no part in creating incentives for them to supply land. On the other hand, the payment made by the user of the land (the firm) ensures that the land is put to its highest-valued economic use. For example, suppose there is a choice acre of vacant land near your school. What should this land be used for—a McDonald's, a massage parlor, a church, or a dump? In a market system, the use will be determined on the basis of who is willing to pay the most. In other words, the market decides between competing uses for the land. If payments to landowners were not made, some kind of planning system would be needed to determine the allocation of land among competing uses.[3]

THE CAPITALIZATION OF RENT

Rent is an income flow to the owner of land in payment for its current use. Often, however, economists speak of the price of land as the lump

---

3. In a mixed economy, zoning commissions or boards may play the role of such a planning system. If they don't allow the most economic use of a piece of land, they are taxing the owner's right to the income from that land.

Henry George may have been the most widely read economist of all time. His book *Progress and Poverty* (1879) sold millions of copies. Measured by per capita sales at the time of publication, this book is the most popular economics book of all time.

Henry George was born in Philadelphia in a lower middle-class environment. He had almost no formal education and went to sea at age fourteen. He ended up in San Francisco and became a journalist. His interests in political economy were fueled by his experience in that job. George ran for the legislature in California but was defeated, mainly because of his strong opposition to state subsidies for railroads.

George loved to read, and he eventually turned his hand to writing about economics and social commentary. Between 1870 and 1886, he published numerous books and articles, but it was *Progress and Poverty* that brought him international fame. In it, George explained rising land values of the time by general economic growth and westward expansion. George's single tax on the site value of land was based on the argument that there was no reason why landowners should get rich because of the simple economics of increased demand brought about by the westward expansion of the U.S. population. The increasing value of the land, George argued, was in no way determined or affected by the owners of the land. In this sense, George was arguing that the rising value of land created a "windfall" profit, much in the same way that President Carter argued that deregulation of oil creates "windfall" profits for holders of oil reserves.

George's book and his idea of a single tax made him immensely popular. In 1886, he re-entered politics. This time he ran as the Labor and Socialist Parties' candidate for mayor of New York City. George was so popular that it took a major coalition of other parties to defeat him. He ran again in 1897 but died during the campaign. The Henry George School of Social Science, which still promotes his ideas, can be found at 5 East 44th Street in New York City.

ECONOMIC PROFILE

HENRY GEORGE
1839–1897

sum at which the buyer and seller exchange title to the resource. There is a simple relationship between the value of a piece of land, or any resource, expressed as a lump sum or a flow. The market price of a piece of land is the capitalized value of the rent. **Capitalized value** is the present value of a stream of future rent payments.

capitalized value
The present value of a stream of future rent payments.

The capitalized value is the amount of money that would earn the annual rent if invested at the current market rate of interest. It can be calculated using the present value technique discussed in the chapter on firms and production. Changes in the stream of rent payments will thus have an impact on the capitalized value. A good example is the value of farmland. For a farmer, the rent from farmland is the income that is produced from farming the land. When farm income falls, the capitalized value of the farmland falls. In some Midwestern states, the selling price of farmland fell by over 50 percent in the mid-1980s. To compound the misery of some farmers (and their bankers), many had used their land, which was falling in value, as collateral for bank loans. They ended up owing banks more than the market value of their land.

LOCATIONAL RENTS

In the chapter on perfect competition, we discussed differential rent theory. The topic arose because firms in perfect competition may appear to be earning economic profits that are actually economic rents to resources owned by the entrepreneur. Perhaps the most basic kind of such a rent is a locational rent. If the seller of a good or service can locate so that the cost of transportation for customers is lower at that location than at the competing locations, the seller can then charge a higher price. If you could find out the location of the interchanges on a new interstate highway, you could buy the land and make a huge profit after the highway is announced. Ocean-front property has a higher market price than does land next to a sewage plant. An acre of land is more expensive in New York City than in Fair Play, South Carolina. These price differences are due to differences in locational rents along interstate highways, on the ocean, and in urban areas.

CAPITAL AND INTEREST

The capital market is the market in which the factor of production capital is exchanged. The term *capital* is, however, used in a number of ways. The economic definition of capital is the tangible equipment, the machinery and buildings, that is used to produce goods and services for consumption. In popular usage, capital consists of the funds (money) borrowed and loaned for the purchase of physical capital. Markets for such funds are close to the extreme of perfect competition.

ROUNDABOUT PRODUCTION

People produce goods so that they can consume. In a sense, therefore, the object of all production is consumption. It is clear, however, that even the most primitive societies make tools to use for production so that they can ultimately increase their output and consume more. These tools are

roundabout production
The creation of physical capital (such as tools) that enhances productive capacity and ultimately allows increased output of consumer goods and services.

capital. The production of physical capital to enhance production instead of final goods for consumption is sometimes referred to as **roundabout production**. That is, roundabout production is the creation of capital goods (such as tools) that enhance productive capacity and ultimately allow increased output. The capital goods that are produced are purchased, or rented by firms, as factors of production. The firm borrows the money it needs to acquire this capital in the market for loanable funds (the capital market).

THE DEMAND FOR CAPITAL

Firms demand capital because it is productive. We can derive a marginal revenue product (MRP) curve for capital just as we did for labor. Such a curve is shown in Figure 2. Just as the demand for labor was a demand for units of input (hours worked), the demand in the market for capital is for physical units. In this example, it is a demand for computers. It is important to realize that the demand for capital is not a demand for money or loanable funds but rather a demand for physical capital.

We can aggregate a firm's demand for all the different types of physical capital it uses by converting this demand into a demand for dollars to purchase (or rent) that physical capital. The price of borrowing money in order to invest is the interest rate. Just as the quantity demanded of computers will increase as the price of computers falls, the quantity of dollars demanded to acquire physical capital will increase at lower rates of interest. You can see this more clearly by examining Figure 3, which shows demand and supply of loanable funds for the firm and in the market for loanable funds. The supply of loanable funds comes from business and household saving. Firms build up a supply of funds out of profits in order to invest them, and individuals save in order to consume more in the future. At higher interest rates, people will save more because present consumption given up will allow greater consumption in the future. As a result, there is an upward-sloping supply curve in the market for loanable funds.

FIGURE 2
THE FIRM'S DEMAND FOR CAPITAL
The marginal revenue product of capital (computers in this case) is the firm's demand for capital.

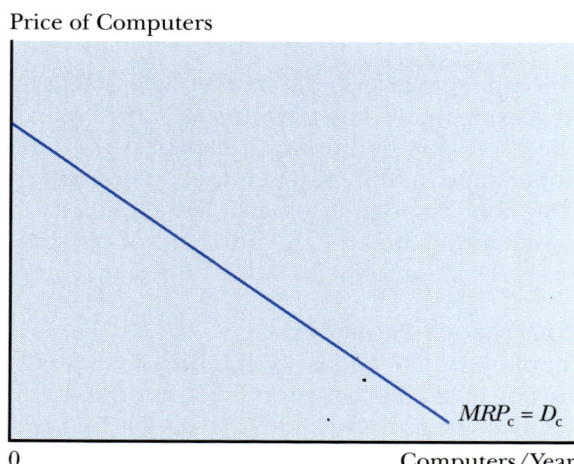

Japanese investors have been buying property and business firms in the United States, making a lot of Americans nervous and angry. When Columbia Pictures was purchased by Sony for $3.4 billion, *Newsweek* lamented that "a piece of America's soul" had been sold. When Mitsubishi purchased Rockefeller Center, *The New York Times* claimed that "a vital piece of American landscape" was sold.

To the economist, this hostility seems strange. That vital piece of American landscape isn't going to be crated up and shipped to Tokyo. It would be hard to imagine that Columbia's new Japanese owners plan to stop making movies in the United States and turn all the firm's resources to making movies of Sumo wrestlers. So why are so many Americans concerned? Does whether Mitsubishi or the Rockfeller family owns Rockefeller Center really matter?

Judging from the press, it seems to matter to a lot of people. Typical is a book called *Selling Out*, which contains chapters such as "Stealing the Crown Jewels," "Colonizing Hawaii," and "The Twenty-Fourth Ward."[a] There are twenty-three wards in Tokyo, and the authors are suggesting that Tokyo is soon to take over Los Angeles. They base their claim on the fact that twenty-eight of the thirty-five most significant buildings in downtown Los Angeles are owned by Japanese nationals. The other seven are owned by Israeli nationals (two), British nationals (three), Korean (one), and American (one). The Japanese claim that they buy high-rise buildings in large cities because people invest in what they are comfortable with, and the Japanese understand high-rise buildings—Tokyo is full of them. Critics seem to think that once the Japanese have the market cornered, they will raise rents and exploit the tenants. These critics don't seem to understand that the previous owners might go out and build some new buildings with the money they got from the Japanese. Another complaint against the Japanese is that they pay too much. This complaint must come from someone other than the sellers!

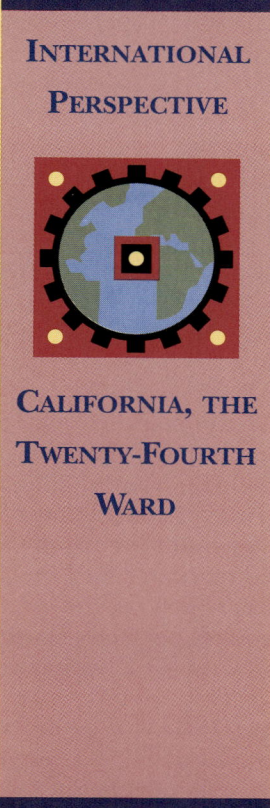

INTERNATIONAL PERSPECTIVE

CALIFORNIA, THE TWENTY-FOURTH WARD

At present, Japanese direct investment in the United States represents about 1.5 percent of all U.S. corporate assets. These investments have grown significantly in the last four years, but they are still lower than those of many other countries. British direct investment in the United States is five times the present level of Japanese direct investment. In 1989, Japanese direct investment in the United States surpassed Dutch direct investment in the United States for the first time. When was the last time you heard someone complain about the Dutch? Furthermore, U.S. citizens still own more assets abroad than foreigners own in the United States.

So why all the fuss about the Japanese? Some Japanese leaders suggest that Americans are racists— that they don't care about a threat from the British or the Dutch but feel threatened by the Japanese. Joseph Nocera, writing in *Esquire*, suggests something different.[b] He suggests that the arrogance of the Japanese offends Americans. The Japanese earn the dollars to invest in the United States because of the trade imbalance between Japan and the United States. The Japanese claim that this trade imbalance is structural, yet they protect their industries from U.S. imports.

The furor over Japanese direct investment in the United States may be indicative of political problems on the horizon. Foreign direct investment is not bad. It is not a sign of U.S. decline. Would you invest in a declining country? The United States is not losing its real estate or its soul. Americans are, however, losing their political patience with the Japanese. American exporters want to be treated fairly and the evidence is that the Japanese do not play fair in terms of granting access to their markets.

a. Douglas Frantz and Catherine Collins, *Selling Out* (Chicago: Contemporary Books, 1989).
b. Joseph Nocera, "Whose Land Is This Land?" *Esquire* (March 1990): 62–63.

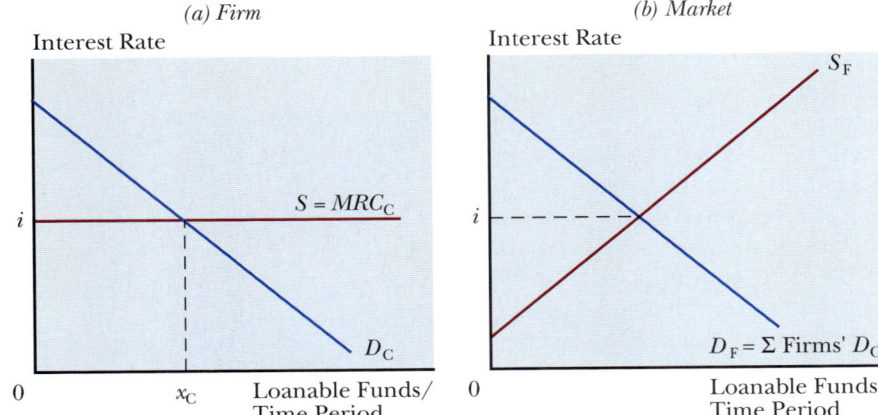

FIGURE 3
THE MARKET FOR LOANABLE FUNDS
The supply of capital to the firm is perfectly elastic at the interest rate set in the market for loanable funds. The firm invests in capital until the marginal revenue product of capital is equal to the market rate of interest.

In Figure 3, the market demand curve for capital is the summation of all the individual firms' demand curves for capital expressed as the demand for loanable funds. The firms' demands are based on their marginal revenue product curves for physical capital. The market rate of interest, i, determines the supply of capital available to firms in the competitive capital market. The firm can borrow all it wants to at the market rate of interest, which means that its marginal resource cost curve (and its supply curve) is perfectly elastic. We can thus determine the amount of borrowing by the firm, which in this case is x_C.

INTEREST RATES, INFLATION, AND RISK

The preceding analysis mentioned only one rate of interest. You know that there are in fact many interest rates, so which one is used for analyzing the capital market? This question is important in both microeconomics and macroeconomics because the interest rate is both a price (a micro variable) and an important aggregate that affects output and employment. In order to answer this question, we have to distinguish between the real rate of interest and the nominal rate of interest. The rate that is observed, or the market rate, is the nominal rate. Of course, we don't observe just one interest rate. We observe a whole family of interest rates. The various rates depend on who the borrower is, how much risk the lender perceives, and how long the repayment period is. Short-term loans ordinarily carry lower rates than long-term loans. Risky borrowers pay more than safe, dependable borrowers. Because there is a variety of interest rates, economists generally use the rate on U.S. Treasury bills (T-bills) as an indicator of how the market is doing. The T-bill rate is the interest rate the government, the least risky borrower possible, pays on its short-term borrowing.

Interest rates generally rise and fall together, so it's reasonable to pick out one important rate and use it to represent the overall level of interest rates. The spreads between rates, however, will vary over the course of the business cycle. As private borrowers begin to look riskier relative to the government, lenders will be more reluctant to lend to them and more in-

Chapter 15 Rent, Interest, and Profit

> **WHAT CAUSES HIGH INTEREST RATES?**
>
> Interest rates are higher:
> - when expected inflation increases,
> - with riskier loans,
> - for longer time periods,
> - when the demand for loanable funds increases,
> - when the supply of loanable funds decreases.

clined to buy T-bills. The rate to private borrowers rises relative to the T-bill rate. The difference between the T-bill rate and the rate to private borrowers for the same length of time is called the risk premium. Risk premiums generally rise during recessions and fall during expansions.

The real rate of interest isn't observed. The real rate of interest is the nominal rate of interest minus the expected rate of inflation. When lenders set an interest rate, they consider inflation as well as risk. If prices are rising, the dollars they are being repaid will be worth less and less with each successive payment. Lenders want to get back, not the number of dollars they lent plus some interest, but the purchasing power they lent plus some interest. On the other side of the market, borrowers are also making calculations of what a loan really costs them, considering that they can repay with dollars that are declining in value. Thus, an inflation premium is included in the nominal interest rate.

COMPETITION FOR CAPITAL

The market interest rate allocates loanable funds among competing firms and among competing uses exactly like the wage rate allocates labor services. Expanding on this idea a little will allow you to see why some economists are so concerned about federal budget deficits. Consider the fact that there are more than just business firms demanding loanable funds. There are two other important groups on the demand side of the market for loanable funds. Consumers demand loanable funds to finance the part of their consumption that is obtained on credit. They borrow to buy homes, furniture, automobiles, and college educations. The other demander of loanable funds is the government. At all levels, federal, state, and local, governments borrow loanable funds. The market for loanable funds is, therefore, composed of three important segments. Demand from all of these is added to give D_F in Figure 4. The market for loanable funds has a supply of S_F and a demand of D_F. The demand curve is the summation of the household demand for loanable funds, the business demand for loanable funds, and the governmental demand for loanable funds. At the resulting interest rate, i, a representative firm adds x units of capital to its capital stock.

What happens, *ceteris paribus*, when the government increases its borrowing? Government demand for loanable funds increases, causing total demand to increase to D'_F. The interest rate rises to i_1. This higher interest rate means that the supply curve for the firm has shifted to the left.

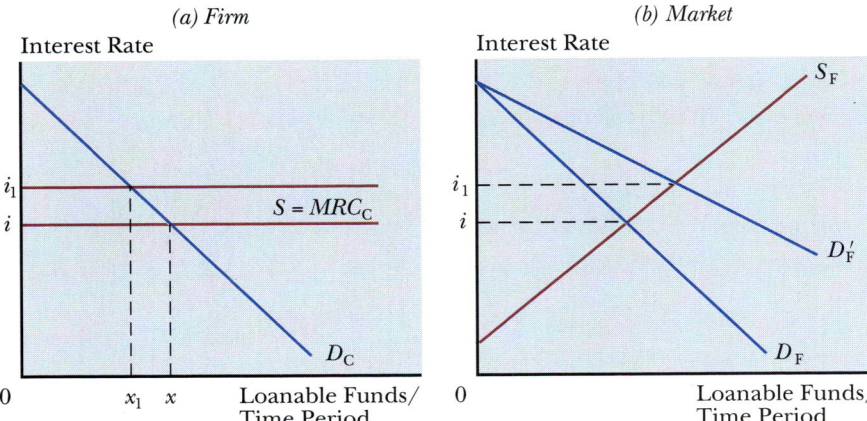

FIGURE 4
CROWDING OUT
The market demand for loanable funds is composed of household, business, and governmental demand. An increase in governmental borrowing will cause the market rate of interest to rise. Firms' response to this increased price of capital is to decrease the quantity demanded. Economists say that firms have been crowded out of the market for loanable funds.

The firm will decrease its investment from x to x_1. The government has crowded some businesses (and households) out of the capital market. Interest rates allocate loanable funds among the three demanders. When the government bids interest rates up, households and businesses will get fewer of these funds.

Many political and business leaders are worried about this crowding out. They believe that this effect is a very real burden of the federal deficit. They argue that the large amounts of borrowing by the government bids up the interest rate and attracts investment funds away from business. When this happens, business investment does not grow as much as it would have and the productivity of the economy suffers. Recall that increases in the capital stock raise the overall demand for labor. Crowding out may also hold down the wages of workers by keeping the demand for labor from growing as fast as it otherwise would have.

ENTERPRISE AND PROFITS

Profits are a residual. They are what's left for the entrepreneur after land, labor, and capital have been paid. This is not to say that profits are not important. As you saw earlier, the quest for profits makes them the prime mover of a market economy. If profits are above normal levels, they will be a signal for firms to enter an industry. If below normal profit is earned, firms will leave the industry. In addition, potential profit is the incentive for innovative activity and risk taking. The entrepreneur takes chances and bets on the future because of the perceived chance to earn profit. Henry Ford installed the assembly line because he thought it would increase efficiency and lead to higher profits. The profit motive drove him to be innovative.

THE SOURCE OF PROFITS

As you have learned, monopoly and other restrictions on markets are a source of profit. Entrepreneurs are therefore very likely to spend a great deal of time trying to monopolize their market. In fact, much of the teach-

A multinational corporation can be loosely defined as a corporation with headquarters in one country and plants in one or more other countries. The essential condition is usually considered to be direct ownership rather than simply financial interest in foreign firms.

Why would a firm go build a production facility abroad rather than export to that country or invest in a local firm there? After all, it can be a hassle to deal with foreign governments and markets that are unfamiliar. It is difficult and costly to get managers to move to foreign countries for long periods of time. Economic theory suggests that the rate of return on investment abroad must be greater by enough to compensate for the additional risks and uncertainty. In fact, if capital markets functioned worldwide as efficiently as in the United States and if worldwide product markets were competitive, there would be no economic rationale for multinational corporations. Exporting would be one alternative. Portfolio investment, or the transfer of capital to foreign entrepreneurs whose knowledge of the local conditions gives them an advantage, would be the second option. The existence of multinationals must therefore be explained by imperfections in product and/or capital markets.

The most obvious explanation is that there isn't free trade and multinationals exist in part to overcome barriers to international trade. Several other imperfections in product markets can be used to explain the existence of multinationals:

INTERNATIONAL PERSPECTIVE

MULTINATIONAL CORPORATIONS

- The investing firm may have patents and technology that it is unwilling to transfer without a great deal of control.

- The investing firm may have a highly differentiated product, such as Pepsi Cola, which gives it some degree of monopoly power. The investing firm can only exploit its brand name capital through direct ownership.

- The investing firm may have control over a raw material or other input that gives it a limited degree of monopoly power.

In all three of these cases, direct ownership would provide the control necessary to exploit any monopoly power that might be present.

There has been a great deal of direct foreign investment by Japanese automakers in the United States. This investment can be explained by some of the above imperfections. First, free trade does not exist. There has been a great deal of "voluntary restraint" of auto exports to the United States by the Japanese. They limit their exports because they are afraid the United States will impose even stricter quotas. It is a good move politically to build plants in the United States because this move dilutes the argument that jobs are lost to Japanese producers. In addition, the Japanese have production and management techniques that are unique. They also produce a differentiated product in that U.S. consumers view Japanese autos to be of very high quality.

ing that goes on in business schools is training in how to differentiate products, develop innovative products, and finance acquisitions. All of these actions are aimed at creating market power and generating profits. Any entrepreneur would choose to be a monopolist, rather than to be in competition. There is, of course, nothing wrong with the search for profit. It is Adam Smith's invisible hand at work. Most monopolies will be temporary, because new entry into the market will erode their success.

The entrepreneur engages in risky activities in search of profits. There is a great deal of uncertainty in the economy. The entrepreneur assumes risk and is rewarded for his or her talent, wisdom, or luck with profit. It is important to note the difference between uncertainty and risk. Many risks are insurable. You can buy auto insurance or fire insurance to protect yourself against risk because insurance companies are able to predict very accurately the average rate of occurrence of auto accidents or fires. The entrepreneur is instead assuming uninsurable risks. These uninsurable risks are the uncertainties surrounding demand and supply. Will a product sell, and can it be sold for a price that is higher than the costs of production? If the answer is yes, the entrepreneur will make a profit for assuming the risk of this uncertain outcome. If the answer is yes *and* other firms can be kept from entering the market, the entrepreneur will have two sources of profit.

The entrepreneur is also involved in innovation. If the entrepreneur can produce a new or better product or find a way to produce an existing product faster or more efficiently, profit will result. Innovations can even include managerial techniques that give a firm a cost advantage. If such innovations can't be patented, and they usually can't, they will quickly be copied by competing firms. Competition will force entrepreneurs to make further innovations, if profits are to be maintained. This race after profits gives the market system its vitality.

Are Profits Too High?

To much of the American public, profit is a four-letter word. It is often combined with an adjective to form phrases with a distinctly negative connotation, such as "windfall profit" or "obscene profit." This attitude toward profit arises from a very common misperception about how high profits are for U.S. corporations. A public opinion poll asked consumers how high they thought profits were in U.S. manufacturing.[4] The average consumer thought that after-tax profits in manufacturing were 37 percent of sales and that a 27 percent profit on sales was "reasonable." The profit level in manufacturing at the time of the poll was only 3.8 percent of sales.

Profits play a very important role. First and foremost, they are the signal of the market system. Second, they reward entrepreneurs for organizing production, monitoring shirking, and coordinating team production. Finally, profits generate the incentive to innovate and strive for greater efficiency.

---

4. Opinion Research Corporation, "Public Attitudes toward Corporate Profits," *Public Opinion Index* (August 1983).

THE DISTRIBUTION OF INCOME

This chapter, in combination with the chapter on labor markets, provides a theory that explains why the distribution of income is what it is. Basically, the theory says that, given private property and competitive market conditions, market forces will produce a certain distribution of income. Labor will be paid according to its productivity, and the owners of capital and land will receive payments according to the productivity of the factors they own. Any event that causes the marginal productivity of a factor to increase will increase the payment that factor receives.

The theory that productivity determines factor income has received much criticism since it was first developed by John Bates Clark. Clark was looking for a natural law to explain how the distribution of income was determined. The criticisms of his marginal productivity theory have almost all been on the grounds of **distributive justice**, a normative argument for a particular distribution of income. Critics argue that the market-determined income distribution is unfair because the old, the sick, the young, and the handicapped, among others, do not receive a fair share since they are not as productive as others. Another normative criticism of marginal productivity theory rests on the premise that social productivity rather than economic productivity should determine income. In a market system, a writer of pornographic novels often earns more than a writer of poetry. Some critics say this is undesirable.

You should recognize such criticisms for what they are—normative, ethical considerations and not positive criticisms of the theory. Think back to our early discussion of the role of theory. A theory is valuable if it provides a good explanation of some aspect of the real world. According to this test, marginal productivity theory stands up quite well.[5]

distributive justice
A normative argument for a particular distribution of income.

INCOME DISTRIBUTION AND THE MARKET

As you have seen, the distribution of income in a market economy is determined by the payments to factors of production, especially to labor. Wages are the largest component of income. However, other sources of income—rent from land, interest on capital, and profit for enterprise—often make the difference between an average income and a high one.

Assume that the market for the factors of production (land, labor, capital, and enterprise) is perfectly competitive. What then determines the distribution of income, and is this outcome just or equitable? The economic theory developed in this chapter offers a clear and positive answer to the first part of this question. Marginal productivity theory allows economists to analyze how factor incomes change in response to changing market conditions. The second part of the question is normative. The distribution of income arising from the market may not be judged satisfactory. Decisions about changing the distribution of income involve value judgments about the "needs" of certain groups, as well as some positive statements about the effects of redistribution on incentives.

---

5. For a review of empirical studies of marginal productivity theory, see David Kamerschen, "A Reaffirmation of the Marginal Productivity Theory," *Rivista Internazionàle di Scienze Econòmici e Commerciàli* (March 1973).

**TABLE 1
THE FUNCTIONAL
DISTRIBUTION OF INCOME
IN THE UNITED STATES**

	SHARE OF TOTAL INCOME				
DECADE ENDING	WAGES AND SALARIES	PROPRIETORS' INCOME	CORPORATE PROFITS	INTEREST	RENT
1920	60.0%	17.5%	7.8%	6.2%	7.7%
1940	64.6	17.2	11.9	3.1	3.3
1960	69.9	11.9	11.2	4.0	3.0
1980	75.9	7.1	8.4	6.4	2.2
1990	73.6	8.9	6.8	10.4	0.3

Source: 1920 to 1980 data adapted from Irving Kravis, "Income Distribution: Functional Share," *International Encyclopedia of Social Sciences*, vol. 7; 1990 data from *Economic Indicators* (Washington, DC: U.S. Government Printing Office, February 1991).

functional distribution of income
The pattern of payments to the factors of production (rent, wages, interest, and profits).

THE FUNCTIONAL DISTRIBUTION OF INCOME

The pattern of payments to the factors of production (rent, wages, interest, and profit) is called the **functional distribution of income**. This distribution (shown for the United States in Table 1) is determined by the supply of and demand for factors of different kinds and qualities. Wages and salaries are the largest single component of income and have increased in relative importance compared to earlier periods.

THE RETURN TO SPECIFIC FACTORS

The demand for any factor of production is derived from the demand for the goods and services that the factor is used to produce. The value of any productive resource depends on the value of what it produces. Differences in factor incomes result from differences in factors' productivity and in the demand for the final products.

Given factor inputs of equal physical productivity, the highest reward will go to those factors employed in the industry whose products are most highly valued in the market. The return to a factor will also be affected by the physical productivity of the other factors with which it is combined in a production process. Thus, it is possible that labor (or another factor) of equal quality will receive different earnings when combined with different amounts and qualities of other factors of production.

Examples of productivity-related differences in factor earnings are easy to find. A piece of land near a new interstate highway will be more valuable than a comparable piece of land elsewhere because of the highway. An engineer employed in a firm with a highly successful new product might receive a higher salary than an equally skilled engineer at another firm. A quarterback on a winning NFL team might receive a higher salary because he was at the right place at the right time with the right set of teammates.

MARGINAL PRODUCTIVITY AND EFFICIENCY

An important advantage of letting the market determine income distribution is that rewards will then be linked to efficiency of resource allocation. *Ceteris paribus*, factors flow to those uses with the highest rewards, that is, those in which their productivity is most highly valued. Such a system rewards and thus encourages higher productivity. In freely operating markets, the returns to factors of equal productivity will tend to be equal (or nearly so). Over time, factors will tend to transfer to their highest-valued use.

The market-determined distribution of income may be unsatisfactory in other ways, however. Not only is this distribution very unequal, but it also involves a great deal of chance. Most individuals will avoid risk unless they can be compensated for assuming it. An individual's future income is subject to a high degree of uncertainty. Most of this uncertainty cannot be shifted or avoided through private effort. Risk aversion reduces the efficiency of allocation of productive inputs, especially labor. The situation creates a demand for government programs to reduce income uncertainty. Government may respond either by reducing the risk itself or by implementing various types of insurance plans. Reducing the risk can take the form of education programs, various types of job security, or mandating of private pension and disability programs. Insurance plans include Social Security, unemployment insurance, deposit insurance on bank deposits, and welfare, all of which were instituted in the 1930s and are collectively known as the "social safety net."

In the next chapter we will consider the normative aspect of income redistribution. There is perhaps no other topic in economics or politics that generates more controversy. How and to what degree should government redistribute income?

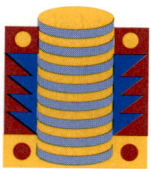

Summary

1. Land is the factor of production that is in fixed supply. Rent is the return to this fixed factor. Economic rent is a payment above the amount necessary to bring a factor into a given use.

2. Henry George proposed a single tax on land. One important problem with this proposal is that if rents weren't paid, a planning authority would have to decide among competing uses of land.

3. Roundabout production is used to describe the production of physical capital to enhance productivity.

4. Capital, like the other factors of production, is demanded by firms because it is productive. The payment to capital is interest. As interest rates rise, the quantity of capital that firms demand will decrease.

5. When an increase in the interest rate as a result of government borrowing reduces private borrowing, economists say that crowding out is taking place in the capital market.

6. Profits are the residual amount that entrepreneurs receive. They can exist because of monopoly power, risk taking, or innovation. In a market economy, profits serve as the signal for firms to either enter or leave a particular industry.

7. Marginal productivity theory explains how the distribution of income is determined in a market economy. It says nothing normative about this distribution.

8. Income distribution is determined largely by forces in factor markets. Wages and salaries are by far the largest component of income.

9. Different types of labor, land, or capital earn different rewards depending on their productivities and the industries in which they are employed.

NEW TERMS

demand-determined price
single tax
capitalized value
roundabout production
distributive justice
functional distribution of income

QUESTIONS FOR DISCUSSION

1. What is economic rent? Have you ever earned economic rent? Would taxation of this rent have caused you to behave differently?
2. What does it mean to say profits are a residual?
3. In what ways are economic rent and economic profit similar?
4. Why is the interest rate called the price of borrowing money?
5. Third World countries often complain that they are "ripped off" by multinational corporations because these corporations earn excessively high profits in host countries compared to their profits in their home countries. Can you think of any economic explanation for these higher profits?
6. When major airports are built in rural areas, commercial and residential buildings often spring up around them. The housing prices are often lower than for comparable houses in other areas. Why? If the residents band together and force planes to use noise abatement methods or follow different landing patterns, what is likely to happen? What does this represent to the homeowners?
7. Why do the activities of city and county zoning boards elicit such strong feelings?
8. The role of entrepreneurs in the production process is often misunderstood. What do entrepreneurs do that makes them so important in a market economy?
9. If your college raised your tuition by $1, would you drop out of school? If it raised tuition by $1,000, would you drop out? How about $10,000?
10. What is meant by distributive justice?
11. What conditions determine wages? What causes some people with equal skills to receive different wages? Would more competitiveness in the economy reduce or increase these differences?
12. What purpose do profits serve? Why do some people think that they are too high?
13. If part of Harrison Ford's earnings as an actor is viewed as a rent, then this part of his pay could be taken away and he would still keep acting. Some people argue that it is necessary to pay such rents in order to ensure a future supply of actors (the same argument could hold for NFL running backs). Explain this argument.
14. What does roundabout production mean?
15. What is meant by the functional distribution of income?

SUGGESTIONS FOR FURTHER READING

Aaker, David A., and Robert Jacobson. "The Role of Risk in Explaining Differences in Profitability," *Academy of Management Journal* (June 1987). A recent study that shows that risk, systematic and unsystematic, has significant impacts on the return on investment.

Herbert, Robert F., and Albert N. Link. *The Entrepreneur.* New York: Praeger, 1982. A good source of ideas about what it takes to be a successful entrepreneur.

Lindholm, Richard W., and Arthur D. Lynn. *Land Value Taxation: The Progress and Poverty Centenary.* Madison, WI: University of Wisconsin Press, 1982. This volume includes papers presented at a symposium commemorating the 100th anniversary of Henry George's *Progress and Poverty.* Many, but not all, of the papers are by present-day economists who support George's view.

AFTER STUDYING THIS CHAPTER, YOU SHOULD BE ABLE TO:

1. Use a Lorenz curve to describe the distribution of income.
2. Describe how poverty is measured in the United States.
3. Identify the groups most likely to be poor.
4. Analyze the effects of discrimination on wage differences.
5. Summarize the arguments for and against the redistribution of income through government.
6. Discuss the advantages and disadvantages of:
   a. promoting equality of opportunity versus promoting equality of results.
   b. redistributing in kind versus redistributing in cash.
   c. redistributing on a centralized basis versus redistributing on a local or state basis.
7. Describe current government transfer programs.

CHAPTER 16

INCOME DISTRIBUTION: POVERTY, DISCRIMINATION, AND WELFARE

INTRODUCTION

No single topic in economics generates more controversy than income distribution and government policies for income redistribution. The market generates an unequal distribution of income. The government is a powerful tool for redistribution, although it does not always redistribute from the rich to the poor. This chapter examines the actual distribution of income, the measures of income distribution and poverty, the effects of labor market discrimination, and the role of government in redistributing income.

As scientists, economists have been reluctant to propose schemes for the redistribution of income. This is because value judgments are necessary to choose among alternative income distributions. However, many economists, philosophers, and politicians have developed normative standards for the distribution of income. Plato was explicit about such a rule. He argued that no one in a society should be more than four times richer than the society's poorest member. In general, there are three major normative standards for redistribution: need, equality, and productivity. The principle of pure communism as put forward by Karl Marx was "to each according to his needs, from each according to his abilities." The principle of pure equality would provide the same income for everyone. The productivity standard is also often referred to as the contributive standard. In a pure market system, this standard is the marginal productivity theory of John Bates Clark, discussed in an earlier chapter.

In the United States, the three standards for income distribution are combined. Productivity is the primary standard. However, there is redistribution to the poorer members of society. Part of this redistribution is done privately through charitable giving and part is done publicly through governmental programs at all levels of government. Income redistribution through government pits one group (taxpayers) against another group (recipients). There is less resistance by taxpayers to income redistribution in a high-growth economy. Society can provide for the poor, the elderly, and other groups out of growing income and output. When economic growth is slow, however, redistribution to some means a reduced share for others. Slow economic growth makes the debate over how and how much to redistribute income much more intense.

THE PERSONAL DISTRIBUTION OF INCOME AND POVERTY

In the last chapter, you learned about the functional distribution of income. The distribution of income in a market economy is determined primarily by the ownership of the factors of production and by the prices paid to the factors of production.

The functional distribution of income is one way of looking at income distribution. Another way of describing income distribution is according to how income is divided, equally or unequally, among individuals or households. This measure is called the **personal distribution of income**.

LORENZ CURVES

A **Lorenz curve** is a graph showing the cumulative percentage of income received by a given percentage of households, whose incomes are arranged from lowest to highest. It is constructed by cumulating the percentage of households on the horizontal axis and the percentage of income on the vertical axis. Figure 1 shows Lorenz curves for three societies. A perfectly egalitarian society would have the Lorenz curve labeled distribution *A*. If incomes were equally distributed, the lowest 10 percent of all households would receive 10 percent of total income, the highest 20 percent would receive 20 percent of total income, and so on. When household incomes are not uniform, the Lorenz curve diverges from the 45-degree line of perfect equality. Distribution *B* in Figure 1 would be found in a less egalitarian society. The greater the difference between the 45-degree line and the Lorenz curve, the greater the inequality in the income distribution. In Figure 1, distribution *C* represents more inequality than distribution *B*.

Lorenz curves for different countries can be used to compare levels of

personal distribution of income
A measure of how total income is divided among individuals or households.

Lorenz curve
A graph showing the cumulative percentages of income received by various percentages of households.

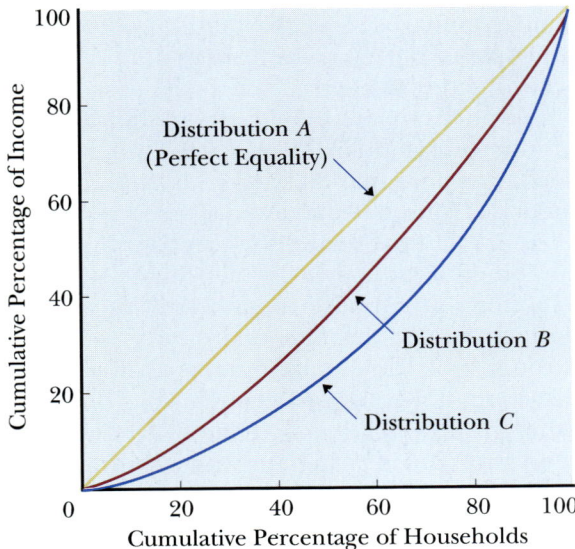

FIGURE 1
LORENZ CURVES
A Lorenz curve shows the percentage of income received by all percentages of households. A perfectly egalitarian society would have a Lorenz curve represented by distribution *A*. Distributions *B* and *C* represent more unequal distributions of income.

income inequality. Sweden's Lorenz curve comes fairly close to the 45-degree line. Less developed countries tend to have curves that are farthest from the 45-degree line. Lorenz curves can also be used to show how the distribution of income changes over time. The data in Table 1 for 1929 and 1988 are graphed as Lorenz curves in Figure 2. Both Table 1 and Figure 2 indicate that the income distribution in the United States has become more equal since 1929.

A Lorenz curve must be interpreted with caution for two reasons. First, Lorenz curves describe the *relative* distribution of income among households. A Lorenz curve might indicate that the lowest 20 percent of the households have only 5 percent of the income, but it doesn't say if this amount of income is high or low in an *absolute* sense. This 5 percent could be enough income to make everyone in the lowest 20 percent well fed, well housed, and well clothed. A Lorenz curve only shows the degree of inequality. By itself, it does not measure either wealth or poverty.

Second, Lorenz curves show how income is distributed among households at a given time. If the households in the lowest 10 percent change over time, the Lorenz curve will give an incorrect picture of relative poverty. The typical household's income changes in a predictable way over time. Income tends to be low when wage earners are young, increases as they reach middle age, and declines in their retirement years. This life-cycle pattern means that households will move around in the income distribution over time.[1] Since the Lorenz curve shows an income distribution at a specific time, it may make income inequality appear greater than it is over time.

One useful source of information on the behavior of income distribution over time is the Panel Study on Income Dynamics (PSID) from the Institute for Social Research at the University of Michigan.[2] The PSID has followed the income and employment history of 5,000 U.S. families since 1968. These data show considerable mobility among income levels. For example, of those who were at the top or the bottom of the income scale in 1971, only about half had been in the same relative position in 1968.

**TABLE 1
INCOME DISTRIBUTION IN THE UNITED STATES, 1929–1988**

Share Received by	1929	1947	1960	1972	1979	1983	1988
Lowest Fifth	3.5%	5.1%	4.8%	5.4%	5.3%	4.7%	4.6%
Second Fifth	9.0	11.8	12.2	11.9	11.6	11.1	10.8
Middle Fifth	13.8	16.7	17.8	17.5	17.5	17.1	16.9
Fourth Fifth	19.3	23.2	24.0	23.9	24.1	24.4	24.1
Highest Fifth	54.4	43.3	41.3	41.4	41.6	42.7	43.7
Highest 5 Percent	30.0	17.5	15.9	15.9	15.7	15.8	16.9

Source: U.S. Department of Commerce, Bureau of the Census, *Statistical Abstract of the United States* (Washington, DC: U.S. Government Printing Office, 1990).

---

1. Morton Paglin found that when life-cycle changes were taken into account, there was about 50 percent less inequality than would be inferred from simple Lorenz curves. Further, Paglin found that adjusting for life-cycle changes revealed a significant trend toward a more equal distribution of income in the United States. See Morton Paglin, "The Measurement and Trend of Inequality: A Basic Revision," *American Economic Review* (September 1975): 598–609.
2. Greg Duncan et al., *Years of Poverty, Years of Plenty: The Changing Economic Fortunes of American Workers and Families* (Ann Arbor, MI: Institute for Social Research, 1984).

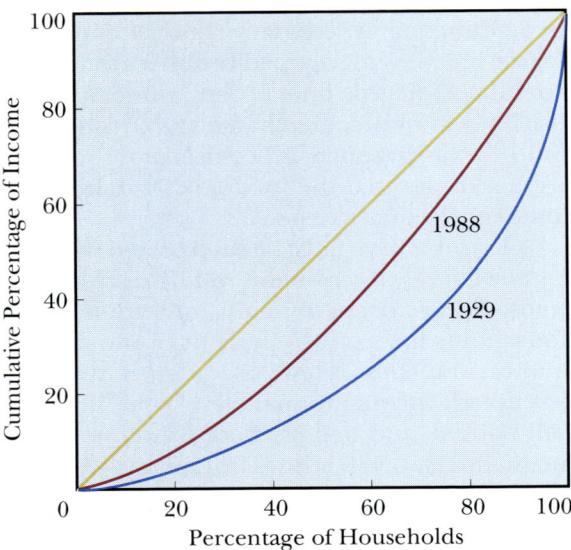

**FIGURE 2
INCOME DISTRIBUTION IN THE UNITED STATES, 1929 AND 1988**
Plotting Lorenz curves for the United States for 1929 and 1988 shows that the distribution of income has become more equal.

Changes in family composition—births, deaths, divorces, marriages, and children leaving home—had the largest influence on relative economic well-being. This finding supports the life-cycle view of income distribution. The PSID data also suggest that the poor may not all be caught in a poverty trap. Many are temporarily rather than permanently poor.

MEASURING POVERTY

Income distribution is not just a relative concept. Statistics on starvation, malnutrition, and disease show that poverty has an absolute meaning as well. Determining the level of income that marks the border between poverty and nonpoverty is difficult, because poverty is both absolute and relative. People who are relatively poor in one country may be well off by the standards of another country or by the standards of the same country at an earlier time.

The U.S. government first established an official definition of poverty in 1964. The definition was based on the cost of a minimally adequate diet. This figure was then multiplied by three, since the typical household spent one-third of family income on food. In 1964, the poverty income level for a family of four was $3,000 ($1,000 for food times 3) or below. In 1988, the official poverty income level was defined as $6,024 or below for a single individual and $12,092 or below for a family of four. The poverty threshold has been adjusted each year for inflation. However, no adjustment has been made for real income growth or for relative poverty. As a consequence, the poverty threshold has fallen from 44 percent of the median family income in 1964 to 31 percent of the median family income in 1988.

Table 2 shows that from 1959 to 1979, the fraction of the U.S. population below the poverty level decreased. Cuts in social programs and high unemployment rates reversed that trend in the early 1980s. By 1988, however, the percentage was back at the 1980 level.

The poverty rate is a rather crude measure of poverty or changes in

YEAR	PERCENTAGE
1959	22.4
1970	12.6
1975	12.3
1980	13.0
1983	15.2
1984	14.4
1985	14.0
1986	13.6
1987	13.4
1988	13.1

TABLE 2
PERCENTAGE OF U.S. POPULATION WITH INCOME BELOW THE POVERTY THRESHOLD, 1959–1988

Source: U.S. Department of Health, Education, and Welfare, *Social Security Bulletin, Annual Statistical Supplement* (Washington, DC: U.S. Government Printing Office, 1987).

poverty because this number gives no indication of how poor the people are. A person whose income is $1 below the threshold is counted as poor, and so is a person whose income is $3,000 below the threshold. If cash transfers bring the first person's income up by $2, the poverty rate falls. If transfer payments raise the second person's income by $2,000, the poverty rate is unchanged. However, these data do provide some indication of how much poverty exists and how it changes over time.

The poverty rate shown in Table 2 has been criticized by some economists because it only counts transfer payments such as Social Security, unemployment compensation, and Aid to Families with Dependent Children. Since 1965, an increasing fraction of programs for the poor have taken the form of in-kind transfers. In 1989, the Bureau of the Census refigured the poverty rate by also counting as income the cash equivalent value of three major in-kind programs: food stamps, housing assistance, and Medicare. These adjustments produced a poverty rate of 10.5 percent in 1988 compared to the 13.1 percent official rate.[3]

WHO ARE THE POOR?

In the United States, the poor come from all parts of the country and every age group. However, it is possible to find certain social, geographic, and racial characteristics of the poor. Geographically, for example, the poor tend to live in the rural South and in Northern cities. Poverty is more common in rural areas than in cities. Table 3 points out some other important characteristics of people living below the poverty line in the United States. Almost 12 percent of the population fell below the poverty threshold in 1985. However, the poverty rate was above 15 percent for certain segments of the population. Nonwhites are much more likely to be poor. Age is also an important factor. Children represent a large fraction of those below the poverty level. In fact, poverty has shifted from being a problem of the elderly to being a problem of female-headed households

---

3. Spencer Rich, "Defining Poverty: A Science or an Art," *The Washington Post National Weekly Edition* (12 November 1989): 31. This article also contains a good summary of how the poverty number was first developed and Congressional criticisms of it.

TABLE 3
POVERTY INCIDENCE IN THE UNITED STATES, 1988

CHARACTERISTICS	PERCENTAGE BELOW THE POVERTY LINE
All Persons	13.1
Adult male in household	10.8
No adult male (female-headed household)	33.6
Household head under twenty-four years old	29.7
Household head under twenty-four years old and black	59.6
Household head sixty-five or older	6.6
Household head sixty-five or older and black	17.1
Households with children under eighteen	
One child	10.4
Two children	9.9
Three children	14.0
Four children	20.8
Less than eight years of schooling	25.0
High school graduate	8.9
Some college (one year or more)	3.5
Employed (50–52 weeks)	3.5
Unemployed (1–49 weeks)	19.4
Did not work	23.9

Source: U.S. Department of Commerce, Bureau of the Census, *Statistical Abstract of the United States 1990* (Washington, DC: U.S. Government Printing Office, 1990).

with small children.

Nonwhites are more likely to be poor than whites partly because of racial discrimination. In addition, nonwhites are also more likely to be poor because a higher percentage are under seventeen, have less education, or live in female-headed households. Whatever the cause of race-related poverty, Figure 3 shows that the nonwhite-white income difference has improved very little for males but a lot for females (white females, however, only earn about 60 to 65 percent of the annual earnings of white males). After some interim improvement, the black-white income ratio was about the same for males in 1988 as it was in the late 1950s.

The figures show that poverty in the United States is greatly influenced by behavior regarding work, education, and marriage. One encouraging sign is that the educational achievement of nonwhites has been increasing. This increase should eventually be reflected in higher income levels. Professor Thomas Sowell argues that monetary returns to education are much higher for minority individuals than for nonminority individuals.[4]

THE REGIONAL DISTRIBUTION OF THE POOR

The share of the population living in poverty varies widely among regions in the United States. For example, in Albany, Georgia, 8.47 percent of all families were headed by females and below the poverty line. The same figure for Sheboygan, Wisconsin was 1.1 percent. In Detroit, Michigan, the figure was 4.9 percent. In Toledo, Ohio, the out-of-state metropolitan

---

4. See Thomas Sowell, *Race and Economics* (New York: David McKay Co., 1975). Sowell's points were discussed in the chapter on marginal productivity theory and labor markets.

Economic Profile

Thomas Sowell
1930–

Thomas Sowell, an economist at the Hoover Institution at Stanford University, has a B.A. from Harvard, an M.A. from Columbia, and a Ph.D. in economics from the University of Chicago. He uses microeconomic theory to analyze race-related problems of income distribution in the United States.

In one study, Sowell examined the impact of affirmative action programs on employment by institutions of higher education. He concluded that such affirmative action programs did not fulfill the intent of the Civil Rights Act of 1964. That law rejected quotas and placed the burden of proving discrimination on the government. In practice, the burden of proof has fallen on the employer, increasing costs for higher education. In addition, Sowell questioned whether such programs were necessary. His data indicate that salaries of black academics equaled or surpassed salaries of white academics with comparable training and credentials before the law was applied in 1971. Sowell's findings also suggest that male-female salary differences at colleges and universities are not primarily the result of employer discrimination but are better explained by social patterns that place heavier family responsibilities on females.

In the book *Ethnic America: A History* (1981), Sowell examined the experience of successive waves of immigrants. He concluded that disciplined hard work and entrepreneurial ability can surmount poverty and bigotry. The impressive record of West Indian blacks suggests that being black is not an overwhelming obstacle to success in the United States.

In all of his work, Sowell uses economic theory to examine social policy questions of considerable interest. He does not shy away from very sensitive questions of race and discrimination. Sowell's ideas and arguments are set forth in *Affirmative Action Reconsidered* (1975), *Black Education: Myths and Tragedies* (1970), *Race and Economics* (1975), *Knowledge and Decisions* (1980), *Ethnic America: A History* (1981), and *Markets and Minorities* (1981).

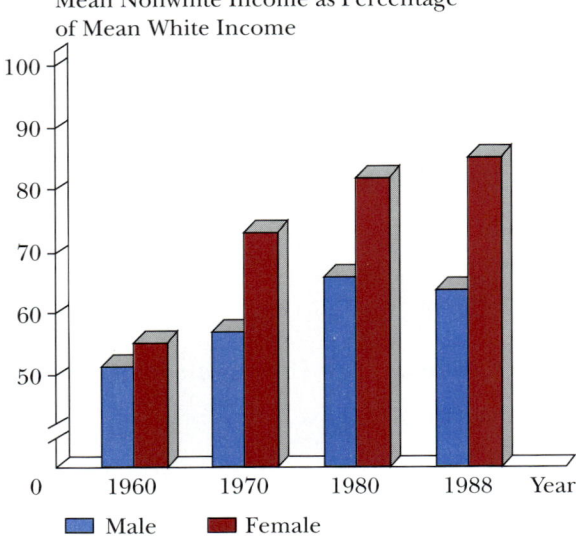

FIGURE 3
NONWHITE-WHITE INCOME RATIOS
Despite some increases in the 1970s, the nonwhite-white income ratio for males improved only moderately between 1960 and 1988. The improvement for nonwhite females, however, was dramatic.

Source: Reynold Farley, "Assessing Black Progress: Employment, Occupation, Earnings, Income, Poverty," *Economic Outlook U.S.A.* (1986) 13: 14–19.

area closest to Detroit, it was 3.8 percent.

Research into these regional differences in poverty rates has led to an interesting economic finding. Low-income, female-headed families respond to economic incentives and move to capture higher welfare benefits. Norman Cloutier and Anthony Loviscek have examined the effects of differences among states in payments for Aid to Families with Dependent Children (AFDC), a transfer program aimed at helping poor children.[5] Their research shows that local economic conditions, especially the unemployment rate, are the most important factors affecting the number of families receiving AFDC assistance. However, metropolitan areas in states with high AFDC benefits located near states with low benefits will experience an increase in the number of their AFDC families. The most recent pair of cities to experience this kind of movement has been Chicago and Milwaukee. Wisconsin raised its AFDC benefits relative to those in Chicago, and AFDC families moved to Milwaukee to capture the increase. This result comes as no surprise to economists. Rational individuals respond to incentives. Welfare mothers are no different from other self-interested individuals.

DISCRIMINATION AND THE DISTRIBUTION OF INCOME

How big a role does race and sex discrimination play in income distribution? Since the Civil Rights Act of 1964, discrimination in employment has been illegal. Many companies, in part to show their compliance with fed-

---

5. Norman Cloutier and Anthony Loviscek, "AFDC Benefits and the Inter-Urban Variation in Poverty among Female-Headed Households," *Southern Economic Journal* (October 1989): 315–322.

eral law, embarked on affirmative action programs in the 1970s. Yet black-white and male-female wage (and income) differences remain high. These differences, however, do not mean that discrimination accounts for the income distribution pattern. Earning differences can be shown to depend at least partly on other influences.

THE DEMAND AND SUPPLY OF DISCRIMINATION

Labor market discrimination today rarely takes the form of setting wages or hiring on the basis of sex or race, which would violate federal laws. Discrimination is usually more subtle, consisting of channeling workers by sex or race into occupations that are "more suitable" for females or nonwhites. As a result of such channeling, certain work categories have a greater supply of workers and lower wage rates than they otherwise would. Traditionally, females were directed into teaching and secretarial work. Many personal service occupations show a high proportion of minority workers. Table 4 shows the concentrations of blacks and females in certain occupations. Females account for 45 percent of the labor force, and blacks account for 10 percent. Females are heavily concentrated in sales, clerical, and private household work. However, they have made progress in recent years in some higher-paying occupations, doubling their representation in medicine and showing impressive gains in law and management. Blacks have also broadened their representation in higher-paying occupations but are still overrepresented in low-paying service and blue-collar occupations.

Figure 4 illustrates the effects of channeling on wage differences. If a majority of workers in some occupations are able to exclude other workers by sex or race, the supply curve of workers for the exclusive occupations will be S'_e rather than S_e. Wage rates for workers in these jobs will be higher than they would otherwise be (W_e rather than W_0). At the same time, the supply curve of workers in minority or female occupations shifts to the right (from S_m to S'_m). The result of channeling is a lower wage rate (W_m rather than W_0) in the minority or female occupations than it would

TABLE 4 EMPLOYED PERSONS BY SEX, RACE, AND OCCUPATION, 1972 AND 1988

	1972		1988	
	PERCENT FEMALE	PERCENT BLACK	PERCENT FEMALE	PERCENT BLACK
Total employed	38.0	9.5	44.7	10.1
Physicians	9.3	2.2	20.0	3.3
Lawyers and judges	3.8	1.6	19.5	3.3
Managers and administrators	19.0	1.6	44.7	6.1
Sales workers	41.6	3.0	48.9	6.1
Secretaries	99.4	6.4	99.1	7.1
Carpenters	0.5	5.0	1.4	5.2
Textile operatives	55.2	15.3	90.1	18.0
Cleaning service workers	32.8	28.6	42.6	23.0

Source: U.S. Department of Commerce, Bureau of the Census, *Statistical Abstract of the United States 1990* (Washington, DC: U.S. Government Printing Office, 1990).

**FIGURE 4
LABOR MARKET
DISCRIMINATION**
(*a*) If workers are excluded from certain occupations, the supply curve will shift from S_e to S'_e. The wage rate will rise to W_e in the excluded occupations. The excluded workers will be channeled into minority occupations. (*b*) The supply curve in the minority occupations shifts from S_m to S'_m, and the wage rate falls to W_m.

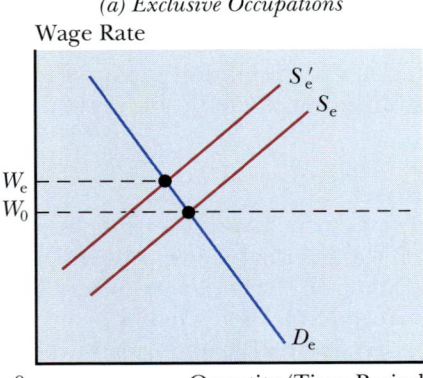
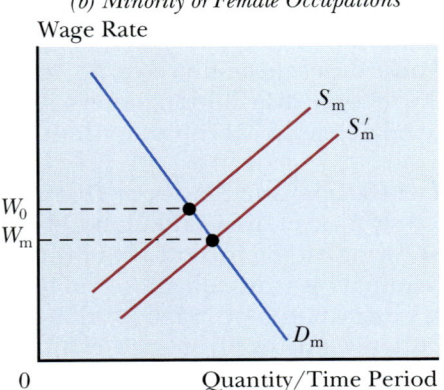

(*a*) Exclusive Occupations (*b*) Minority or Female Occupations

otherwise have been. Such wage differences constitute discrimination only to the extent that they result from workers being excluded from one group of occupations and channeled into another. If there are real productivity differences between the two kinds of occupations in Figure 4 (reflected in different demand curves), market forces would produce different wage rates even in the absence of racial or sexual discrimination. In the real world, productivity differences and channeling effects may coexist in the same markets.

DOES LABOR MARKET DISCRIMINATION EXIST?

In the United States, discrimination in employment is illegal by the 1964 Civil Rights Act and the 1965 Equal Employment Opportunity Act, but wage differences persist. There is some evidence that labor market discrimination exists. For example, in 1989, *Money* magazine reported that blacks earn 10 to 26 percent less than whites with similar educational backgrounds.[6] In addition, a study by Michael Robinson and Phanindra Wunnava showed that female hourly earnings in full-time non-union jobs would be 25 percent higher in the absence of "direct discrimination."[7]

In order to measure labor market discrimination, it is necessary to separate the effects of productivity differences from other reasons for male-female or black-white earnings differences. The first group of differences is called the productivity gap, and the second, the wage gap. Historically, females and minorities have made less investment in human capital (education, training, and job experience) than white males and thus have lower productivity on the average. Studies suggest that about three-quarters of the earnings differences can be explained by differences in human capital, by occupational choice, or by other objective characteristics such as age, health, and geographic location. Do these studies mean that discrimination is not an important explanation for wage differences? No! Consider the effect of discrimination on the incentive to invest in human cap-

---

6. Walter L. Updegrave, "Race and Money," *Money* (December 1989): 152–172.
7. Michael D. Robinson and Phanindra V. Wunnava, "Measuring Direct Discrimination in Labor Markets Using a Frontier Approach: Evidence from CPS Female Earnings Data," *Southern Economic Journal* (July 1989): 212–218.

ital and the effect of channeling on occupational choice. The productivity gap is not independent of the wage gap.[8] Thus, it is difficult to determine precisely how much of current wage differences reflect past and present discrimination and how much would persist even in a discrimination-free world.

OTHER EXPLANATIONS OF MALE-FEMALE EARNINGS DIFFERENCES

A number of recent studies have identified other explanations for male-female earnings differences, besides discrimination. These explanations include career interruptions, role differentiation, relative number of hours worked, and geographic mobility.

CAREER INTERRUPTIONS. Many working females leave the labor force at least once during their lives. Donald Cox examined the effects of such career interruptions, using data from Social Security records.[9] Cox found that lifetime earnings of females are reduced by these interruptions. Income growth is closely linked to job experience, which increases human capital. Interruptions disrupt the acquisition of experience. Cox also suggested that channeling is not entirely based on discrimination, at least for females. Some jobs more readily allow for career interruptions without loss of skills or continuity. These jobs may be more attractive to females because they blend better with bearing and caring for children.

ROLE DIFFERENTIATION. Economist Victor Fuchs argues that much of the observed pay inequality between males and females is the result of "role differentiation."[10] Fuchs uses this term to indicate that society has different expectations for males and females. Fuchs contends that role differentiation begins in childhood and influences the decisions females make about schooling, location, occupational choice, and time spent in the labor market. Role differentiation often encourages a female to choose a job location and job responsibilities that are compatible with her husband's job choice or that lend themselves to career interruptions. Role differentiation is also reflected in hours worked and geographic mobility. Fuchs argues that lower salaries due to role differentiation do not really constitute discrimination in a narrow sense. Instead, they are the result of choices made by females based on widely held social values. In the last twenty years more females have chosen to enter previously male-dominated occupations, and U.S. wage differences between the sexes have begun to fall.

RELATIVE NUMBER OF HOURS WORKED. Females average fewer hours in paid employment than males. Some comparisons of average earnings—such as the popular statement that females earn 60 percent as much as males—do not correct for that fact. And even that 60 percent ratio has begun to change. It is approaching 67 percent. After correcting for differences in hours

---

8. For a discussion of the interaction between the wage gap and the productivity gap, see Thomas D'Amico, "The Conceit of Labor Market Discrimination," *American Economic Review Papers and Proceedings* (May 1987): 310–315.

9. Donald Cox, "Panel Estimates of the Effects of Career Interruptions on the Earnings of Women," *Economic Inquiry* (July 1984): 386–403.

10. Victor Fuchs, "Recent Trends and Long-Run Prospects for Female Earnings," *American Economic Review Papers and Proceedings* (May 1984): 235–242.

worked, the remaining sex-related difference in earnings is even less.[11]

GEOGRAPHIC MOBILITY. Immobility of labor increases any monopsony power in local labor markets. Married females often refuse attractive job offers because of the geographic location of their husband's job. They may limit their job searches to areas close to home. Robert H. Frank has found that such locational restrictions may explain as much as 23 percent of the wage difference between males and females.[12]

One approach to evaluating sex differences in earnings is to compare the earnings of single males and single females. Some studies show that single females, who have the same incentives as males to invest in human capital, to minimize career interruptions, to work longer hours, and to be geographically mobile, earn almost the same wages as males.[13] In fact, Janet Norwood, commissioner of the U.S. Bureau of Labor Statistics, revealed in a speech at Vanderbilt University that "teenage and young adult women have median earnings that are more than 90 percent of the earnings of men of comparable age." She called the narrowing of this gap "quite significant."[14]

DISCRIMINATION AND MARKET FORCES

Some economists argue that racial or sexual discrimination will not persist over time in a market system because it is costly to entrepreneurs. There would be large numbers of minority and female workers who would be earning low salaries but who would have basically the same education and work skills as white male workers. A profit-motivated entrepreneur could hire these minority and female workers and produce goods and services more cheaply than other firms using the more expensive labor. Thus, the profit motive would work to undermine discrimination.

Some economic historians argue that the Jim Crow laws enacted in the South in the late nineteenth and early twentieth centuries were a response to the threat that market forces would undermine racial discrimination. Jim Crow laws were intended to put the force of law behind segregation and discrimination. These laws were eventually overridden by federal legislation. In South Africa, apartheid was needed to maintain a racially segregated system that economic forces would otherwise have undermined.

If market forces work to undermine discrimination and laws penalize discrimination, why do the data show persistent white-black, female-male income differences? One reason is that different sectors of the economy and different occupations adjust to change with different speeds. It is clear that professional athletics has adjusted very quickly to changing laws and customs, and the medical profession has adjusted quite slowly. The presence of monopoly power and licensing as well as the length of time it takes to train for an occupation may influence the speed of adjustment.

Persistent discrimination also reflects an interaction between discrimi-

---

11. Robert Pear, "Earnings Gap Is Narrowing Slightly for Women," *New York Times* (3 October 1983).
12. Robert H. Frank, "Why Women Earn Less: The Theory and Estimate of Differential Overqualification," *American Economic Review* (June 1978): 360–373.
13. See Thomas Sowell, "Affirmative Action Reconsidered," *The Public Interest* (Winter 1976): 47–65; and James Gwartney and Richard Stroup, "Measurement of Employment Discrimination According to Sex," *Southern Economic Journal* (April 1973): 575–587.
14. Frank Swoboda, "Closing the Economic Gender Gap," *Washington Post* (4 December 1989): 22.

Chapter 16 Income Distribution: Poverty, Discrimination, and Welfare   419

nation and characteristics that affect productivity (education, training, experience, and occupational choice). Females or minorities, who expect to be offered lower salaries or to be excluded from desirable occupations, may invest less in human capital. As it became clear in the 1970s that jobs formerly closed to most females and minorities were now accessible, the numbers of females and minorities in those jobs began to rise. The information that provides the basis for such changes is disseminated and absorbed slowly.

Discrimination begets poverty, and poverty begets little investment in human capital. Although discrimination is not the sole source of poverty, it does have a contributing effect. Government can help combat discrimination with laws forbidding employment discrimination and with equal treatment for government employees regardless of race or sex. These policies by themselves, however, are not enough to eliminate poverty. The government may also be called upon to take action that changes the income distribution determined by the market.

INCOME REDISTRIBUTION

Citizens may support income redistribution for a variety of reasons. First, some people have **interdependent utility functions**, which means that their well-being is dependent on the well-being of others. These people would support programs to redistribute income because such redistribution increases their utility. Second, some people might view poverty as a negative external effect, like air pollution—something that makes the environment less appealing. This group would support redistribution to improve their surroundings. They might, for example, support food stamp legislation to help hungry people. Finally, redistribution can be viewed as an insurance policy. People might support redistribution as a safety net, realizing that they might become poor at some time.

interdependent utility functions
Preference patterns in which some people's well-being is dependent on the well-being of others.

PRIVATE INCOME REDISTRIBUTION AND THE ROLE OF GOVERNMENT

Income redistribution in the United States, and many other countries, has been carried out by both the private sector and the public sector. Many public goods or goods with some public benefits are produced at least partly in the private sector. There are private roads, private schools, private outdoor concerts, and other goods and services that generate collective benefits but are privately produced. Income redistribution is another activity with public benefits that is produced at least in part by the private sector. The motives for voluntary redistribution through private charities are the same as those that lead individuals to support public redistribution.

It is not likely that private redistribution alone will achieve the desired level of income transfers. Individuals in a large group will recognize that their contribution is too small to significantly affect total redistribution. Each person has an incentive to free-ride on the contributions of others. If all followed this strategy, there would be no private redistribution. There is not enough private redistribution.

The person who gives to others because of personal satisfaction gained from the act of charity does not experience an incentive to free ride. However, for some people, the nature of the benefit is seeing less poverty in the world. In this case, giving by others diminishes the need for an individual to give, and the free-rider problem can arise.

An important influence on the amount of private redistribution is the size of the group in which redistribution takes place. In a relatively small, homogeneous group, there is likely to be relatively more private redistribution. Think about the Mormon church and the Amish sects, for example, or small towns versus large cities. Greater charity in small groups is consistent with the view that the effects associated with poverty are more significant (observable) when the group size is smaller. Thus, at the national level, a small country with a relatively homogeneous population, such as Sweden, would seem likely to practice more redistribution than a large "melting-pot" country, such as the United States.

Although private redistribution has an important role to play, since the 1930s Americans have expected the government to play a major role in redistributing income and alleviating poverty. For both private and public redistribution, several important questions about the best way to redistribute must be resolved.

EQUALITY OF OPPORTUNITY OR EQUALITY OF RESULTS?

One important question concerns the goal of redistribution. Should this goal be equality of opportunity or equality of results? To the extent that labor market discrimination leads to an unequal income distribution and poverty, there may be a need for policies that create greater equality of opportunity. Such policies would mandate government investment in human capital through technical schools, student loans and grants, or training programs. They might also impose penalties on employers who engage in discrimination that is not based on productivity differences. Such policies should offer the working poor a chance to improve their earnings and escape from poverty.

Government or private programs that reduce unemployment and improve the match between workers and jobs are also indirect forms of poverty relief. Not only do these programs increase total output, they generally improve job opportunities and earnings for workers at the lower end of the wage scale. Anything that the government does to promote economic growth and reduce cyclical fluctuations will also reduce unemployment for all groups. Since the poor are so often the last hired and first fired, they would benefit more than most from such programs. Even programs that reduce the obstacles to working, such as those that improve public transportation or subsidize day care, help the poor who can work.

Programs to alleviate poverty by creating work opportunities and improving the potential to earn result in equality of opportunity. Giving everyone an equal chance at success in the labor market is consistent with the values of freedom, incentives, and individual choice implicit in a market economic system. However, equality of opportunity does nothing to help those who are too old, too young, too sick, too disabled, or too unskilled to participate in the market as workers or those who have to care for very small children. The only programs that will reach these poor are programs that are aimed directly at equality of results.

The fraction of the poor outside the labor force, or not expected to work, has risen dramatically in the last fifty years. In 1939, less than one-third of poor households were classified as composed of persons not able to work for one of the reasons listed above. Today, closer to two-thirds of poor households are headed by a person who is elderly, a student, disabled, or a female with one or more preschool children. These people do not benefit from the rising tide of economic growth and increased job opportunities unless there is a deliberate effort to share those gains through a redistribution program.[15]

IN CASH OR IN KIND?

Once the decision is made to alter the market-determined distribution of income, the next question concerns the form in which payments should be made. Should cash transfers, such as a guaranteed income, be used? Or should income be redistributed through in-kind transfers of goods and services, such as housing, food, or health care?

Many forms of income redistribution, both private and public, are in-kind transfers of specific goods or services. In-kind transfers are popular among private charities. Examples include soup kitchens, shelters for the homeless, and Meals on Wheels for shut-ins. In-kind transfers are based not on a desire to reduce income inequality but rather on a desire to ensure the provision of basics, such as food and shelter. James Tobin calls this motivation specific egalitarianism.[16] Economists tend to be general egalitarians, on the other hand. Most would argue for giving cash instead of specific goods and services because a transfer of cash allows more options and maximizes the freedom of the recipient. This argument is based on the assumption that the goal is to maximize the utility of the recipients. Tobin argues, however, that the majority of people are specific egalitarians. They are concerned with ill-clothed and ill-fed people, not with general inequality. If this observation is correct, there should be more transfers made in kind rather than in cash. For the last twenty-five years most of the growth in government transfers to the poor has been in-kind.

Nobel laureate James Buchanan argues that the preference of voters for in-kind rather than cash transfers simply means that they are maximizing their own utility as donors rather than maximizing the utility of welfare recipients by allowing them freedom of choice.[17] The donor/voter's motive for income redistribution may not be concern for the welfare of the recipients but rather a desire to eliminate some perceived problem—homeless people on the streets, slum housing, or students who disrupt the learning process in public schools because of illness or hunger. Providing specific goods or services is a more direct way of accomplishing that goal.

WHICH LEVEL OF GOVERNMENT?

A final issue in designing an income redistribution program is deciding which level of government should be responsible. Until the 1930s, alleviating poverty was a responsibility of state and local governments. The

---

15. Economic growth as a solution to poverty was criticized on this basis by Sheldon Danziger and Peter Gottschalk, "Do Rising Tides Lift All Boats? The Impact of Secular and Cyclical Change on the Poor," *American Economic Review Papers and Proceedings* (May 1986): 405–410.
16. James Tobin, "On Limiting the Domain of Inequality," *Journal of Law and Economics* (October 1970): 263–277.
17. James M. Buchanan, "What Kind of Redistribution Do We Want," *Economica* (May 1968): 62–87.

Great Depression led to greater involvement by the federal government. In the late 1960s and through the 1970s, strong arguments were made for centralized provision of such programs. Social Security is a federal program, but other programs are shared by levels of government. States that offered high welfare benefits attracted low-income migrants from states where benefits were lower. Thus, some economists argue, states that wanted to offer higher benefit levels were deterred from doing so by fear of attracting more recipients than they could afford. Furthermore, advocates of centralizing welfare argue that the level of income support a household receives should depend on its "needs" (ages, family size, and health) rather than the fiscal wealth of the state in which it is located. Redistribution from richer to poorer individuals would also lead to equalization among states, so even those who lived in poor states but weren't poor would benefit from lower state taxes.

After two failed efforts to centralize welfare in the 1970s (Nixon's Family Assistance Plan and Carter's Program for Better Jobs and Income), it became clear that such plans were not politically feasible. Several reasons have been suggested for this failure. If support for income transfers depends heavily on a desire to eliminate negative external effects (such as crime or blight), then support for redistribution in one's own area will be stronger because the benefits will be concentrated there. Even if taxpayers are interested in increasing the utility of the recipient rather than their own utility, they will still receive more satisfaction from seeing the poverty relief that results from spending in their own area. Thus, if a large part of the benefits of poverty relief are captured at the state or local level, there is reason for a large part of the benefits to be financed at that level as well. In addition, the appropriate level and combination of benefits may vary from state to state. If most of the poor live in rural areas in state A, there may be less need for food programs than in state B. A state with a high proportion of elderly residents or a cold climate will opt to offer more medical care or heat assistance benefits than another state. A state with more children might put more resources into day care or remedial education. Tailoring the benefits to local needs and the preferences of the local electorate is another reason for giving states a major role.

In 1982, such reasoning led the Reagan administration to propose sorting out welfare programs and returning more of the responsibilities to the states. Like Nixon's centralizing proposal, Reagan's proposal was decisively rejected. The proposal was politically unpopular because the funds to pay for the programs would not come from the federal government. After two decades of failed attempts to sort out responsibility for the poor, income redistribution programs in the United States continue to be funded by the federal government, state governments, local governments (in large cities), and private philanthropic organizations.

REDISTRIBUTION TO THE MIDDLE-INCOME CLASS

Not all redistribution is to the poor or for the poor. Nobel laureate George Stigler and Gordon Tullock point out that people try to use government programs as a way to redistribute income to themselves rather than to others.[18] Stigler theorizes that the government will use its power to extract resources that would not be provided by voluntary agreement in the society. Any group that can gain control of the government can then use this power to its own benefit. Stigler argues that the group that controls government is the middle class. Thus, most public expenditures are made for the benefit of the middle class.

Tullock argues that only a small portion of government transfers go to the poor.[19] He argues that, due to the nature of the voting process, relatively more resources will be taken from the rich in taxes. However, it is not entirely clear how they will be distributed. Since the support of middle-income voters is necessary to obtain the authority needed to take resources from other members of society, he expects that money flows from both ends of the income ladder toward the middle.

Both Tullock and Stigler believe that income redistribution tends to be captured by the dominant political group, the middle class. Both of them present examples of redistribution, such as farm subsidies and support for higher education, that mainly benefit individuals in the middle class. Much redistribution is directed to special interests or is absorbed by bureaucracy, and little of that flow benefits the poor.

GOVERNMENT TRANSFER PROGRAMS IN PRACTICE

Until the 1930s, programs to relieve poverty were small scale, provided mainly by local government and private charity. In the Depression, state and local governments were swamped with demands, and the present system of federal and federally assisted income transfer programs was born. These programs include Social Security for workers who are retired or disabled and survivors of deceased workers, unemployment compensation for the temporarily unemployed, and welfare programs for those unable to work.

SOCIAL SECURITY

Social Security, established in 1935, was initially an old-age pension program. It was later expanded to include survivors' benefits (1939) and disability insurance (1950). Social Security was designed to relieve poverty for several major groups of poor persons: the old, the dependent survivors of deceased workers, and the disabled. In 1965, a program of health care for the elderly (Medicare) was incorporated into Social Security. Except for Medicare, Social Security is a cash transfer program with no in-kind benefits.

Social Security payments are financed by a tax on workers and employers, each paying an equal amount. Many workers believe that their employers actually pay the other half of their Social Security payment. Microeconomic theory reveals that at least part of the other half is in fact paid by workers who earn lower wages than they would receive if there

---

18. George J. Stigler, "Director's Law of Public Income Redistribution," *Journal of Law and Economics* (April 1970): 1–10.
19. Gordon Tullock, *Economics of Income Redistribution* (Boston: Kluver-Nijhoff, 1983), Chapter 5.

International Perspective

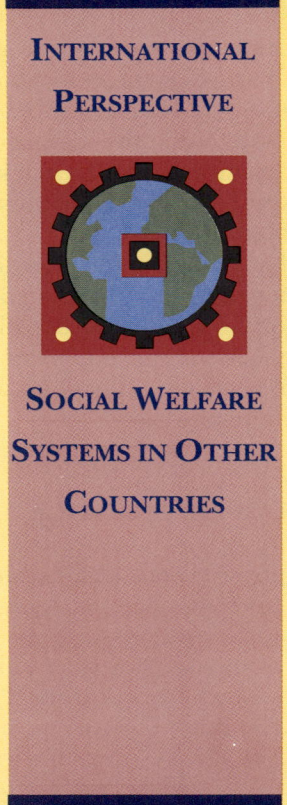

Social Welfare Systems in Other Countries

The social welfare system is a broad term encompassing all of the transfer payments and social services that governments provide to individual citizens. Some of these programs are based on a means (level of income) test and others go to all citizens. Children's allowances in Canada, for example, are provided to all families. Since these grants are taxable income, some of the funds are recovered in tax payments from higher-income families. Education up to a certain level is traditionally provided to all citizens in industrial countries regardless of income. Food stamps and subsidized public housing, however, are subject to an income test.

Despite the hue and cry for welfare reform, social welfare expenditures in the United States are actually low relative to those of most other industrial countries. Only Japan spends a lower percent of its total income on welfare programs. Japanese society places much greater responsibility for welfare on the family. The elderly, for example, are much more likely to live with their grown children than they would be in the United States.

All major industrial countries have some type of publicly funded old age pension system and some provision for unemployment and disability insurance. The nature of welfare benefits varies widely, however. Health care is more likely to be provided at public expense in European nations. Public housing has been an important component of social welfare in the United Kingdom, where until recently 28 percent of the population lived in "council houses" (public housing rented at subsidized rates). In Scandinavian countries, the political consensus is that a basic standard of living is a right. Therefore, certain basic social services and social insurance programs (unemployment, disability, and so on) are provided to everyone without an income test.

The emphasis on individualism and the concern over work incentives that pervade the welfare debate in the United States receive less attention elsewhere, except from the Conservative government in the United Kingdom. Support for the welfare state was at its peak in European countries and in the United States in the 1960s and 1970s. In the 1980s, Japan continued to expand its social insurance programs, but the nations of Western Europe as well as the United States were carefully reconsidering the level of public expenditure on social welfare.

Social Welfare Expenditures (Including Education)

Country	Percentage of GDP	Percentage of Government Spending
Japan	17.5	46.7
United States	20.8	58.3
Canada	21.5	53.4
United Kingdom	23.7	51.0
France	29.5	61.0
Sweden	33.4	52.2

Source: Richard Rose and Rei Shiratori, *The Welfare State East and West* (Oxford, UK: Oxford University Press, 1986).

were no Social Security tax. Figure 5 shows why this is the case. Before the Social Security tax, the supply of labor facing the firm is S_0, and the firm's demand is D. The equilibrium wage is W_0. Adding a Social Security tax equal to $B - A$ (or the length of line AB) shifts the supply curve facing this firm to S_1. If supply is fairly elastic but demand is relatively inelastic, most of the tax falls on the worker. The gross wage (including the tax) rises to W_g, but the net wage taken home by the worker falls to W_n. The actual division of the burden of the tax between worker and employer depends, not on the legislation that says half on each, but on the relative elasticities of supply and demand for labor. Economists believe that most of the tax falls on the worker because the market supply of labor is very inelastic.

Social Security is the largest income redistribution program in the United States. It incorporates some aspects of insurance. Workers must contribute to the program for a specified minimum period of time in order to be eligible for benefits. Workers do not have a choice about participating. With very few exceptions, everyone who holds a paying job earning more than $50 a quarter must pay the Social Security tax, including self-employed individuals. Once workers become eligible to receive benefits, they receive them regardless of how much non-wage income they have in the form of interest, dividends, and/or private pensions. Retired individuals in some age categories face a reduction of benefits if they earn wage income, but not non-wage income. This rule discriminates against poorer retirees, because the only way most of them can supplement their retirement income is with wage income. Higher-income retirees collect interest, dividends, and/or private pensions without loss of Social Security benefits.

Until recently, Social Security benefits were not subject to federal income tax, and even now, most of these benefits are not taxable. Since 1985, Social Security recipients with adjusted gross incomes above $25,000 ($32,000 for married couples) have to pay income taxes on one-half of their Social Security benefits. This rule affected 15 percent of the recipients. Even with this change in the law, a large share of Social Security benefits still

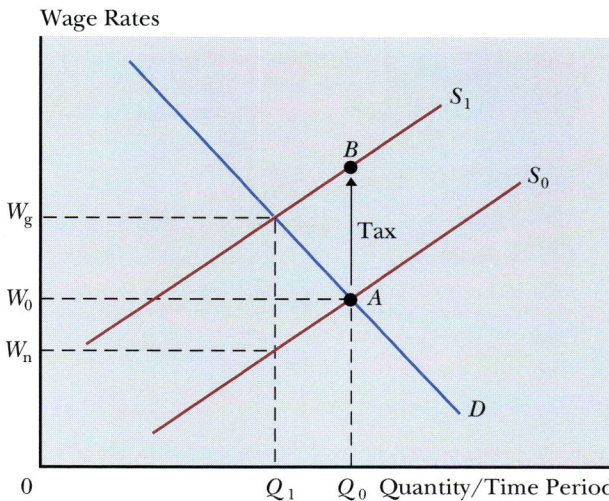

FIGURE 5
WHO PAYS SOCIAL SECURITY TAXES?
The higher price of labor, including the Social Security tax, reduces the number of workers employed from Q_0 to Q_1. The gross wage, including Social Security taxes, rises from W_0 to W_g, but the worker's net wage falls to W_n. The shaded area is the tax burden on workers in the form of lower wages.

goes to people who are not poor. In fact, some of the taxes paid by the working poor are being transferred to the rich through Social Security.

When Social Security was established as a compulsory retirement system, many people believed that their payments went into a trust fund. In fact, the account into which workers and employers pay their taxes is called the Social Security Trust Fund. However, it is simply a fund into which current workers pay and from which current beneficiaries receive payments. No money is held and invested for workers as a pool from which they will later receive income, as true of private pensions and annuities. It is amusing that on a regular basis some enterprising journalist "discovers" that the Social Security Trust Fund is a sham.[20]

The Social Security system is a tax-and-transfer mechanism. Individuals are taxed during their working years to pay benefits to those who are retired, disabled, or surviving dependents of covered workers. In the early years of the Social Security system, the funds coming in were more than adequate because there were many workers and few retired people. However, the age distribution of the U.S. population has changed greatly since that time. Table 5 shows this dramatic shift in the working versus the retired population. In 1950, an individual worker's payments had to support only 6 percent of one recipient's benefits. In 1991, each worker had to be taxed enough to support 35 percent of one recipient's benefits. Coupled with the increasing level of benefits, the changing ratio of workers to beneficiaries has created a heavy burden on workers. In 1980, Social Security taxes represented 30.5 percent of federal tax collections. By 1990, the Social Security share of federal tax revenues had grown to 37.0 percent. That's an increase of 21 percent in ten years. In 1990, Social Security benefits represented 20 percent of federal expenditures.[21]

Can today's workers rely on promised future Social Security payments? Many of today's workers are concerned about whether they will receive the benefits they are being promised. Reforms made in 1985 strengthened the stability of the system. These changes were (1) reducing the growth in benefit levels (including eliminating survivor benefits to college students and delaying retirement ages in the future), (2) broadening the categories of workers required to participate, so there will be more con-

**TABLE 5
SUPPORT FOR
SOCIAL SECURITY
RECIPIENTS**

YEAR	WORKERS PER SOCIAL SECURITY BENEFICIARY
1950	16.0
1960	5.0
1984	3.3
2010	3.0
2034	2.0

Source: The *1984 Annual Report of Board of Trustees of the Federal Old Age and Survivor's Insurance and Disability Trust Funds* (Washington, DC: Social Security Administration, 1984).

20. See, for example, Howard Gleckman, "Social Security's Dirty Little Secret," *Business Week* (29 January 1990): 66–67.
21. See "Bush Faces a Tax Steamroller," *Fortune* (12 February 1990): 8; and "Social Security's Big Fix," *U.S. News & World Report* (2 January 1990) 27–28.

tributors, (3) raising the Social Security payroll tax rate, and (4) raising the income base (the amount of income subject to the payroll tax). These last two changes increased Social Security revenues so much that the deficit turned into a surplus. In 1990, Social Security collected $380 billion in payroll taxes and paid out $249 billion in benefits. By 1993, the annual surplus is expected to grow to over $150 billion. In response to this surplus, Senator Daniel Moynihan has led a movement to reduce the payroll tax and relieve this tax burden on workers.[22]

TRANSFERS TO THE ELDERLY

Earlier in this chapter, we presented the arguments of George Stigler and Gordon Tullock that government is used by organized groups in society to capture income transfers. Since one of the fastest-growing and most politically organized groups is the elderly, that group might be expected to capture an increasing share of government transfers.

Recent experience supports this prediction. In the last several decades, the economic well-being of the elderly has increased greatly in the United States. In 1959, 35 percent of those over sixty-five had incomes below the poverty line, compared to 22 percent for the population as a whole and 27 percent for children under eighteen. The largest segment of the poor in 1959 were those over sixty-five. By 1990, only 12 percent of those over sixty-five were below the poverty line. If in-kind transfers are counted, the number falls to 5 percent. Professor James Schulz observed, "Poverty among the elderly, as measured by the poverty index and adjusted for nonmoney income, has virtually disappeared."[23] Much of this decline is due to the vast amounts of federal resources that are going to the elderly. People over sixty-five make up 12 percent of the population and receive 27 percent of federal spending. If you exclude defense spending, interest on the national debt, and foreign aid, people over sixty-five receive 48 percent of federal spending.

A second factor has also helped reduce poverty among the elderly. The wealth of those over sixty-five has increased dramatically in the last few decades. Professors Daphne Greenwood and Edward Wolff have examined household wealth by demographic group.[24] They report that in earlier decades older Americans consumed the wealth they had built up in their working years, while younger Americans built up their wealth in anticipation of retirement. This pattern changed in the late 1970s and early 1980s. Between 1973 and 1983, the average wealth of those sixty-five to sixty-nine years old increased from $169,366 to $321,562 in constant (1985) dollars. In contrast, in the same time period, the average wealth of those twenty-five to thirty-four years old decreased from $59,624 to $49,046 in constant (1985) dollars. This increase in wealth for the elderly is mainly related to rapidly rising real estate values during the period.

What has been occurring is that income transfers going to the elderly have been increasing at the same time that their wealth is increasing rela-

---

22. See, for example, Paul Craig Roberts, "It's High Time We Retired the Social Security Tax Surplus," *Business Week* (15 January 1990): 13.
23. Subratra N. Chakravarty and Katherine Weisman, "Consuming our Children," *Forbes* (14 November 1988), 223.
24. "Consuming our Children," 223.

tive to those who are paying for the transfers. The transfers to the elderly have become entitlements. Social Security is the biggest entitlement program. As you have seen, Social Security benefits represent 20 percent of federal spending. Benefits are given to all qualified individuals above a certain age, regardless of their financial situation. Medicare is another entitlement of the elderly. When it was established in 1965, this program was projected to cost $8.8 billion in 1990. Even after adjusting for inflation that estimate was far off the mark. In 1990, Medicare cost $111 billion in 1965 dollars.

The trend toward transferring more resources to those who are relatively well off has begun to cause some concern. As demographer Samuel Preston observes, "The United States has become the first society in history in which the poorest group in the population is the children, not the aged."[25] The concern among economists arises from the fact that money spent on children is at least partly an investment in the future productivity of the economy. In contrast, money spent on the elderly generally goes into consumption to make their lives more comfortable.

The solution to this dilemma is simple enough in principle, but borders on the politically impossible. Entitlement to these transfers would have to be abandoned. The original purpose of the Social Security system and related programs was to provide a safety net. Professor Gary Becker has argued that Social Security benefits should go only to the elderly poor. "When all pretense is dropped that Social Security is an annuity system, separate taxes to finance benefits make as little sense as separate taxes to finance the food stamp program."[26] Becker realizes his proposal is politically difficult, but he argues that it will eventually have to be implemented because the present system cannot sustain itself. The political difficulty is easy to pinpoint. The very young can't vote, the relatively young don't vote, and the elderly have the highest voter participation rate. In addition, the American Association of Retired Persons keeps them fully informed about their entitlements.

UNEMPLOYMENT COMPENSATION

Unemployment compensation is a transfer program financed by a tax on employers and administered by the states, which set benefit levels and eligibility requirements. Unemployment compensation is intended to be a temporary replacement of lost income while a worker is between jobs or temporarily laid off. The program has been criticized as providing "paid vacations" while workers go through the motions of searching for jobs. It has also been praised as providing a safety net for unemployed workers while they match their skills to the best available jobs, making labor markets more efficient. Of all income transfer programs, this one is the least criticized because benefits are of a temporary nature.

WELFARE

The group of programs lumped together as "welfare" began in the 1930s with Aid to the Aged, Aid to the Disabled, and Aid to Dependent Children (later Aid to Families with Dependent Children, or AFDC). These pro-

---

25. "Consuming our Children," 231.
26. Gary S. Becker, "Social Security Should Benefit Only the Elderly Poor," *Business Week* (16 January 1989): 20.

grams identify groups of people not expected to work. Costs are shared between the federal and state governments. There are different eligibility requirements and benefit levels in different states. In the 1960s, these programs were expanded and new ones were added as part of President Johnson's War on Poverty. Aid to the Aged, Aid to the Disabled, and several smaller programs were merged into Supplemental Security Income, a federally funded program, in 1972.

In the 1960s, there was an increase in in-kind programs, including food stamps, public housing, Medicaid, legal aid, Head Start for preschool children, and job training programs. These efforts to improve the welfare of the poor were designed to ensure that they consumed the "right mix" of goods and services, especially in the areas of health, nutrition, education, and training.

THE WELFARE REFORM DEBATE

Welfare reform is, of course, high on the political agenda. The ongoing debate was started by the 1982 proposal to return the largest welfare program, Aid to Families with Dependent Children, to the states and also by a controversial 1983 book by Charles Murray, *Losing Ground.* In this book, Murray argued that the current welfare system encourages people to do the wrong things—to avoid working, to have more children, and to become welfare-dependent. Also, the pressures of the budget deficits during the 1980s led to a re-examination of all areas of federal spending, and some of the most vulnerable programs were social welfare programs. Thus, the 1980s debate on welfare reform centered on three issues: the relative roles of the state and federal governments, work incentives, and cost containment.

The issue of how responsibilities should be shared between state and federal governments was at least temporarily put to rest in 1981 and 1982. Although the federal government reduced grants to state and local governments for social welfare programs, states rejected a proposal that they assume full responsibility for Aid to Families with Dependent Children in 1982.

Critics of welfare programs argue that they discourage work. With multiple benefits, it is very likely that a welfare client who takes a job will be worse off. For such welfare recipients, taking a job means losing not only cash benefits but also medical help, subsidized housing, and other benefits from overlapping programs. In order to determine the effects of welfare programs on work incentives, the federal government sponsored four large-scale experiments to measure how various levels of benefits would affect individuals' work efforts. Households in New Jersey, Pennsylvania, rural areas of North Carolina and Iowa, Gary (Indiana), Seattle, and Detroit were studied at various times from 1969 to 1982. The researchers concluded that higher benefit levels did lead to some modest reductions in work effort, especially among females.[27]

---

27. For a detailed appraisal of the results of the income maintenance program, see *Lessons from the Income Maintenance Experiments*, Alicia H. Munnell (ed.), proceedings of a conference sponsored by the Federal Reserve Bank of Boston and the Brookings Institution, 1986.

THE NEGATIVE INCOME TAX

The high cost of maintaining the bureaucracy to administer in-kind programs has led policy makers to search for another solution to the welfare problem. One popular proposal is the negative income tax. A **negative income tax** is a transfer of income from the government to the poor based on a formula similar to the present income tax system. A positive income tax is a transfer to the government from citizens. Milton Friedman first suggested replacing the existing welfare system with a negative income tax in the 1960s.[28] The negative income tax is popular among economists because of its simplicity and positive work incentive.

Under a negative income tax, everyone would be guaranteed some minimum income. Thus, the first problem is to decide what the minimum income should be. This decision is strictly normative. Economic theory offers no clue as to what this level should be. One approach would be to calculate a typical poverty-level budget at current prices as the standard.

In addition to the minimum income guarantee, a negative income tax also must designate a negative tax rate, which is the rate at which transfer payments are reduced per additional dollar of earned income. These two elements determine a third element, the break-even income, which is the level of income at which a household neither pays income taxes nor receives benefits. In Friedman's plan, the minimum income guarantee varies with family size. For example, a family of four might have a guaranteed income of $6,000. Suppose the negative tax rate is 50 percent. That is, for each dollar the family earns, it loses 50¢ of welfare payments. When the household earns $12,000, it will lose its last dollar of benefits and live on earned income only. Since the household keeps part of its welfare benefits when it earns a modest income, work incentives should be stronger than under the present welfare system.

Table 6 gives benefits for four households, assuming a $6,000 income guarantee and a 50 percent negative tax rate. The transfer payment received by a household is $6,000 minus 50 percent of any income earned that is less than $12,000. The amount that a household receives can be determined by the formula

$$W = IG - (t_n \times EI),$$

where W is the welfare payment, IG is the income guarantee, t_n is the negative tax rate, and EI is the earned income. After the household passes the break-even income level, at which it receives no more transfer payments, it starts paying income taxes. With an income guarantee of $6,000 and a negative tax rate of 50 percent, the break-even point would occur at $12,000. Table 6 also shows how another $100 of income would benefit each household.

The relationship between the three elements—the minimum income guarantee, the negative tax rate, and the break-even income—creates some difficult trade-offs. In order to provide a guaranteed income high enough to ensure a minimum standard of living and a negative tax rate low enough to encourage work, the break-even income would be very high. This combination of choices would raise the cost of the system (requiring

---

negative income tax
A transfer of income from the government to the poor based on a formula similar to the present income tax system and implemented with a minimum income guarantee and a negative tax rate.

---

28. See Milton Friedman, "The Case for the Negative Income Tax," in *Republican Papers*, M. R. Laird (ed.) (New York: Praeger, 1968).

TABLE 6 INCOMES OF FOUR HOUSEHOLDS WITH A NEGATIVE INCOME TAX

	HOUSEHOLD			
	A	B	C	D
Earned income	0	$2,000	$4,000	$12,000
Welfare payment	$6,000	$5,000	$4,000	0
Disposable income	$6,000	$7,000	$8,000	$12,000
Increase in income	$100	$100	$100	$100
Earned income becomes	$100	$2,100	$4,100	$12,100
Tax rate	−50%	−50%	−50%	+15%
Welfare payment	$5,950	$4,950	$3,950	0
Disposable income	$6,050	$7,050	$8,050	$12,085

higher positive tax rates above the break-even income) and extend welfare benefits much higher up the income scale. The break-even income could be reduced by lowering the guaranteed income, but a low minimum income would penalize those who are unable to work and totally dependent on transfers—the aged and the handicapped, for example. Alternatively, the break-even income could be lowered by using a higher negative tax rate, but that higher tax on earnings would discourage work.

A major attraction of the negative income tax is that it would provide public funds directly to the poor rather than funneling them through a large welfare bureaucracy. It would, therefore, cost less for the same amount of redistribution because funds would go directly to reducing poverty. Such a system would reduce the cost of administering welfare programs, which have grown to include a vast array of in-kind transfers.

The negative income tax is also attractive to recipients. It is objective and impersonal, allowing recipients to maintain a sense of dignity and entitlement. Instead of cutting off funds to those whose income is just above the poverty level, the negative income tax would provide aid to the nearly poor as well. Perhaps the most important advantage, however, is that the negative income tax does not destroy work incentives as much as the current system, which reduces transfers by 100 percent of any earned income. If a person on welfare earns $1,000, benefits fall by $1,000. A system that allows individuals to keep a portion of what they earn would strengthen work incentives.

Proponents of a negative income tax do not want to see it superimposed on the current system. Instead, they argue it should replace all direct public-assistance programs. This plan is considered by many economists to have decided advantages over other welfare reform proposals. One major obstacle to its adoption is the self-interest of those presently employed in the welfare bureaucracy. Other obstacles include preferences for in-kind programs, concerns about cost, and resistance to centralizing welfare at the federal level.

President Nixon tried to institute a negative income tax (the Family Assistance Plan) in 1971 but succeeded in only two small areas: SSI (Supplemental Security Income) for the aged and the extension of food stamp benefits. President Carter proposed a similar plan in 1978, the Program for Better Jobs and Income, but again it was not enacted. Both plans failed for three reasons: (1) the high cost of a program with an adequate income guarantee and a low enough negative tax rate, (2) opposition to federalizing of welfare, which had always been at least partly a state and local responsibility, and (3) the opposition of the "iron triangle" of congressional committees that oversee programs, beneficiaries, and government bureaucracies that administer existing programs.

WORKFARE PROGRAMS

How to provide work incentives while containing costs was answered in 1986 with the development of a variety of experimental programs at the state level. These **workfare programs** encourage or require welfare recipients who are able to work to take jobs, sometimes in the public sector, or to enter training programs that should lead to jobs, as a condition for continuing to receive benefits. Another aspect of workfare programs is a specification of the point at which mothers of small children are expected to go to work. As more and more women have chosen to work outside the home while their children are still small, the age at which children are expected to be placed in day care so that their mothers can work has been reduced from six years to three. These workfare programs have appeal for both liberal and conservative politicians. They combine the liberal approach of giving where there is need with the conservative approach of giving to those who contribute. In addition, some states have privately contracted the training of workfare recipients for long-term employment. This approach also won support from conservative politicians.

The most celebrated workfare program was established in Massachusetts, where a voluntary program involving training, day care, and help with job searches has produced promising results. The initial cost was high, especially when day care and training programs were involved, but the eventual cost savings from reduced welfare payments were expected to be substantial. The **Family Support Act of 1988** incorporated some aspects of these experimental state workfare programs. This legislation attempted to transform an entitlement into a reciprocal obligation. Getting a welfare check carried the obligation to accept a job or participate in activities to prepare for accepting a job. The results of this reform are only starting to be apparent. Some preliminary analysis of the results is encouraging. With resources and time, it appears that workfare programs can be moderately successful.[29]

workfare programs
State welfare programs that require those receiving welfare who are able to work to take jobs or to participate in training programs in order to be eligible for benefits.

Family Support Act of 1988
A federal law that incorporates some aspects of state workfare programs, turning entitlements into obligations to take jobs or enter job training programs.

THE WELFARE DEBATE IN THE 1990S

President Bush ran his 1988 campaign talking about a kinder and gentler society. To many this vision meant a call for more income redistribution to make society "more fair." Bush seemed to have something other than such redistribution in mind, however. In his speeches, he often refers to his concept as "a thousand points of light." These points of light are private redistributive efforts and voluntarism, such as students giving their time to help the illiterate learn to read or churches sponsoring shelters for the homeless.

---

29. For a review of the studies of transfer programs that require work or training, see Judith M. Gueron, "Work and Welfare: Lessons on Employment Programs," *Journal of Economic Perspectives* (Winter 1990): 79–98.

As you can see, there are conflicting policies and programs in the area of income redistribution. Many of the studies by economists disagree on the extent of the problem with the welfare system and what should be done about it. Thus, we end this chapter with the sentence that started it: No single topic in economics generates more disputes than income distribution and government policies for income redistribution.

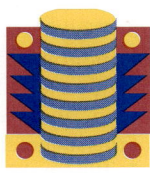

Summary

1. The Lorenz curve measures the relative distribution of income in an economy. The Lorenz curve, however, does not reflect the life-cycle pattern of income earning and may therefore give a false impression of how much income inequality exists over time.

2. Discrimination in labor markets channels certain groups into certain occupations. Some of the inequality that might appear to be the result of discrimination is actually due to differences in productivity or other objective characteristics.

3. To the extent that discrimination exists in the labor market, total output is lower than it could be if all resources were used in the most efficient manner.

4. Market forces will work against discrimination, because discrimination is costly and entrepreneurs can reduce the costs of production by not discriminating.

5. There is some evidence that welfare recipients, like other economic actors, will migrate to areas where benefits are higher.

6. Income redistribution can be viewed as a public good that is underprovided because of free-riding behavior.

7. In-kind transfers have expanded in the last twenty-five years and reduced the incidence of poverty in the United States.

8. Individuals may support income redistribution programs because they have interdependent utility functions, because of an insurance motive, because they view poverty as a negative external effect, or because they are seeking to use the political process to transfer income to themselves.

9. The Social Security system is a tax-and-transfer mechanism. The changing age distribution of the population is putting pressure on the financial viability of the system.

10. The elderly in America are receiving an increasing share of transfers at a time when their wealth is increasing.

11. The United States response to poverty has taken three distinct forms: to provide training and job opportunities, to provide social insurance, and to provide direct assistance to those who are unable to work because of age and health problems.

12. Current welfare reform proposals center on cost control, the federal-state mix in financing and administration, workfare programs, and greater reliance on private voluntary efforts.

13. The negative income tax has been suggested as a mechanism to ensure a minimum level of income while providing work incentives. The trade-offs between the minimum income guarantee, the break-even income, and the negative tax rate make it difficult to design a negative income tax system that is adequate, not too costly, and preserves work incentives.

New Terms

personal distribution of income
Lorenz curve
interdependent utility functions
negative income tax
workfare programs
Family Support Act of 1988

Questions for Discussion

1. How is the official poverty level of income determined? Is it a meaningful measure?

2. Why are some people poor? What would you do if you were in a position to take some action?

3. Do you think a negative income tax would solve the problem of poverty in the United States? Why or why not?

4. Should society be concerned with relative poverty or absolute poverty? How would dealing with absolute poverty differ from dealing with relative poverty?

5. Why do many economists feel that markets will work to undermine discrimination in labor markets?

6. "The social safety net is intended to catch those who fall in, not those who jump in." Discuss the implications of this statement for designing an income support system.

7. Why are there long-term problems with the financial health of the Social Security system? Identify some possible solutions.

8. Find the missing value in each of the three elements of the negative income tax.
   a. Minimum income guarantee, $4,000; break-even income, $12,000; negative tax rate, _____.
   b. Minimum income guarantee, $5,000; negative tax rate, 50 percent; break-even income, _____.
   c. Negative tax rate, 30 percent; break-even income, $9,000; minimum income guarantee, _____.

9. What problems with the welfare system are workfare programs designed to solve?

10. Why does society redistribute income to the poor? Why is private charity likely to be inadequate?

11. Public education is an in-kind transfer to all people in certain age groups. Who benefits more, the poor or the well-to-do?

12. How would George Stigler explain the fact that transfers to the elderly have increased so significantly in the last two decades? Would Gordon Tullock find this surprising? Why or why not?

13. Why do AFDC recipients move? Does it surprise you that they do?

14. Do you favor equality of opportunity or equality of results?

15. How do you think Congress should address the question of entitlement programs for the elderly?

Suggestions for Further Reading

Gabriel, Paul E., Donald R. Williams, and Susanne Schmitz. "The Relative Occupational Attainment of Young Blacks, Whites, and Hispanics," *Southern Economic Journal* (July 1990): 35–46. A recent empirical study that shows that labor market discrimination plays a role in the occupational attainment of black males.

Hurd, Michael D. "Research on the Elderly: Economic Status, Retirement, and Consumption and Saving," *Journal of Economic Literature* (June 1990): 565–637. A survey of recent economic research on the elderly.

Levy, Frank, and Richard C. Michel. *The Economic Future of American Families: Income and Wealth Trends*. Washington, DC: Urban Institute Press, 1991. A look at patterns of income inequality over the last two decades.

Murray, Charles. *Losing Ground: American Social Policy, 1950–1980*. New York: Basic Books, 1984. A controversial book that argues that three decades of well-meaning social programs were a failure. Murray followed it with *In Pursuit: Of Happiness and Good Government* (New York: Simon & Schuster, 1988), which argues that the poor can only be helped by local religious, social, and community organizations.

O'Rourke, P. J. "Octogenarians at the Gate," *Rolling Stone* (19 April 1990): 41–43. A satire about transfers to the elderly.

Penner, Karen. "The Free Market Has Triumphed, But What About the Losers?" *Business Week* (25 September 1989): 178–179. An editorial in a conservative business publication that calls for a more equitable society.

Tullock, Gordon. *Economics of Income Redistribution*. Boston: Kluwer-Nijhoff, 1983. This very readable analysis of governmental transfer policy criticizes a variety of programs.

Market Failure, Government Failure, and Public Choice

5

> **AFTER STUDYING THIS CHAPTER, YOU SHOULD BE ABLE TO:**
>
> 1. Discuss the economic impact of property law, tort law, and contract law.
> 2. Define:
>   a. externalities,
>   b. public goods,
>   c. free riding.
> 3. Diagram cases of both negative and positive externalities.
> 4. State the Coase theorem, and list the conditions under which it holds.
> 5. Explain how free-riding behavior results in the underproduction of public goods.
> 6. Explain how income redistribution and education have some characteristics of public goods.

CHAPTER 17

MARKET FAILURE AND GOVERNMENT INTERVENTION

INTRODUCTION

We have spent a great deal of time examining economic outcomes of market forces. Two of these market outcomes that are often viewed as unsatisfactory are the failure of markets to produce the optimal quantity (and price) of a good when there is monopoly power and the poverty that is often the result of the market distribution of income. Additional instances of market failure exist because of externalities and public goods. In this chapter, we examine the economic arguments for government intervention to correct for market failure.

Even an almost pure market system needs some minimal government to provide a legal system in order to define and protect property rights. We will therefore begin with a discussion of the legal system as the most basic function of government. Then we will examine the existence of externalities and public goods as arguments for governmental intervention into the market.[1]

LAW, ECONOMICS, AND GOVERNMENT

As Adam Smith noted, one of the basic roles of government is to define and enforce property rights. Thus, to an economist, law is the basic framework of any economy. In the United States, government's effect on the allocation of resources is defined by law and the interpretation of law. In recent years, economists have spent a great deal of time extending economic analysis to explain the purposes and effects of legislation (statute law) and judicial decisions (common law).[2] Both types of laws can be analyzed from an economic perspective, although in different ways.

---

1. Recall from Chapter 2 that the functions of government are allocation, stabilization, and redistribution. Stabilization is a topic discussed in macroeconomics. Redistribution was covered in the last chapter. Here we give a closer look at certain aspects of the allocation question.
2. See Richard A. Posner, *Economic Analysis of Law* (Boston: Little, Brown, 1972); and Werner Z. Hirsch, *Introduction to Law and Economics* (New York: McGraw-Hill, 1980).

Chapter 17   Market Failure and Government Intervention   437

Statute law is of interest because of the incentives statutes create and the way they alter existing property rights. *Common law* changes through judicial decisions, and these precedents alter incentives for decision making. Lawyers are interested in the applications of specific decisions to other cases. Economists are more concerned with how these decisions affect the economy by altering incentives.

In analyzing law, economists search for the economic reasoning implicit in legislation and judges' decisions. It is most common to divide laws into three major areas. **Property law** relates to the enforcement of property rights. Enforcement of property rights is one of the basic requirements of any economic system. **Tort law** deals with intentional and unintentional wrongs imposed by one party on another. **Contract law** deals with the enforcement of voluntary exchanges.

The important relationships between economics and law have been studied intensively in recent years by both economists and lawyers. Economics deals with property rights and exchange, which are the most basic elements of a market system. Precedents in common law or changes in statute law will have profound effects on economic activity. Laws (more correctly, the courts' interpretation of laws) determine the private-public mix in our economy.

property law
Law that concerns the enforcement of property rights.

tort law
Law that deals with intentional and unintentional wrongs inflicted by one party on another.

contract law
Law that deals with the enforcement of voluntary exchanges.

PROPERTY LAW

The law in the United States is generally compatible with the economic principle that the economy operates more efficiently under a system of exclusive, transferable property rights. The most important exceptions occur in two areas in which high transactions costs create market failure or interfere with the efficiency of market outcomes.

The first exception concerns incompatible uses of property. Incompatibility exists when the rights of the parties are in conflict. Noise, air, and water pollution are but a few examples. An attractive hazard such as a swimming pool or a construction site is another example. Cases involving incompatible uses are often treated as matters of nuisance. In many of these cases, the court will simply issue an injunction requiring that the party responsible for the nuisance cease and desist. This may appear to be the most fair or equitable solution, but it is not necessarily an efficient solution from an economic viewpoint.

The second exception to property law's compatibility with the principles of a free market is the doctrine of **eminent domain**. The principle here is that government has the legal right to purchase property at "fair market value" if it is deemed to be in the public interest. In these cases, the owner's property right is reduced in value because the owner cannot refuse to sell. Condemnation proceedings are court cases in which the government tries to take property away from an owner by arguing that the government's rights are more important. Governments often invoke eminent domain for construction of public facilities, such as parks, roads, or dams.

eminent domain
A doctrine that gives government the right to buy property at "fair market value" if the purchase is in the public interest.

TORT LAW

A **tort** is a wrongful action (or failure to act) by an individual that causes damage to the person or property of another individual. For example, if reckless behavior on your part injures another person, that person may

tort
A wrongful action (or failure to act) that causes damage to the person or property of another individual.

sue you for damages. Payment of these damages can be justified on the basis of equity. The payment restores the original distribution of income or assets. Payment of damages can also be justified on the basis of efficiency. It makes you bear the costs of your reckless action and thus increases the incentive to be more careful. For example, if you are responsible for any damage your dog may do by biting people or damaging property, you will be more likely to take precautions to keep your dog from inflicting such damage.

The equity principle requires a transfer payment from the wrongdoer to the individual who has been damaged. The impact of the efficiency principle is quite different. The law establishes a precedent for the ownership of property rights. Tort law is used to determine who has the property right when it is in dispute.[3]

CONTRACT LAW

The economics of exchange and contract law are similar in the sense that individuals are presumed to enter into contracts only if they stand to gain. Parties to contracts may end up in court not because the contracts were bad (for either of the parties), but rather because one party failed to satisfy a provision. This most often happens when the contractual exchange fails to take place on time or when the cost/benefit calculation of one party changes.

Contracts usually are not set aside by the courts if the intent is reasonably clear. On the other hand, the courts have set contracts aside if (honest) mistakes have been committed. If one party has been induced to accept a contract through fraud, duress, or incapacity, the court will refuse to enforce the contract.

Contracts, and court decisions under the common law of contracts, are important in economics because contracts, whether they are expressed or implied, form the basis of exchange. Exchange is influenced by contract law, and contract law alters the incentives that affect exchanges. For example, the courts have ruled that a college catalog or a course syllabus represents a contract with a student. This ruling has altered the terms of the production and sale of higher-education services.

EXTERNALITIES

externalities
Costs or benefits associated with consumption or production that are not reflected in market prices and fall on parties other than the buyer or seller.

Externalities are costs or benefits associated with consumption or production that are not reflected in market prices. The cost or benefit is external because it falls on parties other than the buyer or seller. Externalities represent a form of market failure.

The most frequently cited example of an externality is pollution. For example, a firm producing steel must purchase iron ore, electricity, labor, and other inputs. The costs of these factors are embodied in the price of the steel. However, in producing steel, the firm also uses clean air and produces air pollution. Yet the firm doesn't compensate those individuals

---

3. See Chapter 19 of Allan C. DeSerpa, *Microeconomic Theory: Issues and Applications* (Boston: Allyn and Bacon, 1985) for a very thorough and readable discussion of the economics of tort law.

International Perspective

The Japanese Legal System

The Japanese legal system is quite different from the U.S. legal system in that it puts a great deal of emphasis on arbitration and compromise in resolving conflicts. Since most relationships, including economic ones, are considered social relationships in Japan, there is great reliance on informal means of settling disputes. The traditional Japanese citizen views being brought to court as a source of personal shame.

The difference in the two systems is most apparent in the area of tort law. The most common way of resolving a damage case in Japan is for the injured party to renounce its right to indemnity. The wrongdoer comes to offer apologies and offer a sum of money in compensation. The sum offered is often a token amount and is frequently much less than the value of the damages suffered by the victim. The victim is moved by the sympathy and sincerity of the responsible party. It is not the amount of the compensation but the sincerity of the responsible party that is socially important. Sometimes the victim is so moved by the sincerity of the responsible party that all compensation is refused. Even when the victim is not satisfied with the offer of compensation, the courts are avoided. Instead, the victim appeals to someone who has authority to achieve an amicable solution. In this way, both parties are able to save face.

This Japanese attitude about the law extends to contracts. This difference can cause problems in international transactions. The Japanese, with their dislike of the courts' emphasis on conflict, prefer to negotiate a relationship rather than a contract. They can't predict the disputes that may arise but prefer to settle disputes in an informal manner. They dislike the use of the courts because the courts assign fault, resulting in a loss of "face" for the guilty party.

The differences between the United States and Japanese legal systems are striking and are based on differences in the cultures of the two countries. The Japanese legal system is very centralized. There are no local or state laws in Japan. This reflects the strong group orientation and concentration of authority in Japan. In the United States, there is much more individualism and disdain for authority. Americans view the legal system as a way of asserting their individual rights and are much more likely to resort to the courts to resolve disputes. These cultural differences will affect economic transactions and must be addressed when doing business with the Japanese. The Japanese have been quick to understand the U.S. system and have adapted to it when doing business in the United States. Americans have been slower to adapt to the Japanese system of doing business in Japan.

who give up the clean air. As a result, the cost of using the air is not embodied in the price of the steel. This cost is external to the production of the steel.

Many problems due to externalities result from the fact that property rights to certain resources are not clearly defined. Clean air is a resource that is not owned by anyone. Therefore, the steel mill can use clean air and not compensate those who give it up, because there is no clearly defined owner to demand payment.

Externalities can be positive or negative. Air pollution is a negative externality and so is the noise resulting from the use of a snowmobile. The cost that this noise imposes on other individuals may not be taken into account in the price of snowmobiles or snowmobiling. It is external to any economic calculation.

Positive externalities are not so obvious. Inoculations against contagious diseases or spraying to control mosquitoes are examples of activities that generate positive externalities. Benefits accrue to others if enough people are inoculated or enough mosquito breeding areas are sprayed, but these benefits are not considered by those deciding on whether or not to incur the cost. Education is another good example of a positive externality. Society benefits from an individual's education. An individual who is educated is likely to be a better citizen and to be less dependent on others. In addition, that individual is likely to be a more productive person, increasing national income. Yet individuals, in deciding how much education to pursue, do not consider these benefits because they are external to them. The individual is not able to charge those who enjoy the external benefit of his or her education.

To the extent that externalities exist, the market has failed. Private market decisions will result in too little or too much of certain items being produced. Corrective action on a collective basis may be needed. The government can influence production or consumption that creates externalities through taxes, subsidies, or outright prohibitions or by requiring citizens to consume certain goods, such as inoculations and education.

EXTERNAL BENEFITS

In order to analyze the economic implications of a positive externality, suppose Figure 1 represents the market for automobile tires. D_p represents the private demand for automobile tires, and MC represents the marginal cost. Consumers will purchase Q_1 tires at price P_1. Assume that EB represents the marginal external benefits arising from the consumption of new tires. External benefits exist when people consume more new tires, because their cars are safer and the chance of an accident involving others decreases. This greater safety is a social benefit. EB can be viewed as the summation of the demand curves of people other than the immediate consumers of the product. It has a negative slope, like all demand curves.

Adding EB and D_p vertically gives the true demand curve, labeled $D_p + EB$. The two demand curves are summed vertically instead of horizontally because we are interested in marginal benefits of all who gain at various quantities consumed. We are not summing the additional amounts consumers want to purchase but rather how they value these

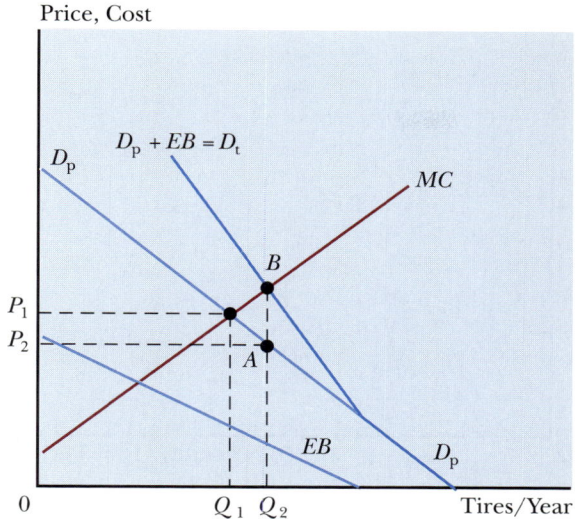

FIGURE 1
THE CASE OF EXTERNAL BENEFITS
External benefits cause the true demand curve, $D_p + EB$, to lie above the private demand curve, D_p. The market outcome, Q_1, is smaller than the socially efficient level of consumption, Q_2.

units. If the external benefits are considered, the combined valuation ($D_p + EB$) indicates that Q_2 rather than Q_1 tires should be consumed. In other words, the existence of the positive externality resulted in this good being underproduced and underconsumed.

It is easy to see how government could correct this market failure. A subsidy to consumers equal to the length of line AB on the graph would reduce the price consumers pay to P_2 and bring about the socially optimal level of consumption, Q_2. This level is the social optimum because it includes the tire production demanded by those who are not counted by the market mechanism. Alternatively, government could require the purchase of Q_2 tires per year. Vehicle inspections, which some states require, are also attempts (rather crude ones) to reach this social optimum.

EXTERNAL COSTS

Earlier, we used air pollution as an example of an external cost. If you live near a steel mill, you are forced to breathe polluted air without being compensated for the fact that the mill is using the air as a place in which to dump some of its debris. The economic importance of this behavior is that the polluting firm avoids paying part of the costs of production. It is quite simple to determine the theoretical effects of such externalities. It is more difficult to determine how to correct them.

Pollution causes damage, or social costs, to those in the general area. **Social costs** are costs that are borne by society or some group without compensation. Negative externalities impose damages, or social costs, on groups in the population. This situation is represented in Figure 2. Assume that the polluter is in a competitive industry that is generating a negative externality. The demand curve is the usual market demand curve for the good or service. The supply curve is the summation of all the individual firms' marginal cost curves (above their average variable cost curves). This supply curve includes all private costs but not marginal social costs. Equilibrium is reached at price P_1 and output Q_1.

social costs
Costs that are borne by society or some group in society without compensation.

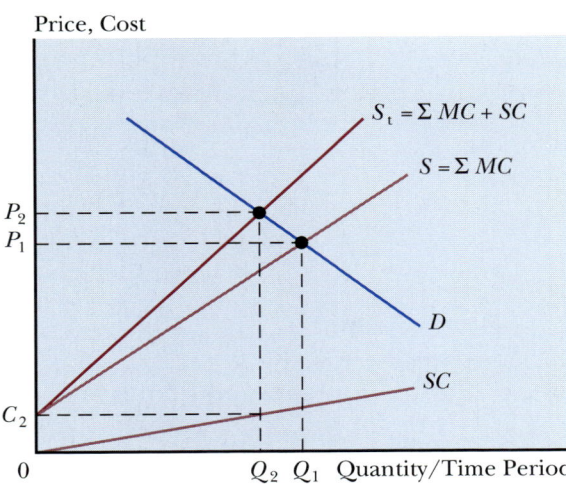

FIGURE 2
EXTERNALITIES AND MARKET EQUILIBRIUM
When the social cost of the negative externality (SC) is added to the marginal cost curves of the competitive firms (S), the true supply curve (S_t) is found. This true supply curve indicates that too much of the good is produced at too low a price, unless the externality is taken into account.

Now suppose we know the value of the marginal social costs generated by the externality, represented by the curve SC. The social costs are zero when no output is produced and are assumed to increase at a constant rate. If we add these marginal social costs to the supply curve, we get the true supply curve, S_t. This curve is the summation of the social costs and the private costs embodied in the firms' marginal cost curves. The socially optimal level of production is not Q_1 but the smaller Q_2. The price associated with efficient production is P_2, which is higher than P_1.

It is clear that when the social costs of production are included, the good becomes more expensive. It isn't that these costs weren't being borne before. They weren't being borne by the producers or the consumers of the good. Instead, they were being paid by those who live near where production is taking place. In failing to take into account the social costs, the firm was producing too much of the good and charging the consumer too low a price because it was not paying some of the costs of production.

In the real world, when production or consumption of a good causes negative externalities, the people who bear those costs subsidize consumers of the product. For example, the people who live in Gary, Indiana, where steel is produced, bear costs that allow consumers of steel to pay lower prices. A person who buys a steel and chrome kitchen set in Orlando, Florida, is subsidized by someone who lives in Gary. If steel producers had to pay for the negative externalities they create, less steel would be produced, and it would be sold for a higher price. The general theoretical conclusion is that when negative externalities exist, the amount of production will not be optimal. Too much output will be produced at too low a price.

It is very important to understand that even if the cost of an externality such as pollution is placed on the buyer and seller of the good or service, this action does not cause the amount of pollution to fall to zero. Only if production of the good or service falls to zero will the resulting pollution fall to zero. In the example in Figure 2, the price paid by buyers rose from P_1 to P_2 when social costs were included, but some pollution and the costs associated with it continued. In other words, there is an "optimum" amount of pollution determined by the market process.

INTERNALIZING NEGATIVE EXTERNALITIES

According to economists, the trick to controlling the social costs of negative externalities is **internalization** of those externalities. This means that producers are forced to take account of the costs they impose on other members of society in their production decisions. When internalized, the externality is incorporated into the market price. In terms of Figure 2, the firm should have to bear the social costs SC so that S_t becomes the supply curve. How can this be done? It would be a simple matter if the social costs could easily be determined. It is easy to analyze the theoretical case, as in Figure 2, but in the real world it is very difficult to come up with a dollar value. You can determine the dollar value of having to paint your house more often because of air pollution, but what is the cost of a certain number of people dying because of respiratory problems? How much is not being able to have a cookout in the back yard worth? If government officials could determine these costs, they could place a tax on the industry that would shift the supply curve up just the right distance (to S_t in Figure 2). The market solution would then be an optimal price of P_2 and an optimal output level of Q_2.

internalization
The incorporation of the social costs of negative external effects into the market price.

Governmental policy makers could also charge firms for the amount of negative externalities they create. Each firm could be monitored and charged for air pollution on a monthly basis. It would be possible to put a meter on each smokestack and measure the pollutants. Then firms could be charged for the air they pollute just as they are charged for the electricity or labor they use. This pollution charge would cause costs to rise and move production toward the socially optimal level. This solution, however, has the same problem as taxation—determining the correct charge per unit of pollutant.

Although there are problems, it can be argued that there is a need for government to intervene in the market process under circumstances when there are negative externalities. When markets don't produce socially optimal results, it may be appropriate for government to step in to attempt to correct for the market imperfection. It is not always necessary for government to correct for social costs, however. Private groups may form in an effort to prevent or limit negative externalities. A good example of such a group is a condo association. Condo associations set up rules of behavior and rules for upkeep of facilities that are designed to limit or prevent residents from creating certain types of negative externalities. By buying a condo, an individual voluntarily limits his or her own behavior.

THE COASE THEOREM AND SMALL-NUMBER EXTERNALITIES. In an article that has had wide influence on how economists think about externalities, Ronald Coase considered cases in which the number of affected parties is small. He concluded that, in such cases, individual maximizing behavior will correct for a negative externality without the need for govern-

Economic Insight

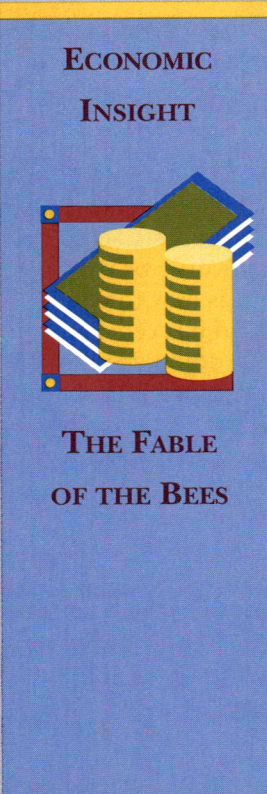

The Fable of the Bees

For years, apples and bees were used as a classic illustration of the externality problem. It was alleged that markets broke down because apple growers' orchards provided a positive externality (nectar) for bee farmers, but the orchard owners received no payment for this nectar. On the other hand, the bees provided pollinating services to orchard owners, but beekeepers were not compensated for this necessary service. As a result, intervention would be needed to make orchard owners grow more nectar-yielding apple trees and beekeepers provide more pollinating bees.

Steven Cheung refused to take this classic illustration of market failure at its face value.[a] He went into apple orchards to determine if these two externalities did indeed produce market value. To everyone's surprise, except perhaps Cheung's, he found that the market worked quite well without government intervention. An active market for beehive placement was in operation. Where the honey yield was great, beekeepers paid the orchard owner an "apiary rent" in order to place hives in these high production spots. When the honey yield was low, the orchard owner paid a "pollination fee" to induce beekeepers to place hives in these places. Cheung even found that beekeepers move hives to different states to pollinate crops in different seasons.

Cheung's study is important because it shows that markets can adapt well and that market failure may be less widespread than might appear. The lesson for policy makers is that they should be very careful in determining whether market failure exists before proposing political or governmental solutions.

---

a. See Steven N. S. Cheung, "The Fable of the Bees: An Economic Investigation," *The Journal of Law and Economics* (April 1973).

ment intervention.[4] The **Coase theorem** states that when there are small numbers of affected parties, a property right assignment is sufficient to internalize any externality that is present. Coase demonstrated that if property rights are clearly defined, the affected individuals will take action to internalize the externality. The only government intervention required to solve the problem is enforcement of property rights.

Consider, as Coase did in his paper, a case where there are only two parties involved in a dispute, a wheat farmer and a cattle rancher. The negative externality is the damage done by cattle roaming on unfenced land. As the rancher increases the size of the herd, the damage done by straying cattle will increase. To approach an optimal result, it is necessary to compel the rancher to take these costs into account, as illustrated by Figure 2. If government intervenes, it is likely to solve the problem by requiring the rancher to pay the farmer for the damage to the farmer's wheat. In this case, the rancher would restrict the number of cattle in the herd until marginal cost equaled marginal revenue (the marginal cost includes the damage to wheat). In Figure 3, $D = MR$ represents the demand and marginal revenue curve of raising cattle, MC represents the marginal cost of raising cattle, and SC represents the marginal social cost, or the cost of the negative externality (the damage to the wheat). Without any internalizing of the social cost, the rancher would raise Q_1 cattle per year, and the farmer would incur a dollar loss to the wheat crop of W_1 for the last (marginal) cow raised. Government intervention would force the rancher to act on the basis of the joint $MC + SC$ curve through some tax scheme or direct regulation. As a result, the rancher would raise only Q_2 cattle.

Coase shows that even if government did not intervene, the same solution would result. According to Coase, all that is necessary is that property rights be defined and enforced. First, assume that the farmer's prop-

Coase theorem
The idea that well-defined property rights are sufficient to internalize any external effect that is present, when there are small numbers of affected parties.

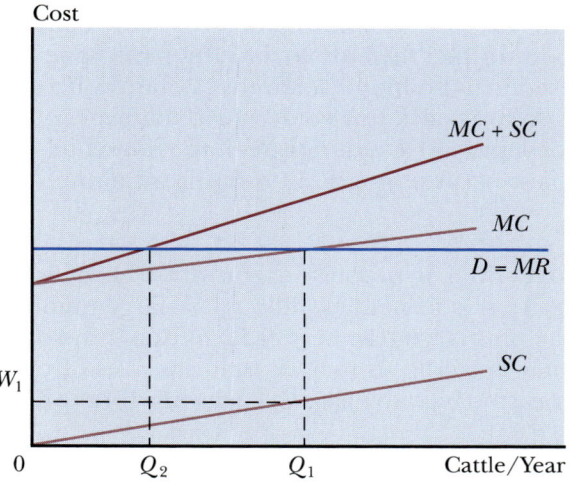

FIGURE 3
THE COASE THEOREM
The Coase theorem shows how externalities are internalized by the assignment of property rights. The social cost (SC) is automatically added to the marginal cost curve (MC) to form $MC + SC$, the true cost of raising cattle. The optimal output, Q_2, will result because a bribe or payment equal to the social cost will automatically come about.

---

4. Ronald Coase, "The Problem of Social Cost," *Journal of Law and Economics* 3, (October 1960): 1–44.

erty rights include the right not to have the wheat harmed. The rancher will then be forced to pay damages, shown by the *SC* curve, and will add these to production costs. The rancher will then raise Q_2 cattle. On the other hand, suppose the rancher has the right to let the cattle roam. The important question then is how much the farmer will be willing to "bribe" the rancher to keep the cattle away. The farmer will be willing to pay the rancher an amount just slightly less than the cost of the damage done by the cattle because this makes them *both* better off than allowing the cattle to damage the wheat. The farmer would pay W_1 for the last cow not raised. The rancher then must include these bribes as opportunity costs because if the cattle are raised, the bribes will not be paid. When these opportunity costs are added to the marginal cost curve, the rancher will raise Q_2 cattle. The result is that Q_2 cattle will be raised regardless of who has the property rights, as long as those rights are defined and the number of people involved is small. Small numbers are necessary because the farmer and rancher must get together and work out a solution.

Note that the Coase solution says only that the allocative results, or the number of cattle produced, will be the same whoever has the property rights. It says nothing about the distribution of income. Assigning property rights does affect who is better off. In the first case, the farmer's income is higher. In the second, the rancher's income is higher. The assignment of rights might have to be resolved by the law or through the political process since it involves an issue of equity, not economic efficiency. It's not really clear whether the rancher is imposing costs on the farmer (by damaging the wheat crop) or the farmer is imposing costs on the rancher (by restricting the grazing range of the herd). That is why there are legislatures to define property rights and courts to interpret and enforce them.

The importance of the Coase theorem is that it draws attention to the role of property rights. Many social problems result from ill-defined or nonexistent property rights. Consider, for example, the case of buffalo and cattle in the Old West. Why were buffalo almost wiped out while cattle thrived? The animals are very similar and roamed the same country. The answer is simple. Nobody owned the buffalo, or rather everyone had a right to shoot them.[5] Consider air pollution as another example. If a copper mine dumped tailings on your yard, you would sue for damages or expect payment for the use of your land as a dump. Yet if the mine polluted the air, you would be helpless because you don't own the air above your land.

LARGE-NUMBER EXTERNALITIES. Even if property rights are well defined, there may still be problems from externalities. If there are large numbers of people sustaining damages or large numbers of firms doing the damage, the Coase theorem may not hold. It may be that the costs of organizing the involved parties are too high to make it worthwhile for the dam-

---

5. For a discussion of how to protect eagles by assigning property rights to them, see Ryan C. Amacher, Robert D. Tollison, and Thomas D. Willett, "The Economics of Fatal Mistakes: Fiscal Mechanisms for Preserving Endangered Predators," *Public Policy* 20, no. 1 (Summer 1972): 411–441.

Chapter 17 Market Failure and Government Intervention   447

aged individuals to sue for damages or organize a bribe. The individuals damaged would have to mount a door-to-door campaign, advertise in newspapers, and form a group for joint action. If the damaging firms are hard to identify, the problem is even greater. In an area with severe air pollution, it would be necessary to determine how much each of many firms contributes to this problem and who should be sued (or bribed). Because the information and transactions costs increase rapidly as the number of parties increases, it is often argued that the Coase theorem cannot fix the market failure that externalities create.

GOVERNMENT INTERVENTION AND EXTERNALITIES. Since the Coase theorem may not work, government intervention may be required to correct a negative externality. Government intervention usually takes the form of direct controls, and such controls often lead to unfairness. Suppose the government requires all cars to have a pollution control device that costs $300. The salesperson who drives a great deal and, as a result, pollutes a great deal pays very little on a per-unit-of-pollution basis. In contrast, the retired couple who drive very little must pay the same $300, although they pollute very little. In addition, government intervention affects the distribution of income. For example, as auto prices rise because of required pollution equipment, the poor are affected more than the rich because the poor spend a higher proportion of their income on cars.

Since government intervention almost always raises costs, it is important that policy makers be sure that the social costs are indeed worth correcting. Sometimes the government makes mistakes when it intervenes in markets, and these mistakes raise costs of production. Mistakes are to be expected because governmental decision making, like private decision making, is carried out by individuals with certain expectations, facing certain incentives. Governmental decision makers aren't incentive-free, they simply face different incentives than private decision makers.

Externalities have received much attention in recent years. This attention may cause some to overestimate their real costs. We have all seen gruesome pictures of oil spills and fish kills. However, this kind of damage seems to be of short duration. This is not to say that such damage is insignificant. However, the cost of correcting for a negative externality may in some cases exceed the damage it causes. Policy makers need to consider these costs before racing headlong into wholesale government regulation of externalities. They also need to consider what form that intervention should take.

The federal government has usually responded to calls to control negative externalities by creating regulations. These regulations impose costs on firms. The regulatory bodies themselves spend large amounts of money on enforcement. The costs imposed on firms are hard to estimate until the required action is actually taken. For example, a regulation to keep copper mines from polluting the air may cause them to close because of increased costs of production. In considering the costs of the regulation, an economist would examine its impact on the affected industry and region. Production may move to a state (or country) that has less stringent regulation. Some geographic regions may compete for industrial growth by offering fewer environmental or economic regulations.

Thus, in attempting to correct for the market distortions caused by negative externalities, government regulation can lead to other distortions.

Each call for regulation should be considered carefully. Some externalities may have already been corrected by market mechanisms. For example, houses near airports sell for lower prices because of airport noise. The people who buy these houses are freely choosing to do so because the lower price compensates for the noise. To change the law because these people don't like the noise would generate a windfall gain for them. It is not surprising that these residents should lobby for such a change, but it cannot be justified economically. The problem is complicated, however, by the fact that some residents may have purchased their homes before the noise became bad. These individuals lose twice. They suffer the cost of the noise and also a reduction in the value of their homes. It might make sense to compensate this group of individuals.

A recent battle concerning negative externalities and the need for government intervention has taken place over cigarette smoking and the rights of nonsmokers. The issues involved in this political battle point once again to the property rights that are at the heart of most such questions. Some states and localities have passed laws prohibiting smoking in some areas (public buildings) and requiring nonsmoking areas in restaurants and other such businesses. Are such laws necessary? If private demand for either smoke-free or smoking areas were high enough, some restaurants and other firms would fill the demand without the need for government action. In fact, some restaurants have done this without the pressure of laws. The recent opening of a motel chain for nonsmokers gives support to the feasibility of a private solution to some problems of negative externalities.

MARKETS FOR POLLUTION RIGHTS

Clean Air Act
A federal law passed in 1970 that empowered the EPA to set emission standards and impose standards on polluters.

More than a century ago, the famous economist John Stuart Mill wrote in his *Principles of Political Economy* (1862): "If from any revolution in nature the atmosphere became too scanty for the consumption, . . . air might acquire a very high marketable value." In the 1980s, he was proven correct as the market began to be used to allocate pollution rights. Economists have long argued for such a system rather than a regulatory approach. In 1970, Congress passed the **Clean Air Act**, which empowered the Environmental Protection Agency (EPA) to set standards for six pollutants and required each state to impose standards that would be met at each emission source. In other words, if emissions were to be reduced by 10 percent, all sources of the pollutant would have to be reduced by 10 percent. This act has since been renewed and extended to more pollutants and greater reductions.

Some economists argued that it would be more efficient to allow the market to solve this problem. Marketing the right to pollute would make it possible to hold pollutants at the desired level and at the same time allocate them to the producers who are willing to pay the highest price. Firms that wished to expand production could do so only if the market value of their product enabled them to purchase the right to use the scarce commodity, air quality. In addition, if pollution rights had a value, firms would have the incentive to search for other ways to produce their

International Perspective

Paying to Pollute in Europe

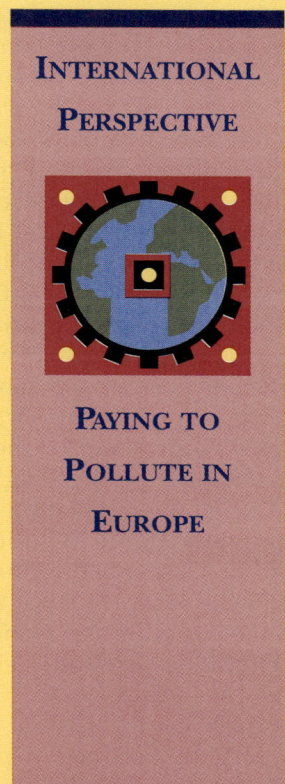

The idea of charging for the privilege of polluting is not unique to the United States. Among the nations that use this approach to controlling water pollution are France, Germany, and the Netherlands. France uses a sewage tax on households and commercial enterprises to fund pollution abatement programs. Because the tax is based on the amount of water used, there is some link between the amount of tax paid and the amount of demand that a customer places on the waste treatment system. Charges to firms, which are also used to raise revenue for pollution abatement, are not linked as closely to the amount of waste discharged. France also uses fees for pollution abatement. By introducing the system through low charges on a few pollutants and gradually expanding coverage and increasing the rates, the French government has encountered very little political opposition to this program.

The German system is similar, except that it is administered by local governments. Charges depend on the type and size of the industry. Like France, Germany earmarks the revenues to pay for water quality improvement. However, economic efficiency only requires that the tax or charge be set so as to reduce the level of emissions to the socially optimal level. It says nothing about how the revenue should be used.

The Netherlands has a system of effluent charges that has been in use for more than three decades. Like France and Germany, the Netherlands earmarks the revenue for pollution abatement. Because effluent charges in this country are much higher than in the other two, however, it appears that the charges have had a significant effect on improving water quality. It is interesting to note that in the Netherlands, environmental groups have supported charges as a method of reducing pollution and industry has lobbied for a regulatory approach. These preferences seem to suggest that the market is the more effective method of pollution control!

Source: Robert W. Hahn, "Economic Prescriptions for Environmental Problems: How the Patient Followed the Doctor's Orders," *Journal of Economic Perspectives* (Spring 1989): 95–114.

products and for ways to control their emissions. If they discovered new methods of emission control, they could sell both the new technology and their pollution rights.

This idea came into use in the 1980s. In 1979, the EPA endorsed a "bubble" concept. The bubble concept allows a group of plants in the same region to adjust their emissions to achieve regional clear-air standards. The economics of the idea is simple. If the plants in the bubble are all owned by the same company, the company achieves the desired level of pollution by shifting emission control from higher-cost to lower-cost sources until the marginal cost of control is the same at each source. This approach minimizes the total cost of pollution abatement. If the plants in the bubble belong to different firms, it is a bit more complicated, but the principle is the same. The plant manager with high costs of pollution control will look for savings by paying neighboring firms in the bubble whose costs are lower to cut their emissions more and sell some of their pollution rights. This approach achieves abatement in the bubble at the lowest cost.[6]

Such bargaining may seem difficult to achieve, but by 1987 there was evidence that a market was working in pollution rights. In California, several plants financed the installation of new technology that saved on emissions by selling their rights to pollute to other companies. These other companies found it less expensive to buy pollution rights than to purchase a more costly technology. In 1984, a private firm, AER*X, was formed to serve as a broker in pollution rights. In 1990, this firm had revenue of more than $1 million a year and was experiencing a rate of growth of more than 30 percent per year.[7]

President Bush's proposals for the 1990s make use of this concept. Acid rain is perhaps the biggest pollution problem the United States presently faces. Bush proposed to solve this problem by setting annual limits on the emission of acid-producing pollutants. Under his proposal, 107 utilities, chiefly in the Midwest, would be allowed to generate a certain level of sulfur dioxide every year based on the level of electricity generation. The utilities would be free to choose how to meet these standards. Those close to Western sources of low-sulfur coal might switch fuels, and others might install anti-pollution technology. Still others might shut down. Beginning in 1995, the utilities would be free to sell their "allowances," regardless of how they had met them. By the year 2000, utilities in areas where more electricity was needed could purchase "allowances" from utilities in slow-growth areas.

PUBLIC GOODS

Public goods have two important characteristics. First, once they are produced, no one can be excluded from consuming them. Second, they are

---

6. For a more detailed discussion on the market for pollution rights and the bubble concept, see Bruce Yandle, "The Emerging Market in Air Pollution Rights," *Regulation* (July/August 1978): 21–28; and M. T. Maloney and Bruce Yandle, "Bubbles and Efficiency," *Regulation* (May/June 1980): 49–52.
7. For a discussion of AER*X, see Michael Weisskopf, "The Pollution Peddlers," *The Washington Post National Weekly Edition* (26 November 1989): 9.

not depleted by consumption. If an individual consumes a public good, this action does not reduce the amount of the good available for other individuals to consume. Economists refer to these two characteristics of public goods as nonexcludability and nonrivalry. Public goods were introduced in Chapter 2. We expand on that discussion here because of the close relationship between public goods and externalities. These concepts are not really two separate and distinct arguments for government intervention. The arguments are actually the same. A public good is simply a good that has very strong external benefits that are nonexcludable and nonrival.

Pure Public Goods versus Pure Private Goods

A pure public good is one that is consumed (automatically) by all members of a community as soon as it is produced. It is impossible to exclude individuals from consumption, and the good is perfectly nonrival. In contrast, a pure private good has a price equal to the full opportunity cost of production, and its consumption provides benefits only to the individual (or group) that purchases the good.

It is, of course, difficult to come up with examples of pure public or pure private goods. No good is purely public because no good can be perfectly nonrival in consumption. Almost any public good, such as a road, a park, or a library, gets congested at some point and loses the characteristic of nonrivalry. At the other extreme, the more private a good is, the easier it is to exclude consumption. The more any individual consumes, the less there is for others to consume. A bottle of orange soda is a good example of a private good. A wilderness park might be an example of a public good if citizens consume the idea of wilderness it embodies even though most of them don't ever visit it. Many of the appeals for the preservation of certain species or habitats are based on this idea. The spotted owl or the rain forest has an appeal for people, even those who do not go out and see the owl or walk in the forest. However, a theme park, such as Disneyland, can clearly be private, and an empty soda bottle on the side of the road is a public good in a negative sense—a public bad.

The Free-Rider Problem

Since nonexcludability is an essential feature of a public good, it is possible for individuals to consume such a good without paying for it. Economists call this behavior free riding. Since it is impossible (or at least costly) to exclude you from consumption of a public good whether you pay or not, you may choose to hide your demand for the good, let others pay for it, and still consume it. Thus, free riding makes it difficult for the market to measure actual demand. An example of a free rider would be a weekend sailor using Coast Guard markers to locate a safe channel into a busy harbor.

Because a public good is nonrivalrous and nonexcludable over a large group, it is likely that the market will not provide enough of the good. It is difficult to free ride in a small group, where everyone knows how much each person contributes and social pressure makes it costly for individuals not to contribute. In many rural communities, this type of social pressure is a way of overcoming the free-rider problem. If you don't help rebuild a barn that has been burned, you can't expect help from your neighbors if you run into problems. The free-rider problem, however, increases as the size of the group increases.

The free-rider problem can be better understood by examining Figure 4. For simplicity, assume that there are only two demanders of national defense. (If this simplifying assumption bothers you, assume that there are two groups that have different demands for defense.) The demand curve of each individual is derived in the same way as demand curves for private goods are derived. The two demand curves reflect the amount each is willing to pay for a given "quantity" of defense. If MC represents the marginal cost of national defense, the private market will produce Q_1 units of defense, which will be purchased by consumer b and consumed by both consumers a and b. However, the marginal benefits of additional units of national defense are determined by a vertical summation of the two individual demand curves. The result is a demand curve, $D_a + D_b$, for the public good national defense. We can now determine the optimal level of production of national defense. At price P_1, Q_2 units of national defense represent the efficient level of production. In this case, individuals have every incentive to hide their demand for national defense and consume amount Q_1.

Government financing of a public good overcomes the strategic holdout part of the free-rider problem. Forced tax collection compels the free rider to pay. It does, however, lead to another problem. In Figure 4, individual demand curves are summed to determine the "correct" demand for a public good such as defense. In reality, this demand is the demand of millions of people for the good. How could all their demand curves be measured? The answer to this difficult problem is that the political process reveals the demand for public goods. Voting for candidate x over candidate y is, at best, a very imperfect mechanism for determining the "correct" level of public good provision.

FIGURE 4
THE MARKET FOR NATIONAL DEFENSE
Since national defense is a public good and thus nonrival, the demand curve for it is found by vertically summing the individual demand curves (D_a and D_b).

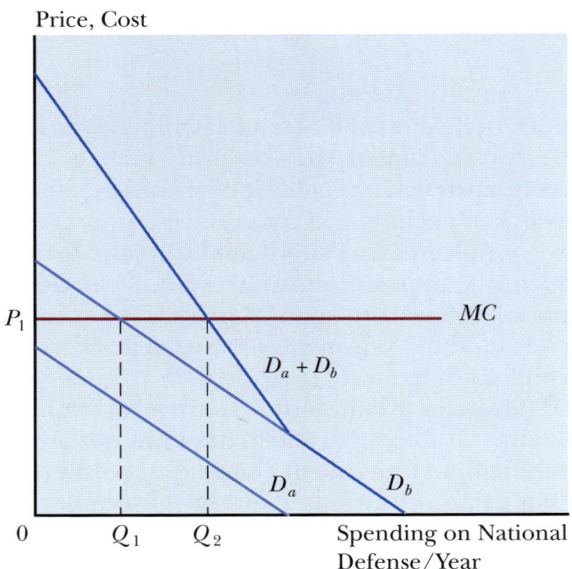

Chapter 17 Market Failure and Government Intervention

MARKET FAILURE AND GOVERNMENTAL REMEDIES

MARKET FAILURE	EXAMPLE	GOVERNMENTAL REMEDY
• Positive externality	Well-maintained houses	Zoning Fines Subsidies Deed restrictions
• Negative externality	Pollution	Prohibitions Fines Selling pollution rights User fees
• Public goods	National defense	Provision
• Natural monopoly	Electric company	Regulation Taxation

Volunteer groups can be more successful than governments in overcoming the free-rider problem and providing public goods under certain conditions. The group must be small—such as a small town, where peer pressure and visibility make free riding difficult. Volunteer fire departments and volunteer recreation programs flourish in small towns. In addition, clubs and associations can be formed to provide public goods. The condo association mentioned earlier does this. For example, some homeowners associations in Arizona require members to have grass in their yards rather than unimproved desert. A second condition that allows volunteer groups to overcome the free-rider problem is the existence of private benefits blended with the social benefits. For example, members of a garden club working for city beautification may derive private benefits from both the companionship of other members and the personal enjoyment of a more beautiful town.

PUBLIC GOODS IN PRACTICE

Economists use the distinction between private and public goods to attempt to determine what projects and activities should be undertaken by the government. The idea is to try to determine which markets might show a more nearly optimal level of output if government intervened in the process. This type of analysis is distinctly different from asking what projects and activities *will* be undertaken by government. In truth, the economic distinction between public goods and private goods has little to do with what goods and services government actually provides. Governments supply many goods that have the characteristics of private goods. At the same time, many goods that at least partly fit the economic definition of public goods are privately supplied, often by volunteer groups, nonprofit organizations, clubs, and, in some instances, the market.

Politicians often incorrectly classify goods as public or private based on who supplies them. For example, garbage removal may be considered a local public good even though it might be better classified in theory as a private good with some positive external effects. In fact, many goods (food, recreation, education, garbage removal, police protection, and so on) could be classed as both private goods and public goods depending on whether they are supplied privately or by government. The supplier may vary from one jurisdiction to another. The economist can ask what determines the goods a political unit will choose to supply. An analysis of the political process as interest-group activity is developed in the next chapter to address this question.

INCOME REDISTRIBUTION AS A PUBLIC GOOD

The argument for government redistribution of income is often based on viewing such activity as a public good. If a society decides that the income distribution resulting from the market is unsatisfactory, it can pursue deliberate redistribution. You know that if income redistribution is a public good, less than the optimal amount of redistribution will take place in the absence of government intervention. Free riders will think that there is no need to help the poor because others will give. Voters, as a result, may decide to redistribute income through government and tax all citizens to achieve a more acceptable outcome than the market-produced outcome. The fact that government does some redistribution of income in most market economies suggests that such redistribution is widely viewed as having at least some characteristics of a public good.

EDUCATION AS A PUBLIC GOOD

It is easy to see how getting a college degree is an investment in human capital. Your income will be higher because you have developed marketable skills that make you more productive. Economists argue that all schooling is investment in human capital. According to this argument, even primary and secondary schooling increases the productivity of the work force. This claim has been supported with a great deal of research that showed the positive effects of education on economic growth. If this is true, some of the return to education does not go to the individual being educated. Therefore, individuals will not invest heavily enough in education.

Much of this theory and empirical work was used to support an argument that education is a public good and should receive increased public financing. This argument was based on the fact that trained and educated workers cannot directly capture all the gain from their education. Some of the benefits spill over to society in general. These positive externalities consist of increased economic growth for the nation, a more informed electorate, greater political participation, improved and extended research, and reduction in crime and other antisocial activity. Since these gains cannot be captured by individuals, they will choose to invest too little in education. Government can correct for this market failure by subsidizing the investment in private education or by direct public production of education (along with compulsory attendance).

WELFARE ECONOMICS

The body of economic theory that concentrated on market failures and sought remedies for them was developed in the 1930s, 1940s, and 1950s in the United States. This body of theory is part of a larger and older branch of economic theory that deals with normative policy prescriptions and is called welfare economics. The market failures were negative externalities, the underprovision of public goods, inequitable distribution of income (which was the topic of the last chapter), and economic instability (which is covered in macroeconomics).

The theoretical conclusions led to the policy approach that government could and should intervene to correct for market failures. Collective choice through the political process would ensure that the society would (1) correct the externality, (2) produce the "correct" amount of the public good, (3) create an "equitable" distribution of income, and even (4) "fine-tune" the economy to a desired level of employment and price stability. This very optimistic theory envisioned collective choice and government operating to make the world a much better place through the use of enlightened economic policies. The next chapter will examine some of the problems associated with government intervention to correct market failure.

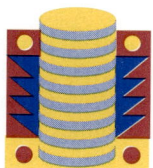

Summary

1. Laws, and changes in laws due to court decisions, have important impacts on incentives. Laws and their interpretation affect the allocation of resources in a mixed economy.

2. Externalities distort market outcomes because a cost or a benefit of the production process is not included in the economic decision-making process. This cost (or benefit) results in underproduction (or overproduction) of the good.

3. The Coase theorem shows that natural market forces can solve problems of externalities if few people are involved and property rights are well defined.

4. Public goods are underproduced because some individuals will free ride.

5. Market failure exists because of monopoly power, externalities, and public goods. Market failure often results in a call for political action to correct the problem.

New Terms

property law
tort law
contract law
eminent domain
tort
externality
social costs
internalization
Coase theorem
Clean Air Act

Questions for Discussion

1. Does air or water pollution exist where you live? What should be done about it? Should the pollution be done away with entirely? How much more in taxes or higher prices for goods would you be willing to pay in order to have less pollution?

2. Is education a public good? If not, why should taxes help to pay for the college education of some individuals?

3. Why are tennis courts sometimes provided as public goods even though it would be relatively easy to exclude free-riding behavior?

4. Does football at Big Ten schools generate any externalities for students who attend these universities?

5. If you happen to live in a dorm or in an apartment populated by students, there is most likely a great deal of noise. Is there a Coase solution to deal with this externality?

6. Distinguish between public goods as defined by economists and goods that governments provide for the public.

7. What is welfare economics?

8. Why are the individual demand curves for public goods summed vertically rather than horizontally like those for a private good?

9. What is free-riding behavior? Have you ever practiced free riding? Did it work? How could it have been prevented?

10. Discuss whether each of the following is a public good or a private good.
    a. National defense
    b. A lighthouse
    c. Income redistribution
    d. Education
    e. An Apple computer
    f. A Buick
    g. Medical care

11. A main idea of the Coase theorem is that parties to a dispute have incentives to settle the dispute through negotiation. This idea has become standard fare in law school discussions of torts, property, and contracts. Professor Coase, in fact, wound up teaching in the law school at the University of Chicago. Can you think of reasons why some lawsuits would end up in court rather than being settled through negotiation?

12. Suppose you were in charge of a government program to charge firms for the right to pollute. How *should* you set the price?

13. Which business firms will take action to reduce the amount they are polluting and which business firms will pay the fee you set in Question 12?

14. Will any of the firms on which you placed fees in Questions 12 and 13 be forced out of business? Which ones?

15. Why do indefinite or poorly defined property rights generate externalities?

SUGGESTIONS FOR FURTHER READING

Browning, Edgar K., and Jacqueline M. Browning. *Microeconomic Theory and Applications*, 3rd ed. Boston: Little, Brown, 1989. An intermediate text that contains discussion of external effects and public goods.

Posner, Richard A. *Economic Analysis of Law*. Boston: Little, Brown, 1972. The standard reference for the application of economics to legal issues.

Stigler, George J. *Memoirs of an Unregulated Economist.* New York: Basic Books, 1988. The memoirs of the Nobel Prize–winning economist provide a witty overview of the impact of theory on policy. Chapter 5 contains a delightful account of the development of the Coase theorem.

Tietenberg, Thomas H. *Environmental and Natural Resource Economics*, 2nd ed. Glenview, IL: Scott, Foresman, 1988. A well-written textbook that deals with solutions to environmental pollution.

AFTER STUDYING THIS CHAPTER, YOU SHOULD BE ABLE TO:

1. Define:
   a. public choice,
   b. rent seeking,
   c. rent defending,
   d. median voter theorem,
   e. logrolling.
2. Explain the biases public choice economists have identified in the political process.
3. Describe how the self-interested behavior of politicians results in rent extraction.
4. Identify the costs of rent seeking and rent defending.
5. Explain why government grows in terms of logrolling and bureaucratic incentives.
6. Explain the bias against new products and new technology that is created by regulation.
7. List some of the methods of privatization.
8. Identify the basic ideas of the Austrian school of economics.
9. Discuss the main themes of radical economic thought.

CHAPTER 18

GOVERNMENT FAILURE AND PUBLIC CHOICE

INTRODUCTION

The last chapter examined economic arguments for government intervention in markets to correct for negative externalities and provide public goods. This chapter analyzes some of the costs of such intervention. Public choice economists have identified ways in which government intervention introduces new problems and biases into the economic system. We will examine these effects and how they might affect the growth of government. Finally, we will examine some other theories about the microeconomic role of government.

PUBLIC CHOICE THEORY

Public choice theory is relatively new. It is perhaps easiest to use the definition provided in the 1988 annual report of the Center for the Study of Public Choice at George Mason University:

"Choice" is the act of selecting from alternatives. "Public" refers to people. But "people" do not choose. Choices are made by individuals, and these may be "private" or "public." A person makes private choices as he goes about his ordinary business of living. He makes "public choices" when he selects among the alternatives for others as well as for himself. . . . While traditional economic theory has been narrowly interpreted to include only the private choices of individuals in the market process, traditional political science has rarely analyzed individual choice behavior. [Public choice theory] is the intersection of these two disciplines; the institutions are those of political science and the method is that of economic theory.

Public choice theory is not as optimistic as welfare economics (discussed in the last chapter) about the potential for government intervention to improve market outcomes. Public choice economists apply the same tools of analysis and simplifying assumptions to the collective choice process and to the private market. These economists recognize that there are market failures. They do not ignore externalities, public goods, unequal income distribution, and macroeconomic cycles. They do, however, argue that collective choice and the intervention of government in the market do not work perfectly either. The weaknesses of the political process mean that government intervention does not work in the ideal way suggested by welfare economists. Public choice analysis begins with the assumption that people who act in a self-interested way when making personal economic decisions are the same people who vote, run for office, or are employed in the bureaucracy. Individuals bring their self-interest to the political process.

Public choice theory is as much political science as it is economics. Public choice analysis seeks to understand how economic incentives and individual self-interest affect political outcomes. For example, public choice economists expect the voter to be ill-informed because the cost of informed voting is extremely high. They view the politician as a vote maximizer, putting coalitions together to attract a majority of voters. Bureaucrats are not profit maximizers but seek instead to maximize budgets and/or to ensure the stability of their jobs. According to the public choice economist, the result of such self-interested behavior in the public sector is that government is an imperfect intervener in its attempt to correct for market failures. One of the most important insights that emerges from public choice theory is that small groups with strong interests will often get their way politically because it is irrational (unprofitable) for the majority to oppose them.

William C. Mitchell has succinctly summarized ten public sector biases that produce this less-than-optimal intervention into the market.[1] This list provides a good foundation for understanding the thinking of public choice economists:

1. Proposals with long-delayed benefits are likely to be adopted only if their costs are unknown or can be deferred or concealed.
2. Proposals offering readily apparent short-term benefits and deferred costs stand a good chance of adoption.
3. Proposals that concentrate benefits and diffuse costs stand an excellent chance of adoption. (A direct majority voting system might induce the opposite, depending on the relative sizes of the individual tax share and benefit.)
4. Proposals to abolish programs or reduce public spending have a low probability of adoption. Electoral rewards go to politicians who propose new programs or expansions and extensions of existing programs.
5. Packages of reform proposals stand a better chance of adoption than individual reform proposals, even if none of the packages' components would be accepted by a majority of voters if considered separately.
6. Direct transfer programs, which clearly designate specific and limited

---

1. William C. Mitchell, *The Anatomy of Public Failure: A Public Choice Perspective*, Original Paper No. 13 (Washington, DC: International Institute for Economic Research, 1978).

When election time rolls around, voters are bombarded with messages concerning their civic responsibility to vote. These statements are often accompanied by complaints about low voter turnouts for U.S. elections.

But think about it rationally for a minute. What are the costs of voting? You must register to vote. You must spend time getting to the polls. You must wait in line at the polls. Most important, you must spend time becoming informed on the issues and the candidates. What are the benefits of voting? It is possible that you might be able to affect the outcome, but the probability of your vote being important is tiny, especially in national elections. Perhaps you vote because you get a feeling that you have done your duty, or you receive satisfaction from participating in civic affairs. These feelings must be important, or even fewer people would vote.

If society as a whole really wanted more people to vote, however, there are ways to make it less costly to vote. (One reason that many states make election day a legal holiday is to encourage voting.) If you don't think costs affect turnout, answer this question: Do more people vote when the weather is nice or when it is bad?

How could the cost of voting be lowered or the benefits increased? Some methods are postcard registration, transportation to the polls, and more voting places so that lines are shorter. Coffee and doughnuts at the polls might lure a few hungry voters, or rock bands might bring in younger voters (but perhaps keep older ones away). If you think about it, perhaps you can suggest even more voter-luring techniques to your local election board.

ECONOMIC INSIGHT

TO VOTE OR NOT TO VOTE— AN ECONOMIC DECISION?

benefits to certain persons or groups, stand little chance of adoption.
7. Proposals that rely on inefficient, complex, multiple revenue sources are preferred over those financed by simple, direct taxation.
8. Proposals that tax market efficiency stand a better chance of adoption than proposals that reward efficiency.
9. Proposals that limit consumption (such as price ceilings and rationing) as a response to product shortages are preferred over proposals that encourage increased production.
10. Policies that protect consumers by restraining producers are preferred over policies that simply improve the information level of consumers.

The implications of such biases for policy analysis are striking. Policy problems exist because two imperfect mechanisms are at work. The market fails because of externalities, underproduction of public goods (including unequal income distribution), and business cycles. The collective political process fails because the participants in that process are responding to incentives other than those assumed by the welfare economists. Policy makers must, therefore, choose between two imperfect mechanisms in attempting to solve any policy problem. The policy maker must examine the biases inherent in both the market solution and the collective political solution. It will not always be clear that the cost of intervention is less than the cost of inactivity. Therefore, the public choice approach may lead to a prescription of no intervention in many cases, on the grounds that the cure could be worse than the disease.

RENT SEEKING

In previous chapters, we discussed the concept of rent. Economic rent is the economic return over opportunity cost. It was defined in the chapter on perfect competition as the payment to any factor of production greater than the amount necessary to bring that factor into productive use. In the chapter on monopoly, we raised the issue of monopoly rent seeking, an additional economic cost incurred by individuals seeking to establish monopolies. Thus, from a societal viewpoint, monopolists "waste" resources (in addition to the deadweight loss of monopoly) by incurring the costs of certain economic activities aimed at establishing a monopoly. If you are uncertain about these two uses of the term *rent*, you should review the relevant sections of the earlier chapters.

We now want to look at the concept of rent seeking in a broader sense. **Rent seeking** is defined as the commitment of scarce resources to capture returns created artificially (by government or quasi-government units). Rent-seeking analysis is used by economists to describe how people or firms compete for artificially contrived transfers. Consider the case in which a government decides to confer a monopoly privilege, for example, the contract to be the sole supplier of food services at a state university. A great deal of effort will be spent to obtain that contract. Lobbyists will work in the legislature, firms will give campaign contributions to legislators, and lawyers will draw up contracts. All these efforts are directed toward seeking a rent that has been artificially created by the state. None of this activity will cause the price of the commodity to fall, as in the case in

rent seeking
The commitment of scarce resources to capture returns created artificially.

which rents are eroded by normal competitive forces. This rent seeking is a real cost to society because competition for governmentally created rents, unlike the "real" rents discussed earlier, does not generate increased supply.

THE COST OF RENT SEEKING

Gordon Tullock, in attempting to measure the costs of rent seeking, was the first to develop the concept.[2] Figure 1 shows a market demand curve D yielding a competitive equilibrium (price P_c and quantity Q_c) and a monopolistic equilibrium (price P_m and quantity Q_m).

As you learned in the chapter on monopoly, the deadweight loss of monopoly is traditionally taken to be the area of triangle ABC in Figure 1. The area of the rectangle P_cP_mAB is supposed to be the transfer from consumers to monopolists in the form of monopoly profits. But Tullock argues that many of the resources represented by that area do not represent a transfer from consumers to producers. The expenditures to capture these profits turn them into a social cost of monopoly. In fact, if competition for the monopoly were vigorous, the area of rectangle P_cP_mAB would be exactly equal to the resources wasted in competition for the monopoly privilege. The using up of economic rent in the "cost of capture" is unproductive in the sense that it uses scarce resources but does not generate any economic activity that lowers price or increases output.

LEGISLATION AND RENT SEEKING

We can use Tullock's concept of rent seeking to explain governmental action as a form of self-interested behavior by politicians and voters. Many actions of government can be explained by this analysis. In fact, it might

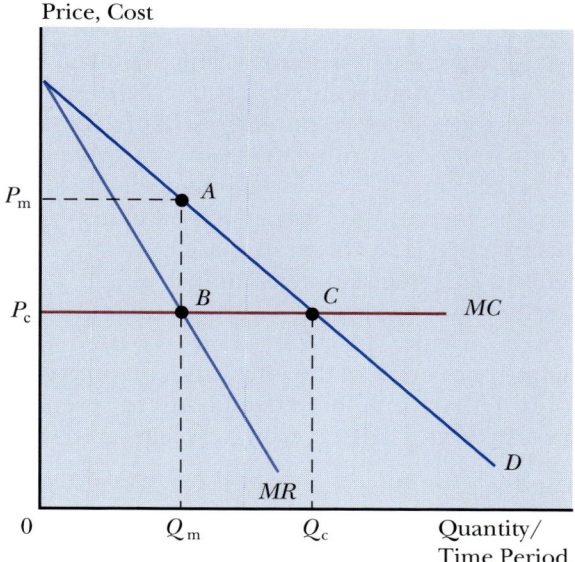

FIGURE 1
THE COSTS OF RENT SEEKING
The deadweight loss of monopoly is the area of triangle ABC, but rent seeking could use up an amount equal to rectangle P_cP_mAB, as rent seekers compete for the monopoly right.

---

2. Gordon Tullock, "The Welfare Costs of Tariffs, Monopolies, and Theft," *Western Economic Journal* (now *Economic Inquiry*) (June 1967).

be argued that an industry of rent seekers exists in most state capitals and most certainly in Washington, D.C.

There are at least two broad applications of this interest-group theory of legislation. The first explains the types of government regulation. George Stigler described the benefits and costs to various interest groups of using the state as a vehicle to increase their own wealth.[3] Some groups, such as agricultural interests, seek income transfers from the state. Other groups, such as automobile producers, use the state to fend off regulation that would have a negative impact on costs and profit. In some cases, management and labor join together to use the state for their mutual benefit at a cost to consumers, such as in attempts to restrict imports.

The second application focuses on the economic behavior of legislatures. In this analysis, the politician is responsible for brokering transfers from one group to another. One can view the politician as an entrepreneur putting together coalitions of rent-seeking groups. Consider the public provision of education as an example. In the United States, education through the twelfth grade is mainly produced in the public sector. A public choice economist would argue that even if education is a public good, there is no reason to believe that representative democracy can create the incentives necessary to internalize the external benefits of education. Instead, such economists expect office holders to broker benefits to certain subsets of the population, including (but not limited to) members of the educational bureaucracy and organized student or parent groups. So, what started as a correction of market failure ends in a solution that is quite far removed from the optimal correction. It might reasonably be called government failure.

POLITICIANS AS RENT EXTRACTORS

In most of the literature on rent seeking, the politician is viewed as a broker for private rent seekers. Fred S. McChesney has focused on the politician as the rent extractor.[4] He sees the politician as an independent actor making demands to which the private sector responds. The politician first threatens to extract private rents through legislation that creates special taxes or new regulations. The private sector responds by striking bargains in the form of campaign contributions or other payments to protect its rent. As long as the cost of protecting the rent is less than the costs imposed by the threatened law, the incentive to strike such bargains exists. McChesney reports that this practice is so common that politicians even have a name for it. They refer to such legislation as "milker bills."

The example that McChesney uses to support his argument is the Federal Trade Commission's "used car rule." In 1975, Congress passed a law that ordered the FTC to initiate regulation of the warranties on used cars. The FTC developed a procedure that would have been costly for used car dealers. While the procedure was being written, Congress legislated itself

---

3. George Stigler, "The Theory of Economic Regulation," *Bell Journal of Economics and Management Science* (Spring 1971).
4. Fred S. McChesney, "Rent Extraction and Rent Creation in the Economic Theory of Regulation," *Journal of Legal Studies* (January 1987): 101-118. For an interesting discussion of the rent extraction and rent defending that took place during the formulating of tax reform legislation, see Laura Saunders, "One Man's Problem Is Another's Opportunity," *Forbes* (March 7, 1988): 105–112.

a veto over FTC action. After the FTC formulated its rule, Congress held hearings. Used car dealers and their trade associations descended on Congress. Congress in turn vetoed the FTC rule. What rent was extracted? McChesney reports that 89 percent of those in Congress who supported the veto and ran again in 1982 received contributions from the National Auto Dealers Association (NADA). The average contribution was over $2,300, and contributions were received by sixty-six members of Congress who had not previously been supported by NADA.

RENT DEFENDING

John T. Wenders has extended the analysis of rent seeking by drawing attention to the fact that consumers also spend resources defending their consumer surplus from rent seekers.[5] Wenders recognizes that this activity might more correctly be called consumer surplus defending, but he prefers to label it **rent defending**. Consumers would be willing to pay an amount represented by the area of rectangle $P_c P_m AC$ in Figure 1 to prevent the market from being monopolized. As you saw in an earlier chapter, that area represents consumer surplus. Consumer surplus is the extra utility that consumers gain due to the fact that they pay less than they would be willing to pay for the item because all units are sold for the price of the last, or marginal unit.

Rent seekers and rent defenders are bidding for the same resources. Rent seekers are bidding for the monopoly privilege. Consumers are willing to spend a similar amount to prevent the rent seekers from acquiring a monopoly. Wenders shows that this situation is analogous to that of Prisoner's Dilemma. If either party spends less, it will lose to the party spending more. This situation ensures that exactly *double* the amount represented by $P_c P_m AC$ in Figure 1 will be spent seeking the monopoly and defending the consumer surplus.

The concept of rent defending expands the analysis of rent seeking. The implication is that in some situations the cost of regulation is much higher than it is traditionally thought to be.

rent defending
Actions by consumers to keep their consumer surplus from being captured by rent seekers.

ANALYSIS OF THE POLITICAL MARKET

According to the self-interest theory of government, the size of government increases as a result of rent-seeking activity by firms and individuals and brokering activity by politicians. There are other forces at work to influence the type of governmental programs that are created by politicians. Still other forces tend to increase the size of government, and at least one tends to reduce it.

THE MEDIAN VOTER THEOREM

The **median voter theorem** predicts that under majority rule, politicians will adopt the positions of voters near the center of the political spectrum. To see why politicians move to the center, refer to Figure 2. Assume that

median voter theorem
A theory that predicts that under majority rule, politicians will reflect the positions of voters near the center of the political spectrum.

---

5. John T. Wenders, "On Perfect Rent Dissipation," *American Economic Review* (June 1987): 456–459.

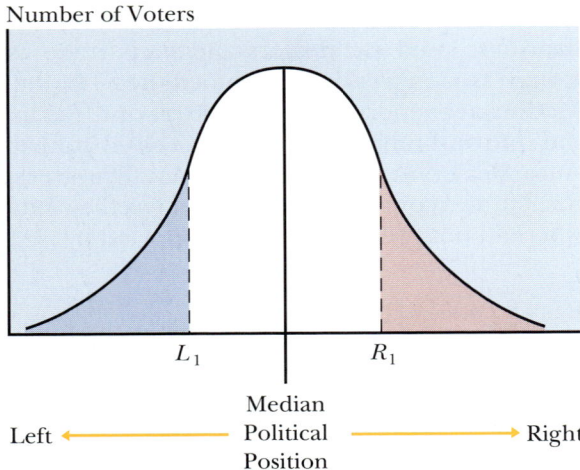

**FIGURE 2
THE MEDIAN VOTER MODEL**
If two politicians are running against one another, they will both move toward the median position to capture votes.

political preferences in society are continuous from left to right and distributed under the normal curve in the figure. If there are two candidates R_1 and L_1 who are at equal distances from the center, they will get the number of votes represented by the area under the curve on their side of the median line. They tie at the polls. Candidate R_1 will realize that he can steal some votes by moving toward the median, because he can count on all the voters to his right. Candidate L_1 will realize what is happening, and she will also move toward the center in an attempt to get a majority of the votes cast. As a result, both politicians will end up near the median political position, where there are the same number of voters to the left and the right.

The median voter theorem can be used to explain why public spending is aimed at groups in the middle of the political stream, especially in a two-party system. Why, for example, do politicians worry more about catastrophic medical treatment for Alzheimer's than they do for AIDS? The median voter theorem is the basis of Stigler's and Tullock's argument presented in the chapter on income distribution—that most of the redistribution of income will be from the rich and the poor to the middle class.

LOGROLLING

When many issues are before a legislative body at the same time, the outcome most preferred by voters on some issues may not result. This failure is due to **logrolling**, which is a form of exchange in which a politician trades support on one issue for support on another issue. Logrolling is the direct exchange of support. The senator from Oklahoma votes for the military base in South Carolina in exchange for a vote by the senator from South Carolina for the water project that will make Tulsa a seaport.

Economists don't know much about the properties of logrolling except that it does not necessarily produce optimal levels of public output. The size of the budget may be too large and its breakdown may be altered as a result of logrolling. The overall outcome depends on the coalitions that surface. It is probably safe to infer that logrolling does not enhance the efficient use of resources.

logrolling
Vote trading in the legislative process.

It often is argued by economists that geographically based representative democracy and logrolling produce too much government spending of the "pork barrel" type. This excess spending results from the fact that citizens see the cost of their local projects being shifted to citizens of other states or districts and reward their elected officials for delivering such projects. With most representatives attempting to be successful at this political "game," logrolling creates larger than desired levels of government spending.

BUREAUCRATS AND BUREAUS

Once a governmental unit has decided how much of a public good to produce and how to pay for it, the legislature and the executive branch (president, governor, mayor) usually turn the job of supplying the good over to a bureau (a government agency or department). In a few cases, governmental units simply purchase privately supplied goods with tax revenue. A classic case of using private suppliers exists in Scottsdale, Arizona, where fire protection is privately supplied and some part of it is purchased by the local government. Garbage removal is also often privately supplied. More often, however, a bureau is responsible for production of a public good.

Bureaus and bureaucrats further cloud the analysis of government intervention because they are charged with the delivery of public goods. The role of bureaus and bureaucracy creates many problems in supplying public goods. The first problem is that it is extremely difficult, if not impossible, to monitor the efficiency of a bureau. Bureaus do not usually produce measurable outputs. Instead, they produce activities. For example, a bureau might produce fire protection, education, or defense. These activities are usually monitored by examining spending rather than by measuring outputs. Citizens may be more interested in output levels. Sometimes there is a partial measure of output, such as the number of students educated or length of response time for fire-fighting units. But how can the value of the outputs of the Department of Defense be measured? The value of such outputs must usually be inferred from the activity of the bureau, and that activity is most often measured by the size of the expenditure on it. Thus, worries over the quality and quantity of education or defense are generally reduced to calls for increased spending on the activity itself.

MONOPOLY PROBLEMS

The problem of monitoring bureaus is further complicated by the fact that bureaus are almost always monopoly suppliers dealing with a single purchaser, the government. This relationship makes the monitoring function of the governmental committee charged with oversight of the bureau difficult at best. The rationale for a monopoly supplier is that it avoids inefficient duplication. This reasoning may or may not be valid. However, the legislative committee charged with supervising the monopoly supplier has no competing information by which to judge its efficiency.

This point has surfaced in recent years in debates concerning the public funding of education. Conservative and Libertarian social critics have suggested a voucher system as a way to introduce competition into public education. Under a voucher system, each student receives a "chit" that can be used for tuition at any school. These social critics argue that the resulting competition would improve the quality and quantity of publicly financed education.

BUDGET MAXIMIZING

Still another problem is created by the way in which bureaucrats are rewarded. As we discussed in a previous chapter, entrepreneurs or hired managers in the private sector generally lay claim to any profit and, therefore, have ample incentive to increase efficiency. In a public bureau, the manager has no such stake. In fact, it may even be that the bureau manager's salary is inversely related to efficiency. This perverse situation can result when salary increases are tied to the size of the budget and the budget grows (in part) because of inefficiency.

There are many possible goals that bureaucrats could substitute for the private manager's goal of profit maximization. Among these other motivations are salary, perquisites of the office, power, public reputation, patronage, bureau output, ease of management, or investment in future private-sector employment. Government officials should keep these competing motivations in mind when they establish bureaus and when they evaluate bureau managers' behavior. All of these motives will give different results from what welfare economists expect to occur with government intervention. Keep in mind that there is an internal contradiction in expecting a government official to try to control the size of a bureau.

THE INHERENT BIAS AGAINST INNOVATION

Government regulation has a built-in bias against new products and new technology. This bias clearly exists in the area of food and drugs and holds generally for any product that faces regulatory approval. The reason is that old products are on the market until they are proven too harmful, but new products cannot be introduced until they are proven safe. This requirement greatly retards innovation in some areas of the U.S. economy. For example, many U.S. citizens routinely travel to Europe or Mexico to receive innovative medical treatment. The list of innovative drugs not available in the United States is very long. Somatotropin for pituitary deficiency, disopyramide for heart patients, propranolol for blood pressure, and sodium valprote for epilepsy were all available in Europe five to ten years before they could be used in the United States.

Similar situations have existed for other products and techniques. For six years, Chemical Waste Management has been seeking permission to burn waste 140 miles at sea. The technique has been used in Europe for more than fifteen years. Also, *60 Minutes* reported on a similar incident in Texas. A firm used a harmless predatory insect to keep harmful bugs out of stored grain. The insect replaced previously approved pesticides that some consumers found unacceptable. The FDA shut the firm down, ruling that the insect was an unapproved additive to the grain, even though its use was recommended by the Department of Agriculture.

Perhaps the most illuminating story about old versus new products relates to sugar substitutes. In 1977, the FDA proposed a ban on saccharin because it had been linked to cancer. Saccharin had been sold in the United States for almost a hundred years. The makers of saccharin fought

Mikhail Gorbachev quickly became a world politician of the first rank. *Time* magazine named him man of the decade in 1989. His agenda of *perestroika* (economic restructuring) and *glasnost* (openness) has created profound change in the Soviet Union and Eastern Europe. So far, glasnost has been much more successful than perestroika.

Property rights and the ability to exchange such rights are essential for markets to function. It is disagreement over such rights that stands in the way of the success of perestroika. This problem is fundamental because the very definition of communism requires collective ownership of the means of production, distribution, and exchange. Marxist-Leninism was built on the contention that private property is theft.

The struggle to reform in the Soviet Union has produced some interesting definitions. In 1988, a "law on cooperatives" was passed. In effect, this law permitted private business. The term "co-op" was used to make private business sound as though it is compatible with socialism.

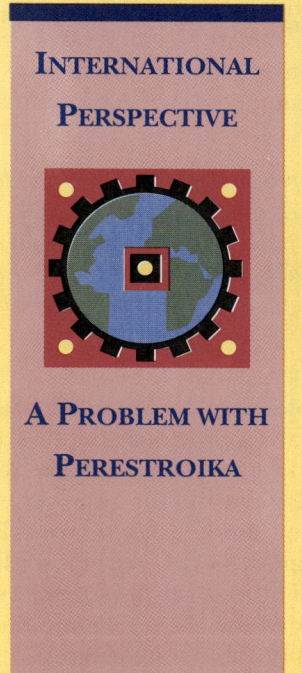

INTERNATIONAL PERSPECTIVE

A PROBLEM WITH PERESTROIKA

Perestroika has also led to some increase in private farming. Private leases on farming land are now available for up to fifty years. There is a great deal of resistance to these private property rights. Again, an imaginative word has been developed to describe this new private property. It is called "citizens' property" to make it compatible with socialism.

The success of perestroika will depend on the development of private businesses and the expansion of private property, not only in agriculture but all segments of the Soviet economy. The development of citizens' property in the agriculture sector has proceeded very slowly. Perhaps the memory of Stalin is still vivid in the Soviet minds. In the 1930s, Stalin "liquidated" some 20 million farmers to destroy private farming and collective agriculture. That collective agriculture has been a failure is not subject to debate, but private farmers have faced continuous obstacles from the Communist bureaucracy. There is now cautious optimism that the failure of the August 1991 coup will allow agrarian reform to move forward more rapidly.

the ban in Congress, and it was overruled. At the same time, it took G. D. Searle eight years and large sums of money to win FDA approval of an alternative sweetener, aspartame. Aspartame might have saved countless lives if it had been approved more quickly.

The moral of such stories is a simple one. Regulation has slowed the introduction of new products. This type of regulation may be having a significant impact on U.S. competitiveness in world markets. Peter Huber commented:

I strongly suspect that if Henry Ford had to bring out his Model T in today's environment, the courts and the regulators would have stopped him. Darn thing was dangerous; why you could break your arm cranking it. Of course, horses were dangerous, too, but as an established technology, horse transportation would have fared better in the courts and regulatory halls than transportation by new fangled flivver.[6]

WHAT IS THE ANSWER?

These problems of government intervention lead to disturbing conclusions. You saw in previous chapters, especially the one on monopoly, that markets do not always produce beneficial results. The chapter on market failure and government intervention added externalities and public goods to the list of market failures. But this chapter showed that political action designed to correct market failure introduces a whole set of new problems. The net result is a messy one. Markets may fail, but governments also can fail. Government and government representatives do not always work in the public interest.

This view of government failure as a parallel to market failure has been widely accepted among policy makers and voters. The important point is that economists can identify market failure and government failure and allow policy makers to sort out the least harmful solution to policy problems that affect everyone.

PRIVATIZATION

One political movement has worked against the tendency of governments to grow. This trend is most often referred to as privatization. **Privatization** is the transfer of governmental activities and/or assets to the private sector. In response to what some observers consider to be excessive growth of government, privatization has been increasing not only in the United States but worldwide. In England, the Thatcher government was very active in a major program of privatizing numerous state-owned industries. In the People's Republic of China, "the reform of the basic tenets of the system" involves elements of privatization. In the United States, privatization has been done mostly by local governments, but the concept may spread to state and federal governments.

The advantages of privatization are that it reduces government spending and is politically feasible because it does not eliminate the service. The spending reductions come from several sources:

1. Privatization introduces competition and the resulting efficiencies.

> **privatization**
> The transfer of governmental activities and/or assets to the private sector.

---

6. Peter Huber, "Who Will Protect Us from Our Protectors?" *Forbes* (13 July 1987): 23.

2. It permits smaller localities to join together into more efficiently sized units for purchasing services.
3. It removes government from labor negotiations and retirement commitments.
4. It transfers revenue-consuming activities to private firms that pay taxes and produce revenues.

U.S. cities and localities have used seven methods to privatize services. These methods are summarized in Table 1. Privatization can also result inadvertently from failure of governments to deliver a quality service. United Parcel Service's (UPS) success in competing with the U.S. Postal Service is perhaps the best example of such a governmental default. Privatization was a hot topic in the 1980s and can be expected to be an even hotter item for state and local governments in the 1990s.

OTHER SCHOOLS OF THOUGHT

Public choice theory, outlined earlier in this chapter, applies microeconomic analysis to the political process. We now draw your attention to two other schools of economic thought that are usually ignored in a beginning economics course. Both offer some useful insights on the appropriate role of government and the nature of government failure.

TABLE 1 METHODS OF PRIVATIZATION

Method	Description	Advantages	Examples
Contracting	Competitive letting of bids	Competitive and can be seasonal	Public works Transportation
Franchises	Grant franchise to operate and charge fee	Can get some revenue without having to provide service	Garbage pickup Airports
Subsidies	Help defray costs of private provider	Cheaper than public provision	Cultural arts Youth activities
Vouchers	Coupon to purchase good or service	Can shop in marketplace—competition	Food stamps School lunches
Volunteers	Ask people to work for free	No-cost services—large pool of people	Tutoring School guards Consulting
Self-help	Variation on volunteerism	No-cost services	Neighborhood watch
Tax incentives	Grant tax concessions	Reduces public need to supply and can be used at federal, state or local level	Income tax credit for child care expenses

Source: Adapted from John C. Goodman, ed., *Privatization* (Dallas: The National Center for Policy Analysis, 1985), 37.

THE AUSTRIAN SCHOOL

The Austrian school has its roots in the work of Ludwig von Mises and Nobel laureate F. A. Hayek.[7] Economists of this school start their analysis from the assumption that policy makers make economic decisions in a state of partial ignorance. Individual consumers and producers plan with incomplete and/or incorrect knowledge of the future. Markets play the role of providing feedback, which coordinates actions as individuals adjust their incorrect plans to changing relative prices. Individuals are frustrated, but by adjusting to changes in relative prices they are better off than they would have been before the adjustment.

The Austrian school is in many ways very close to public choice theory. Economists of the Austrian school argue that political manipulation of the economy is microeconomic in nature, rather than macroeconomic. In their view, politicians do not seek to influence the unemployment rate or the inflation rate, but rather try to influence certain markets for their own gain. For example, one politician may work to create subsidies for farmers. Another may work for aid to urban slum dwellers. The result of these actions is that the size of government increases, with many programs that are difficult to control, much less to reduce.

Economists of this school take a strong stand against governmental planning. This stand is based on four points made by one of the best-known members of the school, F. A. Hayek. The first is that planning always results in more planning because people will circumvent the rules of the planner. As a result, the planner will devise more rules, which lead to more circumvention, which produces still more rules. Hayek referred to this process as "the road to serfdom." Hayek's second point about governmental planning is that no matter how detailed the plan, it can't cover all the specific cases. A bureaucracy will be needed to implement the plan. This bureaucracy will grow powerful and corrupt. Hayek's third point is that high morale is so important to the success of governmental planning that any critics of the plan must be silenced. Hayek's last point is that "the worst get to the top." His point is that governmental planning leads to a dictator. One of the great appeals of Hayek's work is that it so accurately describes the path followed by most countries that have tried central planning. As you will see in a later chapter, the Soviet Union and the People's Republic of China are trying to address some of their internal problems. The Austrian school would argue that these countries' problems are caused by planning, and reforms in the context of planning are doomed to failure.

Perhaps the leading spokesman of the Austrian school in the United States is Murray Rothbard. Professor Rothbard views conservative economists who are suspicious of government intervention as "wimpy moderates" because they do not view *all* government intervention as "not only ineffectual, but also pernicious, and counterproductive."[8] Rothbard and the Austrian school are opposed to any intervention in the macro economy. Although they believe that money matters in the economy, they

---

7. A very good survey of the Austrian school can be found in Thomas Sowell's *Knowledge and Decision* (New York: Basic Books, 1981). In the United States, this school of thought is embodied in the Ludwig von Mises Institute, which has its offices at Auburn University.
8. Peter Brimelow, "No Water Economics," *Forbes* (6 March 1989): 86.

don't think that monetary policy can be carried out because it requires impossibly precise assumptions about the economy.

RADICAL ECONOMIC THOUGHT

Unlike the Austrian school, radical economists are critical of both the market and government in a capitalistic system. Radical economists in the United States draw on the tradition of Karl Marx and Marxist thought, which we will discuss in a later chapter. These economists do add several new lines of attack on capitalism.[9] The basic difference between radical economics and other schools of economic thought is that all other economists (including public choice and Austrian) see a basic harmony in the economic system and believe that most problems can be solved by relying on market forces. Radicals contend that solutions to the problems of modern capitalism can only be found by restructuring industrial capitalism. In addition, radical economists regard orthodox economists as being much too narrow in their analyses.

The main themes of radical economics are monopoly power, state power, exploitation, imperialism, and waste and alienation. Radicals believe that the U.S. economy is dominated by large corporations and that small firms play an insignificant role. These large corporations set arbitrary prices and manipulate consumer wants. The state is viewed as the protector and fostering agent of the powerful monopolies. The radicals see the federal government as controlled by big companies. They believe that the state sets economic policy, including defense spending, in the interest of big business.

Radicals challenge the marginal productivity theory of income determination (discussed in an earlier chapter). They argue that monopolistic firms, unequal opportunity, and the unjustifiable private ownership of capital make this theory defective. They base their description of factor incomes on dual, or segmented, labor markets. **Dual labor markets** result from artificial barriers in labor markets that keep some workers in jobs with low wages. Radicals argue that these two labor markets consist of one in which pay is good and advancements are possible and a second in which pay is low and opportunities for advancement are nonexistent. These dual labor markets are a result of a conscious effort on the part of capitalists to restrict advancement to certain groups in the labor force. As a result, a large fraction of the labor force is doomed to dead-end jobs for life, with low pay, little job security, and no opportunities for advancement.

dual labor markets
The radical economists' idea that there are two labor markets because of artificial barriers that keep some workers earning low wages.

Radicals argue that the main obstacle to third-world development is the imperialism of industrial capitalism. Radicals claim (and here they differ from Marx) that industrial capitalists receive capital from the underdeveloped world and that the terms of trade are exploitive of poorer countries. Radicals would support the New International Economic Order, which was discussed in an earlier chapter, as a way to change these conditions.

Finally, radicals argue that resources are wasted in a capitalistic system. This waste is the amount of money spent on such items as expensive au-

---

9. Most radical economists in the United States are members of the Union of Radical Political Economy (URPE). URPE publishes a journal, *The Review of Radical Political Economics*, which you can check if you are interested in learning more about radical economics.

tos, furs, alcohol, and drugs, as well as the billions of dollars spent on advertising, which radicals claim is used to manipulate consumer wants. Radicals argue that this waste and the power of monopolies contribute to alienation. Since individuals have little control over their destiny, they consume high levels of unnecessary consumer goods and feel alienated from society.

Radical economists have challenged the mainstream to examine more closely some of the weaknesses of capitalism. The response of most economists has been not to take the radicals too seriously (or to ignore them completely). Radical ideas have, however, led to suggestions for "tinkering" with capitalism in some areas, especially in control of monopoly power. The radicals have also provided useful insights into how special-interest groups use government to serve their own self-interests. These insights are not unlike those of public choice economists. The most serious weakness of the radical economic critique of capitalism is that it is negative. The radical analysis identifies problems but does not present feasible solutions.

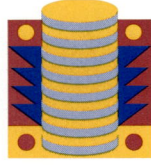

Summary

1. Government often supplies goods that aren't public goods because there is political demand for them.
2. Public choice theory identifies biases in the political process and applies economic analysis to political processes and outcomes.
3. Rent seeking is the economic description of individuals' use of the political process to generate income transfers to themselves or to groups they support.
4. Politicians can threaten to pass taxes or regulations in order to extract rents from private parties.
5. Rent defending is the process by which consumers attempt to defend their consumer surplus from rent seekers.
6. The median voter theorem suggests that under majority rule politicians will adopt positions near the middle of the political spectrum.
7. Logrolling in a legislature increases the size of budgets. Legislators agree to vote for a colleague's project in return for a vote on their project.
8. Bureaucratic decision making is different from firm decision making because bureau managers face a different set of incentives than private sector managers do.
9. Government regulation introduces a bias against new products and new technology.
10. Privatization of government assets or activities permits provision of goods and services to be done more efficiently by relying on market (and other) forces.
11. The Austrian school of economic thought assumes that decision makers proceed on the basis of incorrect and/or incomplete information. The school makes a strong case against economic planning by governments.
12. Radical economics, which is related to Marxism, is based on the belief that monopoly capitalism, protected by government, is manipulative and exploitive.

New Terms

rent seeking
rent defending
median voter theorem
logrolling
privatization
dual labor markets

Chapter 18 Government Failure and Public Choice

QUESTIONS FOR DISCUSSION

1. Should the government intervene in every case in which an externality exists?

2. What is public choice theory?

3. Why do public choice economists argue that direct transfer programs that clearly target a limited group stand little chance of adoption?

4. Why is it so hard to cut public programs once they are started?

5. Why do government programs that concentrate benefits and diffuse costs have a better chance of being enacted than those that benefit many and impose costs on a few?

6. How can politicians be rent extractors?

7. How can logrolling increase the size of government?

8. Is public choice theory pessimistic? What is its criticism of welfare economics (discussed in the preceding chapter)?

9. When Governor George Wallace of Alabama was campaigning for the U.S. presidency, he was fond of saying that there wasn't a "dime's worth of difference between the other candidates." Does his claim make any economic sense?

10. Is it possible for interest groups in Washington to engage in logrolling? How would they do it?

11. Why do bureaucracies not always serve the public interest?

12. Why, according to public choice theory, is it not rational to vote?

13. Why do members of the Austrian school take such a strong stand against central planning?

14. What is the Austrian school's argument against governmental planning?

15. How do radical economists challenge the marginal productivity theory of income distribution?

SUGGESTIONS FOR FURTHER READING

Buchanan, James M., and Robert D. Tollison. *The Theory of Public Choice-II*. Ann Arbor: University of Michigan Press, 1984. This book contains a series of articles related to applications of public choice theory.

Frey, Bruno S. *International Political Economics*. New York: Basil Blackwell, 1984. This book applies public choice theory in an international setting.

Heilbroner, Robert L. *The Nature and Logic of Capitalism*. New York: Norton, 1985. A critical look at capitalism from a (traditional) liberal perspective.

Lee, Dwight R., and Richard B. McKenzie. *Regulating Government*. New York: Lexington Books, 1986. This book uses public choice theory to explain government intervention into the market and why a constitution is needed to restrain government.

Lindbeck, Assar. *The Political Economy of the New Left: An Outsider's View*, 2nd ed. New York: Harper & Row, 1977. Presents a critical review of the radical economics movement.

Vickers, John, and George Yarrow. *Privatization: An Economic Analysis*. Cambridge, MA: MIT Press, 1988. An account of the privatization experience in Great Britain.

AFTER STUDYING THIS CHAPTER, YOU SHOULD BE ABLE TO:

1. Evaluate the following U.S. farm policies:
   a. support prices,
   b. acreage allotment,
   c. marketing orders,
   d. target prices,
   e. Food Security Act.
2. Use a graph to illustrate the farm problems of the United States.
3. Explain optimal city size in terms of economies and diseconomies of agglomeration.
4. Discuss how the provision of local public goods is complicated by spillovers.
5. Explain and evaluate the Tiebout hypothesis.
6. Define and give examples of the tragedy of the commons, and explain why government must either regulate or assign property rights to solve the problem.
7. Identify the problems that can arise when resources are used by several nations.

CHAPTER 19

AGRICULTURE, CITIES, AND THE ENVIRONMENT: CASE STUDIES IN MARKET FAILURE AND GOVERNMENT FAILURE

INTRODUCTION

This chapter applies the theories discussed in the last two chapters to three real-world concerns: agricultural policy, urban problems, and the global environment. You often hear or read about the demise of the family farm and the crisis in agricultural markets. In some areas of the country, traditionally conservative farmers have even used the tactics of protest movements in efforts to draw political attention to their economic problems. The basic tools of economic analysis can provide many insights into the role of market failure and government failure in creating the problems in the agricultural sector.

The issues facing urban America are in many instances not unique to cities but are simply more severe there. For example, pollution and crime are found in all parts of the world, but they are more serious problems in urban areas. Pollution, crime, and other negative externalities associated with living in cities are examples of market failures that government intervention has failed to solve.

Finally, the 1990s have already been labeled the decade of the environment. Reports in the news cause concern about massive oil spills, depletion of the ozone layer, exhaustion of nonrenewable resources, acid rain, the greenhouse effect, the destruction of tropical rain forests, and the pressure of world population on a fragile ecological system. The market system tends not to take a very long view. Critics argue that environmental problems result from failure to plan far enough ahead or to consider the needs of future generations. Governments have attempted to intervene to protect the environment for future generations, but these attempts at correcting market failure bring their own problems.

477

THE FARM PROBLEM

Government involvement in agriculture has a long history in the United States, beginning with the Homestead Act of 1862. During the Great Depression, direct income and price support programs began. Those who favored such government intervention believed that the market failed in agriculture in several ways. The structure of agriculture is very competitive, with a large number of firms (farms). Farmers face unstable prices for their products, so their incomes vary greatly from year to year. Unpredictable weather, international trading patterns that are subject to government influence, and technological changes aggravate the market instability.

U.S. agriculture presents a case study of what happens to well-intentioned government policy as the government becomes part of the problem. Even when it is recognized that policies are unsuccessful, it is politically very difficult to reduce or eliminate the government's role. Professor George Stigler has put it this way:

One finding has been that small groups do better in politics than large groups, certainly per capita and at times in the aggregate. Today American farmers and their families comprise a little over 2 percent of the population but they get about $40 billion in governmental outlays for income stabilization and all kinds of regulations and special programs (restrictions of crops, preferential interest rates, subsidized electrical utilities, etc.). As late as 1950 farmers and their families were about 15 percent of the population and received about $3 billion from total federal government outlays, as compared with $40 billion (about $9.5 billion in 1950 dollars) in the 1980s. That is about a sevenfold increase in payments per farm operator in dollars of stable purchasing power.[1]

In the short run, the farm problem is simple enough to understand. First, agricultural production takes place in a very competitive market that closely resembles the basic supply and demand model developed in Chapter 3. Second, the demand for farm products is price-inelastic. Third, weather plays a significant role in determining the yield of any crop. These conditions together mean that the revenue a farmer receives from year to year can be highly variable.

The irony is that in years of good harvests many farmers may be in worse shape than in years of poor harvests. This situation is depicted in Figure 1. Assume that in the first year farm output sold at a price of P_1, so Q_1 units were sold, and farmers received a total revenue of $P_1 \times Q_1$. The next year, the weather was very good and the crop was large, so the supply curve shifted to S_2. Price fell to P_2, and consumers purchased Q_2 units. Since demand is inelastic, farmers received less revenue than they did the year before ($P_2 \times Q_2$ is less than $P_1 \times Q_1$). The large fall in price brought only a small increase in sales.

The long-run problem for U.S. farmers is largely the result of huge increases in their productivity in the last century. It takes fewer and fewer farmers to produce the same amount of food. In the early nineteenth cen-

---

1. George J. Stigler, *Memoirs of an Unregulated Economist*, New York: Basic Books, Inc., 1988, 118–119.

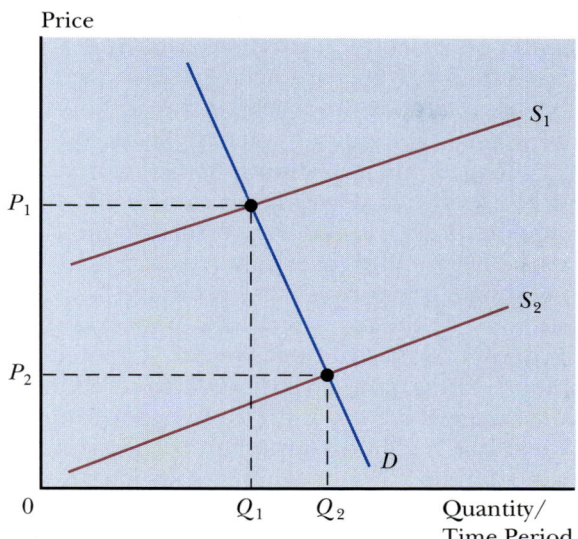

**FIGURE 1
THE MARKET FOR FARM OUTPUT**
The market for farm output has erratic supply (due to changes in the weather) and inelastic demand. Thus, the total revenue a farmer receives in any one year can be highly variable, and an increase in quantity supplied can reduce total farm income.

tury, more than half of the U.S. labor force was engaged in farming. Now less than 2 percent of the work force is employed in agriculture.

Some observers regard the instability of farm income and the decline of opportunities in agriculture as forms of market failure, although they do not fit into any of the categories of market failure identified in earlier chapters. In addition, as you saw in the last chapter, government intervention often does not succeed. One of these failures occurs when government follows policies that benefit special interests even though the costs to society exceed the benefits.

Many of the arguments to save the family farm are intended to stop the trend toward fewer and fewer agricultural workers. Even some nonfarmers support maintaining the current number of farms. They argue that smaller farms are more environmentally benign than huge agri-industry. Farmers have political power, so there has been governmental response to their calls for action. Among the forms of this response have been agricultural price supports and managing production.

SUPPORTING PRICES

Before 1973, the **agricultural support program** consisted of attempts to achieve parity for farmers through the use of price supports. **Parity** is a one-to-one ratio between the average price of farm products and the prices of what farmers buy. In practice, achieving parity means creating **support prices**, or price floors, which are prices maintained above equilibrium levels by the government. The idea behind support prices is to link farm prices to a parity index that maintains the purchasing power of farmers at the level of some base period. For example, if a bushel of wheat bought five gallons of gasoline or two pairs of shoes in the base period, the price of a bushel of wheat should be kept high enough to permit the same purchases today. Highly respected agricultural economist and Nobel laureate T. W. Schultz described parity as "a vulgar economic con-

agricultural support program
Attempts by the federal government to achieve parity for farmers through the use of price supports.

parity
A one-to-one ratio between the average prices of farm products and the prices of what farmers buy.

support prices
Price floors for agricultural products maintained by the government, which purchases any surplus to keep the price from falling.

cept."[2] It is vulgar to Schultz because it does not allow changes in the relative prices of agricultural and nonagricultural products over time.

You saw the effect of price floors in an earlier chapter, so Figure 2 should be familiar. When there is a price floor above the equilibrium price, the quantity supplied exceeds the quantity demanded at the imposed price, and a surplus develops. If the price floor is to be maintained, demand must be increased. However, the government can't sell the surplus on domestic markets, or the price will fall back to the equilibrium price. In the 1950s and early 1960s, the government reacted to this dilemma by building storage bins and storing farm products. The Department of Agriculture sold some of the surplus food to poor countries under the Food for Peace program and distributed some to school lunch programs and welfare recipients. Most of the surplus was just stored, however. At the high point of this storage activity in 1961, the U.S. government had 1.3 billion bushels of wheat and 1.7 billion bushels of corn in storage.

There are some steps that could be taken to dispose of such a surplus. The government could destroy the surplus, but this action would upset those who consider it wasteful.[3] The government could give the surplus away to poor countries, but this might anger other countries who are trying to sell their farm products. The government might distribute the surplus in its own country. In the 1980s, the Reagan administration distributed large amounts of surplus cheese to people over age 65. Some of this cheese went to people who were quite prosperous, including retirees

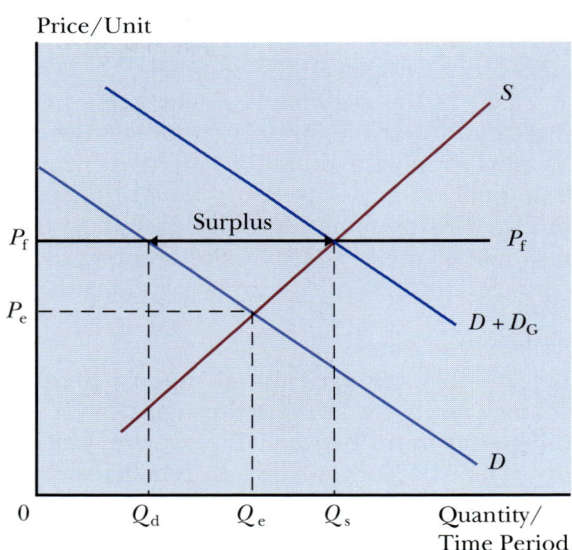

FIGURE 2
PRICE FLOORS IN AGRICULTURE
If the government imposes a price floor (price support) above the market-clearing price, a surplus will result.

2. T. W. Schultz, "Tensions between Economics and Politics in Dealing with Agriculture," Agriculture Economics Paper No. 84:24, Department of Economics, University of Chicago (10 August 1985): 5.
3. The Canadian government once destroyed 28 million eggs. See Patrick Howe, "Unscrambling the Egg Market: A Lesson in Economics," *Common Sense Economics* 2 (Spring 1977): 42–47. For some ludicrous stories of price supports gone amok, see *Fortune* (25 November 1985): 149; (9 December 1985): 150.

with a great deal of accumulated wealth. The government could sell the surplus to other countries if customers could be found. Another alternative would be to retain the surplus for future emergency needs. Regardless of the disposal problems, it is absolutely necessary for the government to buy the surplus it has created.

Managing Production

In the mid-1950s, the U.S. government decided that the purchase and storage of farm surpluses was too costly and that managing production was a better alternative. The new policy called for the government to maintain the price floor by keeping the quantity supplied at lower levels than would exist without government intervention. With this policy, the government was trying to shift the supply curve to the left in order to maintain the higher price without creating a surplus.

The first government attempt to manage production was known as the soil bank program. In the **soil bank program**, which was started under President Eisenhower in the 1950s, farmers were paid to let their land lie idle. A second attempt to reduce production was the acreage allotment. An **acreage allotment** sets a limit on the number of acres that can be used to produce a specific crop. The government must determine who gets what acreage allotment. For tobacco, for example, the decision is based on past levels of production. If your parents had a tobacco acreage allotment and you bought or inherited their farm, you would be entitled to an allotment based on their share of past production.

A long-term government program aimed at reducing supply is the **Conservation Reserve Program (CRP)**. This program pays farmers to remove land from production for ten years or more. In 1990, the total amount of farm land in this program was about 25 million acres. Payments to farmers in the program in that year were over $1.5 billion.[4]

The supplies of many crops that are not directly subsidized by the federal government are controlled by marketing orders. The system of marketing orders started in 1937 with the goal of maintaining farm income and stable marketing conditions. **Marketing orders** establish producer cartels that control the supply of certain agricultural commodities not subject to price supports. The federal government enforces these cartel agreements through a system of fines for growers. Marketing orders are very common in the fruit-growing industry. The influence of these cartels on supply can be enormous. For example, in 1983, 20 million cases of lemons were destroyed to keep them off the market. The amount of lemons destroyed in 1983 exceeded the amount sold to consumers.[5]

The transfer to farmers through marketing orders is a bit different from the transfer through support payments. In support programs, the payment from the government to the farmer represents a transfer from all taxpayers. Under marketing orders, the subsidy takes the form of a federally enforced artificially high price. This subsidy is a transfer from the consumers of specific products to the growers of those products.

soil bank program
Federal agricultural program beginning in the 1950s under which farmers were paid to let their land lie idle in order to reduce the supply of farm products.

acreage allotment
A limit set by the government on the number of acres that can be used to produce a specific crop, based on past production levels.

Conservation Reserve Program (CRP)
A federal program that pays farmers to remove land from production for ten years or more.

marketing orders
A federal program that establishes producer cartels that control the supply of certain agricultural products not subject to price supports.

---

4. Jeffrey D. Karrenbrock, "The 1988 Drought: Its Impact on District Agriculture," *Review*, Federal Reserve Bank of St. Louis (May/June 1989): 8.
5. Doug Bandow, "Federal Marketing Orders: Good Food Rots While People Starve," *Business and Society Review* (Spring 1985): 41.

Attempts to manage farm production directly by reducing inputs have not been very effective because most farmers are good entrepreneurs. Under the soil bank program, almost all farmers took their least productive land out of production with little decline in output. In the acreage allotment program, farmers had an incentive to cultivate the allowed acres very intensively in an effort to produce nearly the same output on fewer acres. Marketing orders have been more effective in reducing quantity supplied. Farmers cannot benefit by increasing productivity and output when the government specifies the maximum allowed output.

INCREASING DEMAND

In addition to trying to restrict supply, another way to raise prices for agricultural products is to increase demand. There have been some governmental attempts to do this. The Department of Agriculture (USDA) has engaged in export promotion. Programs have been created by the USDA and some land grant universities to assist companies in penetrating foreign markets. In other cases, the government has sold agricultural products directly to foreign countries, most often the Soviet Union.

Another demand-increasing program is the food stamp program. In this program, the USDA gives food stamps to the poor to enable them to buy more agricultural products. This program redistributes income at the same time that it increases the demand for agricultural products.

RECENT FARM POLICY

Since 1973, there have been some changes in the system of agricultural price supports. For some products, there are no longer price floors. Instead, the government sets target prices. **Target prices** are prices the government considers to be fair for farmers. The market is allowed to clear, and the USDA then compares the equilibrium price to the target price. The government then pays each farmer the difference between the target price and the market-clearing price. Target prices have less of a distorting effect than support prices because the relative prices of agricultural products are allowed to change. Also, the government does not have to purchase and store the surplus product. Finally, the subsidy aspect is more apparent with target prices than with support prices.

target prices
Prices the government considers to be fair for farmers, used to determine subsidy payments.

During the 1980s, the Reagan administration made some attempts to reduce the price support programs. The first attempt in early 1981 kept a scheduled rise in target prices for milk from going into effect. This move did not do away with supports, but did prevent an increase at that time.

In 1982, President Reagan initiated a **payment in kind (PIK) program**. The idea was to eliminate the overproduction (caused by the existing support prices) and deal with the huge stocks of farm surpluses. For example, the program gave a farmer 8,000 bushels of stored corn, which the farmer would sell, in exchange for not producing 10,000 bushels. The PIK program was similar to the soil bank program, but payment was made in surplus commodities rather than in money. The result was the same as for the soil bank program. Farmers idled 47 million acres of land in 1983, but they put aside their least productive land and worked the best land more efficiently. The percent drop in production was much less than the percentage of land set aside.

payment in kind (PIK) program
A federal agricultural program similar to the soil bank program, but with payments made in surplus commodities rather than in money.

The European Community (EC) maintains a common agricultural policy (CAP) for its member nations. Unlike agricultural policy in the United States, which is based on paying not to produce, CAP says "pay for everything produced." This system of guaranteed payment has produced huge surpluses that are either stored and are rotting or are sold to the Soviet Union at bargain basement prices.

CAP has resulted in what are jokingly referred to as the French wine lake, the European grain mountain, and the great olive oil sea. Great Britain has 150 storage depots that are stuffed full of grain and butter. A junior minister in Margaret Thatcher's government testified in the House of Commons that the cost of storing and disposing of stocks of cereals, sugar, wine, milk, and beef was about $25 million per day. A "rancher" with three or more cows is entitled to a subsidy from the EC! In Germany, many people have become cow ranchers. Bavaria is full of cottages on small plots of land with three cows. Former Prime Minister Thatcher complained, "In Europe, believe it or not, the subsidy for every cow is greater than the personal income of half the people in the world."[a]

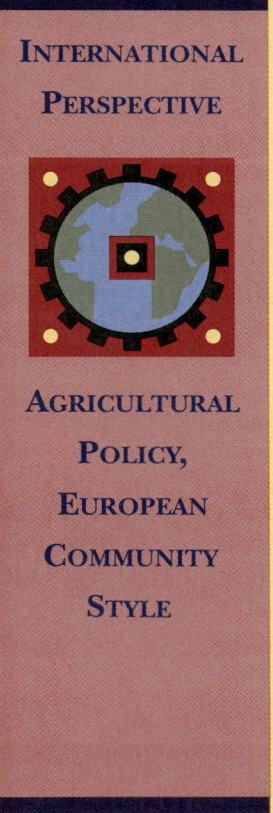

INTERNATIONAL PERSPECTIVE

AGRICULTURAL POLICY, EUROPEAN COMMUNITY STYLE

One of the major beneficiaries (besides the farmers) of this transfer from taxpayers in the EC is the Soviet Union. The Soviet Union has learned to use EC-subsidized surpluses as a way of supplementing its poor agricultural output. Great Britain has sold increasingly large amounts of its surplus output to the Soviet Union. In 1984, sales from Great Britain to the USSR equaled 125,000 tons of products per week, and 35,000 tons per week were sold to Communist countries of Eastern Europe. The prices were deeply discounted from those paid to farmers. Flour was sold at an 80 percent discount; sugar, 72 percent; butter, 60 percent; beef, 88 percent; and wine, 97.5 percent.[b] The Soviets may be taking some lessons from capitalists. At least they know how to profit from the central planning of other governments!

As the EC prepares for complete economic integration in 1992, changes in CAP are high on the agenda. The protection given to agriculture may become a victim of full integration. As economies become more internationalized, the costs of such agricultural subsidies become more visible. The more apparent they become, the more politically vulnerable they will be. CAP will be a political "hot potato" in the 1990s.

a. U.S. News & World Report (30 November 1987): 9.
b. Edward Pearce, "Buying the Farm with the EEC," National Review (18 October 1985): 42–44.

Food Security Act
A 1985 federal law that sets target prices and requires farmers to agree to keep part of their land idle.

THE FOOD SECURITY ACT OF 1985. In 1985, Congress passed the **Food Security Act.** The intent of the law was to make U.S. agricultural products more competitive on world markets. The law eliminated the price support programs that caused their prices to be above world market prices. The Food Security Act sets target prices and requires farmers to agree to keep part of their land idle. Thus, it combines elements of both the target price and soil bank programs. Farmers sell their products at world market prices, and the government pays them a deficiency payment equal to the difference between the target price and the world price. The target price is supposed to be related to the costs of production.

In 1986, the target price of wheat was $4.38 per bushel, and the world market price was around $2.75 per bushel. As a result, U.S. taxpayers had to make a payment of $1.63 for every bushel of wheat sold. As you might imagine, the cost of the Food Security Act is enormous. When Congress debated the bill in early 1985, the cost over its five-year life was estimated at $35 billion. When President Reagan signed the bill in November 1985, his advisers estimated that cost to be $52 billion. In November 1989, the Congressional Budget Office reported that the actual cost for only the first *three* years of the program was $70 billion.

SAVE THE FAMILY FARM ACT. In 1987, Senator Tom Harkin of Iowa and Congressman Richard Gephardt of Missouri introduced the Save the Family Farm Act. The goal of this act was to raise farm prices by drastically decreasing farm output (by more than half). Farmers would be given the opportunity to control production by voting mandatory limits on the amount of farm land that could be put into production. Farmers would face penalties if they did not limit production. However, the bill did not specify what the penalties would be. *Business Week* commented that the Harkin-Gephardt bill sounded "borrowed from a Soviet economic plan."[6]

Supporters of the bill argued that, although prices to consumers would increase, taxpayers would save billions in subsidy payments. One difficulty with this proposal was that, if it were successful in raising U.S. prices, imports would be cheaper and import competition would drive the artificially high U.S. prices down to world market levels. Thus, the program could only achieve its goal with more restrictive tariffs and quotas on agricultural imports than existed at the time. The Save the Family Farm Act did not pass in 1987, but it will be introduced again.

CONFLICTING EFFECTS OF FARM POLICIES

Many of the federal government's farm policies work at cross purposes. Consider, for example, the price support program, which guarantees farmers an unlimited market for grains and dairy products. Farmers expand production because they know they have a buyer to generate the cash flow to meet their payments on expensive machinery and heavily mortgaged land. Thus, this policy works to stimulate production. Other programs, such as the soil bank and marketing orders, are intended to decrease production.

---

6. Michael A. Pollock, "Farmers Will Reap a Bumper Crop of Supports," *Business Week* (12 January 1987): 83.

In 1986, the federal government set out to mop up the milk glut created by price supports and in the process created a new problem. In a sweeping offensive called the Dairy Termination Program, the government sought to eliminate 12.3 billion pounds of milk from the market by buying up dairy herds and selling the animals for beef. In order to participate in the program, farmers had to agree to stay out of the dairy business for five years. Almost $2 billion was spent to get 14,000 farmers out of the milk business. Groups representing beef producers were quick to respond. The program designed to increase milk prices by cutting supply had the opposite effect on beef prices. Prices fell as the supply of beef increased. The California Cattlemen's Association demanded compensation for their losses of from $25 to $60 per head of beef.

Under still another program, the **Soil Conservation Service**, grants were given to encourage farmers to conserve land (rather than produce full tilt) by fallowing fields, contour plowing, and other conservation techniques. (All of these techniques temporarily reduce crop yields.) The price support and the soil conservation programs, both costing taxpayers, work in opposite directions. One creates incentives to expand production. The other offers incentives to contract production.

Soil Conservation Service
A federal program under which grants were given to encourage farmers to contract production by fallowing fields, contour plowing, and other conservation techniques.

STATE REGULATION OF AGRICULTURE

The latest development in government intervention in the agricultural market has been at the state level. In the late 1980s, several states passed legislation that made it more difficult for large corporate farms to operate. Laws passed in Kansas, Iowa, Nebraska, South Dakota, and Minnesota prevent corporations with more than a certain number of stockholders (usually fifteen) from owning land. The intent of such legislation is to preserve the family farm. As Kansas state representative Bruce Larkin said, "The intent of these laws is to keep the family farm in place. Without a family farm structure, rural communities will dry up and wither away."[7] The legislation ignores the economic fact of life that family farms are disappearing. They are being replaced by large-scale corporate farming. Legislation is not going to change this trend.

One outcome of such state legislation has been an economic boon to adjacent states. National Farms, Inc. is building a 1,200-acre hog farm near Brush, Colorado. The company had originally planned to build this farm in South Dakota, but South Dakota passed anti-corporate farm legislation in 1988. The farm produces 300,000 hogs a year and employs 200 farm workers. Maybe some of the unemployed family farmers in South Dakota will move to Colorado to find work!

In early 1990, the state of Wisconsin passed a law prohibiting the sale of milk from cows that had been given a newly developed hormone that dramatically increased milk production. Supporters of the bill argued that health officials were concerned about possible effects of this hormone on humans. Wisconsin lawmakers maintained that they were worried about potential health risks from the hormone. Cynics argued that the lawmakers saw the bill as a way to reduce the potential supply of milk.

---

7. This quote and the facts in the next paragraph from Charles Siler, "Where Did All the Pigs Go?" *Forbes* (19 March 1990): 152–156.

THE FUTURE OF FARM POLICY

U.S. agriculture policy is at a crossroads. The average annual direct subsidy to the average American farmer is more than twice the mean family income in the United States. Two options are open to policy makers. The first is to follow a protectionist, supply management policy. The second option is to confront the challenge presented by other countries in recent tariff negotiations. These negotiations have developed an agreement to negotiate all barriers affecting trade in agricultural products. In 1991, the United States proposed an initiative that would eliminate all agricultural price supports in all member countries by the year 2000. Under this proposal, all government payments to farmers would be "decoupled" from farm production. This change would be drastic in that it would make the payments to farmers into direct welfare benefits rather than transfers through other mechanisms.[8]

Like many social problems, the farm problem cannot be resolved with the tools of economics. These tools can, however, point out some basic options. There are too many resources in the agricultural industry relative to the demand for its output. The resources are encouraged to stay there by transfer payments made to farmers out of general tax revenues. Taxpayers' income is being redistributed to farmers, keeping resources in the farm industry that would otherwise be attracted to other industries. In 1990, the direct budget costs of federal agriculture programs were more than $1,000 for every nonfarm family in the United States. These payments represent a significant share of federal tax revenues and do not include the off-budget transfers to farmers.

The basic tools of economics do not reveal whether this situation is good or bad or predict whether anything will be done to change it. The answer to the first question is a value judgment concerning whether society thinks it is good or bad to maintain the present level of resources in agriculture. The answer to the second question will, in part, depend on the political strength of farmers and the farm constituency relative to other groups.

URBAN ECONOMICS

The study of urban economics also illustrates the problems of market failure and government failure. Government failure occurs when government responds to market failures in a less than optimal way. In this case, market failure consists of the negative externalities associated with population density. These externalities include crime, traffic congestion, environmental pollution, and noise pollution, to name a few. In addition, provision of public goods in many urban areas is complicated by the number of political divisions. In the 1970s, the growth of population in cities was slower than the population growth in rural areas and in suburbs. This trend was seen at the time as due in part to the energy crisis and high gasoline prices. The 1980s saw a reversal of this trend, with population growth

---

8. See E. C. Pasour, "Farm Programs Hurt Everyone—Even Farmers," *The Independent* (Vol. II, No. 1, 1989): 3.

in cities exceeding growth in areas outside of cities. Also during the 1980s, the Reagan administration sharply reduced the amount of federal government transfers that had been going to U.S. cities.

How Large Should a City Be?

Cities come in all sizes, both in population and in land area. There are very small cities that seem to offer their residents a satisfactory collection of public and private goods and services. Very large cities offer a greater variety of services and attractions to residents and visitors. The most desirable size for a city depends on the balance between the advantages and disadvantages of a large population.

Economies of Agglomeration. Urban areas spring up because of economies of scale. Urban economists use the more specific term **economies of agglomeration** to describe the cost savings that individuals enjoy when enough of them locate in one relatively small area. The reasons for these lower average costs are similar to the reasons for cost savings to a firm when economies of scale exist. The savings result because the size of the city yields enough local demand for highly specialized suppliers. In addition, large pools of specialized labor exist in urban areas, again because the demand is large enough to attract enough workers.

> **economies of agglomeration**
> The cost savings that individuals enjoy when enough of them locate close together in or near a large city.

The broadcasting industry is a good example of this principle at work. Broadcasting is concentrated in New York City and Los Angeles. This concentration represents demand for writers, actors, musicians, dancers, technicians, directors, and designers and for firms that specialize in the equipment these individuals use. Start-up costs for new firms are lower because suppliers are close at hand. New firms and new artists locate in these areas in order to take advantage of these cost savings.

Economies of agglomeration usually take the form of efficiencies in production and information gathering. However, agglomeration can also result in a wider variety of consumption alternatives. This wider range of consumption choices can attract residents and lead to further agglomeration. Economists in recent years have gathered data on urban areas to make separate forecasts of economic activity for them. The motivation behind this separation is that macro modeling and forecasting for the whole economy overlooks pockets of economic activity in some areas. In other words, a recession in the United States as a whole doesn't necessarily mean a recession in all parts of the country. A smart entrepreneur needs to know what is going on in the economy at a micro level.[9]

Although some costs are lower as agglomeration takes place, others increase because of **diseconomies of agglomeration**. There are both negative and positive externalities associated with urban growth. The two most obvious negative externalities are crime and pollution.

> **diseconomies of agglomeration**
> The additional costs that individuals must pay when too many of them locate in one city (thus creating negative external effects for one another).

Optimal City Size. Since there are economies and diseconomies associated with agglomeration, there should be some optimal city size. This optimum is the size at which the value of the benefits exceeds the total cost

---

9. John Case, "The Economic Microscope," *INC.* (November 1989): 27.

of the negative externalities by the greatest amount. In terms of microeconomic theory, the optimal size is that for which the marginal agglomeration benefits are equal to the marginal agglomeration (congestion) costs. The optimal size of a city changes as these costs and benefits change. For example, if a technological change made crime prevention cheaper, the model predicts an increase in optimal city size. If technology reduced the diseconomies of agglomeration, optimal city size would increase. In addition, to the extent that demand for the consumption activities supplied by cities is income-elastic, the incomes of residents and potential residents will affect the optimal size of that city. An increase in income will increase the optimal size of urban areas, *ceteris paribus*.

The decision about optimal size will be made by thousands of individuals. Migration out of and into cities will be driven by individual decisions about the value of the positive and negative externalities associated with city size. Differences in tastes and preferences will ensure a variety of sizes of cities. Most economists would argue that such a decentralized process is superior to some governmental decision about how large a city should be. Policy makers can, however, have some influence on city size through zoning, taxes, and transportation systems. They may move a city's size toward or away from the optimum by changing the costs and benefits individuals face in locating there. Both market forces and policy decisions determine the optimal size for each city, and the optimum is always in a state of flux.

SMALL TOWNS AND LARGE CITIES. Large cities in the United States continue to grow, but a large part of the U.S. population still lives in smaller towns and cities that lack both the attractions and the problems of New York, Detroit, or Houston. Many of these smaller towns have lost population. Even those that have grown now enjoy fewer retail services than several decades ago. The booming main streets of the first half of the twentieth century have given way to many empty storefronts since retail outlets have moved to malls that serve a cluster of small towns in a single central location. Economies of agglomeration in retailing have led to the centralization of shopping at the expense of small-town main streets.

NEW SUBURBS. The traditional role of the central city is changing. Historically, suburbs grew away from the central city, but most suburban residents commuted there for work, entertainment, and shopping. This pattern has changed as the information age is decentralizing cities, and it is no longer necessary to commute. All kinds of businesses have moved out of the city and into the suburbs, where, among other things, the rents are cheaper. Barbara Boggs Sigmund, the mayor of Princeton, New Jersey, refers to these new suburbs as "urbanoid villages." Sigmund is critical of urbanoid villages, arguing that they breed traffic, fail to deliver services, and hinder rather than promote community.[10]

---

10. Betsy Morris, "New Suburbs Tackle City Ills While Lacking a Sense of Community," *The Wall Street Journal* (26 March 1987): 1.

Urban Public Goods and the Spillover Problem

Public policy to solve urban problems is complicated by the number of political entities involved in these areas. For example, metropolitan Atlanta has fifty-three separate local governments. These governments do not always cooperate and are often in direct competition for projects and development funds. This competition adds a new dimension to the concept of government failure. It can lessen the potential for government failure by making governments more sensitive to voter demand, but it can also contribute to government failure by making it harder to overcome the free-rider problem.

The problem of supplying public goods is especially complicated when there are many local governments in an urban area. With many political subdivisions, the external benefits of the provision of a public good may spill over into different jurisdictions, making the provision of that public good much more difficult. For example, Figure 3 represents the demand for crime prevention by two groups of citizens in a political subdivision of an urban area. D_a represents the demands of group a, and D_b the demand of group b. Since crime prevention is a public good, it is subject to the free-rider problem discussed earlier. The true demand curve is found by vertically summing the two demand curves. The socially optimal provision of the public good is amount Q_1 at price P_1. Assume for a moment that it is possible to overcome the free-rider problem and that the citizens of the subdivision vote to tax themselves an amount equal to rectangle $0P_1AQ_1$ and supply the optimal amount of crime prevention.

The optimal amount of crime prevention will still not occur if some of its benefits spill into other jurisdictions. In Figure 3, D_c represents the demand of people who live outside the political subdivision for crime prevention inside the subdivision. They have a demand because they come to work and/or shop in the subdivision. In addition, they live close enough to fear that criminal activity might easily spread to where they live. Since they do not vote and pay taxes in the jurisdiction, their demand is not in-

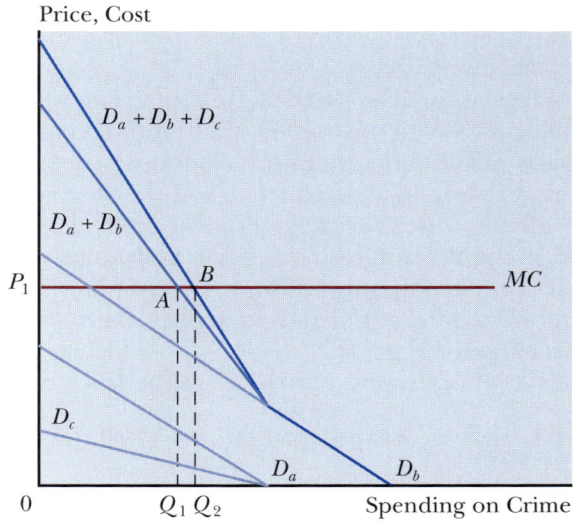

FIGURE 3
THE MARKET FOR CRIME PREVENTION
Crime prevention is a local public good. If D_a and D_b represent the demand of two groups within a jurisdiction, the optimal amount of crime prevention is Q_1. However, if some of the benefits spill into other jurisdictions and the demand of residents there is represented by D_c, the optimal amount of the public good is Q_2.

corporated into the political decision to supply amount Q_1. If it were, the demand curve (again a vertical summation) would be $D_a + D_b + D_c$ and the optimal amount of spending on crime prevention would be equal to rectangle $0P_1BQ_2$. The conclusion of this analysis is that internalizing externalities within a political subdivision becomes much more difficult when the externalities spill across political boundaries.

SOLVING THE SPILLOVER PROBLEM. Revenue sharing, or grants from higher to lower levels of government, is one way to overcome the spillover problem and increase the provision of goods with positive externalities. The state or federal government can help overcome such local urban problems through the use of grants. In the 1970s, this type of grant was very popular. In 1979, 38 percent of the revenue of U.S. cities came from higher levels of government, mostly the federal government. The Reagan administration reduced such grants, forcing urban governments to rely increasingly on their own sources of revenue.[11] By 1985, this type of grant accounted for only 29 percent of local revenues.

Fiscal conservatives are critical of grants from higher to lower levels of government for two reasons. First, they argue that the federal government should not transfer such funds when the federal budget has huge deficits. Second, they argue that these grants make local officials less fiscally accountable than they would be if they had to raise taxes in order to spend. Proponents argue that such grants can redistribute income from richer to poorer areas and compensate cities for some of the positive externalities that are enjoyed by nonresidents.

One possible way to solve the spillover problem without resorting to revenue sharing is through **user charges**, or fees that cover part or all of the cost of a public service. User charges can finance some public goods, at least partially. Local governments can charge different fees to residents and nonresidents. This type of payment schedule works very well for recreational and cultural programs. For example, Greenbelt, Maryland requires proof of residence in order to pay a lower resident fee for swimming lessons and tennis classes at community recreation areas. Most state universities have a tuition schedule that charges less to state residents than to out-of-state students.

THE TIEBOUT SOLUTION. In a famous article, Charles Tiebout argued that the provision of local public goods is best done by small homogeneous jurisdictions.[12] The smaller the jurisdiction, the more responsive the government will be to its citizens. Citizens in an urban area will choose to live in a certain jurisdiction by buying into its package of local public goods and tax prices. For example, in the Washington, D.C. area, individuals can choose to live in the District or five adjacent counties, two in Maryland and three in Virginia. Each offers different tax levels, transportation services, housing quality, and local public goods.

Tiebout argues that a market exists for local public goods in which con-

user charges
Fees that cover part or all of the cost of a public service.

---

11. See Richard P. Nathan and Fred C. Doolittle, "Federal Grants: Giving and Taking Away," *Political Science Quarterly* (Spring 1985): 53–74.
12. Charles M. Tiebout, "A Pure Theory of Public Expenditures," *Journal of Political Economy* (October 1956): 416–424.

sumers "vote with their feet" by moving to areas that provide satisfactory combinations of taxes and services. Further, he argues, the price of housing in an area will reflect the relative desirability of what is offered to the voter-consumers. The **Tiebout hypothesis** is that voters will influence local public goods through their choice of locations. This idea is closely related to the concept of privately supplied public goods discussed in the chapter on market failure. Competition among suppliers of local public services (local governments) forces them to offer more desirable combinations of spending and taxing, since individuals will migrate to those jurisdictions that have the most attractive mix.

Tiebout hypothesis
The idea that competition among local governments as suppliers of local public services will force them to offer the desired combination of spending and taxing to voters, who will migrate to those jurisdictions that produce that combination.

PRIVATIZING: THE CASE OF LOW-INCOME HOUSING

One strategy used by some cities to hold down their tax burdens is privatization, or shifting production of some services to the private sector. Low-income housing is an example. Federally funded programs to provide public housing in the 1960s and 1970s produced very unsatisfactory results in most cities. It was usually easy to identify "the project" by its many boarded-up windows and slumlike appearance. Indeed, in many cities the housing projects built in the late 1960s have been abandoned. Some have even been torn down.

The Local Initiative Support Corporation (LISC), with financing from the Ford Foundation, has tried a different approach—privatizing the process of supplying low-cost housing. The result is low-income housing that has a blend of public and private financing. LISC works with local community groups to determine what is needed in housing. These local groups use public money, foundation grants, and loans from private mortgage lenders to rebuild an area. The group then takes ownership of and manages the housing units. The results have been impressive. Pride of ownership (transferable property rights) has meant better maintenance, and these rebuilt areas have become models that other cities can emulate. The key element has been incentives at the tenant level, resulting in tenant associations that maintain and police the areas.[13]

IS MASS TRANSPORTATION A PUBLIC GOOD?

Many cities are expanding or building new mass transportation systems. These systems can cover an entire metropolitan area, in some cases crossing city or even county lines. For example, the Metropolitan Atlanta Rapid Transit Authority (MARTA) runs bus and train service from distant suburbs into downtown Atlanta. Perhaps the "snazziest" urban mass transportation system is the Metro in Washington, D.C. The system features clean facilities (in contrast to the subway in New York City) with a space-age look. In 1990, the Washington Metro was a 47-mile system. It will cost more than $6 billion when it is complete. Some critics have joked that it would have been cheaper to buy every citizen of the District of Columbia a new Mercedes automobile.[14]

---

13. See James Cook, "Priming the Urban Pump," *Forbes* (23 March 1987): 63–64. On the other hand, privatization has taken some of these properties out of the supply of low-income housing, creating what some view as a "time bomb." See Michel McQueen, "Inadequate Supply of Housing for Poor Could Become Worse, Panel Warns," *Wall Street Journal* (28 April 1988): 10.
14. See David M. Stewart, "Rolling Nowhere," *Inquiry* (July 1984): 18–23.

Are such systems worth the cost? Proponents argue that mass transportation is a public good. Positive externalities are produced by urban bus and subway systems. Low-cost transportation increases population density, which increases the urban tax base. Economic development increases because the dense population attracts businesses. The transportation network also allows the labor force easier access to work sites. Finally, mass transportation reduces air pollution, congestion on the roads, and parking problems. During the energy crisis, an important argument for building mass transportation networks was that they use less of scarce energy resources. Proponents claim that all these positive externalities are of sufficient value to make the benefits of mass transportation exceed the costs of construction.

Critics disagree. They argue that subsidized public transportation transfers income from taxpayers to users of the system. The systems represent a huge subsidy to riders. Critics say that proponents have exaggerated the benefits of such systems and that the costs actually exceed the benefits. For example, the benefits of low-cost transportation in allowing the density of the population to increase are often offset by higher land prices as the demand for urban housing increases. As a result, those who benefit most from public transportation are landowners in the urban area. There is also little evidence that road congestion and air pollution are much improved by such systems. In fact, after the Metro opened, some studies showed that rush-hour traffic into the District of Columbia actually increased.

Transportation, parking, and road congestion are problems facing all urban policy makers. The debate over mass transportation hinges on determining a value for its positive externalities. These benefits must then be weighed against the costs of the project. Conflicting views arise even among economists because it is very difficult to put an accurate monetary value on a positive externality.

The majority of Americans now live in an urban environment. Many are concerned about the spillovers that occur among individuals living close together: noise, pollution, crime, congestion, and other urban problems. As urban populations have grown in the United States and throughout the world, total world population and economic activity have also grown. This growth has created more pressures on scarce resources and more external effects that spread over greater distances of time and space. Concern about these issues has led economists and others to expand their focus beyond rural and urban environments to the global environment.

THE FUTURE OF THE ENVIRONMENT

Many forms of pollution are problems that have market-based solutions based on assignment of property rights. When the negative externalities and the number of people affected are small, it is easier to apply the Coase theorem and resolve those problems through assignment of property rights and negotiation. However, for larger problems, such as acid rain, depletion of the ozone layer, and global climate change, it becomes more difficult to find simple market-based solutions. These problems often extend across national boundaries and over several generations.

In Chapter 2, we presented a spectrum of categories of goods and services that ranged from public goods to positive external effects to private goods to negative externalities to public bads. Most environmental problems lie at or near the public bad end of that spectrum.

THE TRAGEDY OF THE COMMONS

One of the most famous articles of the twentieth century in the field of environmental economics was published in 1948 in *Science* magazine. The author was Garrett Hardin, and the title was "The Tragedy of the Commons."[15] In this article, Hardin addressed the overuse of a **common access resource**, the common grazing land that was found in English villages before enclosure laws assigned such land to specific owners. He pointed out that private owners use their resources at an optimal rate so as to maximize their benefits over time. The same is not true of resources held in common. For such resources, each user has an incentive to overuse the common property to the point where the marginal benefits are zero, because the marginal cost is zero. This overuse is the **tragedy of the commons**.

If a farmer does not put an extra cow to graze on the commons, that farmer does not benefit by having more forage for his other cows or less exhaustion of the common grazing land. The space that farmer doesn't use will be occupied by some other farmer's cow. Since everyone faces the same incentives, the commons will be overgrazed and eventually become useless for all the owners. The benefits from overuse go to the individual, but the costs are spread among the entire group.

The only solution to this problem of overuse of common property resources is to either assign property rights to individuals or have the government or other authority regulate the use in the common interest. If one farmer owns the commons, that farmer will use it at the optimal rate, because all of the costs and benefits will be internalized. If the farmer puts an extra cow to graze, it is that farmer's private property that is being depleted. The future costs will all fall on the farmer and the farmer's heirs rather than on the entire community. Assigning property will thus result in an efficient solution.

As you learned in an earlier chapter, opportunities to assign property rights are more widespread than might be expected. Air pollution rights have been assigned, bought, sold, and traded in the United States. The charging of fines or fees for polluting is quite similar to the purchase and sale of property rights to use the air or water for disposal of wastes. In this case, the property rights have been assigned to the government, which charges for the use of the property. Some common access resources do not lend themselves to assignment of property rights, however. Sometimes it is difficult to identify the individuals who create the problem, the individuals who are hurt by the activities of others, or the possible long-term effects of certain uses of common resources. In other cases, the commons extends across national boundaries, making it difficult for governments to intervene because several governments with different constituencies and agendas are involved.

common access resource A resource that is not owned by any individual but is available for all to use.

tragedy of the commons The overuse of common access resources.

---

15. Garrett Hardin, "The Tragedy of the Commons," *Science* (August 1948): 16–48.

The air, the water, the earth's crust, the ozone layer—all of these are common access resources for everyone on earth. The concern about these global commons is expressed in a variety of ways. Is there a greenhouse effect resulting from too much carbon dioxide emission? If so, the result might be global warming with catastrophic results, such as flooding of coastal cities and creation of deserts where there had been forests and fields. Are human actions destroying the ozone layer that provides protection from the most harmful effects of the sun's rays? Are nonrenewable resources being exploited at a rate that will inflict suffering on future generations? Are renewable resources—trees, fish, whales—being used up at rates faster than they can be replaced? Are humans going to suffocate in their wastes as they pollute the air and water and pile up trash faster than places can be found to put it? These are the major questions posed by those concerned with the use and misuse of the global commons.

THE INFORMATION PROBLEM

Managing the global commons is complicated by two important problems. One is the problem of getting adequate information. In the case of global warming, scientists can determine changes in the gases in the atmosphere, but it is harder to predict precisely how much warming will result and what its impact will be on specific regions. For nonrenewable resources, it is difficult to anticipate improvements in extraction technology and development of substitutes. The same is true to some extent for renewable resources. In the case of hazardous wastes, long delays are common between the disposal of wastes and the recognition of their hazardous effects. At Love Canal in New York, residents ultimately had to abandon their homes because of hazardous wastes beneath their sites. Love Canal is one of the most famous cases of delayed impact in U.S. history.[16]

In statistics, there are two types of error that can be made: accepting a hypothesis as true when it is false and rejecting a hypothesis as false when it is in fact true. Statisticians and scientists tend to pay more attention to avoiding the first type of error, because in their work that type is generally more damaging or costly. In the case of the global environment, however, both types of error are significant. If the dangers of global warming are real and imminent, and this true hypothesis is rejected because it cannot be verified, then the costs will be large and irreparable. Suppose, however, that the hypothesis is accepted, and governments act to restrain economic activity, save the rain forest, and reduce carbon dioxide emissions. Then the forecasts turn out to be wrong, or the forecasts are right but scientists develop a technological solution, or the forecasts are right but the damage is very minimal. In this case, we will have unnecessarily given up output, economic growth, and present consumption.

Many economists point to past experiences to show that the first kind of error, acting on a prediction that turns out to be false or at least overstated, is very common. Nineteenth-century economist Thomas Robert

---

16. Often the discovery of hazardous waste disposal in the land or water resembles a mystery story. For an account of one such story, involving pesticides in the water supply, see "A Tale of Two Towns," *Yankee* (May 1990): 66.

Externalities often spill over national borders. For example, acid rain produced by electric power plants in the United States has destroyed trees in Canada, resulting in political tension between the two countries. However, no environmental event of recent years has produced as many international problems as the Soviet nuclear accident at Chernobyl in 1986.

The accident itself was staggering: 31 people were confirmed as dead, 200 were seriously injured, and 135,000 Ukrainians were evacuated from their homes, perhaps never to return. As serious as these costs are, they were far from the only costs of the accident. Some 1,300 miles from Chernobyl, the Lapps of Norway, Sweden, and Finland were faced with a complete change in their economy and culture.

The reindeer is the core of the Lapp economy and culture. It provides meat, knife handles, glue, and skin for tents, coats, and shoes. Lichens are the reindeer's primary food source. These lichens soaked up so much radiation after Chernobyl that they may not be safe for more than three decades.

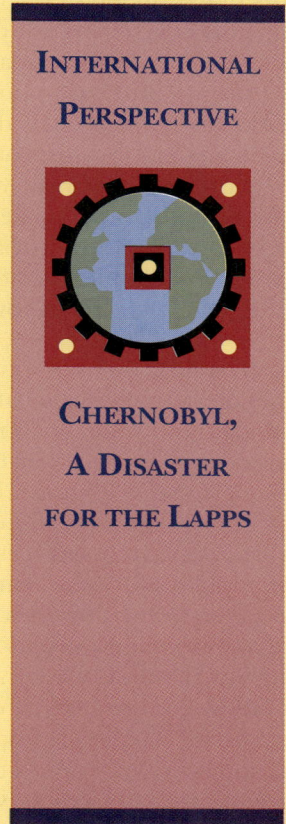

INTERNATIONAL PERSPECTIVE

CHERNOBYL, A DISASTER FOR THE LAPPS

Sweden and Norway averted immediate catastrophe for the Lapps by purchasing all the reindeer meat produced in 1986. Government officials then destroyed the meat or sold it to mink ranchers. This program cost Sweden more than $20 million in 1986. Swedish government officials believe that the Soviets are responsible for the radiation damage, and they are angered at Soviet refusal to compensate the Lapps for their economic loss.

This incident illustrates a growing political problem. Environmental externalities will become increasingly important in the years ahead. Environmental problems within national boundaries can be solved through the political process. Such solutions are difficult enough. Think of the political fighting over site selection for low-level nuclear dumps! What is difficult within a nation, however, becomes nearly impossible when two or more nations are involved. Therefore, increasing levels of international tension over externalities that spill over national boundaries are inevitable.

Source: *U.S. News and World Report* (23 March 1987): 36; (20 July 1987): 14.

Malthus forecasted an imminent crisis of starvation because population was growing faster than the food supply. Advances in agricultural technology proved him wrong. In the middle of the nineteenth century, there were great fears of extinction of the whales, who were valued for whale oil for lighting purposes. Kerosene lamps and then electricity replaced whale oil, and the whales did not disappear. In the 1930s, the fertile farmlands of the Midwest turned into a dust bowl, and some observers thought that farm practices were creating a new desert. Today this land is again highly productive. Even the energy crisis of the 1970s disappeared as higher oil prices led to discovery of new reserves and more conservation. However, the fact that disasters have been averted in the past through technological change or discoveries does not necessarily mean that such solutions will arise in the future. People's positions on environmental issues depend on their faith in technological innovation.

THE SOVEREIGNTY PROBLEM

The second problem that complicates managing the global commons is the fact that the air and water span many nations. Thus, sovereignty over the global commons is divided. The tragedy of the commons does not necessarily represent a market failure. It may be a failure to use the market by assigning property rights or a failure by government to adequately regulate the use of common access resources. The assignment of property rights and the regulation of the commons are responsibilities of governments. However, some of the most important conflicts over the use of common access resources cross national boundaries. England exports sulfur dioxide to Scandinavia, where acid rain damages the forests. Japan continues to kill large numbers of whales, while other nations try to restrain the harvest of whales in hopes of saving them from extinction. Brazil is chopping down its tropical rain forests, which absorb a great deal of carbon dioxide and help to slow the greenhouse effect around the world. The Brazilian government argues that if it were not for the emissions from industrial nations that consume most of the fossil fuels, the rain forest would not be an issue. The United States consumes fossil fuels at a higher rate than any other nation and has been criticized for failing to restrain such consumption with high taxes, as most other industrialized nations do. Even the huge oceans that girdle the globe have shown some serious damage from the disposal of wastes by many nations. Some cooperation between governments in either assigning property rights or regulating use of common access resources is essential in order to find solutions for these problems.

THE RAIN FOREST, CARBON DIOXIDE, AND GLOBAL WARMING

It is difficult to determine whether global warming is occurring. The data on weather and climate that have been assembled over decades, as well as centuries of experience, indicate that weather is highly variable. Some climatologists have argued that the earth is headed for ecological disaster because of clear cutting of the forests—especially tropical rain forests—that absorb carbon dioxide. Figure 4 shows the recent increase in the concentration of carbon dioxide in the atmosphere, mainly due to the heavy use of fossil fuels in the twentieth century. The increased carbon dioxide

Chapter 19 Case Studies in Market Failure and Government Failure   497

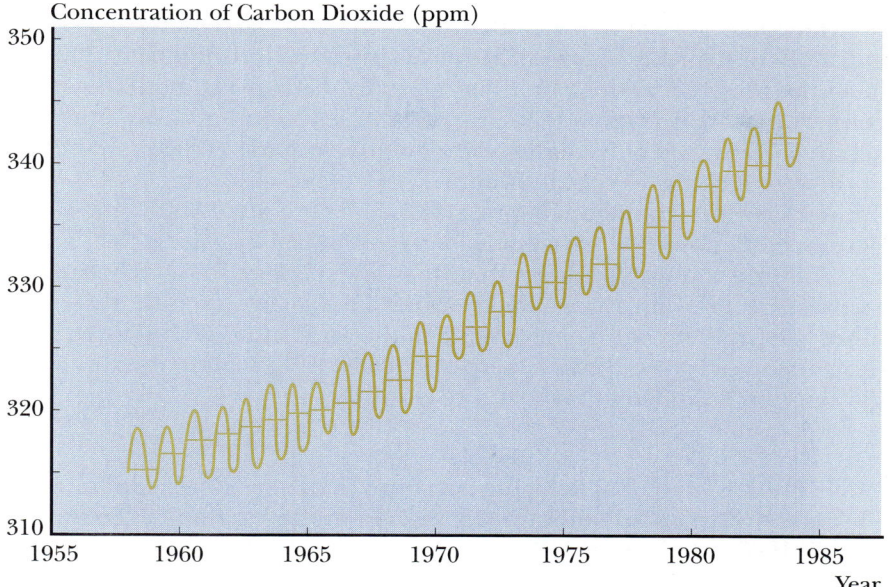

**FIGURE 4
CARBON DIOXIDE IN THE ATMOSPHERE, 1958–1984**
This diagram, based on samples taken at Hawaii's isolated Mauna Loa observatory, shows that there has been a steady increase of about 0.5 percent per year in the concentration of carbon dioxide in the earth's atmosphere.

traps the earth's radiated heat in the atmosphere rather than allowing it to escape. Higher levels of carbon dioxide should result in global warming. However, the amount of increase in global temperature and the resulting effects on weather and climate patterns are uncertain. Effects will be stronger in temperate zones than in tropical zones. The danger of melting of the polar ice caps and flooding of coastal cities is an extreme possibility. The impact of global warming on world food production could also be serious. Changing weather patterns would dry up some areas and provide other, previously dry areas with more water than they could effectively use.

In the United States, there has been no great reduction in forest lands that absorb carbon dioxide, but there has been increased production of carbon dioxide from burning fossil fuels (especially gasoline). Throughout the world, however, population pressures have led to loss of forests. Tropical rain forests are especially effective in absorbing carbon dioxide from the atmosphere, so concerns have focused on those forests rather than on other facets of the problem.

Market mechanisms play a part in both the problem and potential solutions. The demand for tropical hardwoods as building materials in developed countries and the need for more agricultural and grazing land have been powerful incentives for cutting down rain forests. One possible market force in the opposite direction results from the discovery of valuable natural substances in the rain forests that can be used for producing medicines, food additives, and cosmetics.[17] Yet another market force has been the purchase of tracts of rain forest by citizen groups in developed countries. The new owners preserve the trees rather than cut them down. The overall impact of such efforts has been very modest, however.

---

17. "Saving Brazil's Forests," *Newsweek* (1 May 1989): 50.

Individual governments can certainly act to reduce carbon dioxide emissions or to preserve forests. However, just as no individual has enough incentive to preserve the commons, no individual government has an incentive to act to prevent global warming unless other governments also act. In the absence of a single sovereign government to regulate the use of the rain forest as a global commons, the role of governments has been limited to efforts to negotiate preservation. The United States and other developed nations that have made loans to tropical nations such as Brazil have offered to forgive part of that debt in exchange for a commitment to preserve the rain forest. Such efforts have met with little response. Since the problem of carbon dioxide in the atmosphere is linked to both destruction of forests and use of fossil fuels, it is difficult to identify a single cause or a single nation that is responsible.

ACID RAIN

Closely related to global warming is the problem of acid rain. Sulfur dioxide and nitrous oxide combine with water in the atmosphere to create sulphuric acid and nitric acid. When it rains, the rain has a strong acid component that is damaging to plant and animal life. Scientists have documented the negative impact of acid rain on fish and plant life in lakes. The effect of acid rain on forests is not as clearly established.

The problem of acid rain is part of a broader problem of air quality that has been addressed by governments in many nations. Within nations, there is an incentive to clean up air in order to improve the immediate environment and reduce health risks. The battle lines within a country are drawn between those who wish to use the air for the disposal of wastes and those who wish to preserve its quality. What makes acid rain different from other kinds of air pollution is that spillovers between nations are more evident with acid rain than with other types of air pollution.

Certain countries are net exporters of sulfur emissions. The United Kingdom, for example, imports one-fifth of its sulfur and exports two-thirds of its sulfur-based emissions to Western Europe. Net importers of pollutants include West Germany, Austria, and the Scandinavian countries.[18] Within the United States, emissions in the Midwest have their greatest impact in the Northeastern states. Efforts to control acid rain within the country have pitted the producers and users (mainly electric utilities) of high-sulfur coal against environmentalists and residents and firms in the affected areas. Within the United States, the battle over amendments to the Clean Air Act is waged in Congress almost annually. These amendments represent the current trade-offs between the interests of these two conflicting groups.[19] In Europe, the European Community has provided a broader base for discussion and resolution of acid rain spillovers between countries.

---

18. Sandra Postel, *Air Pollution, Acid Rain, and the Future of Forests*, Worldwatch Paper No. 58 (Washington, DC: World Watch Institute, March 1984). This publication provides a good review of the scientific evidence on acid rain.
19. For a discussion of the political battles over acid rain in the United States, see Richard Meyer and T. Bruce Yandle, "The Political Economy of Acid Rain," *Cato Journal* (Fall 1987): 527–545.

Chapter 19 Case Studies in Market Failure and Government Failure

MOUNT TRASHMORE IN YOUR BACKYARD: WASTE DISPOSAL

The disposal of household and industrial wastes has become a major problem for local governments in the United States. Wastes can be grouped into three classes: hazardous, recyclable, and other. Each type presents different disposal problems and potential solutions.

RECYCLABLE AND OTHER NONHAZARDOUS WASTES. Americans—and others—discard an enormous amount of waste each year. Some of this waste has no recoverable value and must be burned or buried in a commons, the local landfill or city dump. New Jersey has an above-ground landfill with the picturesque name of Mount Trashmore! Some household waste is disposed of through the sewer system, especially for households with garbage disposals. A large part of household waste can in fact be reused. Recycling recovers valuable nonrenewable resources (aluminum cans and petroleum-based plastics, for example), reduces the pressure on renewable resources (newspapers and glass), and lowers the amount of space and effort that must be devoted to disposal.

Until recently, most households had little incentive to recycle. It took time and effort to separate the trash and take recyclable items to an appropriate place. There was no penalty for failure to recycle and no rewards for cooperation. In recent years, this situation has changed. Trash disposal is largely the responsibility of local governments, and these and state governments have been innovative and effective in changing the costs and benefits people face in recycling. Local governments took this initiative because of the incentives they faced. Rising land prices, increasing federal regulations on site preparation, and hauling of trash over greater distances created an immediate and powerful incentive to act.

Figure 5 shows the shift in costs and benefits facing the individual household. MB_1 is the marginal benefit curve for recycling in the first year. Perhaps there were a few deposit bottles that could be returned, a small payment for aluminum cans, and some sense of contributing to community well-being. However, the marginal cost of recycling was high, because of the distance the recycler had to travel. Under these circumstances, the representative household only engaged in amount Q_0 of recycling. Then the local government established a recycling center. This act reduces the cost of recycling and shifts the marginal cost curve downward. The local government also started a campaign of education and persuasion that changes preferences, increasing the perceived benefits (MB_1 shifts to MB_2). These actions were typical for local governments in the 1970s and early 1980s. They had an effect on some households, but did not greatly reduce the amount of waste disposal (in the diagram, wastes fell only from Q_1 to Q_2). Effective waste reduction and recycling required more powerful incentives for both governments and citizens.

Further increases in land costs, higher payments for recycled materials, and other pressures caused some local governments to step up their efforts. These efforts shifted both the marginal benefit curve and the marginal cost curve to the right. One city in Oregon used a combination of carrot and stick to promote recycling. Households were given two kinds of containers for waste pickup. The first, general and unsorted waste, carried a fee that increased sharply with added pickups each month. The sec-

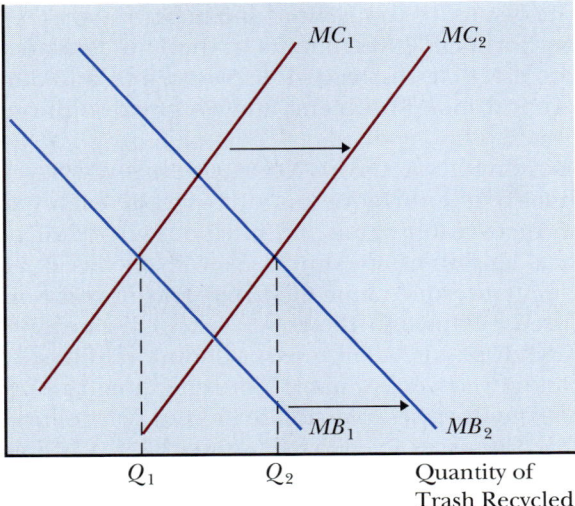

FIGURE 5
MARGINAL COSTS AND BENEFITS OF RECYCLING
With the original marginal cost curve, MC_1, and the original marginal benefit curve, MB_1, the costs of recycling were too high and the perceived benefits too low to result in a very large volume of recycling. The combination of lower costs (a recycling center) and higher perceived benefits (result of an education campaign) shifts the curves. The result is some increase in recycling, from Q_1 to Q_2. Further increases in recycling (to Q_3) can be brought about by making it more convenient to recycle (separation containers, curbside pickup) and more expensive not to (higher pickup fees for unsorted trash).

ond kind of container was separated into color-coded sections for plastics, glass, aluminum, and paper. Pickups from the color-coded containers were free. This plan combined a substantial cash benefit for not using the unsorted pickup with much lower costs of recycling because of the sorting bins and curbside pickup. Other cities have used similar combinations of positive and negative incentives. Recycling is an excellent illustration of how local governments can use market incentives to reduce overuse of a local commons, the city dump.

HAZARDOUS WASTES. Hazardous wastes represent a more serious problem. There is no good way of disposing of such wastes without endangering the air, water, or soil in the area. No one wants to live near the refuse of a nuclear power plant or a chemical plant. In fact, this reluctance to accommodate hazardous waste disposal sites produced a new acronym, NIMBY, which stands for "not in my back yard." Some states have resisted disposal of hazardous wastes, sometimes not even allowing such wastes to pass through en route to another destination. Many states have raised their fees for disposal of such wastes as both a deterrent and a revenue source. As firms find it increasingly difficult and costly to dispose of hazardous wastes, they are forced to seek other solutions. Reuse of waste materials or changes in technology that reduce the amount of hazardous wastes produced are alternatives.

Most of the horror stories about hazardous wastes result from past dumping, when there was less knowledge of the dangers and less government regulation. Hazardous waste problems, chiefly due to industrial wastes, are present in every state and will be costly to clean up. The Environmental Protection Agency's Superfund is earmarked for correcting such past mistakes.[20] Unlike global warming and acid rain, hazardous wastes represent a problem that can be addressed through a combination of market incentives and government regulation.

CHALLENGES FOR THE FUTURE

The environmental issues covered here are not the only ones. For example, the ocean is the ultimate common access resource, and little progress has been made in conserving its bounty or controlling its use as a waste dump. The optimal rate for exploiting renewable and nonrenewable resources will be found only through a combination of market incentives, technological innovation, government regulation, and intergovernmental cooperation. Problems of conserving common access resources, whether local or global, represent a serious and substantial challenge to policy makers. Imperfect information, lack of coordination between nations, and a natural tendency to overuse and exhaust common access resources complicate the problem. It will require innovative strategies, use of market mechanisms, and intergovernmental cooperation to protect the environment for generations to come.

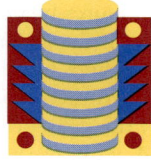

SUMMARY

1. The long-run problem for American farmers is the result of huge increases in productivity in the last century. In the short-run, farmers' problems result from the fact that the farm sector is very competitive, has very inelastic demand, and is affected heavily by the weather.
2. Most federal governmental farm policies are aimed at slowing the trend toward fewer agricultural workers.
3. The various price support programs work primarily on the supply side of the agricultural market. The major programs have attempted to support prices or to manage production, often with conflicting results.
4. Cities are formed and grow because of economies of agglomeration. The optimal city size is where the total benefits of agglomeration exceed the diseconomies of agglomeration by the greatest amount.
5. Supplying local public goods in urban areas is complicated by the division of the area into many political subdivisions. The Tiebout hypothesis is that voters will solve the spillover problem by choosing to live in the jurisdiction that provides the desired combination of services and taxes.
6. The tragedy of the commons is the overuse of common access resources. Each user of such a resource has the incentive to use that resource to the point where marginal benefits are zero. Common access resources must be regulated or assigned to individuals in order to attain efficient use of these resources.
7. Managing the global commons is even more complicated because of jurisdictional and informational problems. Acid rain is a good example of the problems of the global commons.
8. A blend of market incentives and regulation can be effective in addressing many environmental problems.

---

20. The Superfund is financed out of a fee on chemical feedstocks and is used to finance chemical waste cleanups. For a critical review of the performance of Superfund, see T. Bruce Yandle, "Taxation, Political Action, and Superfund," *Cato Journal* (Winter 1989): 751–764.

New Terms

- agricultural support program
- parity
- support prices
- soil bank program
- acreage allotment
- Conservation Reserve Program (CRP)
- marketing orders
- target prices
- payment in kind (PIK) program
- Food Security Act
- Soil Conservation Service
- economies of agglomeration
- diseconomies of agglomeration
- user charges
- Tiebout hypothesis
- common access resource
- tragedy of the commons

Questions for Discussion

1. What are the short-term and long-term problems facing farmers? Why might these problems be considered market failures?

2. Suppose you are a producer in the shoe industry, and you have found that you have to sell 10 percent more shoes this year to buy the same amount of groceries and other items as in the past. How would you go about making a parity argument for supporting the price of shoes? Why would tariffs or other protective measures be needed along with price supports?

3. If the government creates support prices for shoes, will there be a surplus of shoes? If there is, what can the government do about that surplus that is similar to some of the farm programs?

4. Suppose you were sent to a city you had never visited before to determine whether that city needed more residents or already had too many. What criteria would you use to answer that question?

5. Another global environmental problem is the depletion of the ozone layer of the atmosphere, which screens out cancer-causing ultraviolet radiation. The ozone layer is being depleted by the use of chlorofluorocarbons (CFCs) in air conditioners, refrigerators, and spray cans. How is this an example of the tragedy of the commons? How can markets and governments contribute to a solution?

6. How is a common access resource different from a private resource?

7. Suppose you belong to a sailing club, which owns a dock and a boat. Will these be kept in better or worse shape than an individually owned boat and dock? Why or why not?

8. What is the distributional difference between support payments to farmers and marketing orders?

9. Why do programs such as the soil bank and acreage allotment programs have a smaller than expected influence on the supply of agricultural products?

10. In what way is the Tiebout solution for the provision of local public goods similar to the Coase theorem (discussed in the preceding chapter) for dealing with negative externalities?

11. Is a city park a common access resource? How can crowding be controlled?

12. Cattle and buffaloes are very similar animals, yet buffaloes were shot almost to extinction, while cattle were left alone in the same habitat. Why?

13. Today farmers represent about 2 percent of the U.S. population, but they get more than $40 billion in governmental outlays. This is much more than farmers received in 1950, when they were a much larger segment of the population. Does it make sense for farmers to be getting more powerful politically as their share of the voting population decreases?

14. Nobel prize–winning economist T. W. Schultz has referred to parity as "a vulgar economic concept." What did he mean?

15. Should mass transportation be viewed as a public good?

Suggestions for Further Reading

Galston, William A. *A Tough Row to Hoe: The 1985 Farm Bill and Beyond.* New York: Hamilton Press, 1985. This book covers the issues underlying the debate over the 1985 farm bill.

Harden, Garrett, and John Baden (eds.). *Managing the Commons.* San Francisco: W. H. Freeman, 1977. This collection of readings contains classic articles and a variety of perspectives on the issue of managing common access resources.

Heilbrun, James. *Urban Economics and Public Policy*, 3rd ed. New York: St. Martin's, 1987. A textbook that covers urban economic issues in detail.

Chapter 19 Case Studies in Market Failure and Government Failure   503

O'Rourke, P. J. "Manuregate." *Rolling Stone* (12 July 1990): 45–48. A satirical view of the farm problem.

Postel, Sandra. *Air Pollution, Acid Rain, and the Future of Forests*, Worldwatch Paper No. 58. Washington, DC: World Watch Institute, March 1984. This paper and others in the series address a variety of environmental policy issues. A later one is Hilary French, *Clearing the Air: A Global Agenda*, Worldwatch Paper No. 94 (January 1990).

Regulation (Winter 1990). An entire issue is devoted to environmental issues.

Samuelson, Robert J. "The Absurd Farm Bill." *Newsweek* (6 August 1990): 51. An editorial that suggests that the farm lobby is successful because the public considers farmers deserving of the billions of dollars spent to subsidize them.

Smith, Lee. "How to Cut Farm Spending." *Fortune* (10 November 1986): 97–103. An essay that argues that the government should stop paying farm subsidies and adopt a straightforward welfare program for farmers.

Stavins, Robert N., and Adam B. Jaffe. "Unintended Impacts of Public Investments on Private Decisions: The Depletion of Forested Wetlands." *American Economic Review* (June 1990): 337–352. An article that shows how public infrastructure investment in flood control results in private decisions that reduce forested wetlands.

Tietenburg, Tom. *Environmental and Natural Resource Economics*, 2nd ed. Glenview, IL: Scott, Foresman, 1987. A standard textbook that addresses environmental issues.

THE WORLD ECONOMY 6

| AFTER STUDYING THIS CHAPTER, YOU SHOULD BE ABLE TO: |

1. Describe the benefits of free trade.
2. Distinguish between absolute and comparative advantage, and discuss the gains from trade based on comparative advantage.
3. Identify the effects of a tariff and a quota.
4. Discuss the arguments for trade protection.
5. Explain why firms build foreign plants and what the economic effects are.

INTRODUCTION

CHAPTER 20
INTERNATIONAL TRADE

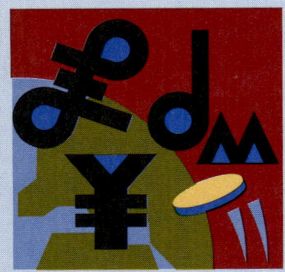

Except for the international perspectives, this book has generally ignored the rest of the world in order to concentrate on how the U.S. economic system operates. Yet the world is increasingly an important part of the American economy. You may drive a Japanese car, drink coffee from Brazil, eat Mexican tomatoes and Honduran bananas, or take pictures with a German camera. Chances are there is a plant of a foreign-owned multinational corporation close to where you live.

Even for a country as large as the United States, where trade with other countries is a relatively small fraction (about 10 to 12 percent) of GNP, international trade has become increasingly important. The percentage of output and sales entering into international trade has doubled in the last 15 years. Foreign competition is important to major industries such as textiles, steel, and autos. Immigration (both legal and illegal), foreign investment in the United States and American investment abroad, and the ups and downs in the value of the dollar are all issues in the news.

International economics is usually separated into two parts: international trade and international finance. International trade deals with the microeconomic questions of who produces what and who trades with whom and why, as well as with multinational firms, tariffs, and quotas. International finance examines the determinants of exchange rates between national currencies, the balance of payments, and the relationship between domestic macroeconomic concerns and the foreign sector.

This chapter covers international trade and the next chapter looks at international finance. You need to recognize, however, that trade and finance are closely related. For example, changes in the price of the dollar affect U.S. imports and foreign demand for U.S. exports. An inflow of investment from abroad can affect output, employment, and interest rates in the United States.

WHY NATIONS TRADE

The reasons for international trade are really no different from the reasons for trade between individuals who live in the same country. It is important to realize that in most cases international trade takes place between individuals and firms. When we speak of trade between the United States and Japan, we are really talking about trade between individuals and firms in these countries. These individuals and firms trade for the same reasons that individuals and firms within a country trade. Trade takes place because of the availability of a better product or a better price or because of an opportunity for profit. Exactly what determines the patterns of trade between nations and how much each nation benefits have been important concerns to economists as long as there have been nation states and economists.

Before Adam Smith, the dominant view was that government should direct many spheres of economic activity, especially international trade. This view, called mercantilism, put heavy emphasis on control of shipping, maintaining colonies, discouraging imports, and promoting exports. Two famous economists are responsible for developing the arguments for a policy of free trade. One was Adam Smith, whose *Wealth of Nations* in 1776 made a strong case for freedom in every sphere of economic activity. The other was David Ricardo, a distinguished nineteenth-century British economist and member of Parliament who was very interested in the practical question of what trade policy England should pursue. He developed the principle of comparative advantage in his classic 1814 book, *Principles of Political Economy and Taxation*.

The Benefits of Exchange

It is easier to envision the processes at work in international trade by focusing first on exchange rather than production. Consider Heather and Peter, who are both stamp collectors. Like most stamp collectors, they expand their collections by trading duplicates of stamps they have. Let's say that Heather has the complete 1938 Presidential series and several extras. Peter has some gaps in that series, but has some extra Canadian stamps that he would like to trade and that Heather would like to have. They work a deal. She trades three Presidential stamps for five Canadian stamps. As an outside observer, you might say that the trade was one of "equal values." That may be true in a market sense, but the stamps weren't of equal value to Peter and Heather. Heather wanted the Canadian stamps more than she wanted the extra Presidential stamps, and Peter felt just the opposite. They both were better off as a result of the trade.

Economists who look at international trade emphasize the **gains from trade**, or the increase in economic well-being that comes from specialization and exchange. The emphasis on exchange is one aspect of the theory of international trade that makes it different from the rest of microeconomics. However, we have to back up one step from exchange to production. Rarely do people trade solely out of existing stocks of goods. People produce in order to trade. The explanation of how people and nations decide what to produce for trade is based on the concepts of absolute advantage and comparative advantage.

gains from trade
The increase in economic well-being resulting from specialization and exchange.

Absolute Advantage

Suppose Heather and Peter are sister and brother, and their parents want the 12 windows in the house washed and the 24 square yards of leaves raked. Heather and Peter estimate their output as shown in Table 1. If this brother and sister divided the tasks equally, they would each have to wash half the windows (6 for Heather, which would take her $1\frac{1}{2}$ hours, and 6

TABLE 1
AN EXAMPLE OF
ABSOLUTE ADVANTAGE

	WINDOWS PER HOUR	SQUARE YARDS OF LEAVES PER HOUR
Heather	4	6
Peter	2	8

for Peter, which would take him 3 hours) and rake 12 square yards of leaves (which would take Heather 2 hours and Peter 1½ hours to complete). At the end of a long afternoon, Heather would have worked 3½ hours, and Peter would have worked 4½ hours. On the other hand, if they each specialized in what they do better, Heather could have all of the windows washed in just 3 hours and Peter could have all of the leaves raked in 3 hours. There would be a clear gain of a valuable ½ hour for Heather and 1½ hours for Peter.

Both Heather and Peter are better off if they specialize, because each has an **absolute advantage**. Heather is more efficient than Peter at washing windows, and Peter is more efficient than Heather at raking leaves. It's not difficult to convince anyone of the benefits of specialization and trade when there is a clear absolute advantage for each partner.

absolute advantage
The ability to produce something using fewer resources than other producers use.

COMPARATIVE ADVANTAGE

Suppose, however, that one partner is better at both. Assume that Heather is better at *both* window washing and leaf raking. The production rates for Heather and Peter in this case are shown in Table 2. Is there still an opportunity for specialization and trade? If they continue to divide the tasks equally, Heather will spend 1½ hours on her 6 windows and 2 hours on 12 square yards of raking. She's through in just 3½ hours. Poor Peter, however, has to spend 6 hours on windows and 3 hours on leaves, for a total of 9 hours of work. Can Heather do something to make Peter better off without spending any more of her own time working?

Suppose they specialize. This time it's not as obvious who should specialize in what. The concept of opportunity cost provides an answer. When Heather rakes 6 square yards of leaves, she's giving up 4 clean windows she could have "produced" in that time. A clean window costs her 1½ square yards of raking. For Peter, a clean window costs 4 square yards of raking. Clearly, Heather's window washing is cheaper than Peter's in terms of alternatives. Heather has a **comparative advantage** in window washing because her opportunity cost is lower in that activity than in the other one. Peter also has a comparative advantage in raking, even though he has an absolute disadvantage in both activities. His opportunity cost of raking leaves is only ¼ of a clean window per square yard, and Heather's

comparative advantage
The ability to produce something at a lower opportunity cost than other producers face.

TABLE 2
AN EXAMPLE OF
COMPARATIVE ADVANTAGE

	WINDOWS PER HOUR	SQUARE YARDS OF LEAVES PER HOUR
Heather	4	6
Peter	1	4

is 4/6, or 2/3. So Peter should specialize in that activity in which he has a comparative advantage, that is, in which his opportunity cost is lower.

Heather and Peter implement a policy of specializing on the basis of comparative advantage. Heather washes all the windows, which takes her 3 hours. Peter rakes all the leaves, which takes him 6 hours. By specializing on the basis of comparative advantage, both of them are better off! They have produced the same "output" (clean windows and a leaf-free yard) with considerably less input. Heather saved 1/2 hour, and Peter saved 3 hours. Both parties gained from specialization.

FROM INDIVIDUALS TO NATIONS. The same principles that determine specialization for two individuals in simple situations apply to more complex situations involving individuals and firms in groups, regions, or nations. Trade between nations is also based on comparative advantage. By specializing, both parties can gain from trade. For simplicity, economists usually use a two-country, two-commodity example. The same analysis applies to situations involving more countries or more commodities.

Suppose there are two countries called Inland and Outland. Before they discover one another, they are producing the products shown in Table 3. Outland, like Peter, is able to produce less of both commodities. This lack of absolute advantage may be due to Outland's resources being less efficient, or Outland may just be a smaller or poorer country with fewer resources. The reason for absolute advantage or absolute disadvantage makes no difference for comparative advantage and the gains from trade.

The output numbers for Inland and Outland in Table 3 represent points on their production possibilities curves. (To keep things simple, both production possibilities curves are assumed to be straight lines as in Chapter 3.) One more piece of information is needed in order to draw the straight-line production possibilities curve for each country. Assume that each country is devoting two-thirds of its resources to steel and one-third of its resources to cloth. This assumption makes it possible to calculate the end points of their production possibilities curves.

If Inland specializes in cloth, the country can produce 225 bolts. If it specializes in steel, it can produce 75 tons. If Outland specializes in cloth, the country can produce 180 bolts. If it specializes in steel, it can produce 30 tons. These points give the production possibilities curves in Figure 1.

Which country should specialize in what product or mix of products? The answer lies in the two countries' opportunity costs. For Inland, the opportunity cost of producing 75 tons of steel is 225 bolts of cloth not produced, or 3 bolts of cloth per ton of steel. For Outland, the same calculation says that 1 ton of steel costs 6 bolts of cloth. Inland's steel is cheaper

TABLE 3 PRODUCTION POSSIBILITIES WITHOUT TRADE

COUNTRY	STEEL (TONS)	CLOTH (BOLTS)
Inland	50	75
Outland	20	60
World Total	70	135

FIGURE 1
PRODUCTION POSSIBILITIES CURVES FOR INLAND AND OUTLAND
The production possibilities curve illustrates the gains from specializing on the basis of comparative advantage. Each country moves from pretrade production and consumption (point A), to output with specialization (point B) and then to consumption after trade (point C).

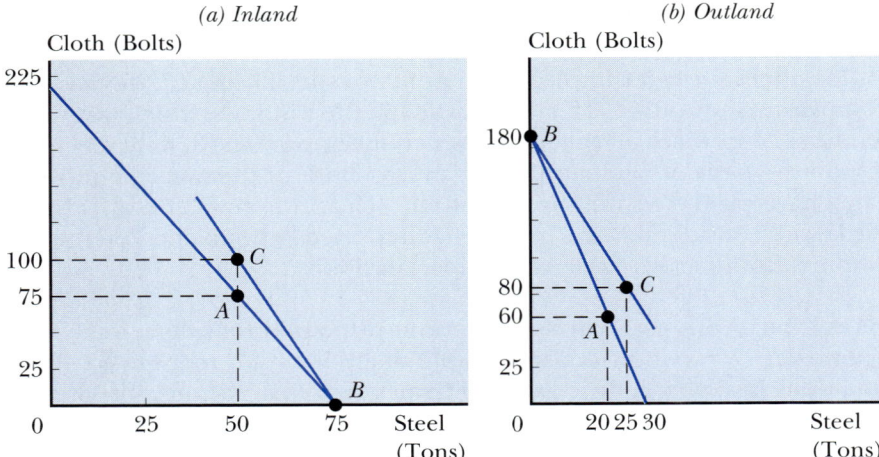

in terms of cloth forgone. Measuring the cost of cloth in terms of steel, on the other hand, gives these results: One bolt of Inland cloth costs $\frac{1}{3}$ of a ton of steel, and one bolt of Outland cloth costs only $\frac{1}{6}$ of a ton of steel. Measured in terms of opportunity costs, Outland's cloth is cheaper. The result of specialization is shown in Table 4.

Total world output has increased, without using additional resources, by 5 tons of steel and 45 bolts of cloth. Are the two countries better off?[1] Not yet. After all, they could have been producing those combinations anyway. It is only after trade that they can be better off.

THE TERMS OF TRADE. At what rate will Inland and Outland trade steel for cloth? Inland will not accept less than 3 bolts of cloth for a ton of steel, because this country can do that well producing its own cloth. Outland will not offer more than 6 bolts of cloth per ton of steel, because more than that would make it cheaper not to specialize. Anywhere between 3 and 6 bolts of cloth per ton of steel should be a mutually acceptable trading ratio. Let's make it 4 bolts of cloth for 1 ton of steel. This ratio is called the **terms of trade**. The exact terms of trade will lie somewhere between the parties' opportunity costs. Exactly where the terms of trade falls between those limits depends on the relative strength of demand for both products in both countries.

terms of trade
The ratio at which one product is exchanged for another.

TABLE 4
PRODUCTION BEFORE AND AFTER SPECIALIZATION

	BEFORE SPECIALIZATION		AFTER SPECIALIZATION	
	STEEL	CLOTH	STEEL	CLOTH
Inland	50	75	75	0
Outland	20	60	0	180
Total	70	135	75	180

1. To be sure that they are better off without knowing anything about their tastes and preferences, we need to be sure that each country has at least as much of one good as before and more of the other.

There are numerous after-trade combinations of steel and cloth that could make both countries better off. One possibility is to let Inland take all of its gains from trade in extra cloth, keeping its steel consumption at the original level of 50 tons and trading away the other 25 tons to Outland for 100 bolts of cloth. That exchange leaves Outland with 25 tons of imported steel and 80 bolts of domestic cloth, a consumption combination that represents more of both goods. The results of trade are summarized in Table 5.

These new consumption points are shown in Figure 1. Point C in part (a) shows Inland consuming 50 tons of steel and 100 bolts of cloth. Point C in part (b) represents a consumption combination of 25 tons of steel and 80 bolts of cloth for Outland. In each graph, this point lies along a "terms of trade" line, or a **consumption possibilities curve**, beginning at point B (total production with specialization) and having a slope of $\frac{1}{4}$ (1 steel to 4 cloth). Each country is able to get beyond its production possibilities curve by separating production (at point B) from consumption (at point C). The gains from trade are the same kinds of improvements in well-being that a country gets from having additional economic resources. Point C in each case represents one of many trade and consumption combinations that makes that partner better off.

consumption possibilities curve
A line showing the consumption combinations attainable through trade.

THE BASIS OF COMPARATIVE ADVANTAGE. What makes Inland better at producing steel and Outland better at producing cloth? For some products, the reasons are obvious. Climate determines the cheapest place to produce bananas, potatoes, and other agricultural products. Mineral resources determine other production patterns. Some products use a high proportion of unskilled labor relative to capital and other inputs. These products will be produced in countries with relatively large amounts of low-cost, unskilled labor. Other products require relatively more skilled labor, capital, or fertile land. These products will be produced in countries where those resources are abundant.

Still other products follow what economist Raymond Vernon called the **product cycle**. When the product is introduced, it will be exported by the country in which it was developed. But as the product and the production process become standardized, production will eventually migrate to other countries with a suitable resource mix. Automobiles, whose production technology was developed in the United States, are now produced almost everywhere. Textile was originally developed in England, but the production of simple cotton textiles (the most standardized part of the industry) has migrated around the globe in search of the inexpensive, low-skill labor that is used heavily in their manufacture.

product cycle
A series of stages, from development to standardization, through which a new product passes.

	BEFORE SPECIALIZATION		AFTER SPECIALIZATION		AFTER TRADE	
	STEEL	CLOTH	STEEL	CLOTH	STEEL	CLOTH
Inland	50	75	75	0	50	100
Outland	20	60	0	180	25	80
Total	70	135	75	180	75	180

TABLE 5
GAINS FROM TRADE

Sometimes the explanation for comparative advantage lies in historical accident. A product starts being produced in country *A* because that is where it was invented, or because its citizens want such a product. Country *A* develops the skills and resources needed to produce that product, including related industries that supply inputs or use the product in making other goods. If *A*'s resources are suited to the production of the good, *A* is likely to have a comparative advantage that it can retain for some time. If the world market is not large, there may be room only for a few suppliers who take advantage of cost savings in large-scale production. The first producer may enjoy a lasting advantage for that reason.

All these factors may explain the existence of comparative advantage. The important point is that it is possible for both partners to increase output and economic well-being by specializing on the basis of comparative advantage, no matter how that advantage originated.

OTHER BENEFITS FROM TRADE

There are at least two other important benefits from trade besides the increased output from comparative advantage. One is competition. The other is economies of scale.

Trade increases the number of competing firms from whom consumers can buy, widening their range of choices of goods and suppliers. This benefit of trade can be very important if the domestic industry has only a few firms. For example, car buyers in the United States have a wide range of choices because of international trade, although there are only a few domestic producers. As a result of foreign competition, domestic producers have responded to demands of some car buyers for smaller, more fuel-efficient cars.

Access to a large world market instead of a smaller domestic one may enable firms to operate at a more efficient scale. Producers of mainframe computers, aircraft, and heavy machinery need a very large market in order to produce at a scale that results in the lowest possible costs per unit.

THE WHY AND HOW OF PROTECTION

With all of these good reasons for free trade, why are some U.S. firms and industries protected from foreign competition? Many arguments are offered by firms that have to compete with imports, but most of these arguments come down to one reason—income distribution. A country as a whole benefits from free trade, but not everyone benefits equally.

Protection of domestic industries is accomplished with two main tools: tariffs and quotas. A **tariff** is a tax on imported goods or services. The tariff can be specific (based on weight, volume, or number of units) or *ad valorem* (figured as a percentage of the price). The average U.S. tariff is less than 5 percent. Many items bear no tariff at all, and a few items have large tariffs.

A **quota** is a quantity limit. It specifies the maximum amount of a good or service that can be imported during a given time period (usually a year). Quotas can be global (limiting total imports of widgets from all foreign suppliers to 1,000 widgets per year) or geographic (assigning quotas

tariff
A tax on imported goods or services.

quota
A limit on the amount of a good or service that can be imported during a given time period.

to specific countries). Quotas also can be combined with tariffs in a **tariff quota**. In this case, a certain amount of a good from one country is allowed to enter another country without a tariff. For amounts in excess of that limit, a tariff is applied.

tariff quota
A combination of a quota and a tariff that allows a certain amount of a good or service to be imported without paying a tariff and imposes the tariff on further imports.

EFFECTS OF A TARIFF

Figure 2 illustrates the effects of a tariff. In this figure, Inland produces, consumes, and imports cheese. The domestic supply curve is S_d. The domestic demand curve is D_d. Because Inland is a small country, its purchases of imported goods do not affect the world price of those goods. Inland can buy all the cheese it wants at the world price, P_w. At P_w, domestic producers are producing A pounds and consumers are buying B pounds. The difference between production and consumption is imports of $B - A$ pounds of cheese.

P_t is the price of imported cheese after Inland imposed a tariff equal to T. Since the tariff drives up the price, consumers buy less. Cheese consumption falls to C. Domestic producers move up along their supply curve to E. They get a bigger share of the smaller market. Imports decrease from $B - A$ to $C - E$.

Who gains? Domestic producers, including their owners, workers, and suppliers. These firms can charge a higher price and have a larger market share, which benefits everyone connected with them. Government also gains some tariff revenue. Who loses? Domestic consumers are paying more and getting less, so they lose. Foreign producers have lost sales. Also, the country imposing the tariff has given up some of the benefits of free trade noted earlier—more output, competition, and economies of scale. Since foreign cheese producers are more efficient than most of Inland's domestic cheese producers, this country is switching from more efficient to less efficient producers.

EFFECTS OF A QUOTA

Quotas are similar to tariffs. In fact, they can be represented by the same diagram. The main difference is that quotas restrict quantity, and tariffs

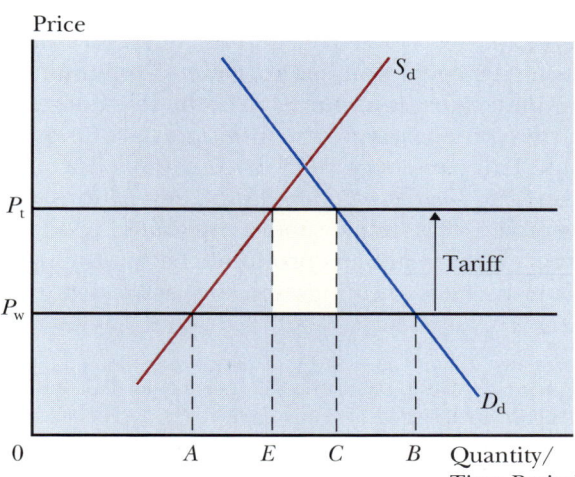

FIGURE 2
EFFECTS OF A TARIFF OR QUOTA
A tariff $T = P_t - P_w$ or an equivalent quota $C - E$ raises prices for domestic consumers (from P_w to P_t), reduces imports (from $B - A$ to $C - E$), lowers consumption (from B to C), and increases domestic output and sales from (A to E).

> **TARIFFS VERSUS QUOTAS**
>
> **A TARIFF**
> - Raises prices
> - Reduces imports and consumption
> - Increases domestic output
> - Produces government revenue
> - Lets imports rise when demand increases
>
> **A QUOTA**
> - Raises prices
> - Reduces imports and consumption
> - Increases domestic output
> - Creates monopoly profits for those with import licenses
> - Makes prices rise when demand increases

work through prices. If, in Figure 2, the government imposed a quota in the amount of $C - E$ on cheese, the effects on price, domestic production, consumption, and imports would be the same as those of the tariff $T = P_t - P_w$. There are a couple of important differences, however.

First, a tariff raises revenue for the government, in the amount of the shaded area in Figure 2. A quota generates no government revenue.[2] All the benefits of a quota go to protected domestic producers and to those importers who manage to get the scarce and valuable import permits used to implement quotas. Permit holders can buy the good at the low foreign price and resell it at the higher domestic price. The difference between the price the importer pays the foreign supplier and the price the importer can charge the domestic consumer ($P_t - P_w$) times the number of units imported is a monopoly profit that comes from having a license to import. Note that this monopoly profit is equal to the revenue the government would have received under a tariff.

Second, suppose demand increased in the country. With a tariff, the quantity of imports would increase. With a quota, only the price would increase. Originally, the tariff T and the quota $C - E$ had the same effect on prices and quantities. As Figure 3 shows, however, when demand shifts from D_d to D'_d under a tariff, imports rise to $H - E$ and consumption rises to H. With a quota, price rises to P_f. Imports remain the same ($C - E = G - F$). Domestic production rises to F, and consumption rises slightly to G.

Several U.S. economists examined the redistributional effects of protectionism in the steel industry, using techniques borrowed from finance and accounting.[3] They examined changes in the value of the stock of steel companies to determine if these firms capture the monopoly profits generated by tariffs and quotas. The owners of steel firms captured a substantial portion of the economic rent created by trade restrictions on steel. Not all firms gained equally. The smaller, more integrated producers gained the most. Those firms that were less profitable before the protection gained the most from it. These findings are consistent with the analysis presented here.

2. In the 1980s proposals were made that would require the government to auction the right to import under a quota to the highest bidder. If this kind of policy was adopted, then quotas could also be used to raise revenue for the government.
3. Stefanie Lenway, Kathleen Rehbein, and Laura Sparks, "The Impact of Protectionism on Firm Wealth: The Experience of the Steel Industry," *Southern Economic Journal* (April 1990): 1079–1093.

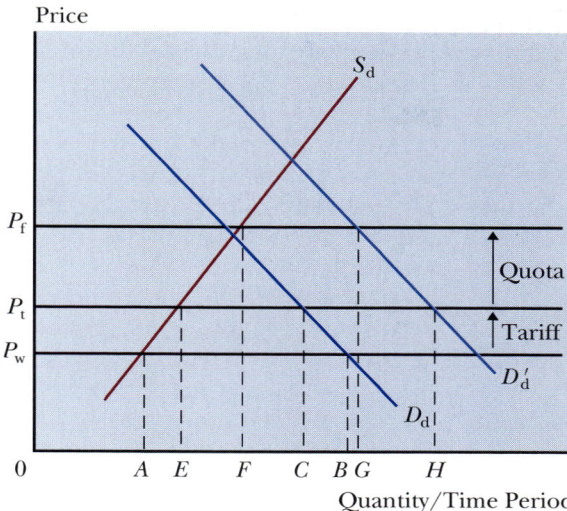

FIGURE 3
EFFECTS OF A TARIFF OR QUOTA WHEN DEMAND INCREASES
Under a tariff, an increase in demand increases the quantity of imports (from $C - E$ to $H - E$) and consumption (from C to H) but leaves the price unchanged (at P_t). With a quota, increased demand leads to a rise in price (from P_t to P_t') and in domestic production (from E to F). Consumption rises slightly (from B to G). Imports are unchanged ($G - F = C - E$).

Most economists prefer free trade to either tariffs or quotas. If they have to choose, they usually consider a tariff less harmful than an equivalent quota. A tariff does allow imports to increase in response to increases in demand. Also, at least some of the tariff revenue goes to the government, which uses it to further the general welfare. Also, a tariff is more visible and therefore easier to eliminate. A quota is less obvious and more likely to remain in place indefinitely.

NONTARIFF BARRIERS TO TRADE

In addition to tariffs and quotas, there are other kinds of government barriers to trade. Domestic laws or policies other than tariffs and quotas that interfere with the free exchange of goods and services across national borders are called **nontariff barriers**. Some of these barriers are intentional. One example is *domestic preference laws* requiring the government to favor domestic suppliers when making purchases for government agencies and programs. Other nontariff barriers are laws or regulations enacted for domestic reasons that make it more difficult for foreign suppliers to compete. For example, it may be difficult for a foreign supplier to comply with U.S. safety standards and labeling requirements. A common form of nontariff barrier is requiring excessive paperwork that adds to costs and reduces profits for foreign suppliers and domestic importing firms. In France, a shortage of customs inspectors constitutes a nontariff barrier because it creates long delays and thus discourages imports.

Sometimes nontariff barriers work the other way. Some U.S. laws and regulations make it more difficult for domestic firms to sell abroad. If American products must meet higher safety standards, for example, the American firm may not be able to compete with foreign producers who do not have to incur those costs.

Another type of nontariff barrier is antidumping codes. Dumping con-

nontariff barriers
Trade restrictions other than tariffs and quotas.

In May 1989, the United States took action against Japan, Brazil, and India for unfair trade practices. The U.S. government demanded that these countries end unfair practices and threatened retaliatory tariffs on selected goods from their countries if action was not forthcoming. Reporting on this development, *U.S. News & World Report* noted that President Bush suggested to one of his economic advisers, "Maybe we ought to take action against a whole bunch of countries—including ourselves."

The United States is a very open market, but there are numerous barriers to trade that its trading partners regard as unfair. These barriers include "voluntary restraints" on automobiles, customs user fees on boats, planes, and trucks, Superfund taxes on petroleum products, quotas on cheese, ice cream, and sugar, a 35¢ per gallon tariff on orange juice, steel restraints, antidumping laws, and consumer preferences for American products. Professor Gary Hufbauer estimates that tariffs, quotas, and nontariff barriers cost American consumers more than $80 billion annually.

Antidumping laws can be a bureaucratic and legal nightmare. A 1989 hearing before the International Trade Commission (ITC) offers a case study. In 1989, Torrington Company, a Connecticut-based maker of ball bearings, claimed firms in eight European countries were engaging in unfair trade practices (dumping). Torrington reportedly budgeted $1 million for the legal battle. The ITC ruled in Torrington's favor that bearings were being dumped in the U.S. market at 60 percent below their home market value. U.S. producers of power tools and machinery were not happy with this ruling. They pointed out that there was a shortage of such bearings in the United States and that Torrington was producing at capacity. They thought the ruling disadvantaged them in export markets because the price of ball bearings they use went up significantly.

Buy American mandates create another barrier that foreign countries claim is unfair. These legal requirements are most commonly found in the defense industry, road construction, and mass transit. Such preferential treatment generally gives American suppliers a price advantage over foreign suppliers. A recent European Community publication refers to these preferences as "permanent discrimination in favor of U.S. products."

Criticism of U.S. barriers to imports by U.S. trading partners conveniently ignores the fact that their barriers are just as irksome to U.S. firms trying to export. As you can see, however, and as Professor Hufbauer reports, the costs of U.S. barriers are significant to American consumers.

ECONOMIC INSIGHT

U.S. BARRIERS TO IMPORTS

Source: Clemens P. Work with Robert F. Black, "Uncle Sam as Unfair Trader," *U.S. News & World Report* (12 June 1989): 42–44.

sists of selling a good at a lower price in a foreign country than in the firm's home country. Firms may dump abroad to get rid of surpluses, to take advantage of differences in elasticity of demand (price discrimination), or to establish a foothold in a competitive market. Most countries, including the United States, have antidumping regulations that forbid this practice as unfair competition. If a foreign firm is accused of dumping (usually by a competing firm in the importing country), the International Trade Commission will hear the case and may impose a duty on the dumped good to counteract the price difference. American firms often claim dumping is being done in order to make selling in the United States more difficult for foreign competitors.[4]

U.S. COMMERCIAL POLICY

The set of actions that a country undertakes to deliberately influence trade in goods and services is its **commercial policy**. For most of its history, the United States has had high tariffs and other trade restrictions. The highest U.S. tariff ever was imposed by the Smoot-Hawley Act of 1930, an average charge of 53 percent.

Since 1934, the United States has greatly reduced tariffs and other trade barriers by negotiating treaties with other countries. Trade barriers were reduced under a series of Congressional acts, beginning with the Reciprocal Trade Agreements Act of 1934. Regular trade negotiations led to reductions in tariffs by the United States and its major trading partners. The latest complete series of trade negotiations, which took place from 1974 to 1979, was called the Tokyo Round. After the tariff cuts agreed to in that round were finally implemented, the average U.S. tariff was only about 4.2 percent. The Tokyo Round also involved some agreements on reducing nontariff barriers. In 1986, a round of negotiations called the Uruguay Round began. In December 1990, the talks broke down over trade in agricultural products. The European countries were unwilling to lower their agricultural supports and the protection necessary to maintain them.

> **commercial policy**
> The set of actions that a country undertakes to deliberately influence trade in goods and services.

THE POLITICS OF PROTECTION

Reducing tariffs does not result in free trade. Quotas still protect autos, steel, textiles, and other industries. Nontariff barriers are still an important impediment to free trade. As the value of the dollar rose from 1981 to 1985, making imports cheap and exports expensive for the United States, pressures for protection rose. These pressures fell, however, as the dollar declined in 1986 and 1987. Critics of free trade point to the success of Japan and Korea, which experienced economic growth with very restrictive trade barriers. The battle between free trade and protectionism is an ongoing one.

Most demands for protection come from industries that once had a

---

4. For a clear, nontechnical review of the different types of nontariff barriers, see Cletus C. Coughlin and Geoffrey E. Wood, "An Introduction to Non-Tariff Barriers to Trade," *Review*, Federal Reserve Bank of St. Louis (January/February, 1989): 32–46.

comparative advantage but lost it when other industries developed even greater relative efficiency. Such demands also come from industries where monopoly or oligopoly conditions allowed them to ignore the need to improve technology and productivity. Shoes, clothing, steel, and, most recently, automobiles are U.S. industries that have asked for protection because they have lost a comparative advantage. Part of the problem with steel and automobiles is that they have been slow to modernize and to respond to changes in consumer preferences.

It is easy to identify gainers and losers from tariffs and quotas. Consumers lose. Foreign producers lose sales. Domestic competitors gain. One loser who does not show up in Figures 2 and 3 is the U.S. exporter. When one country raises tariffs, other countries are likely to do so in response, and the first country's exports fall. Thus, political support for free trade should come from a coalition between exporting firms and consumers, with help from wholesalers and retailers of imported goods. However, such a diverse group is not easy to organize and hold together.

Firms that gain from protection spend large sums of money in lobbying to get or keep a tariff or quota. Consider a tariff on shoes. As a consumer, you may find that the tariff only costs you a few more dollars a year, so it's hardly worthwhile to lobby against the tariff. But if you are a worker whose job in a shoe factory depends on protection or a shoe manufacturer losing sales to imports, you will work much harder to get and keep protection. Even though the total benefits of free trade would exceed the costs, complaints from a few big losers tend to generate far more noise and attention than the lobbying for free trade. If the losers are concentrated in certain regions, the American system of representation by states and districts makes it easier for them to develop "client" relationships with their members of Congress.

COMMON ARGUMENTS FOR PROTECTION

When workers and owners from import-competing firms go to Washington to lobby for protection, they use some tried and true arguments for protection. Some of these arguments have some economic validity. Others have strong political or emotional appeal, but weak economic foundations. We will discuss the most common arguments for protection in this section and then turn to two very sophisticated ones.

INFANT INDUSTRY ARGUMENT
One theoretically valid argument for protection is the infant industry argument. An infant industry is a new industry that is not yet ready to compete with established foreign producers. Given some time (and sheltered conditions) to master the technology, establish a reputation, train workers, and reach economies of scale, the infant industry may eventually be competitive. Comparative advantage can change over time. Temporary protection could give an infant industry the chance to acquire a comparative advantage and "catch up" with established foreign firms.

This argument is only valid if the protected industry will be competitive in time. There is no reason to protect industries that will never be competitive, wasting scarce resources that could be better used elsewhere. There should be no need to protect industries that will quickly become competitive, because entrepreneurs (and lenders) should be able to see past the early losses to profits. The only industries that really qualify are those that generate some kinds of external benefits to society that they are unable to recoup in the early years. Thus, the few deserving infant industries are those that are not profitable by simple cost and revenue calculations, but are worth protecting because they meet two tests:

1. They will eventually be able to compete in the market without protection.
2. They generate benefits to society that are worth the cost of a tariff.

What kinds of external benefits might an infant industry create? Examples include developing roads and power sources that are then available to other industries, training a labor force that may migrate to other firms, or producing a low-cost input that other industries can use. Benefits such as these are likely to be created in less developed countries. It's difficult to make a convincing case for protecting an infant industry in a developed country such as the United States. Even in less developed countries, this argument is easily abused by overstating external benefits and underestimating how long it will take for the industry to be competitive.

NATIONAL DEFENSE ARGUMENT

Another common and economically valid argument for protection is national defense. The product of this industry may be needed in wartime, the argument goes, but the domestic producer can't compete with cheaper foreign producers. Without protection during peacetime, the firm may not be here when war comes and foreign supplies are cut off. This argument gained merit after the War of 1812. England had been the United States's main trading partner and then became an enemy who successfully blockaded the U.S. coast. Again, during World War II, German interference with shipping created problems in obtaining some needed supplies.

However, this argument make less sense for the United States today. The government stockpiles strategic raw materials, and most products needed in wartime are those in which the United States has a comparative advantage, such as heavy machinery, sophisticated electronics, and aircraft. Economists Leland Yeager and David Tuerck argue that the national defense argument only applies in the case of another World War II, what they describe as a "prolonged non-nuclear war of attrition."[5] But, they argue, the more likely kinds of wars—the kind the Pentagon seems to be preparing for—are either "brush fire" wars, such as Panamanian invasion of 1990 and other localized battles, which do not affect U.S. access to supplies, or else all-out nuclear war, in which case there would be no time to resupply. Even the 1991 Gulf War, which was too large to be called a "brush fire," did not affect U.S. access to shipping and supplies.

---

5. Leland B. Yeager and David G. Tuerck, *Foreign Trade and U.S. Policy* (New York: Praeger, 1976).

BALANCE OF PAYMENTS ARGUMENT

Most other arguments for protection have more emotional or political appeal than economic logic. Proponents of protection argue that a balance of payments deficit (or at least that part of the deficit that is accounted for by exports and imports) could be reduced by imposing tariffs and importing less. Up to a point, this argument is correct, but only in the short run. Over time, tariffs encourage the development of domestic industries producing import substitutes, usually products in which the nation has a comparative disadvantage. This policy encourages inefficient use of scarce resources. Furthermore, tariffs usually lead to retaliatory tariffs on the exports of the country imposing the tariff.

EMPLOYMENT ARGUMENT

The employment argument suggests that reducing imports can create jobs producing import substitutes. However, the cost of doing so is high. Protectionism encourages misallocation of resources and tends to lead to retaliation. The tariff-imposing country may gain jobs in import-competing industries and lose them in more efficient exporting industries. Employment may also be lost if domestically produced items cost more or are of inferior quality. Thus, less is demanded and jobs are lost.

CHEAP FOREIGN LABOR ARGUMENT

The cheap foreign labor argument popular among protectionists goes something like this: "We're just as efficient as the foreign competition—we use the same machinery and technology and produce at least as high a quality product. However, U.S. labor costs are at least $7.00 an hour, and firms in some foreign countries have to pay only $1.00 an hour. How can we possibly compete?"

There are several possible answers. One is that cheap labor often means lower productivity. Another is that labor, especially unskilled labor, may be cheap in some countries, but other inputs such as capital and skilled labor are relatively expensive. A country such as the United States should concentrate on producing those products that use relatively more of its abundant (and, therefore, relatively less expensive) resources, capital, and skilled labor.

SOPHISTICATED ARGUMENTS FOR PROTECTION

Two sophisticated arguments from the highly mathematical literature of trade theory are valid arguments for trade restriction. These arguments are so advanced that they rarely appear in beginning economic textbooks. We include them here because we don't want to leave you with the impression that all economists favor free trade in all situations. This section will introduce you to the very basic ideas behind these arguments. You can learn more through the suggestions for further reading if you are interested.

OPTIMAL TARIFF ARGUMENT

If the price elasticity of demand for imported goods is greater than zero and the price elasticity of foreign supply is less than infinite, the imposition of a tariff raises the price of the foreign good by less than the amount of the tariff. The tariff causes the foreign supplier to lower prices in order to maintain sales. The country imposing the tariff then experiences a gain in its terms of trade, because the price of its imports has fallen while the price of its exports remains the same.

This effect on the terms of trade gives rise to the concept of an optimal tariff. An **optimal tariff** is a tariff that maximizes a nation's net gain from altering its terms of trade. At one extreme, if the supply of imports were perfectly inelastic, the optimal tariff would be infinite because the importing country would be a pure monopsonist. At the other extreme, where the import supply was perfectly elastic, the optimum would be zero.

The optimal tariff argument is valid within its restrictive assumptions. The main assumption is that the foreign countries do not retaliate. If other countries see their terms of trade deteriorate and retaliate with an optimal tariff of their own, the flow of trade diminishes. After a series of retaliations and counter-retaliations, world welfare will be diminished. All countries will be at lower consumption levels. Another problem is that application of optimal tariffs would be very difficult in practice. It would require that policy makers know the elasticities of demand for the traded goods. It is difficult to determine these elasticities, and they change over time.

The optimal tariff argument suggests using a country's monopsony power to provide a gain to it by imposing a tariff that causes the rest of the world to suffer a loss. It is likely that such a gain would be only a short-term one, as the rest of the world would soon retaliate.

optimal tariff
A tariff that maximizes a nation's net gain from altering its terms of trade.

THE THEORY OF THE SECOND BEST

The **theory of the second best** is an argument in favor of tariffs as distortions needed to offset other distortions. Monopoly, government policies, and externalities often cause a divergence between private and social costs and benefits, and governmental policy may not be able to eliminate this divergence in order to pursue the first-best policy of free trade. Then a second-best policy of tariffs may be useful to introduce new distortions that eliminate the existing distortions.

theory of the second best
A theory that a second-best policy of tariffs may be useful to introduce new distortions that eliminate existing distortions.

The theory of the second best can be used to justify import restrictions on a selective basis when external effects make the private costs to a domestic producer higher than the social costs to the country. Consider, for example, an excise tax on a domestically produced good, automobile tires. This tax raises the cost of producing tires because that cost will include the portion of the tax that is a transfer from tire producers to the government. As a result, domestic production of tires is lower, and imports of tires are higher than they would be without the excise tax. The country is importing tires at a higher social price than it would cost to produce them at home. An import duty equal to the excise tax would increase the domestic production of tires to the point where the marginal social cost of imported tires and the marginal cost of domestic production are equal.

If government-created cost differences or foreign trade restrictions affected all industries equally, they would not affect comparative costs and distort the efficient pattern of specialization and trade. It is only when these factors affect different industries differently that there may be a distortion of relative prices that justifies some kind of protection. For example, the minimum wage has more impact on costs for industries that use large amounts of unskilled labor than for industries that use primarily highly skilled labor and capital. Thus, the minimum wage raises the costs of the first type of industry more than the second.

The theory of the second best is not limited to trade theory. It recognizes that whenever market prices fail to reflect real opportunity costs, a second-best policy may be appropriate. You should remember, however, that the first-best policy is free trade.

FAIR TRADE AND THE MAINTENANCE OF THE U.S. MARKET

If there are so few valid economic arguments for protection, why does protection exist? There is a group of politically appealing arguments labeled **fair trade**. The concept of fair trade is often described as a "level playing field." If foreign countries erect tariff barriers, nontariff barriers, or quotas that limit U.S. firms' exports to those countries, protectionists argue that the United States should do the same. For example, if the Japanese make it very difficult or expensive for their citizens to buy U.S. automobiles or beef, protectionists say that Americans should treat Japanese exports the same way.

fair trade
The idea that the United States should impose trade barriers equivalent to those that its trading partners place on U.S. exports.

One version of the fair trade argument is called maintenance of markets. Some protectionists argue that it is more costly to operate in the U.S. market than in other markets. U.S. firms pay high corporate taxes, face strict environmental and safety standards, and have to comply with employment regulations such as affirmative action, minimum wage, and overtime pay. Many foreign producers, especially in less developed countries, do not incur similar costs. They can participate in the U.S. market without incurring the costs of maintaining it. This issue has received considerable attention recently because of the proposed free trade area between the United States and Mexico. Mexico has lax environmental standards and few employment regulations.

These fair trade arguments are usually put forward by organized lobbies for industries that are losing sales to foreign competitors. The appeal makes sense to the average voter, because it is couched in terms of fair play and equal treatment. Coupled with arguments against trading with Communist countries and other political enemies, the case for "fair trade" looks even more appealing. International trade differs from domestic trade in that the political dimension carries much more weight. Political concerns help to explain why the economically sound practice of free trade is rarely implemented.

Advocates of protection on the basis of fair trade or maintenance of the U.S. market offer two policy solutions. The more traditional one is a tariff on foreign goods. This tariff would be equivalent to the restrictions placed on U.S. exports by other countries or to the excess cost of maintaining the U.S. market. Computing the appropriate tariff in either case would be a difficult task. For some European nations, with large government sectors and restrictive laws governing employment, the appropriate tariff might actually be negative.

In November 1989, Canadian voters approved the U.S.–Canada Free Trade Agreement (FTA). The FTA called for a ten-year phase-in of complete free trade. Before the pact, about 75 percent of the markets between the two countries had free trade. Autos have been freely traded since 1965. The beneficiaries of this agreement were predicted to be primarily Canadian consumers and U.S. producers, because Canadian tariffs were about three times higher than U.S. tariffs. For example, two months after the agreement was signed, some Harley-Davidson motorcycle models sold for $2,000 less in Canada than they had before the pact.

Freer access to U.S. markets has contributed to a surge of business investment in Canada. The Royal Bank of Canada has reported an increase in plant and equipment investment of more than 28 percent since the signing of the agreement. Canada's Economic Council has estimated that when this investment boom is over, it will have produced more than 250,000 new jobs in Canada. On the American side, business is also booming. Buffalo, New York has reaped some benefits from the agreement, being viewed by those in Toronto as "the cheap side of the border." Shoppers from Toronto head south to purchase computers, clothes, televisions, gasoline, and liquor. Two-way trade between the United States and Canada increased more than 10 percent in the first year of the agreement.

Not everyone is happy with the agreement. Polls in Canada indicate that a majority of the population has turned against it. The Liberal Party has promised to repeal the deal if returned to power. This is understandable because there are winners and losers in free trade. The losers are more visible. Firms that aren't competitive don't survive. The strong Canadian labor unions were opposed to the agreement and still oppose it. Bruce Campbell, an economist with the Canadian Labor Congress, claims that "free trade is a bad deal for Canadians." He would be more correct to say that free trade is a bad deal for Canadian labor union members.

ECONOMIC INSIGHT

THE UNITED STATES AND FREE TRADE PACTS

Free trade of sorts is also booming on the southern border of the United States. *Maquiladoras*, or border plants, are booming along the U.S.–Mexican border. Nearly half a million Mexicans are employed in almost 2,000 plants. These plants receive shipments of parts from U.S. manufacturers and assemble the parts into complete products. Any tariffs are due only on the value added. General Motors assembles auto parts in more than thirty *maquiladoras*. In 1986, this trade amounted to $29.7 billion. It grew to more than $65 billion in 1990.

Mexican President Carlos Salinas de Gortari wants free trade between Mexico and the United States to expand. Mexican and U.S. officials have been exploring a free trade agreement like the one negotiated with Canada. Administration officials look favorably on such proposals, but face tough opposition in Congress. Organized labor in the United States, like that in Canada, is strongly opposed to such an agreement. Labor leaders argue that Mexican firms enjoy an unfair advantage because they do not have to meet the environmental and safety standards that U.S. firms do. Owen F. Bieber, president of the United Auto Workers, argues that a free trade pact with Mexico would mean "there'll be a hell of a lot more empty factories in the United States of America." Perhaps Bieber and Campbell have the same speech writer!

Sources: Stephen Baker, "Along the Border, Free Trade Is Becoming a Fact of Life," *Business Week* (18 June 1990): 41–42; Alan Freeman, "Free-Trade Pact Creates Winners, Losers," *Wall Street Journal* (7 February 1989): A20; Peter Dworkin, "Unhappy Birthday for a Free-Trade Pact," *U.S. News & World Report* (5 February 1989): 54–59.

An alternative solution was suggested by Senator Phil Gramm of Texas (trained as an economist) and former Representative Jack Kemp of New York. Gramm and Kemp are basically in favor of free trade, but are also responsive to political pressures for protection based on fair trade arguments. They propose trading with each country on the basis that it trades with the United States. They believe that this policy would result in freer trade because the U.S. market is so important to other countries that they will lower their barriers rather than see barriers raised in the United States. The appeal of this policy is that it responds to arguments for fair trade and maintenance of the market with economic incentives to promote free trade and specialization based on comparative advantage. This solution demands reciprocity, waving a stick of protectionism in order to get other governments to move toward freer trade.

MOVEMENT OF RESOURCES

If trading countries benefit from the flow of goods and services, what about benefits from the flow of inputs? Labor, capital, and raw materials also move between countries. When they do, objections are sometimes raised by those who are threatened by foreign competition. Foreign competition is unpopular with the owners of factors of production, whether the competition is in product markets or in factor markets. Thus, these owners seek restrictions on the movement of factors as well as on the movement of goods.

Organized labor, for example, opposes immigration of workers and construction of plants abroad. Newly arrived workers compete for jobs and depress wages. An offshore plant of a U.S. firm means more jobs for foreign workers and fewer jobs for American workers. Domestic firms oppose letting their foreign competitors locate inside the country with no tariff wall for protection. Canada is cautious about letting U.S. firms build new plants in that country, and countries such as Kuwait and Japan have even tighter restrictions. Emotional and political arguments are sometimes stronger than economic concerns. Many U.S. citizens are unhappy about the purchase of U.S. banks, farmland, and resort islands by foreign firms and individuals, even when there are no obvious adverse consequences.

The United States puts fewer restrictions than most countries on the inflow or outflow of capital. Except for strategic raw materials (those needed for national defense), there are no restrictions on the flow of natural resources. Exports of natural resources such as oil and copper are often restricted by countries with some market power as suppliers. Some of these countries use controls on exports of these resources to generate revenue for their governments or to attract industries that use the resources as raw materials in manufacturing. Cartels are sometimes formed to take advantage of such market power when that power is shared among a small number of countries.

Immigration policy has been a source of much debate in the United States. After several previous attempts, Congress finally passed a new immigration bill in 1986. The most controversial provisions of that bill centered on illegal aliens, who have come to the United States in large numbers in the last twenty years. The bill made it possible for illegal aliens who resided in the United States prior to 1982 to become citizens but also imposed stiff penalties on employers who hire illegal aliens. The large number of illegal aliens who were residing in the United States when the law was passed was due to past restrictive immigration quotas. Organized labor has generally opposed raising or eliminating immigration quotas because it wants to protect jobs for U.S. citizens.

In general, the movement of inputs between countries can substitute for free movement of goods. If a country is poor in raw materials, capital, or skilled labor, it has two possible remedies. It can import goods that incorporate large quantities of those inputs, or it can import those inputs and produce its own final products. Both kinds of trade should bring benefits. In the absence of artificial barriers, market considerations determine which choice is more efficient—to move the final product or to move the input.

MULTINATIONAL CORPORATIONS

Another important influence on patterns of trade and factor movements is the multinational firm. A **multinational corporation** is a firm with headquarters in one country and plants in one or more other countries. Many large and well-known multinationals are headquartered in the United States, including Ford, General Motors, IBM, and AT&T. (So are many smaller and less-known ones.) Other large multinationals are headquartered in other countries, especially Japan (Honda and Mitsubishi) and European countries (Shell Oil, Nestlé, Michelin, and BASF). Multinationals have been around for a long time, but most of their growth has occurred since World War II.

multinational corporation
A firm with headquarters in one country and plants in one or more other countries.

Why Firms Go Abroad

Why do firms build plants in foreign countries? Why not just export or invest in a local firm that can produce the product? Exporting may not be feasible because of trade barriers, perishability, or a need to produce a product tailored to the local market. Investing in a local firm by purchasing stock or making a loan is sometimes feasible. Often, however, the investing firm wants more control over management, product quality, or patented processes. Sometimes the only way to get access to local resources, especially raw materials, is to build a plant.

U.S. labor unions oppose building plants abroad, arguing that firms are in search of cheap foreign labor. Unions would rather see plants built in the United States and goods exported. However, trade barriers or the unique needs of foreign markets are much more common reasons for building foreign plants than the attraction of cheap labor. Furthermore, U.S. workers have found jobs in the many plants in the United States owned by foreign multinationals, especially Japanese-owned firms. The lower wages and different management style of Japanese companies have meant adjustments not only for their American employees but also for their American competitors.

EFFECTS OF MULTINATIONALS

Multinationals are accused by their critics of stifling competition in the countries in which they locate, creating balance of payments problems, and leading to unhealthy concentration of economic and political power. Advocates argue that multinationals often increase competition, speed up the transfer of capital and technology, and help counteract artificial barriers to trade.

COMPETITION. In some cases, the multinational "shakes up" domestic competitors, forcing them to try harder when they can no longer hide behind a protective tariff wall. On the other hand, multinationals often simply buy out local competitors or keep local competition from developing. Sometimes multinationals increase competition, and sometimes they reduce it. Japanese multinationals and others have generally been regarded as beneficial in the United States. They compete for resources and markets with established American firms that must adjust or decline.

TRANSFER OF TECHNOLOGY. Multinationals expedite the flow of technology between countries. They make available to their foreign subsidiaries processes and methods that they would be reluctant to share with competitors. Less developed countries sometimes argue, however, that this transfer doesn't spill over to other industries for maximum benefit. They also argue that multinationals, which are generally from developed industrial countries, don't try very hard to adapt technology to the local mix of available resources.

LARGE MULTINATIONALS AND SMALL COUNTRIES. Probably the most serious concern about multinationals is that small countries are at a disadvantage in dealing with these large firms. Such a firm may have an annual revenue much larger than the host country's GNP. The multinational may be the largest employer, landowner, and taxpayer in a small country. A multinational represents a threat to the sovereignty of a host country when the firm is larger and more powerful than the government.

Despite these problems, there are real benefits to having multinationals. They provide a way for resources and technology to flow around trade and cultural barriers, which has been very beneficial to the world economy. In most cases, they promote the free-trade goals of more output with less effort that were the concern of classical economists two centuries ago when they formulated the theory of comparative advantage.

Chapter 20 International Trade

Summary

1. Trade takes place because both parties benefit. Trade is based on the principle of comparative advantage, which means that each country produces that product for which its opportunity cost is lower in terms of other production.
2. Specialization increases total output, and trade allows that increase to be shared. Trade also increases competition and allows countries to take advantage of economies of scale for some products.
3. Tariffs, quotas, and nontariff barriers interfere with free trade. A tariff or quota will raise the price, reduce imports, reduce consumption, and increase domestic production.
4. The United States has had high tariffs for most of its history but has reduced tariffs and other trade barriers since 1934.
5. Arguments for protection include protecting infant industries, national defense, balance of payments, employment, and cheap foreign labor. The first two have some validity but must be applied with caution. Most arguments for protection are really thinly disguised requests for income redistribution. The optimal tariff and the theory of the second best are two sophisticated arguments for tariffs.
6. Fair trade arguments call for consideration of the costs imposed on firms by U.S. laws.
7. Movements of resources can substitute for trade in goods and services.
8. Multinational corporations may increase competition in some cases and decrease it in others. They increase the transfer of technology between countries but may have too much power in small, less developed countries.

New Terms

gains from trade
absolute advantage
comparative advantage
terms of trade
consumption
 possibilities curve
product cycle
tariff
quota
tariff quota
nontariff barrier
commercial policy
optimal tariff
theory of the second best
fair trade
multinational
 corporation

Questions for Discussion

1. Consider the following situation for Upland and Downland. Each country devotes half of its resources to producing bananas and half to producing apples, and the figures given are what they produce in the absence of trade.

Country	Apples (Tons)	Bananas (Tons)
Upland	40	80
Downland	60	60

Do these figures indicate an absolute advantage, a comparative advantage, or both? What is each country's opportunity cost of producing apples? By how much will total output rise when they specialize? Can you find a better consumption combination for each country through trade?

2. Represent the information in Question 1 on a graph as a pair of production possibilities curves.
3. Who gains and who loses from a tariff? How do the effects of tariffs differ from the effects of quotas?
4. If you were running a small country, why might you have mixed feelings about the building of a plant there by a big multinational?
5. Among the U.S. industries that have received tariff protection in recent years are textiles and autos. Use one or more of the arguments in this chapter to present a case for protection of one of these industries.

6. Write a criticism of the case you made in Question 5, citing the benefits of free trade.

7. A tariff is proposed on imported pineapple. Economists calculate that 1 million pineapple buyers will incur additional costs of $2 each. Five thousand pineapple workers will earn an additional $100 a year. One hundred unemployed workers will find jobs at an average salary of $10,000. One hundred owners of pineapple packing firms will experience an average income increase of $5,000. What are the total gains to the gainers and the total losses to the losers? Are there other losses not counted in these figures? Do you think the tariff is likely to be enacted?

8. Why do multinational firms go abroad?

9. Why do economists generally prefer tariffs to quotas?

10. Why is an economy's consumption possibilities curve different from the production possibilities curve? How does a consumption possibilities curve help explain the benefits of trade as similar to the benefits of economic growth?

11. Can the government completely eliminate imports of some goods even if there is general agreement that such restrictions are appropriate? How does the experience with illegal immigration and illegal drugs support your argument?

12. Assume that the United States can produce 3 mainframe computers or 3,000 pairs of shoes with one unit of resource, and Italy can produce 1 mainframe computer or 2,000 pairs of shoes with one unit of resource. Could specialization and trade increase world output and consumption?

13. Given the data in Question 12, how will firms in the United States and Italy know what to produce? Who or what will tell them what to produce and what to import?

14. Why might competing domestic producers and importing firms prefer quotas to tariffs?

15. U.S. companies are often criticized as being too focused on the domestic market and not concerned enough with exporting. Business schools in the United States have been blamed for this domestic emphasis and have responded by "internationalizing" the business curriculum. Can you suggest economic reasons why U.S. firms have historically concentrated on the domestic market?

Suggestions for Further Reading

Business Week: Special 1990 Bonus Issue (June 15, 1990). An entire special issue devoted to international trade.

Dertouzos, Michael L., Richard K. Lester, Robert M. Solow, and the MIT Commission on Industrial Productivity. *Made in America: Regaining the Productive Edge.* Cambridge: MIT Press, 1989. A report by an MIT commission on U.S. industrial importance that addresses issues of American competitiveness in world markets. Chapter 2 discusses the U.S. economy in the changing world environment.

Helpman, Elhanan, and Paul R. Krugman. *Trade Policy and Market Structure.* Cambridge: MIT Press, 1989. A highly theoretical treatment of trade policy that demonstrates that when markets are not competitive, government intervention can improve welfare. This argument calls into question the argument for a unilateral free trade policy.

King, Philip. *International Economics and International Economic Policy: A Reader.* New York: McGraw-Hill, 1990. A collection of readings on current issues in trade policy. Includes material on Japan's trade policy, strategic trade, Europe 1992, and multinational companies.

Root, Franklyn R. *International Trade and Investment.* Cincinnati, OH: South-Western, 1990. An intermediate-level textbook covering both international trade and international finance.

Vargish, George. *What's Made in the U.S.A.* Saddle River, NJ: Vargish International, 1988. A book written by a businessman that attacks free trade as a "national catastrophe" and repeats many of the arguments for protectionism discussed in this chapter.

Yeager, Leland B., and David G. Tuerck. *Foreign Trade and U.S. Policy.* New York: Praeger, 1976. This book presents the case for free trade and a criticism of protectionism in theory and practice, with many examples and illustrations from Congressional hearings.

AFTER STUDYING THIS CHAPTER, YOU SHOULD BE ABLE TO:

1. Describe how the market for currencies is different from other kinds of markets.
2. Diagram and explain the operation of the foreign exchange market.
3. Explain what causes shifts in supply and demand for foreign exchange and how countries can deal with persistent disequilibrium in the foreign exchange market.
4. Explain the relationship between the foreign exchange market and the balance of payments.
5. Discuss how the forward market works.
6. Identify the components of the balance of payments accounts and measure the deficit or surplus.
7. Describe how the gold standard and the Bretton Woods system worked, and explain why neither is used today.
8. Discuss the advantages and disadvantages of floating rates.
9. Explain what exchange control is and why countries use it.

CHAPTER 21

INTERNATIONAL FINANCE

INTRODUCTION

International finance seems very unlike other topics in economics. It involves foreign exchange markets, hedgers and speculators, floating rates and gold hoarders, balance of payments deficits and surpluses, the ups and downs of the U.S. dollar, and dealing under the table by international banks to affect currency prices. In fact, the foreign exchange market is really very similar to other markets.

The preceding chapter described international trade in goods and services, but not exchange of currencies or financial assets. One important difference that distinguishes trade *within* nations from trade *between* nations is that people in different countries use different currencies. To pay for goods purchased abroad, a buyer must acquire foreign currency. It is relatively easy for U.S. citizens to purchase foreign currency, but obtaining foreign exchange is more difficult in many other countries.

This chapter looks at the market for currencies and what determines the price of one currency in terms of another (the exchange rate). It also describes the accounting statement for the foreign sector—the balance of payments—and its links to the domestic economy. Finally, we will examine different kinds of international monetary systems to see how they work and how they affect trade between countries.

THE MARKET FOR FOREIGN EXCHANGE

The network of banks and financial institutions through which buyers and sellers exchange national currencies is called the **foreign exchange market**. The foreign exchange market works much like the market for wheat, apples, or skateboards. There is a supply curve, a demand curve, and an equilibrium price and quantity. There are also conditions that are held constant (*ceteris paribus* conditions). When these conditions change, the curves shift and the equilibrium price and quantity change.

foreign exchange market
The network of banks and financial institutions through which buyers and sellers exchange national currencies.

Supply and Demand for Foreign Exchange

Figure 1 represents the foreign exchange market as it appears to U.S. buyers and sellers. In this figure, foreign currencies are represented by the German mark (DM). The price of foreign exchange is measured in dollars.[1] Citizens of other countries supply foreign exchange in order to buy U.S. exports, to travel or invest in the United States, or to purchase U.S. services or assets. U.S. citizens demand foreign exchange in order to import foreign goods and services (including traveling abroad) and to invest in foreign assets.

In Figure 1, the equilibrium price of the mark is 50¢, and the equilibrium quantity is 100 million. At a price of 70¢ per mark (equivalent to 1.4 marks per dollar), there would be a surplus of foreign exchange of 60 million marks. Quantity supplied is 130 million marks, and quantity demanded is only 70 million. At 30¢ per mark (equivalent to 3.3 marks per dollar), there would be a shortage of foreign exchange of 60 million marks (130 million marks demanded less 70 million marks supplied).

Shifts in Supply and Demand

Demand for foreign exchange will increase if something causes U.S. citizens to want to import more foreign goods and services or to invest more abroad. The supply of foreign exchange will increase if foreigners want to buy more U.S. goods and services or invest more in the United States. Recall from Chapter 3 that demand curves shift when the *ceteris paribus* conditions change. Some of those demand shifters, including changes in tastes, population, and income, apply here. Others work a little differently because the foreign exchange market is a macroeconomic market.

The price of a good is affected by changes in the prices of related goods. For example, demand for coffee is affected by the price of tea. In the foreign exchange market, it is aggregate rather than individual prices that matter. Aggregate price changes that can affect foreign exchange are

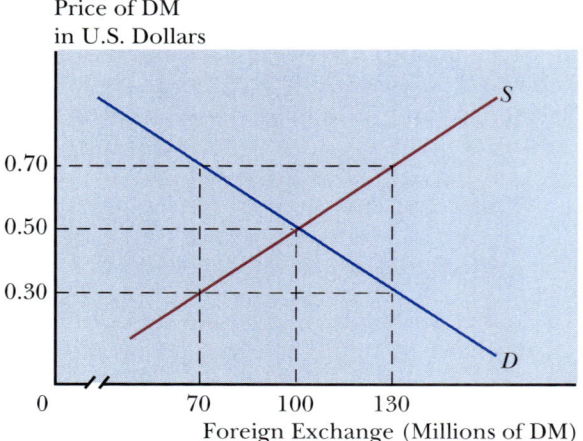

FIGURE 1
THE FOREIGN EXCHANGE MARKET
The foreign exchange market shows the supply of foreign exchange (German marks) from abroad, the demand for foreign exchange by U.S. citizens, and the equilibrium price (50¢ per mark) and quantity (100 million marks).

1. This market can also be represented as the supply and demand for U.S. dollars, but we will focus on the U.S. market for other countries' currencies.

changes in the price level in the United States relative to the price level abroad or changes in the prices of U.S. exports in general relative to prices of foreign goods. Note that the price on the vertical axis in Figure 1 is the price of foreign exchange. Changes in other prices, including the domestic price level, can shift the supply and demand curves for foreign exchange. If the U.S. price level rises more than foreign price levels, imports become cheaper relative to domestic goods, and Americans will want to buy more imported goods. Rising domestic prices shift the U.S. demand curve for foreign exchange rightward. U.S. citizens demand more foreign exchange to buy more imported goods. At the same time, the U.S. supply curve for foreign exchange shifts to the left because foreigners want to buy fewer American exports at higher prices. In fact, economists who forecast changes in exchange rates find that changes in relative price levels are the most significant determinant.[2]

Changes in relative interest rates also shift demand for foreign exchange. If interest rates are higher abroad, Americans will demand more foreign exchange to buy foreign financial assets, such as bonds or bank deposits. From 1981 to 1985, interest rates in the United States were higher than in most other countries, attracting an inflow of foreign capital. This increased supply of foreign exchange drove the price of foreign currencies down, or the price of the dollar up. As U.S. interest rates fell after 1985, the price of the dollar also fell (that is, the prices of marks, yen, and pounds began to rise).

Another source of shifts in demand for foreign exchange is changes in government restrictions on trade, such as tariffs, quotas, and nontariff barriers. These commercial policy tools are often used intentionally to shift the demand for foreign exchange, either to change the currency price or to "cure" a shortage of foreign exchange (balance of payments

SOURCES OF SHIFTS IN SUPPLY AND DEMAND FOR FOREIGN EXCHANGE

Changes in:
- relative price levels,
- relative incomes,
- relative interest rates,
- tastes and preferences,
- population,
- technology,
- input cost and availability,
- tariffs, quotas, and nontariff barriers,
- export subsidies.

---

2. The theory that changes in exchange rates result primarily from changes in countries' relative price levels is called purchasing power parity. Much attention was given to using price level changes to predict exchange rates in the 1970s and 1980s under floating exchange rates. Most studies indicate that purchasing power parity explains long-run exchange rate changes well but not short-run variations.

deficit). Export subsidies and promotions encourage foreign purchases and shift the supply of foreign exchange to the right. Finally, demand for foreign exchange shifts when there are changes in technology or input costs, which can change demand for foreign inputs or foreign products.

The same kinds of factors that shift one nation's demand for foreign exchange also operate to shift other countries' supply of foreign exchange. Changes in a country's relative price level or income, tastes, population, technology, interest rates, and tariffs and quotas all affect the supply of foreign exchange from other countries.

UNIQUE FEATURES OF THE FOREIGN EXCHANGE MARKET

The foreign exchange market has several unique features. First, the operations of this market have important macroeconomic implications. What happens in the market for foreign exchange affects (and is affected by) interest rates, output, and price levels. Second, governments are often heavily involved in setting the price, often in an attempt to limit its fluctuations. Third, a well-developed forward market exists for foreign exchange, where people make contracts for future deliveries of currency at a fixed price. Finally, the foreign exchange market sometimes suffers from persistent disequilibrium.

MACROECONOMIC IMPLICATIONS. U.S. exports and imports, which are heavily influenced by changes in exchange rates, each constitute about 10–11 percent of GNP. In addition, the foreign exchange market supports some large transactions in financial assets, such as stocks and bonds. Exports, imports, and capital transactions affect the domestic economy in many ways. A rise in exports can increase output, but expanding output puts upward pressure on the price level. Rising imports can reduce domestic output but will also reduce inflationary pressures. An inflow of foreign capital can drive up interest rates, the money supply, and prices. The opposite is true for a capital outflow. Thus, any macroeconomic model of the U.S. economy must incorporate the foreign sector if it is to predict output, employment, prices, and interest rates accurately.

Domestic events also affect exports, imports, and trade in capital assets. Changes in output, prices, and interest rates spill over into the foreign sector. Rising output means rising income, some of which will be spent on more imports. A fall in output and income will reduce imports, as it did in the 1981–1982 recession. Rising U.S. prices (relative to foreign prices) encourage U.S. citizens and foreigners to substitute cheaper goods made in other countries for more expensive American products. When the price level rises faster in the United States than abroad, exports fall and imports rise. Falling prices, or prices rising more slowly than in the rest of the world, stimulate exports and discourage imports. Higher interest rates attract capital from abroad, but lower interest rates encourage U.S. capital owners to try to earn a higher return in other countries. All these changes shift the supply and demand for foreign exchange, and thus change currency prices under the present floating exchange rate system.

GOVERNMENT INTERVENTION. Governments have always been heavily involved in the market for their own currencies. Even with floating rates, governments don't always allow the market to completely determine the prices of their currencies. A government may want to keep the price of its currency from falling because of national pride or because of the effect on the terms of trade.[3] Alternatively, a government may want to keep the price of the currency from rising too high because such an increase would make it more difficult for the country's exporters to compete and easier for imports to undersell domestic goods. In small countries where foreign trade is a large part of total economic activity, monetary authorities may be concerned about the effects of changes in the currency's price on the volume of the country's monetary reserves and the money supply. Finally, a government may want to keep the price of the currency stable in order to encourage trade and foreign investment by minimizing risk and uncertainty.

Governments set and maintain prices in other markets, including minimum wages, farm price supports, and rent controls. In these markets, the government usually sets either a floor price or a ceiling price. In the market for foreign exchange, governments historically have set both a floor and a ceiling.

THE FORWARD MARKET. Another special feature of the foreign exchange market is a well-developed **forward market**, in which contracts are made for future delivery of specific amounts of currency at a specified price. Forward (or futures) markets also exist in other goods and services. Probably the best-known forward market is the commodities market, where contracts for the future delivery of corn, wheat, pork bellies, copper, tin, gold, and other metals and agricultural goods are traded.

Traders who try to reduce their risk by buying or selling contracts for future delivery are called **hedgers**. Those who are willing to assume risk in return for the chance of a profit are called **speculators**. Let's look at a simple illustration of how hedgers and speculators interact in the foreign exchange market. Suppose a Honda dealer in the United States receives a shipment of Hondas from Japan. The dollar cost of the shipment is $100,000, but the contract calls for payment in six months in yen. The yen is trading for 150 yen per U.S. dollar, so the dealer owes 15 million yen. What the dealer needs in six months is not $100,000, but however many dollars it takes at that time to buy 15 million yen. Suppose the dealer thinks the price of a dollar in six months will be only 120 yen. Then the payment will cost the dealer more dollars—$125,000, to be precise. There goes the profit! If the dealer can find someone now who will guarantee a reasonably attractive price, say 145 yen to the dollar, that will eliminate the exchange risk. The dealer can concentrate on the business of selling cars and motorcycles.

What about the opposite situation—that of the speculator? Chances are the speculator is a large commercial bank, with many forward transactions in many directions. There is probably some Japanese firm in need of dollars that can be matched with the U.S. car dealer's need for yen.

forward market
The market in which contracts are made for future delivery of specific amounts of currency at a specified price.

hedgers
People who try to reduce their risk by buying or selling contracts in the forward market for currency.

speculators
People who assume risk in the forward market for currency in return for the chance of a profit.

---

3. If the price of U.S. currency falls, then Americans have to pay more U.S. dollars (and therefore more U.S. goods) for foreign goods. Giving up more U.S. goods per unit of foreign good makes U.S. consumers worse off. The ratio of U.S. goods exchanged to foreign goods received is called the gross barter terms of trade.

Some speculators are gambling on changes in currency prices. Perhaps the speculator who offered the car dealer 145 yen per dollar expects the price of yen to go to 160 yen per dollar. If the dealer can buy dollars at 145 yen per dollar and sell them at 160, there will be a profit of 15 yen on each dollar bought and sold.

The forward market in foreign exchange has been around for a long time. Since 1973, when most countries adopted floating exchange rates, the forward market has played an important role in encouraging foreign exchange by reducing risk.

PERSISTENT DISEQUILIBRIUM. If the price of currency is set by the government, it may not be a market-clearing price. If it isn't, there will be a persistent disequilibrium, that is, constant surpluses or shortages of foreign exchange. This situation is shown for the United States in Figure 2. The market shows a shortage of foreign exchange because the price of 40¢ per mark is too low for equilibrium. The quantity of marks demanded exceeds the quantity supplied by 50 million marks.

One way to deal with this problem is to change the price of the currency. Another way is to try to shift supply or demand for foreign exchange in order to make the curves intersect at the official price. A third possibility is for the government to ration foreign exchange. Finally, if the government has some foreign exchange reserves, it may draw on those reserves to meet the shortage, hoping that the shortage will eventually disappear of its own accord.

A shortage of foreign exchange is equivalent to a balance of payments deficit. A **balance of payments deficit** is an excess of a country's foreign spending over its foreign earnings for a given year. In Figure 2, that difference amounts to 50 million marks. (At 2 marks per dollar, 50 million marks translates into $25 million.) A nation can instead have a balance of payments surplus (foreign earnings exceed foreign spending) or an equilibrium in foreign exchange (inflows and outflows are equal). Before exploring the various ways of dealing with disequilibrium, it would be helpful to know a little more about how such surpluses and deficits are measured. The source of that information is the balance of payments.

balance of payments deficit
An excess of a country's foreign spending over its foreign earnings for a given year.

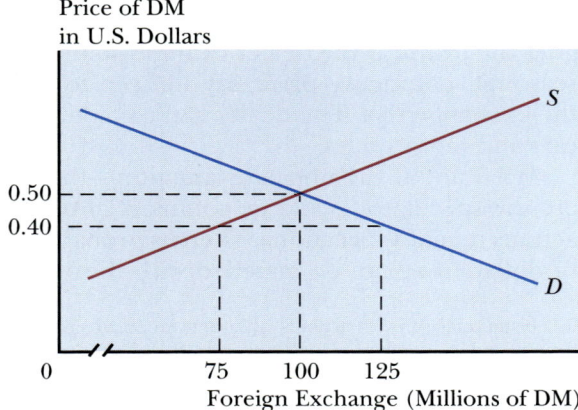

**FIGURE 2
DISEQUILIBRIUM IN THE FOREIGN EXCHANGE MARKET**
At 40¢ per mark, the quantity of foreign exchange demanded exceeds the quantity of foreign exchange supplied by 50 million marks. This gap between supply and demand corresponds to a balance of payments deficit.

Chapter 21 International Finance

THE BALANCE OF PAYMENTS

The yearly summary of the transactions between residents of one country and residents of the rest of the world is that country's balance of payments. The **balance of payments** is an income statement—a summary of the flows of goods, services, and assets in and out of a country in a given year.

The balance of payments was a matter of great concern to the United States from 1945 to 1973. During that period, there was a fixed rate of exchange for the dollar, or a currency price set and maintained by the U.S. government. Every time the U.S. balance of payments was in deficit (which was most of the time), U.S. reserves fell, putting greater downward pressure on the price of the dollar. Since 1973, the balance of payments has been less important. However, it still provides several kinds of useful information. Table 1 presents a simplified summary of the U.S. balance of payments for 1990.

The pluses and minuses in the table have important meanings. A transaction that gives rise to a payment to the United States or a claim to future payment is entered with a plus sign. A transaction resulting in a payment by the United States or a claim for future payment is entered with a minus sign.

balance of payments An annual summary of the transactions between residents of one country and residents of the rest of the world.

TABLE 1
U.S. BALANCE OF PAYMENTS, 1990
(MILLIONS OF DOLLARS)

CURRENT ACCOUNT			
Merchandise exports	+389,286		
Service exports	+130,623		
Merchandise imports		−497,966	
Service imports		−107,699	
Investment income (net)	+7,533		
Unilateral transfers		−21,073	
Balance on current account			−99,296
CAPITAL ACCOUNT			
Changes in foreign private assets in the United States	+56,767		
Changes in U.S. private assets abroad		−62,063	
Changes in government assets other than reserves (net)		−33,749	
Balance on capital account			+28,453
STATISTICAL DISCREPANCY			+73,002
Overall balance			−2,159
SETTLEMENT ACCOUNT			
Changes in U.S. reserve assets	+9,151		
Changes in foreign official holdings of dollars	+47,516		
Balance in settlement account			+56,667

Source: Adapted from U.S. Department of Commerce, *Survey of Current Business* (Washington, DC: U.S. Government Printing Office, March 1991).

COMPONENT ACCOUNTS

The balance of payments provides a lot of useful information. The sum of merchandise and service exports and imports (the balance of trade) indicates how competitive U.S. exports are compared to earlier years. The deficit in the balance of trade in the last decade has been a matter of great concern to policy makers. The buzzword "competitiveness" reflects concern for the big gap between U.S. exports and imports.

The current account, which adds investment income and a few other items to the balance of trade, is roughly equivalent to the part of the national income accounts called net foreign investment. The **current account** is the part of the balance of payments that summarizes transactions in currently produced goods and services, including merchandise, services, investment income, and several smaller items. Note that in 1990 the United States had a large deficit for this account, reflecting an excess of imports over exports. From 1960 to 1971, the United States regularly had a surplus on this account. Prior to the 1980s, the largest deficits in the current account were $14 billion in 1977 and $15 billion in 1978. After some small surpluses in 1980 and 1981, the deficit in the current account reappeared and grew rapidly from $9 billion in 1982 to $46 billion in 1983, $117 billion in 1985, and $161 billion in 1987. These figures set off a wave of alarm about loss of U.S. competitiveness with foreign products. Part of the reason for the current account deficit, however, was the high price of the dollar. The price of the dollar was bid up in foreign exchange markets by a demand for dollars to invest in the United States. The value of the dollar began to fall, and, after a lag, there was some decline in the current account deficit beginning in 1988. The current account is linked to the capital account through changes in the market for the U.S. dollar. In 1990, the deficit fell to $99 billion, a decline of 38.5 percent from the 1987 high.

The **capital account** is the part of the balance of payments that summarizes purchases and sales of financial assets, such as bonds, short-term debts, bank deposits, stocks, and foreign plants. This category showed a surplus in 1990, although the surplus was even larger a few years earlier when high U.S. interest rates attracted foreign capital. The figure of $57 billion in foreign private investment in the United States is enormous compared to past experience. The outflow of private U.S. investment of $62 billion is small compared to levels of investment abroad in previous years. This pattern of a large net inflow of foreign private capital has existed only in the last few years.

The category of statistical discrepancy is often rather large. The **statistical discrepancy** is the part of the balance of payments that reflects unrecorded transactions (such as workers' remittances, smuggling, and other illegal activities) and inaccurate estimates of spending by U.S. tourists abroad or by foreign tourists in the United States. There is a good reason for this entry. Balance of payments accountants do not have perfect information. When the discrepancy is large, as it was in the 1980s, it is believed to consist mainly of unrecorded bank deposits. Thus, a negative statistical discrepancy suggests additional (unrecorded) capital inflows.

SURPLUSES, DEFICITS, AND SETTLEMENT ACCOUNT

The sum of the current account, the capital account, and the statistical discrepancy is the surplus or deficit in the balance of payments. In 1990,

---

current account
The part of the balance of payments that summarizes transactions in currently produced goods and services.

capital account
The part of the balance of payments that summarizes purchases and sales of financial assets.

statistical discrepancy
The part of the balance of payments that reflects unrecorded transactions and inaccurate estimates of spending by tourists.

Chapter 21   International Finance   537

there was a deficit of about $2 billion. At 1990 exchange rates, the demand for foreign exchange in the United States exceeded the supply of foreign exchange by about $2 billion. That figure is not large relative to some of the other sums in the accounts. A moderate balance in the settlement account and a corresponding moderate surplus or deficit in the other three accounts is normal even under a floating exchange rate. When the price of currency is allowed to adjust to clear the foreign exchange market, the small surplus or deficit at the end of the year reflects the fact that the market is moving toward equilibrium but hasn't arrived there. Under a fixed exchange rate, surpluses or deficits would be larger, reflecting the fact that when price is not allowed to adjust, a disequilibrium (surplus or deficit) can be large and persistent.

The **settlement account** is the part of the balance of payments that explains how a deficit or surplus was financed. In 1990, the deficit was settled by selling foreign exchange in the amount of about $2 billion. The Federal Reserve watches changes in foreign exchange reserves closely because they are a component of the monetary base and can affect the size of the U.S. money supply.

Under the present system of floating exchange rates, persistent surpluses or deficits suggest that the price of a country's currency is likely to rise or fall. Under floating rates, a market-determined rise in the price is called **appreciation**, and a market-determined fall is called **depreciation**.

Although the United States and most major industrial countries allow their currency prices to float, many other countries maintain a fixed price for their currencies. However, a floating rate can be either clean or, more commonly, dirty. A clean float means that there is no government intervention to influence the currency's price. A dirty float implies some government involvement in the market to limit fluctuations. This activity has been common in recent years.

settlement account
The part of the balance of payments that explains how a deficit or surplus was financed.

appreciation
A rise in the market price of a currency due to market forces.

depreciation
A fall in the market price of a currency due to market forces.

INTERNATIONAL MONETARY SYSTEMS

Although most industrial countries have floating rates, four different international monetary systems have been tried in the past. Two of them, exchange control and floating rates, continue to be used by most countries. Some economists and policy makers advocate a return to one of the other two systems, the gold standard or the Bretton Woods system. No discussion of international finance would be complete without considering these four alternatives.

Consider what goals an international monetary system might be designed to achieve. Many traders and bankers prefer fixed or at least stable exchange rates. Stable rates reduce much of the uncertainty and the need for hedging in international transactions, making foreign trade more like domestic trade. Another goal that has widespread support is freedom of trade and capital movement, so nations can enjoy the benefits of specialization and trade. Still another goal that many countries want is freedom in domestic monetary and fiscal policy. If the government feels a need to fight recession or contain inflation, it should be free to do so without having to worry about the effects of its policies on the balance of payments or international transactions. Finally, a satisfactory system ensures equi-

International Perspective

Tourism and the Balance of Payments

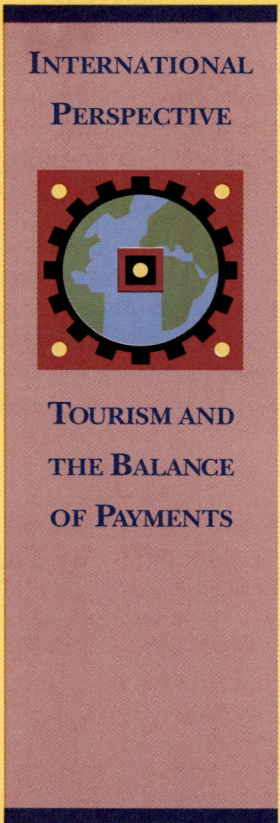

In Dyersville, Iowa, a baseball field was built for the set of the 1989 movie *Field of Dreams*. The baseball field was carved out of a cornfield owned by farmer Don Lansing. It is beautifully groomed and maintained. *Field of Dreams* was a box office smash in baseball-crazy Japan. As a result of the movie's success, a Japanese tour operator began to include Dyersville, Iowa in one of its tours. Lansing hasn't (yet) started charging tourists to see the ball park, but he took donations from the more than 8,500 Japanese who visited in the first twelve months after the tour began to include his farm. Lansing hasn't made so much that he has give up farming, but his experience is an indication that foreign tourism is becoming big business in the United States.

Until very recently, American spending on foreign tourism was greater than foreign spending on tourism in the United States. The balance of tourism trade was positive in 1989, for the first time since the U.S. Department of Commerce started keeping records on tourism. In other words, the United States became a net exporter of tourism for the first time in 1989, when 39 million foreign tourists spent $44 billion in the United States. This total was $1.2 billion more than U.S. tourists spent in foreign countries in that year. As recently as 1985, the United States had a $9 billion deficit in the tourism account. Foreign tourism continues to grow. The number of foreign tourists visiting the United States in 1995 is projected to be four times the number who came in 1985.

Most foreign tourists in the United States (65 percent in 1989), come from Mexico and Canada. However, Japanese tourists account for much of the spending surplus. Although Japanese tourists represent only 8 percent of the foreign tourists visiting the United States, they are big spenders, accounting for 19 percent of tourists' spending. It appears that Americans are buying Japanese autos and selling Japanese tourists greens fees on golf courses and shopping sprees in fancy boutiques in exchange.

Most foreign tourists in the United States follow the same pattern that Americans do when they go abroad for the first time. They go to major cities. As a result, New York, San Francisco, Los Angeles, and Miami are big draws for foreign tourists. Orlando, home of Disney World, is a close fifth. After foreign tourists have seen the cities, they tend to concentrate on the West. Perhaps all those Western movies are now paying off in tourist dollars!

Source: Evan McGlinn, "Good News for the Balance of Payments," *Forbes* (25 June 1990): 36–38.

librium in the balance of payments. The system should have some way of correcting deficits and surpluses. The various international monetary systems attain these goals in different degrees.

THE GOLD STANDARD

From the late nineteenth century until the 1930s, most industrial countries were on the gold standard. The **gold standard** was an international monetary system in which currencies were defined in terms of gold, money supplies were tied to gold, and balance of payment deficits were settled in gold. Gold served as money in most of the world for centuries. Thus, gold was a logical choice for settling accounts between countries with different national currencies. A country on the gold standard was supposed to observe three rules:

1. To define the value of its currency in terms of gold content. Under the gold standard, the dollar price of an ounce of gold was $20.67 from 1837 to 1934, and the price of gold in British pounds was £4.25. The price of each currency in gold automatically determined the exchange rates between the two countries. The British pound was worth $4.86 ($20.67 divided by £4.25).
2. To have its money supply consist of gold or be tied to the gold stock in some fixed ratio. For example, the ratio of gold to currency in the United States was 1:4 in the nineteenth century. The nation's supply of currency could not exceed four times its gold stock. The money supply could be less than the maximum, however.
3. To require its central bank or monetary authority to buy gold from anyone or to sell gold to anyone at the official price.

CORRECTING DEFICITS AND SURPLUSES. These rules, if followed, automatically corrected deficits and surpluses in the balance of payments. When there was a deficit (surplus of U.S. dollars offered for foreign exchange), the price of foreign exchange would tend to rise. As the dollar price of foreign exchange started to rise, U.S. citizens would find that they could get more pounds or francs per dollar by exchanging their dollars for gold at the Fed, shipping the gold abroad, and exchanging it there for pounds or francs. As gold flowed out of the country, the U.S. money supply would shrink, and prices and output would fall.

When prices fall in the United States, exports rise and imports fall. There is a shift in demand and supply for foreign exchange. Foreigners supply more of their currencies to buy more of relatively cheaper U.S. exports. At the same time, U.S. citizens demand less foreign exchange because they want to buy less of other countries' relatively more expensive products. Also, as U.S. output and national income fall, Americans buy less of everything, including imports.

Figure 3 shows these effects. Again, German marks (DM) represent all foreign currencies. The official price of the mark is 40¢, and the cost of shipping 1 mark's worth of gold is 5¢. In a free market, the equilibrium price of the mark would be 50¢. Because the United States is on the gold standard, the price of foreign exchange cannot rise above the official price plus the cost of shipping the gold to Germany. Thus, at the maxi-

> **gold standard**
> An international monetary system in which currencies were defined in terms of gold, money supplies were tied to gold, and balance of payment deficits were settled in gold.

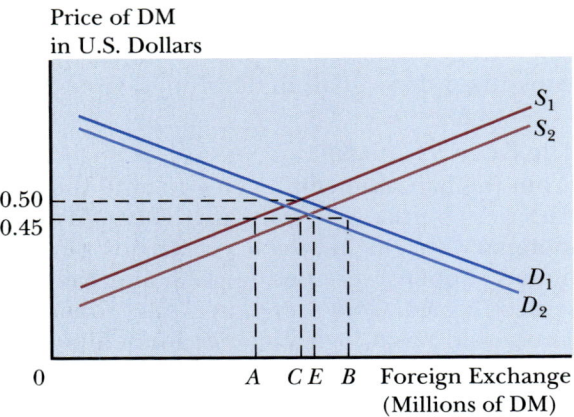

FIGURE 3
AUTOMATIC ADJUSTMENT UNDER THE GOLD STANDARD
At 45¢ per mark, gold flows out of the country to cover the deficit $B - A$. The gold outflow shrinks the money supply, reducing income and prices. Lower income and prices reduce demand for imports (from D_1 to D_2) and increase the supply of foreign currency to buy U.S. exports (from S_1 to S_2). The deficit shrinks from $B - A$ to $E - C$.

mum price of 45¢, amount $B - A$ of gold flows out of the United States. That outflow shrinks the U.S. money supply, lowering national income and the price level and shifting supply and demand for foreign exchange to S_2 and D_2. The deficit falls to $E - C$. This process of gold flows and shifts in supply and demand continues until the official price is restored and the deficit is eliminated.

The effects of the gold flow are reinforced by events in the other country into which gold is flowing. The other country's money supply expands, raising income and prices and further shifting supply and demand in the correct direction. This automatic correction of deficits and surpluses, recognized in the early eighteenth century by David Hume, is called the **specie flow mechanism**. (Specie refers to coined money with a commodity value, such as gold or silver.)

specie flow mechanism The automatic correction of deficits and surpluses in the balance of payments through the effects of gold flows on money supplies.

HISTORICAL EXPERIENCE. The gold standard worked fairly well in the late nineteenth and early twentieth centuries. Numerous discoveries of gold in California, Colorado, Alaska, Canada, and South Africa provided an adequate supply of gold for stock. The gold standard meant that governments could not control their money supplies, but nineteenth-century governments didn't pursue an active monetary policy anyway. There were few major disturbances, such as wars and revolutions, that might have caused shifts in supply and demand so great that they would have been difficult and painful to correct.

World War I marked the end of the gold standard, although some countries (including the United States) remained on it until the 1930s. The gold standard's main attractions were fixed exchange rates and automatic correction. The slow growth in the supply of gold in the twentieth century and the gold standard's restrictions on monetary policy were serious problems that could not be resolved.

The gold standard achieved three of the four goals of an international

The idea of returning to the gold standard has never died. It just went underground, surfacing as regularly as the groundhog every February. Although the Reagan administration never officially endorsed returning to the gold standard, some of Reagan's financial advisers were inclined in that direction. Jude Wanniski, in a popular book on supply side economics, *The Way the World Works*, argued very strongly for a return to the gold standard.[a]

Why does this idea keep returning? In part, it is because gold seems to offer a degree of certainty that paper money does not. When governments have gone down in revolutionary flames, new governments have usually restored faith in the currency by tying it to gold. When refugees leave countries in turmoil, the safest way to transport their wealth is in the form of gold. Fifty years after the gold standard was abandoned, some people still think of gold as the only universal money.

Gold buffs, however, are not sentimental. Most of them are hard-headed profit seekers. Many invested in gold as its price made its dramatic rise from $35 an ounce in 1967 (the official price, maintained by central banks) to over $1,000 an ounce in the mid-1970s in a free market. (Some also had the foresight to get out of gold before its price dropped sharply to under $400 an ounce in the early 1980s.) They didn't invest because of the demand for gold to use for jewelry and dental work. They invested because gold was, is, and probably always will be considered money by a substantial part of the world. The gold buffs would like gold to be *the* money of the world again in the same way it was in earlier centuries.

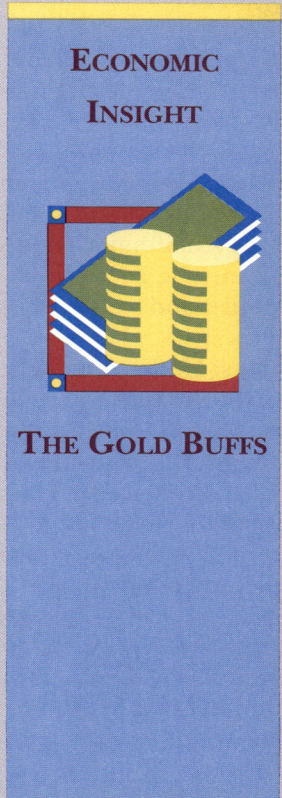

ECONOMIC INSIGHT

THE GOLD BUFFS

Gold buffs usually want to return to the gold standard because they do not trust the government to control the money supply. They would rather have the money supply determined by the impersonal forces of the marketplace and the supply of monetary gold. Give governments the freedom to print money, they argue, and political pressures will sooner or later run up the money supply and the price level.

One argument offered against returning to the gold standard is that the chief advantage of gold is also its chief disadvantage. No one can control the supply of gold. Big discoveries can cause inflation and have done so in the past. Very slow growth of the gold supply relative to growth of output and population can lead to deflation, which can be very painful. Gold buffs argue that at $400 an ounce, the supply is much greater than it was fifty years ago, because an ounce now represents much more money and because there is more incentive to mine gold at the higher price. They admit, however, that it would be necessary to fix the price of gold. Over time, that fixed rate would fail to encourage more gold mining as the cost of finding and retrieving gold increases.

The main reason why gold buffs are unlikely to get their way is that governments don't like to tie their own hands. Returning to the gold standard would mean giving up any sort of stabilization policy. No elected government is going to be willing to give up that option. The argument will go on, but as nations adapt to floating rates, the likelihood of going back on the gold standard gets smaller and smaller each year.

---

a. Jude Wanniski, *The Way the World Works* (New York: Basic Books, 1981).

monetary system: stable exchange rates, freedom of trade and capital movement, and balance of payments equilibrium. It sacrificed independent monetary and fiscal policy. If the money supply is controlled by gold flows, little discretion is left to the monetary authority to use the money supply to change the levels of output, employment, and prices. This drawback, combined with the problem of ensuring an adequate gold supply, makes a return to the gold standard very unlikely.

BRETTON WOODS SYSTEM

From 1945 to 1973, international monetary arrangements were governed by the **Bretton Woods system**, named for the small New Hampshire town where delegates from major countries met to create a new international monetary system. The Bretton Woods system had some of the characteristics of the gold standard and some of the advantages of floating rates.

Bretton Woods system
The international monetary system in effect from 1945 to 1973, based on infrequent changes in currency prices, ample reserves, and the dollar as key currency.

OPERATING RULES. Under the Bretton Woods system, a country defined a par value for its currency in terms of gold. The government was then obliged to keep its currency price within 1 percent of that par value.[4] Central banks bought and sold their countries' currencies in exchange for gold, dollars, or other foreign currencies in order to maintain the currency's price at par value.

The Bretton Woods system differed from the gold standard in that there was no connection between gold, deficits, and the money supply. Countries could pursue independent monetary policies instead of linking their money supply to their holdings of gold. Since there was no automatic correction for deficits and surpluses, a balance of payments disequilibrium might last indefinitely. Because of this problem, the designers of the Bretton Woods system created a pool of **international monetary reserves**, or funds that countries could borrow to settle deficits and repay when they ran surpluses. Reserves consisted of gold, dollars, and other currencies. These reserves were kept at a newly created institution, the International Monetary Fund (IMF). The **International Monetary Fund (IMF)** was the agency that supervised the operation of the Bretton Woods system by recording par values, consulting on devaluations and revaluations, and maintaining a pool of reserves.

international monetary reserves
The pool of gold and major currencies created under the Bretton Woods system, from which countries could borrow to settle deficits and replenish from surpluses.

International Monetary Fund (IMF)
The agency that supervised the operation of the Bretton Woods system by recording par values, consulting on devaluations and revaluations, and maintaining a pool of reserves.

What happened if a country kept running deficits and borrowing from the IMF? The pool of reserves was not intended to sustain deficits forever—just long enough for the situation to get back to normal. If a disequilibrium continued, the Bretton Woods system had a second method for coping with deficits (or surpluses). A country with a persistent deficit could change the currency's price, or the exchange rate. Thus, the Bretton Woods system did not mandate unchangeable currency prices, a central feature of the gold standard. In this respect, the Bretton Woods system was more like floating rates, except that currency prices changed infrequently by large amounts instead of frequently by small amounts.

---

4. The Bretton Woods system, like the gold standard, had both a floor and a ceiling price for each currency. Under the gold standard, the floor and ceiling prices were determined by the cost of shipping gold. Under the Bretton Woods system, the floor and ceiling prices were arbitrarily set at 1 percent above and below the official price.

Chapter 21 International Finance

WHY THE BRETTON WOODS SYSTEM FAILED. The key to the failure of Bretton Woods system lay in the difficulty of finding enough reserves. Since there was not enough gold, the next choice was the U.S. dollar, for two reasons. First, at the end of World War II, the United States had two-thirds of the world's monetary gold stock and was the only nation willing to redeem its currency in gold. Second, the United States dominated world trade as the biggest supplier and the biggest customer. Because dollars were so popular and so useful, they were even used to make payments when no U.S. citizens or firms were involved. A currency that serves as a major reserve asset and is used in transactions between third-party nations is called a **key currency**. The dollar, as the most popular key currency, joined gold as the second major form of international reserves.

key currency
A currency that serves as a major reserve asset and is used in transactions between third-party nations.

Unfortunately, since the Bretton Woods system provided for no built-in corrections, deficits became large and persistent for many countries. Demand for reserves grew rapidly. The United States obliged by creating reserves. To create reserves, the United States ran deficits. The bigger and more frequent these deficits were, the more reserves were created. But the more dollars that were outstanding, the less likely it became that the United States would be able to redeem them from its dwindling gold stock. It became more likely that a devaluation of the dollar would be necessary to correct the deficits. No one wanted to be holding dollars when they were devalued, because of the financial loss. The pending crisis came to a head in 1971, when foreigners started turning in dollars for gold. The United States was forced to suspend the redemption of dollars for gold in August 1971—an event known as the "closing of the gold window." In December 1971, the dollar was devalued by about 8 percent, raising the dollar price of gold from $35 to $38. In February 1973, the dollar was devalued again, raising the dollar price of gold to $42. After the second devaluation, the United States and its major trading partners all switched to floating rates.

The Bretton Woods system was an attempt to have the best of all possible worlds. Nations wanted stable exchange rates, independent monetary policy, and free trade. The Bretton Woods system sacrificed balance of payments equilibrium. The failure of Bretton Woods reminded policy makers that there must be some mechanism to deal with deficits. Once the nations of the world recognized that problem, Bretton Woods could not survive.

FLOATING EXCHANGE RATES

A system of floating exchange rates represents a pure market approach to foreign exchange, in which any shift in supply or demand will change the price of a currency. This system had been tried by some countries, such as Canada, but was not widely adopted until 1973. In February 1973, the United States totally abandoned its commitment to fixed exchange rates. Japan quickly followed suit and allowed the yen to float against the dollar. Within a month, the finance ministers of the European Economic Community announced that they would allow their currencies to float. Most major industrial countries have had floating exchange rates since 1973. Figure 4 shows that the price of the U.S. dollar has fluctuated a great deal under floating rates.

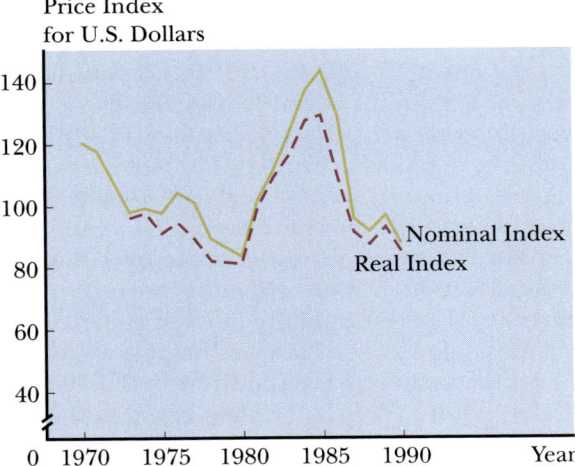

FIGURE 4
THE RISE AND FALL OF THE U.S. DOLLAR
The dollar was devalued in 1971 and again in early 1973. Beginning in 1973, the dollar has floated. Its value has fluctuated in both nominal terms (solid line) and real terms (dashed line—corrected for price level changes) against currencies of the major trading partners of the United States.

Floating exchange rates work on the basic principles of supply and demand. Floating rates support all of the suggested goals for an international monetary system except stable exchange rates. If exchange rate adjustments clear the market, then the balance of payments should always be at or near equilibrium. Thus, there will be no need to shift the curves to intersect at a fixed price or to use restrictions in order to make international payments balance.

When countries first began to use floating exchange rates, there was widespread fear that the volume of trade would shrink because exchange rates would be very unstable. Although exchange rates have been unstable, well-developed forward markets have ensured that this instability does not discourage international trade. One serious problem has been that when a currency's exchange rate falls, it often falls below its ultimate equilibrium before rising back to that equilibrium. In the interim, the exchange rate is still incorrect but it is too low instead of too high. During this time, price signals to importers, exporters, consumers, and producers are distorted. Decisions are made that would not be profit-maximizing at the correct exchange rate.

Floating rates have not resulted in balance of payments equilibrium. Why? Part of the problem is measurement, but another part reflects a basic truth about market equilibrium. Equilibrium is never where the market is, but rather the direction in which it is headed. If supply and demand shift often, the market may always be in the process of moving from one equilibrium to another. However, deficits and surpluses generally have been much smaller under floating rates than they were under fixed rates.[5] In fact, the floating rate system has worked fairly well during severe shocks (major supply and demand shifts), such as the OPEC oil price hike that created large deficits and surpluses and the 1981–1982 recession.

The floating rate system established in 1973 is not a completely free

---

5. The United States has had large deficits in its balance of trade in recent years, but those have been largely offset by inflows of foreign capital.

Chapter 21   International Finance

market in practice. Governments continue to intervene in the market, buying and selling their own currency to limit swings in the price. Countries have not allowed the market alone to determine exchange rates, but they are closer to doing so than ever in the past. Although there is still some unhappiness with floating rates, there is little pressure to return to a fixed rate system. Many government officials are reluctant to go back on the gold standard or to return to the Bretton Woods system because both would limit their flexibility of action.

EXCHANGE CONTROL

The last international monetary system, exchange control, is used by most less developed countries and sometimes by major industrial nations. **Exchange control** means that a country's government requires all earnings of foreign exchange to be turned over to it and then sells the foreign currencies to those who want to import, travel abroad, or invest in other countries.

exchange control
A system in which the government purchases all incoming foreign exchange and is the only source from which foreign exchange can be legally purchased.

Usually, a country adopts exchange control because the currency price is too high and the country doesn't want to change it. Without exchange control, the balance of payments would be in deficit. Typically, the country that uses exchange control has limited reserves and little international credit. By insisting that everyone turn in their foreign currency to the government, which then sells it, the country can make its balance of payments accounts balance.

Exchange control accomplishes three of the goals cited earlier: stable exchange rates, independent monetary and fiscal policy, and no apparent deficit in the balance of payments. However, free trade is sacrificed. In addition, black markets almost always exist. People make side deals in foreign exchange in order to bypass the government. Bribery, smuggling, and falsified reporting of earnings from exports and the cost of imports are regular events in countries with exchange control.

However, exchange control can accomplish other objectives. Often there are multiple exchange rates—different rates for buying, selling, and different uses. Suppose the government wants to encourage factory construction and discourage luxuries. It can charge a low price for foreign exchange to people who want to import machinery and a high price to those who want to buy air conditioners and yachts. Thus, the government can promote specific consumption and production goals. Also, the government can gain revenue for public purposes by buying foreign currencies at a low price and selling them at a higher price.

In some countries, such as China, exchange control involves two kinds of currency. One is used solely by foreigners, such as tourists and approved traders, and the other is used by ordinary citizens. Some stores and service institutions, such as hotels, accept only the first kind. In this way, the government can closely control the use of foreign exchange, deciding who buys imports and who gets the currency that foreigners spend in the country. With this type of exchange control, black markets are less likely, because the country's citizens are not allowed to hold exchangeable currency.

Some degree of exchange control is practiced by all but a few industrialized countries. Total or partial exchange control can coexist with ei-

International Perspective

Watching Currencies Under Floating Rates

One problem of a floating rate system is the difficulty of measuring changes in the price of one currency when others are moving around at the same time. If the price of the dollar is measured in French francs instead of Japanese yen, the picture of what is happening to the dollar may look very different.

One way to obtain a consistent measure of a currency's price is to use special drawing rights (SDRs). These drawing rights are issued by the International Monetary Fund and are only exchanged among central banks. One SDR equaled one U.S. dollar before the 1971 devaluation. This international "currency" provides a constant measuring rod. In the table titled "Currency Units per U.S. Dollar," for example, are the prices of the dollar in March 1977 and February 1991, measured in francs, yen, and SDRs. The SDR price is the most accurate reflection of changes in the price of the dollar because it is the only constant measuring rod. The dollar rose relative to the franc and fell sharply with respect to the yen. The dollar also fell when measured in SDRs. (Note from Figure 4, however, that there were some sharp ups and downs in the interim.)

Measured in SDRs, the dollar and most other currencies have had a lively market since 1973. After the first devaluation (in December 1971), the dollar was worth 0.92105 SDRs. After the second devaluation (in February 1973), the dollar dropped to 0.82895 SDRs. During the ups and downs that followed, the dollar hit a low of 0.74141 SDRs—more than 25 percent below its 1971 price. It rebounded sharply to a high of 1.035 SDRs in 1985 before dropping back to 0.7039 SDRs in February 1991.

Other currencies have seen equally dramatic shifts in prices. The table titled "Currency Units per SDR" gives the high and low values since 1975 for five major currencies. Daily rates (including forward prices) are published in most major newspapers. Long-term trends can be followed in *International Financial Statistics*, a monthly publication of the International Monetary Fund (and the source of these exchange rate figures). Importers, exporters, foreign exchange dealers, lenders, and multinational corporations all follow these figures carefully to make decisions about what to trade, when to trade, and at what price.

Currency Units per U.S. Dollar

	March 1977	February 1991	Percent Change
French franc	4.9780	5.1770	+3.9
Japanese yen	282.7000	132.0000	−53.3
SDRs	0.8639	0.7039	−18.5

Currency Units per SDR

Currency	1971 Value	Low Value (Date)	High Value (Date)
U.K. pound sterling	0.4250	0.8476 (1984)	0.4250 (1975)
French franc	5.6718	9.4022 (1984)	5.2510 (1985)
Canadian dollar	1.0809	1.6703 (1990)	1.1725 (1975)
German mark	3.5481	3.0857 (1984)	2.1378 (1991)
Japanese yen	341.7800	368.4700 (1974)	175.2000 (1987)

ther a fixed rate or a managed float, although fixed rates are more common. The major industrial countries have adopted floating rates, but the majority of nations do not have floating currencies. Most countries still maintain a fixed exchange rate or "peg" their currency to a major currency. For example, many former French colonies in Africa keep a fixed relationship between the price of their currency and the French franc. Since France is still their major trading partner, this link creates a fixed exchange rate for most of their transactions. If the price of the franc falls 10 percent relative to the dollar, the price of a currency pegged to the franc will also fall by 10 percent relative to the dollar. The pegged currency will still have the same relationship to the franc.

A combination of floating rates, managed floats, exchange control, fixed rates, and pegged rates make up the hodgepodge international monetary system of the 1990s. It will be interesting to see how the Soviet Union and the countries of Eastern Europe manage their currency prices as they move from planned economies to market systems.

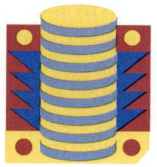

Summary

1. Unique features of the foreign exchange market are the forward market, government price setting, and effects on important macroeconomic variables.
2. U.S. demand for foreign exchange reflects demand for foreign goods, services, and financial assets. The supply of foreign exchange reflects foreigners' desire to buy U.S. exports of goods and services and/or U.S. financial assets.
3. Surpluses and shortages in the market for foreign exchange are equivalent to surpluses and deficits in the balance of payments.
4. Shifts in supply and demand for foreign exchange result from changes in relative prices, incomes, interest rates, tastes, population, technology, and input cost and availability.
5. The forward market reduces the risk connected with changing currency prices.
6. Disequilibrium often persists in the foreign exchange market. Ways in which government can deal with this disequilibrium include changing the currency's price, shifting the supply and demand curves, rationing, and drawing on reserves.
7. The balance of payments is a summary of transactions between U.S. residents and foreigners. It is divided into four accounts: the current account, the capital account, the statistical discrepancy, and the settlement account. The sum of the first three is the deficit or surplus. The settlement account explains how the deficit or surplus was financed.
8. The gold standard relied on movements of gold to settle deficits. Gold flows changed money supplies, affecting prices and income and shifting supply and demand for currency.
9. The Bretton Woods system was established in 1945 to provide some stability in exchange rates. It relied on reserves to settle deficits. It broke down because it was too dependent on a single currency—the dollar—which could not be devalued.
10. Floating exchange rates, determined in the market, have been widely used since 1973.
11. Under exchange control, all sales and purchases of foreign exchange pass through the government. Many less developed countries use exchange control. Usually, black markets in currency develop under this system.

New Terms

foreign exchange market
forward market
hedgers
speculators
balance of payments deficit
balance of payments
current account
capital account
statistical discrepancy
settlement account
appreciation
depreciation
gold standard
specie flow mechanism
Bretton Woods system
international monetary reserves
International Monetary Fund (IMF)
key currency
exchange control

QUESTIONS FOR DISCUSSION

1. Look up the balance of payments for the United States for the last year in the *Federal Reserve Bulletin*. See if you can put it into the simplified format of Table 1 and calculate the surplus or deficit. How has it changed in the last few years?

2. What might shift a country from equilibrium into a deficit in its balance of payments? How would the deficit be dealt with under each of the four international monetary systems—the gold standard, the Bretton Woods system, floating exchange rates, and exchange control?

3. Why is the forward market especially important with floating exchange rates?

4. How do changes in prices and incomes in one country affect the supply and demand for its currency? What about changes in prices and incomes in other countries?

5. Why do some people want to return to the gold standard? What drawbacks does the gold standard have?

6. If interest rates rise in the United States, what happens to the supply, demand, and price of the dollar? Why? How might this affect U.S. exports and imports of goods and services?

7. In what part of the U.S. balance of payments (Table 1) would each of the following transactions be incorporated?
   a. Sale of tractors to Poland
   b. Gift of tractors to Mexico
   c. U.S. citizen's purchase of a restaurant meal in Canada
   d. British resident's purchase of U.S. government bonds

8. How does a recession in one country affect economic conditions in another country?

9. The ways of dealing with a disequilibrium in the foreign exchange market are to change the currency's price, ration, shift the supply and demand curves into equilibrium at that price, or draw on or accumulate reserves. Identify the international monetary system that uses each of these as its primary way to deal with disequilibrium.

10. Why is there a statistical discrepancy in the balance of payments?

11. Do floating exchange rates do away with a country's need to maintain reserves?

12. How would you describe the current international monetary system? How did it evolve?

13. Stories in the press often draw attention to the fact that the balance of trade between the U.S. and Japan is in deficit. In itself, is this bilateral deficit a meaningful number?

14. How would each of the following be likely to affect supply or demand for the U.S. dollar? What should happen to its price?
   a. A recession in Japan, Canada, and Western Europe, the major trading partners of the United States
   b. A fall in the U.S. interest rate relative to that in the rest of the world
   c. More rapid inflation in the United States than in the rest of the world
   d. An export boom in U.S. movies and television shows

15. Graph the foreign exchange market for the zloty, the currency of Poland, to indicate an equilibrium price of 20¢ and an equilibrium quantity of 50 million. Is there a surplus or a shortage at prices of 40¢ and 10¢?

SUGGESTIONS FOR FURTHER READING

Melamed, Leo (ed.). *The Merits of Flexible Exchange Rates: An Anthology.* Fairfax, VA: George Mason University Press, 1988. A collection of articles by eminent economists in support of flexible exchange rates.

Pool, John Charles, and Steve Stamos. *The ABCs of International Finance.* Lexington, MA: Lexington Books, 1987. A simple, nontechnical discussion of current international finance issues, emphasizing the evolution of the international monetary system and the problems of debtor nations, including the United States.

Root, Franklin R. *International Trade and Investment*, 6th ed. Cincinnati: South-Western, 1990. An intermediate textbook on international trade and international finance.

Yeager, Leland B. *International Monetary Relations: Theory, History, and Policy.* New York: Harper & Row, 1976. A classic reference on international finance with a solid treatment of history and policy.

AFTER STUDYING THIS CHAPTER, YOU SHOULD BE ABLE TO:

1. Define:
   a. capitalism,
   b. socialism,
   c. communism,
   d. fascism.
2. Contrast socialism and capitalism.
3. Describe the major features of and the differences in the economic systems of:
   a. the Soviet Union,
   b. the People's Republic of China,
   c. Cuba,
   d. Yugoslavia,
   e. Great Britain.
4. Define:
   a. input coefficients,
   b. shadow prices,
   c. the socialist controversy,
   d. the competitive solution.
5. Discuss prospects for economic reform in China, Eastern Europe, and the Soviet Republics.
6. Identify the unique characteristics of the Japanese economy.

CHAPTER 22

COMPARATIVE ECONOMIC SYSTEMS IN THEORY AND PRACTICE

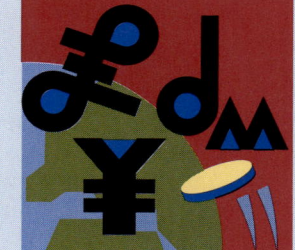

INTRODUCTION

The past few years have seen staggering and revolutionary changes in the world. Political and economic reform has been the order of the day in much of the Communist world. Indeed, many writers now use the words "formerly Communist" when referring to some of the countries of Eastern Europe and the Soviet Union. Few would have thought that on November 17, 1989, Berliners from both sides would be dancing on the Berlin Wall as it came tumbling down, while the East German guards watched. A week earlier, getting close to the east side of the wall would have probably meant death.

This chapter will examine the events of the recent past and speculate on what might occur as these economic and political changes mature. There is much uncertainty surrounding these reforms. The introduction of markets and market mechanisms means choice and uncertainty in countries where security and sameness ruled. To some individuals, this choice and uncertainty will be very unsettling.

To begin, it is important to define some basic differences in economic systems. People often discuss other economic systems without really knowing how to define such terms as capitalism, socialism, and communism. What are the key differences among these systems, and to what degree do these differences affect economic outcomes? Chapter 2 stated that all economic systems are mixed systems and that economic theory can be used to analyze any economic system. That statement was valid because the concepts of opportunity cost, the law of demand, the principle of diminishing returns, specialization, exchange, efficiency, and self-interest do not differ from country to country. Competing ideologies may respond to these concepts differently, but no ideology can eliminate their impact on economic life.

You might ask, if the economics you have learned is good for all systems, why include a chapter on comparative systems? The answer is that politics, cultures, and ideology mix with economics to create widely differing economic-political systems. These different mixes will be important as the various countries of Eastern Europe pursue reform. It is therefore necessary to examine the way economics works in different political and historical settings.

To introduce the subject of comparative economics, we will begin with an attempt to define ideological systems. We will then examine some of the different forms of communism as well as recent changes in a number of countries. Next, we will present a decision-making approach to the analysis of differing systems and discuss advantages and disadvantages of economic planning. Finally, we will examine reform movements in China and the Soviet Union and outline the unique features of the Japanese form of capitalism.

IDEOLOGIES

Chapter 2 divided economic systems into three major groups, labeled traditional, planned, and market. The field of comparative economics subdivides the last two categories, which include all modern industrial economies, in order to classify economies more precisely. A very common approach, and perhaps the oldest, is to classify economic systems according to two criteria: the underlying political philosophy, and the ownership of the factors of production. This might be called the *isms* approach because it concentrates on four major political philosophies: capitalism, socialism, communism, and fascism.

Even this approach oversimplifies the diversity that exists in economic systems. There are numerous economic systems in the world. The term *capitalism* is often applied to the economic systems found in Western democracies, but there are significant differences among economic institutions in the United States, Great Britain, France, and Sweden. Similarly, the economic systems in Eastern Europe and the Soviet Union were labeled communist before the reforms began, but there were important differences in the institutions of the Soviet Union, Yugoslavia, and Romania. This complexity makes it difficult to separate the critical elements of the four basic economic systems. Economists must identify the differences in institutions and then determine if these differences are the reasons for differing economic behavior. The most important factor distinguishing the four *isms* is in the ownership of the factors of production.

CAPITALISM

capitalism
An economic system characterized by private ownership of the factors of production by individuals or groups of individuals.

Capitalism is an economic system characterized by private ownership of the factors of production by individuals or groups of individuals. In pure capitalism, these individuals would be free to use their property as they see fit. Any limitations on the use of the property diminish its value to the owner. Private property holders are at the center of the decision-making process in capitalism.

A system based on private ownership is one in which individuals maximize their own well-being, in terms of either profit or utility. The term *capitalism* is interpreted very broadly to allow for a great deal of government intervention, as long as the primacy of private ownership is retained. It is therefore possible for systems as divergent as the U.S. economy and the British economy to be labeled capitalist.

SOCIALISM

Under a system of **socialism**, the nonhuman means of production are owned by society or the state. Socialism has its theoretical roots in the work of Marx and its real-world roots in various twentieth-century revolutions and their leaders. Socialism shifts the decision-making authority from individual entrepreneurs to a central authority. This central authority makes the major economic decisions. Utopian socialists see this central authority as promoting the "common good," usually greater equality and/or economic development. Critics of socialism point out that this authority may develop into a centralist, personal dictatorship, such as that of Stalin in the Soviet Union or Nicolae Ceausescu in Romania. Fidel Castro of Cuba is a living example of this tendency.

Like capitalism, socialism comes in many forms. There is utopian socialism, such as the Fourier movement in the United States in the early to mid-nineteenth century. Utopian socialists established communes with shared possessions and cooperative labor. Other variations, such as the Social Democratic parties in Western Europe, have become forceful political movements. For instance, François Mitterrand, a socialist, was elected president of France in 1981 and 1988. Because the term *socialism* is used to describe a great variety of people and ideas, it is almost meaningless to label someone a socialist or a set of institutions socialistic.

socialism
An economic system in which the nonhuman means of production are owned by society or the state.

COMMUNISM

To Karl Marx, **communism** was the final stage of the progression from capitalism, with socialism representing the middle stage. Under communism, Marx foresaw the end of scarcity, the end of conflict among the classes, and the creation of a new social order. An ideal member of this new order would no longer be the self-interested individual on which most economic analysis is based. The true communist would put the interest of the larger community above personal self-interest. In the final stage, individuals would receive goods and services according to their needs, and the state would wither away until all it did was administer the economy. The organizational structure that Marx foresaw under communism is not at all clear. Presumably everyone would contribute labor in exchange for goods and services needed. One major problem is how those needs would be defined and determined. A second problem is the motivation that would drive the system and create incentives. In the absence of self-interest, the motivation would have to lie in the development of this new economic order.

communism
The final stage in the theory of Karl Marx, in which the state has withered away and economic goods are equally distributed.

FASCISM

In the countries that have practiced **fascism** (which include Spain, Portugal, Germany, and Italy), monopoly capitalism and private property were combined with a strong authoritarian central government headed

fascism
An economic system that combines monopoly, capitalism, private property, and a strong authoritarian central government.

Political-legal developments in China, Hong Kong, and Taiwan and economic comparisons among them demonstrate much about capitalism and socialism. The varying levels of economic development invite comparison because the areas are similar in many ways, including culture. The essential differences are political and economic.

In 1997, the 100-year lease that the British have for Hong Kong expires, and the territory reverts to Chinese rule. This change is expected to have a profound effect on Hong Kong. There are virtually no government impediments to doing business in Hong Kong. A corporation can be started for a fee of only $250, and there are no reporting requirements. Hong Kong has no currency exchange controls, no tariffs, and no quotas. The entrepreneurs in this prosperous capitalist state are casting a wary eye on 1997 and the arrival of the Communist Chinese. In 1997, the country will go from almost pure *laissez-faire* capitalism to communist rule. Many of Hong Kong's successful entrepreneurs are looking for a haven in Taiwan, Singapore, or other parts of Southeast Asia. Some have moved as far away as Jamaica.

INTERNATIONAL PERSPECTIVE

CHINA, HONG KONG, AND TAIWAN

Taiwan provides another interesting contrast to mainland China. Chinese nationalists who fled mainland China during the Communist revolution in 1949 went to Taiwan. There they dominated the native Taiwanese majority and established a market-directed economy. The People's Republic of China insists that Taiwan is a province of China and that reunification is inevitable. The Taiwanese insist that they must remain independent. A comparison of China and Taiwan seems to indicate that economic development is faster under capitalism than under socialism. In 1950, the socialistic People's Republic and capitalistic Taiwan had basically the same level of development. Today, the average income in Taiwan is about $3,000 per year, more than ten times the per capita income in China. Perhaps this fact is understood in China, where elements of market capitalism are being introduced in the disguise of economic reform.

by a charismatic dictator. This combination promoted monopoly and then imposed "national interests" on that monopoly structure. Fascism lacks both the large degree of personal freedom that is a characteristic of free-enterprise capitalism and the egalitarian ideals of socialism and communism.

USE OF THE *ISMS* APPROACH

The drawback of using the *isms* approach to compare economic systems is that it is too simplistic and does not include many of the keys to determining control over resources. The *isms* approach tends to equate ownership with control and control with decision-making power over the factors of production. This connection is becoming less clear over time. For example, in the Soviet Union, before the reform movement, the leaders of the government did not own much of anything, yet they clearly controlled the system. In the United States, many people own land, but they cannot use it as they please because of zoning or environmental regulations.

All economies are mixed in varying degrees. That is, they contain elements of socialism (or planning) and elements of capitalism (or markets). Therefore, the *isms* approach, though often used in political-economic classification schemes (and political rhetoric), has serious limitations. In fact, applying this classification scheme would be likely to produce just two sets of systems, capitalism and socialism. Yet no serious analyst would consider a scheme that places the United States, France, and Great Britain in one category to be very meaningful. However, capitalism and socialism, like pure competition and monopoly, offer theoretical models to aid in understanding real-world mixed systems.

The *isms* approach remains popular because it is the one almost always used by politicians and journalists. A statement made in 1990 by a member of the Leningrad Communist Party is typical. Pyotr S. Filipov is quoted as saying: "We must hurry away from Marxism-Leninism, through Socialism, to Reaganism."[1] What does this mean and how do the Soviets expect to accomplish such a reform? In this chapter we will try to address these issues so you can give an informed answer to such a question.

CONTRASTING CAPITALISM AND SOCIALISM

Recognizing that there is no such thing as a pure system, we can construct a continuum and attempt to place countries on it. Figure 1 presents such a continuum. On one end is pure, market-directed capitalism, and on the other end is pure, centrally planned socialism. (The Soviet Union and the countries of Eastern Europe have been omitted from Figure 1 because it is unclear what the outcome will be in these reforming nations.) Capitalism and socialism are the two polar extremes of economic systems. Contrasting the distinguishing features of these two types of economic systems will help in evaluating real-world systems.

Private property rights are an important feature of capitalism because they create incentives and make exchange possible. In capitalism, the property rights to resources and factors of production, including labor, are vested with the individual. Workers are free to move about, but they

---

1. *National Review* (29 August 1990): 11.

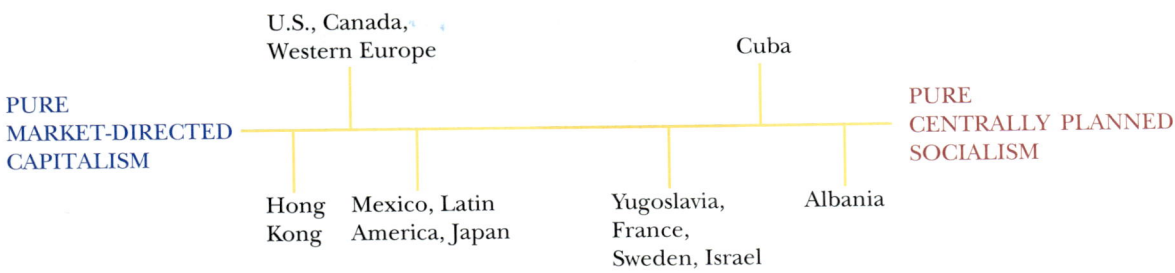

FIGURE 1
A CONTINUUM OF ECONOMIC SYSTEMS
No country has an economic system that represents a pure type. All countries mix market and planning to some degree. It is possible to place countries along a continuum, as shown here, on the basis of their relative reliance on the market or on a plan.

are not guaranteed jobs. In socialism, the state is vested with property rights, including property rights to the individual's labor. As economic reforms proceed in the Soviet Union and Eastern Europe, property rights and who owns what are important issues in these reforms. Government officials in these countries are arguing over the ownership of resources, including a new division between public and private ownership.

Under socialism, especially in China, people are often assigned jobs in certain geographic locations and do not have the freedom to switch occupations or geographic location. The method of job assignment in the U.S. military is similar to that in most socialist states. Workers have greater job security but less freedom to choose jobs than in a market system. Investment decisions follow a similar pattern. Under capitalism, individuals seeking profits make these decisions. Under socialism, a central plan determines the level and composition of investment. Production decisions and decisions that affect the distribution of income are also made by the central planning authority under socialism. These decisions are the *what* and *for whom* questions of Chapter 2.

MARX, MARXISTS, AND MARXISM

Perhaps no other economist has had more effect on the political shaping of the world than Karl Marx, who with Friedrich Engels, published the *Communist Manifesto* in 1848. This book, along with Marx's *Das Kapital*, published in three volumes in 1867, 1885, and 1894, is the philosophical basis for a widely divergent group of economic-political systems. In recent years, almost all communist governments have claimed to be Marxist. Therefore, it is necessary to distinguish between Marx and Marxism (or Marxists).

The central ideas of Marx's economic theory are easy to outline. He believed that every society would evolve through the historical stages of tribal communism, slavery, feudalism, capitalism, socialism, and, finally, communism. The most important transition would come when capitalism decayed because of internal conflict and was succeeded by socialism. The regular cyclical ups and downs of a capitalist economy (the business cycle) would become more and more severe until capitalism finally collapsed. Marx saw the empire building of European countries in the nineteenth century as an attempt to postpone the inevitable failure of capitalism. He believed that when socialism was replaced by communism, scarcity would disappear, and workers would produce without material incentives.

Essential Differences between Capitalism and Socialism

	CAPITALISM	SOCIALISM
• Property rights	Resources are owned by individuals or groups of individuals.	Resources are owned by the state.
• Labor	Workers have a property right to their own labor. They are self-employed or work for private firms.	Workers are employed by the government and are usually not allowed to change jobs.
• Investment	Investment is determined and undertaken by entrepreneurs.	Investment is determined and undertaken by government.
• Production mix	What is produced is determined by market forces.	What is produced is determined by central plan.
• Distribution of income	Distribution of income is determined by market forces, productivity, and ownership patterns.	Distribution of income is determined by central plan.
• Incentives	Labor, management, and entrepreneurs respond to wages, prices, and profits.	Often many nonmaterial incentives are used.

The countries to which communism has spread have been those in which the level of industrialization was very low. This pattern is inconsistent with what Marx predicted. What, then, is the significance of Marx's writings?

The significance of Marx's writings lies not in the accuracy of his predictions but rather in the theoretical, philosophical, and political movements spawned by his work. Communist parties in many countries consider themselves Marxists and appeal to the writings of Marx to justify their views on various issues. In some respects, they are similar. They all condemn the "exploitation" of workers under capitalism and forbid the use of the term *profit*. Countries in which Communists are in power all claim to have full-employment economies and to have overcome the unemployment problem of capitalistic systems. There are also wide differences among Communist countries, however. Countries as diverse as China, Yugoslavia, the Soviet Union, Albania, Romania, and Cuba have all at one time or another claimed to be the true Marxists. Many of the economic reform movements in these countries still use Marxist terminology in their political statements. The significance of Marx is that he was the father of a political, as well as an economic, movement.

LEADERISMS

Socialism was Marx's intermediate stage between capitalism and communism. Under socialism, the decision-making authority shifts from individual entrepreneurs to a central authority, which Marx called the "dictatorship of the proletariat." In practice, the central authority has almost always been personified by a dominant individual. It is thus possible to view many of the offshoots of Marxism as the products of the interaction of Marxist ideas with the personalities of strong-willed leaders. Thus, for example, the Soviet economic and political reforms may have a curious result if they succeed. Gorbachev had to be a strong leader to initiate the reforms, but any success in these reforms will reduce his power. This effect became evident early in his term of office as competition for the right to lead the Soviet Union quickly developed.

LENINISM

Vladimir Lenin (1870–1924) was active in developing the Communist Party in Russia and led that country's successful Bolshevik Revolution in 1917–1918. He claimed to be a follower of Marx but developed new directions for the achievement of communism. Lenin refused to wait for the maturation of capitalism and instead developed a different model for revolution based on four essential ingredients: (1) a small, revolutionary elite, (2) economic underdevelopment (the opposite of Marx's industrialization), (3) a discontented peasantry, and (4) war against an outside force. Lenin's formula worked in Russia and in Yugoslavia, China, Vietnam, and Cuba. In fact, Lenin's formula applies to almost all cases where communism has taken root. The exceptions are those countries of Eastern Europe in which the Soviet Union imposed communism after World War II.

Lenin was the first Communist to be faced with the task of setting up an economic system after the political system was secure. **War Communism** was the economic system that Lenin imposed on Russia immediately after the Bolshevik Revolution. This system instituted rigid administrative control of the economy in an attempt to marshal the resources needed to engage in a civil war with the non-Communist White Russians. Widespread nationalization of industry took place, and all private trading was outlawed. All labor mobility was rigidly controlled, and money as an exchange mechanism almost disappeared. This period is difficult to evaluate. Some economic historians claim that Lenin instituted War Communism only because of the demands of fighting a civil war.[2]

By 1921, the economy had seriously deteriorated. Lenin responded by abandoning War Communism and instituting a program referred to as the **New Economic Policy (NEP)**. This policy was an attempt at market socialism, with planning for only the key industries in the economy. The remainder of the economy was left to respond to basic market forces. There was very rapid economic growth during this period, and the Soviet economy quickly recovered from the protracted civil war. Lenin died in 1924. In 1926, the NEP came to an end for a variety of reasons. One reason was that the move toward a market economy during NEP greatly reduced the power of the Communist Party to channel and direct the course of economic development. Many parts of the current reform in the Soviet Union resemble the NEP.

War Communism
An economic system of rigid administrative control imposed by Lenin in Russia during the civil war following the Bolshevik Revolution.

New Economic Policy (NEP)
A program that replaced War Communism in 1921 in the Soviet Union and was an attempt at market socialism.

2. Others claim Lenin instituted War Communism out of a desire to see such a system evolve as the economic application of communism. For this view, see Paul Craig Roberts, *Alienation and the Soviet Economy* (Albuquerque: University of New Mexico Press, 1971).

STALINISM

After Lenin's death, there was open dispute in the Soviet Communist Party over the direction of development. The **Great Industrialization Debate** was an open debate that took place in the Soviet Union from 1924 to 1928 concerning the correct way to industrialize the economy.[3] The left wing of the party, led by economist E. A. Preobrazhensky, argued that the country should make a concerted effort toward rapid industrialization of key sectors of the economy. This policy would be carried out by the central allocation of investment expenditures. N. I. Bukharin, who was the spokesperson for the right wing, disagreed with this position and stressed balanced growth of the economy. Bukharin argued that all sectors of the economy must grow together because they all support and feed one another.

Joseph Stalin (1879–1953) was both an observer and a participant in the debate. Stalin played one side against the other while forming a power base. At the time of Lenin's death, Stalin allied himself with the right wing of the party in order to counteract the power of Leon Trotsky and the left wing. This alliance allowed Stalin to discredit and weaken the left wing, a task he accomplished by 1927. He then turned on the right wing and, by 1928, had its leaders denounced by the party. Stalin was then in complete control, since he had purged all dissidents.[4]

The planning system that Stalin adopted was centrally directed and was set up in five-year increments. Five years was chosen since it is possible to complete most investment projects in that period. Stalin's first five-year plan was an extreme version of the left-wing industrialization proposal. Its achievement required very centralized planning, investment in heavy industry, and forced collectivization in the agricultural sector, which was expected to supply food and raw materials. Industrialization was very rapid, but the costs of this policy in human terms were great. Millions of people were purged. Many others starved to death because the peasants resisted forced centralization by destroying crops and livestock.

The Soviet Union's rigid system of central planning up to 1989 was the legacy of Stalin. Today, the term *Stalinism* is associated with a ruthless dictatorship as well as with a highly centralized planning structure. However, Stalinism is not openly practiced in any Communist country today.

Great Industrialization Debate
An open debate that took place in the Soviet Union from 1924 to 1928 concerning the correct way to industrialize the economy.

MAOISM

In China, the Communist Party came to full power in October 1949, after decades of struggle. Mao Zedong was the revolutionary leader who took command, just as Lenin's formula for communist revolutionaries had predicted. In the early years of Chinese Communism, the goal was industrialization, much as it had been in the Soviet Union. However, this policy was formulated without the help of Moscow. The Chinese Communist Party, from the very beginning, was fiercely independent of the Soviet Union.

In 1958, the Great Leap Forward was announced. The **Great Leap Forward** was a modernization plan to increase per capita income in China by 25 percent in five years. Many of the programs were ill-conceived, such

Great Leap Forward
A modernization plan that was launched in 1958 to increase per capita income in China by 25 percent in five years.

---

3. See Alexander Erlich, *Soviet Industrialization Debate, 1924–1928* (Cambridge, MA: Harvard University Press, 1960).
4. For an excellent economic history of the Soviet Union, including this period, see Alec Nove, *An Economic History of the USSR* (London: Penguin, 1975).

as the production of steel on a small scale in backyard furnaces. The result was a product of poor quality that was not useful as input to further manufacturing processes. The Great Leap Forward included the collectivization of Chinese agriculture. Mao sought to mobilize the huge underemployed population of China in collectivized agriculture. The result was disastrous. In two years, agricultural production fell by 20 percent and widespread starvation occurred. Mao was ousted from control, and a pragmatic leadership took over. With the aid of revolutionary youth, Mao was able to return to power in 1966 through a political coup.

The period from 1966 through 1969, called the **Cultural Revolution**, represented the high point of Mao's power. The Cultural Revolution embraced revolutionary values. Mao envisioned a completely classless society, organized as a collective operation rather than as a state enterprise, as in the Soviet Union. The motivation for the society was to be completely altruistic, embracing the concept of the "new man" who responds to social rather than to material incentives. The Cultural Revolution almost destroyed the educational system. Professors were sent to work in communes and factories. Education came to a standstill during this period. The Cultural Revolution was also an economic disaster. As a result, in 1969, Mao turned more authority over to Chou En-Lai, who tempered some of the more drastic policies.

The Chinese economy has changed often and in different directions. Not enough information is available to evaluate the success of Maoism in promoting economic development. Several economists who have traveled to China give strikingly different reports. For example, John Gurley argues that China made great strides and has eradicated poverty, but James Tobin claims that there was not much economic progress under Mao.[5] He argues that almost any system that brought peace to the country would have achieved some economic success, since China was torn by revolution and war for several decades before 1949.

After Mao's death in 1976, the new leaders pursued a development strategy that was often openly hostile to Mao's ideas. They attacked the "Gang of Four," Mao's widow and three other radicals. In attacking the Gang of Four, the leaders attacked the ideas of the Cultural Revolution and, in fact, Mao himself, although they were careful not to name Mao. *Newsweek* reported that Chinese officials argued that "Chairman Mao was deceived by the Gang of Four."[6] The Gang of Four were tried and convicted in 1981.

CASTROISM

Fidel Castro, who overthrew the Batista government in Cuba in 1958, learned the lesson of Lenin's formula for revolution very well. He led a small group of committed revolutionaries in an country with a large, discontented peasant class and an underdeveloped economy. The United States served as an outside enemy that he used to unify the diverse elements within Cuba. In many ways, the Cuban system resembles early Chi-

Cultural Revolution
The high point of Mao's power in China, characterized by a radical restructuring of the economy from 1966 through 1969.

---

5. John Gurley, "Maoist Economic Development," and James Tobin, "The Economy of China: A Tourist's View," in Edwin Mansfield, *Economics: Readings, Issues, and Cases* (New York: W. W. Norton, 1977).
6. *Newsweek* (30 October 1978): 50.

nese communism. For example, Castro has placed heavy emphasis on creating a "new man."[7] The goal was to remove all social inequities and motivate workers with moral incentives rather than with material ones. Castro's vision is very close to Marx's view of the final stage of communism. His policy was in large part the work of Che Guevara. The Soviets, who were financially underwriting the Cuban economy, were skeptical of the plan.

Rather than attempt to industrialize the Cuban economy rapidly, Castro concentrated on agriculture and sought to exploit the export potential of the sugar cane industry. This policy required the transfer of labor from cities to rural areas, the exact opposite of what occurred under European Communist regimes. The Cuban economy remains heavily reliant on agriculture. Planning in Cuba is carried out by the System of Budgetary Finance, a centralized planning system that views the economy as a single firm to be rigidly controlled by the central authority.

Castro faces severe problems. The Cuban economy had been receiving more than $5 billion annually in subsidies from the Soviet Union. With reform in the Soviet Union, these subsidies were phased out beginning in 1991. When the Soviet aid declined, the Cuban GNP fell 30 percent. Castro responded by sending 100,000 "volunteers" into the countryside to plant and harvest crops. He called on Cubans to tighten their belts and create a new agricultural class. This move created unrest among the youth, but they appear too apathetic or frightened to protest. Many experts predict that Castro will be the next Communist leader to be deposed. In fact, a group of Cuban-Americans in Miami has drafted a constitution and is planning economic programs for a post-Castro Cuba. The group, called The Cuban American National Foundation, is headed by Jorge Mas Canosa, a successful Florida businessman.[8]

RETREAT FROM SOCIALISM: THATCHERISM

Just as strong leaders have had a significant influence on socialism, some leaders have left a mark on capitalism. Margaret Thatcher led a retreat from socialism through significant reprivatization of the British economy. She served the longest continuous term as British Prime Minister in the twentieth century. In December 1990, Thatcher stepped down as Prime Minister when she was challenged for the leadership of the Conservative Party. Thatcher was often linked with former President Reagan as a proponent of supply side economics and privatization. However, her program aimed at decreasing the size of government was far more successful than Reagan's. Thatcher reduced income taxes in order to reverse the "talent drain" of entertainers and other highly paid individuals from Britain. She convinced Parliament to pass legislation that greatly reduced the power

---

7. For a good review of Castro's Cuba, see Carmelo Mesa-Lago (ed.), *Revolutionary Change in Cuba* (Pittsburgh: University of Pittsburgh Press, 1971).
8. See "Gorbachev Will Soon Make Castro More of an Island," *Business Week*, (16 July 1990): 47; Anthony Daniels, "The Last Days of Fidel Castro," *National Review* (5 March 1990): 29–32; "Soon to Come: Capitalist Cuba", *National Review* (17 September 1990): 19–20. The Council for Inter-American Security sponsored a contest, a pool to predict when Castro will fall from power, and received 300 predictions. Former U.N. Ambassador Jeane Kirkpatrick predicted "by the end of 1991," and Texas oilman Nelson Bunker Hunt predicted October 5, 1993. See "Betting on Fidel's Fall," *Forbes* (1 October 1990): 17.

of labor unions by requiring that they poll their members before calling a strike.

Perhaps the most important element of Thatcherism was the privatization of the British economy. When she became Prime Minister in 1979, the economy was best described as one in which large governmental enterprises were deadlocked with large labor unions. (This situation was referred to as the "British Disease.") During her tenure, she reversed the trend by selling off more than $31 billion in state-owned industries to private investors. These sales included the government's share in British Gas, Rolls-Royce, British Airways, and British Petroleum. Her action and the effect it had on productivity (productivity increases have averaged over 3 percent) inspired similar privatization policies in Italy and France.

ORGANIZATION AND DECISION-MAKING APPROACH TO COMPARING ECONOMIC SYSTEMS

We have been comparing economic systems in terms of how the underlying ideology affects their organization. In many cases, a dominant personality's interpretation of that ideology shaped an entire system. Some of you may have found this an exciting and useful way to categorize the world. Others may have found it frustrating to examine individual systems, rather than developing general principles as to how different systems are organized and how they affect behavior. The first approach has been the way most economists have historically examined alternative economic systems. A second approach is to formulate organizational principles using economic theory as a coherent analytical framework.[9]

THE DECISION PROCESS: DECISION MAKERS, INCENTIVES, AND INFORMATION

To understand an economic system, it is necessary to examine the organizational setting for the production of goods and services *and* the institutional setting for the distribution of those goods and services. The important questions concern the structure of decision making in production and distribution. One such question is which individuals, and at which levels, make the major decisions concerning production and distribution. In the United States, production decisions are made at the entrepreneurial level. In the Soviet Union, these decisions until recently were made at the planning level.

Once the assignment of decision-making responsibility has been made, the next question concerns the motivation for the decision makers. Do the decision makers bear the costs of wrong decisions or reap the rewards of correct decisions? It is also necessary to determine how one person's participation in the decision-making process influences another's. Also, it is possible to change an individual's internal values. In other words, do institutions affect individuals' value systems?

Once these two aspects of the decision-making structure are determined, the informational structure of the economic system can be ana-

---

9. For a comprehensive development of this approach, see Egon Neuberger and William J. Duffy, *Comparative Economic Systems: A Decision-Making Approach* (Boston: Allyn and Bacon, 1976).

lyzed. The informational structure is the way in which individuals learn about their options so they can act on them. In the U.S. economy, prices are an important source of information. In the Soviet economy, the plan plays this role. As decision making becomes centralized, more and better information is critical because the costs of wrong decisions are so much higher. System questions are largely microeconomic in nature.

THE ENVIRONMENT

A country's environment is its social structure, physical conditions, and international situation. Some of the more critical aspects of the environment in terms of possible impact on the economic system are the level of economic development, the size of the country in area and population, the availability of natural resources within the country and from safe allies, the values of the people (religious, cultural, and so on), the political system, the size of the country relative to its near neighbors, the level of development relative to the rest of the world and relative to near neighbors, and the sphere of influence in which the country lies (American, Soviet, or Chinese, for example). These are only a few of the influences on an economic system, but they are representative of the concept of environmental influence.

ECONOMIC PERFORMANCE

The way in which an economy performs is an important evaluation measure. Economists usually focus on the performance of the gross national product (GNP) and examine growth in per capita production, stability of production (business cycles can be socially destabilizing), and equity in income distribution. These measures of performance are mostly macroeconomic in nature.

POLICY CHANGES

Some policy changes can be made within a system without changing the underlying fabric of the system. These changes consist of marginal changes in the system and its environment in order to affect performance. Policy changes can influence the system in a positive or negative way. A "good" system might develop "bad" policies that produce "bad" performance and in turn result in a negative change in the "good" system. For example, a central planning policy decision to consolidate farms into larger units or to shift from corn to wheat can increase (or reduce) productivity and efficiency. Recent policy changes in the Soviet Union and some countries in Eastern Europe affect the entire system.

INTERACTION OF SYSTEMS, ENVIRONMENT, PERFORMANCE, AND POLICY

Of course, all these organizational elements interact in a complex fashion. Using this terminology, however, can help in understanding how economic systems differ and in what ways they are similar. For example, consider a small country with the Soviet Union or the United States as a close neighbor. How would this affect the development of its economic system? Having the Soviet Union nearby had a profound effect on the countries of Eastern Europe, but the Soviet Union has pulled back, even allowing the reunification of the two Germanys in 1990. Similarly, being close to the United States has affected the trade pattern, the output mix, and the level of development in Canada, Mexico, and the Caribbean. What environmental factors caused the Industrial Revolution to spread from England to the United States but not to Russia?

How might performance influence an economic system? Performance is part of Lenin's formula: If things get bad enough, there might be a revolution. On the other hand, if economic conditions stagnate in a Communist country after a revolution, there might be a move toward capitalism or market socialism. There are many complex questions, and the organization and decision-making approach may give you a start in organizing your thoughts. This approach gives some insight into the many and varied forms of capitalism and socialism.

PLANNING

Throughout this chapter, whether we were using the *isms* approach to systems or a more structured organizational approach, we continually encountered the issue of planning. Who directs production, who makes decisions, and who bears the costs for wrong decisions or receives the rewards for correct decisions? Planning is the essence of the problem of understanding systems. The question is not whether planning should take place but rather who should do the planning. General Motors plans, homebuilders plan, wheat farmers plan—and so do you. The key question is the degree of centralization of planning and control. At the market extreme, the answer would be that only individual consumers and entrepreneurs should plan. At the command extreme, the position would be that only the central authority should plan.

THE SOCIALIST CONTROVERSY

Marx had little to say about the actual workings of the economic system under socialism. Instead, Marx criticized capitalism and left the development of the economics of socialism to his followers. In 1922, a professor at the University of Vienna, Ludwig von Mises, wrote a famous article, "Economic Calculation in the Socialist Commonwealth."[10] This article claimed that rational economic calculations were impossible under socialism. Von Mises based his argument on a number of factors, but the essence was quite simple. If the state owned the factors of production (other than labor), it would have to allocate them among competing uses. Without a market to determine prices, this task would be impossible. A simulated market with shadow prices could not supply correct information because of the absence of the profit motive. **Shadow prices** are simulated market prices used by economic planners.

The **socialist controversy** was a debate between von Mises and Oskar Lange concerning the feasibility of planning without markets.[11] Von Mises argued that "the most serious menace to socialist economic organization"

shadow prices
Simulated market prices used by economic planners.

socialist controversy
A debate between Ludwig von Mises and Oskar Lange concerning the feasibility of planning without markets.

---

10. Ludwig von Mises, "Economic Calculation in the Socialist Commonwealth," in F. A. Hayek (ed.), *Collectivist Economic Planning* (Clifton, NJ: Augustus M. Kelley, 1967), 103.
11. For a thorough discussion of the socialist controversy, see Paul R. Gregory and Robert C. Stuart, *Soviet Economic Structure and Performance* (New York: Harper & Row, 1974).

was the lack of rewards for correct managerial decisions and penalties for incorrect managerial decisions. Lange, a famous Polish economist who at the time was on the faculty at the University of Chicago, responded to von Mises by developing a model sometimes referred to as the **competitive solution**. In this model, Lange tried to prove that a socialist economy with a combination of central *and* local decision making can arrive at the same efficiency as attained with perfect competition. Prices are set by the central authority. Local managers are told to maximize profits, although they cannot keep these profits. They are solely accounting profits. If shortages or surpluses develop, the price is changed, and in this way an equilibrium price is finally reached. One of the most telling criticisms of Lange's solution, however, is that in a market system, profits are not merely a measure of success but the *incentive* to succeed.[12]

The debate over the feasibility of centralized planning has never been resolved. Is it possible for a central authority to make the calculations necessary to produce efficiently? In a later article that might be considered an extension of this debate, Nobel laureate F. A. Hayek said no.[13] Hayek argues that information is the friction in the system that causes economic models to diverge from the ideal system of either von Mises or Lange. Information is costly to develop and spread, using up scarce resources that must be taken away from other uses. Hayek argued that market systems are superior because they need less information than do centrally planned systems.

Recall from Chapter 2 what happens in a planned economy and a market economy when an earthquake destroys a copper mine. What happens in each economy? In the market economy, the price of copper will rise, reflecting the decrease in supply. Profit-minded entrepreneurs will substitute cheaper metals to minimize costs. In a planned economy, the planners must first be informed of the disaster. The planners must then make some estimate of the severity of the scarcity. They then inform each user of copper that in the future less copper will be available and that other metals should be substituted. The planners must also contact producers of other metals and tell them to ship to the enterprises that had been using copper. In addition, the planners will have to set priorities for use of the available copper. In the market system, this priority setting was done by the increase in price.

Hayek's position is quite simple: Central planning can never be as efficient as a market system because it requires the use of so many resources in transmitting information. The market system, on the other hand, minimizes the amount of information needed. In 1989, there were severe earthquakes in San Francisco (during the World Series) and in Soviet Armenia. The speed of adjustment in the earthquake zones was much faster in San Francisco, reflecting the positive role that the market can play in speeding the process of economic recovery. Recent developments in planned economies also lead to the conclusion that Hayek was right. The inefficiencies of central planning became too expensive, and market reforms were required to stimulate economic growth.

competitive solution
The model developed by Oskar Lange in an attempt to show that a planned economy could theoretically reach the efficiency of an economy with competition.

---

12. Paul Craig Roberts, "Oskar Lange's Theory of Socialist Planning," *Journal of Political Economy* (May-June 1971): 562–568.
13. F. A. Hayek, "The Use of Knowledge in Society," *American Economic Review* (September 1945): 519–528.

How to Plan

The fact that central planning may be inefficient does not change the fact that it is undertaken. Most socialist countries still rely heavily on central planning to move production in the desired direction. Therefore, we need to look at how planning takes place in a command economy.

First, priorities must be established. Someone has to decide what to produce. In the early years of Soviet planning, such decisions were made at the aggregate level. The first plan was, in fact, called the "State Plan for the Electrification of Russia." Until recently, planning was still done by the state planning commission, commonly called the **Gosplan**. Whether to produce consumer or investment goods was the first aggregate planning decision in the Soviet Union. Since the goal of the early leaders was rapid economic growth, they decided to produce investment goods at the expense of consumer goods. As a result, very few consumer goods were available, forcing consumers to save. This pattern of production permitted heavy investment and very rapid rates of economic growth. There were, and still are, shortages of consumer goods in the Soviet Union.

Once planners decided what to produce, they turned their attention to how much to produce. This is a difficult planning problem because the amount produced depends on the productive capacity of the existing industries and on the resources that will be available during the period. Production uses up resources. Therefore, the planners have to make sure that the resources to be used for the final output will be available. At this stage, the various industries are brought into the picture, and the ministries, one for each major industry, make their plans ahead of the overall plan. Once all plans are finalized, they are communicated to productive enterprises so they can take the necessary action to put the plans into operation. Planning is an ongoing process. Even though the planning period is usually expressed in five-year increments, there is continuous revision and implementation.

The planning process itself used up a great deal of time and productive resources. The individuals who engaged in the planning were highly trained engineers and economists, people taken out of other productive activities in order to plan. It is not, therefore, difficult to understand the burden that planning places on an economy. Ironically, many of the poorest countries, where most Communist revolutions have taken place, are the very ones that can least afford the luxury of planning, because of the high opportunity cost of the resources used in the planning process.

Input-Output Analysis

The complexity of planning led to the development of methods to make it more effective. Input-output analysis, developed by Nobel prize–winning economist Wassily Leontief, shows that everything depends on everything else. These interrelationships are what make planning so difficult, because specific plans must be made as to how much of each good is to be produced, by whom, and for whom. **Input-output analysis** is an attempt to quantify the flows between different sectors of the economy.

Table 1 is an input-output table for a small economy in which there are only a few industries to control. There are only three industries: electric-

---

Gosplan
The state planning commission in the Soviet Union.

input-output analysis
An attempt to quantify the flows between different sectors of the economy for purposes of economic planning.

Chapter 22   Comparative Economic Systems in Theory and Practice

		OUTPUTS				
		Electricity	Trucks	Steel	Consumption	Total Output
INPUTS	Electricity	1,000	1,500	5,000	1,500	9,000 kilowatts
	Trucks	1,000	1,500	2,000	1,000	5,500 trucks
	Steel	4,000	3,000	8,500	3,500	19,000 tons
	Labor	2,000	500	3,000	0	5,500 worker-days

TABLE 1
INPUT-OUTPUT TABLE FOR A SIMPLE THREE-INDUSTRY ECONOMY

ity, trucks, and steel. There is also a labor sector and a category of consumption. The input to labor is consumption. Reading across the rows of Table 1 gives the output of each industry and of labor and shows how that output is distributed. One of the reasons that input-output tables are especially useful in command economies is that physical units are used, and prices of outputs and inputs are not needed for the analysis. The fact that no prices are needed is important in a system where market prices are not available and the prices that exist do not necessarily reflect relative scarcity.

To interpret this input-output table, read across the rows. For example, the steel industry has a total output of 19,000 tons, which is sold or allocated by the central authority to the following sectors: 4,000 tons to the electricity industry, 3,000 tons to the truck industry, 8,500 tons to the steel industry, and 3,500 tons to the consumer goods sector. Reading down a column shows the inputs that are needed to produce the output. For example, in order to produce the 19,000 tons of steel, the steel industry uses the following inputs: 5,000 kilowatts of electricity, 2,000 trucks, 8,500 tons of steel, and 3,000 worker-days of labor. The simple arithmetic of input-output tables can be used to plan future output.

The key assumption in input-output analysis is that production takes place in all industries at *constant* costs. There are no economies or diseconomies of scale. If planners want to double the production of the steel industry, all they need to do is double the inputs. Regardless of the level of output planned, the amount of inputs required per unit of output remains the same. However, for large increases in output, this assumption is very unrealistic.

The numbers in Table 2 can be used to calculate the input needed to produce additional units of output. These numbers are referred to as input coefficients. An **input coefficient** shows the ratio of the amount of an input to the total output of an industry. Each input coefficient in Table 2 can be calculated by dividing each value in a column of Table 1 by the to-

input coefficient
In input-output analysis, the ratio of the amount of an input to the total output of an industry.

		OUTPUTS		
		Electricity	Trucks	Steel
INPUTS	Electricity	0.11	0.27	0.26
	Trucks	0.11	0.27	0.11
	Steel	0.44	0.55	0.47
	Labor	0.22	0.09	0.16

TABLE 2
INPUT COEFFICIENTS FOR THE ECONOMY OF TABLE 1

tal output of that industry. For example, the input coefficient of electricity in the truck industry is 0.27 kilowatts/truck (1,500/5,500). Input coefficients can be used to plan increases in output. Examine the column for trucks. The input coefficient tells what increase is needed from each supplying industry in order to get a given increase in output of trucks.

The input-output information in Tables 1 and 2 can be used to plan for the three-industry economy. Suppose planners want to expand the output of the electricity industry by 2,000 kilowatts. That expansion in output would require 220 kilowatts of electricity, 220 trucks, 880 tons of steel, and 440 worker-days. These inputs are found by multiplying the applicable input coefficients by the desired increase in output. Planners would, therefore, be able to direct these industries to deliver the required inputs to produce the planned output.

You should note that there are feedback effects in this process. In order to produce more electricity, some electricity must be consumed in producing the additional steel and trucks used to produce electricity. Feedback occurs throughout this interdependent system. The example assumes that there is no limit to the capacity of any sector of the economy. In fact, however, this may not be the case. In order to produce more electricity, it may be necessary to build new power generators. Generators require time to produce, causing a delay in fulfilling the plan.

The problems of using input-output analysis for planning stem from the fact that the coefficients are constant and are calculated on the basis of historical experience. In other words, the required inputs are calculated on the assumption that the same input mix as that used in the time period for which the table of input coefficients was compiled will continue to be used.

Problems of Central Planning

The technique of planning seems simple in theory. The calculations for a realistic economy are usually overwhelming, however. Think about the size of an input-output table for an economy with 100 industries, 1,000 industries, or 5,000 industries. The interdependencies between the industries become mind-boggling, or even computer-boggling.

The significant problems of planning begin after the plan has been created. There are the problems of implementing the plan, as well as the problems of creating and maintaining incentives that induce workers and managers to support the plan. Managers have incentives to overstate their "needs" for inputs and to hoard materials, since they do not have to pay for them. It is not surprising that plans are often announced with a great deal of publicity and fanfare, but the poor results are often played down.

REFORMS: ECONOMIC FREEDOM AND POLITICAL FREEDOM

Socialist countries have found through experience that the application of planning has not necessarily improved economic performance. This failure was evident during the Great Leap Forward and the Cultural Revolution in China and is also suggested by the declining rate of economic growth in the Soviet Union. Because of poor economic performance,

Chapter 22 Comparative Economic Systems in Theory and Practice

both the People's Republic of China and the Soviet Union have entered into a series of reforms aimed at introducing market forces into the economy. The difficulty with such reforms is that the economic freedom of markets always produces pressure for other types of freedom, which would reduce the power of the central authorities. The trade-off is easy to see. In order to stimulate economic growth, incentives are needed. Markets are allowed to develop in order to create these incentives. The markets diminish the control of the party and its large and powerful bureaucracy. The problem becomes acute when the economic reforms produce the inevitable demands for other freedoms. Bureaucrats can use the demands for political freedom as an excuse for reversing the economic reforms and, by so doing, restore their diminished power. Each socialist country has to cope with the conflicting goals of economic growth and tight administrative control. It is helpful to examine the reform movements in China and the Soviet Union in greater detail.

THE PEOPLE'S REPUBLIC OF CHINA

After Mao's death in 1976, there was rapid reform in China, affecting almost every aspect of the economy. Much of this reform was due to the efforts of Deng Xiaoping, Party General Secretary since December 1978.

POLITICAL, SOCIAL, AND INTELLECTUAL REFORMS. Many of the holdovers of Maoism disappeared from China in the 1980s. Before then, class labels from before the 1949 revolution were still used. These labels (peasant, landlord, intellectual, and so on) affected such things as how people were treated by the courts and whether they were allowed into schools. In the 1980s, the labels were eliminated. Intellectuals benefited from these changes, a great contrast to the days of the Cultural Revolution. They were encouraged to debate and exchange ideas with Western scholars. The results were sweeping demands for political freedom that culminated in large demonstrations.

A system of laws also evolved in the 1980s. Mao had removed all laws because they interfered with the "dictatorship of the proletariat." The new system of laws replaced the arbitrary power of party secretaries and brought some stability to the country.

ECONOMIC REFORM. The first stage of the economic reforms championed by Deng required the "readjustment" of some priorities. The first shift occurred in the output mix. To establish economic incentives, it is necessary to increase wages *and*, equally important, to produce consumer goods for people to buy with those higher wages. This change was accomplished by setting lower targets for heavy industries and increasing investment in light, consumer-oriented industries.

Most noticeable was the change away from the Maoist principle of self-reliance, that is, independence from other countries. Trade with the rest of the world was greatly expanded. Between 1975 and 1985, China's international trade increased from 3.5 percent of GDP to 16 percent of GDP.

The basic reforms of the economic system had profound effects. In agriculture, the "household responsibility system" assigned land that had been held in communes to individual families. In exchange, these farmers assumed contractual obligations to provide a certain amount of food to the state. Farmers were allowed to sell production in excess of the contracted amounts. The result was dramatic. Production increased sharply, and peasant farmers became some of the wealthiest people in China.

The industrial sector was also radically reformed. Once production goals were met, industrial enterprises could sell any surplus on the open market, or they could barter it for other goods. Profits and losses were used to reward or penalize managers. In some instances, factories that had been making losses were turned over to workers, just as communal farms were divided among households. In addition, the state started to charge industrial enterprises for the investment capital it supplied. In some cases, these "loans" were made with assigned payment schedules and interest charges, just as in capitalist countries.

The changes brought about by Deng Xiaoping were fundamental. They injected a great deal of market influence into the Chinese economy. With the market influence and the rise in foreign trade, there came other observable changes. Western dress, music, and ideas about democracy crept in. These Western influences created a danger. Deng was responsible for the reforms, which were not popular with all party leaders. The frustration of many leaders was understandable, since the freeing of the economy greatly reduced their power and influence. As a result, a political movement to reverse the reforms surfaced. In 1985, some party leaders began to complain about the "excesses" of the reforms and the "spiritual pollution" that had been created. In January 1987, the conservatives in the party finally acted when students demonstrated for democratic reforms, including freedom of expression. The student demonstrations united the police and military elements in the party leadership. The result was that Hu Yaobang, party leader, reform advocate, and likely heir to Deng's power, made a "self-criticism" and was forced to step down. He was replaced by Zhao Ziyang, whose first act was to fire the top security official for being too lenient with the student demonstrators. Zhao was described in the press as a cautious reformer.

The Chinese reform movement was at a crossroads in 1989. The economic reform produced economic gains, which in turn led to political demands. These demands led to the firing of Hu and a campaign against "bourgeois liberalization." Party leaders started stressing central planning, thrift, and reduced consumption. Factory managers remained quiet while party leaders were reasserting their political control. In June 1989, students gathered in Tiananmen Square demanding democracy. The demonstration, which included the construction of a statue copied from the Statue of Liberty, was covered in great detail by the Western news media. On June 4, 1989, the military opened fire on the students to put down what is officially known in China as "the turmoil." Thousands of students died. The commander of the 38th Army who did not obey orders to attack the students received a ten-year prison sentence. The official line is that the student movement was a counter-revolutionary rebellion. During the turmoil, Jian Zemin emerged as General Secretary of the Chinese Communist Party. He told *U.S. News & World Report*, "We do not regret or criticize ourselves for the way we handled the Tiananmen event because if we had not sent in the troops then, I would not be able to sit here today."[14]

The political backlash has restricted further economic reforms. Some Western firms that had been investing in China fear that the crackdown will reverse the economic gains. Others contend that the economic reforms have gone so far that it would be impossible to reverse them.

THE SOVIET UNION

Recent changes in the Soviet Union have been staggering. Before 1989, planning was the major feature of the Soviet economy. Gosplan supervised the planning and the implementation of the plan through approximately fifty ministries. Each ministry represented a segment of the Soviet economy. The changes were spawned by the Soviet Union's lackluster economic performance. In Stalin's time, growth rates were high. But a succession of general secretaries, including Brezhnev, Andropov, Chernenko, and now Mikhail Gorbachev, have acknowledged the poor economic performance in their speeches.

Concern focused on several areas. First and foremost, economic growth has been slow. Coupled with this slow growth were "imbalances" (shortages) in consumer areas. Wages increased, but the production of consumer goods was too low. As a result, workers had few production incentives. In addition, both shortages and surpluses were common because the plan did not adjust to changes in supply and demand. As Soviet consumers became relatively better off, they resisted purchasing shoddy merchandise, creating surpluses of some products.

The reasons for the poor performance are not hard to pinpoint. The centralization of economic decision making, based on detailed, explicit plans, led to mistakes. There was no good mechanism for channeling feedback from consumers into the plans. Ultimately, the managers of enterprises were only concerned with satisfying the central planners in the relevant ministry. This concentrated central planning, coupled with enterprise security (the firms faced no competition) and employment security (workers faced no job-loss threat), created few incentives to increase productivity or to be more responsive to consumer preferences.

REFORMS. In March 1985, Mikhail Gorbachev was made general secretary of the Soviet Communist Party following the death of Konstantin Chernenko. Gorbachev, in his fifties, represented a change from rule by elderly men from the Stalin era. His first steps in the direction of economic reform were taken in early 1987. The economic reforms are referred to as *perestroika*. Political reforms are known as *glasnost*, or openness.

Perestroika represents the first steps in economic reform. Reform was not easy to accomplish because every step toward markets and efficiency was a step away from central planning. *Glasnost* and *perestroika* are dramatic changes from earlier periods when the Soviet Union intervened first in

perestroika
Restructuring, economic reforms in the Soviet Union.

glasnost
Openness, political reforms in the Soviet Union.

---

14. Emily MacFarquhar, "Back to the Future in China," *U.S. News & World Report* (12 March 1990): 41. This issue of *U.S. News & World Report* contains three very good articles on China.

International Perspective

Reform in East Germany, Poland, Hungary, and Czechoslovakia

While the Soviets struggle with the political aftermath of the failed coup, some of the Eastern European countries are moving much faster in the area of economic reform. It must be kept in mind that these countries differ greatly from the Soviet Republics. For most of these countries, the main obstacle to reform was the Soviet Union. When they realized that the Soviet Union would not intervene militarily as it had in Hungary (1956) and Czechoslovakia (1968), the reform movements gained momentum.

The success of reforms in Eastern Europe is based on many factors. To begin, most of these countries have escaped the ethnic unrest that has been so devastating in the Soviet Republics. In addition, their economies were in better shape than the Soviet economy when the reforms began.

East Germany was the most developed of the Soviet bloc countries. Its reform movement has been greatly helped by its reunification with West Germany. The financial aid from the West German economy is so important that East Germany is a special case by itself. Even there, however, there have been problems. Unemployment has been high, and buyers for state enterprises have been hard to find.

Poland moved toward capitalism in a bold step. Poland's Finance Minister Leszek Balcerowicz is a former economics professor with an MBA degree from St. John's University in New York. He is an admirer of Milton Friedman. With the help of Professor Jeffry Sachs of Harvard University, Balcerowicz drafted a plan for Poland's economic reform. In 1990, inflation dropped to an annual rate of around 30 percent, compared to 3,000 percent in 1989. The stores are well stocked with agricultural products from local farms and high-tech consumer goods from West Germany and Hong Kong. All restrictions on new enterprises were lifted in the fall of 1989, and 80,000 new companies sprang up in the first year. It was expected that 45 percent of all goods and services would be produced by firms in the private sector by the end of 1991.

Problems remain. Unemployment is high and consumers spend most of their income on food and shelter. The main obstacle to continued success in Poland is political. Lech Walesa and Prime Minister Tadeusz Mazowiecki fought for control of the ruling Solidarity movement in November and December of 1990. Walesa won the election and became Prime Minister in December 1990. Critics worry that his political ties to labor will undermine the reforms. Since his election, Walesa has been uncharacteristically silent about his plans.

Hungary is pursuing a very sophisticated reform package, loosely based on a Thatcher-like gradual selling of government-owned enterprises. The ability to attract foreign capital will determine its success. By the end of 1991, 45 percent of the Hungarian GNP was produced by privately owned firms.

The Czech reform is proceeding more slowly. Czech reformers do not want to sell government assets directly to foreigners or to Czech citizens. They favor a gradual approach. The Czech plan calls for vouchers to be given to citizens, who could use them to buy equity in state-owned enterprises. About 10 percent of the Czech economy had been privatized by the end of 1991.

Hungary, then in Czechoslovakia, and finally in Poland to make sure that economic reform did not mean a slide toward capitalism. In 1989, the Soviet Union did not intervene when radical change swept Eastern Europe. The most dramatic event occurred in East Germany where the Berlin Wall came down, but change also occurred in Romania, Hungary, Czechoslovakia, and Poland.

The reforms in the Soviet Union have not gone smoothly. The once powerful Red Army is in disarray. In the first half of 1990, when only 26 percent of the drafted young men showed up, the government chose not to crack down on the draft-dodgers. To complicate the military situation, several independent armies emerged in ethnic republics, including Georgia, Armenia, and Azerbaijan.[15] In August 1991, Gorbachev was the victim of a coup, but he was rescued when Boris Yeltsin's political support defeated the coup.

The reforms face at least eight problems:

1. There is no experience with markets, property rights, and exchange. There is widespread distrust of market processes.
2. Pollution is rampant in the Soviet Union (and the countries of Eastern Europe). An emerging environmental movement is demanding that more attention be paid to the environment. This will be expensive at a time when other matters are more pressing.
3. There is growing ethnic unrest. Independence movements have succeeded in the Baltics, the Ukraine, Moldavia, and Georgia. Fighting has erupted between Armenia and Azerbaijan.
4. There is growing labor unrest. Miners are the most organized and violent. They threaten to strike unless their demands are met.
5. The military is in turmoil. Senior military leaders are unhappy about their loss of status in the political apparatus.
6. Agriculture is in disarray. Although bumper harvests, the best in fifteen years occurred in 1990, food rotted in the fields because the distribution network is not adequate.
7. The economic reformers demand faster and more radical economic changes. At the same time, there is strong resistance from bureaucrats and consumers who fear higher prices.
8. Finally, the economy is in chaos. The widespread shortages are aggravated by panic buying from consumers afraid of higher rates of inflation. An illegal black market thrives. Economic conditions are likely to deteriorate before they get better.

To address these growing problems, Gorbachev teamed with his rival Yeltsin in August 1990 to announce a new 500-day program to replace the failed reform of the previous year. Under the 500-day program, the government's huge subsidies to industry were to end. The twenty remaining industrial ministries would be substantially cut back, further freeing the economy to market forces. Workers, the public, and even foreign investors would be permitted to buy state assets. The republics were to be given more control over their own resources. Most have already declared such

---

15. See "The Enemy Within?" *National Review* (17 September 1990): 7.

control.[16] The future is difficult to predict. The failed coup in August 1991 ended communist rule. The Communist Party and the KGB were shut down in Russia by Yeltsin. Other republics quickly followed suit. It is unclear what the political structure of the former Soviet Union will be.

CAN REFORMS SUCCEED IN THE SOVIET UNION? The next few years will determine whether reforms succeed in the Soviet Republics or are halted by a conservative backlash. The twin forces of *perestroika* and *glasnost* can cause opposing changes. In China, the democracy movement created a setback for the economic reform movement. In some Soviet Republics, the same result could occur.

A major problem that market reform faces is the attitude of consumers. Consumers want the standard of living that capitalism produces, but they like the safety of governmental regulation. If such attitudes prevail, it will be very difficult to institute market reforms in a democratic setting. The breakup of the Soviet Union into a loose federation of republics could be the cause for optimism. The various republics will go their separate ways, and markets may have a better chance with decentralization and the shock destruction of the centralized political power.

JAPAN

In Japan, great strides have been made in a modified capitalistic structure in the last forty years. The Japanese "miracle" is of great interest to developing countries and industrial managers in the United States. The interest stems in part from wanting to borrow those elements of the Japanese success that can be transplanted into other economies.

In 1950, Japan was starting to recover from the devastation of World War II. The U.S. Commerce Department reports that Japanese per capita income in 1950 was only about an eighth of that in the United States. Thirty-five years later, in 1990, the per capita level of income was four-fifths of that of the United States. In the 1950s, the phrase "Made in Japan" implied cheap, shoddy copies of U.S. products. In the 1990s, "Made in Japan" implies the finest of automotive and high-tech products. This rapid economic growth occurred in a country smaller than the state of California with few natural resources (Japan imports almost all of its oil) and a population half as large as that of the United States.

TAXES

Compared to Western Europe and the United States, Japan has very low taxes. Japan's taxes are around 25 percent of national income, compared to 30 percent in the United States, 35 percent in the United Kingdom, and almost 40 percent in West Germany.

---

16. See "This Time, Gorbachev May Really Turn the Economy Upside Down," *Business Week* (27 August 1990): 8; "Out of Stock," *The Wall Street Journal* (23 July 1990): 1; "Moscow's Bumper Crop of Troubles," *U.S. News & World Report* (3 September 1990): 27–28; "Who's in Charge Here?" *Forbes* (3 September 1990): 32–33; Anthony DeCurtis, "Anarchy in the Soviet Union," *Rolling Stone* (26 July 1990): 29–34; "Yeltsin's Shadow Just Keeps Getting Longer," *Business Week*, (17 September 1990): 28; and "500 Days," *Business Week* (1 October 1990): 29–30.

Supply siders in the United States argue that low taxes are an important reason for growth. They note that the tax structure in Japan is not used to redistribute income. Until very recently, there was no social insurance system, and even now it is very limited. The pre-tax distribution of income is about the same as the post-tax distribution. As a result, there are powerful incentives to engage in risky, entrepreneurial activity.

INVESTMENT AND SAVING

The Japanese people save about 20 percent of their annual incomes. These savings find their way into capital investment, which creates future income. The high rate of Japanese saving is the result of two powerful influences. The first has already been mentioned. Since only a very limited social insurance system exists in Japan, workers must save for their retirement. Second, the tax system is structured in such a way that tax credits are given for saving. In contrast, in the United States, dividends and interest—the returns to saving—are taxed, and Social Security reduces the incentive to save for retirement.

LABOR-MANAGEMENT RELATIONS

Perhaps the aspect of the Japanese economy that has generated the most interest in the U.S. business community is the labor-management relationship. Great loyalty to the firm exists in Japan. Many workers in the manufacturing sector enjoy lifetime employment to age fifty-five, when mandatory retirement occurs. These workers belong to company unions that cooperate with management in setting goals, work schedules, and plans for the company.

Certain aspects of this labor-management relationship are being tried by U.S. businesses. **Theory Z** is the idea that employees are not motivated by negative incentives, such as threats, or by monetary incentives, such as raises and promotions, but are motivated by being included as active participants in the management process. The use of quality circles is one of the tools of a Theory Z style of management. In **quality circles**, workers organize themselves into units to try to improve quality by discussing production problems and suggesting solutions. A quality circle is a kind of activist, organized, suggestion box.

Theory Z
A management theory that workers are motivated to perform if they are made part of the management process.

quality circles
Groups of workers organized to improve quality by discussing production problems and suggesting solutions.

HAS JAPAN PEAKED?

Many observers feel that the Japanese economy may have peaked in the mid-1980s.[17] They point to the fact that Japanese exports have dropped and industrial production has fallen. Other observers have predicted that younger workers in Japan will grow restless because of long working hours and high consumer prices. They will demand higher standards of living, rather than increased investment and production through higher levels of saving.

The Japanese Ministry of International Trade predicts that Japan will lose 560,000 manufacturing jobs by 2000. Some of this loss is due to the increasing tendency for Japanese firms to produce in foreign countries rather than producing in Japan and exporting. Approximately 20 percent

---

17. See "To Have and Have Not in Japan," *U.S. News & World Report* (13 February 1989): 41–42.

of Japanese manufacturing is expected to be "offshore" in 2000, compared to 5 percent in 1987.

The Japanese response to the changing economic position will be important. If Japan opens its market to foreign trade, it will be able to live off its investments rather than its production. This openness will be a challenge because changing the pattern of economic development has been disturbing to Japanese leaders. These leaders have tended to support protectionist policies in the past. In the face of rising production costs at home, a rise in protectionist policies may follow. These trends could represent a cloud on the Japanese horizon.

Still another cloud on the Japanese horizon is growing discontent among Americans about the trade relationship between the United States and Japan. Forty-four percent of Americans say they do not trust the Japanese, and sixty-one percent believe Japanese imports into the United States should be restricted. These negative attitudes are unlike the attitudes of U.S. voters to trade relations with other foreign countries.[18]

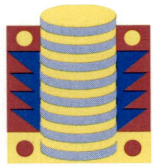

Summary

1. The study of comparative systems allows economists to analyze different environments and institutions to determine how they can affect economic outcomes.

2. The most common approach to comparative economics is to classify systems according to dominant ideology. This approach is not very useful. Almost all systems can be labeled as either capitalist or socialist but differ widely within these general categories.

3. Marx's writings provide the basic political framework on which all socialist systems are based. The economic systems of these countries are, however, widely divergent. The variation in the systems has been, in many cases, the result of dominant political leaders. Thus, it is possible to distinguish among Leninism, Stalinism, Castroism, and Maoism as separate forms of socialism.

4. Another way to analyze different economic systems is to examine their organizational and decision-making differences. This approach looks at the level at which decisions are made, the informational requirements and the motivations of the decision-making units, and the interaction of system, environment, performance, and policy.

5. Planning is carried out in all economies. The key difference between systems is the level at which planning is carried out. The higher the level of planning, the greater the informational requirements of the system.

6. Central planning requires the determination of what to produce. In the Soviet Union, such planning resulted in rapid growth because the central authority decided not to produce many consumer goods. This decision generated high rates of investment.

7. Central planning relies on input-output analysis. Input-output analysis starts with historical data on the amounts of inputs necessary to produce a given output. Those data are used to determine what inputs are necessary to produce a desired output. Input-output analysis assumes that the historical production record will continue to hold.

8. After all the technical problems of planning are worked out, it is necessary to put the plan into operation. Implementation requires transmitting the plan to the production units and creating the proper incentives.

9. China and the Soviet Republics face reform movements. Economic growth in each case will depend on whether these reforms are continued or reversed.

10. The Japanese "miracle" is based on low tax rates, high saving rates, and labor-management harmony.

---

18. Lee Smith, "Fear and Loathing of Japan," *Fortune* (26 February 1990): 16.

Chapter 22 Comparative Economic Systems in Theory and Practice

NEW TERMS

capitalism
socialism
communism
fascism
War Communism
New Economic Policy (NEP)
Great Industrialization Debate
Great Leap Forward
Cultural Revolution
shadow prices
socialist controversy
competitive solution
Gosplan
input-output analysis
input coefficient
perestroika
glasnost
Theory Z
quality circles

QUESTIONS FOR DISCUSSION

1. How did the trade union Solidarity threaten the Communist Party in Poland? Why was the Soviet Union so interested in developments in Poland?

2. How did Lenin change the theories of Marx? Which of the two appears to be more important as the inspiration of communist revolutions?

3. Is planning an important function in all economies? Is it more important in market or command economies?

4. How would allowing the input coefficient to vary complicate input-output analysis? Is the assumption of fixed input coefficients a damaging one?

5. List as many problems of maintaining proper incentives under a central planning system as you can. Do these problems exist only in centrally planned economies?

6. How do you evaluate the performance of the Japanese economy? Are there lessons for the U.S. economy?

7. What are the weaknesses of fascism?

8. What was the period of the New Economic Policy in the Soviet Union?

9. Evaluate the two sides of the socialist controversy.

10. What is the connection between economic freedom and political freedom?

11. How can political freedom undermine economic reform in Eastern Europe, China, and the Soviet Union?

12. What are the primary obstacles facing the reform movement in the Soviet Republics?

13. Which reform movement in Eastern Europe has been the most successful? Why? Are there any lessons in this for the rest of the world?

14. Cuba is the last of the Communist countries to continue rigid planning. What are prospects for reform in Cuba?

15. Do the events of the past five years signal the death of communism and the victory of capitalism?

SUGGESTIONS FOR FURTHER READING

Doder, Dusko, and Louise Branson. *Gorbachev: Heretic in the Kremlin.* New York: Viking, 1990. A book billed as the story of how "Gorby got to the top." The authors final prediction: "It is entirely possible that Gorbachev ultimately will be rejected by the nation in a free election."

Galbraith, John Kenneth. *Economics in Perspective.* Boston: Houghton Mifflin, 1987. A fast-paced economic history that extends from Adam and Eve to the present.

Gray, Francine du Plessix. *Soviet Women.* New York: Doubleday, 1990. Looks at the reform movement through the eyes of Soviet women and describes the problems they face.

Kahn, Joseph F. "Better Fed Than Red," *Esquire* (September 1990): 186–197; and "Inside Quin Cheng Prison," *Harper's* (August 1990): 17–19. Two accounts of what happened to different groups of students after the Tiananmen Square protest in China. The first chronicles the life of student leader Wu'erkaixi after his escape to Paris. The second describes life in prison for some of the arrested students.

Kotkin, Stephen. *Steeltown USSR: Soviet Society in the Gorbachev Era.* Berkeley: University of California Press, 1991. Shows how difficult Soviet reforms will be, based on interviews in a steel-producing city.

Winiecki, Jan. *The Distorted World of Soviet-type Economies.* Pittsburgh: Pittsburgh University Press, 1988. A book by a respected Polish economist that outlines the problems that faced Soviet-type economies on the eve of the reform movement.

Yoshino, M. T., and Thomas B. Lifson. *The Invisible Link: Japan's Sogo Shosha.* Cambridge, MA: MIT Press, 1986. Examines how the Japanese general trading houses coordinate trade and production.

GLOSSARY

absolute advantage The ability to produce something using fewer resources than other producers use.

accounting profit The difference between total sales and explicit costs.

acreage allotment A limit set by the government on the number of acres that can be used to produce a specific crop, based on past production levels.

administered prices Prices that are relatively rigid, or changed only infrequently.

AFL-CIO Organization formed by the merger of the American Federation of Labor and the Congress of Industrial Organizations in 1955, which gave labor a more unified political front.

aggregates Quantities whose values are determined by adding across many markets.

agricultural support program Attempts by the federal government to achieve parity for farmers through the use of price supports.

allocation Any activities by government or its agents that affect the distribution of resources and the combination of goods and services produced.

allocative efficiency The use of resources to produce the goods most desired by society. Free markets allow allocative efficiency.

American Federation of Labor (AFL) An exclusive union for skilled workers founded by Samuel Gompers in 1886 as the first business union.

American Federation of State, County, and Municipal Employees (AFSCME) A union of public employees that was one of the few unions that grew in the 1970s.

appreciation A rise in the market price of a currency due to market forces.

arbitration Third party intervention in a dispute consisting of hearing the arguments of both sides, studying their positions, and rendering a decision. In binding arbitration, both sides must abide by the decision.

arc elasticity The elasticity at the midpoint between two points on a demand curve.

association-causation fallacy The false notion that association implies causality.

average fixed cost (AFC) Total fixed costs of production divided by number of units of output.

average physical product (APP) The total physical product (output) divided by the number of units of a factor used.

average revenue (AR) Total revenue divided by the quantity sold, or the revenue per unit sold (the price).

average total cost (AC) Total costs of producing a level of output divided by the number of units of output.

average variable cost (AVC) Total variable costs of production divided by the number of units of output.

backward-bending supply curve A labor supply curve that slopes back to the left at the point where the income effect dominates the substitution effect.

balance of payments An annual summary of the transactions between residents of one country and residents of the rest of the world.

balance of payments deficit An excess of a country's foreign spending over its foreign earnings for a given year.

bar chart A graphic representation that expresses data using columns of different heights.

barriers to entry Natural or artificial obstacles that keep new firms from entering an industry.

bilateral monopoly Market structure in which monopolies deal with each other as buyers and sellers, such as when an inclusive union sells labor to a monopsonistic firm.

black markets Markets in which people illegally buy and sell goods and services at prices above government-imposed price ceilings.

board of directors The individuals elected by the stockholders of a corporation to select the managers and oversee the management of the corporation.

bond An interest-earning certificate that is issued by a government or corporation in exchange for borrowed funds and has a fixed face value, annual interest payment, and maturity date.

Bretton Woods system The international monetary system in effect from 1945 to 1973, based on infrequent changes in currency prices, ample reserves, and the dollar as key currency.

budget constraint A given level of income that determines the maximum amount of goods that may be purchased by an individual.

business firm An organization formed by an entrepreneur to combine inputs in order to produce marketable outputs.

business union According to Samuel Gompers, a union that works for economic goals without wanting to change or destroy the business organization or the political environment in which it functions.

capital The durable inputs into the production process created by people. Machines, tools, and buildings are examples of capital.

capital account The part of the balance of payments that summarizes purchases and sales of financial assets.

capitalism An economic system characterized by private ownership of the factors of production by individuals or groups of individuals.

capitalized value The present value of a stream of future rent payments.

cartel A group of independent firms that agree not to compete but rather to determine prices and output jointly.

Celler-Kefauver Antimerger Act A federal law that strengthened the Clayton Act in 1950 by making it illegal in certain circumstances for a firm to merge with another by purchasing its assets.

ceterus paribus assumption The assumption that everything else will remain constant, used for most economic models. (*Ceterus paribus* is Latin for "all else being equal.")

ceterus paribus fallacy The false notion that arises because an observer fails to recognize that variables other than the one in question have changed.

chiseling Cheating on a cartel agreement by lowering prices in an attempt to capture more of the market.

circular flow model A visual representation of the relationships between the factor market (in which income is obtained) and the product market (in which income is used to purchase goods and services).

Clayton Act Federal law, passed in 1914, prohibiting the acquisition of the stock of a competing company if such an acquisition would "substantially lessen competition."

Clean Air Act A federal law passed in 1970 that empowered the EPA to set emission standards and impose standards on polluters.

closed shops Firms where workers must be union members before being employed.

Coase theorem The idea that well-defined property rights are sufficient to internalize any external effect that is present, when there are small numbers of affected parties.

coefficient of price elasticity of demand (E_d) The numerical measure of price elasticity of demand, equal to the percent change in quantity demanded of a good divided by the percent change in its price.

coefficient of price elasticity of supply (E_s) The numerical measure of price elasticity of supply, equal to the percent change in the quantity supplied of a good divided by the percent change in its price.

collusion Agreements between firms in an industry to set a certain price or to share a market in certain ways.

command economy An economy in which the three basic questions are answered through central planning and control (also called a planned economy).

commercial policy The set of actions that a country undertakes to deliberately influence trade in goods and services.

Commodity Credit Corporation (CCC) A U.S. government agency that makes loans to farmers as part of federal price support programs.

common access resource A resource that is not owned by any individual but is available for all to use.

communication Firms' ability to signal their intentions to each other.

communism The final stage in the theory of Karl Marx, in which the state has withered away and economic goods are equally distributed.

comparable worth A standard for determining wages that calls for equal pay for jobs that require similar levels of training, responsibility, and skills.

comparative advantage The ability to produce something at a lower opportunity cost than other producers face.

comparative statics A technique of comparing two equilibrium positions to determine the changing relationships between variables.

competitive fringe The smaller competitors in informally coordinated markets with one large, dominant firm.

competitive solution The model developed by Oskar Lange in an attempt to show that a planned economy could theoretically reach the efficiency of an economy with competition.

complementary goods Goods that are jointly consumed. The consumption of one enhances the consumption of the other.

concentration ratio A measure of the distribution of economic power among firms in an oligopolistic market.

conglomerates Firms that perform many unrelated operations or produce many unrelated products or services.

Congress of Industrial Organizations (CIO) An affiliation of industrial unions that was organized when the AFL decided not to move into mass-production industries.

Conservation Reserve Program (CRP) A federal program that pays farmers to remove land from production for ten years or more.

constant cost industry An industry in which expansion of output does not cause average cost to rise in the long run.

constrained sales maximization The hypothesis that managers' primary goal is to increase the sales of the firm because they will be rewarded by stockholders for increasing the firm's relative share of the market.

consumer surplus The extra utility derived from a purchase that has a value to the consumer greater than the market price.

consumption possibilities curve A line showing the consumption combinations attainable through trade.

contestable markets Markets composed of large firms that are nevertheless efficient because easily reversible entry into the market is possible.

contract law Law that deals with the enforcement of voluntary exchanges.

coordinates The values of x and y that define the location of a point in a coordinate system.

coordination Firms' ability to relate their production decisions to those made by other firms in an industry.

corporation A form of enterprise in which stockholders are the owners of the firm but have limited liability.

cost-plus pricing The form of price regulation that allows firms a markup that is a percentage of average costs of production.

countervailing power The offsetting power possessed by both sides of the market in a monopoly.

craft union A union composed of specific kinds of skilled workers, such as plumbers or carpenters.

cross elasticity of demand The measure of the responsiveness of changes in the quantity demanded of one good to changes in the price of another.

Cultural Revolution The high point of Mao's power in China, characterized by a radical restructuring of the economy from 1966 through 1969.

current account The part of the balance of payments that summarizes transactions in currently produced goods and services.

deadweight loss The lost consumer surplus due to monopolistic restriction of output.

decrease in demand A shift in the demand curve indicating that at every price, consumers demand a smaller amount than before.

decrease in supply A shift in the supply curve indicating that at every price, a smaller quantity will be offered for sale than before.

decreasing cost industry An industry in which expansion of output causes average cost to fall in the long run.

demand The desire and ability to consume certain quantities of a good at various prices over a certain period of time.

demand curve A graph representing a demand schedule and showing the quantity demanded at various prices in a certain time period.

demand-determined price A price that is determined solely by changes in demand because supply is perfectly inelastic.

demand schedule A table that shows quantities demanded at various prices during a specific time period.

dependent variable The variable, usually plotted on the vertical axis, that is affected or influenced by the other variable.

depreciation (1) The decline in the value of an asset, such as a machine or factory, over time. (2) A fall in the market price of a currency due to market forces.

derived demand Demand for a productive resource that results from demand for a final good or service. For example, the demand for labor is derived from the demand for the product that the labor produces.

diamond-water paradox The fact that diamonds, although less useful than water, are more expensive than water. That is, things with the greatest value in exchange (price) often have little value in use.

differentiated oligopoly An oligopoly that produces heterogeneous products that are very close substitutes.

differentiated product A good or service that has real or imagined characteristics that are different from those of other goods or services.

discounting The technique of calculating present values by adjusting for interest that would be earned between now and some specified future time.

diseconomies of agglomeration The additional costs that individuals must pay when too many of them locate in one city (thus creating negative external effects for one another).

diseconomies of scale Increases in long-run average cost that are due to increased plant size.

disequilibrium An unstable situation in which variables are moving toward equilibrium but are not yet at equilibrium.

distributive justice A normative argument for a particular distribution of income.

dominant firm The most influential firm in an industry, usually the largest firm.

dual labor markets The radical economists' idea that there are two labor markets because of artificial barriers that keep some workers earning low wages.

dumping The practice of selling in foreign markets at lower prices than in domestic markets (a form of price discrimination).

economic efficiency The least-cost method of production.

economic profit The difference between total sales and the total of explicit and implicit costs of production.

economic rent A payment to a factor of production in excess of its opportunity cost.

economics The study of how people and institutions make decisions about production and consumption and how they face the problem of scarcity.

economies of agglomeration The cost savings that individuals enjoy when enough of them locate close together in or near a large city.

economies of scale Declines in long-run average cost that are due to increased plant size.

elasticity The measure of the sensitivity or responsiveness of quantity demanded or quantity supplied to changes in price (or other factors).

eminent domain A doctrine that gives government the right to buy property at "fair market value" if the purchase is in the public interest.

endogenous variables Variables that are explained or determined within a model.

enterprise The input to the production process that involves organizing, innovation, and risk taking.

excess capacity The unutilized part of existing production facilities by a monopolistically competitive firm.

exchange control A system in which the government purchases all incoming foreign exchange and is the only source from which foreign exchange can be legally purchased.

excise tax A tax that on the purchase of a particular good, such as liquor, cigarettes, or electricity, or a broad class of goods, such as food.

exclusive union A union that restricts the supply of labor and maintains a higher-than-competitive wage for its members by excluding workers from a trade or occupation. Craft unions are exclusive unions.

exogenous variables Variables that are determined outside of a model and affect endogenous variables.

expectations Feelings that individuals have about future conditions.

explicit costs Accounting costs or money outlays.

externalities Costs or benefits associated with consumption or production that are not reflected in market prices and fall on parties other than the buyer or seller.

factor market Set of markets in which owners of the factors of production sell these to producers.
factors of production The inputs of land, labor, capital, and enterprise that a firm uses to produce outputs.
fair rate of return The normal profit that a regulated industry must earn in order to stay in business.
fair trade The idea that the United States should impose trade barriers equivalent to those that its trading partners place on U.S. exports.
fallacy of composition The false notion that what holds for the parts holds for the whole.
Family Support Act of 1988 A federal law that incorporates some aspects of state workfare programs, turning entitlements into obligations to take jobs or enter job training programs.
fascism An economic system that combines monopoly, capitalism, private property, and a strong authoritarian central government.
featherbedding The maintenance of jobs that management claims are unnecessary or redundant.
Federal Trade Commission Act A federal law passed in 1914 that set up the Federal Trade Commission (FTC) to police unfair and deceptive business practices.
fixed factors The factors of production that cannot be varied in the short run.
Food Security Act A 1985 federal law that sets target prices and requires farmers to agree to keep part of their land idle.
foreign exchange market The network of banks and financial institutions through which buyers and sellers exchange national currencies.
45° line A line in the first quadrant, passing through the origin, with a slope of +1, which divides the quadrant in half. If the scales on the axes are the same, the value of the x-variable is equal to the value of the y-variable along the 45° line.
forward market The market in which contracts are made for future delivery of specific amounts of currency at a specified price.
free riders People or business firms who consume collective goods without contributing to the cost of their production.
functional distribution of income The pattern of payments to the factors of production (rent, wages, interest, and profits).

gains from trade The increase in economic well-being resulting from specialization and exchange.
game theory A mathematical theory about rational decision making under conditions of uncertainty that can provide insight into oligopolistic behavior.
glasnost Openness, political reforms in the Soviet Union.
gold standard An international monetary system in which currencies were defined in terms of gold, money supplies were tied to gold, and balance of payment deficits were settled in gold.
Gosplan The state planning commission in the Soviet Union.
Great Ind᠎ ᠎alization Debate An open debate that took place in the Soviet Union from 1924 to 1928 concerning the correct way to industrialize the economy.
Great Leap Forward A modernization plan that was launched in 1958 to increase per capita income in China by 25 percent in five years.

Hart-Scott-Rodino Antritrust Improvement Act A 1970 federal law amending the FTC Act to require firms to report mergers or acquisitions to the FTC and Department of Justice before the fact.
hedgers People who try to reduce their risk by buying or selling contracts in the forward market for currency.
Herfindahl Index A summed index of concentration that takes into account all the firms in an industry.
holding companies Firms set up for the sole purpose of owning and thus controlling other firms.
horizontally integrated firms Firms that perform many similar production operations in the same industry.
human capital The investment made to improve the quality of people's labor skills through education, training, health care, and so on.
Humphrey-Hawkins Act A 1978 amendment to the Employment Act of 1946 that set specific targets for output, employment, and prices.

implicit costs Costs measured by the value of alternatives given up.
inclusive union A union that attempts to organize all the workers in an industry and to maintain a strong bargaining position with respect to management.
income-consumption curve A curve that uses parallel budget lines to show changes in consumer equilibrium when income changes.
income effect An increase in demand for a good (or service) when its price falls, *ceteris paribus*, because the household's real income rises and the consumer buys more of all normal goods.
income elasticity of demand The measure of the responsiveness of quantity demanded to changes in income.
increase in demand A shift in the demand curve indicating that at every price, consumers demand a larger amount than before.
increase in supply A shift in the supply curve indicating that at every price, a larger quantity will be offered for sale than before.
increasing cost industry An industry in which expansion of output causes average cost to rise in the long run.
increasing opportunity cost The principle that as production of one good rises, larger and larger sacrifices of another are required.
independent variable The variable, usually plotted on the horizontal axis, that affects or influences the other variable.
indifference analysis An approach to analyzing consumer behavior based on ranking the utility of choices relative to one another.
indifference curve A plot of all combinations of goods that the consumer is indifferent among.
indifference map A set of indifference curves. Higher curves represent higher levels of utility.

indifference set Any number of combinations of goods among which the individual consumer is indifferent (has no preference).

industrial union An inclusive union that gains power by organizing all (or a large share) of the workers in an industry.

Industrial Workers of the World (IWW) An international union that organized U.S. steelworkers after World War I and was viewed as a socialist organization, which contributed to its demise.

industry A group of firms producing similar or related products.

industry studies Investigations of specific industries to determine the degree of competitive behavior.

inferior good A good for which demand decreases as income increases.

injunctions Court orders to cease some activity, such as ordering labor to stop a strike or walkout.

input coefficient In input-output analysis, the ratio of the amount of an input to the total output of an industry.

input-output analysis An attempt to quantify the flows between different sectors of the economy for purposes of economic planning.

insatiable wants The needs and desires of human beings, which can never be completely satisfied.

interdependent demand Demand that depends on another type of demand. For example, a firm's demand for labor depends on the amount of other factors that the firm plans to use.

interdependent utility functions Preference patterns in which some people's well-being is dependent on the well-being of others.

interest The return to capital, one of the factors of production.

internalization The incorporation of the social costs of negative external effects into the market price.

International Monetary Fund (IMF) The agency that supervised the operation of the Bretton Woods system by recording par values, consulting on devaluations and revaluations, and maintaining a pool of reserves.

international monetary reserves The pool of gold and major currencies created under the Bretton Woods system, from which countries could borrow to settle deficits and replenish from surpluses.

interpersonal utility comparisons Attempts to compare the utility of one individual with that of another (or others).

investment Purchases of real, tangible assets, such as machines, factories, or inventories, that are used to produce goods and services.

invisible hand The idea advanced by Adam Smith that individuals pursuing their own self-interest direct the market system toward socially desirable outcomes.

isocost line A line that shows the amounts of two inputs that can be purchased with a fixed sum of money (a firm's budget line).

isoquant A curve that shows all combinations of two inputs that can be used to produce a given output.

key currency A currency that serves as a major reserve asset and is used in transactions between third-party nations.

kinked demand curve A demand curve with a bend in it at the price settled on in an oligopolistic industry because other firms' price cuts, but not price increases, are matched.

Knights of Labor Organized as a secret organization by Uriah Stevens in 1869, it won the first major strike in the United States against the railroad industry but had political reformist goals that led to its demise.

labor The physical and mental exertion that human beings put into production activities.

land Natural resources that can be used as inputs to production.

Landrum-Griffin Act An act passed in 1959 and aimed at curbing union power by making unions more democratic, restricting Communist Party members and convicted felons from union leadership, and making picketing illegal under certain circumstances.

law of demand The quantity demanded of a good or service is negatively related to its price, *ceteris paribus*.

Lerner Index of Monopoly Power (LMP) An index that evaluates the gap between price and marginal cost as a measure of monopoly power.

limited liability The fact that the stockholders of a corporation cannot be sued for failure of the corporation to meet its obligations.

local monopoly A firm that has monopoly power in a geographic region because of the large distance from other suppliers of its product (or substitutes).

logrolling Vote trading in the legislative process.

long run The period of time in which all inputs, including plant and equipment, can be varied.

long-run average cost (*LRAC*) curve A curve tangent to all the possible short-run cost curves and representing the lowest attainable average cost of producing any given output.

long-run profit maximization The argument that even if managers seem to behave in accord with satisficing or constrained sales maximization, they only do so because it leads to higher profits in the long run.

Lorenz curve A graph showing the cumulative percentages of income received by various percentages of households.

macroeconomics The study of the economy as a whole or of economic aggregates, such as the level of employment and the growth of total output.

marginal analysis A technique for analyzing problems by examining the results of small changes.

marginal cost The change in total cost from producing one more (or one less) unit of output.

marginal cost pricing A policy tool for forcing a monopoly to behave more like a competitive firm by regulating the monopoly price so that it is equal to marginal cost.

marginal physical product (*MPP*) The change in total output that is produced by a unit change in a factor of production.

marginal productivity theory An explanation of how the distribution of income is determined in a market system. Each factor is paid according to its contribution, or its marginal productivity.

marginal rate of substitution *(MRS)* The trade-off ratio along an indifference curve.

marginal resource cost *(MRC)* The cost of each additional unit of a productive resource.

marginal revenue *(MR)* The change in total revenue from selling one more (or one less) unit.

marginal revenue product of labor *(MRP_L)* The amount that an additional unit of labor adds to a firm's total revenue.

marginal utility *(MU)* The amount of utility that one more or one less unit of consumption adds to or subtracts from total utility.

market A place where buyers and sellers meet to exchange goods, services, and productive resources.

market-clearing price The equilibrium price, which clears the market because there are no frustrated consumers or suppliers.

market concentration doctrine The hypothesis that the degree of concentration in an industry is a reliable index of monopoly power and that a high concentration ratio is likely to be associated with undesirable monopoly behavior.

market demand curve The sum of all of the individual demand curves. A market demand curve shows what quantities will be demanded by all consumers in a specific time frame in a certain market at various prices.

market economy An economy in which the three basic questions are answered through the market, by relying on self-interested behavior and incentives.

market equilibrium A point at which quantity demanded by consumers is equal to quantity supplied by producers. The price at which this occurs is the equilibrium price, or market-clearing price.

market power The ability of buyers or sellers to affect price.

market supply curve The sum of all of the individual supply curves. A market supply curve shows what quantities will be supplied by all firms at various prices during a specific time period.

marketing orders A federal program that establishes producer cartels that control the supply of certain agricultural products not subject to price supports.

maximum The point on a graph at which the *y*-variable, or dependent variable, reaches its highest value.

median voter theorem A theory that predicts that under majority rule, politicians will reflect the positions of voters near the center of the political spectrum.

mediation Third-party intervention in a dispute consisting of attempts to keep the parties together and talking by offering suggestions and clarifying issues.

microeconomics The study of individual market interactions, focusing on production and consumption by the individual consumer, firm, or industry.

minimum The point on the graph at which the *y*-variable, or dependent variable, reaches its lowest value.

mixed economy An economy in which the three basic questions are answered partly by market forces and partly through government.

model A set of assumptions and hypotheses that is a simplified description of reality.

monopolistic competition The market structure in which a large number of firms sell differentiated products.

monopoly The market structure in which there is a single seller of a product that has no close substitutes.

monopoly power The ability to exercise some of the economic effects predicted in the model of monopoly by restricting output.

monopoly rent seeking The efforts and resources expended by those attempting to establish monopolies to earn monopoly profits.

monopsonistic exploitation The difference in wages paid by a firm that has monopsony power, compared to what would be paid in a competitive market.

monopsony A market structure in which there is a single purchaser of a factor of production.

multinational corporation A firm with headquarters in one country and plants in one or more other countries.

name brand capital The value that consumers place on a product because of experience, reputation, or image.

National Labor Relations Board (NLRB) A board established by the Wagner Act in 1935 and empowered to investigate employer unfair labor practices and to determine the legitimate bargaining agent for labor when there are competing unions.

National Labor Union The first successful national union in the United States, founded in 1867 by William Sylvis.

National Recovery Administration (NRA) A major New Deal program that was aimed at business recovery but was anticompetitive since it allowed and encouraged agreements between firms. It was eventually declared unconstitutional.

natural monopoly A monopoly that emerges because economies of scale mean that there is room for only one firm in the market.

negative externalities Harmful spillovers to third parties that result from production or consumption of certain goods.

negative income tax A transfer of income from the government to the poor based on a formula similar to the present income tax system and implemented with a minimum income guarantee and a negative tax rate.

negative relationship A relationship between two variables in which an increase in the value of one is associated with a decrease in the value of the other.

New Economic Policy (NEP) A program that replaced War Communism in 1921 in the Soviet Union and was an attempt at market socialism.

nonprice competition Competing with rival firms through advertising, style changes, color changes, and techniques other than lowering price.

nontariff barriers Trade restrictions other than tariffs and quotas.

normal good A good for which demand increases as income increases.

normal profit The opportunity cost of capital and enterprise, or the rate of return that is necessary for a firm to remain in a competitive industry.

normative statements A set of propositions about what ought to be (also called value judgments).

Norris-La Guardia Act A law passed in 1932 that vastly strengthened the power of labor unions by limiting the court's use of injunctions in labor-management disputes.

(not quite) law of supply The quantity supplied of a good or service is usually a positive function of price, *ceteris paribus*.

number equivalent A measure of the theoretical number of equal-sized firms that should be found in an industry (the reciprocal of the Herfindahl Index).

oligopoly The market structure in which a few firms compete imperfectly and recognize their interdependence.

opportunity cost The value of the other alternatives given up in order to enjoy a particular good or service.

optimal-size plant The plant represented by the short-run average cost curve with the lowest attainable per-unit costs.

optimal tariff A tariff that maximizes a nation's net gain from altering its terms of trade.

origin The intersection of the vertical and horizontal axes of a coordinate system, at which the values of both the *x*-variable and the *y*-variable are zero.

parity A one-to-one ratio between the average prices of farm products and the prices of what farmers buy.

partnership A form of enterprise in which there is more than one owner, and the firm does not have a legal existence separate from the owners.

payment in kind (PIK) program A federal agricultural program similar to the soil bank program, but with payments made in surplus commodities rather than in money.

perestroika Restructuring, economic reforms in the Soviet Union.

perfect competition The market structure in which there are many sellers and buyers, firms produce a homogeneous product, and there is free entry into and exit out of the industry.

perfectly elastic demand Demand represented by a horizontal demand curve with a coefficient of price elasticity of demand that is equal to infinity. The quantity demanded responds in an infinite way to a change in price.

perfectly inelastic demand Demand represented by a vertical demand curve with a coefficient of price elasticity of demand that is equal to zero. There is no response in quantity demanded to changes in price.

personal distribution of income A measure of how total income is divided among individuals or households.

pie chart A graphic representation in the shape of a pie that expresses actual economic data as parts of a whole. The sizes of the slices of the pie correspond to the percentage shares of the components.

planning curve The long-run average cost curve used in the planning stage.

point elasticity The elasticity at a particular point on a demand curve.

positive externalities Spillover benefits to third parties (free riders) that result from production or consumption of certain goods.

positive relationship A relationship between two variables in which an increase in one is associated with an increase in the other and a decrease in one is associated with a decrease in the other.

positive statements A set of propositions about what is, rather than what ought to be.

predatory pricing The act of selling below cost to destroy competitors.

present value (*PV*) The value of a future payment or series of future payments discounted to the present.

price ceilings Upper limits on prices imposed by a governmental unit. The ceiling is a price that cannot be exceeded.

price clusters Groupings of prices for similar, but not homogeneous, products.

price-consumption curve A curve that shows changes in consumer equilibrium when the price of one good on an indifference curve changes.

price discrimination The practice of charging different prices to different consumers or to a single consumer for different quantities purchased.

price elasticity of demand The measure of the responsiveness of the quantity demanded to changes in price.

price elasticity of supply The measure of the responsiveness of the quantity supplied to changes in the price.

price floors Minimum limits on prices established by a governmental unit. The floor is a price that cannot be undercut.

price leadership The form of tacit collusion in an oligopolistic industry in which one firm, the price leader, sets the price or initiates price changes and the other firms follow that lead.

price searcher A firm that sets price in order to maximize profits and thus has monopoly power.

price taker A seller (or buyer) in perfect competition that has no influence on price and can sell any amount at the market-clearing price.

primary effect The dominant or immediate effect of a change in an economic variable.

principle of comparative advantage The idea that output will be maximized if people specialize in producing those goods or services for which their opportunity costs are lowest and engage in exchange to obtain other things they want.

principle of diminishing marginal rates of substitution The fact that as more of one good is consumed, more and more of the other must be given up to maintain indifference between the two.

principle of diminishing marginal utility The fact that the additional utility declines as quantity consumed increases. Less satisfaction is obtained per additional unit as more units are consumed.

principle of diminishing returns The fact that as more

and more units of a variable factor are added to a set of fixed factors, the resulting additions to output eventually become smaller.

privatization   The transfer of governmental activities and/or assets to the private sector.

product cycle   A series of stages, from development to standardization, through which a new product passes.

product group   A market for a set of goods that are differentiated but have a large number of close substitutes.

product market   Set of markets in which goods and services produced by firms are sold.

production   The process of transforming inputs into marketable outputs.

production function   A description of the amounts of output expected from various combinations of inputs.

production possibilities curve   A graph that depicts the various combinations of two goods that can be produced in an economy with the available resources.

profit   The return to enterprise, one of the factors of production. Profit is whatever remains after all other factors have been paid.

property law   Law that concerns the enforcement of property rights.

property rights   The legal rights to a specific piece of property, including the rights to own, buy, sell, or use in specific ways. Markets can exist and exchanges can occur only if individuals have property rights to goods, services, and productive resources.

public bads   Negative external effects of production or consumption that impact a large number of individuals—for example, acid rain.

public goods   Goods that are nonrival in consumption and not subject to exclusion.

pure oligopoly   An oligopolistic industry that produces a homogeneous product.

quality circles   Groups of workers organized to improve quality by discussing production problems and suggesting solutions.

quota   A limit on the amount of a good or service that can be imported during a given time period.

redistribution   Actions by government that transfer income from one group to another.

rent   The return to land, one of the factors of production.

rent control   A price ceiling imposed by a governmental unit on housing rents.

rent defending   Actions by consumers to keep their consumer surplus from being captured by rent seekers.

rent seeking   The commitment of scarce resources to capture returns created artificially.

representative firm   A typical firm in perfect competition, one of the many identical firms in the market.

residual claimant   Individual, or group of individuals, who shares in the profits of an enterprise.

right-to-work laws   State laws that allow people to hold jobs without belonging to unions.

Robinson-Patman Act   A federal law that amended the Clayton Act in 1936, making predatory pricing illegal.

roundabout production   The creation of physical capital (such as tools) that enhances productive capacity and ultimately allows increased output of consumer goods and services.

S corporation   A hybrid type of corporation that passes income directly to the owners, avoiding the double taxation of corporate profits.

satisficing hypothesis   The argument that managers do not seek to maximize profits but rather seek target levels of output and profits that are satisfactory to the ownership interests.

scarcity   The central economic problem that there are not enough resources to produce everything that individuals want.

scatter diagram   A graph that plots actual pairs of values of two variables to determine whether there appears to be any consistent relationship between them.

secondary boycotts   Union actions to stop an employer from doing business with other firms.

secondary effects   Effects indirectly related to the immediate effect, often smaller and felt after some time.

self-interested behavior   A basic assumption of economic theory that individual decision makers do what is best for themselves.

separation of ownership and control   The idea that large firms are run (controlled) by hired managers, not the owners, and the managers might have different goals from those of the owners.

settlement account   The part of the balance of payments that explains how a deficit or surplus was financed.

shadow prices   Simulated market prices used by economic planners.

shared monopoly   The model of oligopoly that says that oligopolists coordinate and share markets to act as a monopoly.

Sherman Antitrust Act   The first federal antitrust law in the United States, passed in 1890. Section 1 of the act declared every contract, combination, or conspiracy in restraint of trade to be illegal. Section 2 made it illegal to monopolize or attempt to monopolize.

shirk   To put forth less effort than agreed on.

short run   The period of time that is too short to vary all the factors of production.

short-run supply curve   The supply curve for the period in which the size of the plant cannot be varied (in perfect competition, the same as the short-run marginal cost curve).

shortage   The amount by which the quantity consumers wish to purchase at some price exceeds the quantity suppliers wish to supply at that price. A shortage can occur on a lasting basis only when a price ceiling is in effect.

shutdown point   The minimum point on the average variable cost (AVC) curve, or the level of output at which a firm minimizes its losses by ceasing operation.

single tax   A tax proposed by Henry George to capture the economic rent on land.

slope   The ratio of the change in the dependent variable (y) to the change in the independent variable (x).

social costs   Costs that are borne by society or some group in society without compensation.

social science An academic field that studies the behavior of human beings, individually and in groups, and examines their interactions.

socialism An economic system in which the nonhuman means of production are owned by society or the state.

socialist controversy A debate between Ludwig von Mises and Oskar Lange concerning the feasibility of planning without markets.

soil bank program Federal agricultural program beginning in the 1950s under which farmers were paid to let their land lie idle in order to reduce the supply of farm products.

Soil Conservation Service A federal program under which grants were given to encourage farmers to contract production by fallowing fields, contour plowing, and other conservation techniques.

sole proprietorship A form of enterprise in which no legal distinction is made between the firm and its owner.

specialization Limiting production activities to one or a few goods and services that one produces best in order to exchange for other goods.

specie flow mechanism The automatic correction of deficits and surpluses in the balance of payments through the effects of gold flows on money supplies.

speculators People who assume risk in the forward market for currency in return for the chance of a profit.

stabilization Actions by government to reduce changes in output, employment, and prices.

Standard Industrial Classification (SIC) system A code devised by the U.S. Census Bureau for classifying industries using about 400 four-digit numbers.

statistical discrepancy The part of the balance of payments that reflects unrecorded transactions and inaccurate estimates of spending by tourists.

stock A certificate of ownership in a corporation.

stockholders The owners of a corporation.

substitute goods Goods that can be interchanged. The consumption of one replaces the consumption of the other.

substitution effect An increase in the quantity demanded of a good (or service) because its price has fallen and it becomes a better substitute for all other goods.

supply The quantity of a good offered for sale at various prices during a certain time period.

supply curve A graph representing a supply schedule and showing the quantities supplied at various prices in a certain time period.

supply schedule A table that shows quantities offered for sale at various prices over a particular time period.

support prices Price floors for agricultural products maintained by the government, which purchases any surplus to keep the price from falling.

tacit collusion Unorganized and unstated attempts by informally coordinated oligopolies to practice joint actions.

Taft-Hartley Act Act passed in 1947 to reverse some of the Wagner Act's favoring of labor by shifting some legal rights back to employers.

tangent line A straight line just touching a curve (non-linear graphic relationship) at a single point. The slope of the tangent line is equal to the slope of the curve at that point.

target prices Prices the government considers to be fair for farmers, used to determine subsidy payments.

tariff A tax on imported goods or services.

tariff quota A combination of a quota and a tariff that allows a certain amount of a good or service to be imported without paying a tariff and imposes the tariff on further imports.

tax incidence The place where the burden of a tax actually falls after all shifting has occurred.

teams Groups of employees that work together to produce something.

technical efficiency The basis for minimizing the physical inputs to a production method according to some specific rule (an engineering concept).

technologically determined demand Demand that depends on techniques of production and technological progress. For example, the demand for labor will be affected by the introduction of new technology in a firm or industry.

terms of trade The ratio at which one product is exchanged for another.

testable hypothesis An inference from a theory that can be subjected to real-world testing.

theory A set of principles that can be used to make inferences about the world.

theory of the second best A theory that a second-best policy of tariffs may be useful to introduce new distortions that eliminate existing distortions.

Theory Z A management theory that workers are motivated to perform if they are made part of the management process.

Tiebout hypothesis The idea that competition among local governments as suppliers of local public services will force them to offer the desired combination of spending and taxing to voters, who will migrate to those jurisdictions that produce that combination.

tort A wrongful action (or failure to act) that causes damage to the person or property of another individual.

tort law Law that deals with intentional and unintentional wrongs inflicted by one party on another.

total cost (TC) The sum of all the costs of production for a given level of output.

total fixed costs (TFC) The costs of the fixed factors of production, which can't be avoided in the short run.

total physical product (TPP) The amount of output that a firm produces in physical units.

total revenue (TR) The amount of money a firm takes in, equal to the quantity of the good or service sold multiplied by its price.

total variable cost (TVC) The total of costs that vary directly with output, increasing as more output is produced.

traditional economy An economy in which the three basic questions are answered by custom, or how things have been done in the past.

tragedy of the commons The overuse of common access resources.

transactions costs Costs associated with gathering information about markets (prices and quantities supplied) for consuming or producing.

trusts Organizations set up to control the stock of other companies through boards of trustees.

tying contracts Agreements between producers and retailers that call for the retailer to stock certain items in return for being allowed to stock other items.

unintended effects of policy Results that are unanticipated by policy makers but become evident through careful economic analysis.

union shops Firms where union membership is necessary for a worker to remain employed.

unit elastic demand Demand represented by a demand curve that is a rectangular hyperbola with a coefficient of price elasticity of demand equal to one. The quantity demanded responds at the same rate as any change in price.

United Mine Workers (UMW) The industrial union for mine workers.

user charges Fees that cover part or all of the cost of a public service.

util An arbitrary unit used to measure individual utility.

utility The satisfaction that an individual expects to receive from consuming a good or service.

utility function A relationship expressing a consumer's desire to consume differing amounts of a good.

utility maximization The process by which a consumer adjusts consumption, given a budget constraint and a set of prices, in order to attain the highest total amount of satisfaction.

value of the marginal product of labor (VMP_L) A measure of the value of the additional output that each unit of additional labor adds to a firm's total, found by multiplying the marginal physical product by the price at which the firm can sell the product.

variable factors The factors of production that can be increased or decreased in the short run.

vertically integrated firms Firms that perform many sequential steps in a production process.

wages The return to labor, one of the factors of production.

Wagner Act A law passed in 1935 that gave employees the right to organize and bargain collectively and outlawed certain unfair labor practices by employers.

War Communism An economic system of rigid administrative control imposed by Lenin in Russia during the civil war following the Bolshevik Revolution.

Wheeler-Lea Act A 1938 federal law amending the FTC Act to make unfair or deceptive acts or practices in commerce illegal.

wildcat strikes Local strikes that are unauthorized by the national union.

Worker Adjustment and Retraining Notification Act (WARN) An act passed in 1988 that required all firms with more than 100 employees to give sixty-days' notice before shutting down or laying off workers.

workfare State welfare programs that require those receiving welfare who are able to work to take jobs or to participate in training programs in order to be eligible for benefits.

x-axis The horizontal line in a coordinate system that shows the values of the independent variable; the horizontal axis.

x-inefficiency The inefficiency associated with the "slack" management of monopoly firms because of the lack of market discipline.

y-axis The upright line in a coordinate system that shows the values of the dependent variable; the vertical axis.

yellow-dog contracts Contracts that require employees to agree to refrain from union activity as a precondition for employment and that allow firms to discharge workers who violate that agreement.

INDEX

Abowd, John M., 373–375
absolute advantage, 507–508, 509. *See also* comparative advantage
accounting profit, 210, 211–212
acid rain, 498
acreage allotment, 481–482
Adelman, M. A., 311
administered prices, 314–316
advertising, 166, 287–289
  by oligopoly, 300–302
AFDC (Aid to Families with Dependent Children), 414, 429. *See also* transfer payments; welfare programs
AFL (American Federation of Labor), 377
AFL-CIO, 381
  involvement in international affairs by, 384
agglomeration, 487
aggregates, 2–3
agricultural support program, 479–480
agriculture
  cartels in, 481
  effects of government policies on, 484–485
  government management of production in, 481–482
  increasing demand in, 482
  market failure in, 478–479
  policy on in European Community, 483
  price supports and, 479–481, 482
  recent government policies on, 482–484
  state regulation of, 485
airline industry, deregulation of, 332–333, 387–388
Alchian, Armen, 186, 275
allocation, 55–57, 90–93,
  nonmarket, 103
allocative efficiency, 90
Aluminum Company of America (Alcoa), 253, 259, 326–327
American Federation of Labor (AFL), 377, 380, 381
American Federation of State, County, and Municipal Employees (AFSCME), 381–382
antitrust laws

abroad, 325
  economic consequences of, 330–331
  enforcement of, 326–330
  in the United States, 323–326
appreciation, 537
arbitration, 380–381
arc elasticity, 132
Asch, Peter, 330
association-causation fallacy, 20–21
Austrian school of economic thought, 472–473
average fixed cost (AFC), 213
average physical product (APP), 197–198
average revenue (AR), 231
average total cost (AC), 213
average variable cost (AVC), 213

backward-bending supply curve, 345–346
Bailey, Elizabeth, 278
Bain, Joe, 316–317
balance of payments, 529, 535–537
  protectionism and, 538
  tourism and, 538
balance of payments deficit, 534
Balcerowicz, Leszek, 570
banking, competition in, 247
bar chart, 37, 38
barriers to entry, 258, 303, 310
  artificial, 259, 260
basketball "crime," economics of, 102
Battalio, Ray, 167
Baumol, William, 275
Baxter, William, 328
Becker, Gary, 101, 428
bees, fable of, 444
Bieber, Owen F., 523
bilateral monopoly, 370
black markets, 103, 105–107
blood, supply of, 92
board of directors, 189
bonds, 189
Bretton Woods system, 542–543, 545. *See also* international monetary systems
Briggs, Everett, 384
Britain
  privatization in, 54, 560
  taxation in, 561

Brozen, Yale, 317
Buchanan, James, 421
budget, maximizing of, 468
budget constraints, 157, 173–174
Bukharin, N. I., 557
bureaus, 467, 468
Bush, George
  antitrust policy of, 328–329, 331
  deregulation of natural gas industry by, 115
  income distribution under, 432
  industrial policy of, 333–334
  pollution rights and, 450
business firms. *See* firms
business union, 377

Canada
  comparable worth in, 361
  trade with, 523
capital, 41, 42, 358, 395. *See also* human capital
  competition for, 399–400
  demand for, 396–398
  interest rates and, 398–399
capital account, 536
capitalism, 550–551, 552
  contrasted to socialism, 553–554, 555
capitalized value, 395
cartels, 291–296
  in agriculture, 481
  commodity, 293
  examples of, 292–296
Carter, Jimmy
  antitrust policy of, 328
  energy crisis and, 111–116
  negative income tax and, 431
  welfare programs and, 422
Castro, Fidel, 558–559
Celler-Kefauver Antimerger Act, 324, 326
ceteris paribus, 15
  fallacy of, 21–23
Chamberlin, Edward, 281, 282, 283
change, responding to, 47
Chernobyl, 495
Cheung, Steven, 444
China, 552, 557–558
  reforms in, 567–569
chiseling, 291–292

I-1

Choi, Dosoung, 330
Chou En-Lai, 558
cigarettes, elasticity of demand for, 139–141
CIO (Congress of Industrial Organizations), 380
circular flow model, 48–52
  adjustments to, 50–52
  foreign sector and, 51–52
  government and, 50–52
  income in, 341
  injections or leakages in, 50–52
  two-sector, 49–50
cities, problems of, 486–492
Clark, John Bates, 342, 343, 362, 403, 407
Clarkson, Kenneth, 191
Clayton Act, 324, 326, 379
Clean Air Act, 448
closed shops, 380
Cloutier, Norman, 414
Coase, Ronald, 185, 443, 445
Coase theorem, 443–447, 492
coefficient of price elasticity
  of demand (E_d), 128
  of supply (E_s), 142–143
collusion, 291, 296
commercial policy, 517
Commodity Credit Corporation (CCC), 108
common access resource, 493
common agricultural policy (CAP), 483
communication, 291
communism, 551
comparable worth, 360–362
comparative advantage, principle of, 62–64, 508–512. *See also* absolute advantage
comparative economics, 549–550
  ideologies as basis of, 550, 553
  organizational principles as basis of, 560–562
comparative statics, 84
competitive fringe, 296–297
competitive solution, 563
competitiveness, national, improving, 333–334, 335
concentration, and performance, 311–317
concentration ratio, 309–310
conglomerates, 185
Congress of Industrial Organizations (CIO), 380
Conservation Reserve Program (CRP), 481
constant cost industries, 240–241
constrained sales maximization, 275

consumer choice
  assumptions about, 152
  indifference analysis and, 170–173
consumer surplus, 266–267, 465
  deadweight loss and, 271–272
  tariffs and, 165
  utility theory and, 164–166
consumption possibilities curve, 511
contestable markets, 277–278
contract law, 438
Cooper, Michael, 92
coordinates, 30
coordination, market, 291, 296–298, 302–304
corporations, 187, 189
  managers of, 273–276
cost
  explicit, 209
  implicit, 209
  long run, 216–220
  production function and, 215–216
  short run, 212–216
  types of, 212–213
cost constraints, 205
cost curves, 213–216
cost-plus pricing, 322
countertrade, 270
countervailing power, 318
Cournot, Antoine Augustin, 135, 137, 138, 255, 298
Cox, Donald, 417
craft union, 368
crime, economics of, 98–102
cross elasticity of demand, 142
crowding out, 400
Cuba, 558–559
Cultural Revolution, 558
culture, and enterprise, 238
Culver, Anthony, 92
current account, 536

deadweight loss, consumer surplus and, 271–272
death penalty, economics of, 100
de Beers Company of South Africa, 259
decreasing cost industry, 242–245
demand, 69–76. *See also* elasticity; income elasticity; price elasticity; supply; supply and demand
  for capital, 396–397
  changes in, 85–86
  cross elasticity of, 142
  elastic, 130
  foreign, 81
  for foreign exchange, 530–532
  indifference analysis and law of, 180–181

  for labor, 341–345, 386
  law of, 70, 85
  marginal utility and law of, 159–160
  market, 70–71, 73
  monopoly and, 254–255
  nonprice determinants of, 72–76
  perfectly elastic, 129
  perfectly inelastic, 128–129
  shifts in, 71–76, 85–86
  unit elastic, 130
demand curve, 70
  kinked, 299–300
demand-determined price, 391
Demsetz, Harold, 186, 331
Deng Xiaoping, 567, 568. *See also* China
dependent variable, 31
Depository Institutions Deregulation and Monetary Control Act, 247
depreciation, 537
deregulation. *See also* regulation
  of airlines, 332–333
  of natural gas, 114–115
  political problems of, 114–115
  unions and, 387–388
derived demand, 341
diamond-water paradox, 152–154, 162
differential rent theory, 249–250
differentiated oligopoly, 290
differentiated product, 282
DiLorenzo, Thomas, 275
diminishing marginal rates of substitution, principle of, 173, 204–205
diminishing marginal utility, principle of, 155–156
diminishing returns, principle of, 196–197
disasters, economics of, 119–121
discounting, 225. *See also* Federal Reserve System
discrimination. *See also* comparable worth
  income distribution and, 414–419
  in labor markets, 416–418
diseconomies of agglomeration, 487, 488
diseconomies of scale, 487, 488
disequilibrium, 80. *See also* equilibrium
distributive justice, 403
dominant firm, 296–297
dual labor markets, 473
Dukakis, Michael, 385
dumping, 269–271, 515–517
DuPont, 327

earthquake relief, 119–121
Eastern Europe
　markets in, 89
　reforms in, 570
economic development
　culture and, 238
　economies of scale and, 218
economic efficiency, 193–194
economic fallacies, 20–23
economic models, 14–15
　of crime, 98–102
economic profit, 210, 264
economic rent, 392
　differential rent theory and, 249–250
　in perfect competition, 248–250
　representative firms and, 248
economics. *See also* comparative economics
　advertising and marketing and, 166
　basic elements of, 17–20
　basic questions of, 43–44
　definition of, 2, 3
　industrial organization as subfield of, 207
　international, 22
　policy analysis and, 23–24
　urban, 486–492
　welfare, 455
economies of agglomeration, 487, 488
economies of scale, 218, 219, 220
　as barriers to entry, 258–259
　international trade and, 512
economy. *See also* capitalism; communism; socialism
　changes in, 47
　command, 45
　market, 43–44, 45–46, 47
　mixed, 47–48
　traditional, 44–45
　types of, 43–48
Edgeworth, F. Y., 170
education
　investment in, 358–359
　public choice analysis of, 464
　as public good, 454, 467–468
efficiency, economic, 193–194, 273
Einhorn, Henry A., 312
Eisenhower, Dwight D., antitrust policy of, 328
elasticity, 125, 126–127. *See also* demand; income elasticity; price elasticity
　arc, 132
　point, 132
elderly, transfers to, 427–428
eminent domain, doctrine of, 437

employment, and protectionism, 520
energy crisis, 111–116
Engels, Friedrich, 554
enterprise, 41, 42–43
　culture and, 238
　profits and, 400–401
entrepreneur, 402
environment. *See also* acid rain; global warming; pollution; property rights; waste disposal
　economic, 561
　global, problems of managing, 494–496
equilibrium. *See also* disequilibrium
　disequilibrium and, 80–84
　market, 80, 544
　in monopolistic competition, 282–285
　in perfect competition, 245–247
European Community (EC)
　agricultural policy in, 483
　monopoly in, 315
excess capacity, 286–287
exchange control, 545, 547
exchange rate, 529. *See also* international monetary systems
　floating, 543–545, 546
　imports and exports and, 532
excise tax, incidence of, 145–148
exclusive union, 368–369
exogenous variables, 84
expectations
　demand and, 75–76
　supply and, 79
experimental economics, 166–167
explicit costs, 209
exports, 51
　elasticity of demand for, 136
　exchange rate and, 532
externalities, 438–440. *See also* public goods
　government intervention and, 447–448
　international, 495
　negative, 56, 57, 441–447
　positive, 56, 57, 440–441

factors of production, 41–43. *See also* capital; enterprise; labor; land
　fixed, 194–196
　variable, 196
faculty offices, allocation of, 92–93
fair rate of return, 323
fair trade, 522, 524
fallacy of composition, 21
Family Support Act of 1988, 432
farming. *See* agriculture
Farrow, Mia, 104
fascism, 551–553

featherbedding, 366–367
Federal Trade Commission, 311
Federal Trade Commission Act, 324, 326
Feinberg, Robert, 330
firms
　activities of, 185–186
　economic efficiency and, 193–194
　forms of, 186
　households as, 184–185
　labor-managed, 188
　nonprofit, 190–193
　philanthropy of, 195
　price changes and, 208
　as price searchers, 253
　as price takers, 230
　separation of ownership and control in, 273–276
fixed factors, 194, 196
Flach, Alexander, 315
floating exchange rates, 544–546
flood relief, 119–121
Food Security Act, 484
Forbes, M. S., Jr., 384
Ford, Gerald, antitrust policy of, 328
Ford, Henry, 139
foreign exchange. *See also* exchange rate, floating; international monetary systems
　supply and demand for, 530–532
foreign exchange market, 529, 532–534
foreign sector, 59–61, 81
　benefits of trade with, 61–62
　in circular flow model, 51–52
　privatization in, 54
　size of, 60, 61
45° line, 36
forward market, 533–534
France, pollution rights in, 449
Frank, Robert H., 418
free riding, 55–56, 451–453
free trade, 523. *See also* protectionism
Freedman, Audrey, 385
freedom, in economic markets, 90
Friedman, Milton, 17, 18, 19, 295, 430
Fuchs, Victor, 417
full employment, 12, 382
functional distribution of income, 404

gains from trade, 507
Galbraith, John Kenneth, 290, 291, 318–319
game theory, 299
Garbade, Kenneth, 331
Gary dinners, 298
General Electric, 294, 319

George, Henry, 392–393, 394
Gephardt, Richard, 484
Germany
  antitrust policies in, 325
  pollution rights in, 449
glasnost, 569–572
global warming, 496–498
gold standard, 539–542. *See also* international monetary systems
Goldfarb, Robert, 109
Gompers, Samuel, 377
goods
  complementary, 74–75
  inferior, 74
  normal, 74
  public, 55–56, 57
  substitute, 74–75
Gorbachev, Mikhail, 378, 469, 556, 569–572
Gosplan, 564
government
  allocation and, 55–57
  bureaus of, 468
  in circular flow model, 50–52
  economic role of, 46, 52–59
  exchange control by, 545–547
  externalities and, 447–448
  federal system of, 57
  intervention in markets by, 91–93
  logrolling in, 466–467
  management of agricultural production by, 481–482
  market failure and, 453
  market for currency and, 532–533
  median voter theorem of, 465–466
  nonprofit firms in, 192
  redistribution and, 57–58
  role of in income redistribution, 419–420, 421–422
  stabilization and, 58–59
Gramlich, Edward, 109
Gramm, Phil, 524
Grange, the, 323–324
graphs, 29–39
  abstract ideas and, 36–37
  descriptive, 37–39
Great Industrial Debate, 557
Great Leap Forward, 557–558
Greenwood, Daphne, 427
Gurley, John, 558

Hamilton, Alexander, 218
Hand, Learned, 326
Harberger, Arnold C., 272
Hardin, Garrett, 493
Harkin, Tom, 484
Hart-Scott-Rodino Antitrust Improvement Act, 324, 326
Hayden, Tom, 104
Hayek, F. A., 472, 563, 564

health care industry
  price controls in, 117–118
  supply and demand in, 116–119
hedgers, 533
Herfindahl Index, 310–311
Hodel, Donald, 111
holding company, 323
Hong Kong, 552
horizontally integrated firms, 185
households, as firms, 190–191
housing, 491
How to Lie with Statistics (Huff and Geis), 39
Hu Yaobang, 568
Huber, Peter, 470
Hufbauer, Gary, 516
human capital
  comparable worth and, 362
  heredity and, 374
  investment in, 358–359
  race and, 359–360
Hume, David, 540
Humphrey-Hawkins Act, 382
hurricane relief, 119–121
hypotheses, 14

IBM, 327
illegal parking, economics of, 100–102
immigration, 524–525
  supply of labor and, 348
implicit costs, 209
imports, 51
  elasticity of demand for, 136
  exchange rate and, 532
  unions and, 388
inclusive union, 369–371
income, in circular flow model, 341
income-consumption curve, 177–178
income distribution, 403–405, 407. *See also* income redistribution
  discrimination and, 414–419
  functional, 404
  personal, 408
income effect, 162–163
income elasticity of demand, 141–142
income redistribution. *See also* income distribution; poor, the; poverty; transfer payments; welfare programs
  forms of, 421
  goal of, 420–421
  middle class and, 422–423
  normative standards for, 407
  private, 419–420
  as public good, 454
  role of government in, 419–420, 421–422
increasing cost industry, 241–242

increasing opportunity cost, 11
independent variable, 31
indifference analysis, 170–173
  budget constraints and, 173–176
  law of demand and, 180–181
  maximization of utility and, 176–179
indifference curve, 171
indifference map, 171–172
indifference set, 170
industrial organization, 207
industrial policy, arguments in support of, 333–334
industrial union, 369
Industrial Workers of the World (IWW), 377, 379
industry
  constant cost, 240–241
  decreasing cost, 242–245
  definition of, 307–308
  increasing cost, 241–242
  structure of, 309–311, 387
industry studies, 207
infant industry argument, 218, 518–519
inflation, unions and, 375
information
  in economic systems, 563
  environmental problems and, 494
injunction, 379
innovation, 468, 469
input coefficient, 565–566
input-output analysis, 564–566
inputs, optimum combination of, 206–208
insatiable wants, 4–5
interdependent demand, 341, 343
interdependent utility functions, 419
interest, 42
interest rate, capital market and, 398–399
internalization, 443
international finance, 506
International Monetary Fund, 542
international monetary reserves, 542
international monetary systems. *See also* balance of payments; Bretton Woods system; gold standard
  exchange control as, 545–547
  floating exchange rates as, 543–545, 546
  goals of, 537–539
international trade, 506. *See also* multinational corporations; protectionism
  benefits of, 61–62, 507, 512
  factors of production and, 524–525
  fair trade arguments and, 522–524

nontariff barriers to, 515–517
reasons for, 507
terms of, 510–511
International Trade Commission (ITC), 516, 517
interpersonal utility comparisons, 163
investment, 42, 50
in human capital, 358–359
"invisible hand," 63, 90. *See also* Smith, Adam
isocost line, 205–206
isoquant curve, 203
marginal rates of substitution and, 204–205

Jackson, Maynard, 382
Jacobs, Barry, 92
Japan
antitrust policies in, 325
capitalist economy of, 573–574
intervention in oil industry by government of, 113
investment in United States by, 397
legal system in, 439
Jensen, Michael, 313
Jevons, William Stanley, 153, 154
Jian Zemin, 568–569
Johnson, Lyndon
antitrust policy of, 317, 328
War on Poverty and, 429

Kagel, John, 167
Kemp, Jack, 524
Kennedy, Edward, 117
Kennedy, John, antitrust policy of, 328
key currency, 543
Keynes, John Maynard, 4
kidneys, market for, 92
kinked demand curve, 299–300
Klebanov, Vladimir, 378
Knights of Labor, 376
Koch, Ed, 104
Koop, C. Everett, 139–140
Koryagin, Anatoli, 378
Kotkin, Joel, 315
Kotter, Manfred, 315

labor, 41–42
demand for, 341–345
elasticity of demand for, 354–355, 386
market for, 343–347
shifts in demand for, 355–357
supply of, 345–347
labor market
discrimination in, 416–418
dual, 473

in monopoly, 347–350
poverty and, 419
labor movement. *See also* unions
prior to WW II, 376–380
since WW II, 380–385, 386
land, 41, 42
Landrum-Griffin Act, 381
Lange, Oskar, 562, 563
Lansing, Don, 538
Lapps, and Chernobyl, 495
Larkin, Bruce, 485
law
contract, 438
in Japan, 439
property, 437
tort, 437–438
Leibenstein, Harvey, 273
Lenin, Vladimir, 556, 562. *See also* Soviet Union
Leontief, Wassily, 564
Lerner Index of Monopoly Power (LMP), 322
leveraged buyouts, 313–314
Lewis, H. Gregg, 371, 372
Lewis, John L., 380, 381
limited liability, 189
loanable funds, demand for, 399
local monopoly, 265–266
logrolling, 466–467
Long, William, 330
long run, 196, 216–220, 237–245, 284–285
long-run average cost ($LRAC$) curve, 217–218
long-run profit maximization, 275–276
Lorenz curve, 408–410
lotteries, 224
Loviscek, Anthony, 414

macroeconomics
definition of, 2
issues in, 12
Malthus, Thomas Robert, 494–496
management, Japanese style of, 573–574
Mao Zedong, 557–558, 567. *See also* China
marginal analysis, 84
marginal cost (MC), 213
marginal cost pricing, 320
marginal physical product (MPP), 197–198
marginal productivity theory, 343, 362
criticisms of, 403, 473
marginal rate of substitution, 173–174, 208
isoquant curve and, 204–205
marginal resource cost (MRC), 347

marginal revenue (MR), 221–222
for a monopoly, 254–255
marginal revenue product of labor (MRP_L), 344–345
marginal utility (MU), 155–156, 159–160
market concentration
doctrine of, 314, 317
prices and, 314–316
profit levels and, 316–317
ratio of, 309–310
studies of, 311–312
market power, 230
market structure, 304. *See also* monopolistic competition; monopoly; oligopoly; perfect competition
determinants of, 309–311
market system, drawbacks of, 90–91
marketing orders, 865, 866
markets
as allocation mechanisms, 109–111
black, 103, 105, 106
equilibrium, 80
factor, 48, 49, 50
freedom in, 90
for pollution rights, 448–450
product, 48, 49, 50
Marshall, Alfred, 127, 154, 277–278
Marx, Karl, 243, 407, 473, 551, 554–555, 563. *See also* socialism
mass transportation, 491–492
Mattila, J. Peter, 360, 362
maximum, 34–35
Mazowiecki, Tadeusz, 570
MacAvoy, Paul W., 112
McChesney, Fred S., 464–465
McCormick, Robert E., 102
McLaren, Richard, 328
McLeod, Rex, 385
Means, Gardiner, 311, 314, 316
Meany, George, 381
median voter theorem, 465–466
mediation, 380
Medicare, 423, 428
Medoff, James, 373
Menger, Carl, 154
mercantilism, 507
mergers
between U.S. and European firms, 315
in the 1980s, 312–313
in the 1990s, 313–314
Mexico, trade with, 523
microeconomics
definition of, 2
in social policy analysis, 119–121
Mill, John Stuart, 448

Miller, James C., III, 328
minimum, 35
minimum wage, 108–109, 353–354
Mitchell, William C., 460
Mitterrand, François, 551
model, 14
monopolistic competition
  excess capacity and, 286–287
  long-run equilibrium in, 284–285
  resource allocation in, 289–290
  short-run equilibrium in, 282–284
  theory of, 281
monopoly, 253. *See also* antitrust laws; deregulation; market concentration; regulation
  Alcoa as, 253
  arguments in support of, 318–319
  bilateral, 370
  compared to perfect competition, 260–263, 265
  costs of, 271–273
  effects of regulation of, 322–323
  in European community, 315
  facts and fallacies about, 276–277
  by government bureaus, 467–468
  labor market and, 347–350
  local, 265–266
  long run, 264
  multinational corporations as, 261
  natural, 220
  price discrimination and, 266–271
  price and output decisions under, 255–260
  profits and losses of, 263–264
  regulation of by prices, 319–321, 322–323
  regulation of by taxes, 321–322
  state trading and, 270
  supply curve and, 257–258
  unions and, 386
monopoly power, 253
  Lerner Index of, 322
monopoly rent seeking, 273
monopsonistic exploitation, 352
monopsony, 350–354
Morck, Randall, 313
Morgenstern, Oskar, 299
Mueller, Willard, 302
multinational corporations (MNCs), 401, 525–527
  as monopoly in foreign country, 261
Murray, Charles, 429

name brand capital, 302
national defense argument, 519
National Farm Organization (NFO), 294

National Labor Relations Board, (NLRB), 379–380, 381, 382
National Labor Union, 376
National Recovery Administration (NRA), 328
natural gas industry, regulation and deregulation in, 111–116
natural monopoly, 220
negative externalities, 56, 57, 441–447
negative income tax, 430–432
negative relationship, 33
Netherlands, the, pollution rights in, 449
New Economic Policy (NEP), 556–557
Nixon, Richard
  antitrust policy of, 328
  negative income tax and, 431
  welfare programs and, 422
Nobel Prize for Economics, winners of, 7
nonprice competition, 288, 300, 302. *See also* advertising
nonprofits, 190–193
nontariff barriers, 515
normal profit, 210
normative statements, 17
Norris–La Guardia Act, 379
Norwood, Janet, 418
(not quite) law of supply, 76–77, 85
number equivalent, 311
Nutter, G. Warren, 312

oil industry
  in Japan, 113
  OPEC and, 294–296
oligopoly, 281, 290
  categories of, 291
  characteristics of, 297
  game theory and, 299
  market coordination by, 302
  price leadership and, 296, 297–298
OPEC, 294–296
opportunity cost, 5, 9, 63
  choice and, 6, 8
  comparative advantage and, 508, 510
  increasing, 11
optimal-size plant, 219
optimal tariff, 520–521
Orazem, Peter F., 360, 362
organ donations, 91–92
origin, 30
output, and monopoly, 255–258

Panel Study on Income Dynamics (PSID), 409–410
Pareto, Vilfredo, 170

parity, 479–480
Parsley, C. J., 371–372
partnership, 187
PATCO (Professional Air Traffic Controllers Organization), 382
payment in kind (PIK) program, 482
perestroika, 469, 569–572
perfect competition
  characteristics of, 229–230
  compared to monopoly, 260–263, 265
  economic rent in, 248–250
  equilibrium in, 245–247
  example of, 247
perfectly elastic demand, 129–130
perfectly inelastic demand, 128–129
personal distribution of income, 408
philanthropy, corporate, 195
physical product
  average, 197, 198
  marginal, 197, 198
  total, 197, 198
Physiocrats, 48
pie chart, 37, 38
planning
  in command economies, 564, 566
  in economic systems, 562–566
  input-output analysis in, 564–566
  socialist controversy in, 562–563
planning curve, 217
plant size, 216–220
Plato, 407
point elasticity, 132
politicians, as rent extractors, 464–465
pollution
  property rights and, 492–493
  rights to, market for, 448–450
poor, the. *See also* income redistribution; poverty; transfer payments; welfare programs
  characteristics of, 411–412
  regional distribution of, 412–414
positive externalities, 56, 57, 440–441
positive relationship, 33
positive statements, 17
Posner, Richard, 329, 330
poverty. *See also* income redistribution; poor, the; transfer payments; welfare programs
  discrimination and, 419
  measurement of, 410–411
predatory pricing, 324
Preobrazhensky, E. A., 557
present value, 223–226
Preston, Samuel, 428

price ceiling, 102–107. *See also* price floor
    rent control as example of, 104–105
price clusters, 290
price-consumption curve, 178–179
price discrimination, monopoly power and, 266–271
price elasticity of demand, 128
    college students and, 141
    imports and exports and, 136
    for labor, 354–355
    smoking and, 139–140
    substitutes and, 134
    time and, 134
    total revenue and, 135–139
price elasticity of supply, 142–145
    coefficient of, 142
    factors affecting, 144–145
    production costs and, 144
price floor, 102, 107–109. *See also* price ceiling
    minimum wage as example of, 108–109
    support prices as, 479–480
price leadership, 296–298
price searcher, 253
price taker, 230
prices
    functions of, 88–90
    income effect and, 162–163
    market concentration and, 314–316
    monopoly and, 255–258, 319–321, 322–323
    regulation of monopoly with, 319–321, 322–323
    substitution effect and, 162
    theory of formation of, 85–88
primary effect, 85
Prisoner's Dilemma, 299
privatization, 470–471
    in Britain, 54, 560
    in urban areas, 491
producer choice, 203–208
product cycle, 511
product differentiation, 282, 285–289
product group, 282
production, 184
    factors of, 41–43
    management of, 481–482
    roundabout, 395–396
production function, 194
    cost and, 215–216
    inputs and, 198–200
production possibilities curve, 8–11, 13
    comparative advantage and, 510
    shifts in, 12–13

profit, 43
    accounting, 210
    concentration and, 316–317
    economic, 210
    monopoly, 263–264
    normal, 210–211
    source of, 400–402
profit maximization, 221–222
    alternatives to, 273–276
    long-run hypothesis of, 275–276
property law, 437
property rights, 46, 53–55, 553–554
    pollution and, 492–493
protectionism
    common arguments for, 518–520
    optimal tariff argument for, 520–521
    political pressures for, 517–518
    theory of the second best and, 521–522
    tools of, 512–515
public bads, 56, 57
public choice theory, 459–460, 471, 472
public goods, 55–56, 57, 450–454. *See also* externalities
    government bureaus and, 467
    mass transportation as, 491–492
    Tiebout hypothesis of, 491
    in urban setting, 489–491
pure oligopoly, 290

quality circles, 574
Quesnay, François, 48, 50
quota, 512, 513–515

radical school of economic thought, 473–474
rats, experiments on, 167
Reagan, Ronald
    agricultural policies of, 482, 484
    antitrust policy of, 328, 329, 331
    energy crisis and, 111
    gold standard and, 541
    labor and, 382, 383, 384, 385
    urban policies of, 487, 490
    welfare programs and, 422
recycling, 499–500
redistribution, 57–58
regulation. *See also* deregulation
    as inhibitor of innovation, 468–469
    of monopolies, 319–323
    of natural gas industry, 111–114
    of oil industry in Japan, 113
regulatory agencies, 331
rent, 42, 391. *See also* economic rent
    capitalization of, 393–395
    functions of, 393
    locational, 395

rent control, 104–105
rent defending, 465
rent seeking, 462–465
    in monopoly, 272–273
representative firms, 232, 248
residual claimant, 191
Reuther, Walter, 381
revenue
    marginal, 221
    total, 221
Ricardo, David, 243, 507
right-to-work laws, 380, 387, 388
Rill, James F., 329
robbery, economics of, 99–100
Robinson, Joan, 281, 283, 285
Robinson, Michael, 416
Robinson-Patman Act, 324, 326
Roosevelt, Franklin D.
    administration of, 327–328
    unions and, 379
Roosevelt, Theodore, 327
Rothbard, Murray, 472
roundabout production, 396

S corporation, 189
Sachs, Jeffry, 570
Salinas de Gortari, Carlos, 523
Samuelson, Paul, 17, 18
Santa Monica, rent control in, 104–105
satisficing hypothesis, 275
Save the Family Farm Act, 484
saving, in Japan, 573
savings, 50
scarcity, 4
scatter diagram, 31–33
Schramm, Richard, 330
Schultz, T. W., 479–480
Schulz, James, 427
Schumpeter, Joseph, 318
Schwarzman, Stephen, 313–314
Scully, Gerald, 352–353
secondary boycott, 380
secondary effect, 85
self-interest, 15–17, 63, 246
    in analysis of crime, 98–102
Seligman, Daniel, 140
Seneca, J. J., 330
separation of ownership and control, 273–276
settlement account, 537
shadow prices, 562
shared monopoly, 290
Shepherd, William, 312
Sherman Antitrust Act, 324, 327–328
shirking, 186, 191
Shleifer, Andrei, 313
short run, 196, 212–216, 230–237, 282–284
short-run supply curve, 232
shortage, 102

shutdown point, 234, 235
Siegfried, John, 330
Sigmund, Barbara Boggs, 488
Silber, William, 331
Silk, Leonard, 313
Simon, Herbert, 274
single tax, 392–394
slope, 33–34
Smith, Adam, 62, 63, 90, 152, 162, 230, 507
Smith, James P., 359–360
Smith, Vernon, 166–167
social costs, 441–442
social science, 3
Social Security System, 51, 58, 423–427, 428. *See also* transfer payments
socialism, 551, 552, 555–556. *See also* Lenin; Mao Zedong; Marx; Soviet Union; Stalin
  competitive solution and, 563
  contrasted to capitalism, 553–554
socialist controversy, 562–563
soil bank program, 481
Soil Conservation Service, 485
sole proprietorship, 186–187
Soviet Union, 556–557, 564, 567
  reforms in, 953–956
  strikes in, 378
Sowell, Thomas, 413
special drawing rights (SDR), 546
specialization, 61–62
specie flow mechanism, 540
speculators, 533
spillover, 489–490
sports, monopsony in, 352–353
stabilization, 58–59
Stalin, Joseph, 557
Standard Industrial Classification (SIC) System, 308–309
states
  agricultural policies of, 485
  antitrust enforcement by, 329
  industrial policies of, 334
  welfare programs of, 422, 429
statistical discrepancy, 536
Steiger, Janet D., 329
Stevens, Uriah, 376
Stigler, George, 90, 301, 302, 316, 422–423, 464, 466, 478
stock, 189
  effects of unions on prices of, 373–375
stockholders, 187
students, recruitment of, 141
substitutes, elasticity of, 134
substitution effect, 162
Sununu, John H., 334

supply, 69, 76–80. *See also* demand; supply and demand; supply curve
  changes in, 77–80, 86
  foreign, 81
  of foreign exchange, 530–532
  of labor, 345–347
  market, 77
  (not quite) law of, 76–77
  price elasticity of, 142–144
supply and demand, 3, 125–126. *See also* demand; supply
  health care industry and, 116–119
  model of, 69, 82, 85
  taxes and elasticity of, 145–148
supply curve
  backward-bending, 345–346
  market, 237
  monopoly and, 257–258
  short run, 232
support prices, 479–480
surplus, 107
  consumer, 164, 165, 266–267
Sweezy, Paul, 299, 301
Swierenga, David, 332
Sylvis, William H., 376

tacit collusion, 296–298
Taft-Hartley Act, 380, 381, 382
Taiwan, 552
tangent line, 34
target prices, 482
tariff quota, 513
tariffs, 512, 513, 514–515
  consumer surplus and, 165
  optimal, 520–521
tax incidence, 146–148
taxes, 50, 58
  elasticity of supply and demand and, 145–148
  excise, 145
  incidence of, 146
  in Japan, 573
  negative income, 430–432
  regulation of monopoly with, 321–322
  utility theory and, 163
taxi industry, 91, 260
teams, 186
technical efficiency, 194
technologically determined demand, 343
terms of trade, 510
testable hypothesis, 14
Thatcher, Margaret, 559–560
theory, 14
theory of the second best, 521–522
Theory Z, 574
Thompson, Earl, 191

Tiebout solution, 490–491
Tobin, James, 421
Tollison, Robert D., 102, 330
tort, 437–438
tort law, 437–438
total cost (TC), 212
total fixed costs (TFC), 212–213
total physical product (TPP), 197–198
total revenue (TR), 135–139, 221–222
total variable costs (TVC), 213
tourism, 538
trade. *See* international trade
tragedy of the commons, 493
transaction costs, 87–88, 185
transfer payments, 51, 58, 411, 414, 423–429. *See also* AFDC; welfare programs
  the elderly and, 427–428
  in other countries, 424
Truman, Harry, 380
Trump, Donald, 104
trusts, 323
Tuerck, David, 519
Tullock, Gordon, 422, 423, 463, 466
twins, study of, 374
tying contracts, 324

unemployment, 11, 12
unemployment compensation, 428
unintended effects of policy, 119
union shops, 380
unions. *See also* labor movement
  business, 377
  craft, 368
  economic effects of, 371–375
  effects on stock prices of, 373–375
  elasticity of demand for labor and, 386–387
  forces that strengthen, 386–387
  forces that weaken, 387–388
  future of, 385
  goals of, 365–367, 386
  industrial, 369
  inflation and, 375
  in Soviet Union, 378
  types of, 367–371
unit elastic demand, 130
United Auto Workers (UAW), 385, 388
United Mine Workers (UMW), 381
urban economics, 486–492
user charges, 490
U.S. Steel, 298, 326
util, 154
utilities, 323
utility function, 154–155, 419
utility maximization, 159

utility theory, 154–160
    applications of, 160–164
    consumer behavior and, 156–157
    consumer surplus and, 164–166
    problems of, 161
    progressive income tax and, 163

value of the marginal product of labor (VMP_L), 344–345
variable factors, 196
variables, 29–30, 31
    endogenous, 84–85
    exogenous, 84–85
Vernon, Raymond, 511
vertically integrated firms, 185
Vietnam War, 12, 15
Vishny, Robert, 313
von Mises, Ludwig, 562, 563
von Neumann, John, 299
von Stackelberg, Heinrich, 281
voting, costs of, 461

wages, 42
    effect of union activity on, 367, 371–373
    minimum, 353, 382
    monopsony and, 353–354
Wagner Act, 379–380
Walesa, Lech, 570
Walras, Leon, 154
Wanniski, Jude, 541
wants, 4–5
War Communism, 556
waste disposal, 499–501
Wealth of Nations, The, 62, 63. *See also* Smith, Adam
Welch, Finis, 359
welfare economics, 455
welfare programs, 428–429
    reform of, 429–433
Wenders, John T., 465
Westinghouse, 294
Wheeler-Lea Act, 324, 326
White, Lawrence, 331
Wills, Robert, 302
Wolff, Edward, 427
Worker Adjustment and Retraining Notification Act (WARN), 385
workfare programs, 432–433. *See also* welfare programs
Wunnava, Phanindra, 416
Wurf, Jerry, 382

x-axis, 30
x-inefficiency, 273

y-axis, 30
Yeager, Leland, 519
yellow-dog contract, 379
Yeltsin, Boris, 571
Yugoslavia, firms in, 188

Zeman, Morton, 359
Zhao, Ziyang, 568

Year	GNP (Billions of Dollars)	Consumption (Billions of Dollars)	Investment (Billions of Dollars)	Government Expenditures (Billions of Dollars)	Exports (Billions of Dollars)	Imports (Billions of Dollars)	Annual Growth Rate (%)	GNP (1982 Dollars)	Real GNP Growth Rate (%)	GNP Deflator (1982=100) Index	GNP Deflator (1982=100) % Change
1950	288.3	192.1	55.1	38.8	14.5	12.3	10.7	1,203.7	8.5	23.9	2.0
1951	333.4	208.1	60.5	60.4	19.8	15.3	15.7	1,328.2	10.3	25.1	4.8
1952	351.6	219.1	53.5	75.8	19.2	16.0	5.5	1,380.0	3.9	25.5	1.5
1953	371.6	232.6	54.9	82.8	18.1	16.8	5.7	1,435.3	4.0	25.9	1.6
1954	372.5	239.8	54.1	76.0	18.8	16.3	.2	1,416.2	-1.3	26.3	1.6
1955	405.9	257.9	69.7	75.3	21.1	18.1	9.0	1,494.9	5.6	27.2	3.2
1956	428.2	270.6	72.7	79.7	25.2	19.9	5.5	1,525.6	2.1	28.1	3.4
1957	451.0	285.3	71.1	87.3	28.2	20.9	5.3	1,551.1	1.7	29.1	3.6
1958	456.8	294.6	63.6	95.4	24.4	21.1	1.3	1,539.2	-.8	29.7	2.1
1959	495.8	316.3	80.2	97.9	25.0	23.5	8.5	1,629.1	5.8	30.4	2.4
1960	515.3	330.7	78.2	100.6	29.9	24.0	3.9	1,665.3	2.2	30.9	1.6
1961	533.8	341.1	77.1	108.4	31.1	23.9	3.6	1,708.7	2.6	31.2	1.0
1962	574.6	361.9	87.6	118.2	33.1	26.2	7.6	1,779.4	5.3	31.9	2.2
1963	606.9	381.7	93.1	123.8	35.7	27.5	5.6	1,873.3	4.1	32.4	1.6
1964	649.8	409.3	99.6	130.0	40.5	29.6	7.1	1,973.3	5.3	32.9	1.5
1965	705.1	440.7	116.2	138.6	42.9	33.2	8.5	2,087.6	5.8	33.8	2.7
1966	772.0	477.3	128.6	158.6	46.6	39.1	9.5	2,208.3	5.8	35.0	3.6
1967	816.4	503.6	125.7	179.7	49.5	42.1	5.8	2,271.4	2.9	35.9	2.6
1968	892.7	552.5	137.0	197.7	54.8	49.3	9.3	2,365.6	4.1	37.7	5.0
1969	963.9	597.9	153.2	207.3	60.4	54.7	8.0	2,423.3	2.4	39.8	5.6
1970	1,015.5	640.0	148.8	218.2	68.9	60.5	5.4	2,416.2	-.3	42.0	5.5
1971	1,102.7	691.6	172.5	232.4	72.4	66.1	8.6	2,484.8	2.8	44.4	5.7
1972	1,212.8	757.6	202.0	250.0	81.4	78.2	10.0	2,608.5	5.0	46.5	4.7
1973	1,359.3	837.2	238.8	266.5	114.1	97.3	12.1	2,744.1	5.2	49.5	6.5
1974	1,472.8	916.5	240.8	299.1	151.5	135.0	8.3	2,729.3	-.5	54.0	9.1
1975	1,598.4	1,012.8	219.6	335.0	161.3	130.3	8.5	2,695.0	-1.3	59.3	9.8
1976	1,782.8	1,129.3	277.7	356.9	177.7	158.9	11.5	2,826.7	4.9	63.1	6.4
1977	1,990.5	1,257.2	344.1	387.3	191.6	189.7	11.7	2,958.6	4.7	67.3	6.7
1978	2,249.7	1,403.5	416.8	425.2	227.5	223.4	13.0	3,115.2	5.3	72.2	7.3
1979	2,508.2	1,566.8	454.8	467.8	291.2	272.5	11.5	3,192.4	2.5	78.6	8.9
1980	2,732.0	1,732.6	437.0	530.3	351.0	318.9	8.9	3,187.1	-.2	85.7	9.0
1981	3,052.6	1,915.1	515.5	588.1	382.8	348.9	11.7	3,248.8	1.9	94.0	9.7
1982	3,166.7	2,050.7	447.3	641.7	361.9	335.6	3.7	3,166.0	-2.5	100.0	6.4
1983	3,405.7	2,234.5	502.3	675.0	352.5	358.7	7.6	3,279.1	3.6	103.9	3.9
1984	3,772.2	2,430.5	664.8	735.9	383.5	442.4	10.8	3,501.4	6.8	107.7	3.7
1985	4,014.9	2,629.0	643.1	820.8	370.9	448.9	6.4	3,618.7	3.4	110.9	3.0
1986	4,231.6	2,797.4	659.4	872.2	396.5	493.8	5.4	3,717.9	2.7	113.8	2.6
1987	4,515.6	3,009.4	699.5	921.4	449.6	564.3	6.7	3,845.3	3.4	117.4	3.2
1988	4,873.7	3,238.2	747.1	962.5	552.0	626.1	7.9	4,016.9	4.5	121.3	3.3
1989	5,200.8	3,450.1	771.2	1,025.6	628.2	672.3	6.7	4,117.7	2.5	126.3	4.1
1990	5,463.0	3,658.1	745.0	1,098.0	670.4	708.4	5.0	4,155.8	.9	131.5	4.1

Year	Money Supply (Billions of Dollars)		T-Bill Interest Rate (%)	Value of U.S. Dollar (1973=100)	Federal Revenue (Billions of Dollars)	Government Expenditures* (Billions of Dollars)	Surplus (Deficit) (Billions of Dollars)	National Debt (Billions of Dollars)
	M1	M2						
1950			1.2		50.4	41.2	9.2	256.9
1951			1.6		64.6	58.1	6.5	255.3
1952			1.8		67.7	71.4	(3.7)	259.1
1953			1.9		70.4	77.6	(7.1)	266.0
1954			1.0		64.2	70.3	(6.0)	270.8
1955			1.8		73.1	68.6	4.4	274.4
1956			2.7		78.5	72.5	6.1	272.8
1957			3.3		82.5	80.2	2.3	272.4
1958			1.8		79.3	89.6	(10.3)	279.7
1959	140.0	297.8	3.4		90.6	91.7	(1.1)	287.8
1960	140.7	312.3	2.9		96.9	93.9	3.0	290.2
1961	145.2	335.5	2.4		99.0	102.9	(3.9)	292.9
1962	147.9	362.7	2.8		107.2	111.4	(4.2)	303.3
1963	153.4	393.2	3.2		115.6	115.3	.3	310.8
1964	160.4	424.8	3.5		116.2	119.5	(3.3)	316.8
1965	167.9	459.4	4.0		125.8	125.3	.5	323.2
1966	172.1	480.0	4.9		143.5	145.3	(1.8)	329.5
1967	183.3	524.3	4.3	120.0	152.6	165.8	(13.2)	341.3
1968	197.5	566.3	5.3	121.1	176.9	182.9	(6.0)	369.8
1969	204.0	589.5	6.7	122.4	199.7	191.3	8.4	367.1
1970	214.5	628.2	6.5	121.1	195.4	207.8	(12.4)	382.6
1971	228.4	712.7	4.3	117.8	202.7	224.8	(22.0)	409.5
1972	249.3	805.1	4.1	109.1	232.2	249.0	(16.8)	437.3
1973	262.9	861.0	7.0	100.0	263.7	269.3	(5.6)	468.4
1974	274.4	908.5	7.9	101.4	293.9	305.5	(11.6)	486.2
1975	287.6	1,023.2	5.8	98.5	294.9	364.2	(69.4)	544.1
1976	306.4	1,163.7	5.0	105.6	340.1	393.7	(53.5)	631.9
1977	331.3	1,286.7	5.3	103.3	384.1	430.1	(46.0)	709.1
1978	358.5	1,389.0	7.2	92.4	441.4	470.7	(29.3)	780.4
1979	382.9	1,497.1	10.0	88.1	505.0	521.1	(16.1)	833.8
1980	408.9	1,629.9	11.5	87.4	553.8	615.1	(61.3)	914.3
1981	436.5	1,793.5	14.9	102.9	639.5	703.3	(63.8)	1,003.9
1982	474.5	1,953.1	10.7	116.6	635.3	781.2	(145.9)	1,147.0
1983	521.2	2,186.5	8.6	125.3	659.9	835.9	(176.0)	1,381.9
1984	552.1	2,371.6	9.6	138.3	726.0	895.6	(169.6)	1,576.7
1985	620.1	2,570.6	7.5	143.0	788.7	985.6	(196.6)	1,817.0
1986	724.7	2,814.2	6.0	112.2	827.9	1,034.8	(206.9)	2,120.1
1987	750.4	2,913.2	5.8	96.9	913.8	1,071.9	(158.2)	2,345.6
1988	787.5	3,072.4	6.7	92.7	972.4	1,114.2	(141.7)	2,600.8
1989	794.8	3,221.6	8.1	98.6	1,052.9	1,187.2	(134.3)	2,867.5
1990	825.5	3,323.3	7.5	89.1	1,111.7	1,273.0	(161.3)	3,206.3

*In national income and product accounts.